THE UPPER NILE PROVINCE
HANDBOOK

A Report on
Peoples and Government in the
Southern Sudan, 1931

ORIENTAL AND AFRICAN ARCHIVES · 3

THE UPPER NILE PROVINCE HANDBOOK

A Report on
Peoples and Government in the
Southern Sudan, 1931

compiled by

C. A. Willis

with contributions from
A. H. Alban, C. L. Armstrong, J. Beavan, G. P. Cann,
T. F. G. Carless, P. Coriat, G. K. Hebbert, J. K. Maurice,
E. C. Tunnicliffe, H. G. Wedderburn-Maxwell,
and J. W. G. Wyld

edited by

Douglas H. Johnson

Published *for* THE BRITISH ACADEMY
by OXFORD UNIVERSITY PRESS

Africa World Books Pty Ltd,
P.O. Box 130 Wanneroo, WA 6065, *Australia*

ISBN 9780994363107

© *Douglas H. Johnson, 2015*
First published by Oxford University Press for the British Academy, 1995

British Library Cataloguing in Publication Data available

Transferred to digital printing 2015

All rights reserved. Except as permitted by current legislation no part of this work may be photocopied, stored in a retrieval system, published, performed in public, adapted, broadcast, transmitted, recorded or reproduced in any form or by any means without the prior permission in writing of the copyright owner

Phototypset by J&L Composition Ltd, Filey, North Yorkshire

Contents

List of Plates	vii
Preface	ix
Acknowledgements	xiv
Note on Editing	xv
List of Abbreviations	xviii
Glossary	xix

Editor's Introduction: The Upper Nile Province: An Historical Overview

From Military to Civil Administration, 1898–1926	1
The Administration of Governor Willis, 1926–31	14
The Ethnography of Native Administration: The Governor's View	19
The Ethnography of Native Administration: The District Notes	22
Issues of Development	28
Epilogue	31

THE UPPER NILE PROVINCE HANDBOOK

Chapter 1: *C. A. Willis*, INTRODUCTION	39
Chapter 2: *C. A. Willis*, MAIN REPORT AND PROPOSALS	73
Chapter 3: *J. Beavan*, NORTHERN DISTRICT	142
Chapter 4: *G. P. Cann*, SHILLUK DISTRICT	154
Chapter 5: *C. L. Armstrong*, NASIR DISTRICT	176
Chapter 6: *E. C. Tunnicliffe*, AKOBO DISTRICT	198
Chapter 7: *J. W. G. Wyld*, BOR-DUK DISTRICT	208
Chapter 8: *G. K. Hebbert*, YIRROL DISTRICT	250
Chapter 9: *A. H. Alban*, ABWONG DISTRICT	268
Chapter 10: *H. G. Wedderburn-Maxwell*, ZERAF VALLEY DISTRICT	289
Chapter 11: *P. Coriat*, WESTERN NUER DISTRICT	296
Chapter 12: *T. F. G. Carless*, MALAKAL TOWN	312
Chapter 13: *J. K. Maurice*, GAMBEILA ENCLAVE	321

Chapter 14: C. A. Willis, SOME SUGGESTIONS FOR THE FUTURE	330
Appendix 1: K. C. P. Struvé, Handing-Over Notes, July–August 1926	350
Appendix 2: C. A. Willis, Report on possible effects of the Sudd Project of Irrigation on Local Populations, 1928	377
Appendix 3: Biographical Notes	411
Appendix 4: Steamer Transport in Upper Nile Province, 1926–31	432
Archival Sources	434
Bibliography	437
Maps	
The Anglo-Egyptian Sudan, 1933	448
Upper Nile Province, 1927, from 'The Anglo-Egyptian Sudan (Tribal)', *Military Report on the Sudan*, 1927	450
Sketch-map to show distribution of the Eastern Jikany tribal sections (arrows point from area of villages to dry season camps) after Mr. C. L. Armstrong (from Evans-Pritchard, *The Nuer*, p. 58)	452
Index	453

List of Plates

Between pages 252 and 253

Captions in quotations are taken from the original collections.

1. Governor Willis with Shilluk guard of honour, on the Kodok light line (Willis). Sudan Archive, University of Durham (SAD) 210/14/192.
2. Governor Willis on trek, 1927 (Coriat).
3. Shilluk review (Willis). 210/14/195.
4. Murle at Akobo, 1928 (Coriat).
5. 'A Dinka near Khor Fulus mouth on the road to Fadding', c.1928 (Romilly). SAD 788/1/2.
6. Nuer building thatched roof over namlia (Willis). SAD 210/14/137.
7. Nuer building road, Coriat and Willis in background, 1928 (Willis). SAD 210/14/165.
8. Coriat, Wyld, Maxwell at Tied Wiot, Khor Atar (after 30 hours march), 1928 (Romilly). SAD 788/1/12.
9. Captain Romilly (Gaweir March 1928) with 'daughter of sword and honour bloke [chief Guer Wiu]' (Romilly). SAD 788/1/28.
10. Gaawar 'who gave false information and had been definitely antigovernment being flogged', Gaweir March, 1928 (Eastwood).
11. Coriat, Romilly, Maxwell, 'looting a hippo harpoon', Nuer cattle camp, Gaweir March, 1928 (Romilly). SAD 788/1/13.
12. 'Women prisoners on the march with goods & chattels & babies on their heads—one baby was born en route', Nuer Settlement, 1929 (Eastwood).
13. Pulling car on a raft across Khor Woat, 1930 (Coriat).
14. Yoynyang Roman Catholic mission, 1930 (Coriat).

Preface

This handbook has been selected for publication by the British Academy's Oriental and African Archives Committee. Their invitation to me to edit the handbook came shortly after I had returned from my first visit to the province since the outbreak of the Sudan's second civil war in 1983. Contrasting the state of Upper Nile in 1930, at the end of the period of imperial pacification, with what it is now, in the middle of a civil war, I was struck by the similar problems which confronted two essentially military governments—the British and the Sudan People's Liberation Army—as they each sought to establish civil administration in very different circumstances. It is for this reason that I willingly accepted this invitation to take a more thorough look at an earlier period in the province's history.

The Upper Nile Province was always considered by British administrators as one of the most remote areas of the vast territory of the Anglo-Egyptian Sudan. Appearing to possess only zoological and ethnographic interest, it remained essentially undeveloped throughout the entire period of British overrule. To publish now a handbook describing this province at the end of 1930, mid-way in the Condominium period before what little that was achieved had even begun, may seem to many readers a perverse decision, offering documents of only esoteric value. Yet, for all its remoteness Upper Nile Province was, and remains, a problematic territory for the Sudan. It was here that Britain successfully contained the advance of rival European imperialisms, and here where the Fashoda Incident (according to Sellar and Yeatman, the only 'memorable' Incident in History) took place. The last pacification campaign anywhere in British Africa was fought against one of the peoples of Upper Nile (the Nuer) surprisingly late in imperial history (1927–30). Much of the Sudan's long international border with Ethiopia runs along the eastern edge of the province and has been the site of tensions—alternatively creative and destructive—in the recent history of both nations. The Upper Nile has long been known for its abundance of water, but to that now can be added most of the Sudan's known, if as yet untapped, oil reserves. And just as oil and water rarely mix anywhere else, so in Upper Nile the attempt to control these vital resources has fuelled the ferocity of the second civil war. The future development of the Sudan, in whatever form, will depend considerably on the security and tranquillity of the territories found within the borders of the old Upper Nile Province. As of this writing we can look forward to that tranquillity with far less assurance and confidence than the British officials whose reports appear in this volume. And if more rests on that future peace now than they were aware of then, the overview they provide of the Upper Nile at a pivotal period in its earlier history will help current observers attain some perspective on the region's problems and potential.

This handbook was intended for publication. It was compiled in part as an extended handing-over note on the province by the out-going governor, Charles Armine Willis. The production of handbooks on the Sudan before the First World War had been a major activity of the Intelligence Department, of which Willis was the eccentric head from 1915 to 1926. What distinguished the earliest handbooks from those few which appeared after the war was the central editing of the former as opposed to detailed participation of local officials in the writing of the latter. There was a substantial improvement in the quality of information thus presented; the very first handbooks had an almost comic quality about them.

It is amazing, given the international interest in the exploration of the Nile basin in the mid-nineteenth century, how little the incoming British administrators knew of the Upper Nile and the Southern Sudan when these regions were re-occupied following the battle of Omdurman in 1898. A small handbook, based on exploration literature and the surveys of American officers in the Egyptian army had been issued somewhat optimistically in 1884 for use by the advancing Gordon Relief Expedition, and it summarized what was then known about the geography and ethnography of the entire country. The quality of its ethnography can be judged by this comment on the 'red-brown' skinned Bongo of Bahr el-Ghazal: 'it would seem that the soil they inhabit has a marked bearing on the colour of the races. Here the red iron rock prevails, while, in the low-lying dark alluvial flats, we find the Denka and Nuehr of a deep black tint'.[1]

That handbook was revised by the Intelligence Division of the War Office in 1898 in time for the final advance on Omdurman. Its compiler admitted a certain incompleteness to the book, but dismissed most changes since 1884 as 'mainly historical' and asserted that 'it can hardly be expected that important changes can have taken place in the territorial aspect of the countries dealt with.' He was confident that the geographical account 'will be found to be accurate.'[2] Even this assumption of geographical reliability proved complacent. Before the first year of re-occupation was over a supplement to the handbook had to be issued. Reports by the new administrators had revealed an unanticipated geographical confusion. The new supplement cautioned that, 'owing to the fact that no two

---

[1] Intelligence Branch, Quartermaster-General's Department, Horse Guards, War Office, *Report on the Egyptian Provinces of the Sudan, Red Sea, and Equator* (London, 1884): 94–5.

[2] Captain Count Gleichen, Intelligence Division, War Office, *Handbook of the Sudan* (London, 1898): p.iii.

descriptions (whether *per* map or report) of the same bit of country or river agree as to distances or spelling, several discrepancies as to mileage, &c., will be noticed. An attempt has been made to strike an average between the various authorities, but it is not expected that the result will be entirely satisfactory . . .'[3]

As regards the political organization of the Southern Sudanese peoples, that most essential concern of administrators, virtually nothing was known. This was in distinct contrast to the Northern Sudan where the Egyptian Army Intelligence Department had made many contacts with local leaders in the years leading up to the overthrow of the Mahdist state. Of those peoples who came directly within the Anglo-Egyptian sphere of influence in the Southern Sudan, only the Shilluk had previously been described by travellers in any detail. About the Dinka and Nuer, the two largest groups who confronted the new administration, there was almost complete ignorance. The 1884 handbook had merely repeated Schweinfurth's comment that 'the Nuehr are a warlike tribe somewhat formidable to the Denka', and the only advance on this statement in 1898 was a modernization of the spelling.[4]

Subsequent handbooks were compiled from the route reports forwarded to Khartoum by all itinerant inspectors, and from the lengthy special reports which sometimes appeared in the appendices of the *Sudan Intelligence Report*. The first set of province handbooks, including Bahr el-Ghazal but excluding the other southern provinces, was issued in 1911.[5] All suffered from a remoteness which distance from the centre imposed on understanding local conditions. It was L. F. Nalder, governor of Fung (later Blue Nile) Province who compiled the first locally produced guide with his mimeographed *Fung Province Handbook*, in c. 1929. His more ambitious *Equatorial Province Handbook*[6] was, perhaps, a model of what province handbooks should have become: briefly covering all aspects of administration and natural history, complete with statistics, written by local officials, and including references to the writings of missionaries, professional ethnographers and linguists.

It is against this background that we can judge Willis' own intentions for this handbook. It was, in the first place, a policy document, both explaining and justifying to his successor, and to his superiors in

---

[3] Major Count Gleichen, CMG, Intelligence Division, War Office, *Supplement to the Handbook of the Sudan* (London, 1899): p.iii.
[4] *Report on the Egyptian Provinces of the Sudan*: 100; *Handbook of the Sudan*: 121.
[5] Intelligence Department (S.G.), *The Bahr el Ghazal Province*, Sudan Handbook Series No. 1 (London, 1911).
[6] *Volume I. Mongalla*, Sudan Government Memoranda (New Administrative Series), No. 4 (Khartoum, 1936).

Khartoum, the reasons why he had proposed the policies he had (the most controversial being the suppression of the Nuer). It outlined what he thought he had achieved in systematizing the new principles of Native Administration which had been brought in after the Milner Report of 1921 and were broadly similar to the theory of Indirect Rule propounded by Lord Lugard in Nigeria. This accounts for the district by district focus, the paucity of general statistics on rainfall, river transportation, cotton production, schools, etc., and the lack of academic precision. Unlike Nalder, Willis had an Orientalist's lack of interest in ethnography. Very little had been written on the peoples of Upper Nile by 1930; what there was had either been published in German by Austrian missionaries, or had been produced by American missionaries, for whom Willis felt a deep and personal distaste. He displayed a similar hostility towards the professional anthropologist, Evans-Pritchard, who arrived in the province early in 1930. This handbook, therefore, rests its opinions on the authority of 'the man on the spot', and focuses exclusively on practical problems of administration.

Willis forwarded a copy of this report to the Civil Secretary's office in Khartoum,[7] but it was not, in the end, published. The project was half-heartedly revived in the 1930s and 1940s by a two of Willis' successors, A. G. Pawson and F. D. Kingdon, but then it was always abandoned for more pressing matters, and only the notes and rough drafts survive.[8]

The lack of an official overview of Upper Nile at any time during the Condominium is an unfortunate gap in the published literature. Despite the perceived remoteness of the province there is an extensive list of publications on the languages, livelihood and ethnography of its peoples, its topography, hydrology and natural history, not to mention its development potential (a selection of which is given in the bibliography). An account of Upper Nile at the end of 1930 not only helps to fill the gap in official publications, it provides an important historical context for subsequent anthropological and development research: in 1930 Evans-Pritchard's field-work among the Nuer had only just begun, and plans for the Jonglei Canal were still at an embryonic stage. With almost all traces of previous administrative structures now obliterated by war from the landscape of the rural Upper Nile, a description of the beginnings of civil administration

---

[7] Where it can be found in the National Records Office (NRO) under Civsec 57/2/8. Willis' was the first Upper Nile Province governor's handing-over notes to be deposited in Khartoum. He retained the only copy of his predecessor, K. C. P. Struvé's notes to him, which appear here in Appendix 1. No handing-over notes of any governor of Upper Nile before 1972, British or Sudanese, were to be found in the government offices in Malakal in 1983, the last year in which provincial files were transfered to the Southern Records Office in Juba.
[8] 'Upper Nile Province Annals', NRO UNP 1/44/328–329.

may even be of use in future administrations. Far from being remote in time and place, the contents of this handbook are of immediate interest.

The handbook, as Willis intended it, forms the core of this volume. It is preceded by an introduction which gives a summary account of the administrative history of the province up to 1926, Willis' own period as governor, a comparison between Upper Nile Province at the end of the Condominium period and now, and an analysis of the handbook as an historical and ethnographic source. For the sake of completeness, as well as to provide additional contextual material, two separate documents are included in the appendices: Struvé's own handing-over notes and Willis' critique of the Egyptian irrigation schemes for his province, the precursor of the Jonglei Canal. In this way I hope that readers both from within and without the Sudan will gain greater familiarity with such a little known but so problematic a region.

Douglas H. Johnson
Oxford

PREFACE TO THE PAPERBACK EDITION

The Upper Nile Province Handbook was first published in 1995 by the British Academy as the third volume in their Oriental and African Archives series. At that time Sudan's second civil war was being fought out very largely in 'Greater Upper Nile', whose territory is described in this book, and the early administrative record of Upper Nile and the Southern Sudan was largely inaccessible to scholars and South Sudanese alike. The publication of the Handbook was intended mainly for use by researchers, and as such had a limited circulation before being put out of print. Since the end of that war in 2005 there has been a growing demand for the book from a new readership inside South Sudan and in the South Sudanese diaspora around the world, especially those from Upper Nile itself. Scholarly editions of primary sources rarely reach a popular readership; therefore, it is with great satisfaction that a paperback edition of this book is now available for the audience who will appreciate it most.

DHJ
Oxford
June 2015

Acknowledgements

My thanks go first to Professor Peter Holt and the Oriental and African Archives committee of the British Academy for inviting me to edit the Upper Nile Handbook; to the British Academy for supporting the project; and to Mr. J. M. H. Rivington, publications officer of the British Academy, for steering the manuscript through to its final transformation. Thanks are also due to Lesley Forbes and Jane Hogan of the University of Durham Library for their unfailing assistance in providing materials from the University of Durham's Sudan Archive. As always there is a debt of gratitude to Professor Richard Hill for either identifying obscure names mentioned in the text, or pointing me to the right sources for identification. Dr. Peter Garretson shared with me his vast knowledge of sources for the history of the Sudan-Ethiopian border. Heather Bell, of Nuffield College, Oxford, gave useful advice on locating information on civil and military medical personnel. Ken Osborne, the Records Manager/Archivist of the CMS very kindly answered my enquiries about missionaries and mission sources, as did Mrs. Ellen Theobald (née Smith), and the Rev. Keith Black, Director of Action Partners (SUM), Australian and New Zealand Headquarters. Grateful acknowledgement is given to Mrs. Honor Baines, Mrs Jean Eastwood and Mr P. B. Dawson for permission to reproduce photographs from the collections of Percy Coriat, Brigadier Gerald Arthur Eastwood, and Capt. H. A. Romilly. Finally, gratitude is due to Robin Hodgkin for his admonitory comments about footnotes; it is my fault, not his, if they fail to reach his standard of interest.

Note on Editing

The principles of editing are greatly simplified by the fact that most of the manuscripts included here were intended for publication in some form. This relieves the editor of any obligation to faithfully retain all misprints and omissions, or leave obvious errors uncorrected. There has thus been an attempt to be consistent in headings, spelling, capitalization and punctuation throughout, applying modern conventions where appropriate. There is an inconsistency in the writing of Sudanese names. Willis' own style varied in the documents published here: for instance, he alternates between Gawer and Gaweir for Gaawar, Garjo and Garjok for Gaajok, etc. To avoid confusing readers who are not familiar with variations in Anglo-Egyptian orthography I have tried to adopt the most common spellings used in 1930, the date of most of these manuscripts, and have applied them throughout. These are in fact the forms used by the district commissioners in their reports (the exception being J. W. G. Wyld, whose spelling of English and Dinka was always idiosyncratic). Where the administrative forms of names of groups differ from modern spellings popularised in the classic ethnographies of the region, the latter are given in brackets under the appropriate entries in the index.

Place names present another problem. Southern Sudanese geographical names have undergone a progressive anglicisation and arabicisation. Most of the place names on the Sudan Survey 1: 250,000 maps were derived from surveys undertaken in the first quarter of this century, without reference to any standard form of phonetics, and are usually only rough approximations of what was heard. The Lou Nuer village of Cith, for instance, appears on all Sudan maps of the area as Shit. In languages where 'f' and 'p' are often interchangeable there will always be alternate readings; though it seems that the preponderance of the 'Fa' prefix (rather than 'Pa') on maps south of the Sobat has something to do with the tendency of early surveyors to use the dialect of local Dinka guides rather than Nuer. In many cases the original meaning of a place name is completely obscured by the permutations which appeared on successive maps. Thus Pacota (the village of the hornless cattle) has been irretrievably lost to history as Fashoda. Khor Pul luth (the pool of the lungfish) appears variously as Khor Filus, Fullus, or Fulluss, but only rarely as Fulluth. Duk Paiwel (the village of Aiwel) has appeared as Duk Faiwel, Faiywil, or Fayuil. Arabicisation has added to the confusion, due to the paucity of vowels in Arabic script and the different ways some letters can be transliterated in roman script. The roman 'g' has done duty for both qaf, in its

Sudanese colloquial pronunciation, and *jim*, following an older Egyptian convention. Thus *qoz* becomes 'goz', but *jabal* frequently appeared as 'gebel' on the earlier Anglo–Egyptian military maps. This confusion was never completely tidied up on later maps and places such as Fangak were transformed by the pronunciation of map-reading officials. Fangak (or Pangak) in Dinka means the place (*pan*) of the crow (*gak*). British officials often assumed that the 'g' on the map represented *jim*; 'Fangak' thus became 'Fanjak' in administrative-speak, and this Anglo–Arabicised form is growing in use even among Southern Sudanese who do not come from the area. The combination of Arabic geographical terms with local names produces yet another level of confusion. Meshra el-Rek, the landing place of the Rek Dinka, is fully arabicised beyond recognition in modern books on the Sudan, either as Mashra' al-Raqq or Mashra' al-Riqq. Who such authors think they are writing about is open to question.

There is no easy solution. There has been no attempt to standardize the phonetic system used for African place names on Sudanese maps. Many current maps employ the anglicised spellings used on maps which appeared at independence. Other modern atlases and gazetteers give a roman transliteration of the Arabic now officially used in the Sudan; thus moving even further from the original approximations of African names appearing on maps contemporary with this handbook. It would be an historical anomaly to standardize all names by either a modern or a more purist transcription, yet readers must be enabled to locate place names on other maps. Therefore, the most common contemporary spelling is used consistently throughout the handbook; where that differs substantially from the spelling used on the Sudan Survey 1:2,000,000 1:1,000,000 and 1:250,000 maps (still the most detailed of accessible maps), the latter will be given in brackets after its first appearance.

There is a temptation to over-annotate a manuscript of this sort. I have tried to limit footnotes to simple identifications, corrections of fact or cross references to other documents or recent studies which amplify (or clarify) specific points. Willis made a few marginal comments on the district notes. These have been retained in the body of the text, marked by an asterisk and contained within brackets. It has not been possible to identify all of the persons mentioned in the manuscript. Those for whom I have more information than is found in the handbook have been grouped together in a section of biographical notes, which immediately follows the introduction. A separate list of steamers mentioned in the texts follows the biographical notes.

The order of the manuscripts follows that of the copy in the Sudan Archive at the University of Durham, with the following minor exceptions. MS page 212/13/4, on the Atwot, was found in the section on administrative staff and clearly was displaced from its original position under native administration. It now follows MS page 212/13/16. Similarly, MS pages 212/13/23–26 appear to have been placed out of order and now follow MS page 212/13/3 in the administrative staff section. MS pages 212/14/12–13 (Northern District Census) were filed in reverse order in the archive copy. The ordering of the district notes is the same in both the Durham and Khartoum archives, with the tribal districts coming first, followed by the two non-tribal districts (Malakal town and the Gambeila enclave).

List of Abbreviations

ADC	Assistant district commissioner
BD	Bor District
BGP	Bahr el-Ghazal Province (the 'BOG')
Civsec	Civil secretary's files, NRO
CMS	Church Missionary Society
Dakhlia	Department of interior files, NRO
DC	District commissioner
EA	Egyptian Army
ED, END	Eastern District, Eastern Nuer District
EID	Egyptian Irrigation Departmen
ENRC	Eastern Nuer Rural Council
Intel	Intelligence department files, NRO
JAH	*Journal of African History*
JRAI	*Journal of the Royal Anthropological Institute*
£E	Egyptian pound, currency of the Sudan until 1956, roughly equivalent to £1.0 s. 6 d (£1.25).
LND	Lou Nuer District
LPS	Local Provincial Service
MI	Medical inspector
M.I.	Mounted Infantry
m/m; m/ms	milleme; one thousandth of an Egyptian pound
MO	Medical officer
MP	Mongalla Province
M.P.	Mounted Police
MPMIR	Mongalla Province Monthly Intelligence Report
NMP	Nuba Mountains Province
NRO	National Records Office, Khartoum
OC	Officer commanding
PRO	Public Records Office, Kew
Pt	Piastre; one hundredth of an Egyptian pound
PWD	Public Works Department
SAD	Sudan Archive, University of Durham
SCR	Strictly confidential report
SDF	Sudan Defence Force
SG	Sudan Government
SGR&S	Sudan Government Railway & Steamers
SGS	Sudan Government Steamer
SIR	*Sudan Intelligence Report* (1898–1920)
SMIR	*Sudan Monthly Intelligence Report* (1921–28)
SMR	*Sudan Monthly Report*, N.S. (1929 on)
SMS	Sudan Medical Service
SNR	*Sudan Notes and Records*
SRO	Southern Records Office, Juba
UNP	Upper Nile Province
UNPMD	Upper Nile Province Monthly Diary
WNP	White Nile Province
ZV, ZVD, ZVR	Zeraf Valley, Zeraf Valley District, Zeraf Valley Region

Glossary

araki	(Arab., *'araq*), distilled alcohol,
ardeb	(Arab., *ardabb*) measure of capacity equalling 198 litres
bash shawish	(Turk., *baş çavuş*) rank of sergeant major in army and police
bimbashi	(Turk., *binbaşi*) rank of major in the army
debba, dubba	(Arab., *dabba*) low alluvial mound of silt or sand
doleib	(Arab., colloq.) *Borassus flabellifer* var. *æthiopum*, a type of palm tree
dura	(Arab., *dhura*) *sorghum vulgare*
effendia	(Turk., *efendi*) from the honorific title 'effendi', in this case referring to educated Egyptian officials as a group
feddan	(Arab., *faddān*) land measurement, 1.038 acres
felucca	(Arab., *falūka*) a type of sailboat used on the Nile
ferik	(Arab., *farīq*) a group; colloquially a herd of domestic animals
ferrash	(Arab., *farrāsh*), waiter
fiki	(Arab., *faqih*), Muslim holy man or religious teacher
ful, fula	(Arab., colloq., *fūla*) large pool of water (in Nuer *ful* /*pul* also means pool)
gellaba	(Arab., *jallāba*) itinerant traders
ghaffir	(Arab., *khafīr*) watchman, caretaker
goz	(Arab, *qoz*) stabilized sand dune
hafir	(Arab., *ḥafīr*) a dug pit used as a water reservoir, *fula*
hakim	(Arab., *ḥakīm*) doctor, also medical officer or dresser
hamla	(Arab., *ḥamla*) transport animals, baggage train
harimat	(Arab., *ḥarīmāt*) wives of soldiers and police; women's quarters
hashab	(Arab., colloq.) *Acacia verek*, a type of gum tree
heglig	(Arab., colloq., *hijlij*) *Balanites ægyptiaca*
hiker	(Arab., *ḥikr*) land rent tax
hosh	(Arab., *ḥawsh*) enclosure, courtyard
jebel	(Arab., *jabal*) mountain
kadi	(Arab., *qāḍī*) judge of Islamic law
kaimakam	(Arab., *qā'mmaqām*) rank of lieutenant-colonel in the army; the immeidate source is the Turkish (from Arabic), *kaymakam*.
kantar	(Arab., *qinṭār*) measure of weight equalling 100 rotls or 99.05 lbs
khor	(Arab., *khawr*) seasonal watercourse
kujur	(Arab., colloq.) derogatory term applied indiscriminately to pagan religious and spiritual figures, equivalent to English 'witchdoctor'
lau	(Nilotic, *loua*) cloth worn knotted over one shoulder
luak	(Nilotic) cattle byre, barn

malakia	(Arab., *malakiyya*) the 'civilian' area of former garrison towns
mamur	(Arab., *ma'mūr*) junior civil administrative official in charge of a sub-district (*ma'muriyya*); post held by Egyptians and Sudanese
merisa	(Arab., colloq. *marisa*) beer brewed from sorghum and other grains (a drink Egyptians originally associated with Maris, i.e. northern Nubia)
merkaz/merakiz	(Arab., *markaz/marākiz*) district headquarters, office
meshra	(Arab., *mashra'*) landing place on a river
miralai	(Turk., *miralay*) rank of senior colonel or junior brigadier in the army
mudiria	(Arab., *mudiriyya*), province; province headquarters
murasala	(Arab., *murāsala*), messenger
nafar	(Arab.) rank of private in army and police
namlia	(Arab.) mosquito-proof house
nas	(Arab.) 'people'
ombashi, onbashi	(Turk., *onbaşi*) rank of corporal in army and police
osta	(Arab., colloq., *usta*), artisan, foreman
rais	(Arab., *ra'īs/rayyis*) river boat pilot or captain
rakuba	(Arab., *rākūba*) open shelter providing shade
Ret	(Shilluk, *reth*) king
rotl	(Arab., *raṭl*) measurement of weight, roughly one pound
ruba	(Arab., *rub'*) measurement of capacity, equal to 8.25 litres
saigia	(Arab., *sāqiya*) water wheel
sarraf	(Arab., *ṣarrāf*) government storekeeper
shawish	(Turk., *çavaş*) rank of sergeant in army and police
shen, shieng, shyeng	(Nuer, *cieng*) a territorial or social unit of indeterminate size, applied to the family homestead, lineage segment, or tribal territory
sol	(Turk., *sol kol ağasi*) rank of warrant officer in army and police
sudd	(Arab., *sadd*) obstacle or dam; general term applied to the vegetation blockages in the central swamp region of the upper Nile
suk	(Arab., *sūq*) market
sunt	(Arab., *sanṭ*) Acacia arabica
talh	(Arab., *ṭalḥ*) Acacia seyal, a type of gum tree
tukl	(Arab., colloq.) round hut of wood, mud and thatch
tumargi/tumargia	(Perso-Turkish, *timarci*) medical orderly; male nurse
toich	(Nilotic, *toic*) seasonally flooded pastureland
ushur	(Arab., *'ushr*) one-tenth; tax on cultivable land
wakil	(Arab.) deputy, agent
wakil ombashi	(Turk.) rank of lance corporal in army and police
zaptieh	(Turk., from Arab. *ḍabṭiyya*) district or station gaol for short-term prisoners
zariba	(Arab., pl. *zarā'ib*) thorn hedge enclosure, fortified camp
zeer	(Arab., *zīr*), earthen water jar

EDITOR'S INTRODUCTION

The Upper Nile Province: An Historical Overview

FROM MILITARY TO CIVIL ADMINISTRATION, 1898–1926

The region which later became Upper Nile Province confronted the incoming Anglo-Egyptian army with a series of international problems when, on 19 September 1898, General Kitchener arrived at Fashoda by riverboat after his decisive victory over the Mahdist army of the Khalifa Abdallahi at Omdurman. Not only was a small French force under the command of Captain Marchand entrenched at the old Turco-Egyptian headquarters of Fashoda, but further up the Nile the Belgians at Rejaf and Lado claimed yet another chunk of what had been the Egyptian Equatoria Province; and to the east the emperor of Abyssinia, Menilek II, not only claimed all the lands from the Abyssinian foothills to the White Nile, he had sent an expeditionary force along the Baro and the Sobat to plant his flag and so strengthen his claim with 'effective occupation'. It was this competition of various imperial powers which established the administrative limits to the new Fashoda administrative and military district. The old Egyptian outposts of Nasir and Bor were hurriedly re-occupied by Sudanese troops of the Egyptian Army to secure these places against the Ethiopians and Belgians. Marchand was withdrawn and the Belgians contained by European diplomacy, and Menilek, too, settled his borders by negotiation—though it took some years of further filling in the map before anyone was certain just where these borders lay. Once these limits had been agreed Upper Nile Province (as it was renamed) ceased to be of any great concern to the government centred at Khartoum. It became little more than a place to get through on the way to the Bahr el-Ghazal, the Congo and Uganda, where the main river channels had to be kept clear of vegetation blockage, but where little money could be spent because very little revenue was expected.

Upper Nile Province's reputation as a backwater was gained early, but this belied a history of constant activity, a complicated balancing of relations between many different peoples, and the persistent influence of Ethiopia just across the invisible borderline. In the history of the province during the first quarter of this century we can see the themes of the transition from military to civil administration, and the development of an 'ethnographic' approach to the governing of African peoples.

Upper Nile Province grew out of the Fashoda Military District, created during the Anglo-French confrontation. Major H. W. Jackson was appointed the district's first commandant on 19 September 1898, with a garrison of one battalion of infantry, four guns and a gunboat. The following day a second, smaller outpost was established at the mouth of the Sobat. The old Egyptian fort at Nasir was re-occupied early in December, and shortly thereafter the French garrison at Fashoda withdrew up the Sobat into Abyssinia.[1]

Fashoda, now no longer contested, remained the capital of a district whose boundaries took some time to define. Its western boundary was set when the Bahr el-Ghazal was occupied by a military force in 1901 and subsequently became a separate province. The eastern frontier with Abyssinia was finally agreed in 1903. The southern limits of the province were further defined in 1906 when Bor and Mongalla were hived off to form Mongalla Province, though the provincial border was not fixed until 1910 when it was made to coincide with the ever-changing 'tribal' boundary between the Nuer and Dinka. This arrangement soon proved to be more trouble than it was worth. Nuer-Dinka affrays very nearly escalated into inter-province wars, and during the period coinciding with World War One the governors of the two provinces were scarcely on speaking terms as each began to side with the perceived interests of his own subjects.[2] Finally, in 1926 the northern half of Bor District, containing those Dinka who directly bordered the Nuer, was transferred to Upper Nile Province as the Dinka-Nuer District, with its headquarters at Duk Fayuel and subsidiary police posts at Duk Fadiat, Kongor and Jonglei. The Bor and Aliab Dinka, living along both banks of the Bahr el-Jebel, were administered by Bahr el-Ghazal Province until 1928, when Bor was rejoined to Duk Fayuil in Upper Nile. The Aliab Dinka were incorporated into Yirol, which continued to be part of Upper Nile until 1936.

While the outlines of the province gradually took shape, the administrative details of the interior were sketched in as old garrison sites were reoccupied or new police and customs posts were established. A police post was created at Renk in 1901; another post was established at Abwong on the middle Sobat and a trading enclave was carved out at Gambela on the Baro in 1904; the old government post at Bor was revived in 1905; and a small seasonal boundary outpost was sited at Jokau on the Abyssinian border in 1906. In 1903 'Fashoda' disappeared from administrative nomen-

---

[1] *SIR* 60 (25 May to 31 December 1898): 10–11.
[2] Johnson (1982a).

clature when the town was renamed Kodok and the district was redesignated Upper Nile Province—'Fashoda' being thus returned to the Shilluk for their exclusive use as the name of their royal capital. The military headquarters were separated from the civil in 1910 when the army office was transferred to the main military camp across the river at Taufikia, Sir Samuel Baker's old camp. The two headquarters were re-amalgamated in the new provincial capital of Malakal in 1914, and Taufikia was ultimately abandoned altogether.[3]

The core of the province having been established by the time of the outbreak of World War One, there were still large stretches of administrative no-man's land to the east and west which were not fully incorporated until the 1920s. The Anuak and Murle, with whom the Nuer and Dinka had considerable dealings as well as conflicts, remained unadministered for nearly a decade and a half. The Anuak used their position astride the international boundary to arm themselves with modern rifles from Ethiopia, for use mainly against the Nuer. The Murle were less well armed, but their remoteness from any centre of imperial authority (Ethiopian or British) enabled them to raid the Dinka of Bor District with relative impunity.[4] In 1912 two patrols were sent out, one against the Adonga Anuak and the other against the Murle. The military results were ambiguous, but a fort was built at Akobo as the headquarters of a new Pibor River Province, created that same year, with boundaries extending from Nasir south to Uganda and east to Abyssinia. Another military outpost was established at Pibor Post to observe the Murle. This was the last example of direct military administration in the Sudan. Pibor River Province subsequently changed its name to Sobat-Pibor District (Military Administration), which in 1922 was contracted further to Pibor District (Military Administration). In 1925 it was handed over to the civil administration of Upper Nile Province, and Akobo became an inspectorate of the Eastern District, administering both the Anuak and Murle.

The Nuer living west of the Bahr el-Jebel were also unadministered by any province for the first two decades of the century. Nominally part of the Bahr el-Ghazal, the northernmost Nuer were briefly included in the Nuba Mountains Province, and in 1913 Upper Nile Province proposed to include all the Western Nuer in the civil administration of the Zeraf Valley District. Nothing came of the plan except for the establishment of a small outpost—nothing more than a steamer stop—at Hillet Nuer (Adok) in 1915, which reportedly upset the Nuer. No official made any further contact with the Nuer until 1921, when they were formally included in the

---

[3] GGR 1914: 65.
[4] Johnson (1986b); Garretson (1986).

administrative jurisdiction of Rumbek. In 1924 the Nuer and Dinka of the Nuba Mountains were transferred to the Eastern District, Bahr el-Ghazal, which now contained all Western Nuer. No permanent administrative headquarters was built in the district at this time, and the district commissioner toured aboard his floating office, the SGS *Kerreri*. In 1926 it was decided to amalgamate all the Nuer of the Sudan within one province, but the murder of the district commissioner, Captain Fergusson, in 1927, and the subsequent punitive operations in 1928 delayed the transfer of the Eastern District from Bahr el-Ghazal to Upper Nile until 1929.[5]

With this slow territorial advance of civil government in Upper Nile administration remained *de facto* in the hands of military officers for a very long time. The first commandants of the Fashoda garrison also served as administrators of Fashoda District. When the district became a province in 1903 the administrator became the governor, but he was still officer commanding the provincial garrison, and was entered as such in the yearly Egyptian Army lists. The duties of governor and commandant in the province were separated only in 1919, when the first civilian governor, K. C. P. Struvé was appointed, and Lt.-Colonel C. R. K. Bacon continued in his dual role as OC troops UNP and Sobat-Pibor District, and administrator Pibor District. Upper Nile Province was slightly in advance of the other southern provinces in establishing civilian control over the civil administration as the others retained their soldier-governors longer: Mongalla until 1920, Nuba Mountains until 1928 (soon after which it reverted to Kordofan), and Bahr al-Ghazal until 1934.

All of the province's first administrative officials were drawn from the officers (British, Egyptian and Sudanese) serving in the Sudanese battalions. Even when the Sudan Civil Service was formed in 1899, most of its members were short-term contract officers drawn from the Egyptian Army, where British officers, already on secondment from their home regiments, served from the rank of bimbashi (major) on up. The history of the Sudan Political Service (an informal distinction originally made between the civil administration and the technical departments) has been written almost exclusively in terms of its university graduate members. Prior to World War One the majority of men serving in the civil administration of the Sudan were soldiers. Even at the end of Willis' governorship in 1931 the number of 'contract' officers (most of whom were seconded or retired soldiers) outnumbered the permanent members of the political service in all three southern provinces by nearly two to one (see below, chapter 14). The military character of administration continued at the lower levels. The mamurs and sub-mamurs who served under British inspectors were all

---

[5] Johnson (1994: ch. 7).

originally 'native officers' (Egyptian and Sudanese) from the army. Even the civil police in the province prior to the 1920s were mainly recruited from discharged Sudanese soldiers. Given the itinerant role of the British inspector throughout the first two decades of Condominium rule, the character of 'government' was more often defined for the rural peoples of the Sudan by these native officers than by their British superiors. This was certainly the case in the Upper Nile where Dinka and Shilluk soldiers were posted to the districts as police officers and mamurs, where Nuer, Dinka and Shilluk policemen and soldiers served as government interpreters, and where Egyptian officers made a much earlier start in learning vernacular languages and studying local customs than their British colleagues.[6]

The province administration was constructed from the bottom up in the following way. At the most basic level army or police garrisons of varying size were found in outposts along the rivers or in the interior of the province. The police progressively took over the duties of the army in the rural areas until by 1926 (the year Willis took over as governor) the only two remaining army garrisons were at Malakal and Akobo. Both police and soldiers were 'Sudanese', a term which, even as late as the 1930s, denoted racial and class (rather than national) status. They were mainly of southern origin, but were all from the Arabic-speaking, Muslim, black, ex-slave class.[7] Some, indeed, came from one of the main language groups of the province (especially Shilluk or Dinka). In the remoter outposts the main government representative was usually the senior NCO in charge. Police posts in the rural areas were frequently occupied throughout the year, and even though garrisons were regularly rotated the police and their families often constituted a permanent colony of 'government' influence throughout the year, living in neat, orderly rows of huts, and paying visiting government officials public, and even ostentatious, respect. In the early 1920s the small inland post of Ayod was inhabited almost exclusively by the police and their families. Their commanding sergeant, Sabah al-Khair (literally 'Good Morning'), was used to being left in charge for months on end. He won the gratitude of the British inspector, who noted with relief that 'I could desert the post without misgivings as to the quiet continuance of its internal life', and described the exuberant reception given him on his return after several months' absence. 'My excellent Shawish Sabah El Khair welcomed me at the head of his small force

---

[6] Johnson (1986a; 1991a)
[7] Only the mounted police and a few foot police in towns such as Malakal were northern or 'Arab' policemen. For Willis' attitude towards the Sudanese ex-soldiers, see his comments under 'Labour' in ch. 14, below.

with the effusion usually bestowed on a triumphant potentate, and the reception generally accorded me by male and female populace alike was in its sheer enthusiasm very gratifying even if quite devoid of any reasonable cause.'[8]

Above the police NCOs were the mamurs, who resided in the most important outposts of the province and were in charge of their sub-districts (mamuriyya). These, too, were very frequently the most senior government officials on hand throughout the year. They were in charge of collecting taxes and fines and trying minor cases (all major cases being referred to the inspector).[9] Often they were in their posts during much of the rainy season, when British officials were either confined to provincial headquarters or were on leave. Mamurs also frequently reinforced their ties with the community by marrying locally, polygamous marriages being no obstacle for Muslims (though *de facto* polygamy did not always deter British officials from taking local wives, either).

By contrast, British inspectors supplied little continuity in the rural administration of Upper Nile Province until after World War One. Assigned to one district, and responsible for the administration of justice and the supervision of their mamurs, they were often required for duty in other districts. The career of Captain H. H. Wilson, while perhaps not typical, is certainly instructive. Having been lent by the army to the civil administration of Fashoda District in 1901, he served in various capacities until being appointed inspector at Renk in 1903–04. During those years he toured the Zeraf (twice in 1903), the Sobat (1904), and the Ethiopian frontier (1903, 1904), scarcely setting foot in his inspectorate the whole time. Even his successor soon abandoned Renk and was sent off to explore the Pibor River.[10] K. C. P. Struvé, the first civilian assigned to the province (1906–10) did spend much more time touring his own inspectorate of Dinka and Nuer from Khor Atar to the southern provincial boundary, but with no permanent district headquarters in which to reside he remained a tourist, not a resident. The senior inspector was, if anything, even more peripatetic than the inspector, acting as the governor's emissary at border negotiations or in meetings with important chiefs.

There was even less continuity during World War One when inspectors returned to the army, or were rapidly rotated in and out of civil and military duties. It is indicative of the distance which continued to separate the British officials from their Sudanese subjects in Upper Nile that it was only in 1922 that a British administrator is reported to have become

---

[8] 'Ben Assher' (1928: 152–4, 182, 257).
[9] Warburg (1971: 71–2).
[10] Comyn (1911: 71–9). Wilson's reports on his tours can be found in *SIR*.

conversant in a local language.[11] Even as late as 1926 Struvé mentions only two DCs by name as men 'who know the language' (see below, Appendix 1).

It was partly to close this distance that the principles of native administration, as suggested in the Milner Report, were formally adopted as policy at the end of 1921. Nomenclature changed with inspectors becoming district commissioners and assistant district commissioners (the distinction was mainly a matter of seniority). Senior inspectors were renamed deputy governors and, in Upper Nile at least, became more bound to the province headquarters and the office than their predecessors had been. In practice the district commissioner was to work directly with local native authorities in his district, the role of the mamur being reduced, and in many cases altogether eliminated. This was, in fact, one of the intentions of the reforms, to reduce the influence of Egypt in the administration of the Sudan. With the expulsion of the Egyptian Army from the Sudan following the mutinies of 1924, not only were Egyptian officers excluded from the administration, but even Sudanese mamurs were increasingly recruited from the civilian sector rather than from military ranks.[12]

The legacy of 1924 can be found in both Struvé's and Willis' papers published here. Struvé voices a continuing distrust of the mamur and the government interpreter, those obstacles interposing between the British rulers and their subjects, though this is qualified by sympathy for old Sudanese soldiers of proven loyalty (Appendix 1). Willis, as director of Intelligence in Khartoum in 1924, was in the thick of the mutiny (which cost him his job). Running right through his reports are expressions of the lingering fear of potential Egyptian and Muslim influence in this non-Muslim province. His highly prejudiced comments on the residual colonies of Arabic-speaking Sudanese in the towns (chapter 14) are revealing of his failings as director of Intelligence; for these were the class of people represented by the Sudanese officers in the White Flag League, men for whom Willis had no understanding, sympathy, or respect. More especially, the arguments he mustered against the Egyptian Irrigation Department's plans for the province (Appendix 2) must be read in the context of the Sudan government's long established political ambition to restrict Egyptian influence in the Sudan, if not remove it altogether.

The logic of native administration, which ultimately led in 1930 to the

---

[11] *SMIR* 341 (December 1922): 4. Both Wilson (1905) and Stigand (1923) produced vocabularies, but these are little more than word lists. Wilson's Dinka vocabulary was written with the close collaboration of a Dinka-speaking Egyptian mamur. Internal evidence suggests that Stigand's Nuer vocabulary was compiled through the aid of the Nuer-speaking Dinka interpreter at Nasir (Johnson (1993a: p.xx, n.3)).
[12] Daly (1986: 289–90, 354).

formulation of the Southern Policy of separate development between North and South, was that much routine administration could be done through local authorities, using customary structures and law, in so far as these could be co-opted by government.[13] Much of this had been implicit in administration from the start; everywhere 'legitimate' chiefs had been sought out, especially in the North, to replace the functionaries of the Mahdist regime, which was characterised as having usurped the authority of traditional rulers. Even in Upper Nile a code of Dinka 'law' had been produced in the province as early as 1906.[14] Much of the administrative activity throughout the Sudan in the 1920s and early 1930s was spent in regularizing what had gone on before by providing the legal and administrative framework for a devolution which was still to be closely supervised by British officials. But in the Upper Nile (as in many other parts of the South) the previous two decades had been spent in subordinating the very indigenous rulers which the new theory of native administration now required to be propped up. The autonomous power of local leaders had to be suppressed before it could be co-opted, and in practice the greater the potential power the more vigorous was the suppression.

One of the leaders who, institutionally at least, had potential power and who might therefore have posed a rival authority to the new government was the Shilluk king (*reth*). When Kitchener arrived at Fashoda he found that reth Kur Nyidok had already signed a treaty of alliance with Marchand's French. He had earlier been installed in office with the aid of the Mahdist government, who had killed the previous reth. Fortunately for the British there were other claimants to the kingship, and within a few years of occupying Fashoda they removed Kur and replaced him with one of his rivals—an action which from the perspective of 1930 already looked distinctly illegal and of doubtful political value (see below, chapter 4). It is true that the reth's power was often more symbolic than actual, but he did stand at the head of an indigenous hierarchy, and both his office and his person commanded a respect not often demanded by or accorded to Southern Sudanese leaders. So much so that the government's hand-chosen reth, Fadiet Kwathker, at first behaved in the company of government officials 'in a manner inexplicable to one accustomed to the deference shown elsewhere to the British officer.'[15] In order that his absolute subordination to the government be brought home

---

[13] This policy was explicitly stated as early as 1922 in 'Policy in the Southern Sudan', 1922 (note attached to S/Adm/2629 from civil secretary to governor, UNP), SRO UNP 66.E.4. See Daly (1986: 396–419).
[14] O'Sullivan (1910); it originally accompanied O'Sullivan, 'Lau Nuers', 13 March 1906, NRO Dakhlia I 112/13/87. Also Johnson (1986a).
[15] Comyn (1911: 79).

to him, and to the Shilluk, guide-lines were drafted which ordered that the reth reside in the province headquarters rather than the royal capital, and restricted his rights to travel independently of the governor, hear cases, or collect taxes. It was also decreed that 'when the Mek [king] is found with the Governor, the tribe should not salute the Mek, but salute the Governor, who represents the Govt'.[16]

The subordination of an entire people through the co-optation of their central ruling institutions was the exception rather than the rule in the Southern Sudan during the early twentieth century. Only the Shilluk and the Azande were organized into kingdoms. In Upper Nile Province most indigenous leaders wielded an authority which was derived as much from their personal abilities as from the institutions which they represented or were in the process of creating. Among the Dinka, the Nuer, the Anuak and the Murle individual leaders were frequently described as 'paramount chiefs' or 'meks' (kings) by administrators during the first two decades of the century, and became objects of government favour or disfavour as a result. Those who refused to be reconciled to the government's presence, or failed to respect its demand of submission, were removed—or at least the attempt was made to remove them. The application of force through a punitive patrol was not always the result of an active show of hostility by the targets of the patrol; nor did the display of force always have unambiguous results. Where an indigenous leader was identified as the source of disaffection, his death or capture and exile was usually one of the main objectives of the expedition. Even when successful this direct subjugation of local leaders did not lead inevitably to a more tractable attitude on the part of their people. Thus the districts described in this handbook saw more than a dozen punitive patrols in the first quarter-century of Anglo-Egyptian rule: starting with the Lou Nuer in 1902, the Atuot in 1907 and 1910, the Murle and Anuak in 1912, the Gaawar Nuer in 1913–14, the Lou Nuer and Atuot again in 1917–18, the Aliab Dinka in 1919, the Eastern Jikany Nuer in 1919–20, the Twic Dinka in 1921, the Dok and Nyuong Nuer in 1923 and 1925, and the Jagei Nuer in 1925. Three more campaigns against the Lou, Gaawar and Nyuong Nuer were completed before the 1920s drew to a close.

This catalogue of defiance earned the people of the province a reputation for innate truculence. It could as easily—and more accurately—have been taken as proof of the failure of administrators and their policies. After the inconclusive results of the province's first punitive patrol against the Nuer in 1902 the new governor, Major G. E. Matthews, initiated a policy of administrative penetration which attempted to involve his officers directly in the judicial life of the people they governed. Eschewing regular

---

[16] 'Duties of Shilluk Mek', n.d., SRO UNP 40-1.

demonstrations of force as much as possible, Matthews proposed that government could demand tribute only if it first provided some tangible benefit. By the end of his tenure he was even suggesting that the benefits government could offer were very few indeed: 'Government is a necessity, of course, if we are to occupy their country', he wrote of his subjects, 'but in some ways it is not an unmixed blessing, therefore one is probably not far wrong in saying that those tribes are best off which have as little of it as possible.'[17]

This turned out to be too radical an approach to administration and was abandoned by his immediate successors. Government by persuasion was replaced by government by demonstration. From 1910 until 1922 the main function of the British official in most of the province's districts was not so much to keep the peace and dispense justice, as to lead tribute collecting patrols. Increasing amounts of force had to be exerted to collect tribute in cattle. The army and even the Slavery Department mounted police often being brought in, so that by 1913 there was very little to distinguish these 'administrative patrols' from the punitive patrols of the military. By 1916 their futility was recognised by virtually all provincial administrators—most of whom were still military men—but having been introduced to establish government prestige, they were continued lest government prestige be further diminished by the abandonment of its only visible administrative activity. The opportunity to rebuild civil administration in the province came only after the end of the World War and the appointment of the first civilian governor, K. C. P. Struvé.[18]

Struvé had served under Matthews and rose to be his last senior inspector. He returned to Upper Nile Province as governor in 1919, in time to preside over an ambitious military expedition against the Eastern Jikany Nuer, deferred since the outbreak of World War One, and set in motion by his predecessor. As far as Struvé was concerned this campaign was the proof of the failure of the policy of administration by patrol. The expense of the operation, involving as it did the dispatch of gunboats, artillery and even the RAF, and following on so closely the campaigns of the previous three years against the Lou in Upper Nile Province and the Atuot and Aliab Dinka in Bahr al-Ghazal and Mongalla Provinces, also convinced Khartoum that a different administrative approach was needed. Given the caricature of Struvé's administration which Willis gives in this handbook, it is perhaps time that Struvé's reputation as an administrator is rehabilitated.

Towards the end of 1920, after the conclusion of the campaign against

---

[17] 'Annual Report. Upper Nile Province, 1908', *Reports on the Finance, Administration, and Condition of the Sudan, 1908* (Khartoum, 1909): 655.
[18] Johnson (1982a; 1986a; 1994: ch. 1).

the Eastern Jikany, Struvé explained to Khartoum his objections to the previous method of administration among the Nuer and Dinka. 'I do not consider that the old system of sending an inspector round the country with a small patrol collecting cattle during the dry season can be called administration at all, and I have no intention of reverting to that system.' The alternative to tribute patrols was to get the government away from the rivers, into the countryside to be seen, and to be seen governing. To this end he advocated the building of a road to the newly established post of Ayod among the Gaawar, and the use of Ford cars to bring a year's supplies to Ayod during the dry season so that it could function throughout the year. A track was cut through the bush to Ayod, but no Ford cars were allocated to the province for several years to come.[19] Civil administration among the Nuer began only with the appointment of two men—John Lee at Nasir and Percy Coriat at Ayod and Abwong—who quickly learned to speak Nuer and came to know their districts and their people well (see Struvé's comments on both men in Appendix 1). Despite Khartoum's refusal to allocate the resources needed to attempt Struvé's experiment with Ayod, Coriat spent three months of his first rainy season in 1922 there, an experiment in wet season administration of the Nuer which had never been tried before.[20]

The problem of taxation throughout the province took longer to reform. Struvé's first deputy governor, H. C. Jackson, slowly introduced a section-by-section tax for the Nuer, to replace the general tribal herd tax. Struvé discovered that he was obliged to continue sending police patrols to collect tax among the Nuer because the neighbouring Shilluk and Dinka, who already paid tax, would refuse to do so if taxation was not universal. By the end of his term of office in 1926 Struvé had managed to introduce a low percentage tax on Nuer and Dinka herds, and even reduced it for the Nuer and Dinka of Duk District. He was never happy with the taxation patrols, considering that they functioned 'to the detriment of any other form of administration', and he even proposed to suspend taxation of the Nuer throughout 1923 in order to allow administrative officials to concentrate on devising a sounder scheme of tribal organisation and administration.[21]

In 1922 Jackson proposed the creation of a series of Nuer 'parliaments', composed of a variety of important men. Struvé endorsed it as being an amplification of the accepted general policy of 'encouraging self-administration among the tribes through their chiefs', which he judged had already been a success among the Shilluk and a moderate success among

[19] Governor UNP to civil secretary, 12 Sept. 1920, SRO UNP SCR 14.A.5.
[20] Coriat (1993: 6–11); Johnson (1993a: pp.xxv–xxviii).
[21] K. C. P. Struvé to civil secretary, 12 March 1922; K. C. P. Struvé to civil secretary, 2 Dec. 1922; 'Notes of a Meeting held at Akobo', 2 March 1926, all in NRO Civsec 1/2/6.

the northern Dinka. But the civil secretary gave Struvé little leeway to devise a structure of administration for the Nuer in line with the general policy, and turned down his request to devote 1923 to devising an ideal administration in lieu of tribute collecting.[22] The creation of a system of administration based on tribal leaders thus proceeded much more slowly than Struvé wanted. Khartoum's financial strictures hampered him throughout his administration, slowing the pace of reform, and giving the impression (at least to some of his subordinates) of a tired conservatism dominating the governor's office.[23] Despite the restraining hand of Khartoum some progress was made. By 1923 Coriat and Lee had done enough preliminary work in their districts to begin organising chiefs into specific sectional courts. In 1926 the travelling chiefs' court was introduced among the Lou Nuer and proved a popular success. Even though money was not forthcoming for the chiefs' police who were to support the chiefs' courts, Coriat had begun the informal recruiting of such a force almost as soon as he arrived in his district.[24]

Fiscal restraint came to the support of administrative theory in one respect, that of internal security. The civil government at Khartoum wanted no more expensive punitive campaigns, nor policies which would lead to them. Upper Nile Province's long border with Ethiopia meant that nearly anyone in the province who wanted could obtain a relatively modern rifle and a supply of ammunition. The Anuak of Akwei-wo-Cam had shown what they could do with their rifles in 1912 when in one engagement they killed 2 British officers, 3 Egyptian officers and 42 soldiers (including an entire detachment of mounted infantry).[25] The army, which until 1925 administered much of this border, was understandably worried about the continuing arms trade between Ethiopia and the Upper Nile. Struvé's assessment of the potential danger presented by the growing circulation

---

[22] H. C. Jackson to governor Malakal, 24 Nov. 1922; Struvé to civil secretary, 2 Dec. 1922; civil secretary to governor Malakal, 18 Dec. 1922, all in NRO Civsec 1/2/6.

[23] 'Ben Assher' (1928: 83); Coriat to his wife, 8 Jan. 1927 and 2 March 1927, Coriat MSS, Rhodes House, MSS Afr. s 1684. Jackson later claimed that he was transferred out of UNP because of his dispute with Struvé over the tribute collection policy (Jackson to Butts, 15 Nov. 1927, NRO Civsec 5/3/10), but the contemporary record clearly shows that Struvé and Jackson were in fundamental agreement on this point. Their disagreements appear to have been entirely personal. Jackson was both excitable and suspicious, while Struvé was formal and reserved. Jackson (a civilian) had managed to get himself attached to the military intelligence office in Egypt during the war, receiving three campaign ribbons which he wore every chance he got; thus earning Struvé's rebuke for having departed for war 'in a cloud of petty glory', leaving the burdens of the day to his colleagues. ('Ben Assher' (1928: 185–6)).

[24] Johnson (1993a: p.xxviii–xxix).

[25] SIR 212 (March 1912): 3. It was later said that this was the highest loss of Anglo-Egyptian troops in battle since Omdurman. As late as 1940, when it was proposed to mark the site of this battle with a simple monument, the district commissioner protested against reminding the Anuak of 'their success against the Government' (Upper Nile Province Diary (June 1939), SRO BD 57.C.1; DC Pibor District to governor UNP, 21 April 1940, SRO Pibor 2/16/51).

of arms was that the presence of firearms did not *in itself* constitute a major threat to security; rather any rising would come about only through discontent over some other issue. It was the business of civil administration to make sure that such discontent did not materialize.[26] In this he was in agreement with his immediate predecessor, Major Stigand, who had made the same point ten years earlier.[27] He thus dismissed the army's fears as exaggerated and resisted the urging of the district commissioner of Duk District, Major Wyld, to systematically disarm the Nuer (see Appendix 1). As a former inspector in the area who had drawn the boundary which still divided the Nuer of Ayod from the Dinka of Duk, he had an entirely pragmatic approach to Nuer-Dinka arguments, preferring to set up the mechanism by which disputes could be settled, rather than allowing the government to be drawn in on one side or the other, as it had been before the war.

Struvé thus had many solid achievements to his credit when he retired in the summer of 1926. He had begun the transformation from administration by patrol to administration through groups of chiefs; under him his district commissioners spent more time travelling in their districts getting to know their people, and had made systematic contact with the most important local leaders (especially the Nuer prophets Guek Ngundeng and Dual Diu); taxation was in the process of being reformed, and even reduced; the last military district in the country was finally incorporated into the civil administration; the Dinka of Duk District were transferred to the province, making the settlement of cross-border disputes much easier; and above all, none of Struvé's policies had provoked determined resistance or an armed uprising anywhere in his province.

The news that his successor was to be C. A. Willis came as a shock to Struvé. Willis was the former director of the Intelligence Department who had been removed from this position partly because of the events of the 1924 Mutiny in Khartoum, but mainly because of a general dissatisfaction with the way he ran his department.[28] After a short spell writing a report on slavery in the Sudan, Willis was sent to Upper Nile Province as the most suitably distant post from Khartoum in which to await his scheduled retirement. Struvé considered Willis to be the antithesis of all that he had stood for in civil administration, and he may have interpreted the appointment as criticism of his own policy and method.[29] Uncharacteristically for so a reserved man, Struvé left Willis detailed notes on the province with warnings about specific potential problems and advice on

---

[26] K. C. P. Struvé to civil secretary, 17 May 1926, NRO Civsec 1/2/6.
[27] C. H. Stigand, 'Report on Sobat Valley Nuers', May 1916, NRO UNP 1/12/101.
[28] Daly (1986: 276–8, 329–32).
[29] Adrian Struvé, personal communication.

how to handle them: especially on matters concerning the Nuer-Dinka border, the proliferation of firearms, and the use of the police (Appendix 1). It is against this advice that Willis' own actions as governor should be judged. Having thus done all he could do to preserve his gains, Struvé left the province, and the Sudan, a deeply disappointed, almost distraught man.

THE ADMINISTRATION OF GOVERNOR WILLIS, 1926–31

The contrast in style and method between Struvé and Willis could scarcely have been greater. Whereas Struvé, an intensely private man, left very little record of his administration, Willis wrote volumes. Where Struvé, perhaps overburdened by Khartoum's constraints, worked gradually to build up the internal structures of native administration, Willis was an interventionist. While Struvé was content to give his district commissioners considerable leeway, Willis was determined to set his own seal on the administration of his province.

The change in style brought some immediate benefits. Finance for the province had always been a problem. Governor Matthews' plans had been thwarted because of the low priority of his province in Khartoum's budget. Struvé, too had been disappointed in this respect. Willis understood the ways of Khartoum enough to do some hard bargaining, and his initial horse-trading was promising. Struvé, as outgoing governor, proposed that the army garrison at Akobo could be replaced by police, but Willis raised objections until Khartoum agreed to provide money both for the police needed to replace the army, and a new road to Akobo on which the army and police could move.[30] This seemed to justify one district commissioner's anticipation that Willis 'is either clever enough or popular enough to get Khartoum to agree in spirit and money, money underlined' to his new proposals.[31] The anticipation was ultimately disappointed: Willis was certainly not popular. He succeeded in getting some money for road-building and financing chiefs' courts and chiefs' police (whose ultimate justification was that they would replace province police in the rural areas and thus *reduce* expenditure). A more ambitious bid for money to finance expanded road-building, increased administrative staff, and increased central control within the province was turned down by Khartoum early

[30] 'Minutes of meeting in Kaid el 'Amm's Office', 24 Jan. 1927; C. A. Willis to Civil Secretary, 28 May 1927, both in NRO Civsec 1/2/6.
[31] Coriat to Kathleen, 8 Jan. 1927, Coriat MSS, Rhodes House, MSS Afr. s 1684.

in Willis' administration, in a series of decisions between April and June 1927.[32] This forced Willis into new arguments for finance: one being the security threat allegedly posed by the Nuer, and the other being the other type of threat posed by the Egyptian Irrigation Department's proposals for the province (see Appendix 2), to which we will return later.

Willis' personal style of dealing with his subordinates provoked mixed reactions. Coriat was at first enthusiastic about both the new governor and his wife. This feeling changed when Coriat's own wife came to the province and was subjected to the full force of Willis' social snobbery.[33] Christopher Tracey, who was district commissioner Renk when Willis arrived (see Appendix 1), also had mixed feelings about Willis, whom he later described as a disappointed man on leaving Khartoum. 'He blundered about in the unfamiliar world of the Upper Nile: and blamed me for allowing the brother of the Mamour Melut to set up in trade there. Such a thing showed no political sense—until I quoted his Khartoum letter ordaining the arrangement—which I had obeyed. He had the grace in reply to my letter by sending me a telegram saying "You win—Chunky". I liked him—a cheerful somewhat bibulous extrovert.'[34] Captain V. H. Fergusson, the district commissioner of the Eastern Province, Bahr el-Ghazal, which was scheduled for transfer to Upper Nile in 1928, had a more unsettling confrontation. Having read Fergusson's report on his district Willis stated bluntly that he did not believe a word of it. His subsequent criticisms appeared to Fergusson as a flood of words without lucid explanation. Following Coriat's visit to the district and his favourable report Willis then 'gave in all along the line and agreed to adopt [Fergusson's] methods, but wanted no advice and was quite sure that he knew exactly how to set about it'[35] By the end of 1928, in the middle of the operations against the Nuer, another district commissioner, H. G. Wedderburn-Maxwell, applied for a transfer to another province, stating that he felt unable to maintain an 'attitude of loyalty and confidence towards his Governor', a serious breakdown in working relations considering Wedderburn-Maxwell's growing importance in Nuer administration at that time.[36] Willis' well-known

---

[32] Collins (1983: 120–3); Daly (1986: 400–1).
[33] Johnson (1993a: p.xxxvii).
[34] Christopher Tracey to the editor, 11 Aug. 1978.
[35] Fergusson (1930: 282–6)).
[36] Governor to civil secretary, 18 Dec. 1928, NRO Civsec 5/3/12. Wedderburn-Maxwell had his own reputation for speaking out of turn, and was rebuked by the civil secretary for it. Shortly before his request for a transfer Willis wrote, '. . . had to go & see Maxwell, & incidentally try & restrain him from being so impetuous in speech, which was a situation not without its humours for me. However I am sorry to say, I wasn't very effective, as he promptly went off the deep end again.' (Willis to 'D', 2 Dec. 1928, SAD 209/12). Willis put Wedderburn-Maxwell's request down to strain, and the transfer was not processed.

ability to alienate those around him continued throughout his governorship, especially as the province capital began to fill up with district commissioners' young wives. These he almost invariably disapproved of and kept a running commentary on their failings in his letters home to his sister: one committed the sin of revoking at bridge, and another was 'thoroughly unsound on "serviettes"—you know the type well. . .'[37]

The question of personality aside, greater problems arose from his approach to administration. As director of Intelligence he had involved himself in many aspects of native administration, a role more properly belonging to the civil secretary. His attempted interference in provincial affairs angered many governors, and his method of gathering and assessing information was criticised in the Ewart report, which stated:

> The Intelligence Department amasses a vast amount of inchoate detail, which, tested by the experience of the Director enables the latter to form opinions upon the problem as a whole. The value of such opinions would be greatly enhanced if their information had been influenced by a wider and more general knowledge of the subject, and by the informed views of equally experienced Provincial officials.[38]

Willis was to apply much the same method of judgement as governor of Upper Nile, especially in the formulation of a policy of Nuer administration. Given Ewart's criticisms of his failure to make use of the 'views of equally experienced Provincial officials', it is notable that in the end Willis relied relatively little on the judgements of his Nuer district commissioners. He tested what they reported against his own (extremely limited) understanding of Nuer customs and leadership. To a very large extent he favoured the proposals of Major Wyld, whose Dinka district bordered the Nuer. As many Nuer leaders along the border included large numbers of Dinka among their followers, Wyld saw his main task as creating a Dinka administrative structure opposed to and in competition with that of the Nuer. To this end he was an early advocate of disarming the Nuer and repatriating the Dinka to live under his chiefs. This is one reason why Struvé cautioned Willis that Wyld might be 'too prone to force the pace' (Appendix 1). With Willis he got a more sympathetic hearing, and Wyld's own proposals ultimately formed the basis for Willis' 'Nuer Settlement' plans.

The campaigns against the Lou and Gaawar, the suppression of their

---

[37] Willis letters, SAD 209/13.
[38] 'Report of Mr. J. M. Ewart, Indian Police, on the Organisation of Public Security Intelligence in the Sudan, 8 June'. This report was widely distributed, and a copy was sent to Malakal (where I first consulted it in in 1975). Its specific criticisms of Willis would have only confirmed Struvé's dismay.

prophets, and the segregation of the Nuer from the Dinka were the events which defined Willis' term as governor: he began planning the removal of the Lou prophet Guek Ngundeng as early as 1927, and the removal of all Dinka living among the Nuer was still not complete by the time he left the province in 1931. As these events have been described in detail elsewhere,[39] only an outline is given here.

Under Struvé the province administration went to some length to contact the most influential religious leaders among the Nuer—the prophets—and incorporated them into the embryonic structure of native administration. Jackson visited Guek Ngundeng of the Lou and Coriat did much to secure the personal goodwill of Dual Diu among the Gaawar. In the end Guek remained shy of the government and unwilling to play an active role within the new hierarchy of chiefs, while Dual was a whole-hearted participant and was confirmed as paramount chief of the Bar-Gaawar primary division. It was through such contacts that Struvé managed to introduce more settled administration among the Lou and Gaawar and reduce tensions between the Nuer and Dinka. Prophets, along with all other 'kujurs' (the colloquial Arabic equivalent of 'witch-doctor') fell under the Sudan government's general suspicion of inspired religious figures.[40] The local accommodation of prophets was seen as both temporary and expedient, but it was flexible enough to treat favourably any 'kujur' who willingly submitted to government authority, and it allowed the administration to advance beyond its automatic paranoia concerning prophets.

Within a year of arriving in the province Willis reverted to the pre-war hostility to 'kujurs'. In June 1927 he declared that the Lou were the model of all the Nuer and the most advanced in native administration. Also in June the last of three of his proposals for expanded programmes and additional funding was turned down by Khartoum. By August he discovered that the security of the province and the future of its administration was under threat from the intransigence of the Lou Nuer 'kujurs' (see below, chapter 1). To combat this threat he required the central government to commit some of the resources to his province it had only just refused. Because the application was made under the argument of security, it could scarcely be turned down.

The evidence of this prophetic conspiracy rested on the reaction of Guek Ngundeng to the plans to use Nuer labour to construct a motor road through Lou Nuer territory—roads being the keystone of Willis' administrative policy. The labour gangs were to be organized by the chiefs, who

---

[39] Coriat (1993: 99–152); Johnson (1994: chs 5 and 6).
[40] Johnson (1981; 1994: ch. 1).

had only recently been organized into courts. The Nuer in general were not enthusiastic about this new corvée, but the chiefs all owed what new powers they possessed to the recognition and support of the government, and were reluctant to oppose a programme which the government was determined to implement. Guek was urged by many persons—some chiefs among them—to voice their objections to road-building. This he did in a meeting with Coriat in June. Coriat then left the province on home leave, and Wyld provided Willis with information from his Dinka sources that Guek was planning to oppose the road by force. In this way Guek's reluctance was translated into rebellion, a rebellion which Willis seems to have welcomed, seeing in it a chance to reinforce native administration with an unmistakable demonstration of government power.[41] Military preparations were well underway by the time Coriat returned from leave and he witnessed some of the Nuer's own preparations for the conflict they knew was to come. The army and the RAF were used to attack Guek's village, the Lou dispersed into the countryside, and the army conducted several sweeps to round up fugitives. These sweeps were extended to the Gaawar, including Dual Diu, who had remained loyal up to this time. In response Dual raised a rebellion, attacking the government and its Dinka allies in the latter half of 1928. Both the major prophets (and a number of minor ones) remained at large for several months.

To bring this situation to an end Willis proposed the 'Nuer Settlement', whereby the Lou and Gaawar would be ordered to concentrate in small accessible areas during the dry season of 1929, with all those found outside the concentration areas being treated as in rebellion and attacked. A no-man's land would be created between the Dinka and the Nuer and all Dinka extracted from the Nuer area and returned to Wyld's chiefs. Both Nuer and Dinka would be further organized under the authority of government chiefs, and some attempt would be made to introduce veterinary and health services, as well as new economic activity, to induce the Nuer to settle down. Willis was to get his administrative programme very nearly fully funded after all. Guek was killed in battle in 1929, Dual Diu was captured in 1930, and the Nuer Settlement was declared a success. It was on the results of the Nuer Settlement that native administration for a large part of the Nuer and Dinka was founded.

---

[41] 'Extract from a letter from Mr. Willis . . . to [the governor-general] Sir John Maffey', NRO Civsec 5/2/10.

An Historical Overview

THE ETHNOGRAPHY OF NATIVE ADMINISTRATION: THE GOVERNOR'S VIEW

Willis' initial comments on native administration in Upper Nile Province are found in his August 1927 letter to Khartoum (chapter 1) and do not deviate from the broad principles agreed upon and enunciated by government since the Milner Report. He assumed, however, that there was an office of 'chief' among the Nuer which had been undermined or usurped by the 'kujurs' (an assumption subsequently exploded by Evans-Pritchard's research). Once the confrontation which he initiated with the Nuer gathered pace, he elaborated on this theme in a number of reports, attempting to prove just how far the 'kujur' had transgressed their proper inspirational bounds—though his arguments were received with growing scepticism by Khartoum, who feared the consequences of an ill-thought out general anti-kujur crusade.[42] The suppression of 'kujurs', however, did not lead to a re-emergence of chiefs from the background, and Willis began to qualify his earlier statements about the existence of traditional chiefs. By 1928 he was beginning to admit that the idea of an executive chief was itself imported by government. 'It is the object of the Government to develop a native administration', he declared, 'the idea of which is inevitably preconceived from the more organised and less individualistic peoples both North and South. In fact it wants a Chief who can give an order on any subject and ensure its execution, with an organisation of Sub-Chiefs etc. ultimately spreading over the whole populace.'[43]

By 1929 he was frankly advocating invention, but still in the name of custom. His policy in the Upper Nile, he explained to the civil secretary 'is the growth of native administration by the development of tribal institutions and the strengthening of tribal customs and law, and in general to build up on native foundations.' He concluded, without apparently recognizing a contradiction, that 'I am . . . convinced that the building up of a native administration on the foundations of tribal custom and organization is the only sound method of tackling these tribes, even to the point of inventing an organization where, as with the Dinka, they have lost their own.'[44]

Willis was not unique in thus blending tradition with invention, either in the Sudan or in other parts of British Africa.[45] His comments do throw

---

[42] Johnson (1985a).
[43] C. Armine Willis, governor UNP, 20 April 1928, Nasir END 1.F/1&2 vol i.
[44] Governor, UNP to civil secretary, 'Nuer Policy', 18 Feb. 1929, NRO UNP 1/44/329.
[45] Terence Ranger, 'The Invention of Tradition in Colonial Africa', in Eric Hobsbawm and Terence Ranger (eds), *The Invention of Tradition* (Cambridge, 1983).

some light on the process by which the government defined, or redefined, legitimate authority in the structures it was creating. Willis professed to want executive chiefs, but he was inconsistent about how much autonomous power they were allowed to wield. In 1927 he praised the Western Nuer chiefs for their establishment of 'a tribal discipline that surpasses anything to be found elsewhere among the Nuer' (chapter 1), but in 1931 he complained that these same chiefs were too powerful and needed to be curbed (chapter 11).

In practice Willis' vision of tribal societies was one of ever-refined particularities. Each tribe was to have its own tribal territory: Nuer were to live with Nuer and Dinka with Dinka, rather than mix together. They were to be ruled by their own chiefs, whether invented, as with some of the Dinka, or reduced in power, as with some of the Nuer. They were also to be governed according to their own custom which, whether it was rediscovered or reinvented, was to be free of contamination from outside sources. The Shilluk, Dinka and Nuer were each to have their own tribal religion, uninfluenced by each other, or by any other competing source of inspiration. Tribal custom ceased to be natural once it crossed tribal boundaries and inevitably became perverted and subversive once it was transported.[46]

Thus administration was to proceed on ethnographic lines, with administrators learning vernacular languages and investigating local customs and institutions. In fact there was often a tension between the practising administrator and the professional anthropologist. The former was not always convincing, even to his colleagues, when pronouncing on the behaviour of primitive man, especially if that behaviour too conveniently met the requirements of administrative theory or practice. When Willis represented the Nuer 'kujurs' as anti-social, revolutionary charlatans, he did so to support his claim that he needed greater autonomy of power from Khartoum in order to meet this disruptive threat within his own province. His marshalling of ethnographic data in support of his administrative bid prompted Harold MacMichael, the civil secretary, to minute to the governor general:

> I cannot controvert the Governor's facts, but neither can I admit that I am convinced we have got to the bottom of the matter. A whole class of tricksters does not appear in a primitive society, subsist upon 'a combination of ventriloquy sleight of hand & charlatanism' and obtain all the power & respect which these 'kujurs' have, unless there is something in the beliefs of the people which, so to speak, gives them a warrant.
>
> I believe the fact of the matter is that to obtain an understanding of the

---

[46] Johnson (1979; 1985a; 1994: ch. 1).

recesses of the savage mind one must either be a savage or a very highly trained anthropologist of wide technical knowledge on the one hand and of a broad human sympathy on the other. At present we fall between the two stools.[47]

It fell to Evans-Pritchard to provide both the wide technical knowledge and the broad human sympathy, and he was sent—very unwillingly—to the Upper Nile in 1930 to begin his research into Nuer political and social organization. Willis at first thought Evans-Pritchard 'a knowledgeable sort of man' when the two had met briefly in Renk in 1927,[48] but that was before his own problems with the Nuer. He certainly resented having Evans-Pritchard inflicted on his province and did much to impede his progress.[49] Willis had excluded anthropological research from his 1928 proposals; such investigations were part of an administrator's normal duties and did not need a technical expert. In some ways this handbook, being a presentation of *his* experts in the field, was a rebuttal of Khartoum's decision to send Evans-Pritchard to his province to carry out redundant investigations.

Willis also had little time for missionaries, those other competitors for expert knowledge of the native. He was particularly critical of the Australian and American missionaries. As early as 1926 he noted that the latter 'need to be herded and watched.'[50] His main complaint was that they had made little progress in their language work, and produced students who were of very little use to the government. For those who may find in Willis' strictures against Muslim influence evidence of a Christian design on the Sudan, the dismissiveness of Willis' official pronouncements on the missionaries, and the hostility of his private comments will come as a surprise. Willis may have given his expression freer reign than many other administrators, but again he was not altogether untypical. There was always an uneasy relationship between the Sudan government and the missions.[51] Once native administration became the foundation of local

---

[47] Minute page, NRO Civsec 36/2/4.
[48] 'Renk. January 21st. 1927', SAD 212/9/84.
[49] Johnson (1982b).
[50] Willis, 'Missions', 1926, SAD 212/9. Willis had a particularly strong loathing for America and Americans. Describing one missionary at Doleib Hill he wrote, 'he ... has fallen under the spirit of the Middle West which is so admirably and cleverly described in Main Street and Babbitt, books which I read with appreciation of their skill and horror of their facts.' ('Christian Missions in the Upper Nile Province', June 1927, NRO UNP 1/14/119). Of America in general he declared, 'The U.S.A. is a terrible place, the general population is grossly ignorant, politically dead & morally weak—they have the only merit, it if isn't a serious demerit, of enormous numbers—& they ought to be a standing example of the horrors of democracy.' (Willis to 'D', 22 Feb. 1929, SAD 209/13).
[51] Sanderson and Sanderson (1981).

government, Christianity came to be seen by many administrators as a disruptive force of 'detribalisation'. In Upper Nile for many years after Willis left all that the majority of British administrators wanted were a few natives literate *in their own languages* to assist in keeping records for the chiefs. Anything more than that was strictly unnecessary.

Willis' version of native administration was not continued by his successor, A. G. Pawson, who eventually reversed the policy of repatriating the Dinka living among the Lou and Gaawar to one Dinka district. The policy did not work as many Dinka refused to stay in their new district under their new chiefs.[52] Pawson relaxed the no-man's land, and by the time he left the province himself in 1934 he advised against the single tribe district, advocating instead including more than one tribe in a district 'as it improves the relations between them and enlarges the outlook of the individual administrator.'[53] Struvé would have agreed.

THE ETHNOGRAPHY OF NATIVE ADMINISTRATION: THE DISTRICT NOTES

The ethnographic approach to administration required that rural administration be conducted in a vernacular language, rather than English or Arabic. Acquisition of vernacular languages proceeded slowly. Of the twelve district commissioners providing reports for this handbook over half had some command of a vernacular language: Alban (Nuer), Cann (Shilluk), Coriat (Nuer), Tiernay (Nuer), Tunnicliffe (Anuak), Wedderburn-Maxwell (Nuer) and Wyld (Dinka). Hebbert appears to have spoken Dinka, and Armstrong was learning Nuer. Cann, Wyld, Coriat, and Armstrong all had left the province by the end of 1931, and Hebbert and Tiernay left in 1932. Of these men only Coriat's replacement (Captain H. A. Romilly) already spoke the main language of his district upon his appointment (having previously served as ADC under Alban and Coriat).

It will be clear from reading the district chapters here that by 1931 there still was no common administrative vocabulary to describe indigenous political systems in the Southern Sudan. The wide variety of political organizations, each derived from specific historical experience, inhibited such generalizations; though the word 'chief' certainly did duty for a number of different figures of authority. Experience gained in one part of the province could only with difficulty be applied to another part. The majority of the peoples of Upper Nile belong to the Western Nilotic

---

[52] Johnson (1982*a*).
[53] 'Handing Over Notes by Mr. A. G. Pawson, Governor Upper Nile', NRO Civsec 57/2/9.

language family: the Shilluk, Anuak and Meban speak Lwoo languages (related to the Acoli and Luo of East Africa), while the Dinka, Nuer and Atuot speak very closely related (though distinct) languages within the broader family. Even among the Dinka, however, there are wide dialectical variations, and the vernacular of the Bor Dinka is very different from that of the Dinka of Bahr el-Ghazal or even northern Upper Nile. Along the Ethiopian frontier, bordering the Nuer, Anuak and Meban, are remnants of a much earlier and older language family, the Koman-speaking peoples, which include the Koma and Uduk. Further south along that frontier the Murle (neighbours to the Anuak, Nuer and Dinka) represent one of the Surma languages, related to the Didinga and Larim further south in Equatoria, and to the Mursi, Bodi and Kwegu of southwest Ethiopia. But language affinity does not bring with it similarities in political or social organization. The Meban are more like the other 'Burun' peoples (Koma and Uduk), with whom they are generally classed, than the Shilluk, whose language is close to theirs. The Shilluk and the Anuak share many social values with the Nuer and the Dinka, but their political systems are quite different.

The Shilluk, as indicated above, were the only people to present the type of territorial kingdom and dynastic politics which the British could easily comprehend, not only from their own historical experience, but from their imperial experience elsewhere. With the only reigning 'king' left in the Sudan, the Shilluk provided the British with a territory which seemed to fit all the requirements for indirect rule. Out of deference to the reth's rank the district commissioner was referred to by the exalted title of 'resident', more in keeping with the nomenclature of the Indian princely states and northern Nigerian amirates (it was a style which did not survive the 1930s). The Shilluk kingdom was already divided into territorial political sub-units, whose leaders played a significant role in the selection and support of the king. In fact the Shilluk had long experience of succession disputes becoming civil wars between the northern and southern halves of the kingdom, a political opposition which is reenacted in the rites of installation of each new king. The Anuak also appeared to have a similar institution of kingship, but it was a mobile, circulating kingship which lacked a kingdom. Among the Anuak there are two tiers of authority: that of the headman (*kwaaro*), who reigns over a village or collection of villages; and that of the prince (*nyieya*) whose possession of the emblems of nobility entitles him to be king. Yet in the early part of this century the Anuak appeared to have no use for entrenched leaders: headmen were often ousted from their villages and replaced by other contenders through regular 'village revolutions'; and until the proliferation of firearms made the creation of private armies among nobles a possibility, the royal emblems circulated from prince to prince so frequently that kingship was largely symbolic. By 1930 the British were still struggling to produce a fixed set of rulers among the Anuak through which some form of administrative continuity could be developed; yet such continuity had so far eluded them.[54]

For all their unpredictability the Anuak still appeared to be far more organized than the Murle, their neighbours living between the Khor Geni and the Boma Plateau. The Murle of the Pibor river and its tributaries had divided themselves into four territorial 'drumships', each represented by a sacred drum, whose guardians ('drum chiefs' or 'red' chiefs) came from specific clans, to which other clans attached themselves. The drum chiefs certainly had a spiritual importance, but they scarcely wielded the executive authority the British were looking for. Unlike the other peoples of the province, whose chiefs were being given administrative authority through judicial duties in the newly created chiefs' courts, the Murle scarcely saw the need for courts in 1931; therefore they scarcely saw the need for administrative chiefs. The principles of Murle territorial and political organization were only vaguely appreciated by administrators at this time. It was not until the 1940s, when two district commissioners (B. A. Lewis and R. E. Lythe) learned the Murle language that indigenous terminology and concepts began to appear in administrative writings.[55]

The Dinka of Upper Nile Province in 1931 also presented wide contrasts. The northern Dinka had a recent history of flight, subjugation and the involvement of external governments in internal disputes. It is for this reason that they are described here as a people somewhat arbitrarily divided into territorial sections, with no families of 'hereditary' chiefs having clear and undisputed rights to leadership. Further south in Bor District the Dinka there had also experienced a history of dispersal, which gave the administration the opportunity to attempt to fashion a number of clearly defined 'tribes' out of disparate groups. Here 'chiefs' were also in the process of being created as the focal point for the new tribes. It is only across the river in Yirol that the description of 'tribal groups', as a somewhat fluid combination of groups of agnatic kin, bears any resemblance to the now classic ethnographic description of Dinka political organization.[56] Here the figures the British were able to make use of as administrative chiefs were the 'spear-masters' (or 'masters of the fishing spear'); men of spiritual authority who came from specific families around which other groups attached themselves. That the Dinka of Yirol, alone of those Dinka

---

[54] For Shilluk see Hofmayr (1925), Pumphrey (1941), Howell (1952a); for Anuak see Evans-Pritchard (1940c: ch 3), Lienhardt (1955 & 1957–58).
[55] For Murle see Lewis (1972: ch 4).
[56] Lienhardt (1958).

described in the district chapters, are familiar to us should come as no surprise; for the main ethnographic presentation of the Dinka is derived from the western Dinka of the Bahr el-Ghazal, a point often overlooked in anthropological commentary. The district chapters in this handbook both describe and document some of the essential differences (as well as some of the many similarities) between the three main groupings of northern, southern and western Dinka.

It is in the four chapters on the Nuer districts where, surprisingly, we find the least agreement in the description of indigenous political organization. In Nasir we find one Nuer 'tribe' described as consisting of three divisions. In Abwong the Lou Nuer are said to consist of two sections, divided into 'shyengs' and 'sub-shyengs'. In the Zeraf Valley the Lak, Thiang and Gaawar are described as 'clans', whereas in Western Nuer the terminology alternates between 'clan', 'sub-tribe' and 'tribe'. There are also some hints at the wide variety of authorities covered by the term 'chief'. Evans-Pritchard was to bring a scholarly precision to this administrative muddle in his earliest articles on the Nuer published in *Sudan Notes and Records*.[57] He distinguished between the terminology of kinship and the terminology of politics (though in fact the Nuer often used the word *cieng* to denote either lineage or territorial affiliation). The word 'clan' was relegated to the discourse of kinship, whereas 'tribe' defined a political unit, the largest unit which combined for offence or defence. Evans-Pritchard also distinguished between spiritual and social leaders, and tried to identify the role each had, or could, play in political organization. The hereditary spiritual leaders included the earth-master (*kuaar muon*), who Evans-Pritchard termed the leopard-skin chief or priest, and the cattle-master or man of cattle (*wut ghok*). The former mediated in cases of homicides and feuds, while the latter organized the seasonal movements of cattle. In addition to these were various non-spiritual leaders, the 'bulls of the cattle camp' (*tut wec*) who represented the interests of the sub-sections and sections. Administrators were to adopt Evans-Pritchard's terminology (though not always his analysis of Nuer politics) with gratitude. Throughout the 1930s and 1940s there was a conscious effort to build up a hierarchy of chiefs from among the tut wec rather than the masters. Evans-Pritchard's terminology for the Nuer lineage system was also applied, perhaps with less justification, to the Shilluk and Murle.

Native Administration after 1931 was built up gradually, and claimed its greatest achievements in those districts where the district commissioner resided longest. Administrators attempted to integrate themselves in the social as well as judicial life of the people. Each was given his own

[57] Evans-Pritchard (1933–5).

honorific 'ox-name', describing the colours and horn formation of their special name-ox presented to him by the chiefs of his district. Many married local women (contrary to the public image of the Sudan Political Service as composed almost exclusively of chaste boy scouts): in fact Captain Alban used to regularly advise new arrivals that the best and quickest way to become fluent in Nuer was to marry a Nuer girl from a respectable family. Captain Alban's manner of administration was given this approving description in 1933 by governor Pawson, Willis' immediate successor:

> Captain Alban has his own methods of dealing with these people and they appear to be most successful—his servants, grooms, dairy men and even his official interpreter are all ordinary Nuer dressed (or rather undressed) in the tribal beads etc. His chukker-out a powerful young Nuer with a red mane and cheerful disposition gives him an occasional half hour alone, but normally he is surrounded by Nuer always ready to crack a jest and greatly appreciative of his ready wit.[58]

Elsewhere the concentration on stripping administration back to the bare essentials was also seen to have a positive effect in providing administrators with knowledge of 'true native methods'. In Yirol there was a steady effort to abandon 'the so-called native customs' introduced in the recent past by government clerks and other agents brought in from outside the district as advisers to the courts. Patient investigative work by the district commissioner in Akobo eventually led to the restoration in 1934 of some of the Anuak royal relics, hidden by one of the absconding kings since 1927; thus enabling him to regularise further the 'temporary enthronement' of royal claimants.[59]

For all the emphasis on practical knowledge, the administration at this time just did not have the ability to produce reliable data in a number of areas. Population figures, so necessary in order to appoint chiefs, assess taxes, and assign labour duties, were only just being collected in the late 1920s. They were based on lists of adult male taxpayers, not on full censuses. The figures given at various times in this handbook reveal just how uncertain the government was about the size of the political units it was trying to organize. Tribal censuses in these days were very rough and ready, and there was very little improvement throughout the rest of the Condominium period. Discrepancies in lists of tax-payers—a 20% decline of taxpayers among the Bar Gaawar between 1926 and 1935, a 25% increase among the Twic Dinka between 1927 and 1938—were accounted for in a number or ways, but it was usually accepted that such changes were

[58] Upper Nile Province Monthly Diary, May 1933, SRO BD 57.C.1.
[59] Upper Nile Province Monthly Diary, September 1933 and March 1934, SRO BD 57.C.1.

Table 1: Population Estimates

GROUP	1930	1954	1955-6
Anuak	25,000	–	8,106
Atuot	31,195	45,900	58,147
Abialang Dinka	4,496	6,300	8,846
Aliab Dinka	13,670	14,850	12,408
Bor Dinka	16,846	58,139	62,231
Cic Dinka	23,495	38,250	31,087
Dungjol Dinka	15,000	8,550	9,554
Ghol Dinka	4,248	9,956	11,058
Ngok Dinka	6,949	15,300	19,943
Nyareweng Dinka	2,316	9,856	12,447
Paloic Dinka	12,279	9,000	13,124
Rueng/Atar Dinka	7,360	16,150	16,175
Rueng/Bentiu Dinka	9,000	32,399	31,641
Twic Dinka	17,728	45,641	43,399
Koma	2,000*	–	6,313
Murle	50,000	4,395† (taxpayers only)	44,595
Bul Nuer	10,924	31,599	33,893
Dok Nuer	11,063	27,400	31,296
Gaawar Nuer	18,000	36,040	42,490
Jagei Nuer	5,195	13,896	20,539
E. Jikany Nuer	92,000*	86,500	102,089
W. Jikany Nuer	6,974	20,583	32,248
Lak Nuer	18,000	36,103	31,763
Leek Nuer	11,473	26,059	24,552
Lou Nuer	19,825	67,275	102,982
Nyuong Nuer	7,421	13,234	16,111
Thiang Nuer	7,750	12,785	16,374
Shilluk	116,000	120,000	90,738

* Figures from A.G. Pawson's Handing-Over Notes (1934), NRO Civsec 57/2/9
† Figures from Murle Census 1949-50, BAL 1/2/14 (ISCA, Oxford)

due mostly to a greater accuracy in counting.[60] Table 1 compares the population figures given in the district chapters here, with the census of taxpayers used in the 1954 Jonglei Investigation Team report, and then with figures of the first systematic national census to use a uniform methodology, just before independence. The frequently wide variations between the 1954 taxpayers' lists and the 1955-6 census indicates just how unreliable lists of taxpayers were for demographic purposes; thus throwing further doubt on the first such lists used to compile the figures in this handbook.

[60] Upper Nile Province Monthly Diary, December 1935—January 1936, SRO BD 57.C.1; Bor District Monthly Report, February 1938, SRO BD 57.D.2; JIT (1954 i: 229).

The strongest criticism later levelled against the policy of native administration throughout the Southern Sudan was that it restricted economic, social and political development, placing British officials in the role of caretakers of an anthropological zoo. While we can see from the district reports reprinted here that there was nothing inherently static about native administration, and administrators often saw themselves as progressive reformers rather than as tribal reactionaries, there was little in the way of planning for the internal economic development of the province. This was partly because the central government did not see the province as having any great economic potential, and partly because what little economic planning there had been was discussed within the broader context of the political and economic relations of Egypt and the Sudan, issues which are discussed in chapter 14 and appendix 2.

ISSUES OF DEVELOPMENT

The economic development of Upper Nile Province had always been a problem. Government investment in development of any form was always limited. Governor Matthews felt he had no choice but to acquiesce in this during the formative years at the beginning of this century. In 1906 he described the year's work as 'more give than take', and 'as a sacrifice of our own special Province interests for the good of the whole polity.' Despite lack of progress in his 'own patch of the Southern Sudan' he could find 'comfort in the remarkable achievement of the Nile-Red Sea Railway as a sufficient cause for lack of progress in his own immediate sphere of work. In other words, money was very properly spent where prospects of success were brightest.'[61]

The province was always seen as a cattle province with an untested potential for agricultural development. Most of Willis' own proposals, whether in 1927, 1928, or 1931, reflect this thinking, as do the proposals made by his district commissioners in their district notes. Willis very rightly saw the improvement of overland communication as essential before the economic potential of the province could be either tested or developed. His original intention was to open up the province through a system of roads, and then bring in Arab merchants to develop markets in dura, cotton, cattle and ivory.[62] The only area where such commercial activity was already well established was along the White Nile, especially

---

[61] 'Annual Report. Upper Nile Province, 1906', *Reports on the Finance, Administration, and Condition of the Sudan, 1906* (London, 1907): 723.
[62] Coriat to Kathleen, 8 Jan. 1927, Coriat MSS, Rhodes House, MSS Afr. s 1684.

around Renk, where the river offered good transportation to distant markets, and where Arab merchants were already investing extensively in agricultural production.[63]

Egyptian proposals for a sudd-diversion canal, to be constructed somewhere through Upper Nile Province, introduced a new set of mainly political issues into the question of the province's economic future. Willis was not the first member of the Sudan administration to object to the proposals, but his contribution to the debate over the canal (appendix 2) is the first time that the interests of the province itself were raised.

The Egyptian proposals, long in the making, coincided with the crisis in Anglo-Egyptian relations over the Sudan. By the end of 1924, when the Egyptian Army had been expelled from the Sudan and Egyptian officials withdrawn from almost all administrative positions, the Egyptian Irrigation Department became the most important remnant of Egyptian interest and influence in the Sudan. In May 1925 it produced a proposal for a canal from Bor to the Bahr el-Zeraf, and a remodelling of the Zeraf channel. In August 1925 this proposal was approved by the Egyptian council of ministers and £E 1 million appropriated for it. Only in December 1925 was the Sudan government informed, and protested immediately. It was only in October 1926 that Willis, newly arrived in Malakal, learned of the proposal, and he too objected, but mainly on the grounds that the Egyptian Irrigation Department's behaviour and activities infringed on his authority as governor. He prohibited any EID employees to travel south of Lake No.[64]

In the confrontation which developed over the canal scheme Egypt agreed that construction of any canal would not proceed without the agreement of both the Sudan and British governments. It also backed away from the original Bor-Zeraf cut proposal, offering a variety of alternative schemes instead, and agreeing that a study be undertaken on the likely effects of the canal on the local inhabitants of the Upper Nile. The man appointed to undertake this study was an engineer, W. D. Roberts, the sacked inspector-general of the EID in the Sudan who had proposed the Bor-Zeraf Cut in the first place. In contrast with later investigation teams set up in the 1940s, 1950s and 1980s to study the environmental and social effects of proposed canals, whose research took many specialists and many

---

[63] Because of this extensive investment by Northern merchants Renk was excluded from the Closed Districts Order of 1922, which was applied to the rest of the Southern Sudan and some adjacent areas.
[64] Howell, Lock and Cobb (1988: 33–4, 83–4); Collins (1990: 170–2). Collins is somewhat confused over the chronology of events, claiming that Willis found out about the laying of beacons for the canal line when he invited the British employees of the EID to dinner in Malakal in December 1925. Willis was still in Khartoum at that date and was not appointed governor of Upper Nile until August 1926.

years, Roberts gathered his information entirely from administrative officials, and mainly by questionnaire, spending less than a year on his report.

Willis' claim in 1931, given at the beginning of his contribution to this handbook, that 'the grant of a considerable sum of money by the Egyptian government for the examination of irrigation schemes in Upper Nile Province appeared to me to make a more progressive [native administration] policy essential' (chapter 1) is clearly a *post hoc* justification for some of his more expensive proposals. There is no mention of this urgent need in his 1927 or 1928 proposals reprinted in chapter 1. His own contribution to the Roberts report in 1928, reprinted here as appendix 2, also makes no mention of the need to advance tribal administration swiftly. Quite the opposite, for he states that he viewed 'with apprehension any scheme which involved unduly hastening the stages of development of these tribes.' His response was essentially political, concerned with the re-introduction of Egyptian influence after it had been so drastically curtailed in 1924 during his tenure as director of Intelligence in Khartoum. To combat that potential threat he employed several arguments, all calculated to strengthen the Sudan government's hand in the assertion of its responsibilities.

Willis' initial objections concerned security, a style of argument he had already used in his confrontation with central government over the Nuer and his plans for increasing his own independence of action. The people of his province needed time, he said, to adjust to 'new ideas', otherwise disturbances were likely. The second argument was that the canal scheme undermined the ruling orthodoxy of native administration by increasing contact between the 'pagan negroids' and a Northern Sudanese workforce. It also raised questions of who would exercise authority over the scheme, and what sort of law would apply in this part of his province (all surrounding areas being subject to customary law and the Sudan Penal Code). His objections based on the impact of the canal on the livelihood of the people were linked to all of these arguments. His information concerning the environmental impact came from his district commissioners' responses to the Roberts questionnaire (especially Major Wyld's typically detailed reply). Willis gave the original proposal for a Bor-Zeraf cut his qualified approval, but he was shrewd enough to use the proposal itself to argue for other gains for his province, such as increased expenditure on local fuel and power supplies. It is something of an exaggeration to claim Willis, on the basis of this report, as 'a remarkable if not improbable environmentalist', or to conclude that his principal objection, 'about which he wrote with genuine conviction, was his fear for the way of living of the people of the Upper Nile.'[65] His concern for the livelihood of the people may have been

---

[65] Collins (1990: 172, 175).

genuine enough, but his arguments had more to do with the consequences for the provincial government and the rival authority which such a concession to the EID would represent. The environmental arguments were presented both to support and to mask the political objections. He was not against large-scale economic projects in principle; not only was he an advocate of compulsorary cotton cultivation, but in his final recommendations for the economic development in the province (chapter 14) we find him advocating 'opening up some large economic scheme' and also exploiting the province's growing labour reserve, though not in a way which would mean 'the sacrifice of the tribal ideals.'

In the end Willis did not develop a coherent economic policy for the province. Economic development of any kind had to be tailored to the requirements of ruling policy of government, native administration. This considerably restricted the available options. While looking forward to a distant time when tribesmen might be shopkeepers, very little was done, in Willis' day or later, to help bring this about. Even more recently the external approach to the region's development has rested on the exploitation of its labour reserves and its natural resources by some outside agency, rather than the encouragement of indigenous commercial activity. The continuation of this approach, with the full backing of the national governments of Egypt and the Sudan sixty years after Willis, contributed greatly to the Sudan's second civil war, which began in May 1983, at Bor.

EPILOGUE

Willis' retirement from the province in 1931 was met with general relief, and his replacement, A. G. Pawson, won instant approval from DCs, DCs' wives and even the odd anthropologist in the province.[66] Willis had written extensively about the theory of native administration, but to those in his province it seemed clear that the DCs—Coriat and Wyld especially—had done the real work in laying its foundations.[67] Some years later it was Pawson, rather than Willis, who was given credit for the transformation of the province's administration.[68]

Willis' achievements as governor are difficult to assess. He has left behind a much more extensive record of his work than any of his predecessors or successors, and for that reason he has had a far greater influence as a source on historians. Yet the weakness of his method as

---

[66] Johnson (1993a: p.xxxvii; 1982b); Kay Coriat MSS, Rhodes House, MSS Afr. s 1684 (1).
[67] Coryton, quoted in Johnson (1993a: p.xlvi).
[68] Upper Nile Province Monthly Diary (June 1934), SRO BD 57.C.1.

director of Intelligence is evident in the reports he compiled in the Upper Nile, and in some of what is published here. We know from the testimony of many of his subordinates that he appeared reluctant to acknowledge his reliance on their experience and advice. What he wrote is thus frequently a misrepresentation or misinterpretation of what was known locally: whether it was his characterization of Struvé's governorship, or his descriptions of the succession of the Shilluk king, the history of government relations with Nuer 'kujurs', or the 'traditional' authority of Dinka chiefs. He could, however, be influenced by his DC's, and more often than perhaps he wished to publicise, their proposals were the foundation of his own: especially so in his response to the Egyptian Irrigation Department proposals and in the formulation of the Nuer Settlement. He could also, like any experienced civil servant, argue both sides of a case: for instance arguing for restrictions to the Egyptian Irrigation Department's plans, and later using their proposals as a justification for his own; or referring to the alarming prevalence of firearms as evidence of the need for a punitive campaign in 1927 (chapter 1), but dismissing the reported existence of 10,000 rifles in Nuer hands along the border as being of no security threat when giving a summary of his own administration's achievements in 1931 (chapter 14); or insisting on the use of custom as the foundation of native administration, to the point of sanctioning the invention of 'custom' where it did not exist.

Willis' own writings are less reliable as descriptions of his province than are the reports of his DCs. Yet his notoriety within his own service should not be used to dismiss his few achievements out of hand. Willis rightly saw an improvement in communications as the first plank of any administrative policy. Where Struvé failed to get Khartoum to agree to this, Willis succeeded in implementing the first road-building project in the province. Where Struvé had bowed to Khartoum's financial restrictions over the development of a system of native administration, including the creation of the chiefs' police, Willis used arguments of financial prudence in support of both. Willis' one real achievement, in the words of one of his successors, was to put the Upper Nile Province on the map as far as Khartoum was concerned.[69]

Willis kept up his connections with the Sudan after his retirement, becoming an adviser to Sayyid Abd al-Rahman al-Mahdi ('S. A. R.'), whose political rehabilitation after World War One Willis had assisted. With the re-election of the Conservative government in Britain in 1951 Willis emerged from retirement freely offering advice to the Foreign Office, the Colonial Office, and even Buckingham Palace, all with the

---

[69] John Winder, personal communication.

hope of enhancing Sayyid Abd al-Rahman's political standing in the negotiations between Britain and Egypt concerning the Sudan's independence. In the Foreign Office he was quickly identified as sympathetic to the Mahdists, 'even to the point of bias'. In Khartoum the Sudan government deplored both his past and his current activities on behalf of S. A. R., and the Foreign Office finally replied to his overtures in terms designed to 'choke Mr. Willis off'.[70] He attempted no further role in Anglo-Sudanese relations after independence. He is certainly not on record as having lobbied for any special consideration for the Southern Sudan in pre-independence constitutional discussions, unlike one of his fomer DCs, Major Wyld, who was a frequent, if discrete lobbyist on behalf of the Southern Sudanese.

Upper Nile Province remained one of the Sudan's least developed provinces throughout the Condominium period. More effort was put in the further evolution and refinement of native administration than in educational or economic development. It was only after World War Two, with the Sudan's independence looming over the near horizon, that both educational and economic advancement were accelerated. District commissioners now positively pressed the chiefs to send boys to school. The revival of the sudd-diversion canal proposals (renamed the Jonglei Canal) led to the first extensive economic surveys of the province in the reports of the Jonglei Investigation Team, and then in the report of its successor, the Southern Development Investigation Team. But these surveys led to very little economic planning before independence.

Very few persons from Upper Nile were represented in the army, police or civil service by the time of independence in 1956. The police and prison warders who mutinied in Malakal in August 1955, following the news of the Equatorial battalion mutiny in Torit, were recruited mainly from outside the province. The Upper Nile was drawn into the Sudan's first civil war relatively late, only in the mid–1960s, when semi-autonomous groups of 'Anyanya' guerrillas were formed among the Dinka and Shilluk, and later among the Nuer. As the war progressed more and more men from Upper Nile began to take leading roles in the guerrilla forces, and the Upper Nile's long border with Ethiopia enabled many of its people to seek refuge from the war itself. In fact, when the war came to a negotiated end in

---

[70] See (PRO) JE1017/56 in FO 371/9011, JE1051/323 in FO 371/96910, and FO 371/96936, 'Circumstances Surrounding the Presentation of a Golden Sword to King George V by Sayed Abdel Rahman, son of the Mahdi in 1919; Question of Relevance to Present Relations with Sudan'.

1972, it was in Upper Nile Province that some of the most active resistance to the terms of peace was found.[71]

During the eleven years of peace which followed the Addis Ababa Agreement of 1972 people from Upper Nile continued to make a significant contribution to the political life of the Sudan. Abel Alier, a Bor Dinka (and graduate of Malek school), the leader of the government delegation at the Addis Ababa peace talks, was twice president of the High Executive Council of the Southern Regional government in Juba, and for many years a vice-president of the republic. To many in the Southern Sudan it sometimes seemed that the people of Upper Nile, the Bor Dinka in particular, had a disproportionate influence in government. There were many reasons for this appearance. Malek school was the oldest school in any Dinka district, producing more graduates than any other similar school by the time of independence. It has been suggested that the economic prospects of Bor District have always been so bad that educated persons have been forced to leave the district, and even the province, to find work elsewhere; thus the surprisingly high percentage of people from Bor (relative to their own numbers) in various branches of the civil service. The floods of the 1960s added to the emigration of the Bor Dinka, many of whom left with their herds, moving southwards into Equatoria. For many years in the 1970s they were the main suppliers of meat to the regional capital of Juba, and while the meat was welcomed by townspeople and local farmers, the herders and their cattle were not.

It was the near simultaneous revival of the Jonglei Canal project and the discovery of oil in Bentiu and other parts of Upper Nile in the 1970s which brought the province into the political frontline between the Northern and Southern Sudan. The disregard for local needs and feelings which accompanied the beginning of the construction of the canal generated considerable local grievances against both the central and regional governments. The various attempts in Khartoum to assert control over the oil fields to the detriment of the Southern Region was the source of a much wider grievance throughout the South. Deteriorating relations between the Sudan and Ethiopia meant that the Ethiopian government was willing to offer sanctuary and support to Sudanese dissidents. By the 1980s Upper Nile Province had become the political fault line between North and South. Southern guerrilla units began operating in the province from bases across the border as early as 1980. The Bor Mutiny of 1983 marked the renewal of civil war, a war in which access to Ethiopia through Upper Nile was of crucial importance to the guerrilla movement of the Sudan People's Liberation Army.

---

[71] Alier (1990: 139–40, 154–7).

Gambela and the Baro salient became the economic and political centre of the SPLA; for it was at Itang that the largest refugee base was established where Southern Sudanese came to escape the attacks of the Sudanese army and their militia allies, where SPLA soldiers settled their families, and through which supplies were channelled to the SPLA and to adjacent territories along the border. It was also in camps in Gambela district that new recruits were gathered and trained. For many years the administration of this part of Ethiopia was largely in the hands of the SPLA, until the fall of Mengistu in May 1991 led to the sudden evacuation of the Sudanese refugee camps and the flight of the SPLA out of Ethiopia into Upper Nile. This precipitated a crisis within the SPLA itself, culminating in a split in the movement led by the SPLA commanders based at Nasir in August 1991.

Since 1991 the Upper Nile has become the site of a major political fault line within the Southern Sudan: John Garang, Riek Mashar, Lam Akol, William Nyuon Bany, Martin Majier and Arok Thon—major players in internecine fighting within the SPLA—all came from Upper Nile. The peoples of the Upper Nile have been affected more directly by the split than any other Southern Sudanese. The movement of Gaajak Nuer and Anuak into Ethiopia accelerated during the war, contributing to political tensions within Gambela, even after the removal of the SPLA from the region. Prior to the split the SPLA appeared to be the protectors of numerous border peoples caught up in the war. After the split the Nuer of the SPLA Nasir command (later renamed SPLA-United) became the predators and exploiters of the Meban, Koma and Uduk. The Shilluk were at first divided within themselves between those loyal to John Garang's leadership and those favouring the Nasir commanders, but the death of the reth in 1993 and the installation of a new reth (a grandson of Fadiet Kwathker) enabled the Shilluk to negotiate some autonomy respected by both the government and the local SPLA, removing them, at least temporarily, from active participation in the war. The main fighting between the two SPLA factions has been in the border region between the Gaawar and Lou Nuer and the Nyareweng and Twic Dinka, with the Dinka of Kongor and Bor Districts and the Nuer of Ayod and Waat being particular targets. The power struggle within the SPLA-United has also been organized around different groups of Nuer. The perception that the SPLA split is little more than a power-struggle within Upper Nile meant that both major factions faced difficulties in rallying enthusiastic support in other parts of the Southern Sudan. Yet, an obscure province no longer, in many ways Upper Nile now holds the key to the wider region's future.

THE UPPER NILE PROVINCE HANDBOOK

A Report on
Peoples and Government in the
Southern Sudan, 1931

CHAPTER 1

Introduction

C. A. WILLIS

The Upper Nile Province has for some years been going through a progress of accretion. During my predecessor's tenure he took over the Sobat-Pibor Military Administration and the year I took over he added Duk and Bor Districts from Mongalla Province.

Since then, what was the Eastern District of the Bahr el-Ghazal has been added, (what are now the Yirrol and W. Nuer Districts), and negotiations are proceeding for a cession of territory from Bahr el-Ghazal and from Kordofan.

A suggestion has been put forward to transfer Rumbek District to Upper Nile Province in order to effect economies of staff, but is, I hope, to prove abortive, though I am recommending the addition of Tali and the Mandari to Yirrol District.

It was inevitable that the system of administration holding in those districts that were freshly added to the province should differ both in principle and in practice from the main body of the province.

The policy of my predecessor may be shortly described as the maintenance of adequate security at the lowest possible cost. He did not demand a high degree of security, e.g. he disregarded inter-sectional fights and casual affrays amongst the tribesmen provided that the matter was not the cause of too many casualties or if blood-money were paid up and peace restored in due course.

The system of taxation by ushur and herd tax was found to be unreasonably laborious and a tribute was imposed on the Shilluk and northern Dinka based on the average taxes over some years, whilst the Nuer paid (or did not) a nominal tribute of cattle.

The incidence of taxation was very variable. In some cases the tribute worked out at 35 Pt a head, in others as low as 25 m/ms. These figures however were based on a very rough census and in most cases were guess work.

The probable effect of the irrigation schemes on the province had not then been taken into consideration. Thus as Mr. Struvé saw no likelihood of an economic return from the province, and no necessity to develop administration beyond the barest limits of security, and as the introduction of mechanical transport had not yet been shown to be feasible, he was more concerned to keep expenditure down than to elaborate a constructive administrative policy.

The grant of a considerable sum of money by the Egyptian government for the examination of irrigation schemes in Upper Nile Province appeared to me to make a more progressive policy essential.

If extensive works were to be constructed in the province, inevitably the tribesmen would come into contact with civilization much more quickly and extensively than they would in normal conditions. Moreover the possibility could not be overlooked that the irrigation schemes might seriously alter local conditions and upset tribal customs and habits; and since the tribesmen were practically primitive and somewhat truculent, it was urgently needful that they should be organized and disciplined and taught to adapt themselves to new circumstances.

In these circumstances the right line to follow appeared to be to study first what the existing conditions were and then to use them as the foundations of a constructive policy which should make the fullest use of any existing institutions, gradually eliminating elements adverse to government and insinuating such benefits of sanitation, education and progress as could be absorbed.

The latter part of 1926 was spent in visiting all parts of the province accessible by water and in 1927 I was able to go over a very considerable part by land and so observe on the spot the administrative problem before me.

It was clear that in almost every case assistant district commissioners had leaned to a system of 'Devolution' by working up a tribal organization to deal with tribal cases and discipline. The degree of success varied very greatly according to the capacity of the assistant district commissioner, the amount of existing organization in the tribe concerned and their amenability to the idea. By the end of 1927 the need of a definite policy for the administration of the Nuer became an issue of immediate importance as the wizard Gwek Wanding [Guek Ngundeng][1] set himself up as a law unto himself in the Lau Nuer[2] in opposition to the government, and unless the government was prepared to allow any self styled wizard with a gift of sleight of hand to impose any rules on the tribesmen that took his fancy, it had not merely to eliminate the 'wizards' but to find a tribal system acceptable to the people and to insist on it being carried out.

---

[1] Willis was never able to spell Guek Ngundeng's name correctly. 'Ngundeng' is Nuer for 'gift of Deng'; 'Wundeng', the version which appeared most often in administrative records, is the Dinka pronunciation of the name; 'Wanding' is a mishearing of the Dinka.

[2] The MS here reads 'set himself as a law unto himself up in the Lau Nuer'.

Introduction

In February 1928 I compiled a memorandum to headquarters putting forward a general scheme for the province, embracing both political and departmental needs and proposing a scheme of cooperation to put the province on a basis which might ultimately lead to economic stability as well as material security [see below, pp. 58–72].

At the same period I circulated letters to the assistant district commissioners of Nuer districts laying down general lines of policy with the object of gradually bringing the different districts into one system.[3]

From a political point of view patrol S8 in 1928 was a failure: although the pyramid of Gwek was destroyed, he and his immediate followers remained at large and the whole of the Lau clan continued in a state of divided loyalty.

It had been arranged for troops to march through Gaweir in the latter part of the dry season of 1928, as there was reason to apprehend an extensive raid by the clansmen on the Dinka to the south.

Actually the ADC of Zeraf Valley [H. G. Wedderburn-Maxwell] accompanied by an officer of the Equatorial battalion (Capt. H. A. Romilly) whilst preparing food dumps for the march surprised the tribesmen in the course of preparation for a raid under a certain Kurbiel [Kerbiel, or Gatbuogh Yoal].

The effect of the march was to stop the raid at the moment but incidentally it caused Dwal Diu an important chief to secede violently from the government owing to the confiscation of some 23 rifles, and in August, when all movement by trained troops was impossible, a large number of Gaweir assisted by young men from Lau in search of loot raided the Dinka of Duk Faiwel District, killing many people and removing cattle; and they finally attacked the police post at Duk Faiwel where however they met with a reverse.

It was arranged that the E. District of the Bahr el-Ghazal comprising W. Nuer and Yirrol Districts should be transferred to the Upper Nile Province at the beginning of 1928.

Early in December 1927, the district commissioner Captain Fergusson was killed at Lake Jorr (more properly a Dor [Ador]). The governor of the Bahr el-Ghazal Major M. Wheatley who was retiring at the end of 1927 stayed on to clear up the situation and to act as political officer to Patrol S9. The patrol captured a large number of cattle and collected a certain number of the population, but the actual murderers of Capt. Fergusson were not caught, and a chief who was imprisoned as being accessory to the murderer was subsequently found to have had no part in it though he had been guilty of grave irregularities in other ways.

---

[3] The correspondence on this subject can be found in NRO UNP 1/44/329.

Major Wheatley handed over in April 1928: the situation though superficially peaceful was by no means satisfactory.

The murder of a British official by Nuong [Nyuong] the continued defiance of Gwek Wanding and his satellites to any authority in Lau and the raid on the Dinka by Gaweir and Lau ending in an attack on a government post showed an accumulation of indiscipline that demanded strong measures and the patrols had not apparently produced sufficient effect.

His excellency the governor general [Sir John Maffey] came to Malakal at the beginning of January 1929 with the kaid el amm [General H. Huddleston], the civil secretary [H. A. MacMichael], and Wing Commander Reid, and discussed with all the assistant district commissioners of Nuer districts the solution to the problem.

As a result of these discussions 'Nuer Settlement' was evolved. This was in effect the confirmation of the policy already outlined, but every assistance was professed to bring it into being as speedily as possible. The object was to bring the tribesmen in to government and so get hold of their tribal organization and so strengthen it that lawlessness could be checked and defiance of authority could be dealt with at its first appearance before it was a serious matter.

Additional British staff was provided and the SDF supplied help in all forms, providing M.I. to cooperate with or take the place of mounted police, garrisons from Equatorial battalion, mechanical transport for the delivery of supplies etc., medical staff and wireless and expert engineering advice.

The preliminary process of reducing the tribesmen to discipline has occupied two seasons' work. It has been complicated by the reorganization and enlargement of the police throughout the province and the speeding up of 'native administration' in tribes other than the Nuer.

At the present time it is probably fair to say that the machinery has been set up but has yet to be run in, and it is not to be expected that some misfires backfires and undue heating from friction can be wholly avoided.

The form of this memorandum follows logically from that of February 1928. In that I put forward communications as the first essential to the establishment of administration, and once a sound system were established and capable of working without undue effort the province should be capable of economic development. The period of administrative growth provided the time required for research and experiment into economic possibilities.

Attached to this introductory note are copies of correspondence of August 6th 1927 outlining the general situation in the province and my note of February 1928 putting forward a more or less comprehensive scheme for the policy of the province.

As communications formed the first 'plank' of this policy, they form the subject of the first section of the body of the handing over note.

The second comprises notes on the administrative staff and on departments.

The third consists of notes by the assistant district commissioners on their districts with comments where necessary.

The fourth contains confidential reports [not included in copies deposited in Khartoum and Durham].

1927 PROPOSALS

Malakal, 6th August, 1927

Civil Secretary, Khartoum

Now that one may review the season's work, it should be possible to outline the next steps to be taken in the establishment of a native administration among the negroid tribes of this province.

Nuer

I have taken the opportunity to discuss with Captain Fergusson the method he has adopted with such success in his section of Nuer (population roughly 60,000) and I sent Mr. Coriat assistant district commissioner, Abwong with Captain Fergusson to see these methods working, in order to see how far he could bring his own and Captain Fergusson's methods into line. The discussions both before and after this visit were most useful, and not only were various misconceptions and misunderstandings cleared away but they have put me in a position to go rather further in my conception of the next steps to be taken.[4]

Captain Fergusson had the advantage of taking over a country previously unadministered, which was surrounded either by deep rivers or almost impassable marsh, so that the natives were more or less confined to this area and they had not a long record of patrols against the government, which in other parts of the Nuer country had taken the form of raids capturing cattle and burning villages.

For several years he followed a policy of 'peaceful penetration', till

---

[4] For Fergusson's impression of these discussions see above, editor's introduction, p.15.

1923 the persistently obstructive attitude of certain kujurs (rain makers and jujumen) compelled him to apply for troops. But the knowledge he had obtained of the tribesmen and chiefs enabled him to restrict the action to the guilty sections. The patrol of 1923 was practically a failure, and was followed by another in 1924 against the same combination of kujurs. In this case again though casualties were inflicted, both kujurs escaped. Finally in December 1925 the kujur again wished to try conclusions with the government and collected the support of all other kujur they could and attacked the government troops and received very heavy casualties including practically all the kujur; since then the sole remaining kujur has become a staunch supporter of the government.[5]

The destruction of the influence of the kujur has made possible the development of the chiefs' authority, and the establishment of a tribal discipline that surpasses anything to be found elsewhere among the Nuer. Not only do the chiefs get their orders obeyed but they take a pride in their position and are keen to maintain it.

There are certain inferences to be drawn from the above that are of importance in considering native administration. One is that although Captain Fergusson has no police or armed force in his district, the organization he has built up was made by force of arms, more especially by the last patrol when some 400 casualties were caused in a few minutes by machine gun fire.

Secondly, the influence of the kujur is anti-government and has to be broken if the government chiefs are to execute their proper authority. The kujur are comparable to the 'hedge fikis' of the Northern Sudan, now a fast disappearing type as education spreads. They exploit the superstitions of the people and their position and wealth depend on keeping the people ignorant and frightened of their supposed supernatural powers; and in the nature of things they must be reactionary and opposed to a policy of progress such as the government proposes.

Thirdly, on the elimination of the kujurs, the chiefs can acquire and use authority over their people.

The introduction of money and the means of making money have no doubt had a great effect in bringing these Nuer into line. Their one desire is cattle, and they find that by growing cotton they can buy cows, and so much is the fact appreciated that a chief can and does fine a tribesman who refuses to grow cotton.[6]

---

[5] This is not a summary of Fergusson's views. Fergusson, like all other administrators, wanted eventually to replace the authority of the prophets with that of the 'chiefs', but he repeatedly expressed satisfaction with the administrative work of individual prophets in his district. In 1927 at least three of his appointed chiefs were also prophets.

[6] Enforced cotton growing was, in fact, unpopular among the Western Nuer and was abandoned late in 1931. See below, ch. 11.

How far have these principles been followed with the rest of the Nuer and how far are they applicable?

Starting eastward from the Nuer under Captain Fergusson, the next block is the Lak 20,000 and the Thiang 10,000 who inhabit the Zeraf Island. The Thiang extend eastward of the Zeraf as well. The conditions of these people are comparable to the Nuong in that they are completely surrounded by rivers, so that they could have markets on a line of communication.

The people are fairly biddable, and pay up their tribute without trouble, but they still continue to have 'shen' fights, and it is reported that they have been acquiring a certain number of rifles. They gave some trouble in 1926 in killing a couple of wood cutters and it must be admitted that their tribal discipline has still a long way to go.

They are administered from Fangak, which is itself rather remote from settlements of Nuer and is on the east bank of the Zeraf and the local population of some 200 Dinka are refugees from elsewhere.

I have no information as to whether cotton will grow, but have no reason to suppose it will not.

The people grow a certain amount of dura but they depend largely on luck for their crops, as they may get washed out or water-logged.

The post at Fangak consisting as it does of the district commissioner's house and office and the local police post, and a couple of 'gellaba', has no clerk or sarraf or official staff, and (as will appear later) might very well be relieved of the unmounted police who do nothing but guard their own arms, watch the tribute cattle vicariously and do a little rather ineffective gardening.

The Gaweir Nuer 23,000 also fall to this district. Their headquarters is at Rufshendol and they move south in the dry weather and have to be carefully watched to stop them encroaching on the Dinka who lie south of them and have for several generations been looked upon as their natural prey.

These people have a good many rifles, are almost without discipline, and although they have one or two good chiefs, they will take a lot of handling before such can be done with them. They get a certain number of elephants the ivory of which they exchange for rifles smuggled from Abyssinia, and they are the only section of the tribe that is behind hand with tribute.[7]

This is partly due to Captain Pletts' transfer to Gambeila as he was

---

[7] For ivory and rifles see Coriat (1993: 23–5, 43), and Johnson (1986b; 1994: 220–1). Struvé had a less alarmist view about the security risk of rifles among the Nuer, a view which Willis shared by the time he left the province (see below, ch. 14).

unable to make a second tour through their country, but these Gaweir are one of the difficult spots in the Nuer.

Between the Zeraf and the Pibor is a huge plain almost devoid of any distinguishing mark. The pyramid of Deng Kur is its chief feature. This is about 8° N/ 32° 15' E and is a monument to the influence of kujur. Except in the corner by the mouth of the Zeraf into the White Nile, the Nuer are cut off from the Sobat for a long way up. Roughly speaking, the Gun Lau Nuer inhabit the western half and Mor Lau the eastern half. South of the Lau lie people who were originally Dinka but were conquered by the Nuer and they are gradually drifting back to their Dinka beginnings and will probably end by being merged with them entirely, as long as the government protects the Dinka from the Nuer.[8]

The Gun Lau are the most advanced and amenable of the Nuer in the province; it will be observed that they inhabit an area remote from any main lines of communication, there are no markets or money and no produce (except cattle) for which money could be given. It would never pay to bring out e.g. cotton by road, assuming that cotton would grow. No Agricultural inspector has visited the area to determine what might be grown. Though I am arranging for one to go as soon as the roads are open next season.

The Mor Lau are less amenable, partly because they are more difficult to get at than the Gun and partly because they are influenced by the kujur Gwek Wunding who has been anti-government since the beginning and is now reported to be making propaganda against the road-policy of the government; and, as the making of roads means work, he is getting some hearing. For the rest the conditions described for the Gun apply to them, only more so.[9]

Lastly there are the Jekaing, consisting of the Gaajok population 100,000 and Gaajak population 100,000, sections north of the Sobat, divided by the Machar marsh.

The Gaajok are the more advanced, chiefly because they have not got the facilities the Gaajak have of disappearing into Abyssinia. The system of chiefs' courts has been adopted by both sections and they have all paid up their tribute this year without any trouble, but the degree of their discipline is distinctly qualified.

They are reputed to have 10,000 rifles, and though ammunition is short, every rifle has a few rounds.

---

[8] Here Willis is referring to the Rumjok section of the Gun Lou, who lived intermixed with the Nyareweng, Ghol and other Dinka.
[9] In fact Guek lived among the Gun Lou and had far less influence among the Mor. The Mor were also largely unaffected by the road-making scheme,which passed mainly through Gun territory.

Introduction

The Jekaing grow a considerable quantity of dura, but it is almost entirely consumed locally, as the difficulty of getting it across the considerable khors to the Sobat bank precludes ramping of the best areas, and the fact that the Sobat is not navigable at the time of year when trade is possible provides a further obstacle to economic development.[10]

These people have so far shown a marked objection to growing cotton—the basis of their dislike to it being that it leaves them dependent on others for their food supply, and if it were to be grown, it should be only as an addition to the dura crop.

The method which has been followed in bringing the Nuer under administration has been more or less parallel to that adopted by Captain Fergusson i.e. first the district commissioner got in touch with the people, found out what organization existed and built on it, introducing as much discipline as they could. It must be remembered that in the case of these Nuer, the natives were not unreasonably suspicious of the government; for years they only knew the government as armed raiding parties seizing cattle indiscriminately and often burning down villages as well. The patrol against Lau Nuer [in 1917] did this to such a degree that the Lau were made uncomfortable and were disinclined for a repetition of it but the kujur responsible for the attitude that led to the patrol still remained at large and is still giving trouble.[11] The patrol against the Jekaing in 1919 destroyed a lot of houses, but as many of the owners were away in Abyssinia, the moral effect was not as such as was anticipated, and it is difficult to deny that in their inner hearts the Nuer are not convinced that the government would get the better of them in a fight.

One great disadvantage that the district commissioners of this province have to compete with in dealing with the Nuer, is the vast area which the tribe is spread, something like 15,000 square miles south of the Sobat and almost as much north of it.

Secondly the distance from any main line of communications and the consequent difficulties of economic development make the application of Captain Fergusson's methods for the introduction of money impracticable at any rate at present.

Thirdly, up to the present the chiefs can only settle cases with the backing and at the instigation of the district commissioner and they are

---

[10] The Jikany were exporting grain by 1930. As early as 1932 the whole of the Sobat valley exported 120 tons of grain by steamer, and 421 tons of grain were exported in 1934 (SDIT (1955: table 49)).

[11] Pok Kerjiok, the prophet who was the target of the 1917 patrol, had been quite eclipsed by Guek Ngundeng by this time, and his influence was confined mainly to his own section. As Pok was virtually unknown to the administration by 1927 it is likely that Willis is here confusing him with Guek. See below ch. 9 and Appendix 3, Biographical Notes.

not yet strong enough nor sufficiently imbued with a sense of their position to enforce decisions of the courts or their own orders but there is a noticeable improvement. For instance there have been no crimes of violence in the last season by the Lau Nuer, and a great mass of old cases have been settled up.

In discussing native administration there is a distinction of considerable importance to be made with regard to the Nuer.

In the normal course, there is a paramount chief or sultan who is the acknowledged head: he has his ministers, kadis and his organization of sheikhs etc. under him, his system of taxation etc. and to some degree his army and police, and the government representative advises his administration.

With the Nuer there is no reason to suppose there was ever a paramount chief, even over the larger sections, such as the Jekaing or Lau. The basis of the tribal organization is the family and in each 'shen' (this word is variously transliterated shen sheng shyeng and I adopt the simplest). There is a family from which a hereditary chief is selected: in the case of very large shens, there may be subdivisions with hereditary chiefs, and no main chief.

There are also the chiefs of the land and the leopard skin who also go by families. They are really restricted to certain functions i.e. the settlement of land cases and mediation in murder cases with a view to settlement by blood money but the possession of these functions does not necessarily mean that a land or leopard chief can extend his authority in other directions. If the Nuer are to administer themselves, they will do it through the medium of a considerable number of chiefs, selected from the proper families in each 'shen'.[12]

Within his 'shen' the chief should manage his own case by forming a court of heads of families and should acquire sufficient authority to enable him to carry out the decisions of the court and any government orders.

Interrelations of 'shens' are largely determined by combined courts of chiefs, I have in previous correspondence had to draw a distinction between *chief*'s and chiefs' courts. Ultimately these courts will become a kind of witenagemot of which it may be a titular head will be found, but in the meantime we have to deal with the chiefs as they are: and as their number must be fairly large, the district commissioner will be concerned to supervise their relations and will probably have to deal much more directly with administration than he would with the normal form of native administration.

So satisfactory has been the progress of the Lau Nuer that Mr. Coriat

---

[12] For a fuller account of earth masters (*kuaar muon*), or 'leopard-skin chiefs' see Evans-Pritchard (1933–5; 1940a). See also below, ch. 14, n.5.

Introduction

(ADC Abwong) is prepared to go a step further towards native administration, by eliminating his foot police and clerical staff, provided certain modifications can be arranged. The first necessity is the abolition of the kujur influence by the capture of Gwek Wonding and his removal temporarily at least, and the destruction of the pyramid of Deng Kur. This is, I think entirely necessary, and I had intended arranging for it in view of Gwek's propaganda against the road making or obeying any government orders.[13] Whether it would be necessary to employ troops of Sudan Defence Force or only police I will discuss separately.

Secondly, provision for watchmen, ferrash, gardener etc. will have to be made as the station at Abwong must be looked after and kept in order.

Thirdly, some modification of the system of accounts must be made so that the assistant district commissioner can deal with them in English on the simplest possible lines.

He gives as his financial requirements:

100 chiefs' police	£ 180
Station gardener	18
2 garden boys	10
10 herdsmen	25
6 station employees	30
2 interpreters	40
General: to cover remuneration for agricultural work, tumargia, school, casual labour	200
Remuneration of chiefs	100
School teacher	36
Reserve	50
	£ 689

Of these all but the six station employees, the school teacher, general and reserve can be provided for in the budget as it stands. Remuneration of chiefs presents slight difficulties. Hitherto the Dinka of that district have received their remuneration in cash and have paid their tribute latterly in cash. The Nuer have received occasional small gifts, paid for against remuneration and generally the subject of correspondence with the Accounts Section of the Finance Department who want to know exactly how much the chief in question is paid, and as he is paid cattle, the exact

---

[13] There is no evidence in the surviving official record or in Coriat's personal papers that Coriat himself saw either the removal of Guek or the demolition of the Mound as necessary for progress in his district. Major Wyld, in the neighbouring district, however, was keen on both proposals. This proposal was written while Coriat was away on home leave (Coriat (1993: documents 1.5 and 3.2) and Johnson (1994: 186–91)).

price cannot be traced. This is a matter about which I have written to the Finance Department separately but it is very important for the district commissioner to be able to remunerate a chief in the most effective way the chief knows i.e. by the gift of a cow, the value of which in cash is normally considerably less than the cash remuneration that the chief might get and would not be grateful for. Even if the remuneration to chiefs exceeded the percentage allowed on the tribute, I should recommend letting the district commissioner have a free hand, as it is necessary to give the chiefs an adequate quid pro quo for their trouble and responsibilities and the remuneration is not merely for tribute paying but all the business of administration. It is not thought advisable to put chiefs on to a regular pay and so reducing them to being the paid hirelings of the government, but a good gift for services rendered can meet the case, and may reasonably be left to the discretion of the man on the spot.

The incomings Mr. Coriat makes at:

Fines	£ 100
Medical fees	100
	£ 200

Apart from the tribute which he estimates at £900. There would also be the saving of sixteen foot police, roughly £480 p.a., and an accountant sarraf at £96.

There is a very genuine saving on the total expenditure and I think the experiment is well worth making.[14] The only difficulty I foresee is over the accounts, as we experience quite enough difficulty already in answering fiddling little queries based on a state of affairs that does not exist and regulations that cannot be made to apply. The whole success of the scheme turns on finding a way out of the complications of the accounts. One way would be to withdraw certain sums from the Province and Local Provincial Service budget, and transfer them to 'native administration', which would then be completely independent of Finance regulations, and the district commissioner would then administer these sums on behalf of the native administration and periodically his accounts would be examined and a reserve built up if possible.

I would have been glad to apply the same experiment, to Fangak, but I do not think it is right to do so until the new assistant district commissioner of that district has had time to get the personal knowledge of the people and the country that are essential prior to making administration changes.

[14] For the results of these changes in Abwong District see Coriat (1993: document 1.5), and below, ch. 9.

Introduction

Moreover the system of chiefs' police which exists in Lau has not yet been started on the Zeraf Island, or only in so elementary a form as to be negligible; but if the experiment at Abwong proves successful, and if Mr. Maxwell whom I am putting at Fangak succeeds in getting into sufficient touch with the natives I should hope to be able to extend the experiment to that district—the saving in that case would be only twelve police (unmounted), as there is no clerical staff there. But the withdrawal affects the question of the Bor and Yirrol as compared with UNP police to which I shall refer later.

Captain Fergusson has attained his ends by following peaceful methods as long as he can but when they fail giving the culpable natives a severe beating with the aid of troops and repeating that process until he can return to peaceful methods.

The Upper Nile Province has followed a similar method, but has used a far lesser degree of force, and the reaction of enforcing discipline on the native has been correspondingly less.[15]

The principle is however the same; the Nuer are a warlike tribe with all the conceit of the African, and unless they know that they dare not attempt conclusions with the government, they may break out at any moment. It is not many years since the governor of the province had a spear thrown at him by a Nuer.[16]

I am not suggesting a series of punitive expeditions against this tribe, and should be the last person to do so: but I think that an occasional show of force e.g. route marching through a tribe in a perfectly peaceable manner, would have a good effect, and what is needed is a small but swiftly moving and well armed force which can pursue, catch and deal with any recalcitrants. In the words of Mr. Kipling 'It is punishment not war'—and the mounted police have constantly shown their ability, to do this on a small scale, and a mounted constabulary with machine guns, on mules, would seem to be the desideratum.[17]

There is a point with regard to the native administration of the Nuer which has a wider application and I cannot omit it. I have already laid stress on the necessity of the district commissioner acquiring a personal

---

[15] This is a curious statement given the scale of the 1917 campaign against the Lou and the 1919–20 campaign against the Jikany. Both patrols involved far more troops than were used against the Western Nuer at that time; the latter patrol included the use of gunboats, artillery and aeroplanes.

[16] A possible reference to the 1910 annual report which recorded Struvé's experience as an inspector on tour when, placing his hand on a Nuer's shoulder 'to intimate that he might lend a hand with some game which had been shot for them, two spears were thrown at him.' ('Upper Nile Province. Annual Report, 1910', *Reports on the Finance, Administration and Condition of the Sudan, 1910*: 414).

[17] See Johnson (1991) on policing.

knowledge of the people before he can venture to administer. The time taken to do this must be considerable, and then the native administration has to be started, put into running order and kept going until the chiefs and people have learnt to like it and to carry it out of their own accord. Until that state has been reached, any change of the staff means going back right to the beginning. I am given to understand that the chiefs of Captain Fergusson's original district, (for he has had recent accretions) have reached the point when a change could be made without the authority of the chiefs' suffering. Mr. Lee who has reduced the Jekaing from active opponents of the government to passivity is retiring next February, and I hope that Mr. Tiernay will be able so to get into touch with the chiefs through the help of Mr. Lee that he can have at least a good start, but I hope he can then remain for a period of some years.[18] The same applies to Mr. Wedderburn Maxwell at Fangak—I hope to give him all the assistance I can to be introduced to the chiefs by Mr. Coriat who knows especially the Gaweir.

At present our hold over the Nuer is such as it is largely dependent on a few individuals. If the proposals I envisage are successful, the native administration would be a thing in being and cease to be the personal influence of some particular man—but until that has been attained, I hope you will see your way to leaving those employed in this area until either they fail to produce any result in which case I shall be the first to ask for a change or they have produced the final result, when changes will not matter.

The Dinka

The Dinka suffered very severely at the hands of the slave raiders from the North, and also from the Nuer who [cut?] through their country. The word for slave in the Nuer language means Dinka.[19] The result has been that whatever tribal organization originally existed has been permanently destroyed. The Dinka are an imitative people, and they have tended to

---

[18] Lee stayed on until 1929, when he was invalided out of the service. Tiernay remained as ADC until after February 1930, overlapping with Armstrong, Lee's successor, by only two months. Armstrong complained that the nature of his transfer meant that a fresh start had to be made to attempt to progress (C. L. Armstrong, 'Eastern District, Upper Nile Province, Taking-over Notes', 8 April 1930, NRO UNP 1/51/4).

[19] The Nuer use of the word *jang* (Dinka) has a variety of connotations, some derogatory, some not. Today when applied to other Nuer it indicates a person of foreign (though not necessarily Dinka) origin. The Nuer adopted numerous Dinka captives and refugees into their families, or incorporated them into their lineages, often forcibly, but they did not practice slavery or the ownership of other human beings.

adopt the customs of those around them. Thus in the North there has been a tendency to ape the Arabs, and in the South they follow the customs of the Nuer.[20]

Now that they have security and can rely on protection from their more powerful neighbours, some of the better chiefs are making great efforts to remake the tribes, Yol Kur in the north and Deng Malwal in Duk Faiwel District are men of exceptional character and intelligence, of whom much may be made. The Dinka differ from the Nuer in that they are more susceptible to new ideas. They take to clothes with avidity and adopt anything that they think will give them a higher social status. For this reason they are easily Arabicised, but the result is deplorable. It is noteworthy that quite a number of the leaders of the White Flag League were Dinka (notably Ali Abdel Latif the head of it).[21] It seems particularly desirable in the circumstances to keep the Dinka developing along their own lines and not adopting alien customs. In the Northern District the Dinka have been greatly reduced in numbers and wealth, and the Arabs encroached a long way into them.

Efforts have been made and are still being made to prevent further encroachment, but the Dinka in that area are too poor to stand up for themselves.

They have their chiefs' court which originally sat monthly, but now sits as and when required.

It is dominated by Yol Kur, and but for him would be of little use. There is not much to be done to develop Dinka administration in this district till they have acquired more wealth. With better and more markets that may occur, and steps have been taken to provide markets and more are contemplated.

The Dunjol Dinka are almost entirely isolated. The district commissioner, Central District reports that although the chiefs' courts

---

[20] Willis' only direct experience of the Dinka, prior to coming to UNP, was of the Ngok Dinka of the 'Arab' Kordofan Province before the First World War (see his 'Notes on the Western Kordofan Dinkas', *SIR* 178 (May 1909) Appendix C: 16–18).

[21] Ali Abd al-Latif, founder of the pro-Egyptian early Sudanese nationalist White Flag League, was born in an army garrison in Egypt, his father was a Nuba soldier and his mother was a Dinka slave. Because he was brought up by his mother's people he was usually referred to as a Dinka. Most of the pre-1925 Sudanese officer corps were similarly part of the old slave-soldier community, very few having been born in the South or having strong contacts with the peoples of their parents or grandparents. Contemporary British administrators classified them as 'detribalized', and it was this 'detribalization' which was thought to make them susceptible to new political movements such as nationalism or pan-Arabism. Willis was Director of Intelligence in 1924 when Ali Abd al-Latif's arrest and imprisonment provoked a mutiny in some units of the army.

had great difficulty in getting their decisions carried out, there has been improvement.

Consciously or not, the government has in the Dunjol Dinka a section of the tribe that does for all intents and purposes administer itself; owing to its remoteness and inaccessibility the tribe is little visited, but it pays up its tribute readily and gives no trouble. The tribe numbers about 5000.

The Dinka in Abwong District consist of the Ngok (pop. 5,000), Jureir (3,000) and Ballak (300).

The Ngok and Ballak have a more or less permanent court, which now manages its own sittings without requiring the assistance of the district commissioner.

The Jureir are being put on the same lines as the Ngok.

These people are well placed as they have good land and are close to the main line of communications. They get cash for their crops and pay their tribute in money. They will form part of the area in which the experiment of native administration is to be made, and they are a valuable part of it, as they already manage their affairs and make an example for others to imitate.

The Dinka of Duk Faiwel District fall roughly into two parts, the Nyarreweng [Nyareweng], (pop. 10,000), Gol [Ghol or Hol], (pop. 10,000) and Dwar [Duor] (3,000) on the north side and the Twi [Twic] (70,000) on the South. The northern lot suffered very badly from the raids of the Nuer and they are considerably mixed up. The Nuer have a fancy for Dinka women. It is not uncommon to find Dinka with a Nuer chief and vice versa. The Nyarreweng are said to be the aristocracy of the Dinka, and for that very reason they suffered the most from Nuer raids. They have the advantage of a particularly intelligent chief, Deng Malwal, who will probably end by being paramount[22] chief in this area. They are staunch adherents of government as they know that without government protection the Nuer would overrun them, and they can be relied on to give valuable information. But all Dinka information has to be sifted very carefully, as they delight in getting the government to go and bully their enemies.

The Twi have a reputation for truculence, and they told me that if they had horses and rifles they would be as good as the government. That is typical of the Dinka.

However they have come to hand in the last two years.

There was a mass of intertribal cases, the results of old raids and fights, a very large number of which have been settled, and it should be possible soon to make a time-bar and refuse to hear old cases, and then the chiefs should be able to manage.

---

[22] Typed as 'permanent' in the manuscript.

The Twi have an outlet on the river at Jonglei on the Khor Atem. Experiments in cotton and dura are now being made and there is some hope that trade might be worked up in this area. There are general characteristics favourable to the extension of the 'native administration' to this district. There are points of difficulty in removing the police in toto, as the Posts and Telegraph Office at Kongor would probably not consent to be left without some sort of guard. But the police in this district already present a problem. The police at Bor which will be added to the district on 1.1.1928 are paid on Bahr el-Ghazal rates, i.e. from 35 Pt plus a ration upwards. The police at Duk Faiwel are paid at the normal rates of Sudan government police and come under the police pension scheme. More over they are mostly old soldiers, to whom the Sudan government is under some obligation.[23]

I have been in consultation with Captains Kidd and Richards and they tell me that they can spare respectively ten and five men. If therefore four additional men can be taken on at Bor, or Duk Faiwel, on Bahr el-Ghazal government rates, the 19 can be posted at Duk Faiwel and Kongor in lieu of those now there, who would be withdrawn to Malakal, and strength of the mounted police reduced accordingly. That would tide over until it is possible to say whether the experiment in the Abwong District can be extended.

Shilluk

The chief obstacle in the way of the development of native administration among the Shilluk is the lack of discipline. The chiefs cannot control the young men, who at the instigation of their leaders will line up for a fight on the smallest provocation; and a chief who tried to follow the lines of e.g. Captain Fergusson's Nuer, would certainly get a spear into him very soon.

The only way to cure this is to round up refractory characters immediately; and they fly off into the bush, as soon as they suspect any government official coming for them; and probably the only way to catch them is to picket their villages and prevent them getting any food until they surrender. No great force is needed, but speed is the main thing.

Apart from the lack of discipline of the young men, there is also the fact that many of the chiefs are not sufficiently interested to follow the government policy. It is true there is the remuneration for tribute, but they detect in every government order a new form of tribute. Cotton

---

[23] The police in Bahr el-Ghazal Province had originally been raised as an 'irregular' force (*jihadiyya*), paid at a lower rate than the regular army or police, were given a regular ration, but otherwise required less equipment and fewer supplies than the regulars.

growing was looked upon as a new form of impost and education of the boys another.

With so much suspicion about, the Government needs to have the certain support of the chiefs, and that can best be obtained by making the position of chief desirable.

Much may be done by bringing the young men under the chiefs' authority, but the gift of a few cows from time to time would be extremely effective.

If moreover they had been immunized to cattle-plague at the serum station, it would serve as propaganda for that as well. The effect would be greater production, as a good chief sees that his people get on with their cultivation, so that the government should get back any expenditure indirectly. There are thirty main sections of the Shilluk, and a considerable number of sub-chiefs, as is only natural for a population of 90,000, so that the provision of rewards for services rendered would be likely to run to several hundred pounds. It would however be a good investment, if it brought the Shilluk into control. If the government could see its way to allotting, say, £300 for this purpose, I believe it would be well worth a trial. I should suggest putting it under the heading of native administration and adding it to the figures assessed by Mr. Coriat for his native administration.

Conclusion

There is nothing very sensational in the proposals put forward: but they do to some degree define the outlines of the future administration of these negroid tribes.

I assume that the objective is a tribal administration cleared of all influence from the Northern Sudan which will run itself with the supervision of British officials. That this can be done on the relatively small scale, Captain Fergusson has proved, but it is important that it should be recognized that his system was really established by force, and that the native character requires not to be cowed but to be restrained by the knowledge that the force exists, ready to act if need be.

The question is whether the general lines of Captain Fergusson's administration can be worked on a scale ten, fifteen or twenty times as big. My suggestion is to make an experiment, on a larger scale than Captain Fergusson's but still not too large to involve final commitments. It is to be expected that there may be backslidings, as there were with Captain Fergusson, and they would have to be dealt with promptly and efficiently but they will not be proof of failure. As the experiment progresses other areas can be prepared for the same or similar treatment.

As soon as the tribes have enough discipline there is little difficulty in getting lads for training in agriculture, and dressings, and as time goes on, all the other departments of life.

As things progressed, a headquarters organization to deal with the native administration could be recruited from the districts; and though that is looking very far ahead, it would ultimately mean the re-organization of headquarters in method, staff and arrangement.

One essential of the whole scheme is disarmament. The natives have bought their rifles and they will not give them up willingly, and establishment of tribal discipline must come first as there would be some hope of getting in at any rate many rifles without trouble, once the discipline is there.

The proximity of the Abyssinian frontier and the large number of rifles available then adds to the difficulty, but once the native learns that a rifle is too expensive to be worth buying, the trade will cease. The Nuer especially strike me as a particularly hard-headed lot when it comes to a deal.

The proposals are as follows:

1. Removal of Gwek Wunding and destruction of Deng Kur's pyramid.
2. Experimental 'native administration' of Abwong District by:
    Withdrawal of the mounted police and sarraf accountant.
    Substitution of local natives for merkaz staff.
    Transfer of certain sums to a separate account to be entitled 'native administration account' which would be managed by the district commissioner subject to the approval etc. of the governor, and possibly a special grant in aid.
3. Strengthening the position of the chiefs by a system of rewards for services rendered and by supporting their authority, if necessary by force.
4. Examination of the agricultural possibilities of these areas.
5. Permission to troops to move about the province in area where their presence is likely to have a sound political effect.
6. Disarmament of the tribesmen by gradual process, section by section.

C.A.W.
Governor, Upper Nile Province

Chapter 1

NEW PROPOSALS 1928

7th February 1928

The Civil Secretary, Sudan Government, Khartoum

I send herewith notes on new proposals. They comprise the following subjects:

1. The improvement and increase of native cattle by breeding and Veterinary assistance.
2. The distribution of staff throughout the province, its immediate requirements and probable expansion.
3. Roads and mechanical transport.
4. River transport.
5. A general survey of the needs of the province from the point of view of medicine, agriculture and forestry.
6. The need for research.

I am forwarding them all together to you because these subjects all affect the administration of the province closely and need to be considered as a whole, but I am sending copies for the departments concerned, and I shall be obliged if you will forward them to their several destinations. It must be remembered that whilst in the North the departmental official can carry on his work more or less independently of the political officials, in the South he has to keep in the closest possible touch with the DC or ADC and in the initial stages needs the actual presence of the political official to give authority to his instructions.

It may seem that I am making heavy demands on the finances of the country for a province, the economic possibilities of which have yet to be proved. Ostensibly that is so, but if the cost of the patrols that have taken place in the province since the beginning of the Sudan government were added to the actual cost of administration, I believe it would immediately be clear that some revision of the system is desirable, and an increase of direct expenditure on administration should more than compensate for the reduction if not the total elimination of military patrols.

The system of native administration is yet in its infancy, and during its early growth, it will require constant attention, but that period can also be used to prepare the way for the development that should normally follow in administration, production, and in all sides of government activity.

Governor, Upper Nile Province

Introduction

New proposals I

The administration of the negroid tribes of this province presents a difficulty in that the government has very little to offer the natives which attracts them and might stimulate them to produce.

Medical treatment has provided only a partial solution; for, whilst the natives are grateful for treatment it is the sick who receive it and they are presumably those least capable of production.

The administrative development of the province has had to follow the lines of least resistance; i.e. the district commissioner introduces any part of the general lines of native administration that he finds he can get adopted.

Thus in the Western Nuer the chiefs' courts are comparatively forward but the chiefs' police have yet to be organized. In the Lau Nuer the police are more forward, with moderately good chiefs' courts, and among the Shilluk the police are extremely useful whilst chiefs' courts (apart from the Ret's) hardly exist.

Thus the development, is rather uneven, and although this is to be expected in the early stages when the system is first introduced it is obviously desirable, so to organize the administration that the different sections be brought into the same level all round.

With all the negroid tribes the ruling passion is cattle, especially cows. The Nuer who form the largest part of the population depend almost wholly on milk and meat for their sustenance and at a pinch can survive on blood extracted from their cattle. The boys acquire their names from their special bulls, which become an integral part of their personality so that the 'name bulls' are their most important possession. Bulls are used for sacrificial purposes and for dancing and in effect the whole tribal life is centred on cattle.[24] The same applies in a lesser degree to both Shilluk and Dinka.

The obvious line of approach to the confidence or cupidity of the native is through cattle.

The wealth of cattle actually owned by the tribes is largely a matter of guess work and varies considerably.

The Dinka of Renk and Melut District for instance who number some 23,000 people have only some 8,500 cattle, and there is reason to believe the number of cattle has dropped appreciably in the last ten years. The Shilluk with a population of some 90,000 have 40,000 cattle. The Lau Nuer with a population of about 100,000 have only 25,000 head of cattle, though they had double that number some years ago.

---

[24] Where Willis writes 'bulls' he should mean oxen. Very few bulls are left intact; the 'name bulls', 'dance bulls' and sacrificial animals are castrated animals.

On the other hand the Nuer of the late Captain Fergusson's district are said to have some 300,000 head of cattle or about 5 to 1 head of population.[25]

Some of the Twi Dinka are also rich in cattle, whilst the Gol, Dwar and Nyarreweng are poor. On the whole the cattle population of the province is far below the numbers that the country could stand, and is not really sufficient to maintain the people, according to their normal customs. Apart from actual numbers, the milk production of the local breed of animals is very poor, giving an average of about 1 lb. a day through the milking season. An improvement of the stock should do much to increase the food supply of the tribesmen and render them less liable to disease and more capable of work.

It may be assumed therefore that:
(i) The cattle population is very low
(ii) The most effective appeal to the tribesmen is by increasing their herds whether (a) by improved treatment and breeding,
or (b) by accretions as rewards for services rendered.

To that should be added:
(iii) The price of cattle is unduly high and will remain so until the tribal needs are met by increase of tribal herds.
(iv) As a result, any genuine development of cattle trade must await the time when there is a true surplus of cattle above the needs of the tribesmen.

The government has hitherto been dependent upon 'malakia' labour (Sudanese colonists), for any work that was required.

The supply of these is limited, and their employment precludes the use of the tribesmen who thus are not being introduced to new ideas and methods from the performance of new tasks.

It is noteworthy that there is no Veterinary inspector in any of the Southern Provinces.

My suggestions are that (i) a Veterinary inspector should be provided to investigate the problem on the spot and determine the best steps to take to increase the existing herds, improve the stock, and immunize them from disease, and train suitable tribesmen to assist in this service, on the same lines as the Medical Service pursues in its work.

(ii) To start one or more government farms on which cattle would be bred, if possible from improved stock;[26] the farms should provide stud

---

[25] These guesses were wide of the mark. Evans-Pritchard's impression in the early 1930s that the ratio between human and cattle populations was roughly 1:1 was generally confirmed twenty years later by the Jonglei Investigation Team. In 1954 the total cattle population for all the Nuer districts was placed at just over half a million. See JIT (1954 i: 230–1) and Howell (1954: 239).

[26] For the fate of some of the bulls introduced to the districts to improve stock, see below, ch. 9.

bulls to serve native cows, and it would also provide a considerable number of calves, immunized from cattle plague, which would prove a valuable incentive to natives to work. Then if the system adopted by Captain Fergusson of fining delinquents in heifer calves be maintained and widened, there would be a considerable number of animals obtainable yearly which could be either merged into the farm for breeding purposes or used as rewards for the services rendered.

(iii) The depot for making serum which is being started at Malakal this February should increase its out-put to cover the amount likely to be wanted for use in the Southern Provinces.

(iv) It might be possible in time to introduce fairs and shows.

(v) The possession by the government of a commodity which the native wants would not only facilitate provision of labour but would encourage the introduction of the use of money.

(vi) Subject to modifications for technical reasons the obvious line would be to have one stock farm among the Shilluk, say at Kodok, where it might be under the supervision of the Agricultural inspector, one adjacent to the Nuer wherever a reasonably accessible and healthy place could be found, and one among the Southern Dinka who have suffered so greatly from Nuer depredations that they are very short of cattle. It is possible that assistance could be given by the Agricultural inspector in these two cases also.

(vii) The chief difficulty I anticipate is in the adaptation of theory to the peculiar conditions of the province, especially under the fierce light of native criticism; as the natives consider that they know all that can be known about cattle management in these parts, and they have in fact learnt by experience a great deal. They will only accept new ideas if they are proved useful, e.g. the Shilluk are already asking for anti-vaccine against cattle plague, and one failure is disproportionately damaging to the spread of a new idea.

(viii) I have not attempted to consider the possible cost of this proposal, as that must largely depend upon the technical opinion of the Veterinary Department.

New proposals II

The distribution of the staff indicated by the Quarterly Returns of Officials up to end of 1927 has given a fallacious impression in that it appeared that there were triple inspectorates, i.e. three assistant district commissioners in one main district could interchange. In practice they could not do so by reason of difference of tongues and customs of their people and the remoteness of their respective district headquarters.

The addition of the Eastern District of Bahr el-Ghazal to the Upper Nile Province should be of value in bringing the whole of the Nuer under one administration and as the Nuer represent a large part of the whole province, and possibly the most difficult, the organization of their administration may be used as a basis on which the province staff can be arranged.

There are:

1. The Western Nuer (i.e. those of the late Captain Fergusson's district) population	60,000
2. The Lak and Thiang in Zeraf Island	30,000
3. Gaweir	23,000
4. Lau (Mor and Gun)	100,000
5. Jekaing (Gaajok and Gaajak)	200,000

It would be possible and convenient to make of these three double districts 1 & 2 making the first, 3 & 4 the second and 5 the third. The district commissioners and assistant district commissioners should be so distributed that some continuity could be relied upon, and the senior man would be transferred as the junior one had acquired the knowledge and experience needed to enable him to carry on and to teach a more junior man.

This will make the normal period of service in the South at least five years before transfer.

The rest of the province is divided into (I) the northern part, with the Shilluk tribe holding all the west bank of the Nile, and some settlements on the east, and further north again some sections of Dinka, who about finally on the Arabs. (II) the southern part, consisting of the Bor and Duk District on the east bank and the Aliab and Cic Dinka with the Atwot on the west bank.

Owing to their remoteness and their differences of dialect etc. it is impossible to combine the Dinka under one set of district commissioners and assistant district commissioners.

The Shilluk on the other hand are a united tribe, with their villages strung parallel to the river from Tonga to Kaka and from Nagdia up the Sobat to some miles north of Malakal on the west bank.

They are so far the most productive people in the province, and grew approximately 12,000 kantars of cotton in 1926–27, besides exporting a considerable quantity of dura, but their chiefs are mostly feeble, the young men are undisciplined, and they need constant handling, which in view of

Introduction

the length of country over which they are distributed is difficult even with motor transport.

Among the Shilluk a double district would be a great help, when the assistant district commissioner, Malakal could take over the management of the southern Shilluk under the district commissioner, Kodok, and the two districts made interchangeable.

This makes three double districts of Nuer and one of Shilluk, and three single districts of Dinka of which (1) one (Yirrol) has hitherto been a double district; (2) another (Bor & Duk) being in the area of the irrigation schemes and fairly highly populated is likely to require to be a double district at some future date, and (3) the Renk and Melut District in the north.

There remains the Akobo District which nominally includes the whole of the SE portion of the province down to the Boma plateau, but in fact extends to the Anuak residing within the borders of the Sudan and to some degree the Beir [Murle], further south, whilst the rest of the district is unadministered and much of it is empty.

There is also the Daga Valley where a patrol along the Abyssinian frontier is maintained during the dry season. Gambeila owing to its

	Staff required	Population
Nuer		
District No. 4	2	100,000 ?[a]
" 2	2	130,000
" 3	2	200,000
Shilluk	2	90,000[b]
Dinka (Bor & Duk)	1	120,000)
{Aliab Cic Atwot	1	100,000 ?}[a]
(Renk & Melut	1	30,000)[c]
Akobo	1	50,000 ?
Daga Valley	1	2,000[d]
Gambeila	1	
	14	

[a] Rough estimate similar to those made of the existing districts of Upper Nile Province, but probably low.
[b] Ligwe [?] not including either Rueng Dinka or Dunjol Dinka who fall into that administration.
[c] Including some 6,000 Arabs and Sudanese whose administration is the same as that followed further north.
[d] The main business of the assistant district commissioner Daga Valley is to patrol the Abyssinian frontier. Hitherto he has also managed the trading from that area, but it is desirable to let that lapse to merchants. Ostensibly the second assistant district commissioner in Jekaing should be able to do this patrolling, but practically he cannot.

inaccessibility employs an assistant district commissioner all the time. This work is rather economic than administrative. The existing staff of the province (including that of Eastern District of Bahr el-Ghazal) besides the governor and deputy governor is twelve district commissioners and assistant district commissioners and one assistant district commissioner on loan.[27]

At present assistant district commissioner Malakal does the work of commandant of police. This prevents him from having adequate time to assist in the administration of the Shilluk, as between the police work and the local business of Malakal town his time is fully occupied. If a commandant of police were appointed in connection with the re-garrisoning of Upper Nile Province, a solution to this problem would be found.

The nett result however is that one additional assistant district commissioner has to be found for Nuer area, and somebody to patrol he Daga Valley. Later it would be reasonable to foresee the doubling of the two southern Dinka districts.

New proposals III. Roads & communications

The existing roads are as follows:
   Geigar to Gelhak
   Kaka to Tonga
   Malakal to Khor Fullus
   Khor Fullus to Nyerol & Mwot Did
   Mwot Did to Duk
   Duk to Bor
   Melut to Nyeda
Roads to be constructed:
   Malakal to Nasir
   Nasir to Akobo
Additional roads required:
   Gelhak to Kurmuk
   Gelhak to Melut
Roads partially cleared:
   Mwot Did to Akobo
The existing allotment of cars is:
   One touring car
   Three lorries
   A further lorry under consideration

---

[27] Captain H. F. Kidd, Fergusson's replacement, was on loan from Bahr el-Ghazal.

One lorry is in use in the Bor and Duk District. Owing to the distance of this district from headquarters, this lorry is not available for other services even if it were not in constant use by the DC of that district.

One lorry works on the Shambe-Yirrol road and is fully employed there.

One lorry has been lent to SDF for a time, previously it was working in Malakal chiefly to assist PWD and it has returned to that work.

It is needed to work on the Kaka-Tonga road in conjunction with DC Kodok.

One lorry is needed at Renk to enable the ADC to visit Gelhak and Geigar with despatch. He cannot manage the Gelhak market unless and until he has some means of motor transport. Owing to the distance from headquarters, this car would very rarely be available for work in other districts.

The touring car is used as a general utility car e.g. it has taken a Medical inspector from Melut to the Dinka villages to enable him to vaccinate the population against a scare of smallpox, it has assisted DC Kodok in providing a 'flying column' to arrest a dangerous native, it has taken the governor to meetings with officers on patrol etc.

Thus all cars already allotted are earmarked, and no car is available for the Fullus Mouth-Nyerol-Mwot Did road, which is one of the most important as it enables the ADC Abwong to get into swift communication with the Lau Nuer.

Also the maintenance of communications with Nasir and if possible with Akobo should be carried out by car as soon as the road can get through.

Two box Fords or lorries should be allotted for these services. The box Fords are slightly cheaper but the lorries have the advantage of being able to carry much more, and as they are likely to be used for a great variety of purposes, such as bringing in sick for treatment, distributing cotton seed or the like as well as transporting the ADCs and their kit, a certain latitude in carrying capacity is desirable.

It will be observed that all these cars are working singly. This is not really sound, as in the event of a serious breakdown at a distance from district headquarters, a DC might have great trouble in getting home, whilst on some stretches e.g. the Mwot Did-Akobo section owing to the lack of water on the road a breakdown might mean great risk of dying of thirst.

There should be a reserve of, say, one touring car and one box Ford, which could be despatched to accompany a DC when he was going over a dangerous bit of road at a great distance from headquarters.

To enable cars or passengers and their baggage to get across rivers, four ferries would be needed. One across the Sobat at Fullus Mouth, one at

Malakal to reach the main Shilluk (Kaka-Tonga) road, one at Melut, and one at Nasir to cross the Sobat to the Akobo side.

I am informed that ferries suitable for use on khors are supplied by Sudan Government Railways & Steamers to Bahr el-Ghazal Province at about £60 each. Whether these would be practicable for the main Nile, I cannot say, possibly enquiries could be more swiftly made direct from Khartoum on this subject.

The Minkeman bank would complete a circuit from Shambe to Yirrol and thence to the river again opposite Malek, and would provide a connection between the main Bor-Malakal road with the west bank. A ferry would be necessary here too unless CMS Mission would undertake to find one.

The provision of these services should make a network of roads over the Upper Nile Province which would enable the officials concerned to deal more swiftly with their work, to keep in closer touch with the outlying sections of the tribes and to spread the spirit of discipline which can only come by constant handling of the native. It is the first and most potent safeguard that can be employed to preclude the repetition of conditions which lead to expensive patrols.

For strategic and administrative reasons these recommendations can be justified and economic development must depend on improved communications.

The effect would be that in the dry season travel would be mainly by land and not by steamer, and therefore some saving could be effected in the hire of steamers and cost of firewood.

Some additional allowances would have to be made for water transport, during the dry weather, but it would be trifling as compared to the saving that might be effected.

New proposals IV. River transport

1. Whatever steps may be taken to increase communications by land, certain areas will continue for years to come to be only practicable by the use of steamers.

The Western Nuer District is one: and it has been supplied with the SGS Kerreri for some years. If this district be combined with the Zeraf Island, as a double district, some additional steamers or barge accommodation would be required for the second assistant district commissioner in the district. Hitherto the assistant district commissioner has been based on Fangak and has had the use of a province steamer from time to time either to land him at one side of the island and evacuate him some days later at the other side or to enable him to cross and recross the Zeraf from one set of cattle camps to another.

With the redistribution of districts suggested in my earlier note assistant district commissioner Zeraf Island would not be occupied with natives east of the Zeraf, and would assist assistant district commissioner Western Nuer in the administration of the Nuer on the west bank of the Jebel river.

Thus the provision of the Kerreri for one ADC and a tug and barge for the other ADC would seem the only practicable method until some more convenient means of accommodation can be discovered.

As the steamer is the sole residence of the assistant district commissioner it has to provide room for the servants of the official as well as himself, for animals both cattle and mules, and often a number of natives. It is necessary that the steamer should provide proper protection for servants, crew and animals against mosquitoes, heat and rain on a scale that is not normally provided.

The same would apply to the tug and barge.

2. The river transport required for this district is particularly important because the ADCs have no other residence than the steamer or barge.

At the same time the steamers actually hired to the province are very constantly in use and when in use are equally the residence of the officials on them a review of their conditions and accommodation they give deserves notice.

Apart from the Kerreri already mentioned and only transferred to Upper Nile Province in 1928 the province steamers are the Hafir, the Shabluka, the Culex and the Eland. The two Agricultural inspectors in the northern part of the province have one tug and barge. The Agricultural inspector in Western Nuer District also has a tug and barge and the conservator of Forests has a tug and barge except in the rains when he gets a steamer. The Margaret is hired to the province for the rainy season.

The Hafir is a good boat, with two cabins and a mosquito house. On the barge there is a mosquito house, which is commonly used by an ADC as a living room when accompanying the governor. As this exposes him in all the more intimate business of dressing and washing to the gaze of the crew, police, servants and others who may be on the boat there is felt to be a need for a cabin on the barge. There is a mysterious doghole about five feet square sometimes used by Mohammedan wives of police but it cannot be called normal human accommodation. The barge is always on the point of sinking.

There is no protection to the crew or servants against mosquitoes. The engine is adequate, the rais knows the river and his work and keeps good discipline with his crew.

The Shabluka has two small cabins, and is so designed that it is almost impossible to find anywhere cool enough to sleep. The barge is a double decker with no room or house on it. The engine is so old that the ship is often unable to progress against the wind. The rais is long past his work and has lost his nerve and cannot manage his crew. This steamer and barge has no protection to crew and servants whatsoever.

The Culex has a single cabin, and whilst it can be made to manage on the main Nile, the conditions up the Sobat or in the sudd make life on it almost impossible, as the mosquitoes cannot be kept out. There is a single decker barge, which is so small it is of little use, as it hardly takes the mules of an ADC and no police. The engine is not quite so bad as that of the Shabluka, but that is the best that can be said of it. The rais is a fool, and cannot manage his crew.

The Eland has the great merit that it draws very little and can go up the Sobat when nothing else can. It has a well, between the engine and the boiler and the steampipes running over head and the heat is like a Turkish bath. A mosquito house has been put, at private expense, on the single decker barge, as it was inhuman to send British officials e.g. up the Baro without some protection. There is no kitchen and no latrine.

Actually the Eland is not meant to be a passenger vessel, but in practice in this province we have to use what we have got to the best we can manage. The bottom of the Eland is mostly cement and sailor's shirts. We have much to thank the Eland for, but I fear she cannot go on very much longer. The engine seems relatively stronger; the rais is excellent, knows the Sobat extremely well and manages his crew well.

The Margaret is used by tourists during the season: she is extremely unhandy and district commissioner Nasir prefers any boat to her because of this. She is also so shaky it is impossible to write on her.

Of the tugs and barges I know little except one of the Agricultural barges only has a native latrine.

I think it is sufficiently shown that the steamer accommodation is rough, and not designed to suit the climatic conditions. It must be remembered that when a DC or ADC is travelling on a steamer, he is proceeding on a further trek inland and has to be accompanied by an escort of police besides his own mules. Besides this he generally has assistant Medical officer, some sick and very possibly Public Works Department stores etc. till natives are found clinging to the roof rafters like bats.

It is difficult to make a definite recommendation on the subject of steamers because one does not know what is obtainable. But I believe that one good boat like the Hafir with a properly fitted barge for the climate and conditions, one strong tug (not a seagoing tug drawing six foot of water) capable of shifting heavy barges and of moving by itself to pick up and drop barges in swift succession, and one shallow draught launch similar to the Thornycroft possessed by the American Mission up the Sobat would make a more efficient and cheaper service for the requirements of the province other than the Western Nuer District. Before fitted for the climatic conditions would be required e.g. for PWD partly and for general work. It might also be necessary to hire a steamer to work up the Sobat for a few months between July and December when movement by land is impossible and I should not like to commit myself to dispensing with the possibility.

I assume that the Shabluka, Culex and Eland must shortly be scrapped, and my proposal should present possibilities of economy and the scheme offers at least a basis of discussion.

3. Any proposal for the reduction of steamer transport, or the partial substitution during the dry weather of mechanical transport means that much of the work now done by province steamers would have to be done by postboat. This implies a certain elasticity in the capacities of the postboats both for passenger carrying and barge shifting.

I know that the Sudan Government Railways and Steamers is building up a new fleet and must be embarrassed in the transition period, especially when the expansion of passenger traffic has outstripped expectation: but there are certain points that strike us dwellers in the swamps which we hope will be taken in the spirit of helpful criticism in which they are made.

The schedule appears to be based on an ideal almost unattainable for it is quite the exception for a postboat to reach Malakal either from north or south on time. This is no doubt due to the boats trying to take more barges than they can drive at the required pace to keep up to time. Great improvement in the distribution of barges and organization was noticeable when there was a British official of the SGR&S in Malakal to keep touch with the movements of vessels, but he has unfortunately gone sick. The need of such an official has, I hope, been established. If so, accommodation should be found for him both as residence and office, he should presumably have a wide latitude of responsibility in dealing with river traffic on the White Nile.

The new vessels, such as the Lord Kitchener and Sir R. Wingate, are disappointingly slow, and present little hope to the layman of maintaining the schedule.

If boats like the Anuak, admittedly cargo boats, are used for passenger traffic the temporary provision of mosquito houses for the sleeping accommodation of passengers is essential.

The engineers on the boats require versatility, they not only have to ensure the proper working of the engine, but are responsible for discipline of the crews, cleanliness of the ship, efficiency of catering, supercargo work, and the general comfort of the passengers. It seems doubtful if the terms offered by the Sudan government are attracting the right kind of men; verbal complaints by passengers on one or other of these points are not uncommon. If one may be allowed to say so, the boats, posts or otherwise, are not fitted for the special conditions of the Southern provinces, and there seems to be some lack of appreciation what the conditions are. When one has been waited on at dinner by a servant literally dripping blood on the shoulders, because of the onslaughts of mosquitoes between the cook house and the dining room, (a personal experience) one felt that some system of protection of crew and servants would be humane (e.g. something in the nature of an adjustable wire frame work which could be put up when required). A tourist who had hired a steamer from the Sudan government somewhat ruefully remarked that the price did not apparently include a better light than candles, admittedly a small point but it is the small things that accumulate to a feeling of general grievance.

Without multiplying instances let it be enough to say that there is felt to be a need (1) for a fuller examination of the local conditions and the adaptation to them of the steamers of all sorts, and (2) for a closer adherence to the schedule and (3) for the provision of permanent senior staff up the White Nile to organize the traffic and maintain an efficient inspection and control with authority to deal with minor matters which trifling in themselves tend to be exaggerated into grievances.

New proposals V

A general survey of the needs of the province:

One of the most satisfactory features of the province is the great expansion of Medical and Agricultural work. This has been done by the close co-operation of the officials of the department concerned with the political service, and the gist of this proposal is not to suggest anything new but to co-ordinate, systematize and extend what already exists.

The distinguishing principle of work in the province and perhaps in the whole of the South is opportunism or if it be preferred, following the line of least resistance. Innovations have been introduced to the natives not systematically but by taking advantage of any opportunity offered or any facility that existed. Because cotton was being heavily 'boomed' in the Sudan, the cultivation of cotton was pressed in the UNP without a previous examination of the soil and conditions or needs of the people.

It appears to me to be time to ask for a general survey of the province from an agricultural point of view, to show what areas are suitable to this or that type of cultivation, and to collate this information with the actual condition of the people, e.g. whether they have an adequate, excessive or

Introduction 71

inadequate food supply, what labour is available, what means of removing produce, till the government is in a position to concentrate efforts on the most effective and economic objectives. There are still areas which have not been visited by an Agricultural inspector; and as it happens that there is a short cotton crop to collect this year, so that the Agricultural inspectors will not be so engrossed as usual in this work, there is an opportunity for the collation of the information needed.

The work of the Medical Service is inestimable, and the Medical inspectors untiring, and DCs and ADCs assist not only by their influence but with their personal efforts. The population however is so large, the area so extensive, and the conditions of life so hard, and the medical problems are so numerous that much effort may be wasted unless the work is approached systematically and with an eye to all the conditions and not merely those of health. For this purpose there is needed a general survey of the province dealing with each area in some detail, and showing not only the incidence of disease and the possibilities of alleviation or cure but also the facilities of communication available and the chances of an economic return for increased efficiency. For instance the best method of improving the health of the area may be to supply the services of an Agricultural inspector to assist in increasing the food supply and so giving the native greater resistance to disease, whilst in another place the further economic development may await the successful eradication of some disease.

I have in a previous correspondence described the need of bringing re-afforestation schemes in relation to the native administration, and I hope that that will succeed sufficiently to allow the Forestry authorities opportunity to examine the forest possibilities and needs of the province.

Such a survey of the Medical, Agricultural and Forestry requirements of the province, concentrated into a whole in relation to the political situation would prove of the first, I would rather say essential, value in forming the policy of the future. It would have to be worked out with consideration of the native staff to be obtained and trained, and so would interconnect with the educational and missionary policy of the government.

I recommend therefore that (1) the existing data be collated and put on record; and (2) where there is a hiatus in our information, steps be taken to fill it.

New proposals VI. Research

The previous section referred to the systematic examination of facts in the field. It is a question whether the time is not arriving, if it has not already arrived for the establishment of a nucleus of research to co-operate with the work in the field. The extent of the Medical work already being done in the province would appear to justify the establishment of a centre of research in the South. The presence of the material actually at its doors should assist the work of research, besides giving great help to the work of the Hospital. The existence of a station for the making of serum against cattle plague in the vicinity of Malakal indicates another need for a research base and it is reasonable to suppose that the opportunity of access to precise instruments and scientific assistance could not but be of great value both to the Agricultural and Forestry.

I suggest that it might be possible for the [Wellcome] Research Laboratories to open a branch at Malakal. It would no doubt refer much to Khartoum where greater facilities would be available, and this would keep it to the form of a mere outpost of research, but it should be of value not only to the province but also to the Central Research Laboratories in widening the field of scientific enquiry and bringing the remoter areas of the Sudan into closer touch with the main organization.

CHAPTER 2

Main Report and Proposals

C. A. WILLIS

COMMUNICATIONS

Land

Roads

'In 1920 the Government decided to open a road from Bor to the main White Nile and a track was cleared from Bor through the lines of the Duks to a point in the Nile near the mouth of Khor Atar. The Northern half of this, from the Duk Fadiat to the Nile fell into what was then the Upper Nile Province. The road was remote from villages, or camps, it served no economic purposes and was practically useless and after being kept up at considerable trouble and expense for two years, it was allowed to disappear and now there is no trace of it.' (See Ben Assher, 'A Nomad in the South Sudan', Witherby, London 1928).[1]

A road had also been opened from Melut eastwards to the line of the Dinka villages about eighteen miles out and thence east again into the Fung Province.

Owing to the fact that no one ever used it this road fell into desuetude and my predecessor put it in record that the maintenance of roads in Upper Nile Province was impracticable [see below, appendix 1].

In 1925 he actually took over the Duk and Bor Districts from Mongalla Province so had the maintenance of the southern half of the road already referred to.

Notwithstanding his pessimism I was so strongly impressed with the need of communications as a first step in administration that in 1926 I obtained a small grant for experimental purposes and in 1927 was given a Ford touring car, to see if it could be used effectively, and it was tried on a track in the Shilluk country on the west bank of the Nile at Melut to the Dinka villages, and from Fullus mouth to Nyerol.

The result of these experiments was sufficiently reassuring to justify a

---

[1] This is not a direct quotation from 'Ben Assher' (1928), but a summary of chs. 6 & 7.

scheme of roads (1) through the Shilluk on the west bank from Tonga to Kaka; (2) a road on each side of the Sobat in Abwong District and from Fullus mouth to Lau; (3) a small piece of road from Jokau to Kigille to make the coffee trade of the Daga Valley capable of development.

In 1928 patrol S8 occurred in Lau, and the Sudan Defence Force brought down an old grader from the Darfur Patrol 1916 and used it to improve the Nyerol road. It was only a qualified success as the soil was too hard, for the most part, to respond to treatment. Still the practicability of mechanical transport could be re-tried (that it had been tried before, was proved by a car laying derelict since 1919 between Abwong and Nyerol).

In 1929 began Nuer Settlement, and the development of communications was recognised as an integral part of policy. Funds for opening new roads and for improving those that existed were generously provided, and a more ambitious scheme initiated:

1. Tonga-Kaka road
2. Geigar to Melut
3. Malakal to Bor via Fathai
4. Fathai to Akobo
5. Malakal to Akobo via Nasir

In 1928 the Upper Nile Province took over the Eastern District of Bahr el-Ghazal (Yirrol and Western Nuer Districts). This involved the Shambe-Yirrol-Rumbek road and later a complete road system connecting all tribal centres of the district with the Shambe-Yirrol road.

Meanwhile the Egyptian Irrigation Department had been exploiting the use of mechanical transport for its own purposes and had been using modern graders but unfortunately not in the best manner; i.e. they merely scraped a smooth track out of the surface of the earth, thus leaving a depression, instead of lifting soil from each side of the road and raising the level, so as to form a cambered road. They subsequently modified their method, but in opening the Malakal-Nagdia section the old way was used and much of the track became water-logged in rain.

They also cut a road from Malek to Pibor and thus opened up the possibility of reaching the Pibor Post in dry weather and raised the question of trying to find a track from Akobo to Pibor.

In 1930 assistant district commissioner Western Nuer (Mr. P. Coriat, MBE) examined the Western Nuer District and found that the villages of the 'Jebel Island' could be reached throughout its length if a means were found of crossing the Khor Waad inland of Adok and a pontoon was sent out up to make this possible. This road is now in use from Ameij in the southern Nuong [Nyuong] to Bentiu on the Bahr el-Ghazal.

If it proves practicable to make a track from the Tonga-Eliri road

Main Report and Proposals

westward and thence south to Yoynyang or thereabouts, the Jebel Island will be connected with the whole province road system.

A proposal to connect Ameij with the Yirrol road system has been put forward; one line suggested vial Luel and Akot involved a bank of some twenty miles, but a new scheme has not been proposed to cut a road due west from Ameij to cut the Rumbek-Pakkam road at Anong.

Subsequently it was found possible to ramp the khor and dispense with the position which was not of sufficient displacement to take a loaded lorry.

A track from Malakal north to a point opposite Kodok has been cleared and a scheme has been mooted to extend this across the Khor Adar at a point some twenty miles up it and on through the ten Dinka villages to connect with the Renk-Melut road and so make it possible to go right through from Khartoum to Nairobi.

It is hoped to connect Fangak with the Fullus-Fathai road, but so large a part of the Zeraf Valley District goes under water from flood and rain that road making in that district especially east of the Zeraf is fraught with great difficulty.

A road running N & S through the Zeraf Island is also contemplated. It would connect with Buffalo Cape on the Jebel river and Barboi or thereabouts on the main White Nile, go through Lak southwards to the Thiang and so on through Lai Kaich to the southern Gaweir villages. Preliminary work for this road is being put in hand.

In 1930 the Public Works Department supplied a grading party of three graders, three lorries and a tourer under a British mechanic (Mr. Colebourne). After some experimental work at Malakal, the party proceeded to Fullus and thence southward. 1929 had been a very wet year and the old alignment of the road was found to be under water and a new line was selected by Bimbashi G. Kavanagh via Ket where a natural landing ground was found, across the Lior (erroneously called the Kwanjor) and so on to Mwot Did, and thence to Duk Fadiat.

In 1930 the temporary bank at Lior was found to be inadequate and had to be enlarged, and it still needed to be strengthened and straightened at the southern end. A new alignment of part of the road along the Upper Fullus also had to be made, to keep clear of water.

Owing to the delays involved in getting across the Lior and re-aligning sections of the road the grading party was unable to complete its work to Bor and is returning to Bor in November 1930 to work up from that end.

The road from Malakal to Nasir was cleared by the province and the Egyptian Irrigation Department undertook to grade it in 1930, but owing to casualties to machines the work was not finished until the beginning of the rains. It has however been re-opened immediately after the rains, and except in the immediate vicinity of Nasir was passable in November 1930.

The Egyptian Irrigation Department proposes to re-open the Malek-Pibor road and then to grade a road from Pibor to Akobo: and an Egyptian Irrigation Department party is examining the possibility of connecting Nasir and Akobo by road: the alternatives under consideration are from the wood-station near the mouth of the Nyanding parallel to the Nyanding to meet the Fathai-Akobo road, or from old Nasir southwards to the east to Ngwer on the Pibor and thence to Akobo.

The rains and flood of 1930 were both indifferent, so that the country dried up exceptionally early, and it is not therefore possible to say, finally, whether the grading system is a success or not. It cannot be denied that the Malakal-Bor road has become open to traffic at the end of November, and Mr. Colebourne went through from Malakal to Kongor in under eleven hours, including the passage of the Sobat.[2]

It must not however be overlooked that an alternative experiment has been under trial between the Shambe-Yirrol and the Bor-Kongor road. This involves the construction of banks up to three feet in height with culverts at intervals, going across country which is liable to be flooded with a definite stream.

An irrigation lorry and car did the return journey to Nasir from Malakal in ten hours in December 1930.

Graders cannot at present bank to the height required, but they can probably be usefully employed in improving the banks when made.

Yirrol district differs from all others in the province; in that it has available iron stone which can be used to metal the roads, and the actual soil over a large part of the district makes a good and hard surface which requires comparatively little labour to make into an adequate road.

It is hoped as funds become available it may be possible to metal all those parts of the Yirrol-Shambe road which require it, to make the road passable at least for light traffic all through the year.

Unfortunately it is not practicable to carry the iron stone away and use it as metal elsewhere.

A sketch map [not included] shows (1) the roads cleared and graded (2) those cleared only but known to be capable of taking mechanical transport (3) those cleared but not tried and (4) contemplated roads.

A grant was made for a bank from the Nile bank opposite Malek to Minkeman and so connect the Bor and Yirrol Districts.

Unfortunately the work is one which would involve very great expense

---

[2] This is an impressive record. Even in the 1970s the journey by four-wheel drive car from Malakal to Ayod could take all day, and it was only with the construction of the Jonglei Canal road in the early 1980s that one could reasonably expect to make the journey between Malakal and Kongor within the daylight hours.

	Miles
Cleared and Graded	
Malakal-Mongalla boundary	348
Malek-Pibor (old type grading)	115
Malakal-Nasir	150
Cleared and Available for MT	
Tonga-Nun	150
Malakal-opposite Kodok	40
Yirrol road system	220
Geigar-Melut	120
Nuong-Leiro-Bahr el-Ghazal	140
Fathai-Akobo	109
Fullus-Kormayom	60
Abwong-Nyerol	37
Nasir-Akobo	70
Contemplated	
Akot-Ameij on Anong Ameij	
Akobo-Pibor	
Fangak-Lior	
Khor Nyanding-Akobo	
Tonga-Yoynyang	
Zeraf Island N-S	

and labour as there are big khors at a considerably lower level than the Nile at that point, filled up from a point down stream.

Ultimately if the Egyptian government desires to make any scheme involving the sudd area it will almost certainly have to make a barrage at a point either there or at Gameiza, so that this work ultimately is likely to be done without expense to the Sudan government, but it will certainly not be undertaken for some years.

Even without this, if the connections proposed can be carried into effect, it should be possible to reach all district headquarters, (with the possible exception of Fangak) and to work extensively in all districts by the use of MT.

This should mean the possibility of saving considerable expense in steamer transport at least during the dry weather, and the reduction of compensation for the loss of animals, in groom and forage allowance. For instance if the road system in Western Nuer can be connected with Malakal and Shambe, the steamer used as the residence of assistant district commissioner Western Nuer would cease to be necessary at any rate in the dry weather; again if assistant district commissioner Akobo can reach Pibor Post in a few hours by lorry, it would be possible to manage the district with one dry weather (Pibor Post) and one wet weather (Akobo) headquarters and save the maintenance of the other post; this would be advantageous from various points of view, and would make an economy of 25 [police] NCOs and men southern type.

It is necessary to lay stress on the point that economies are dependent on the successful completion of the road system, and the ferries required at various points.

There is reason to hope that the Akobo-Pibor connection will materialize this season.

If money were available the Western Nuer system might at least be aligned and cleared and the requirements of banks and culverts or ferries determined.

The road from Melut southwards has been cleared to a point near Rom, but until a practical means of crossing the two khors there is discovered, traffic cannot go through. As however this would mean opening up a through route from end to end of the province, the expense of supplying the necessary ferries should be justified.

A short road from Jokau to Kigille post was maintained for several years, to enable the coffee imported from Abyssinia to be brought to the Baro and stored till the river opened; unfortunately the Ethiopian government has put an embargo on this trade and so the road has been discontinued. With some engineering it might be extended to Daga. Beyond Daga to the Yabus is extremely waterless, but it is conceivable that a connection might be made with roads in southern Fung, e.g. Melut-Nyeda road, if it were required.

Suggestions have now been made from time to time e.g. by the Ethiopian Transport Company at Gambeila to make a road from Gambeila to Nasir—the chief difficulties about this are that the whole river bank from Jokau to the mouth of the Pibor goes under water at flood time, thus involving the re-making of the road annually. Moreover the khors Jokau, Machar and Makeir involve considerable bridging.

Culverts

Corrugated iron culverts were tried in various places but always gave trouble, notably that at Gelhak causeway.

Experiments were made with the ARMCO type and they appear to stand the stresses of the local conditions satisfactorily. The main trouble is that it is impossible to pack the heavy cotton soil properly round, and especially at the lower part of the culvert to give it the necessary support, and the corrugated iron ones invariably buckled under the strain of e.g. a lorry going over the road above and the culvert ceased to function.

A considerable number of culverts have been put in in various places, e.g. from Fullus to Fathai and through the Tonga-Nun road. It is likely that in the latter case culverts of an unnecessarily large size have been obtained, thus causing excessive expense.

An alternative to ARMCO culverts was used in the Shambe road, concrete slabs resting on concrete supports, but it is doubtful if they have sufficient foundation, and the flood in passing through tended to undercut the concrete and bring the whole structure away.

In Malakal three bridges have been put in on the main road ('Sharia Coryton') [see below, appendix 1], over khors and drains, besides two biggish bridges of EID. On the road along the river bank are also bridges which are not up to heavy traffic nor very successful as drains and it is proposed to substitute culverts for the latter wherever possible and to put in small 8″ culverts in various places where otherwise a bridge would be needed.

Considerable care has to be used in sorting out culverts when delivered; there are tops and bottoms and end pieces and the correct number of each has to be sent with the appropriate number of bolts etc. The instructions sent with the culverts would be thought to be fool-proof but are not in the Sudan and great confusion has been caused not only by wrong delivery from the Khartoum agents here or wrong distribution from here but also in the accounts where the identity of individual culverts was not known and they were charged for against the wrong item.

Nevertheless the ARMCO culverts or its British equivalent with which experiments are now being made seem to supply a solution to some of the difficulties of road making and drainage.

Wells

In view of the large amount of river and marsh in the province it may be a matter of surprise that there should be any need of wells. In point of fact once away from the rivers, the water supply becomes very precarious in the dry weather as it depends on the maintenance of pools filled up during the rains: the water is generally foul, since even where it is not used by cattle it is rendered undrinkable by water fowl; moreover the localities in which the natives put their camps vary from year to year and a water hole reported as good one year may be found to be exhausted early in another season through the presence of cattle camps.

Deep wells, reaching the Nubian sand stone, have been opened at Kongor and Yirrol and at Rest House No. 3 on the Shambe road. There is a well at Ayod which however was found to be empty in 1929.

A well was sunk east of Melut by the SDF many years ago but has not had water in it for years.

An attempt has been made to sink a well at Gurbana, the NE corner of Renk District, but so far water has not been reached.

Probably the immediate solution of water supply in e.g. the Lau plain is the control of khors and improvement of existing pools. The natives already do a certain amount of digging out existing pools and sheltering the water from evaporation by grass. It remains to be seen what effect the banks across the Lior and Fullus at Fathai may have. They are culverted, but it should be possible to retain a considerable volume of water if necessary.

Gaweir presents difficulties over water as when the flood drops and the natives go down to the 'toic' it is almost impossible to travel inland owing to the difficulty of getting water. It will probably be necessary to sink a deep well somewhere in the neighbourhood of Mayom at the N end of the Duk ridge in order to maintain communications with the road system further east.

Wells with helical pumps for getting clear drinking water exist at Abwong and Akobo and Western Nuer. Similar pumps should be installed at Nasir and similar small district headquarters as they enable a small vegetable garden to be maintained at slight expense.

A well was made at Gambeila to enable the assistant district commissioner to get clear water to drink. Unfortunately it turned out brackish. This is also a good case for a helical pump, when good water is found.

As the 'malakia' village at Malakal extends gradually eastward, it will become increasingly needful to find water, not only for domestic purposes but for the conservancy system of which the pits must lie further east than the village. Whether it may be possible to obtain water at a kilometre or more from the river has never been ascertained and borings would be useful. It is worth noting that even on the river bank where digging for water to 'earth' the WT cables, holes had to be dug to the depth of low Nile level before the soil was found sufficiently damp for the purpose. It is questionable whether water can be found; and on the other hand borings might discover sand or even gravel from some ancient river bed, or indeed water.

Borings in connection with the construction of sanitary pits hit very hard soil at about six metres: probably very heavy yellow clay. As this clay is impermeable water cannot be found without going through it.

Main Report and Proposals

Rest houses

Apart from the Shambe-Yirrol road which is a means of entry to the Bahr el-Ghazal Province there was no line of road communication which needed rest houses until the Malakal-Bor road was completed and even then the number of people using it other than officials on duty and presumably supplied with tentage was negligible.

On the other hand, the formation of temporary bases in Lau and Gaweir in 1927, 1928, 1929 and 1930 brought home the need of mosquito and fly protection on an extensive scale, in any Nuer country. Even when there are not mosquitoes the flies are so bad that it is almost impossible to eat or have any respite from them during daylight. A number of mosquito houses were brought down for Nuer settlement by SDF in 1929, and proved so successful that more of them of slightly improved pattern were constructed and are being distributed at such places as require them.

They can be taken to pieces and removed and re-built. They consist of wooden frames of mosquito wire, fitting into a frame work with a wooden floor and a penthouse roof, the whole resting on steel bases. There is a mosquito trap and a food hatch.

These are being put up at selected places like Fathai in Lau Nuer, Duk Fadiat, Jonglei, Ajwong etc. but also at each of the meshras of Western Nuer to provide the assistant district commissioner with a temporary rest house where he can deal with business. These are also being used to form the nucleus of a temporary station such as Megaga and have also been used to accommodate e.g. a foreman of work when erecting a cotton shed at Yodni.

Rest houses of that checkarts [?] with a mosquito proof room have been erected at every stopping place along the Shambe-Yirrol road.

A rest house at Kodok was originally built for the sub-mamur and has since been permanently occupied by the Agricultural inspector, a purpose for which it is not adequate.

The assistant district commissioner Renk has a rest house at Melut where he has a couple of brick tukls and one old and one new mosquito houses.

The house formerly occupied by the school master at Renk is available as a rest house there.

With the exception of Malakal, and Bor about which more will be said later, there are no rest houses available at any district centre except those mentioned at Kodok and Melut, one at Tonga and one at Shambe which is full of bats and of which the mosquito house recently fell down after a violent rain storm on the head of a British official sleeping within. Moreover the houses of the assistant district commissioners at places like Abwong, Nasir, etc. do not permit of entertaining guests.

At Bor there is a rest house belonging to the Egyptian Irrigation Department which has been so grossly misused that it is now reserved for the EID only. There is also a two roomed house generally known as the P&T rest house for the use of the inspector of P&T when he visits the place. It will be occupied in the immediate future by the Agricultural inspector (Mr. Broadhurst) as he has no other home except the mosquito houses at Duk Fadiat which are hardly suitable for European furniture.

At Malakal there has been a rest house for some time: it consisted of two rooms and a mosquito house with no verandah and it was so hot and stuffy that it was difficult to bear. A room was added, in order to enable us to cope with the number of people who were prone to arrive to stay in Malakal and in 1930 a verandah was added to it and it will be much better without being luxurious. This rest house is kept for use of British officials and in fact has at times been the permanent residence of a Medical or Veterinary inspector. There is no rest house for government employees, and when an accountant or translator arrives with family, furniture and all complete awaiting transfer to some post which is not dealt with by the SGR, he finds great difficulty in discovering what to do with himself or any of his belongings. As transfers are fairly frequent owing to ill health, this hardship seemed to me oppressive, and I applied for one extra quarter as rest house, but it was not granted.

The chief accountant is supposed to visit the merakiz and audit the accounts. Should he do so, he has no where to live unless the local man is a bachelor and can put him up: and the situation would even so have its awkwardness.

The only course of reasonable economy seems to be to provide a mosquito house in connection with a thatched rest house of quite a simple kind at every administrative centre: and then to see that the quarter is not misused. A ghaffir would be needed also.

It has not been necessary so far to deal with this problem, but I anticipate that it should be faced in the near future.

Mechanical transport

CARS

The growth of the use of mechanical transport has been as rapid as the roads allowed. The distribution of the cars and lorries of the province is shown in attached schedule [see above p.65].

It will be noted that there are two tribal lorries, one a Morris belonging to the Shilluk (see roads supra) and the other bought by the Cic Dinka round Shambe. This is definitely an ambulance car for the use of the sick.

In both cases the government has taken over the expense of providing a driver and maintenance.

Apart from the province cars, the Agricultural inspectors, one at Kodok and one at Bor and Duk Districts have lorries and the Medical Service proposes to have three in 1931. The Veterinary Service has been urged to provide MT for both the serum Veterinary inspector and the province VI. A great deal of work is done both for PWD (against payment) and for P&T (not at present paid for but the subject of correspondence), by province transport.

The SDF used six wheeler Thorneycrofts with great effect for shifting heavy loads of supplies from Fullus to Fathai and elsewhere, and it is likely that the provision of some of this type of heavy lorry will be needed as MT gradually takes the place of river transport. The difficulty of finding drivers for such cars and the necessity of developing on cautious lines makes it premature to ask immediately for them but the provision of, say two in 1932 would be judicious.

DRIVERS

The question of the provision of drivers has been fraught with many difficulties. The arrangement laid down in principle, i.e. the employment of policemen drivers proved a complete failure as the men sent for training learnt little and lost all discipline and the fact is that the type of Sudanese employed as a policeman in UNP is not the type suitable to be a driver.

Again an Arabic-speaking Northerner, when driving over roads in country inhabited by Shilluk, Dinka or Nuer is incapable of making himself understood, does not know the roads and has to be supplied with an interpreter if he is to carry on, thus using up accommodation. The obvious thing to do is to train local natives, preferably tribesmen, to do the work; and in fact there are a few Shilluk mission-trained boys who drive cars in the Shilluk area, there are also some Nuer and Dinka who have some but not very much idea of driving, and we are trying to train some lads locally, but the linguistic difficulties are great, as Arabic is not really a good language for the explanation of internal combustion engines and 'Mongallese'[3] is hopeless. The only course at the moment seems to be to make use of local Malakal 'malakia' with a few Northerners, and to train on tribesmen as and when opportunity offers, but a proper organization for their training, preferably in English, is much needed.

There is an arrangement with the Egyptian Irrigation Department whereby we do not take their apprentices or they ours, without mutual

---

[3] i.e. Southern colloquial Arabic (also called 'Nubi'), the precursor of 'Juba Arabic', the language now spoken by most Southern Sudanese drivers and mechanics.

knowledge, so as to avoid these young gentlemen exploiting the two governments.

STORES

Another trouble in connection with MT is the care and issue of stores and spare parts. The mudiria storekeeper deals only in Arabic and the technical terms of the spare parts of a Ford car are not known to him, and it is therefore almost impossible for him to keep a proper check. The log books provided are no doubt admirable for literate drivers but will, I fear, be kept somewhat vaguely by the local type.

So far, the commandant of police, Malakal has had the business of looking after the province cars and drivers thrust upon him. It should not, properly speaking, be his work but one has to do what one can.

The RAF has a petrol store on the landing ground. The Shell Coy has a temporary thatched hut for benzine pending the building of a proper place beyond the new EID dockyard.

Local requirements are drawn from the Shell Coy.

The RAF has had some trouble over their petrol supplies, and there has been put forward a suggestion that a more highly trained storekeeper possibly British, is required to protect their interests.

GARAGES

A garage was erected in Malakal in 1930. Previous to that all cars were put under the verandahs of the officers, during the rains, a system not congenial to efficiency.

Outside Malakal temporary shelter with thatched roofs have been erected in some merkaz, but actually the lorries are so constantly on the move in the dry weather that garage is unnecessary and the bulk of them are sent in to Malakal for re-fitting in the rains.

As the roads improve and the period over which they can be used extends it will probably be necessary to provide garage accommodation, e.g. at Yirrol, Bor this has now been built (January 1931), and Renk. At Kodok the district commissioner has been accustomed to use the 'chiefs court' (really an old EA store) as a garage.

Animal transport and carriers

HORSES

When my predecessor left there were two horses in the province, as there was a theory that horses would not survive and were not able to stand local conditions. Actually 'fly' (tsetse) occurs only on the Abyssinian frontier, and though casualties occur mainly from 'sarraga' (epizootic lymphangitis) improved stabling and care show marked decrease in losses.

Towards the end of 1926 it was possible to start polo at Malakal, and there has been a steady increase in the number of horses used. The experience of the Cavalry and M.I. in 1929 and 1930 definitely proved that with proper acclimatization pony troops were more efficient than mules, and the police are now to have two troops mounted on ponies and if the Equatorial battalion is withdrawn from Malakal, a further two troops on ponies. The question of further substitution of ponies for mules has also been put forward for the consideration of the authorities, as difficulty is found in getting mules at a reasonable price.

At present the police are mounted on second class remounts but it is proposed to have a proportion (20%) of the first class remounts to enable the heavier men to have suitable mounts.

Stabling throughout the province is either lacking or inadequate. It has indeed in many cases not been asked for owing to other needs being more pressing. But considerable demands are being made in 1931/32 programme.

It is to be hoped that with a Veterinary inspector there will be a further reduction in casualties.

MULES

Before the province acquired the large proportions it now has, it carried on with two troops of police on mules, and the assistant district commissioners then had an allowance for six mules only: but in practice many had to keep more in order to carry the supplies etc. they require for protracted journeys. The supply was maintained partly from purchases by SDF or SG Veterinary officer at Gallabat, and partly from local purchases and the prices varied from £4–7. Latterly however the price has risen very greatly and the actual cost of a mule delivered from Gallabat to Malakal is £11, and local purchases can no longer be made.

The casualties were very high, more than one third of the mules dying every year.

During the rains the police mules were kept at Kodok in what had been an old barrack room. They were terribly over-crowded and though I had the place burnt out with blow lamps three times 'sarraga' continued to break out.

It was inconvenient to have the mounted police at Kodok away from headquarters and the only course was to bring them in to Malakal.

With improved stabling and more supervision the casualties have been reduced. Three stables were erected on a plan modified from that recommended by the province and the modifications spoiled them. Subsequent stables on a better plan have been erected.

Standings for the mules also had to be made.

The assistant district commissioners have an allowance of ten mules and two horses in cases where they have heavy travelling. As each mule's saddlery costs £10.715 and the mule £10, the capital expenditure for an ADC joining the province is very high.

DONKEYS

Donkeys are almost useless for transport. The Equatorial Coy at Malakal still has twenty donkeys to carry rations, water etc., but it is known that in practice the animals are useless.

The wood stations use donkeys for carrying wood from the forest to the wood station but are finding it difficult to keep up establishment.

Over cracked cotton soil a donkey breaks his legs in the cracks and over mud he sticks and practically has to be carried.

BULLS

An assistant district commissioner at Kodok (Mr. Pollen) some years ago persuaded the government that he should have a bull hamla, though I have never discovered that he used it as such, and always suspected that they were actually employed on the sagia in Kodok garden.

The natives unfortunately have too much pride in their bulls and bullocks to use them as transport or for draught; but it is to be hoped that in time they will take as much pride in their draught animals as they do in the 'dancing' or 'name' bulls.[4] Assistant district commissioner Bor has started training bulls to the plough. An abortive effort was made a few years ago to use a 'cultivator' with bulls at Taufikia. An attempt was made to resuscitate some old bull harness at Malakal, but somebody made away with the original and the matter was dropped. If however native produce such as cotton, grain etc. is to be put cheaply on to the market, it is almost essential that bull transport should be made fashionable. It is a matter for experiment and training and it is to be hoped that the Veterinary and Agricultural inspectors can approach the problem in a practical spirit.[5]

CAMELS

Camels have occasionally been brought down by SDF on patrols. They invariably die, and it can be taken as a rule that a camel's condition varies inversely to its distance south of latitude 12°.

---

[4] Nuer will still say that they respect their cattle more than the Arabs do, when asked why they do not use their oxen for transport in the same way as the Arabs in Kordofan.
[5] There have been numerous attempts to introduce ox-ploughing, in one form or another, to the cattle-keeping peoples of the Southern Sudan. All have failed.

Main Report and Proposals

CARRIERS

There has been an assumption that negroids, because they wear no clothes, carry loads. It is quite erroneous. The tribesmen of this province hate carrying loads. Partly they look on it as women's work: but mainly they are not the build for carrying loads and though they can on occasions carry a load of sorts, it is never a full one. 'Casemen' i.e. tribesmen who have a case to be heard by chiefs' court outside their own sub-section commonly carry small loads 'to oblige', and an assistant district commissioner can generally get things shifted, because he can make the tribesmen understand that it is for their own good the stuff is to be shifted, but such jobs as shifting telegraph poles and heavy stores over long distances are really beyond their capacity.

I have circulated to persons concerned that carriers cannot be produced from Duk and Bor District, as there was a tendency to call on unlimited carriers there, and I had had several complaints from the natives, and they seemed justified. A few carriers can sometimes be obtained from Shambe, from the Cic Dinka, but his is only due to poverty and as they improve in general condition, they will be more difficult to obtain for the service.

There is little doubt that in the past the excessive impressment of carriers had much to do with the aggressive attitude of the tribesmen to the government, and one of the strongest arguments for the development of mechanical transport should be the abolition of porterage except over short distances or in cases of extreme emergency.

Store sheds

When I took over in 1926, I found that there had been considerable damage to government and private property owing to lack of store sheds. E.g. at Renk a quantity of gum left on the landing stage for shipment had been destroyed by rain and at Melut cotton bales awaiting transport had been re-baled three times with considerable loss of lint owing to rain.

A particularly hideous structure which forms the nucleus of Kaka indicated that store sheds were a possibility though that one was not a good criterion, as, having no cement or concrete floor, it was almost impossible to protect goods from white ant.

A proposal to Khartoum to build sheds was referred to SGR&S on the ground that it was their peculiar privilege to build sheds and they did actually put one up at Jokau. The fact that they sent a moulder to erect a steel and corrugated iron shed at a season of the year when the whole area was under water indicated some unfamiliarity with local conditions which has been subsequently confirmed.

At Malakal I found a system whereby merchants paid a rate of 5% on every article stacked on the foreshore. In return for this imposition they got the services of a ghaffir who was quite incapable of guarding all the dumps on the shore, and it struck me that a shed for storage was appropriate. The correspondence has now been going on for three years and is not without its humours, and the shed is no nearer materialization than it was; but the situation has changed, as it is now the SGR that is keen to get the shed erected, in order to store goods in transit for Meshra [el-Rek] etc., whereas local trade has not of late years shown sufficient expansion to justify any urgency in the matter.

There are two sheds at Shambe, inherited from the Egyptian Army, that provided useful accommodation.

A shed was erected in 1930 at Renk, to deal with the gum question and is very useful as a garage in the rains, as it contains nothing, once the gum is cleared.

Otherwise there are no sheds, and as the rain rains in most districts from April to October inclusive, and as the storage accommodation provided as a routine matter for standard offices etc., is never adequate, there is a real need for store sheds almost any where, and if any economic results are obtained from the province, there will be further need.

It is to be hoped therefore that the construction of sheds can be restored to its normal place in the building hierarchy, and dealt with on the lines of local requirements and conditions.

Light lines

1. For the light line at Malakal see note on Malakal Town [below].
2. At Renk there is a light line from the landing stage to the merkaz and thence to the assistant district commissioner's house—some 2000 metres in all. It is of great use both for shifting material from and to the landing stage and at present in carrying water to the merkaz. It is hoped to substitute a tank and tower and pipe line for the latter service.

An additional 300 yards of line to connect the gravel pits to the landing stage is to be laid by disconnecting the branch running through the market.

The gauge is 18" and the rolling stock limited and hard to replace.

3. Kodok has a light line from the landing stage to the merkaz. It carries water for distribution and shifts all heavy objects including cotton bales to the landing stage.
4. The Egyptian Irrigation Department contemplated laying a length of light line (said to be about five kilometres) from Jebel Zeraf to the river to shift stone:[6] but the expense of running the plant for the amount of stone

---

[6] The three granite outcroppings at the mouth of the Bahr el-Zeraf are the only source of stone in the province south of the Sobat, other than the remote Boma plateau.

required proved to be expensive, and until the demand for stone at or near Malakal increases very much higher than seems not likely to materialize.

Water

Steamers and barges

STEAMERS

Before the UNP took over the Duk and Bor Districts and the Eastern District of Bahr el-Ghazal it was concerned only with the main White Nile, the Sobat and its tributaries and the Zeraf river; the fleet consisted of: Hafir, Margaret, Shabluka, Culex, Eland.

Sometimes the Culex was hired to the PWD and sometimes to the province, but in practice all boats executed any services that were necessary, without distinction of department.

There was also a tug and barge for the Agricultural inspector.

The Lady Baker was employed permanently on medical work.

When the Bor and Duk Districts were added no addition was made to the fleet. When the Eastern District of Bahr el-Ghazal was added, the Kerreri came with it, as it was the residence of district commissioner Western Nuer. There was also a tug and barge for the use and residence of the Agricultural inspector of the southern part of the province. These additions to the province fleet did not however make up for the additional work required to cope with the considerable amount of river involved, and as the volume of the work increased owing to larger forces of police, increased activity and incidentally the pressure of 'Nuer Settlement', the difficulty of coping with requirements became almost insuperable.

My report of February 1928 dwelt at length on the situation at that time, i.e. before we had incurred the liabilities of Yirrol and Western Nuer Districts.

Meanwhile the boats were not becoming any more efficient with age. The Shabluka could not go down stream against the wind, the Kerreri had been condemned in 1925 but apparently nothing was done at the time to ensure renewal, and the tug and barge of both Agricultural inspectors were withdrawn.

In 1929 the Atbara, a new boat on the lines of the Metemma was supplied in lieu of Culex; as the latter boat had no mosquito protection, I did not consider it fit for use in these parts. The Shabluka was also withdrawn and scrapped, unmourned.

The Kerreri still continued in service although she leaked so badly that she was not fit for human habitation in rain, and the same applied to the Lady Baker.

The fleet in 1930 consisted of: Hafir (now fitted with electric light), Atbara (fitted with electric light), Margaret, Kerreri, Eland.

There were also in the province, employed on departmental work only, the Lady Baker, Medical Service, in a state of disrepair, the Beatrice or similar boat for the Forest superintendent, the P&T launches at Taufikia and Bor.

The new Kerreri is due to arrive in February 1931 and will it is hoped be a real improvement, so that further remarks on the old one are unnecessary.

The Atbara was rather a disappointment. She was expected to solve all problems and satisfy all tastes and she did not. She is so designed that she cannot go astern as her rudders do not then function, and this makes her useless when sudd or heavy grass has to be dealt with. She is very noisy and vibrates a lot, so much so that the mosquito house built in her stern as an office and sleeping place is useless for either purpose. This was particularly unfortunate as she had been built on lines approved by various authorities who might have been expected to know, but the fact was that the old vessels were mostly so bad that any improvement was accepted with enthusiasm and the opportunity to find a still better plan was lost.

Meanwhile a new design for the cabin work on a similar steamer has been made and has been the subject of correspondence.

The question is not easy to solve and has unfortunately been dealt with largely by persons whose experience of malarial districts was either non-existent or lost in the vistas of memory.

The Hafir on paper has a cabin, a saloon and a mosquito house. In practice it has a cabin, a combined cabin and office, and the saloon is protected by bullet proof steel, a relic of the days when the Hafir was a gun-boat. This makes it intolerably hot, and the vibration is often bad.

The mosquito house has been enlarged and thereby greatly improved. A serving hatch is still needed and a mosquito trap would be an advantage if it could be worked in. The Hafir still remains the best boat of the fleet although the oldest.

The Margaret belongs to the Princess class, and is probably the best of them, e.g. it is possible to write on her but not legibly; on the others you cannot write at all. She steers wildly and so is an awkward boat for narrow and curly rivers. It is hoped that she will be the next for substitution by a new ship.

This privilege should really belong to the Eland. She is really hardly bigger than a launch and to live in her would be to be parboiled as with the boiler at one end, the engine at the other and steam pipes over head (she has no upper deck) her well is insupportable. But she draws only 18" and so can go to Gambeila and Akobo etc. when nothing else can. Her single cylinder engine however is not strong enough to get her out of trouble. She had a new boiler in 1929. In her way she is a most valuable vessel, but if a similar but slightly less crudely engined vessel could be made to tow a small barge, it would be a very valuable asset. As it is, the Eland works, and one is grateful for her, but she cannot last very much longer and steps should be taken to design another craft of the same draught and size, but preferably better. By the time the design is achieved it will be full time to accelerate the construction.

BARGES

The subject of barges is complicated by the fact that the department has dealt with barges by their individual number and not as part of a unit with a steamer. Thus each of the steamers in the province fleet in 1926 was a different size, and each had a barge in proportion to its size, and no interchange was really possible, but occasionally an additional barge was hired for special purpose such as the trooping season.

The first barge to go was that of the Hafir and a substitute for it was sent up with no housing on the upper deck whatsoever. It was pointed out that the old barge had had a mosquito house and a small wooden cabin, and poor as this accommodation was it did provide something for an assistant district commissioner to live in, when (as was constantly liable to be the case) he was travelling with the governor on inspection. This problem was solved by the provision of a third class barge No. 51 which has a mosquito house and four small cabins with wooden bunks on them: they provide some privacy for assistant district commissioners travelling with the governor and also some accommodation for servants who otherwise have no room and no mosquito protection.

It was an improvement on the original barge, and although it still left a good deal to be desired, it was gratefully accepted—not without a struggle.

The Margaret barge was the next to go; and this was condemned out of hand at Kosti and a single-decker barge quite inadequate to the work of the Margaret was substituted. Then the Atbara was sent for the first time with two barge-loads of bricks and no barge of her own, although the Shabluka and Culex were both returned to the department with their own barges; and finally the old Shabluka barge found itself back in the UNP attached to a steamer too large for it; thus the steamer was unable to cope with the calls that were made upon it, owing to lack of barge room.

This was at a moment when all province steamers were occupied in transferring Cavalry and M.I., mounted police, SDF stores etc. up the Zeraf, Bahr el-Ghazal and Sobat in connection with 'Nuer Settlement', and a trooper barge was hired temporarily to enable the steamers to do the necessary work.

The position at the moment of writing (November 1930) is that the Hafir has a fair barge No. 57, the Atbara has now got barge No. 70, which renders this unit efficient.

The Kerreri has been supplied with a good third class barge and though it is rather heavy for her, it is a great improvement.

The Margaret after various vicissitudes has two single-decker barges which takes the place of one double-decker (at double the price) and they are not capable of taking a lorry owing to low clearance and being too narrow.

The Eland barge is a single-decker affair on which a mosquito house was erected by the province to give officials some protection and the Steamers Department, after protesting that it was not a passenger ship added a latrine. There is no pretence at comfort, but the ship can get an official to his station when he can go by no other means.

Meanwhile a design for a so-called province barge was carried out and the first specimen sent up to take the place of an old barge to carry the Agricultural inspector (Mr. Porter) in the Jebel and Ghazal rivers. As the complement of a tug it was a complete failure as the accommodation for fuel was so short that if the barge was loaded with sufficient fuel to take the launch from one wood station to the next there was no room e.g. for cotton seed or whatever happened to be the cause of the move.

The barge itself was very cramped and the cabins so small as to be incapable of taking any furniture. There was naturally a good deal of protest, and it was urged that the general design of vessels and barges should be passed to the province before it be assumed that the result would acquire any merit locally.

Actually a design for a barge was put forward in August 1930, and was signed, very reluctantly, by me, as it was still a bad hull, and, to my mind, dangerous, but as my suggestions with regard to cabin work had been met, I felt constrained to sign.

There are other designs under consideration, and every endeavour has been made to provide the department with the data on which to base its designs. It is admittedly difficult to conceive from the N. Sudan the conditions common here, e.g. (a) that it is by no means uncommon to have to steam some hours up or down a river in order to cross it: (b) the menagerie of mules, horses and cattle that must inevitably accompany an assistant district commissioner and the numbers of tribesmen who get temporarily attached to a boat in connection with cases, or for medical treatment etc.; or (c) that an assistant district commissioner is commonly based on a steamer for months at a time and must therefore have more accommodation than is required for a journey of two nights which would be normal in N. Sudan.

There are one or two simple facts which have to be borne in mind when considering barge requirements. One is that with the exception of the Eland which would be overweighted with a double-decker barge, all steamers are constantly carrying men and animals and to accommodate them a double-decker barge is necessary. The number of animals that constantly accompany an assistant district commissioner is anything from 20 to 45, so that adequate flat space on the lower deck must be available. As there is no accommodation for servants on any steamer, and as the health of an official largely depends on the health of his servants, a little accommodation is required for, say, two servants on the barge. Wood is made up in lengths nominally a metre square, if wood is to be put in it easily; also the shifting 200 lbs of dura in a sack through a small hole is slow and laborious, so hatches should be made amply wide. Gangways should be provided strong enough to take cattle or a lorry.

There should be adequate room for a lorry to be taken on board if necessary stanchions should be removable. I should like to place on record my appreciation of the efforts of Major Mulholland to meet the needs of the province in the teeth of great difficulties.

Launches, small boats, feluccas, etc.

Feluccas are supplied by SGR at Renk, Melut, Nasir and Bor. There were also feluccas at Abwong and Fangak, but they were withdrawn as unduly expensive.

The P&T has a launch at Taufikia and another at Bor. They can tow a small barge in which the inspector contrives to exist though the accommodation is very poor.

The SGR has had a launch on trial at Malakal. It has been condemned by every authority for the purpose of an inspection boat for SGR superintendent though it might have uses in other ways.

The assistant district commissioner at Bor has got an outboard motor which he can attach to his felucca, and this gives it far more mobility. Sails are of little value in the very narrow channels of the khors that this type of boat is wanted for and towing is very laborious.

Assistant district commissioner Akobo had a small boat and outboard motor as a loan from the governor, and found it of great value in enabling him to visit villages at a season when travelling was impossible.

Unfortunately the outboard motor was dropped in the Fullus and never recovered. He has since been using a made up affair with a Ford engine in it to propel his felucca.

A small boat capable of shifting loads from the mainland to the mainstream is wanted at Papiu; without this the place as a port of entry to the Aliab is impracticable.

A collapsible tub was lent to assistant district commissioner Western Nuer (Captain Masterman) when approaching the Bul Nuer, as the only known line of approach was intersected with many khors and much water. It proved helpful but was on too small a scale to do much more than relieve the assistant district commissioner from constant swimming.

Ferries

Ferries present two problems, (a) the type of ferry or pontoon which will take a lorry or mules or baggage across a small river or khor and (b) a ferry for the same purpose across the main Nile.

For the first purpose native boats have been obtained, boarded over with a platform, and they are handled across by a rope. In Yirrol District they have two old pontoons, which are however both too small and are too rusted with age to last much longer. A new type of pontoon has been put in on Khor Gurr near Ajwong and on Khor Waad inland from Adok but as it is reported that some fifty or sixty natives are required to hold the pontoon down whilst a lorry is put on, it seems that something rather larger is needed.

For ferrying across the main Nile no solution has been reached. Anything that is sufficiently substantial to stand the wind and waves liable to be met is prohibitively expensive. Such are wanted at Malakal, chiefly, and if the road from Malakal to Melut materializes there will be need for one at Kodok. The number of places is restricted by the fact that it is rare to have approachable bank on each side of the river at any one point.

Banks and landing stages

At nearly every place along the river, a bank has to be made across a piece of marsh from the true main land to the negotiable river bank: e.g. Renk, Kodok. In the stations of Western Nuer and Zeraf Valley Districts these banks are frequently of great length e.g. at Ajwong the bank is 600 yards long and up to ten feet height in places; at Adok there is a big bank for something over a mile and a small one for some miles further.

At the river end of the bank a landing stage is made to enable steamers to come along side with ease.

Such landing stages and banks are at:

Renk, Kodok, Abwong, Ajwong, Shambe, Adok and Laikaich and Tithbel and Gwogol.

At Papiu a bank reaches some way towards the river but there is no landing place and a boat has to be used: at Lake Jorr (which is more correctly a Dorr [Ador]) there is a landing place of sorts on the west side of the lake but no bank. At Nuong, approach has to be made some miles up a fairly swift khor.

The landing stages where post boats call e.g. Shambe and Renk are liable to be worn away by the boats bumping into them and though some material such as old rails and corrugated iron have been provided to protect the stage, the result is not wholly satisfactory and owing to the difficulty of providing an effective foundation this is hardly to be avoided.

The inland banks such as that from Ajwong to Rufshendol by Khor Gurr are primarily a question of labour. Their object is to enable the line of villages and higher ground to be reached from the river without wading for miles. They are particularly needful in Zeraf Valley where approach from inland involves a very long journey which is barely feasible in the rainy season or high flood.

Sudd

The rise and fall of the flood, and sometimes the effect of storms, break away large masses of grass and papyrus growth in the marsh areas and drive them into the main channel. There they drift unless caught by wind or a local shallow. If they remain stationary they collect other masses of grass till the whole river is blocked and a sudd is formed. Then if the grass can get its roots to the ground it can take root and give a good deal of trouble. For many years sudd cutting was done systematically until the channel was made so open that its 'sudding' was unusual and the methods of dealing with it and the material required were neglected.

In 1927?[7] there was a big block south of Shambe at the seven bends known as the Seven Sisters. The block was nearly ten miles deep and took some weeks to break, owing to the fact that every lump of grass removed had to be towed down stream to a point where there was sufficient stream to float the lump away. The method of extraction is simple. Anchors known as 'Nyam Nyam'[8] are lodged in different places in the grass and connected to a steamer by wire ropes; the steamer then backs down and tears out the

---

[7] The manuscript has '192', with the final digit left blank. The date given here is suggested by information found in John Winder's 'Notes and Queries', SAD 541/9.

[8] So named because of the pointed 'teeth' of the anchors, reminiscent of the filed teeth of the Azande and other alleged cannibal ('nyam-nyam') peoples of western Equatoria and Bahr el-Ghazal.

lump, whilst the sailors hack at the line of cleavage with bill hooks and saws to get the piece away.

The sailors get a good deal knocked about by the grass and require constant first aid or the abrasions caused by the grass fester.

It is obvious that a steamer must be able to go astern effectively to do this kind of work. Some, like Atbara cannot,[9] because her rudders are so placed that she cannot steer backwards.

There does not appear to be any rule of the road about sudd and if one is to judge by the behaviour of certain vessels in recent times it is 'sauve qui peut'.

There is no Conservancy Board on the Nile nor any authority responsible for the maintenance of the fairway and the banks etc. Possibly the Egyptian Irrigation Department may arrogate to itself that position, but it has never done so; and I doubt if its claims would be accepted by the SG if it did.

The Steamers Department naturally does not go out of its way to look for a job of sudd clearing, and where a sudd occurs off the line of mail boats e.g. up the Pibor the work falls on province boats unless the Egyptian Irrigation Department will give a hand.

In practice the Egyptian Irrigation Department will help to clear a block if it looks like interfering with the flow of water. Otherwise it is not interested.

As a result the northern Jonglei channels have been blocked for two years and nothing has been done.

As the SG has not, apparently, an effective dredger of its own, it is doubtful if it could cope with a really difficult block unassisted.

A supply of tools for sudd clearing is now kept at Malakal, SGR&S depot.

Air

The RAF was employed in UNP in 1920,[10] but it has been in 1928, 1929 and 1930 that it has been employed to an increasing degree in the province.

In 1928 it did some bombing work in Lau and tried without much success to burn down Gwek Wanding's settlement by the pyramid.[11]

---

[9] The original line was garbled, reading, 'Some, like others cannot, like Atbara'.
[10] In the operations against the Eastern Jikany (the 'Garjak Patrol').
[11] The first bombing run against Guek's village was on 19 December 1927, when 20 lb bombs were dropped on the Mound itself and incendiary bombs were dropped on the village. As the bombs dropped on the Mound failed to explode (or were muffled by the thickness of the Mound's earth), and the incendiaries went off at some distance away, the Lou were reconfirmed in their belief in the protective qualities of the Mound itself. Ground troops were later sent in to burn the village and blow up the Mound (see Johnson (1994: 194)).

Main Report and Proposals

In 1929 [*sic*, 1928] it bombed the Nuong Nuer heavily and did some bombing work in Lau and Gaweir, but was also much occupied in reconnaissance work. In 1930 the RAF did no offensive work but proved its value to an increasing degree by enabling assistant district commissioner and others to go over country in a short time and so save weeks of fruitless 'trekking'. Float planes were first tried in 1929 and the first experiments were not wholly successful, but by improved floats and with more experience the float planes have shown that they are particularly well adapted to work in UNP during the rains. They still require at least half a mile of straight water to rise in, and this makes it dangerous for them to land in some of the smaller rivers such as Pibor, as they cannot get off again.

There are landing grounds at Renk, Melut, Kodok, Malakal, Duk Fadiat, Ket, Akobo, Nasir, Daga, Pibor Post, Wangkai, Kongor, Bor, Yirrol, and a landing ground can be made at Faddoi and elsewhere in Lau plain if required.

Thus both in dry and rainy weather the bulk of the province is accessible by air, and will become more so as technique improves.

My own belief is that in time, say ten years, the transport of governor or assistant district commissioners to district headquarters or tribal centres will be almost wholly by air, within the limits of the district mechanical transport will be widely used, and if that is impracticable, it will be a case of walking with carriers as it is now.[12] But that would only be in cases of emergency which should become increasingly rare as tribal organization and discipline improve.

By means of the air, the remoter parts of the province such as Boma plateau and the Beir can be brought into touch without considerable additions of staff; and if it be that aerial troop carriers materialize into success under local conditions, there should be good hope of removing expensive and rather difficult garrisons and frontier posts.

So far, through the good offices of the RAF a considerable variety of work has been performed: the transport of nurses from Khartoum to Malakal, the transport of governor on inspection duty, the carriage of urgently needed medical stores, the survey of the best line of the route

---

[12] The prediction proved wildly off target. Air transportation never became so widespread within the province during the Condominium period. One of the complaints of the independent Sudanese authorities against foreign missionaries in the 1960s was the latter's use of small planes for internal transport while the government lacked such facilities for its own use. The closest fulfilment of Willis' prediction has been the extensive use of air transport by external relief agencies involved in Operation Lifeline Sudan (beginning 1989), but it was the disruption to overland and river transport by war that has made this reliance on aircraft necessary.

for troops or for a road, the search for refugee tribesmen, apart from definitely punitive action, such as bombing.

Granted the principle of applying air transport to administrative needs; it remains to organize and develop the service and provide effective means of economy in other directions e.g. water transport and land transport, and immense saving in time which is equally a saving of money.

Post and telegraphs

Offices:

Renk	Post and telegraph	
Kodok	"	"
Malakal	"	"
Nasir	"	and wireless telegraph
Akobo	"	"
Gambeila	"	"
Kongor	"	and telegraph
Bor	"	"
Shambe	"	

Post

The postal service to Abwong, Nasir and Akobo, after the last Gambeila boat, is dependent on province steamers till the roads are sufficiently dry for mule or mechanical transport to Nasir.

Akobo and Gambeila mails go thence by canoe.

Mails at stations such as Pibor Post, Daga and Kigille, Duk Faiwel are arranged by assistant district commissioners concerned.

Telegraph

Land line runs from the northern boundary along east bank of Nile to Melut were it crosses the river by cable and a leg connects with Kaka. The line crosses by cable again at Malakal, and thence goes each side of the river on the west, connecting at Tonga with Talodi and Kordofan circuit and on the east up the Zeraf river to Kongor and Bor and so on to Mongalla Province. The line from main White Nile to Tithbel is hard to maintain, from Tithbel to Duk Faiwel is worse still as it is cut off from the river by bad khors and marshes and difficult of access.

Telephone stations exist at Khor Atar, Fangak, Kilo 175 and Awoi, which communicate daily with Malakal or Kongor to report conditions on the line.

A superimposed telephone has been installed to connect Malakal with Fangak but it has been disconnected for some time as it very rarely worked and it is to be removed.

Telephone between Malakal and Kodok, Malakal and Tonga and between Renk and Melut works tolerably.

Wireless stations are at Malakal, Nasir, Akobo and Gambeila. Temporary stations have been at Fathai and Duk Fadiat in 1929 and 1930 in connection with Nuer Settlement. A new engine etc. was installed at Malakal and Nasir in 1929 and a new one is being set up at Akobo in 1931.

The difficulty and expense of maintaining the land line from Malakal and Bor has caused a scheme to be mooted for the substitution of wireless telegraph stations south of Malakal.

Melut post and telegraph station was closed down on 16th October 1930.

ADMINISTRATIVE STAFF

Upper Nile Province non-British officials

Name	Appointment	Grade	Remarks
Fuad Eff. Bishara	Chief clerk	V	retiring
Awad Eff. Girgis	Translator	VI	
Atia Eff. Tadros	"	VI	
Tayeb Eff. Mukhtar	"	VII	on leave
Mohammed Eff. Safwat	"	VIII	
Mustafa Eff. Bakri	"	VIII	
Mohammed Eff. Fahmi	"	VIII	
Abdulla Eff. Ahmed Ibrahim	"	VIII	
Mohammed Eff. Ismail	Store keeper	VII	
	Accounts Section		
Fuad Eff. Araman	Chief accountant	V	
Fuad Eff. Dagher	Accountant	(contract)	"
Lewis Eff. Marroum	"		
Zaki Eff. Faris	"	VIII	
Zein El Abdein Eff. Gaafar	"	VIII	
Osman Eff. Nurel Medina	"	VIII	on leave
Ibrahim Eff. Zaki Shawki	"	VIII	"
Sadik Eff. Ali	"	VIII	
Mohd. Eff. Mahd Abu El Naga	Sarraf	VIII	
Hassan Eff. Sid Ahmed	"	VIII	contract
Abdel Rahman Eff. Abdalla	Translator	VIII	

Name	Appointment	Grade	Remarks
	Police Section		
El Shafia Eff. Ahmed	Police officer	VI	
Mohd. Eff. Abdel Rahman Burhan	" "	SPOG	
Abdel Mutalab Eff. Mustafa	Store keeper	(contract)	
	Malakal District		
Sagh Ahmed Eff. Okeil	Mamur		
Yuz. Abdel Radi Eff. Murjan	Sub-mamur		
Awadel Kerrim Eff. Osman El Karm	Accountant	VII	now at hq
Mudather Eff. Gabr el Dar	A/accountant	VIII	
Abu Bakr Eff. Ali Tayeb	Translator	VIII	
Ahmed Eff. Mohd. Ali	"	VIII	on leave
Ibrahim Eff. Said	Sarraf	VIII	duty at Kodok
Billal Eff. Allagabu	Clerk	Ungraded	
Abdel Rahim Eff. Abdalla	"	"	
Abdel Gelil Eff. Omer	Sanitary overseer	"	
	Kodok District		
Capt. Said Eff. Abdel Rahman	Sub-mamur	VII	
El Sayed Eff. Ahmed El Hag	Sarraf	VIII	on leave
Ali Eff. Ibrahim	Weigher	Ungraded	
	Renk District		
Amer Eff. Mohd. Bashir	Mamur	V	
Mahmud Eff. Osman El Sheikh	Sub-mamur	VI	
Abdel Gadir Eff. Lutfi	Accountant	VII	
Mohd. Eff. Hamdi	Translator	VIII	
Mohy el Din Eff. El Geneidi	Sarraf	VIII	
Abbas Eff. Saleim	Weigher	Ungraded	
Abdel Nabi Eff. Fadl el Mula	"	"	
Abdel Wahab Eff. Mahmud	"	"	
Osman Eff. Abdel Wahab	"	"	
Bellal Eff. Ahmed	"	"	
	Melut District		
Abdel Aziz Eff. Hamad Hassoun	Sub-mamur	VI	Duty at Bor Dist.
Mohd. Eff. El Sayed El Hanafi	Sarraf	VIII	
	Abwong District		
Ismail Eff. Hashem	Sarraf	VIII	
	Nasir		
Mustafa Eff. Khalifa	Sarraf-accountant	VIII	
	Akobo		
Mubarak Eff. Nasr el Din	Sarraf	VIII	

Main Report and Proposals 101

Name	Appointment	Grade	Remarks
	Gambeila		
Fahim Eff. Hanna	Sarraf-accountant	VII	
	Bor		
M.A. Farag Eff. Ismail	Sub-mamur		
M.A. Nayel Eff. Ali	" "		on leave
Agaibi Eff. Fam	Sarraf	VIII	
	Yirrol		
Mahdi Eff. Omer	Translator	VII	
Sir el Khatm Eff. Hasan Taha	"	VIII	
Aziz Eff. Michael	Sarraf	VII	
Girgis Eff. Buctor	"	VIII	on leave

An examination of the distribution of staff in the province [above] indicates that there are two different systems of administration working. For instance a relatively small district like Renk has a mamur, sub-mamur, translator, sarraf and accountant (these last two are to be combined in to one) and weighers as well whilst in a big district like Western Nuer there is no staff at all.

Roughly the need of clerical or accounting staff and sub-mamurs depends primarily on the presence of 'malakia'. i.e. Arabic-speaking Sudanese of Mohammedan or quasi-Mohammedan belief and custom. Thus at Renk and Malakal where there are some thousands of 'malakia' there has to be a complete staff.

At merakiz headquarters where the post boats call and there is a certain amount of traders and traffic, and the normal legal process is understood, there is need for a sub-mamur as a minor magistrate; and so a sub-mamur is found at Melut, Kodok and Bor.

A sub-mamur was placed at Akobo, as long a company of Equatorial Corps was stationed there, so that there should be some authority to deal with petty cases; but the reduction of business makes it possible to substitute a sarraf-accountant for a sub-mamur there.

A sub-mamur is appointed to Duk Faiwel as the district is remote and has been attacked by Nuer, and a fairly responsible person is needed to visit Kongor and occasionally Jonglei in the absence of the assistant district commissioner, e.g. during the rains, to pay the police and keep accounts etc.

Otherwise the standard staff of a district is a sarraf-accountant. He remains necessary as long as the present system of accounts is maintained; but some districts e.g. Western Nuer and Zeraf Valley do not have even that.

It is clear therefore that where there are no 'malakia' and little if any intercourse with the outside world a different system of administration holds. The only point in common between them is accounts, and that is really illusory.

In those districts where a normal staff exists the policy is common to other places where such staff is used for the administrative material for which it is designed, and further comment on it is unnecessary.

Accounts[13]

The principle underlying the system of accounts in the Sudan government is that one man keeps the accounts and another keeps the cash or stores, and one is checked against the other. As soon as two functions are merged in one person i.e. the sarraf-accountant, the principle is lost.

Among the primitive tribesmen of Upper Nile Province money is rare, and all transactions of moment are made in terms of cattle. The bulk of such transactions as affect the government are made through the assistant district commissioner who keeps his own records and carries out his work on tour, and if any record is made in the merkaz books, it is probably only the nett result of his transactions.

The consequence is that tribute for instance is paid in to the assistant district commissioner and disposed of; and no record is to be found in the merkaz monthly return to check against the entry which is ultimately recorded from the assistant district commissioner's direct report to the mudiria. Assuming the assistant district commissioner sent a copy of his report to his merkaz headquarters, the sarraf-accountant would not be able to embody it in his accounts because he would not be able to read it, being in English, and I doubt very much if he would understand it if he could read it.

It must be remembered that in districts like Abwong, Akobo and Nasir the assistant district commissioner is commonly absent from his headquarters for weeks and months at a time.

The total number of payments in and out a month at a district headquarters like Abwong is very small, perhaps a dozen, but in order to comply with financial regulations a sarraf-accountant is kept to record them. As he has no knowledge of the district or the names of places therein, he is liable to make the record wrong and the staff at headquarters has no means of checking his error. E.g. the cost of making a new road may be entered by the sarraf-accountant as maintenance, and it is only when the maintenance allotment is exceeded and enquiry made, that it is discovered that debits

---

[13] The sections on accounts and stores (MS pp. 212/13/24–26) were placed immediately before the section on tribal workshops (below, MS pp. 212/13/27–28), but clearly should follow the preceding section (MS p. 212/13/3).

have been entered against the wrong item and by that time it may be almost impossible to unravel which item is which. By the time an accountant has learnt the difference between Yirrol and Nyerol or Abwong and Ajwong he is just about ripe for transfer to another province.

In the case of W. Nuer,[14] where there is no clerical or accounting staff, the assistant district commissioner periodically comes in with his accounts and the chief accountant then works out all the necessary certificates, payment orders etc. that are necessary and the assistant district commissioner signs. This works quite well in practice but is rather a tedious process and in actual fact evades the whole system of check that is supposed to exist.

Assistant district commissioner Zeraf Valley has a similar system but the mudiria usually sends an accountant to him; so his accounts show as going through the merkaz; but as the accountant goes about once in two months, it is in fact the assistant district commissioner who keeps the account.

Actually the monthly accounts of these small merakiz could be put on one sheet of paper quite easily. But by the time all the bits of paper have been added, to satisfy regulations, it makes quite an imposing packet. As this packet is liable to be factitious, I think it should be eliminated, but I do not wish to decide for the director of accounts what is the best system.

This question of accounts also has a bearing on the type of sub-mamur required, as in some cases the staff consists solely of a sub-mamur, and the capacities of a sub-mamur to keep accounts and store books vary. It is disappointing to find how few SDF officers can do so with any accuracy. Civilian sub-mamurs especially those who have been through clerical routine in the Sudan government are often better, but if they are properly trained to the work of a sub-mamur, it is really wasting them to use them on what is really less skilled work.

The present chief accountant, through his experience of work in Khartoum and by dint of considerable personal effort, has cleared up the Augean stable left by his predecessors to a working degree, but the amount of correspondence required to keep the Khartoum office contented seems to me disproportionate, and I doubt if we could find another man with sufficient dexterity to maintain the accounts in their present state of efficiency; so unless he is condemned to Upper Nile Province for the rest of his service, reform is needed.

The provision of English-speaking accountants at headquarters is one desideratum; probably a smaller but more highly trained staff would be more efficacious than the existing one.

---

[14] The MS reads 'E. Nuer', but from the above it is clear he means 'W. Nuer'.

Stores

Equally in the matter of stores, the present situation is unsatisfactory. In principle the police stores are defined and limited by the exact requirement of the police. In practice not only are the requirements of the police liable to vary from the normal but there are constant demands from assistant district commissioners for urgent needs in the way of saddlery and equipment, besides small stores varying from a pound of nails to a spool of thread which would normally be obtainable in the market but do not exist in their remote stations.

As far as police go, the reason is that the mounted police are continuously on tour for six or seven months at a time and the wear and tear on kit and equipment is very heavy.

It may be argued that assistant district commissioners should order their requirements direct from the Stores and Ordnance, but a brief examination of the complications involved and the delay that would occur should immediately dispose of this argument.

Then there are motor spares. The ordinary Arabic-speaking storekeeper is completely fogged by these and has some justification in expressing ignorance of the identity of the different spares.

The two current accounts for cattle and dura are also a constant source of trouble. It is not as easy to count a biggish mob of cattle as it sounds; I have watched and assisted two assistant district commissioners check a herd of some 180 cattle, and it took some hours to get the three officials to agree within one animal.

The herdsmen of course know all the beasts by name and would know if one were missing but cannot count up to large numbers.

In practice the cattle accounts are kept by the assistant district commissioners and they send in periodic returns which are checked against the corresponding items of tribute, fines etc., but it is not to be expected that complete accuracy can be reached.

The dura account is complicated by the various ways in which dura can be issued. It may be part payment of chiefs' police, maintenance of chiefs' courts issues to medical patients, or forage for officials or mounted police. Considerable amounts are issued as famine relief against payment, mostly in kind or in work. The payments are made practically entirely on tour and the only record of issue is normally the certificate of the assistant district commissioner.

EDUCATION

When I took over the Upper Nile Province I found that there had been a good deal of correspondence on the subject of education in the South but by some remarkable oversight the governor of UNP had not been consulted. As the tribesmen of UNP present a more difficult problem than that in any other province, the omission was in some ways unfortunate.

Actually there are four Roman Catholic Missions, stations of which three are in the Shilluk and one at Yoynyang for Nuer up the Bahr el-Ghazal, each having a school of sorts. There is an American Presbyterian school at Doleib Hill for Shilluk and at Nasir for Nuer.

The CMS has a school at Malek for Dinka and started a school at Akot adjacent to the Yirrol District boundary in 1929. There is a scheme for a CMS Mission station and school in the Jebel island and Archdeacon Shaw proposes to prospect for a site in the Zeraf Valley this season.[15]

Until the government started to take an interest in these schools they can hardly be said to have produced any appreciable results. Such boys as were taught were absorbed into the missions as teachers; a few were adopted by the Medical Service and trained as sanitary hakims and have done fairly well.

The stimulus supplied by government has had a good effect up to a point, but there is still much to be done to get the missionaries to stick to the curriculum and syllabus laid down.

For instance the Americans disregard the appointed holidays when it suits them, and the Roman Catholics seem to try to keep their pupils for an unduly long time without holidays, thus annoying both parents and pupils.

Handicrafts which should be a most important part of the education are mostly inefficiently and inadequately taught, but where suitable staff is available, the results are gratifying. For instance Mr. Price at Malek trained three Dinka boys to look after and drive a car and they have since been attached to Mr. Colebourne of PWD grading party and two of them have done very well. This may reasonably be attributed to the fact that Mr. Price is fully equipped to teach such work. The chief trouble with the missionaries is that they are prone to be amateurs in the crafts that are to be taught and so do not teach well enough.

Two incidents of importance have occurred recently: at Yirrol the tribesmen of a certain section refused to select as their chief the son of their old chief because he had been educated at a mission school and had thereby from their point of view become detribalized.

---

[15] A station and elementary school was opened by the CMS at Ler in 1931, and another at Juai Bor on the Zeraf Island in 1936.

At Bor on January 23rd the head chief of the Bor Dinka [Deng Col] complained that the boys educated at the mission, including his own son [Joseph Deng Col], were too superior to do their share of work with the other tribesmen.

These two cases show how important it is that education should not be allowed to dissociate the school boys from tribal obligations and is I think support for the theory that a merely literary education is to be avoided but should be accessory to a training in some specific trade of value to the tribesmen, whether it be medicine, veterinary work, motor driving or anything else. There is a tendency in some cases to try and teach natives a craft that can be of no obvious application to their own needs e.g. brick making, and this is to be deplored. In education as in administration the line of development must be along native ideas. That the tribesmen can adapt themselves to new ideas that are of use to them is shown by the quickness with which they appreciate the value of mechanical transport or the most up-to-date treatment of disease by tropical research.

To deal with the districts in detail: in Renk District there was a small and inefficient elementary Arabic school, which was closed down at the end of 1930 as the pupils did not appear to be learning anything. No educational facilities are available either for Renk or Melut Dinka.

The mission station at Rom in Dunjol Dinka does no educational work.[16]

In the Shilluk, the Detwok school is doing fairly well owing to the keenness of Father Pschorn, but attendance is not good.

The school at Lul has done practically no educational work for months and merely supplied suitable 'eye wash' for inspection purposes. Pupils who mean business ask to go elsewhere.

Tonga school is beneath contempt.[17] Doleib Hill is hampered by the local feuds which are so bitter that if boys from one village go to school those of another are not allowed to go by their parents. In the Nuer, the American school at Nasir has been goaded partly by government and partly by unexpected reactions of the native to a much larger proposition than the

---

[16] On visiting Rom in 1926 Willis wrote that Dr. Trudinger's 'idea is to give the native just enough reading and so on to enable him to read the Gospel and to go home and read it. It seems to me he would soon tire of his literature and lapse to his original condition. However there is something to be said for the idea, but meanwhile the few natives who show a desire for education even of the mildest sort are worth pushing into jobs where they can spread a few ideas among their fold.' (SAD 212/9/27).

[17] Willis' first impression of the Catholic missions had been altogether more favourable. Shortly after taking over as governor he wrote, 'The Roman Mission is the most important in the province, partly because it has more stations, and partly because it is more successful both with the Government and the natives. They are not ultra Sabbatarian, as the others are, and they seem to have a better appeal to the native than any other.' (SAD 212/9/73).

missionaries really care about. This school depends for its drive mainly on the ladies of the mission.[18]

The Yoynyang school has not been going very long, and the candidates for education supplied by the missionaries are mostly local hybrids, but ADC Western Nuer has sent a number of boys. The missionaries did the school a great deal of harm by keeping their pupils after the time that they had promised to send them home, notwithstanding a definite arrangement to the contrary.

No educational facilities exist in Akobo or Abwong districts. In the latter, pupils are sent to Nasir. In the former nothing has yet been done but an Acoli teacher could possibly be obtained from the CMS for the Anuak.[19]

In the Bor and Duk Districts the Malek mission supplies a school. The Dinka of Duk District always ask for a school in their own neighbourhood, and it is to be hoped that this may materialize when CMS can supply a teacher. Malek school is much the best we have in UNP but it is very difficult to get pupils away once they have gone there; the real difficulty is that the pupils are often efficient up to their lights in knowledge but deficient in moral and religious training and are therefore detained at school when they might be usefully employed. It is a matter on which sooner or later missionary education must come into conflict with the lay mind. Western Nuer and Zeraf Valley Districts are under consideration. Yirrol can send pupils to Akot.

The following table shows the number of pupils in the different schools. The number do not indicate any immediate fear of creating an 'intelligenzia', with no means of employment and too expensive ideas. At the same time too much stress cannot be laid on the importance of diverting education to practical ends and not allowing any school boy to

---

[18] After his first visit to the Nasir mission in October 1926 Willis wrote, 'I thought the whole affair amateur and rather inefficient, and I commented on the fact that in ten years they had made but little progress with the language, but the fact is that people who mis-pronounce English as badly as Americans of this type are hardly likely to appreciate the niceties of native intonation and pronunciation. However they seem to have a working knowledge of the tongue, and they say they are about to produce a grammar and vocabulary. The pupils do a certain amount of work for the mission, and the whole establishment appeared to be run on Mr Squeers' line without the ferocity. It was all rather feeble and ineffective, and the missionaries are not of the class to impress anyone. ... I urged on Smith the need of identifying the interests of the mission with those of the Government. I held that unless he could or would do that, the mission could never have the position in the eyes of the natives that it should have....I observed that Smith had an idea in his head that employment in the Govt. put a native under severe temptations, a notion I can only suppose he brings from the United States.' (SAD 212/9/49–51).

[19] Acoli and Anuak are closely related Lwoo languages. The CMS opened a station among the Acoli at Opari only briefly in 1920–1.

think that the rudiments of education absolve him from his tribal duties and obligations.

At Malakal there is a combined 'Fiki' school and elementary school, on the usual lines of education in the Northern Sudan. It is not quite good enough for the children of officials and better class merchants and is too good for the 'malakia'. There seems to be little reason however for either officials or merchants to expect to educate their children in an unhealthy place like Malakal when they all have relations and domicile in the Northern Sudan, and I favour the reduction of the school to a standard suitable to 'malakia' and its re-siting to that end.

Pupils in Upper Nile province schools, 1930

Malek	77
Tonga	17
Yoynyang	38
Lul	24
Detwok	36
Doleib Hill	42
Nasir	62
	296

MISSIONS

The missions in UNP are the CMS, the Italian Catholic Mission, the Presbyterian (American) Mission and the Sudan United Mission.

1.	CMS	Station	Malek (Dinka)
		"	contemplated at Leiro [Ler] (Western Nuer)
2.	Italian Catholic	"	Detwok (Shilluk)
		"	Lul "
		"	Tonga "
		"	Yoynyang (Nuer)
3.	American Mission	"	Doleib Hill (Shilluk)
		"	Nasir (Nuer)
4.	Sudan U. Mission	"	Melut (Dinka)
		"	Rom "

For educational work see under Education.

Main Report and Proposals

1. CMS is in charge of a small leper station at Malek. There are a few boys from Malek who have gone on to the higher school (Nugent) at Loka [Mongalla Province]; and a number of the Malek pupils were sent as a nucleus of a new school at Akot which is just outside the UNP on the Yirrol-Rumbek road and should be of some use for Atwot pupils. [Note: The incidence of tuberculosis among the Dinka pupils at Loka is found a serious deterrent to their education there.]

A scheme to start a new post inland of Adok in Western Nuer has been mooted and should be useful.

It has been suggested that a post might be placed with advantage in the Zeraf Valley and that the present merkaz at Fangak might be used for a nucleus of it, and a new post found for the merkaz close to the Nuer.

The general tone of the CMS is good but the mission keeps its pupils for a very long time in order to establish them well in the faith. As a result output has been very small so far.

2. The general standard of the Catholic missions is low; Yoynyang is probably the most go ahead, though it is still on the small side. Detwok has improved greatly under Father Pschorn.

The object of the missions is apparently to get as many converts as possible and not to expect too high a standard from the individuals. It is alleged that over 600 Shilluk communicate twice yearly. Only a very few mission boys have managed to attain a standard of education fit to qualify them for employment by government.

There is a tendency to squalor in the Catholic mission (notably Tonga), which reacts unfavourably on their work. The three northern stations come in the Khartoum Episcopate and Yoynyang under that of Wau. Archbishop Hinsley gave the impression that he would alter this and put in a special man for the UNP preferably an Englishman.

3. The American mission at Doleib Hill is handicapped by the fact that there have been very violent feuds between the villages near the mission and the Shilluk carried their animosities to the point that family enemies would not allow even their children to be taught in the same school.

The medical work of this mission has been negligible since the decease of the mission doctor and his wife some six years ago. Apart from a school there is a little kindergarten and mothers' welfare work but the whole work of the mission is on a very small scale.

The Nasir mission had a qualified doctor who had been through the Tropical School of Medicine, but he went to the Abyssinian branch of the mission two years ago and the dispensary has not been very active. One of the chief difficulties is the insistence of the missionaries on the principle of 'No Hymn, No Drug'. Some friction has been caused at times with the

ADCs in getting treatment for emergency cases, venereal and for Mohammedans.[20]

The school is doing very well, primarily because ADC Abwong supplied a number of pupils and in 1930[21] the Gaajak suddenly were converted to education and the Gaajak chiefs started sending their sons for education.

4. The Sudan United Mission at Melut is supposed to be a medical mission and Dr. Trudinger is in charge. No educational work is done and not much medicine, and the mission is a rather depressing failure. There is a dispensary and mission at Rom, east of Kodok, which is by way of working among the Dunjol Dinka. The dispensary has done some useful work, but the Dinka complain that the missionaries seem to think that giving medicine or anything else enables them to interfere in native affairs.

The disappearance of both Melut and Rom stations would be little loss. These posts are not within the mission spheres as distributed in the early days of the SG between the different societies. The spheres were originally designed to provide the mission societies with plenty of scope without interfering one with another. It is a system detestable to the missions, but has proved a great boon up to date. The spheres however were very arbitrarily fixed in days when but little was known of the distribution of tribes, and it is probably high time the situation were reviewed and the spheres readjusted. The obvious thing to do is to grant each mission as its basis posts and places where it can show that it has in fact produced results. The remainder which would amount to 90% of the total at least, could then be dealt with piecemeal by application of the missions and subject to conditions of service and efficiency sufficient to preclude the dingy deficiency of the last thirty years.[22]

Meanwhile, and it will take a considerable time to get any readjustment of the spheres, the only thing to do is to try and keep the standard of work up, and possibly by a spirit of emulation, possibly by the somewhat

---

[20] American mission medical treatment was the target of numerous, sometimes contradictory criticism by British officials. In 1920 the missionaries were condemned for allowing a white woman to treat syphilitic natives, an exposure which was alleged to have led her to fall in love with a (non-syphilitic) Shilluk Christian convert (SRO UNP SCR 30.5, 'Miss Marie Tuan American Mission Nasir').

[21] Here the MS reads 'and date in 1930'.

[22] The school at Rom was begun in 1924, originally for the children of mission employees, but had grown sufficiently to be recognized as an elementary school by 1937. The school at Melut had begun as early as 1914 but had never been successful. By 1938 the SUM wished to concentrate its activities at its main station in the Nuba Mountains, and the fundamentalist North American-based Sudan Interior Mission (recently expelled from Ethiopia by the Italians) was granted a sphere in northern Upper Nile in 1938, founding stations among the Meban and Uduk that year, and taking over Melut from the SUM in 1939 (Sanderson and Sanderson (1981: 240–1)).

material lure of a government subsidy, endeavour to get out of the missions sufficient education to meet our more pressing needs. Their medical work is not so necessary as the government organization is better, bigger, and more acceptable than anything the missions seem to be capable of supplying.

NATIVE ADMINISTRATION

The great bulk of the work of the Upper Nile Province is concentrated on establishing a system of native administration which will enable the tribes to manage their own affairs along their own lines.

In the Northern Sudan the general lines of native administration are well defined, both language and customs are known; but with the Nilotics, languages are little known and customs are obscure, and our knowledge of the religion and morality of the people is very limited.

In the past assistant district commissioners frequently settled cases for the tribesmen and there is little doubt that their decisions, though given in good faith, were contrary to native ideas, and therefore only led to trouble.[23]

Moreover custom appears to be extremely fluid. In Colonel O'Sullivan's pamphlet on Dinka Laws and Customs [O'Sullivan (1910)] the impression is given of a hard and fast law, but in practice the law, if realized at all as such, is used as an ideal principle, and each case is settled on its special merits.

The tribal conditions in different districts vary considerably so that the degree to which the administration has been worked up and even the lines on which it is worked, vary.

In theory, however, the foundation is based on established custom; and our object is to eliminate objectionable customs and encourage and develop those which improve the conditions or strengthen the organization of the tribesmen. It is essential however, that any new idea be a genuine growth from existing custom and not an innovation imposed from outside. It has been to a great extent the direct interpolation of alien ideas from the North that has kept these people so backward and remote from government.

For this reason it is important to avoid the use of such words as sheikh and omda as these have implications which are not actually to be found in the local tribal organization.

It is true again that individual leaders have arisen from time to time to

---

[23] For further discussion of the conflict between customary law and the Sudan Penal Code see Johnson (1986*b*).

combine large bodies of the tribesmen, but that does not mean that they have established a dynasty, and their tenure of power depends wholly on public opinion. For instance there are men who were reported as being very influential and powerful some years ago in Gaajak and are now of no importance and devoid of followers.

This does not mean that anybody can set himself up as a chief if he has enough brains and personality, as there appear to be certain 'chiefly' families from which chiefs derive, but the person of those families in whom authority may rest at any time gets that authority by the backing of public opinion; and whilst government naturally endeavours to support influential men in the control of their people, it has to avoid backing a man who has in fact lost his hold over them.

It has been our endeavour to ascertain the divisions, and sub-sections of the clans and to get chiefs, sub-chiefs and headmen to be responsible for their respective units; the chiefs and sub-chiefs administer the tribal custom in court to settle matters of dispute and their chiefs' police to assist in the working of the courts both in collecting the required persons for the case and seeing to the execution of the decision afterwards.

A few notes on the different districts may be explanatory.

Dinka

In the Renk and Melut Districts, the Dinka are a very small population and those at the northern end are much Arabicized and quite a number pretend to be Moslems and go through the externals of being Moslems. In early days individuals were chosen as their 'sheikhs and omdas' who played up to the Arab element and incidentally assisted, there is not much doubt, in the slave trade.

Fortunately one strong man emerged, Yol Kur, who though he had been terribly harried by the Dervishes, kept his independence and did his best to maintain the Dinka as a people. Placed as they are, however, in close juxtaposition to Northerners of greater intelligence and initiative, they need a good deal of support. They have their courts, which used to sit regularly once a month but owing to paucity of business now sit when required.

The Melut Dinka consist of four clans, of whom three of the chiefs are doing well and the fourth is apparently the best available.

The strength of the tribal discipline has greatly improved in the last two years and these people are beginning to show some capacity for looking after their own affairs. The tribesmen have comparatively little to do with Arabs except a certain amount of poaching, congenial to both parties.

South of the Melut Dinka lie the Dunjol Dinka who come under Kodok District and receive very little attention owing to lack of transport at the disposal of district commissioner Kodok and the inaccessibility of the people. They give little trouble, but the chiefs have some difficulty in getting their decisions carried out. This was partially due to an effort on the part of a chief to assume to himself a function in customary law which belonged to someone else. This was discovered and put right, but it is worth recording as an instance of how careful it is necessary to be to avoid offending tribal susceptibilities by not knowing some detail of procedure, the lack of which nullifies the value of all the preliminary effort, whilst any attempt to compel acceptance of the result without the proper ritual can only lead to chaos. A similar instance can be found among the Nuer, where a feud cannot be legally finished until the sacrificial bull has been duly speared by the proper functionary and torn to pieces by the assembled multitude.

South of Dunjol and lying on each side of the Sobat in the Abwong District are the Ngok Dinka. They have some thirty chiefs (which is too large a number) but they settle their own affairs, and have periodic courts, and give no trouble at all; and, owing to their good dura, pay their tribute in cash without difficulty.

Recently there has been an attempt by one section to refuse to combine with the other sections of Dunjol. The matter is under investigation.

The (so-called) Jureir to the south of the Ngok are really parts of the clans further south in the Duk District and they are being repatriated.[24]

The section of Rueng Dinka who live up the Khor Atar give little trouble but need more attention than they get, so that the tribesmen may obtain the advantages of the chiefs' courts. They pay up their tribute on demand and with more handling should clear up their old cases and settle down to a quiet life.

The Dinka of Duk District are much reduced in numbers by the Nuer raids of the past. It is stated that the Nyarreweng used to number 100,000 but they are now not more than 7,000, and the Dwer and Gol are still smaller.[25] The Twi round Kongor are a rich and numerous clan and the Bor south of them though relatively timorous are a fairly strong clan. These Dinka have been worked up to a considerable degree of organization and two outstanding chiefs, Deng Col and Deng Malwal, and though they have been compelled to adopt a certain amount of Nuer custom because they have lost their own traditions they are progressing favourably and an

---

[24] For the failure of this repatriation policy see Johnson (1982a).

[25] Major Wyld was probably the source of this very dubious claim. All estimates of past populations must be treated with extreme caution (see above, editor's introduction).

enormous amount of work has been done in clearing off old disputes and establishing a time bar to prevent the raising of unreasonable claims of the past.

Captain Routh described the Twi as a lot of truculent and unmanageable savages, but in practice they have responded to the method of treatment and show more adaptability to new ideas than people like the Nuer, though that does not mean any very liberal state of mind.

The Aliab Dinka who lie inland from the west bank of the Nile opposite Malek are a fine people, physically, and have recently been very hard hit by rinderpest. They have voluntarily made roads, and seem to have given up their intransigent attitude which led to the death of Major Stigand.[26] They tend to mix with the Mandari who appear to be acquiring cattle-owning characteristics. The Yirrol District system has not yet been brought wholly into line with the rest of Upper Nile Province, but both the Aliab and Cic should respond to it readily.

The Cic Dinka are very likely not Dinka. They are a much more sheepish and timorous people than the normal Dinka; but this may be due to oppression, raids, and poor physical conditions. It is probably that they only took to cattle-owning fairly recently so that their tradition in that form of life is not strong. They have however a working organization, and the important point is to ascertain that it is built up on genuine tradition and is developed on the right lines.

The basis of the system is that each chief runs his own section, and can settle disputes by his own authority. Intersectional quarrels go to a chiefs' court, the members and president of which are liable to vary according to the origin of the disputants. The decision once reached is carried out immediately and it is up to the court to see that the proper ritual, if any, is performed. Appeals amongst the Dinka are expensive as otherwise no decision is ever accepted. They are heard, as a rule, by the assistant district commissioner with a board of chiefs as assessors who can state the custom but sometime the board of assessors can be, or must be, left to deal with appeals. They are incidentally a test of the probity of the chiefs in settling their internal affairs and of the sectional courts and so have a real value.

The chiefs' police normally work under their chief, fetch defendants and witnesses in cases and keep order in court. They can at a pinch be combined to go and collect any tribesman who refuses to obey. They are also a source of information to the assistant district commissioner. During 'Nuer Settlement' they were used as scouts and messengers etc., but in peaceful times their duties are not onerous.

[26] During the Aliab Patrol of 1919 when both Major C. H. Stigand (governor of Mongalla Province) and Major F. R. White (OC Equatorial battalion) were killed in an Aliab ambush.

Atwot[27]

The Atwot talk a species of Nuer but do not show other signs of Nuer origin. It seems possible that they are an agglomeration of people originally fish-eating or iron workers who acquired cattle and nomadic habits possibly under the domination of the Nuer.[28] Their chiefs have been constantly influenced by medicine-men who urge them to rebel against government and they are treacherous and difficult people. The removal of one particularly malevolent medicine man Afuki had a good effect. It was astonishing to think that a decrepit and blind old man could have so much influence as he had, but even the province police treated him with reverence and awe. He has been sent to Rumbek to end his days.

For the last two years there has been an improvement in the Atwot, but the occurrence of locusts and cattle disease and changes in province staff are liable to have a baleful effect, and there are rumours of a recrudescence of the old troubles of 'Bir' and Allah water which caused difficulties some ten or twelve years ago.[29]

Shilluk

The Shilluk administration has not advanced proportionately to that of other tribes in the province. This is partially due to the disproportionate amount of attention to the Nuer and partly to the fact that they had advanced up to a point which, superficially examined, appeared more satisfactory than it really was.

The Shilluk are peculiar in having the Ret who as the living embodiment of the tribal spirit has great authority. He is not however an absolute monarch. First of all, he is tied by tradition and he cannot go against it. Modifications of custom can be and have been made by the Ret after consultation with the chiefs in the annual council.

The very fact of the Ret's existence and authority however tends to weaken the chiefs who are unwilling to give decisions for fear of trespassing on the Ret's preserves, and if they develop too much authority, arouse the Ret's apprehension that they are preparing to oust him and take his place.

---

[27] This section on the Atuot (MS p. 212/13/4) was found between the sections on non-British staff and education, but clearly should follow the section on the Cic Dinka (MS p. 212/13/16).

[28] Atuot now claim that it was the Nuer who took their language and 'twisted it'. For more on the Atuot see below, ch. 8, and Burton (1981a & b; 1987).

[29] For the history of the Biri society, a closed association of Zande origin, see Johnson (1991c); for the Atuot 'holy lake' (mistakenly confused with the Yakan or 'Allah Water' cult of the Lugbara in Uganda) see Fergusson (1922).

The Shilluk provide an interesting example of the necessity of working through native custom. No chief can be accepted as a man in authority until he has been invested by the Ret with a piece of clothing. Thus a government-appointed chief without the sanction of the Ret is powerless.

Another difficulty in the Shilluk is the fact that there are two royal families and the Ret is chosen, normally, alternatively from each family.[30] During the reign of a representative of one family, the members of the other family are so to speak 'His Majesty's Opposition'. For instance at the present time there is often difficulty with the people of Fanyikang where the opposition family resides. The Ret naturally dislikes going there as his position is anomalous and involves some personal risk. The normal method of succession in the past has been the killing of the Ret by a man with the necessary qualifications to become Ret.

The existing Ret has slain two people with his own hand attempting to kill him, and to some degree lost prestige by killing them with a revolver instead of a spear.[31]

The Shilluk country is divided into areas, each of which is under a chief who has under him a number of headmen. The young men are extremely insubordinate, and do not obey the headmen and the latter sometimes encourage, when they should stop, fighting.

At the present moment there are nine serious inter-village feuds which need to be set right, but the tribesmen require considerable pressure to come in and settle their differences.

Efforts have been made to establish minor courts under certain hereditary exponents of Shilluk tradition, and they have done some work, but they have still to be worked up to a much greater degree of efficiency. There is a certain amount of prejudice against them as taking away from the authority of the Ret.

The chiefs' police among the Shilluk were the first to be started and formed originally a body guard of the Ret and were extended to provide a local representative of law and order in the different areas. This was appreciated sufficiently for a 'gloss' to appear in the tribal dance representing a battle over cultivation rights. The chiefs' police intervene to keep the peace and are overpowered and the battle begins.

There is a good deal of work still to be done to get the distribution of the chiefs' police more even. At present some places have a number of

---

[30] There were, in fact, three branches of the family from which candidates were chosen. See below, ch. 4 and notes.

[31] For Willis' own account of one of these incidents (written when he was director of Intelligence) see Willis (1922).

police and some have none. Probably some police can with advantage be diverted to training as veterinary retainers. For over a year now they have taken over the guarding of the merkaz at Kodok by night, but they cannot guard prisoners, as these escape from them unless they have firearms, and an armed province policeman sleeps with the guard at night in case of emergency.

A useful gauge of the tribal situation among the Shilluk is the state of the buildings at Fashoda and other holy places of the tribe. If they are allowed to fall into disrepair, it is an indication that all is not well, and enquiry should be made into the cause.

Nuer

Lau

The chiefs' courts of Lau were begun in 1927 in the form of itinerary courts travelling with the ADC. Though these courts cleared off a great many old disputes, they needed a good deal of help from the ADC, but they were progressing favourably till the trouble arising out of Gwek Wanding and the subsequent 'Nuer Settlement' kept the clan in such a state of unrest that no courts could be held. In 1930 they were started afresh and their organization included the sections previously attached to Duk District; two sessions were held up to January 1931, and the chiefs are working the system with reasonable success.

A strong point is made of the presence of all the chiefs so that all the tribesmen can be dealt with. The decisions given at the last court can be reviewed and if they have not been carried out the chief concerned is available to explain why—and steps taken to see that they are. This has the effect of impressing on the chiefs their responsibility to carry out decisions and goes to strengthen their authority over their sections. Any fresh cases can be dealt with and decisions given for execution. The courts deal with an average of twelve cases a day and generally sit for about five or six days at a time, and should sit about every two months throughout the dry weather.

Jekaing

The courts in Nasir District were started after those of Lau. Gaajok adopted them fairly readily; but the Gaajak were shy of them, partly from distrust and partly owing to a big feud which rent the clan in twain. In 1930 Gaajak suddenly came to the conclusion that the idea was a good one and suggested certain alterations, e.g. in the method of appointing chiefs' police, and the courts are acquiring some authority.[32] The fact that a large part of Gaajak go into Abyssinia in the dry weather whilst they are inaccessible in the wet makes the opportunities for dealing with them few, and they can so easily retire out of reach if they are pressed that their administration and control can only be carried out by the exercise of great tact and patience.

The effect of trying to insist on any line of policy inacceptable to the chiefs and tribesmen would only be to lose all the work already done and establish a permanent source of trouble on our Abyssinian border.

It is to be hoped however that they will in time appreciate the benefits the government can provide so much that they will not dare risk losing them. This would apply specially to Veterinary work once they have learnt the advantages that can be gained by treatment of their cattle.

Lak, Thiang, Gaweir

In the Zeraf Valley, the system of chiefs' courts and chiefs' police is still less developed as it has practically only been started in the last two years and has been much hampered by the upset of 'Nuer Settlement' but as the object of that was to establish them, it is gratifying to find that the chiefs are beginning to deal with cases through the courts. But in Gaweir for instance the recovery of blood-money for the Dinka presents great difficulties.[33]

In general, however, in the districts of Nasir, Abwong and Zeraf Valley there is a common system of chiefs, chiefs' courts and chiefs' police and though they are at different stages of development they should ultimately turn out the same.

Western Nuer

In the Western Nuer District a different system was started and worked up to a considerable degree. The whole district was divided into areas, and in each area was a chief who through sub-chiefs and headmen administered his people, and the areas so administered had a considerable population sometimes exceeding 10,000 persons.

There were no courts and no chiefs' police, but the chiefs made use of

---

[32] The Gaajak acceptance of chiefs' courts, especially the distinction between chiefs and sub-chiefs, is reported in some detail in C. L. Armstrong, 'Jekaing. Progress Notes', 8 April 1930, NRO UNP 1/51/4.

[33] These were all due from cases resulting from Dual Diu's raids against the Dinka in the rains of 1928, which were provoked by the army's sweep through Dual's village during the 'Gaweir March' in the previous dry season (see Johnson (1994: 224–8)).

Main Report and Proposals

some of their young men to carry out their orders. They fined any tribesmen who disobeyed orders and these fines were sold and provided the funds necessary to pay for the chiefs for clothing, rations, medicine etc.

Since Mr. P. Coriat took over the district, he has been endeavouring to adapt its system so as to develop along parallel lines with those in other parts of the Nuer. Whilst in other parts chiefs are possibly too many and it would be desirable to merge some of them into sub-chiefs under another chief, those in Western Nuer are probably too powerful and it may be necessary to split up the areas. There is reason to think that the chiefs are or have been oppressive, and a chief who claims and obtains the backing of the government to oppress his people must sooner or later create a situation of great difficulty. One source of oppression was cotton growing as every tribesman who failed to grow cotton was fined a calf: but now that cotton growing is being dropped this particular source of trouble is eliminated.[34]

The merits of having one big chief to deal with instead of a number of small ones is obvious, but unless he is checked by tradition or public opinion he almost inevitably goes wrong. A good check on him is the holding of cases in open court, where any miscarriage of justice is not only liable to cause immediate murmurings but is practically certain to reach the ears of the ADC. But the government has to take care that the government chief does not attempt to usurp powers that properly belong to special hereditary functionaries.

A typical instance of the risk of putting authority into the hands of one man was the so-called court of appeal at Yirrol, which was run by a certain [name left blank]. He came originally from Rumbek District and he must have been a man of considerable intelligence. When the district was handed over to Upper Nile Province he was given a glowing character. Subsequent experience however disclosed that he never gave a decision without being paid for it and his decisions had often been biassed and unfair, and he ended up being tried and found guilty of taking bribes, and there are still cattle to be recovered from his property and returned to the lawful owners.

Akobo district

The Anuak have a princely family and an elaborate tribal tradition in connection with the two royal thrones and certain emblems. No man of the princely family can rule the Anuak unless he has sat ceremonially on the thrones so that the possession of the thrones is of great importance. By an agreement made by the assistant district commissioner with the 'Niyya'

---

[34] For further details on corruption and competition among Western Nuer chiefs (and the contribution of such internal rivalries to the murder of Captain Fergusson) see below, ch. 11, and Johnson (1994: ch. 7).

or princes, the thrones and emblems are put in the custody of one of them every year and the custodian arranges for applicants to sit as required.[35]

The 'Niyyas' have adopted the custom of settling cases by court and in practice many Anuak from the Abyssinian side come to get redress through the courts.

There are chiefs' police attached to the chiefs on the same lines as among the Nuer.

The Beir have only recently shown any desire to come into touch with government but the benefits of medicine and famine relief were appreciated by them and they came in and proferred tribute. Their chiefs are hereditary and appear to have some authority but their administration is still in an amorphous state.

TRIBAL WORKSHOPS

Reference has been made to the proposal to find a 'handy man' who could undertook the supervision of province works including MT bridging and building so-called 'semi-permanent' accommodation.

One of the chief difficulties ADCs experience is the entire lack of skilled or semi-skilled staff. The tribesmen are roughly speaking in the pre-bronze age. The introduction of spears of metal from the North has given them one tool to work with and this they use for every conceivable purpose from cutting their toe nails to making canoes. It is of course very laborious work and wastes much time, and as the tribesmen appear to have a natural knack for anything mechanical, it seems obvious that means should be found to train a certain number of them as mechanics, carpenters, smiths etc. The complete lack of any 'ostas' in Malakal other than those already employed by PWD and EID prompted me to apply for and obtain a small workshop and carpenter and smith at Malakal, and there is to be a small saw mill in charge of a carpenter at Yirrol; but Malakal is not a good milieu for training negroid tribesmen, nor is Arabic a convenient language to do it in, especially when it comes to training men to drive and look after lorries.

So far, the handicrafts encouraged by the missions have been rather futile in design and execution and it is doubtful if they would individually be in a position to run separate schools for teaching this kind of thing, and they would be unlikely to agree to combine in a common school.

It should however be possible to find quite a considerable proportion of

---

[35] There was only one 'royal' stool. For further details see below, ch. 6 and notes.

boys being taught in the elementary mission schools who would be better fitted for some kind of 'trade' than for clerical or other similar work.

It is suggested that there might be an opening for the expenditure of some of the Stack Memorial Funds on an institution for training tribesmen in arts and crafts. It would of course have to be in close connection with the mission schools without being incorporated in any one of them.

It should be placed sufficiently far away from such places as Malakal for the learners to grow up in their own appropriate surroundings, free from Northern influences, but near enough for fairly continuous supervision to be exercised and for encouragement to be given.

It would have to be near enough to the main line of communication for supplies etc. to be easily attainable and to ensure that tribesmen could reach it from their homes with comparative ease, as one of the most curious characteristics of these tribesmen is their homesickness and a separation of as much as 100 miles from their homes appears a remote exile unless they can return to visit their friends every few months.

POLICE

Until the Upper Nile Province took over the Eastern District of Bahr el-Ghazal in 1929, all the police of the province mounted and dismounted were on Northern rates and were recruited mainly from discharged Sudanese soldiers or Sudanese from the North.

Yirrol provided a centre from which considerable numbers of natives of the types of the soldiers of Equatorial Battalion could be recruited at a lower rate than the Northern, and a scheme was made to substitute the Southern type of police for unmounted duty for all stations South of Malakal.

The mounted police and the unmounted police for the districts of Malakal, Kodok, Melut and Renk continued to be recruited as before and to be paid at the higher rates, (see distribution attached).

The gradual extension of the province and the withdrawal of Equatorial Battalion garrisons has meant a great increase in the numbers of mounted police, and the successful use of Cavalry and Mounted Infantry in Nuer Settlement has established that ponies are as good as, and generally better than, mules. Thus the mounted police have developed into a considerable force run on semi-military lines whose duties have little to do with normal police work. For instance it has been impressed on all assistant district commissioners that their mounted police are a personal escort and must not be allowed to work independently of a British official's control. In the event of trouble they become a small but effective striking force which lapses again into an escort as soon as the work is done. This limitation of the use of mounted police has been proved to be necessary as the Northern Sudanese cannot be trusted not to loot, rape, and generally misbehave when let loose on people they call 'Abid' [Arab., 'slaves'].

The mounted police are still in the process of growing and the unmounted police southern type are only recently organized and still require a good deal of training. The unmounted police (Northern type) have suffered from lack of training and musketry as until recently it has been impossible to have them at full strength to enable a small nucleus for training to be kept at Malakal.

In view of the increased work the government has approved the appointment of a commandant of police and native officers at Malakal and the same at Yirrol, and it is to be hoped that a period of quiet training and organization can now be anticipated so that the police can be rendered fully efficient.

The large number of posts fed from Yirrol involves a steady system of reliefs and continuous training at Yirrol, and the shipping arrangements to meet these demands will always need careful staff work.

Equally when the mounted police go out of their stations in November and return from them about May or June, there is a heavy call on the province transport.

One side of police work that has caused a quite disproportionate amount of trouble is stores and equipment. It is desirable that a better and more highly trained type of storekeeper be found but it is doubtful if there are any such on the list who can be spared from the central depot in Khartoum North.

In many ways too it is very inconvenient to have to run what is really in practice a military force on the lines of police, and it is to be hoped that in time a more elastic system can be devised which can allow for the peculiar conditions of the province. In no other province, for instance, are mounted police on continuous patrol away from headquarters for six months at a time.

One of the least satisfactory sides of police work is the maintenance of isolated posts such as Daga, Kigille, Pibor Post, Shambe where there is no administrative official to supervise them and see that discipline is properly maintained. In principle I believe such posts to be unsound, and I hope that it may be found possible gradually to abolish or alter them.

The question of Daga and Kigille is one involving our relations with Abyssinia and has a special history and it is now the subject of correspondence with the authorities in Khartoum.

It should be possible to make Akobo and Pibor alternative posts, for wet and dry weather respectively and so have only one garrison always posted

Main Report and Proposals

at the place which is for the time being the headquarters of the assistant district commissioner. But the tradition of the need of a large force handed on from the days of the Sobat-Pibor-Military Administration dies hard. With improved communications and mechanical transport it should receive the coup de grace.

In the mounted police the tendency is undoubtedly to substitute ponies for mules, and the liabilities involved thereby are the subject of correspondence.

It will be observed that there is no specific allotment of mounted police to the northern districts. This is because the Shilluk area is served by roads capable of taking mechanical transport, and the villages are along the road.

In Renk District the casualties to animals were very high and in any case mules were an unsuitable form of transport for the more arid parts of the district, and in fact the work in that district is more in the lines of true police than the semi-military organization that the Upper Nile Province police have become.

Mechanical transport to practically all parts of the district is now possible and it is hoped that the ADC can dispense with mounted police though he can at any time call on reserve in Malakal.

It is worthy of note that the Shilluk tribal police have taken over the mounting of the guard at Kodok for a considerable time and thereby reduced the need for unmounted police Northern type.

They cannot however without firearms deal with alarms or run away prisoners, and the final development in this line will turn on the time it takes from the tribal police as an integral part of native administration to be merged into the government. Presumably this is the government objective but I do not think that the implications involved have been fully appreciated or even considered.

Upper Nile province police distribution under 1931 budget

Mounted	Sol	Sergt. Major	Sergt.	Corporal	Constable	TOTAL
Hdqrs.	1	1	3	2	2	9
6 Troops	–	2	4	12	156	174
TOTAL	1	3	7	14	158	183

Distribution—mounted police 1931 provisional programme

1 Mule Troop (dismounted) &	in Malakal
1 Horse Troop	
1 Mule Troop –	Akobo
1 " " –	Nasir
1 " " –	Fangak
1 Section Mule –	Bor
1 " " –	W. Nuer
1 " " –	Abwong

The W. Nuer section will later be withdrawn and replaced by one pony troop, when animals have been received from the dismounted troop.

Southern foot

	Sol	Sergt. Major	Sergt.	Corporal	Constable	TOTAL
H.Q. Yirrol	–	1	4	–	1	6
Yirrol	–	–	1	6	77	84
Duk	–	–	–	1	19	20
Bor	–	–	1	1	23	25
W. Nuer	–	–	1	1	28	30
Daga	–	–	1	1	8	10
Kigille	–	–	–	1	9	10
Nasir	–	–	–	1	11	12
Fangak	–	–	–	1	11	12
Abwong	–	–	–	1	11	12
Akobo	–	–	1	1	28	30
Pibor	–	–	1	1	22	24

Northern foot

	Sol	Sergt. Major	Sergt.	Corporal	Constable	TOTAL
Malakal	–	1	2	5	57	65
Renk	–	–	1	1	16	18
Melut	–	–	–	1	11	12
Kodok	–	–	–	1	11	12
Gambeila	–	–	–	1	11	12

CHIEFS' POLICE

The first tribal police to be started in Upper Nile Province were Shilluk, and their appointment arose, I believe, in the first instance owing to attempts on the life of the Ret by possible successors, and the need of supplying him with some kind of bodyguard.

Out of this grew a body of men selected mainly for good physique and intelligence who kept in close touch with Kodok and could be relied on to send or bring information of impending breaches of the peace.

They had a uniform of a blue 'lau' with scarlet belt and an arm badge carrying the sign of one of the Ret's totems. They were paid half an ardeb of dura and 50 Pt in cash a month except in the case of literates or men of exceptional value who received twice that amount.

They developed a good deal of esprit de corps and their function as the protectors of security was so fully recognized that glosses have been introduced into the tribal dances to bring them in.

The idea of having one or more police attached to each chief was later applied to the Lau Nuer, with considerable success. The selection of suitable men was supposed to be in the hands of the chiefs but had to be carefully supervised by the ADC.[36]

As a result a body of extremely useful scouts was organized who were of great help for intelligence purposes and as a screen in front of a moving column during patrols, and in peace time they had a divided allegiance partly to chief and partly to the ADC. Their reliability was severely tested in the operations against Gwek Wanding, but only one man went wrong.[37]

This system was reproduced simultaneously or shortly afterwards in the Bor and Duk District among the Dinka and in the Nasir District among the Jekaing, whilst a few police were found for the Dinka of Renk and Melut and the Dunjol and Rueng Dinka of Kodok District, and also among the Anuak.

The transfer of the Eastern District of Bahr el-Ghazal to Upper Nile Province included a number of chiefs' messengers having no responsibility of their own.

In 1930 the Gaajak clan of the Nuer having previously held off from the establishment of chiefs' police convinced themselves of the need of them subject to certain conditions which were not merely reasonable but based

---

[36] In fact, Coriat began recruiting young men into an informal chiefs' police among the Gaawar at Ayod as early as 1923–4; see Kulang Majok, quoted in Johnson (1993a: pp.xxviii–xxix).
[37] Nyith Guer, a chiefs' policeman of the Goal-Tiang sub-section, Lou (see Coriat (1993: 80)).

on their own conception of the tribal organization, and the tribal system of Nasir District was appreciably strengthened.[38]

Although, as mentioned above, some of the Atwot and Dinka chiefs of Yirrol District had chiefs' police when the district was transferred to Upper Nile Province, the Nuer of that district (Western Nuer) had none. But both in these districts and in the Zeraf Valley they are being introduced: the process is rather slow owing to the need of getting just the right men.

It is interesting to find that the chiefs' police of Bor district have trained themselves in English drill, through a retired soldier of the Equatorial Battalion,[39] and nearly all the chiefs' police (i.e. omitting Renk, Melut and Dunjol Dinka) make an attempt to organize themselves together as a body.

As however they are very democratic and no one of them would permit it to be suggested that another was better than he, it is an organization without NCOs and it is indeed remarkable that they cohere as much as they do.

AGRICULTURE

Food crops

Practically the whole province starves for several months in a year and a large part of it for much more. This is due partly to the fact that no means of storing grain has been discovered so that all supplies are consumed or sold immediately, partly to the fact that large parts of the province are inhabited by people who for one reason and another do not cultivate enough (e.g. certain clans of the Nuer amongst whom cultivation is almost certainly limited to the women), partly to the devastation of birds and occasionally locusts. The tribesmen are saved by the fact that they can live for long periods on fish and heglig nuts (lalob), and they depend also on milk, meat and blood, though the supply of these is not adequate to the population.

People like the Gaajak cultivate extensively and not only dura but maize, and a good deal of maize has been introduced among the Shilluk; it is the merit that the seed is too large and to solidly fixed for the birds to eat it, and the Australian maize is extremely popular.

Owing to the fact that the soil and the white ants make storage

---

[38] See C. L. Armstrong, 'Jekaing. Progress Notes', 8 April 1930, NRO UNP 1/51/4.
[39] The soldiers of the Equatorial Battalion drilled in English, unlike the old Sudanese battalions of the Egyptian army, or the northern units of the SDF.

impossible, there is the absurd result that there is generally a considerable export of dura, although the province cannot feed itself, and of late years steps have been taken to divert dura in the direction that is required within the province and so reduce the import of famine relief.

The habit of merisa drinking accounts for a considerable part of the dura crop, but this again is partially explained by the inability to store and the people think they may as well drink what they cannot keep. Moreover the negroid merisa is a very light drink and though they can get drunk on it, it is not the social pest that it is further north.

Vegetables, apart from government gardens, are hardly known, though the Shilluk are beginning to take a mild interest in paupaus and native vegetables.

The Dinka are the best food producers in the province. Those of Bor and Duk fail through birds, unseasonable rain or flood, but they generally manage to feed themselves; they have had bad luck in the last few years. The Ngok Dinka of Abwong get big and valuable crops of good white dura which they sell to advantage. The Melut Dinka and the Dunjol Dinka both get big crops of white dura, much of which is paid to the government in kind and is used for the maintenance of the police etc. The Shilluk are roughly self-supporting and the Nuer always (with the exception of Gaajak) in want. The Anuak can get two good crops but cannot export for lack of means of transport even if they could justifiably do so, which is doubtful.[40]

Money crops

Cotton has been very strongly pushed in certain parts of the province, i.e. the Shilluk and Western Nuer and Yirrol and, to some degree, among the Bor Dinka.

With the Shilluk, the cotton is of good quality and has saved the people from starvation several years when their dura crop failed.

The cotton of Yirrol and Western Nuer and Bor is not of such good quality and in Yirrol District the return per feddan does not justify its growth, though the tribesmen like growing it as an easy money crop with which they can pay their tribute. Actually, however, owing to the cost of transport to Shambe, it is doubtful whether there can ever be any real profit in it.

---

[40] The Nuer appeared to be 'always in want' throughout the period of Willis governorship because the punitive operations he initiated co-incided with periods of extensive flooding, locust infestation and cattle plague; see Johnson (1991b). For a more detailed survey of agriculture throughout Upper Nile Province see Sherwood (1948), JIT (1954 i: ch. 5), and Howell, Lock and Cobb (1988: ch. 13).

Efforts have been made to interest the natives up the Sobat in cotton but their profits in dura were obviously better and the need for dura greater.

The Melut Dinka grow some cotton but here again the transport to the river is laborious and the trouble disproportionate to the result.

Now that the price offered for cotton is only 20 Pt a kantar it can be safely anticipated that the growth of cotton will cease, and hardly any distribution of seed will be made in 1931.

From what chiefs have said about cotton, it is improbable that any natives south of the Shilluk will ever attempt to grow cotton again, except under very considerable pressure: and this will react adversely on their capacity to pay tribute in cash which they have hitherto obtained from cotton.

Ful Sudani [groundnut] is a very successful and valuable crop in the goz land, inland of Geigar (Renk District); it is largely maintained by natives of the White Nile Province who come south for the purpose. Provided that these immigrants do not acquire any rights over land or in any way interfere with the development of Dinka tribal organization in Renk there is no reason to interfere. Unfortunately the Dinka organization in Renk District is weak and the tendency of the Arab to reduce the negroid to a lower social position is very strong, so that there are objections to an unfettered development of this type of agriculture. It solves itself on an economic basis as over production is easily reached.

Ful Sudani is being tried in the light soil of Yirrol District, but has turned out an unfortunate investment, owing to a heavy slump. The only use for it in such an area is really as a food crop but it is not sufficiently familiar for this purpose and any way does not make beer.[41]

Experiments etc.

Valuable experiments have been made at Yirrol on local seeds to determine which are the kinds best suited to be developed. No less than seventeen different sorts were identified in the local seeds and the probability is that this mixture has been evolved so that whatever the conditions something comes up and has a chance to escape from the birds, who are responsible for the greatest loss of food supply.

An experiment was started in the rains of 1930 at Duk Fadiat and Fathai to try different duras and manioc, the latter as a last resort in time of

---

[41] Geigar remained the main production area of groundnuts in UNP throughout the Condominium period, but Tonga, too, began exporting large quantities of groundnuts in the 1940s (SDIT (1955: table 44)). Groundnut cultivation (as a food crop) did expand in the sandier soils of the duks and riverine areas after the end of the first civil war (1972).

famine. 'Ajak' dura was found to do well and has been extensively adopted in the Duk and Bor Districts.[42]

In the Shilluk area local natives have been trained to sort, weigh and pack the cotton, and local people have been taught methods of cotton growing for propaganda work in the villages. In Western Nuer on the other hand this work has been given to Arabic-speaking natives from Shambe, and the work was not dealt with tribally. Steps were being taken to remedy this but presumably cease in the present circumstances.

There still remains a great deal of work to be done to bring up the local food supply to requirements by improved seed, better methods of cultivation and new introductions.

A most interesting experiment on a small scale was started by ADC Bor and Duk on the river bank opposite Bor. An area of some five acres was walled in, cleared of grass and sown with cotton, sugar cane, vegetables and a few trees. Notwithstanding a barricade of barbed wire a hippopotamus managed to get in and ate practically the whole of the sugar cane. It was however abundantly clear that the land was exceptionally rich. Banana trees planted in May 1930 were over twelve feet high and bearing extensively by January 1931.[43] Half an acre of cotton produced a return of seven kantars.

Rice was also grown with success, and a good crop of maize was raised and garnered.

It is within the bounds of possibility that large areas of 'sudd' could be reclaimed and turned into paying crops. Such a scheme would probably need to be directed by Europeans and the product, whatever it might be, reduced to a form suitable for transport at relatively cheap rates.

Whether the proper line to follow is the production of sugar cane to make spirit for motor transport with all the by-products of molasses etc. or whether some other plant can be found more paying, or whether to rely on the possibilities of pure 'sudd' as an alternative to wood pulp or again as a basis of cellulose, are all matter for research: but in view of the possibility of irrigation schemes which may render these 'sudd' areas more amenable to habitation, it would seem a matter of some urgency to determine the

---

[42] *Ajak* (*jak* in Nuer) is a tall, slow-maturing, relatively flood-resistant strain of dura which was originally the staple of the Shilluk and Dinka along the White Nile and Sobat. Because it can withstand some flooding it can be planted in open grassland. During the severe disruption to Nuer and Dinka cultivations during the early 1930s, due to forced dislocation by the Nuer Settlement, flooding, and locusts (Johnson (1991*b*)), *ajak* began to be used more and more among the Nuer and Dinka south of the Sobat. By the 1950s it was being taken up by the Western Nuer and was described as the best yielding dura in the Jonglei area (JIT (1954 i: 367–8)). Also see below, ch. 9.

[43] See below, ch. 7, n.27.

possibilities of the land. Ploughs are being used in the government garden in Kodok and on the experimental plot in Bor. In both cases some difficulty is experienced in obtaining bulls to pull the ploughs though there should not be any real trouble in training them.

An attempt to use a 'cultivator' at Taufikia failed as the ground was too hard.

FORESTRY

A certain amount of controversy has been going on for some years on the subject of forestry, the contention of the governor being that the true function of the department was to grow more and better trees and it was prostituting itself to the production of wood fuel and not replacing capital losses.

That this was true in the main was undeniable, and the Sudan government at long last resuscitated the Forestry Department, went in to the figures of wood fuel and discovered that even assuming the gradual alteration of mail steamers to coal or oil fuel for wood, the demand for wood fuel could be met by careful husbanding of existing assets and reproduction when possible.

After many years of rather futile efforts to grow 'sunt' trees along the White Nile and an entirely disproportionate result for the effort and expense involved, it appears to be agreed now that the best plan for reproduction of forest is fire protection from the grass fires to enable the local type of tree to grow to maturity. These might be increased by the additions of seedlings and young trees from other sources but the main supply must be natural.

The protection of the areas should be done, not by imported labour, but by local tribesmen on the same lines as dressers and chiefs' police.

Nothing on this line has yet been done, as the Forest superintendent is fully employed in the supervision of wood stations.

Apart from the Yirrol District where a lighter soil is helpful, the province is not well off for good forest tree, and there is a dearth even of the light timber required for native 'luaks' and huts.

Tentative efforts to grow bamboo have been only partially successful and more might be done in this matter.

The Shilluk have shown considerable keenness for trees if only for domestic shade in their villages and a scheme has been proposed to issue seedlings to be planted round their cultivation. This should mean that the trees would be established by the time the land is tired and a new lot of trees can then be started on the new plantations until there came to be a regular cycle.

The Egyptian Irrigation Service has a scheme for an experiment of timber growing just outside Malakal, but there are various sanitary problems to be tackled, and owing to lack of funds the scheme has been dropped.

The wood-cutting stations in the province are:

Main Nile	River Sobat	Bahr el Ghazal
Wad Akona		
Torakit		
Zarzur	Nasir	Tonga Malwal
Barboi		
Shambe		
Kenisa (condemned)		

Regeneration work has been done at Zarzur as well as Taufikia. The station at Kenisa is very unhealthy and the wood is poor and the station is to be moved.

There is a proposal to run a tractor at Shambe and cut wood some twelve miles inland and bring it to the river. Whether this is really an economic proposition seems doubtful, as the tractor could only work for a limited period of the year. The area available for stacking at Shambe is restricted and great deterioration from boring beetles occurs if wood is left for long in stacks.

There used to be an assistant conservator of Forests in the province as well as a superintendent and a clerk, but the first of these was economized. The superintendent is fully occupied in visiting the wood-stations to check the amounts cut and paid for and if necessary to shift the wood station elsewhere.

As a result he has little time to give to regeneration and experimental work.

The wood-cutters are mainly 'Sudanese' and were recruited originally from the old slave class. As these are now dying off, their places are being taken by labour from Omdurman often of a distinctly undesirable type.

Unfortunately the local tribesmen could not, at any rate yet, be persuaded to go on cutting wood all the year round: a few weeks of it and they would be pining to get away to their cattle or their hunting.

Whether it may be possible in the future to organize tribal labour has yet to be seen, but without rather an elaborate organization to enable reliefs to be provided at short intervals, it is difficult to see how to avoid the continuance of the introduction of this undesirable Northern labour.

Considerable opportunities for illicit gain lie in the hands of the forest overseers: a case was tried in 1930; unfortunately the accused though undeniably guilty escaped on appeal from the penalty of his misdoings.

IRRIGATION

All irrigation work in Upper Nile Province is done by the Egyptian Irrigation Department.

There are domestic problems of irrigation likely to appear when the Egyptian government decides which of its numerous schemes it proposes to carry into effect.

The schemes will all affect large areas of grazing land and possibly cultivation and the best way to make use of the new conditions entailed by the irrigation schemes will be a matter for the Sudan government to decide.

Moreover the conditions of life for instance in Gaweir are so hazardous and unhealthy that in the long last they must either have their conditions ameliorated by reclamation and drainage or be allowed to migrate to better areas which may or may not be brought into existence by the Irrigation 'schemes'.

The whole matter is a tricky and special subject: and the sooner it is made the subject of enquiry the more likely the Sudan government is to be in a position to express its needs to Egyptian government when schemes materialize.

Egyptian irrigation department

The Egyptian Irrigation Department has an allotment of a kilometre square in Malakal. They were in fact the first people to settle in the place. The boundaries of the colony are marked out, and mapped.

Within their area they are more or less independent; we only ask for plans etc. in connection with the sanitary system. The narrow gauge railway in the area belongs to them but they let the SG truck etc. run over it. It is a heavier line than ours.

They have an 18' pump and an installation for providing clean water and distribute water and electric light to the colony and the hospital: since October 1930 they have also supplied the British officials with drinking water, taken from the hospital tap.

Notwithstanding the fact that the EID pays rates for all houses in the colony, it provides its own roads and does a good many services which might reasonably fall on the rates: in fact if the Egyptian government chose to demand a return for rates other than sanitary, the LPS would be hard put to it to provide the requirements, and could only plead that the EID had set up a higher standard than could be met out of the funds available. E.g. they have macadamed a certain amount of their roads.

The annual programme of the department varies and the inspector writes in annually to give a general outline of what he proposes to do.

At the present time owing to the financial stringency field work outside Malakal is limited to the taking of sections and other data and making roads from Malek to Pibor and Pibor to Akobo, and from the wood station near the Nyanding mouth southwards to Akobo.

A barge is stationed near the [Zeraf] Cuts taking statistics: and there has been one at the Pibor mouth doing the same. Rest houses have been built at Bor and Renk for the same purpose but are not at present in use.

Gauges for Nile readings are situated at all district headquarters on rivers, and kept up by anyone with sufficient intelligence to do so.

At Gambeila the ADC gets a monthly allowance and the use of a launch for taking the discharge twice a week.

The schemes contemplated by the EID are the subject of a long printed report to be found in SCR files.

LANDS

Owing to the variety of provinces that have contributed to the UNP different systems of lease and tenure were to be found in different areas. They have now been brought into a common system, so that shops are leased at 2 m/ms per square metre per annum except in Malakal where there is a higher rate of 5 m/ms and 10 m/ms.

A great deal of confusion was caused by the fact that hikr was collected as if it were house tax, though the House Tax Ordinance does not apply to UNP. At Malakal itself, a flat rate was collected to cover hikr and rates and was supposed to be, but was not, adjusted in the accounts.

In the Renk District, some kind of levy which may or may not have been rates or hikr was collected on villages near Renk without any reason that could be ascertained.

The whole thing is rather complicated and obscure, but I think it has been at last cleared up.

Leases for shop sites are now being formally issued. Notwithstanding instructions to issue them, none had been made out for years.

On the other hand an effort to register the sites and holdings of all the tukls in the malakia village at Malakal has been resisted, as involving enormous labour without adequate return.

The Egyptian Irrigation Department holds its land as elsewhere in the Sudan not on a formal lease but by the interchange of letters with the Lands Department.

It has a site of one kilometre square at Malakal and there are boundary posts to mark the corners. Sites for houses e.g. at Bor and Renk are granted in the same way. In the case of Renk, the department had to be reminded that it must ask before it builds. In view of the extensive schemes possible for irrigation purposes, it is desirable to keep an eye on the matter.

All land other than town land is government land held by tribesmen without any system of tenure. I.e. land which is tribally held by Nuer cannot be appropriated by Shilluk without some mutual arrangement being reached. But as between one Nuer and another in Nuer land, the matter is settled by the land chief, unless (as is liable to occur) the government has to call on the chiefs' court to determine grazing or other rights between sections, to avoid fighting.

The missions hold their land on lease with a nominal rent. They are demarcated by the Surveys Department with concrete posts and were checked in 1928.

A site for the Shell Coy's benzine and oil store at Malakal has been allotted just south of the serum station, it is classed as second class land (i.e. 5 m/ms per metre).

Imperial Airways have applied for sites at Malakal and Shambe. The former is on the river bank just north of the northerly WT mast between two small khors. It is for a restaurant and includes a dining and sitting room, lavatory and latrines with servants' quarter and kitchen. But if they contemplate anything like a hotel this site is definitely not suitable. Probably the best site for a hotel would be south of the hospital block adjacent to the road on the top of the river bank. The plot at Shambe is for a rest house and petrol store and ADC has been instructed to demarcate.[44]

A scheme to put Malakal under the Town Planning Ordinance is under consideration. It is somewhat hampered by the lack of an up to date map of the town, but it is necessary if there are to be developments by commercial firms.

MEDICAL

Much of the most important work ancillary to administration done amongst the tribesmen has been the medical work. Captain H. A. Crouch, OBE, MC travelled all over the province and without making a detailed survey got a

---

[44] These arrangements were for the Imperial Airways Flying Boat service which followed the Nile to Lake Victoria.

sufficient general knowledge to enable him to work out the needs of the province. He had at his disposal a hospital at Malakal of nominally 75 beds, and the Lady Baker. By the use of the 'catacombs' and temporary tukls and tents he has been able to look after a steady average of 200 patients in the Malakal Hospital and the Lady Baker has been not only of the highest value as a peripatetic hospital for the evacuation of cases in and out of the Malakal Hospital but was a training establishment for selected boys mostly mission trained, as sanitary hakims. These when trained take charge of dispensaries which are placed in suitable tribal centres and are the connecting link between the tribal dressers and the hospital and expert surgical treatment.

An examination of the staff of 'native administration' will show to what extent the system has been developed.

The general scheme is to have tribal dressers working under the chiefs who deal with simple 'first aid' matters and by providing antiseptic treatment to small wounds in good time check the stream of cases requiring long treatment in hospital.

The dressers forward cases beyond their scope to the sanitary hakims who are established at suitable places in dispensaries which are generally supplied with a little accommodation for sick to live whilst they have their treatment.

These dispensaries are under the Medical Service and the SMI arranges to evacuate the cases for operation and treatment in hospital.

In the early stage it occurs almost inevitably that a certain proportion of the 'dressers' are not sufficiently intelligent or well-trained or energetic to do their work properly and it is to be anticipated that the numbers of dressers will be considerably reduced. On the other hand those that remain will be so fully employed that the normal wage of 5 Pt a month that they mostly get will not suffice them and the nett result financially will be the same.

In the earlier years treatment for e.g. yaws was not systematic, the main object being to get in infectious cases and treat them, later it was proposed to work through specific areas and deal with all cases thoroughly and so eliminate the disease from that area and then proceed to the next. Owing to the 'Nuer Settlement' this work has been interfered with but a great deal of medical work was done in the course of the 'Nuer Settlement' and the basis of the medical system established.

A medical survey of the Shilluk was carried out by Dr. L. Henderson in 1929, 1930 with useful results and he is to continue on these lines.

In my opinion, in view of the large population east and west of the Nile south of the Sobat and Bahr el-Ghazal, the government will find it necessary to establish hospitals probably in both areas, but without doubt on the east side, where there is a vast population both of UNP and Bahr el-Ghazal which is at present dependent on the Lady Baker or Wau (both very remote) for expert surgical or medical treatment.

I do not say that these hospitals are needed immediately or that there is sufficient data to show where they should be placed and I think therefore that the new Lady Baker will prove a useful stop-gap until a more comprehensive policy is devised.

There is considerable opening for research work in the province and it has been urged that an 'outpost' of the Research Laboratory should be placed at Malakal. A design for laboratory was made but was unfortunately so reduced and man-handled in the course of discussion that it was made futile. The matter has been re-opened and a new plan put forward which it is hoped will materialize. Stress must be laid on the fact that research work is sui generis and the man in charge of it must not be expected to take on duty e.g. in charge of a hospital. Equally research laboratory must be adequate to research needs, and not a makeshift.

One of the most interesting things in the medical work is the proof it has given that suitable boys can be taught in English to a satisfactory level of medicine in a few months. The same mutatis mutandis can presumably be done in other subjects provided that the necessary effort is made. The argument that the tribesmen cannot learn enough English (which has been put forward by an educational authority at the time in Uganda) is disproved; and equally the theory that the natives are mentally not equipped to learn to a sufficient standard.

Distribution of medical staff

Malakal
Medical inspector	1
" officers	2
Laboratory assistant	1
Dispensary hakim	1
Sanitary hakims	2
Bash tumargis	2
Tumargis (male)	15
" under training	10
" (female)	4

Dispensaries
1	Renk	Sanitary hakim
2	Melut	Run by Dr. Trudinger, Australian mission
3	Kodok	Sanitary hakim
4	SGS Kerreri	" "
5	Shambe	" "
6	Yirrol	Dispensary hakim

7 Bor	Sanitary hakim
8 Duk Faiwel	" "
9 Fangak	" "
10 Abwong	" "
11 Nasir	" "
12 Akobo	" "
13 Gambeila	Dispensary hakim
14 Lady Baker	MI and two tumargis

Dressing station
1 Torakit	Sanitary barber
2 Detwok	Christian tumargi
3 Rom	(run by Dr. Trudinger)
4 Lul	Christian tumargi
5 Tonga	" "
6 Yoynyang	" "

Proposed dispensaries
1 Fathai or Faddoi	Dispensary hakim
2 Pibor	Sanitary "

Proposed dressing stations
1 Doleib Hill	Christian tumargi

Proposed travelling dispensaries
1 Sanitary hakim with Mr. Tiernay	
1 " " " Captain Romilly	
1 " " " Mr. Bacon	

PUBLIC WORKS DEPARTMENT

In 1926, housing at Malakal for political officials consisted of the governor's house and the old mess, and there was a rest house of great discomfort and heat. There was no accommodation for MI, for Veterinary staff, WT inspector. The foreman of Works had an indifferent house adjacent to the prison. The Agricultural inspector at Kodok, the Forest overseer and the P&T inspectors were nominally housed at Taufikia. There was only one stable of one stall built ad hoc in Malakal.

In the districts houses had been built of semi-permanent kind at Nasir, Akobo, Abwong and Fangak.

The ADC Renk lived in a wooden hut which was very hot and full of mosquitoes. Kodok house consisted of two rooms only and there was a very small and inconvenient rest house originally meant for the sub-mamur. At Yirrol the district commissioner's house was ill built and the effendia quarters too dark to be habitable and had no mosquito protection.

By the end of 1930, the housing at Malakal had been almost completely re-organized, new houses had been erected for the DC, ADC and commandant of police, the Medical inspector, and a double quarter for two Veterinary inspectors; the rest house had been enlarged and provided with a proper verandah, a new store room and a garage built, and a new post office enabled accommodation to be given to clerical staff in the zaptieh. The mudiria had two offices added and other alterations to find room for staff. The effendia were housed in a type of house originally called Bollard quarters but much improved by making the rooms rectangular and adding mosquito traps and the hoshes were wired in and privacy provided by grass matting. A new WT station in the 'defensible' area had been erected with accommodation for the staff adjacent.

The old native officers mess had been converted into a RAF rest house. Three quarters for British officials were also in course of construction.

In the districts, proper house for ADC Renk was constructed in 1929, and steps for improving the water supply were under consideration. The Kodok house was to be enlarged and improved. The Abwong house was enlarged by a verandah.

At Nasir a new house for the ADC was under construction and various improvements and additions to store rooms, prison etc. were proposed.

At Akobo accommodation for the WT staff and sanitary hakim was being built, and various alterations to fit in with the transfer of the Equatorial Coy elsewhere. At Bor the ADC's house had been practically rebuilt. At Yirrol the DC had built himself a fairly good house, a second was under construction for ADC and the old Agricultural house pulled down and rebuilt on sound lines for commandant of police. Proper quarters were also built for three effendia.

A number of minor works of all sorts have been done and the general situation in relation to buildings has been put on to a much better footing.

There is still housing needed for the Agricultural inspector in Kodok, and the one in the south of the province has no house at all, being temporarily housed partly in a two-roomed hut at Bor and partly in a rest house at Duk Fadiat.

The roads, drainage, light and water system and the river front at Malakal are problems for future work. It will be almost certainly necessary to build a house for SMI at Malakal.

What buildings if any may be required in Western Nuer District and Zeraf Valley remain to be determined.

In view of the malignant type of mosquito found at Yirrol, extension of the mosquito wire to include the verandahs is desirable. The Medical Service is inclined to view that Yirrol is unsuitable as a government post—but as this is the third post selected, any change must be carried out with great care.

Stabling at Malakal has yet to be provided both for the police and for officials. Indeed stabling is an almost universal need.

Apart from Medical buildings and those put forward in the 1930 and 1931 building schemes there should not be a great deal of permanent building to be done.

Bor buildings are under Juba and Shambe under Wau. The latter in view of the position of Yirrol seems rather absurd, and re-acts unfortunately on the buildings there.

Maintenance has been a matter of some difficulty in the past and the department does not allow special maintenance staff; and so any men needed for maintenance have to be taken off works under consideration. Moreover owing to the peculiar conditions of the province some places have to be dealt with in the rains, as only then are they accessible.

A regular organized inspection followed by a maintenance party is what is needed, so that the whole province could be dealt with in the course of the year.

The PWD has taken charge of road grading. An experiment on a large scale was started in 1930 and is to be completed in 1931 (see Communications).

The PWD nominally claims to supervise all engineering work in the province: in practice however it does not do so. E.g. MT is under commandant of police. Various pumps are erected at Renk, Kodok and Bor without PWD supervision.

A suggestion was made in 1928 to find a handy man with sufficient engineering knowledge to do the supervision of the 'works' in the province, including the control of mechanical transport, the improvement of so called 'mud buildings', erection of bridges etc. It did not however lead to any result.

An important point is the need of a nucleus of training of smiths, chauffeurs, buildings etc. from the local tribesmen. Malakal is not a good centre owing to the Arab influence and the temptation of town life. The question is mixed up with that of education Q.V.

There is a good deal to be done yet to bring the PWD into close co-operation with the political service so that there is mutual advantage and economy. The importation of trained men from the North is inevitable as long as work is urgent, but the aim should be to train local people to learn to carry out all unskilled and semi-skilled work. It must however take time to attain this.

SURVEY

The river system of the province has been pretty fully mapped, and when the latest additions and corrections provided by EID are incorporated they should be very accurate.

The areas lying away from the main rivers are rather sketchily done, as they are compiled from compass sketches fitted to a few fixed points.

The addition of a few more fixed points, say, two on the Fullus-Bor road would be a great help to correcting the existing maps, and this would be of particular assistance to aviators who use this road as a guide to fly by.

There appears to be some error also in the Yirrol District which might with advantage be corrected.

Town survey in Malakal is out of date, and it is desirable to get a good large scale map of the town completed to date.

The mission sites are all surveyed and marked out.

A sketch plan of every district headquarters is needed to enable sites to be fixed and sanitary problems dealt with at headquarters.

VETERINARY

In my memo of February 1928 I drew attention to the need of a Veterinary inspector in the province. The larger part of the province is inhabited by cattle owning people, but the cattle population is far below the normal requirements of the people and there can be no hope of a cattle trade on sound lines until the cattle population is over local requirements. Much could be done by reducing disease, and if the losses from rinderpest and bovine pleuro-pneumonia were eliminated this alone would bring the number of cattle somewhere within the limits of local needs. There are at least two if not three types of cattle in the country and the inferior kinds are ousting the better and will do so until much more selection is used for breeding. The obvious line to follow is to train veterinary dressers and 'hakims' on the same lines as the medical ones and to provide the tribesmen with drugs and treatment, at the same time to endeavour to improve breeding by selection. Whether anything can be done to improve local breeds by outside blood has yet to be proved and in any case involves much time and expense.

A Veterinary inspector was appointed in the province in November

Main Report and Proposals

1930[45] and it is hoped to provide him with experimental herds at Abwong and Fangak and to start training natives through these.

The serum station has now been working for three seasons and is being built on a permanent basis. Serum is required for use in the Gezira and elsewhere in the North Sudan, but is hoped that a sufficient surplus can be made annually to meet local production.

The provision of the cattle needed for serum production should be a routine affair of transfer from tribute cattle to the Veterinary Department but the maintenance of these cattle in health till they are required has proved difficult, and it be one of the first duties of the Veterinary inspector.

Veterinary boxes are issued to each troop of mounted police and there are five veterinary police at Malakal.

The cattle come from Nasir district but run to ridiculously high prices.

Sheep are bred by the Beir but sheep breeding as a general business will depend largely on the development of forestry, as sheep require shade.

The Dinka in Melut and Bor Districts breed a certain quantity of sheep, for which their country is very suitable. They exchange the sheep for cattle with the Arabs of Fung Province.

Some pigs are being bred at Abwong experimentally and appear to thrive.[46]

The Nuer look on chickens as verminous and will not have anything to do with them, and many of the Dinka think the same. Among the Shilluk eggs are effeminate food, but the Shilluk are beginning to keep a few chickens to sell the eggs.

District commissioner, Kodok had some clutches of English eggs, the progeny of which were popular.

Since the arrival of the Veterinary inspector in November 1930 he has been practically continuously in work combating pleuro-pneumonia and rinderpest and is already acquiring a reputation among the natives. They held off at first and later were anxious to get treatment. He is also training a few veterinary dressers but his activities are hampered by lack of transport.

---

[45] A post of Veterinary inspector was allocated to UNP for the first time in 1930 but remained vacant until the beginning of 1931. A. B. MacIntyre (Veterinary Service, 1928–31), temporarily filled this post for the first half of 1931, and W. H. Glanville (who also joined the service in 1928) came to the province at the end of the year (after Willis had retired) and held the position from 1931 to 1934.

[46] See Coriat (1993: 74); and below, ch. 11.

CHAPTER 3

Northern District

JOHN BEAVAN[1]

BOUNDARIES OF THE DISTRICT

The Northern District boundaries are as follows. To the north is the White Nile Province, the line cutting the Nile at about lat. 12° 14′ N and thence running almost due east to Goz Nabbuk, circling Sahlat Um Dilwis and so south to the old government well on the Renk-Gule road at 33° 12′ E. From there the boundary runs to a point 33° 16′ E on the Gelhak-Ulu road, bordering with the Fung Province, thence south as far as the marshes of the Upper Khor Adar and so west to the river at about lat. 10° 2′. On the south are the Dungjol Dinka.

This is divided into two districts by the Khor Miakwe, the northern one being administered from Renk and the southern from Melut. There is also on the west bank of the Nile an area of country running as far north as Geigar. The Dinka do not use this at all: the only people who come into it are the Seleim Arabs with their herds from the White Nile Province. Wad Akona wood station administered from Renk is on the west bank.

The White Nile Arabs are continually attempting to encroach on the Dinka country from the north for 'harig' cultivation[2] and for cattle and sheep grazing.

DISTRIBUTION OF POPULATION

A complete census of the Northern District has just been made and I attach herewith the figures for all inhabitants.

All the Taaisha and the great majority of the Malakia live at or north of

---

[1] Dated 12 January 1931.
[2] *Hariq* cultivation is the burning off of old and new annual grasses together, both to clear land for sowing and conserve soil moisture. As a system in Upper Nile it was practised mainly in the Meban, northern Shilluk and Paloic Dinka areas. The areas under *hariq* cultivation expanded markedly in the early 1950s before independence, especially around Paloic, as part of the growth of mechanised agriculture, financed and managed by Northern Sudanese merchants (JIT (1954 i: 329–31)).

Renk.³ The Taaisha villages are at Goz Fami, about ten miles inland from Geigar.

The Bawom, Akon and Giel Dinka are spread along the river from Geigar to Khor Miakwe. The Melut Dinka live inland and bring their cattle to the river in the dry weather for grazing.

GENERAL TRIBAL ORGANIZATION

Each section of the Dinka has a head chief, with sub-chiefs under him but the whole of the Abialang are to some extent under Yol Kur, chief of the Bawom section.

The names of these chiefs are as follows:

Bawom	Yol Kur
Akon	Ajang Ajwang (Ibrahim)
Giel	Deng Kak
Abuya⁴	Malek Agweir
Ageir	Oweit Shol [Awet Col]
Beir	Dal Aiwel
Niel	Lual Wal

There is a chiefs' court established at both Renk and Melut and these work fairly well. Yol Kur is the president of the Renk court and Dal Aiwel unofficially of the Melut court. The other chiefs and their wakils are entitled to sit on the court but generally it is only the chiefs who do so.

Recent history

In the old days probably 150 to 200 years ago all the Renk and Melut Dinka and the Dungjol Dinka of Kodok District were founded by a large force of young warriors who came with their women folk from the Twi, Bor and Ngok Dinka, with a few from other tribes, Aliab, Cic and Agar, on the east bank of the Nile.⁵

---

³ These were the remnants of the Ta'aisha Baggara from Darfur who had been resettled on the Nile by the Khalifa Abdallahi during the Mahdiyya.
⁴ The following four sections were administratively separated from the Abialang in the mid–1930s to form the Paloic Dinka.
⁵ For an earlier account of the Dinka occupation of the White Nile see 'Report by Bimbashi H. Wilson on the Dinkas of the White Nile', Appendix C, *SIR* 104 (March 1903). Wilson dated the earlier events at around 1775. Neither he nor Beavan gave their reasons for the dates they chose for the Dinka invasion of the White Nile, though Wilson may have been relying on James Bruce's near contemporary account of the Fung Kingdom of Sennar.

At that time the Fung owned this country as far south as the Sobat and the Dinka drove them back from the river as far north as Geteina. Later when the Dinka did not pay tribute in the Turkia they were driven back as far as Khor Adar whence they retired on the Dungjol country opposite Kodok where they were left alone. Soon they decided to pay their tribute and were allowed to return to lands north here as far as Geigar where a post was established to protect the Dinka from the Arabs.

At the time of the Mahdia the Abialang all ran away to avoid military service and sat down at Rom of the Abuya south of Khor Miakwe.

Then chiefs Areng Chom and Kak Akwei went to Omdurman and asked permission to return to their country which was allowed.

The Bawom and Akon came right north and the Giel stayed south as now. Then Kak Akwei and Areng Chom went back to Khartoum for the Khalifa to decide which should be the chief and Kak died there. Areng returned to find Akol Kak, eldest son of Kak Akwei had been made chief of the Giel, Areng being left with the Akon and Bawom. Akol Kak's uncle complained about the boy being made chief whereupon Akol killed him. The people then complained to Zaki[6] at Kaka and he beat them all up so that the Giel scattered among the Akon, Bawom and Ageir. Areng became chief then of the Bawom, Akon and northern Giel. Bakhit Nyok was his wakil in the Akon, Deng Akwoi in the Bawom and Deng Akol in the Giel.

When the Khalifa's officers came up and enquired for Areng Chom at Renk, Areng sent gifts to them by the hands of his wakils. Soon it came to his ears that these wakils in handing over the gifts said that he, Areng, was not here at all and that the gifts were personally from them. This enraged him and he took all their cattle with him and retired to Melut area where he raised the Ageir, Niel and Beir and fought the Giel and Akon as far as Tong just south of Renk. The wakils Bakhit Nyok and Deng Akol with the Akon and Giel ran away to the Mangnok section of the Bawom just north of Renk. Areng asked for the wakils to be given up but the Bawom refused and fought, calling in the assistance of the Khalifa's troops. Areng and his supporters were driven back to the Ageir country, five of them being killed. Areng later on raised the forces there again. Then Bakhit Nyok, Deng Akol, Deng Akwoi and Goc Deeng (Mangnok) went to the Khalifa and complained, asking for assistance. The Bawom ran away before Areng's forces as far as Tayiba where they were caught up and a fight took place and Areng being defeated, again retired to the Ageir.

Areng was then taken to the Khalifa who gave him gifts and told him to go back to his own country and to live there in peace. Areng intending to do

---

[6] Al-Zaki Tamal, commander of the Khalifa's riflemen, and commander of the expedition to the White Nile in 1891–2 which devastated the Shilluk and the Dinka.

this went off to the Ageir country in order to bring back his family and his flocks to Renk but in a personal quarrel there he was speared and killed by a man of Piti. His family took his clothes with them and went to the Khalifa to complain and he sent up a force to deal with the murderers. The chiefs of the Ageir gave up to them all the cattle of the Piti section and told them that the murderer had been killed by the Niel.

On its way back to Omdurman this force was met at Renk by Kitchener's force which was en route for Kodok and was beaten there.[7]

In settling the question of chief General Jackson, then at Kodok, appointed Areng's son Padiet Areng, chief of the Bawom and Akon and Salem Banga chief of the Giel. Both Padiet Areng and Salem Banga were soon turned out by government. Padiet was followed by Oweir [Awir] Areng who only lasted two months[8] and the following chiefs were appointed:

Yol Kur of the Bawom, Bakhit Nyok of the Akon and Wiao Kak of the Giel. The last named was dismissed but is still alive and was followed by Shan [Can] Kak who died and was succeeded by Deng Kak who is now chief there; all these Giel chiefs were of one family.

Bakhit Nyok of the Akon was turned out in 1928 and Ibrahim Ajwang was appointed in his place.

Yol Kur, who is of the Mangnok section of the Bawom, thus has little hereditary right to his post and has no right at all to chieftainship over the whole Abialang. If such a post were made the chief claim would be that of the Giel chief, Deng Kak.

REVENUE

Dinka tribute. The last assessment of Dinka tribute was much too high and for the last three years has been reduced from its original figure by about 10% to the following amounts:

Bawom		£E 337
Akon		233
Giel		288
	Total Renk	£E 858

---

[7] Kitchener arrived at Renk on 15 September 1898, where he met and defeated the Mahdist force under the *amir* Sa'id Sughaiyir. The Mahdist force had been camped at Renk since the end of August, after its attack on Fashoda had been repulsed by Marchand (*SIR* 60 (25 May to 31 December 1898): 8–9).

[8] In fact, Awir was appointed before Padiet; the former was dismissed in 1902 and the latter in 1913 (see Biographical Notes).

Abuya		£E 158
Ageir		419
Beir		281
Niel		376
	Total Melut	£E 1234
Total Dinka tribute		£E 2092

A new assessment is now being made and I shall suggest a total likely to work out at about £E 369 for Renk and £E 732 for Melut a total of £E 1101.

All residents, who are not tribal Dinka, are taxed ushur on their crops and pay herd tax.

A number of White Nile Arabs cross the northern boundary and cultivate within the Northern District: these also pay ushur.

The figures on these items for the past two years are as follows:

	1929–30	1930–31
Ushur	£E 849.552 m/ms	101.620
Herd tax	112.800	

The balance of the revenue is made up as follows:

	1929	1930
Hikr	124.050	16.650
Local rates	70.628	61.597
Traders licences	59.500	78.000
Traders tax	12.000	3.000
Permits to trade	44.350	47.000
Liquor licences	35.250	39.750

ROADS

The Northern District is now well supplied with roads: there are some 340 miles altogether as follows:

Renk district

(1)	White Nile boundary to Renk	40
(2)	Geigar to Goz Fami & Gerbanat	26
(3)	Renk to Gelhak town	60
(4)	Renk to Gule second well	27
(5)	Gelhak to Atakdok	50
(6)	Gelhak causeway to Khor Miakwe	25
		228

Melut District

(7)	Khor Miakwe to Melut	56
(8)	Paloc to Mialek (approx.)	57
		113
	Total	341

The last named road is now being cleared. This goes nearly as far south as Kodok and it might be possible to join this up with a road to Malakal and go south.

The main road from White Nile Province boundary as far south as Khor Miakwe is for the most part very good, and so is the road to Goz Fami and Goz Gerbanat.

The west and east roads to the Fung boundary from Renk and Gelhak are bad and are not likely to improve. The roads from Khor Miakwe to Paloc and Paloc to Mialek are also bad but with use and time they will probably improve a good deal. The Paloc-Mialek road runs through many villages and the use which the Dinka will make of it when clear will be sure to consolidate and level the surface.

There are embankments and bridges at Khors Doleib, Gelhak, Bibban, Meriok and Miakwe and another will have to be made over Khor Adar on the new Paloc-Mialek road.

Wells are few and far between. The cultivators at Gerbanat make hafirs. At Goz Fami there is good well water.

There are also wells in Melut District at Katalok and Paloc.

There are ferries, run by contracts over the Nile at Geigar, Rek and Gelhak. The amounts paid for these contracts in 1931 are £E 6–4–3 respectively.

Chapter 3

ECONOMIC DEVELOPMENT

Renk district

The paying crops in Renk District are ful sudani [groundnuts], on the Gozes, 'harig', dura and gum. There is a strong possibility that the Dinka will soon take to tapping hashab for themselves without Arab assistance. The very high price of gum last year and the very poor crops of dura and ful this year have encouraged them to do so lately and I hope that this will continue to develop. For this reason it is to be hoped that some gum gardens at any rate will always be reserved for the Dinka and not handed over to the Arabs of the White Nile. One of the main difficulties of the Dinka in developing this is the lack of transport for which they have to rely on the Arab camels. Donkeys are becoming more common both in Renk and Melut and these will assist for gardens close to water. Without the Arab assistance however such development can only be very slow.

Cattle trade will not do any good in Renk District owing to 'fly' [trypanosomiasis] but the older Dinka are wisely pushing the rearing of sheep for which the grazing is excellent. The young men are difficult about this and it is a sad thing that the Arabs of the Fung have been allowed to bring cattle to Renk for exchange as the young men rush in with their sheep, against the advice of their elders, and hand them over to the Arabs for a few cattle instead of increasing their flocks. It would be a very good thing if the bride price could be payable in sheep and I have discussed this with the chiefs. The flocks of sheep among the Dinka have certainly increased in the last year and this should be encouraged.

Melut district

The Melut Dinka grow very good crops of excellent dura but there is little likelihood of their increasing their cultivations. A few of them collect talh and hashab[9] opposite Kaka but no development is probable.

The cattle in Melut are much better than in Renk, as 'fly' had not penetrated there until last year with some trespassing Arabs from the Fung.

---

[9] The gum produced by hashab was the best commercial value. See Broun & Massey (1929: 170–1).

BUILDINGS

The following buildings are on Public Works charge in the Northern District.

Renk

31	Zaptieh (a)
32	Zaptieh (b)
33	Kadi's quarter & Mahkama sharia
34	Sarraf's house
35a	Postmaster's house
35b	Translator's house
36	Dura store (once a stable)
37	Sub-mamur's house
38	Mamur's house
39a	Dispensary hakim's house
39b	Kadi's clerk house
40	District commissioner's house
41	Accountant's house
42	Rest house
–	Dispensary
–	Garage

Melut

Zaptieh (a)
Zaptieh (b)
Sub-mamur's quarter
Postmaster's quarter
Sarraf's quarter

The mud buildings are as follows:

Renk

Schoolmaster's quarter
School, brick building
School, kurnuk, zeer house, latrine
Police, 21 quarters
Police, 2 latrines
Females' prison
Prison cookhouse

Suk rakuba
Employees' kitchens, etc.
Old Mahkama sharia

Melut

Rest house
Dispensary
Temporary stable
2 tukls for sailors
Police quarters and latrines
Employees' latrine etc.

The grants for mud buildings in Renk and Melut 1930 were £E 80 and 28 and have been budgeted for in 1931.

FORESTRY

No afforestation has been done in these districts, either Renk or Melut, but it has been proposed to start work at Torkwac north of Melut, in the bend of the river between there and Kaka.

Just south of Melut boundary at Zarzur in Kodok District there is a small plantation.

There is a wood cutting station at Wad Akona on the west bank just south of Renk and it has been proposed to start one south of Jebel Ahmed Agha.

GARDENS

There are merkaz gardens at Renk and Melut, with a pump at Renk which is now being installed and I hope that when this is working there will be a supply of vegetables and fruit for Renk itself and saleable to steamers stopping here.

The garden at Melut is small—there are seldom any prisoners there to do the watering and it just supplies green stuff to the merkaz.

Merkaz cattle

The following show the numbers of cattle in Renk and Melut herds on 31.12.1930.

Renk 27
Melut 23

The cattle in Renk are very poor and give but little milk—the comparison with cattle in Kosti in this is very great. Sometimes the milk falls as low as 5 rotls per day which is insufficient for merkaz demands and it would be a good thing to bring in some new blood.

OFFICIALS EMPLOYED IN THE DISTRICT

In accordance with the covering letter I am forwarding Confidential Reports on the classified staff under separate cover.

The staff is divided as follows:

Renk

Mamur	Mohd. Eff. Sabir Idris
S/mamur	Mahmud Eff. Osman El Sheikh
Translator	Mohammed Eff. Ali Hamdi
Accountant	Abdel Gader Eff. Lutfi
Sarraf	Mohy El Din Eff. El. Geneidi

Melut

*S/Mamur	Abdel Aziz Eff. Hasoun [*Sent temporarily to Duk & Bor March 1931.]
Sarraf	Mahmud Eff. El Sayed El Hanafi

In addition to the classified staff there are the following unclassified officials, all weighers, their posts and their pay per month being shown after their names.

Abdel Wahab Mahmud	Renk	£ 3.000
Billal Ahmed	Renk	£ 2.500
Abbas Seleim	Geigar	£ 3.000
Osman Abdel Wahab	Geigar	£ 2.500
Abdel Nabi Fadl El Mula	Gelhak	£ 3.000

The police establishment at Renk is 18 and at Melut 12.

NORTHERN DISTRICT CENSUS 1930

Dinka

Renk District

	Houses	Men	Women	M/C	F/C	Youths	Old Folk	Total
Bawom	417	219	271	372	400	151	138	1551
Akon	337	175	271	315	305	94	66	1226
Giel	425	244	325	438	443	142	127	1719
Total Abialang	1206	638	867	1125	1148	387	331	4496

Melut District

	Houses	Men	Women	M/C	F/C	Youths	Old Folk	Total
Abuya	261	183	219	138	171	91	45	847
Ageir	638	388	488	495	539	281	146	2337
Beir	448	268	351	451	445	243	144	1902
Niel	759	407	542	791	610	173	174	2697
Total Melut	2106	1246	1600	1875	1765	788	509	7783

Total

	Houses	Men	Women	M/C	F/C	Youths	Old Folk	Total
Total Dinka	3312	1884	2467	3000	2913	1175	840	12279

Non-tribal inhabitants

Renk District

Tayiba	52
Geigar	283
Goz Fami (Malakia)	177
Goz Fami (Taaisha)	415
Gerbanat	64
Magara	204
Khershawal	271
Renk, Kumshowar	178
Radif	24
Suari	168
Gabarona	331
Goz Ajwang	134
Goz Gelhak	71
Gelhak Island	106
Total Renk Dist.	2478
Melut District	351
Total Non-Tribal inhabitants	2829

Northern District

Total Tribal Dinka	12279
Total Non-Tribal	2829
Grand Total	15108

CHAPTER 4

Shilluk District

CAPTAIN G. P. CANN

BOUNDARIES OF THE DISTRICT

The 'Shilluk' or Central District, UNP is bounded as follows:

ON THE NORTH:
(On the west bank of the Nile) by the 11th parallel of latitude as far as the Kordofan/Upper Nile boundary.

(On the east bank of the Nile) by a line drawn from the junction of 10° 15' North parallel with the Nile to the apex of the Fung/Upper Nile boundary at the junction of 9° 30' latitude and 32° 45' longitude.

ON THE SOUTH:
From the apex of the Fung/Upper Nile boundary (mentioned above) to a point on the Sobat River (marked Shilluk/Dinka boundary) between Nagdia and Banglai, thence to Wunakir on Khor Fullus, thence to Jebel Zeraf and the Zeraf River mouth, thence to Lake No Irrigation Nile Gauge (claimed by Shilluk), the White Nile being the boundary.

ON THE WEST:
From Lake No Nile Gauge along the Kordofan/Upper Nile boundary northwards to the 11th parallel North.

DISTRIBUTION OF POPULATION

N.B. Figures are approximate, but I do not consider more in error than 15%.

Shilluk: 116,000

Distributed along the west bank of the Nile from Fafoijo in the south west to Tworokit—opposite Jebel Ahmed Agha—in the north, along the east bank of the Nile from the Zeraf River mouth in the south to about opposite Kodok on the North.

Shilluk also reside along both banks of the Sobat from its mouth to Nagdia, and along Khor Fullus from its mouth to Wunakir.

Dunjol Dinka: 15,000

Scattered over the area enclosed by a triangle formed roughly by Khor Adar in the north east, Sobat River in the south, and the Nile, except that they do not reside within 20 miles radius of Malakal or on the banks of the Nile or Sobat.

Rueng Dinka: 6,000

Scattered over the inland area which is roughly bounded by a line drawn from Khor Fullus mouth to Jebel Zeraf on the south and the north by Khor Atar.

Arab and Nuba: 2,000

In the area west and north west of Kodok called Fama and Atara.

Non Provincial Sudanese: 9,000

At the main towns, Malakal, Kodok, Tonga, Taufikia, and Kaka, also at wood stations Zarzur and Tworokit.

Europeans: 50

Including government officials of Sudan and Egyptian services at Malakal, Taufikia, and Kodok, and missionaries at Detwok, Lul, Rom, Tonga, and Doleib Hill.

Egyptians: 50

Employees of Egyptian service and clerks and Post Office officials of Sudan service.

Floating population: 500

Eliri [Nuba Mountains] and other Arab labourers coming in from Kordofan in search of work at Malakal, fishermen and native crews etc.

TRIBAL ORGANIZATION

Shilluk

The organisation of this tribe may be traced back to the period—about 300 years ago—when the tribal 'ancestor', Nyikang, invaded and conquered the

156   Chapter 4

terrain that is now occupied from the 'Funy' (probably the present Fung tribe).[1]

Since the 'passing' (Shilluk kings do not 'die'!) of Nyikang the chieftainship, or 'Retship' has been held only by direct descendants of this 'ancestor' and thus the Ret holds an almost divine position amongst his people, and so he becomes the natural and supreme authority of the Shilluk.[2]

It is inevitable that during the past 300 years the original family has divided into several branches—though all directly of the seed of Nyikang—and to overcome the confusion natural under these conditions it has been tacitly agreed by the tribe that the successions to Retship should follow in turn to each branch of the family: to make this a little more plain the following list of nine recent Rets shows how elections were made:

Akoic [Akoc]	
Nyadok [Nyidok]	
Kwatkeir [Kwathker]	
Ajang	son of Nyadok
Kweikun	son of Kwatkeir
Yor	son of Akoich
Kur	son of Nyadok
Fadiet	son of Kwatkeir
Fafiti	son of Yor

At the present time I think that the sons of Kur and Fadiet are the only elements to be considered in the event of the 'passing' of the present Ret, as it is most unusual for the Retship to pass from father to son direct, though of course after the position has been held by the Kur and Fadiet family the Fafiti family is next for appointment.[3]

---

[1] The date for the foundation of the Shilluk kingdom is probably taken from Westermann (1912: li-lii), who arrived at a date in the first quarter of the 16th century by multiplying the Shilluk king list by an average regnal length of thirteen and a half years. Hofmayr's king list (published in German) was subsequently accepted as more accurate than Westermann's, and placed the first three mythical kings in the late sixteenth century (Hofmayr (1925: 58–64)). For the Shilluk and the Funj kingdom of Sennar see R. S. O'Fahey and J. L. Spaulding, *Kingdoms of the Sudan* (London 1974), 25–6, 61–3. For the Funj see James (1977).
[2] Through the ethnography of Westermann (1912) and Hofmayr (1925), and through the interpretive work of Seligman (1911) and other early anthropologists, the Shilluk *reth* became the best known living example of 'divine kingship' in twentieth century Africa. For a criticism of this interpretation see Evans-Pritchard (1962). The ceremonies attending the death and installation of successive reths have been well reported (Munro (1918), Howell & Thomson (1946), Howell (1953a)).
[3] The system by which the election to reth alternated between the three families of Akoc, Nyidok and Kwathker dates back to the beginning of this century. From roughly the mideighteenth to the mid-nineteenth century the kingship was held in succession by members of

The system, while perfectly fair to branches of the Nyikang family, is unsatisfactory from an administrative point of view; for it becomes impossible to train up the natural heir apparent by the district commissioner, as such a course—over and above being extremely distasteful to the ruling Ret—would certainly make the pupil swollen-headed, and lead him on to overt action against the reigning Ret at every occasion.

The uncertainty of heirs to the Retship until the actual time that they may be called upon to take up their duties therefore is a great incentive to their good behaviour.

The Ret therefore, guided by the district commissioner, holds supreme* control over the tribe [*subject to the limitations of tribal custom and common sense and decency, not to mention the higher authority of the SG], and decides all tribal cases that do not call for trial under the Sudan Penal Code. The trial of petty cases—chiefly civil claims—is delegated to some eight court chiefs who are appointed by the Ret in accordance with ancient custom.

Appeals against decisions of court chiefs are decided by the Ret.

Tribal police—of an approved strength 150—are appointed with the Ret's approval and are usually able to perform the duties of province police except against determined resistance.

Such police are available for assisting the station authorities in keeping order, find the station guard by night at Kodok (reinforced by one province policeman, armed), and should now attend chiefs' courts to render assistance.

The tribe is divided up into about forty main divisions, each under a head chief who should be held responsible for any occurrences in his division. These head chiefs all assemble for a tribal council meeting on King's Day each year,[4] and generally pay at least one ceremonial visit annually to the Ret at Fashoda.

Generally speaking these head chiefs are weak, and unable to control the actions of the fighting men—more especially as they are in sympathy in cases where tribal custom dictates warlike action in preference to reporting cases of sudden and grievous provocation to the DC—but the discharge of

---

the same line: Kudit and his son and grandsons. As only those sons of the reth who are born while his father is actually reigning are eligible for succession, this limited the number of potential successors during the short reigns of Anei, Akwot and Awin. By the time of the death of the long-lived Nyidok his sons Akoc and Kwathker were both eligible, and the succession was constantly manipulated by interventions by the Turco-Egyptian and Mahdist governments. When Kitchener arrived at Fashoda in 1898 there were three contenders from the three families listed above, and it was as much an administrative as a Shilluk decision to limit future successions to them in strict rotation. The next three reths after Fafiti Yor were Anei Kur Nyidok, Dak Fadiet Kwathker and Kur Fafiti Yor (see Biographical Notes).

[4] King's Day was held each January to commemorate the visit of King George V to Port Sudan in 1912.

old and appointment of new chiefs is not a matter to be lightly taken by DCs unless backed up by the Ret.* [*And is governed by tribal custom, discharge being dependent on certain conditions and appointment requiring 'investment' by the Ret.]

Each division has recognised battle leaders, and these men are followed unquestioningly by the young men in battle, the chief seldom leads his men.

Now that reasonably serviceable motor roads exist throughout the district, and an ADC is to be permanently stationed at Malakal District, there should be little difficulty in obviating inter-village fighting of any severity, as news of impending fights is quickly passed through to district headquarters.

The main incidents of importance in the tribe in recent years:
Ret Kur Nyadok deposed by government in 1903.
Ret Fadiet appointed Ret in 1903.
Ret Fadiet died 1917.
Ret Fafiti Yor appointed February 1917.
Severe smallpox epidemic 1919.
1st Shilluk Council held 18th January 1925.
Shilluk police inaugurated 1925.
Chiefs' courts definitely established at the council meeting 22nd January 1928.

Dunjol Dinka

The organisation of the Dunjol Dinka is by no means as satisfactory as that of Shilluk, for—though the Dinka have a useful code of laws—they lack a personality to dispense justice among them.

For some years these Dinka relied upon the decisions of Yuzbashi Ahmed Eff. Ragab, an Egyptian mamur who interested himself in the laws and customs of the Dinka, spoke their language fluently, and proved a most capable and faithful interpreter of Dinka law. Since his departure in 1925 the experiment in delegating legal powers to court chiefs under the presidency of chief Aiywel [Aiwel] Akwei has proved fairly satisfactory until in 1928 Aiywel incurred the jealousy of the lesser chiefs who demanded an equal voice in hearing cases. This demand has now been met by the appointment of chief Deng Shol [Col], of another Dunjol division, as court chief with power to sit as president of courts.

There are six main divisions of Dunjol Dinka, with a small section of Niel Dinka attached.

The Dunjol also have their complement of native police, 14 in number, who compare favourably with the Shilluk police. (Armlets are required for these police.)

The Dunjol Dinka are generally peaceable and pay up their tribute promptly, mostly in grain which they grow in great quantity on the fertile inland soil. This season has unfortunately been unsatisfactory owing to lack of rain and the ravages of locusts, and a remission of the usual tribute will be necessary—estimated at 33%.

The most noted character of the Dunjol was a wizard by the name of Ajak Tor Bil, who after being the cause of trouble in 1916 and assisting the Gaajak Nuer in their resistance of government in 1919 and 1920, gave himself up at Melut at the end of 1920. This man died in July this year, and no other wizard of consequence remains in that area.

Rueng Dinka

There are five small clans of Rueng in the Khor Atar vicinity, none of the chiefs of which merit great comment; and of whom it was found in the past to be impracticable to make any one of them head of the others—owing to jealousy.

These Dinkas pay a small tribute of about £E 120 annually in cash or bulls at Malakal; otherwise they are seldom seen except by the district commissioner on trek.

They are extremely fond of litigation and in the days of the police post at Khor Atar used to take their cases to the sol who was in charge, or even to the onbashi who succeeded him! And when this police post was withdrawn the Rueng continually petitioned for its re-establishment.

The Rueng some years ago had a serious fight and one section ran away to a mythical placed called 'Fanaru' (somewhere between Lake No and Talodi, and said to be three days hard trekking through swamps from Tonga.)[5]

The Rueng have been instructed in holding chiefs' courts by district commissioner Malakal and have an establishment of chiefs' police.

REVENUE

The main source of revenue of the district is tribute, which is paid by the Shilluk and Dinka tribes as under:

Shilluk tribute	
Malakal District	£E 1,383
Kodok District	£E 1,552

---

[5] Panaru is a real place in Bentiu district, north of the Bahr el-Ghazal river and near the Kordofan-Upper Nile border. It was occupied then, as now, by the main body of Rueng Dinka, of whom those along the Khor Atar were only an offshoot.

Dunjol Dinka tribute

Kodok District	£E 1,120

Rueng Dinka tribute

Malakal District	£E 124
Total tribute	£E 4,179
Ushur from non-tribal element	£E 22
Herd tax from non-tribal	£E 31
NB. Ushur and herd tax figures for Kodok District only.	
Hikr at Kodok only	£E 29
Traders' tax and licences Kodok District only	£E 110
Rent of government houses at Kodok only	£E 100

ROADS AND COMMUNICATIONS

Since 1926, when the district commissioner commenced using motor transport, preparation of roads throughout the district has progressed until in 1930 reasonably serviceable dry season roads exist as follows:

Moro (north of Kaka) through to Fafoijo (to the southwest of Tonga), or about 180 miles.

Tonga to Khor Ragaba, about 20 miles.

Kaka to Id el Haluf, about 18 miles.

Kodok to Adawado Nyerur and Atara, 25 miles.

Malakal to Nyingaro (east bank), 25 miles.

Malakal to Doleib Hill and thence to Nagdia on Sobat River, about 37 miles.

Malakal to Nagdia (direct Irrigation road), about 17 miles.

A total length of some 320 miles.

These roads are cleared of grass yearly by local villagers without remuneration, but an annual grant is made for heavier repairs as may be necessary.

In order to obtain an additional couple of months use of these roads in the earlier and later parts of the rains 47 Armco culverts* were purchased in 1928 and 1929 and these are placed longitudinally in khors with embankments leading to them from either side. [*These culverts were

Shilluk District

extravagantly large and some could be replaced by smaller ones. The banks mostly need extra work.]

An additional 18 of such culverts have been asked for to complete an additional programme of roadmaking in 1931.

No roadmaking material such as stone exists in the district, and the formation of camber by ditching is too costly to carry out by manual labour, so it is hoped that one of the graders (used on the Malakal-Bor road) may be used in this district in the near future.

Embankments leading from the mainland to the Nile exist at Tonga, opposite Malakal* [*the Irrigation tiebank], Kodok, and are maintained by province funds.

Embankments at Lul and Detwok are maintained by the Roman Catholic Mission.

The Financial Secretary when visiting Kodok in 1930 discussed the possibility of forming a system of meshras (by dredging through the swamps from the Nile to the mainland) for the purpose of assisting cotton purchase, but the matter has been dropped temporarily owing to the Steamers Dept. being unable to find the necessary vessel and staff at present.

Wells. Native wells are kept up by Arabs and Nubas in the Fama and Atara locality. They are merely pits sunk in drying up Khors.

Ferries. There was a government ferry at the Sobat opposite Khor Fullus mouth for transport of motor vehicles across the Sobat.

Natives run ferries across the Nile at Kodok by canoe, and at Malakal by canoe and native boats.

ECONOMIC DEVELOPMENT AND POSSIBILITIES

Agricultural

The only outstanding development in the past five years has been the cultivation of rain grown cotton.

The cotton growing industry was revived in 1923, and by 1925 was becoming firmly established in Kodok District, and steady progress in yield has continued in that district up to the 1929–1930 season: 1930–1931 crop however will be a light one owing to insufficient rains and in some cases to attack by locusts.

Kodok District has now come to understand the value of cotton growing as a money crop with which tribute may be easily paid in cash, and thus is of great value administratively.

There seems to be little prospect of this district being capable of producing more than about 15,000 kantars of seed cotton even in a good cropping season, and further development should be looked for by fostering this industry in Malakal District—from which but small crop is obtained to date.

The Dunjol Dinka are far too valuable a food crop tribe, and I think it would be a mistake to divert their energies to cotton growing, as Kodok District, and to some extent the province headquarters rely upon Dunjol grain to provide rations for their staff of police and animals.

Dura amongst the Shilluk is generally grown in sufficient quantity to meet tribal requirement, except in the Sobat River area where the crops are generally in excess of local wants and merchants are able to purchase about 2,000 ardebs yearly.

The Shilluk District generally suffers from great variation of crop annually—owing to the length of the district—and divisions in want of grain are accustomed to purchase their requirements from their more fortunate neighbours.

For this reason there is usually little or no Shilluk grain for sale to merchants on the west bank of the Nile, and reputable merchants are beginning to recognise this fact, though there is always a demand for petty traders to be allowed to open small shops at trading posts in that area (such applications being refused as much as possible).

The Dunjol Dinka are exceedingly good dura producers, and grow no other crops, and it is usual for government to take some 1200 ardebs annually in kind as tribute, while merchants are still able to purchase a further 1500 to 2000 ardebs from this source. In years of famine in the Kodok Shilluk District the Dunjol can generally supply enough to save the situation, even after the merchants and government have taken their requirements.

NB The Dunjol crop for 1930/31 happens to be poor for the first time in many years.

Simsim is grown by the Arabs and Nubas at Fama and Atara, but not in any great quantity.

Veterinary

Considering the raids made on the district herds during the Mahdia it is surprising that the Shilluk and Dinka have herds at all; and though I would not call the Dinka or the Shilluk rich in cattle, they have quite sufficient for their local needs—though they have no surplus for export.

Despite the efforts of the Veterinary Department who have on frequent occasions sent Veterinary officers for brief tours of the district, the prevalence of cattle plague and pleuro-pneumonia amongst Shilluk herds is increasing, and I feel will continue to do so as long as Arabs from Kordofan Province are able to effect entry into the district.

At least 50% of the hides purchased and exported from the district are those of cattle that have died of disease; so transport figures of hides exported from the district are apt to be misleading as indicating that Shilluk sell their cattle which is not the case.

My rough observation of the herds of these tribes is that the Dinka herds are increasing but the Shilluk herds are decreasing in the past seven years.

Spasmodic efforts at inoculating cattle in past years have been made by the district commissioner, and for one period carried out by El Kaimakam Ellison Bey, but such efforts are insufficient for the urgent need of the whole Shilluk country and a resident Veterinary officer with a staff of Veterinary police is an essential to the well being of the cattle.

Traders

The district suffers from an excess of petty traders, and has quite enough men of financial stability to develop such trade as offers in the district.

It is generally difficult to persuade the principal merchant to do his own trading at traders' posts, as he prefers to stay in one of the towns and send out unsatisfactory and dishonest agents.

Itinerant traders are not allowed in the district.

Various Shilluk have tried their hand at trading in the past, but they usually fail for lack of funds and trading instinct and fall into the hands of the Northerner who, by means of advances of goods or cash eventually breaks the native.

Although it is popularly supposed that the Shilluk is invariably cheated when he deals with the merchant, this is only the case when he purchases luxuries such as beads, oil, etc.—the native is capable of driving a very hard bargain when he wishes to sell his products.

BUILDINGS

The following permanent buildings exist at Kodok station, remarks as to suitability and condition added:

Station offices. 4 rooms used as offices for DC, inspector of Agriculture, mamur and accountant. Good repair, roof of DC's & inspector of Agriculture plank lined newly in 1930. Accommodation adequate.

Prison block. 5 rooms used as arms store, prison (women), prison (men), hospital ward, and dispensary. In good repair. Store and prisons suitable, but hospital and dispensary should be moved away from this block when new accommodation approved: these two rooms could then be utilised for chiefs' courts.

Motor garage. One large building without any dividing walls, very suitable for garage of two lorries and two cars. Used annually as Shilluk council house.

Grain store. Two store rooms opening out into a large granary, in good repair and suitable for grain storing.

Stable block. Giving accommodation for 100 mules in one large chamber, with store room for harness and equipment & small guard room. Walls and floor in good order but roof requires attention to make it bat proof. Very suitable as stables and was originally used for housing the mounted police animals. Now used for storing cotton, and the remaining animals of the inspector of Agriculture.

DC's house. Three roomed house, of which the two living rooms are knocked into one, bathroom, W.C., and pantry, namlia verandahs north and south, and mosquito house on the roof. Kitchen and servants ironing room attached, enclosed by namlia wire. Requires annual repairs, and another bedroom is about to be built. Suitable for purpose.

Sarraf's house. Two rooms joined by central mosquito house, repaired in 1930, is quite suitable for a single man.

Mamur's house. Two rooms, store, and bath room, with small namlia on east, in fair order but very hot from corrugated iron roof. Suitable for the purpose.

Resthouse. At present used by inspector of Agriculture. Two roomed building with small bath (no bath provided) and store, with a small and unfitted kitchen and W.C. built away from the house. This house has now been fitted with mosquito wiring along the east and north sides. The eastern wall and room are sinking and the wall is badly cracked, though it was shored up by PWD in 1930.

AMO's house. A Bollard double tukl quarter with central namlia, repaired in 1930, and suitable for present occupant.

Native accountant's house. A Bollard double tukl quarter with central namlia, repaired 1930, and suitable for present occupant.

Agriculturalist's house. An iron framed building consisting of two rooms joined by namlia hall, kitchen tukl and E.C. outside. Suitable for present occupant.

Postmaster's house. Similar to that of the agriculturalist's house above. Suitable for present occupant.

Post Office. Two roomed building built in 1930 and suitable for the purpose.

Bungalow resthouse. Two roomed wooden house of bungalow type raised on short piles, & kitchen, E.C., and tukl for servants built of brick. The corrugated iron roof harbours bats despite repairs by the PWD in 1930. Unsuitable for European occupation, and owing to high rent unoccupied by Sudanese officials.

Building at Tonga

Resthouse. Two roomed building, iron framed, with mud brick walls and corrugated iron roof. Has two small namlias under the open verandah roof. Requires some repairs, building a kitchen was approved. Suitable as rough accommodation for a short stay by Europeans.

Mud buildings at Kodok

In order to effect future economy in the heavy cost of upkeep, of native mud built tukls for police and junior unclassified staff, two iron frame tukls with burnt brick walls have been built this season, and six police tukls are in course of erection in burnt brick.

There are eight tukls occupied by female patients at hospital, hospital cook house, tumargia: six old tukls occupied by police pending completion of their new houses, & four tukls used to house the station herd of cattle.

With the exception of the Agricultural inspector's, agriculturalist's, postmaster's and DC's, and bungalow resthouse, kitchens are built of mud or brick and maintained by the annual grant for mud buildings.

FORESTRY

The Forestry Section of the Department of Agriculture have certain areas at Zarzur and Taufikia devoted to re-afforestation, sunt is chiefly grown and does extremely well near the Nile banks but growth is slow further inland and difficulty is experienced in protecting these plantations from fire in the dry season.

Efforts are being made—notably at the Shilluk council—to encourage afforestation tribally and the inspector of Agriculture has agreed to plant suitable seed in nursery so that young plants may eventually be given out for planting at village areas.

The provision of firewood for domestic use at towns (especially Malakal) becomes increasingly difficult and is mostly done by local Shilluk who charge heavily for this commodity.

Charcoal burning is also a very profitable industry in the hands of the Shilluk.

SUNDRY

Gardens

The production of vegetables at Kodok in sufficient quantities to supply the needs of the station and provide a surplus to Malakal was the object in view when a pumping plant was allowed to replace the old iron sagia which was unable to supply the larger area involved by the necessity to break up new soil. The results obtained from the new area taken in have however been very disappointing owing to the extreme hardness of the soil—though it was ploughed and reploughed, treated with plenty of manure, and sand was added to lighten the soil.

A new fruit garden has however been established of about half an acre, and young grapefruit, orange, mango, guava, custard apple, and 'bullock's heart' trees are flourishing. The Agricultural inspector is invaluable as he gives all his spare time to the garden, and obtains good results from a garden that he opened in 1929/30 season on the island in front of the station: the soil on this part is excellent and vegetables grow well, but beetles and hippopotami are a source of anxiety.

The staff employed consists of two Shaigia [Shaygiyya] men, of reasonably good experience, one of whom acts as an engine driver, and a Shilluk who has some experience, and two boys or a man (employed casually) for weeding and ploughing work as required. This staff is to be reduced to either three men or two men and two boys in 1931.

The cost of running the garden cannot at present be met by the sale of produce, and a loss of some £E 70 to £E 90 per annum is inevitable: but by concentrating on growing vegetables on the island soil, and further planting of fruit trees in the old garden should tend to reduce the loss. This is the opinion of the inspector of Agriculture to which I am in agreement.

The difficulty of transporting vegetables in fresh condition to Malakal at regular intervals is ever present: steamers are used whenever possible and a trial was made of a bicycle orderly and cars going to Malakal from Kodok are sometimes practicable, but quickly perishing produce such as lettuces usually arrive in such a limp condition as to be unsaleable.

The engine driving the pump requires fixing in a concrete bed and should be done by PWD masons on their next visit to Kodok. The overhead flume leading from the top to the old sagia well to the higher part of the garden is insufficient to carry water and can be delivered by the pump, and it is necessary to obtain about 90 feet of a good type of flume pipe. This has been estimated for in 1931 budget proposals.

Station cattle

In May 1928 the station herd of cattle which stood at 20 head was increased by receipt of 262 cows and calves from Shambe ex-Patrol S9.[6]

These cattle were valued at £E 711 and were issued to Shilluk and Dinka tribesmen against payment either cash or credit: a great many of these cattle died later and the collection of the accounts due became difficulty but £E 567 has come to hand and a balance of about £E 144 is still outstanding.

A cattle herd book is being handed over in which are entered all transactions in cattle received in fines from Shilluk and Dinka—as well as the account of Patrol S9 cattle.

On returning from leave this year I found a number of cattle had died of disease, these cattle however were fines cattle that should have been sold by auction as soon after their receipt as possible. The mamur however felt that he had not the authority to sell cattle while I was on leave.

There are four ploughing bulls in the herd all getting old having completed eight years of sagia and ploughing work.

A proper cattle 'luwak' [*luak*] is necessary as the cattle are accommodated at present in old tukls vacated by police when the establishment of the station was reduced.

Medical staff

Excluding the native staff under training at Malakal hospital, and village dressers in that district, Kodok dispensary is under charge of a Shilluk sanitary hakim named Savario Yukwan who is paid by Medical Department: he is able to give injections, perform simple operations without anaesthetics, and generally diagnose cases. Two dressers work under him

[6] The punitive patrol against the Nyuong Nuer following Captain Fergusson's assassination.

at Kodok, and a 'nurse' who has been trained at Malakal hospital and specialises in the treatment of women suffering from gonorrhea.

A woman cook is regularly employed making native food for the patients, which generally average eight men and six women in-patients.

The male patients are accommodated in one room of the prison block, next door to the dispensary, and the females are provided with ordinary native tukls near the police lines.

This accommodation is unsatisfactory, and either a new hospital block or buildings is necessary, or the old mule stables might be converted into a hospital.

Detwok Mission station has two dressers who work in harmony with the sisters, having a good dispensary building and accommodation for patients. These dressers and sisters visit outlying villages regularly and are a great help in reporting outbreaks of disease.

Aviation

A landing ground is marked on the open plain about 500 yards north of the DC's house, for which an allowance of £E 5 per annum is generally granted.

This area requires burning off, some small bushes clearing, and re-whitening of corner and centre marks.

Education

The Roman Catholic Mission stations of the district at Detwok, Lul, and Tonga, are supposed to provide education for Shilluk, but suffer from inability to retain pupils for a continuous course of teaching, which causes the inspectors of Southern Education to make bitter complaint whenever they pay visits to these stations.

I recommend that a more thorough understanding of the conditions and difficulties of these missionaries should be attained by one or other of these inspectors staying at one of these missions—preferably Detwok—for a least one month in 1931 to study the question.

The Shilluk tribe as a whole are not as interested in education as it was hoped that they might be. Individuals who volunteer for study are generally found to be clever, but the urge of tribal life and village duty frequently cuts short the education of very promising material.

Definite orders by government that boys should attend schools is met by obstinacy on the part of parents and chiefs, who fear an ulterior motive, but much may be done persuasively e.g. by refusing to employ youths as artisans etc. unless they are ready to go to one of the missions to learn to read and write.

A school started at Kodok and under the care of Odhok—the native office clerk—in 1929 was extremely popular, some ten pupils male and female attending. This school can be re-opened at any time but requires the influence of the DC to ensure regular attendance.

The Sudan United Mission at Rom[7] works with the Dunjol Dinka, has a small school, and dispensary under Mr. Kippax who is a qualified chemist. Dunjol chiefs are rather jealous of the fact that Mr. Rimmer has succeeded in claiming quite a number of followers.* [*Their complaint is that he interferes in administrative matters and needs watching.]

When Mr. Rimmer returns with his wife from New Zealand to assist Mr. and Mrs. Kippax this mission should be very successful.* [*This is an optimistic view.]

Criminal

The main offences committed by Shilluk and Dinka are murder, manslaughter, adultery, and on rare occasions rape, and unless such crimes of necessity be tried by Sudan Penal Code native laws provide recognised punishments which can be administered by chiefs' courts. My experience has been that murder is very seldom committed, by this I mean the grosser forms such as waylaying with intent to kill, killing for pecuniary gain, or killing of women or weak persons: of such killings I can quote the example of Adung Okeich of Nejok, on the Sobat, who shot his first cousin and an uncle with a rifle in 1926 (this man still has evaded arrest after many efforts to catch him).

The ordinary killing occurs in defence of property whether cattle or women, or in battle.

Native law however makes no distinction in murder, manslaughter, or purely accidental killings, and native law is purely one of compensation—human life having a defined value.[8]

The following villages have had feuds in past years which might break out afresh:

---

[7] Founded on the site of an old Turco-Egyptian *zariba* in 1924, the station at Rom replaced Melut as the SUM's main centre of work in the UNP in June 1928, and a hospital (consisting of a dispensary, operating room and wards) was built in 1929. In 1938, following the expulstion of the Sudan Interior Mission from Ethiopia by the Italians, the SUM handed over its stations at Melut and Paloich to the SIM and confined its efforts to Rom (the SIM eventually closed Melut in 1943). By their own account, the SUM made very few converts in the 1920s, the first Dinka convert at Rom being made in August 1928. See Spartalis (1981: 34–9).

[8] For a fuller summary of Shilluk customary law see Howell (1952a).

Nybodo vs Aiyadajo, Tonga division
Fakwar vs Niyiyar, Fanyikang
Tworo vs Oashi, Dettim
Awarajok vs Atokong, Awarajok
Falo vs Manam, Fanyidwai
Agordo and Twolong vs Yoing, Biu, Abanima, of Lul division
Fabur vs Nyngaro and Bol
Fashoda vs Nygir
Gulbaing vs Fadiang
Kodok vs Gaulo
Kwoishung of Fabiu vs Allel, Detwok
Abiangyai vs Ogon
Damawt vs Atoadwai
Nyuyudu inter alia
Nyuyudu vs Delal Ajak
Akurwa vs Aburu, Maomo

The position in these villages is usually perfectly quiet at present, but any news of ill feeling between either opponents should be carefully investigated and settlement made at the earliest possible moment so that conflict may be avoided.

The safeguard against serious fighting is that provided the DC has the confidence of the Shilluk he will receive information of impending fighting in plenty of time for him to get to the scene and settle the grievance and avoid bloodshed, but promptness is the essential factor.

The presence of the Ret or the DC will be sufficient to stop fighting provided the opponents have not yet joined battle.

Fights usually take at least 24 hours to materialise, and night battles are not generally indulged in, the usual time for the joining of battle is from 8 to 10 am but villages in close proximity may commence soon after dawn.

Lunatics or idiots

The following list of idiots usually seen round Kodok civil village may be useful:

Mohamed Ahmed. See CD/67.B.14. Said to be dangerous when in drink, but never convicted.

Gwer. Harmless but cunning and a beggar.

Mohd. El Dinkawi. Is idiotic and dances on all occasions, said to threaten his wife but has done no harm as yet.

Fatma. An Arab married to Shilluk spends most of her time abusing Shilluk and gellaba, sings a great deal, harmless.

Nyatuk. Appears to be a sexual degenerate, harmless.
Nyalwingi. Similar to Nyatuk, but is willing to work.

Liquor

Kodok has always held a reputation as premier town for wine and women south of Khartoum, but since the departure of the mounted police this reputation is being lost, nevertheless 'araki' can generally be obtained here despite heavy sentences of fines and imprisonment meted out to all found brewing this spirit, but fines are readily paid up and imprisonment does not deter the distillers. Deportation while being greatly feared is hardly fair on the authorities of the future place that distiller proceeds to inhabit.

A very large quantity of merisa is brewed here for consumption by Shilluk or Dinka visitors to the town.

Police

The province foot police establishment of Kodok station is 9, but the original police are at present firing their annual musketry course at Malakal and the relief is not permanent so I am not reporting on them.

The station police escort parties of prisoners, attend office daily, go out in company with the DC or mamur when necessary, and one man is detained to reinforce the Shilluk station guard at night.

Stores

The stores of dura are in charge of the mamur who holds the key. Station tools are issued and kept by Faragalla Fleet.* [*since discharged.] The artisans' tools are kept in charge of the head mason but require checking by the DC.

The dura store requires disinfection of sus yearly, burning sulphur appears the best way of destroying these insects.

Sugar contractors

Khawaga Yakoub Apkarian [Armenian merchant] and Ali Abdel Rahman are recommended to provide 15 sacks of sugar each monthly in 1931. They have been middlemen in the past and never caused any trouble.

Transport

The station now possesses a Morris Lorry, purchased by Shilluk Funds in the past but now taken over for repair and maintenance by the province.

This lorry requires some repair, and the chief mechanic of Malakal will be sent here shortly to overhaul it and the garden engine and pump.

The Ret bought a car from Mr. G. R. Davies which is now getting past, so he has bought my car and will thus be in possession of sufficient spares to make one reasonably useful car for his work.

The Morris lorry is intended for use primarily on medical work in the Shilluk District, and there is a province lorry due to this station in the future.

Veterinary

Now that I understand that there is a province Veterinary officer it would be well worth while for him to give as much time as possible to the Shilluk herds—the Dunjol Dinka do not want him!

The great thing is to get news of cattle plague and pleuro-pneumonia as early as possible through the Shilluk police and chiefs who do not usually advise one of these outbreaks unless questioned on the matter.

Although not quite a veterinary matter the governor wishes some Shilluk police to be trained as locust destroyers, and bran could be obtained form Malakal for training purposes.

Artisans class

The nucleus consists of a mason who does rough carpentry, and native blacksmith, and they have ample tools for their work. I have not yet got the class formed for 1931 so that my successor may choose youths that he may think fit and worth training.

NOTES ON OFFICIALS EMPLOYED AT KODOK DISTRICT

CAPT. SAYED ABDEL RAHMAN, DCM. A Shilluk of Gulbaing division. Served in the King's African Rifles for 21 years, awarded the DCM for gallantry in the Great War, retired with a gratuity in 1919. Appointed as police officer in UNP serving at Kodok, Renk, Daga Valley, for short periods, then about three years in charge of Pibor Post after which posted to Kodok. This officer has great personality, is highly respected by the Ret and Shilluk tribe as also by Dunjol Dinka, bears an exemplary character in every way, and is capable of executing any order given him by his DC. Unfortunately he is illiterate and has to rely on others in matters of correspondence, and naturally has no knowledge of the Ordinances of Sudan Penal Code procedure so that he cannot be classed with the present standard of mamurs and police officers.

SAYED EFF. AHMED EL HAG—ACCOUNTANT SARRAF. A Mereifabi of Berber. Entered government service as an unpensionable official in November 1928 and served at Wau being transferred to Kodok in 1929. This official bears an excellent character during his service at Kodok, appears to be a neat and accurate accountant, and has taken pains to learn English since coming here. I beg to recommend him for appointment at pensionable service as soon as a vacancy may occur.

ALI IBRAHIM—WEIGHER. A Shilluk of Fama district. Entered unpensionable government service as weigher at Renk district. Was transferred to Kodok in same capacity in January 1930. Owing to his knowledge of Arabic and Shilluk is very useful here, is of very good character, willing and very anxious to make good. It is hoped that in time he may be absorbed into permanent service.

FARAGALLA FLEET—DEVOLUTION ACCOUNTANT. A Shilluk of Lemme, who after a good many years service in the stores at Malakal was retired on pension and given a salary under Devolution budget. This official is getting old and does not do a great deal of work except in assisting Capt. Sayed Abdel Rahman with his correspondence: he has the advantage of getting on well with the Ret, and is respected locally. He will presumably be superseded by a more active official when such an one can be trained for the work.

ODOK DEDIGO—SHILLUK-ENGLISH CLERK. A Shilluk of Faniyidwai division. Educated at the American Mission at Falo was sent here for trial in 1929. He is a good type of Shilluk youth, very well behaved and does his best to get on. He is still rather raw but is gradually learning typewriting and simple filing. A further course of English would help him towards efficiency.

* * *

Governor,
Upper Nile Province,
Malakal

Your 48.J.4 of 19th November, 1930.

I do not propose to add very much to the report made out by Capt. Cann on handing over the Shilluk District, as his report also refers to Malakal District.

REVENUE. Attached statement explains the position to date.

GARDENS. The gardens of officials' houses run on a communal basis, in that all vegetables grown therein are the property of the community. The staff consists of one mechanic, two gardeners, and prison labour. The head gardener is a prisoner. The crop is collected by head gardener and brought to the merkaz where it is sold under the supervision of the mamur. A secondary garden which has been very successful was started last year on the west bank.

MERKAZ CATTLE. These are the result of fines. Their milk is sold to the British officials as far as it will go round. The herd ought to be enlarged and properly housed. Milk being a most important commodity to Europeans from the point of view of health, and for many months of the year very difficult to obtain in Malakal.

OFFICIALS. A separate report will be submitted in due course.

Kodok, 9th December 1930

T. F. G. Carless
A/District Commissioner, Malakal

Shilluk District

ITEMS	Rabt £ m/m	Supplementary £ m/m	Total £ m/m	Amounts collected up to Oct. 1930 £ m/m	Uncollected amount £ m/m
Tribute	1,994.085		1,994.085	1,023.600	970.485
Ushur	28.936		28.936	28.723	0.213
Animal tax	19.010		19.010	18.820	0.190
Hikr	424.120	3.240	427.360	349.706	77.654
Traders tax	90.000		90.000	90.000	000.000
" licences	000.000		000.000	138.000	000.000
Rent of govt. houses	653.730	50.873	704.603	413.222	291.381
Water	35.933	3.525	39.458	24.413	15.045
Firewood				30.100	
Fines				95.000	
Stamped papers				16.650	
Court fees				29.750	
Various				137.920	
Native liquor				147.000	
Gardens				35.716	
General rate	365.492	5.863	371.355	313.505	57.850
Conservancy rate	469.065	34.000	503.065	346.567	156.498
Market fees				81.810	
Slaughtering fees				118.100	
Morada				155.788	
Meat market rent	36.500		36.500	29.900	6.600
Tawkilat fees				2.500	
Firearms licences				0.500	
Milk				19.860	
Duplicate fees				0.250	
Miscellaneous				1.050	
Ivory rates				0.788	
Straying animals				4.580	
Money order fees				0.080	
Shadufs dues				1.100	
Total	4,116.871	97.501	4,214.372	3,654.998	1,575.916

Amounts collected from assessed items £ 2,638.456 m/m
"   "   "   unassessed items £ 1,016.542 m/m
TOTAL £ 3,654.998 m/m

CHAPTER 5

Nasir District

C. L. ARMSTRONG

The following notes are statements of facts and therefore, to those who are acquainted with the subjects discussed, will appear as obvious as the multiplication table.[1]

They are intended, however, for those who do not know the district or, perhaps are acquainted with only one aspect of it.

It is hoped that corrected or amplified as time goes on they may give a slight picture of this district and so provide a framework for further inquiry into any particular subject or policy.

August 15th 1930

BOUNDARIES

The boundaries of the district are:

NORTH

The river Daga valley and the Machar swamp.

EAST[2]

The Abyssinian Frontier.

SOUTH

Not very clearly defined but approximately a line running west from the river Pibor between Koratong and Dengjok on N. Lat. 8° 00' to Fula Lak.

---

[1] These were Armstrong's notes written prior to going on final leave from the district, and prior to Willis' request. Apparently Tiernay forwarded only extracts from the notes: according to the internal numbering on the pages of the report there is a gap of ten pages between the end of the section on history and the beginning of the section on Nasir village, a gap of another ten pages between the section on taxation and the section on native administration, and a gap of one page between the sections on Jekaing Nuer and tours (though in fact the latter follows logically from the former, and the missing page is probably the absent sketch map).

[2] In the manuscript west was written for east, and east for west.

WEST
a) Line running due north from Khor Luing on river Sobat 8° 59', 32° 26'.
b) Line running south east from Wegin on river Sobat 8° 50', 32° 32', to Mankaith on Khor Nyanding 8° 27', 32° 37'.
c) Line running south east from Mankaith to Yor 8° 17', 32° 55'.
d) Line running south to Fula Lak 8° 00', 32° 50'.

TRIBES

The tribes inhabiting the district are: Jekaing Nuer, Khoma Burun, Anuak, Abyssinian refugees.

Jekaing Nuer

The district is essentially a Nuer one. The Jekaing are divided into two main divisions, the Gaajok and the Gaajak, though a third has been recognised i.e. the Gaagwang.[3]

The Gaajok occupy the country west of the great Machar swamp and the Gaajak the east: the Gaagwang have a small area between the two.

Khoma Burun[4]

The Burun inhabit the afforested belt between the plain and the Abyssinian hills and are naturally confined to the valleys where permanent water is found.

---

[3] The Gaagwang are one of the three original primary divisions of the Jikany. In the east they are very much smaller than either the Gaajok or Gaajak, each of whom also include a secondary section of Gaagwang (Jal (1987: 21)). Prior to 1930 the Gaagwang were administered as a secondary section of the Gaajok. Evans-Pritchard classified each of these primary divisions of the Eastern Jikany as 'tribes', because of the apparent autonomy they displayed in relation to each other (Evans-Pritchard (1940a: 140)).

[4] 'Burun' is the name given by Arabs to a group of loosely-related peoples living along the Ethiopian border between the Upper and Blue Nile Provinces. The Nuer, Dinka and Shilluk call the same group of peoples 'Cai'. They include the Meban, Jum Jum, and Hill Burun (Western Nilotic speakers), and the Uduk, Ganza, Kwama, Koma, and Shyita (Koman speakers). Between 1937 and 1953 all but the Jum Jum and Hill Burun were included in Upper Nile Province. After the 1953 boundary changes only the Meban and some of the Koma remained in the province. See James (1979).

Anuak

There are tiny colonies of Anuak at Nasir and Ajungmir near the mouth of the Pibor and some, fleeing from Abyssinia, are settling on Khor Lau.

Abyssinian refugees

Scattered in the Burun area are to be found villages and colonies of refugees from Abyssinia and Khogalli's [Khojali] territory.[5]

Neighbouring tribes

The following diagram explains why relations with neighbouring tribes do not play a large part in affairs.

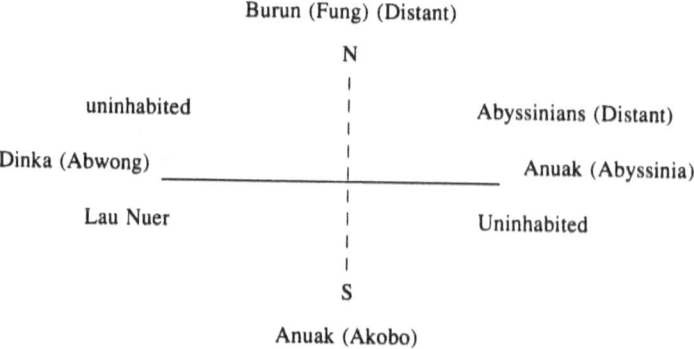

Relations both with the Anuak of Abyssinia and of Akobo used to be unfriendly.

The Burun and Dinka were looked upon as natural prey.[6]

Relations with the Lau Nuer seem always to have been friendly.[7]

---

[5] Khojali al-Hassan, ruler of Asosa and much of the border region of Bela Shangul from the turn of the century to about 1935. He was actively involved in the arms trade, as well as raids against the border peoples, at one time attempting to enlist the aid of the Nuer in his attacks on the Koma (Zewde (1976: ch. 3); Johnson (1986a: 229, 237–40)).

[6] The Dungjol Dinka in fact had generally close relations with the Jikany (see above, Northern District); and some sections of the Gaajak also protected groups of Meban and Koma from raids by Abyssinians or other Nuer (Johnson (1986a: 239)).

[7] The Mor Lou Nuer accompanied the Jikany in their initial occupation of the Sobat valley in the early nineteenth century. Even after settling south of the Sobat the Mor continued to intermarry with the Jikany, the Gaajok especially.

Nasir District

PHYSICAL CHARACTERISTICS

Except for the rivers Sobat, Baro, and lower Pibor in the south and the river Daga in the north there is only one other feature of note—Jebel Gemi (6840 feet) lying on the eastern boundary.

The district consists of a vast cotton soil plain with most of it level but a few inches above the flood level of the rivers. Where the level rises for a few inches are found the permanent villages; where it sinks are khors which drain into or fill up from the rivers impartially; where the depressions are large there are swamps—the largest of these being the Machar swamp which effectively cuts the district into two.

The western edge is very slightly higher than the western centre and is sparsely wooded on the plain with thicker belts along the khors.

The centre is mostly featureless grass plain or swamp according to the season. Fifteen miles east of the Machar swamp the ground again rises and is wooded until finally on the foothills of Jebel Gemi there are well defined torrent beds with dense forest and bush intermixed.

The normal cycle is as follows: About May the Sobat has risen sufficiently to hold back the Pibor and to stop drainage from the khors. The local rainy season follows and as there is no drainage all low lying areas get filled up. About November-December the Sobat falls sufficiently to allow the khors to drain and the surface water is carried away sluggishly. There is thus an excess of water between June and January and scarcity for the remainder of the year which forces the natives to the rivers.

It is most unfortunate that the rivers form the boundaries, as with the Adura, Gila and two Makwais so invitingly near most of the natives pass over to them.

COMMUNICATIONS

External

Nasir itself is well served as it lies on the river Sobat which needs no description.

Commencing, according to the state of the river, about June the Gambeila service runs until about September.

In September the province steamers run to Nasir and Akobo until about January when the river is too low and recommence as soon as it rises about the end of April.

From January to May urgent communication can be on the motor road to Abwong which is cleared as soon as the rainy season ends definitely. Dates are uncertain as there are various depressions which have to dry up.

A motor road is cleared to Akobo but without heavy expenditure it should be considered more of a potential means of communication than an actual one.

A motor road is also cleared from Jokau to Kigille.

Mails and telegrams

Mails, when the river is open are by the steamer service. During the dry season either by mules or car to Nasir and then by canoe service (arranged through Ajungmir Anuaks) to Akobo and Gambeila.

Telegrams are by wireless linked to Akobo and Malakal.

Internal

By mule transport (see note on 'Administration. Tours' below). A steel whaler and crew is attached to the merkaz but as the river is twisty and the wind during the dry season generally from the north* it is only useful for making dumps and ferrying. [*Said to blow from the north for a fortnight only.]

Air

There is a landing ground at Nasir and Daga.

HISTORY

Singularly little information is available on this subject and the following notes stand in need of confirmation or correction.

The district appears to have been almost untouched until the middle of the last century when slave raiding took place at intervals up to the Mahdia.

One of the advanced posts was chosen by an Egyptian named 'Nasir' on a dabba called by the Nuer 'Noor'.[8]

---

[8] Nasir Ali (probably a Dongolawi, not an Egyptian), an agent of the trading firm Küçük Ali, who was moved from his *zariba* on the Bahr el-Zeraf in 1874 by Gordon, and then employed in Egyptian government service to establish a fort on the upper Sobat to cut the slave trade between the Sobat basin and Fadasi (M. F. Shukry, *Equatoria under Egyptian Rule* (Cairo, 1953), 155–8, 202–3, 205, 317). Junker somewhat improbably claimed that Nasir was named not after the man, but his rank, *nazir* (W. Junker, *Travels in Africa 1875–1878* (London 1890), 219). Nor (or Nordeng) was so called because of the palm trees (*noor*) there. In 1991 it was the site of a highly overcrowded camp of Southern Blue Nile returnees evacuated from the Sudanese refugee camp at Itang after the fall of the Mengistu government in Ethiopia.

After the battle of Omdurman this post was occupied by a detachment of the XIII Sudanese who found a French flag flying and promptly lowered it.[9] The Gaajok area seems to have been a sort of no-man's land between the Sobat-Pibor Military District and the Province headquarters at Taufikia and the Gaajak area was untouched. Administration seems to have been confined to tax collecting expeditions by steamer led by the inspector Sobat river, governor, or anyone else available. These expeditions were little more than raids to show the power of the government.

In 1912 the XIII Sudanese moved from 'Noor' to the site of the present Nasir [on the right bank] leaving the police post at Old Nasir. In 1918 the garrison was reduced and in 1920 the stations were exchanged and later (1925) the troops were withdrawn.

Sometime about 1910 the old tribute collecting raids began to die down and some effort was made to distinguish between friend and foe and administer the people, though the tribute collection was still described as a patrol and sometimes allotted an official number.[10]

The Gaajok about 1918 were paying tribute fairly regularly but the Gaagwang and distant Gaajak paid it when they pleased. Various raids by the latter led to the Gaajak Patrol of 1920.* [*This is all rather sketchy and leaves out of account the Sobat Pibor administration which is sketchier still.]

In consequence of the attitude of the Gaajak a police post was formed in the Gaagwang area in 1919 before the patrol and another at Nyerweng in 1920 subsequent to the patrol but both these were withdrawn about 1923. The Gaagwang Post was in charge of an inspector during the patrol itself.

During the regime of Captain Stigand as governor the army officers in charge of the district began to hear cases among the Nuer and at the end of 1919 a civil inspector was appointed.[11] After the patrol the district became under the sole charge of the civil inspector and the next seven years were devoted to peaceful penetration.[12] About 1924 the practice of settling cases on the advice of the native interpreter alone ceased and chiefs were consulted as assessors, a practice which developed into chiefs' courts. The mamur was also withdrawn.

---

[9] Raised there by the Bonchamps expedition which entered the Sobat valley from Ethiopia in an unsuccessful attempt to link up with the Marchand expedition. For a contemporary account of the reoccupation of Nasir (where there is no mention of the French flag) see 'Major Maxse's Report on the Sobat River', Appendix 53; and 'Major Hill Smith's Report on the Sobat', Appendix 56, both in SIR 60 (25 May to 31December 1898): 86–90.

[10] In fact, the official 'cattle snatching' patrols continued right through the years of World War One.

[11] J. F. H. Marsh.

[12] From 1921 under John Lee, who very quickly learned to speak Nuer.

In 1927 a district commissioner was appointed for the Burun area but on the report of his successor in 1928 the appointment was abolished and the district joined on to Nasir.[13]

1928 and 1929 were somewhat troubled years owing to the reactions caused by the activities against the Nuer elsewhere but however much the Eastern Jekaing may have sympathised with the others they did not join in—a lot of ground was however lost by having to treat the Nuer as potentially unfriendly.

The district commissioners were increased to two in 1929[14] and this is the present establishment.

NASIR VILLAGE

There is little of interest in Nasir which seems to have been chosen because it was an inch or two higher than the surrounding country near Old Nasir.

Commencing from downstream there is:

The American Mission. The mission hold a block on lease from the government and form a community by themselves.

The Market Area. This was burnt out in February 1930 and laid out afresh with as little disturbance to old claims as possible.

It consists practically of one street of shops with a second line at right angles at the upstream end.

The Malakia Quarter. The malakia consists of a few old soldiers and a number of rifraff who should be cleared out.

The Market and Government Employees Area. This is the worst laid out as huts have been built to avoid puddles and are therefore scattered all over. It is hoped to re-organise them and add a native administration quarter which is at present entirely lacking.

The District Commissioners' Quarters. These require no comment.

Buildings

The government buildings at Nasir are definitely bad and have been so stigmatised since 1917.

Permanent buildings are:

---

[13] H. G. Wedderburn-Maxwell, followed by Capt. A. H. Alban.
[14] With the appointment of J. F. Tiernay as ADC.

1. District commissioner's quarters (not yet built).
2. Assistant district commissioner's quarters. Two rooms, 5 × 4 m, 5 × 3 m, verandah mosquito proofed 13 × 2½ m, store 2 × 2 m, bathroom 2 × 2 m, outside kitchen 2 × 2 m, latrine.
3. Mamur's quarters (occupied by sarraf-accountant). Two rooms and mosquito house, latrine.
4. Post office.

Semi-permanent buildings (brick walls, thatch roof):
A. Office block.
B. Store block.
C. Shoona block.[15]
D. Dispensary block.
E. Inspector's house at Old Nasir (unoccupied).

Red brick tukls:
(1) Post office officials' quarters. 4 tukls.
(2) Police. 12 tukls.

The remaining buildings are very inferior grass huts except the old post office which is a wooden shanty. Owing to the perpetual lack of timber repairs are like to 'pouring wine into old bottles' especially as the district commissioner is absent during the whole of the repair season.

Building materials

1. Red bricks of fairly good quality are burnt by merchants at Dordeng about 8 kms downstream. The kilns are under water at high river. Transport is not undertaken by merchants. Average cost Pt 150 per 1000 for large contracts.
2. Sand is obtainable from sandbanks exposed at low river. The nearest is at monkey island about 20 kms upstream. Average cost Pt 50 per m^3.
3. Building timber is unobtainable locally and must be cut and transported from the forests near Khor Nyanding.
4. Building grass and gassab [*qassab*, cane stalks from dura and maize] is plentiful in the dry season.

---

[15] Arab., *shuna*: warehouse, magazine, barn.

Chapter 5

STAFF AND STATION WORK

Staff

1	sarraf-accountant
1	murasla-ghaffir
1	sanitary man
3	gardeners
–	cattlemen and milkers
–	mule grooms
3	felucca crew
–	medical staff
2	native interpreters
–	native chiefs' court clerks
–	native administration clerks
–	chiefs' police

NOTE: A dash (–) opposite an item indicates number variable.

Station work

The sarraf-accountant has no executive authority and his work is confined purely to non-native affairs.

Owing to the post office and the presence of some 60 northern merchants and agents his regular attendance in the office is necessary i.e. he is of little use in supervising gardens, buildings, etc., etc. during the working hours.

The district commissioners do their own typing, filing, registering, etc. and on tour issue forage and rations and keep accounts of police and followers.

They also control completely the native administration.

As all tribute is paid in bulls and fines in cattle the accommodation accounting and disposal of government cattle is an important item. During the tribute collection season a chief with his own followers is generally co-opted to help.

POLICE

The system in force is one of having very small garrison of foot police and of supplementing them by mounted police during the dry weather.

The present establishment is:

Nasir	1 wakil ombashi and 11 nafars
Kigille Post	1 ombashi and 10 nafars
Daga Post	1 shawish and 10 nafars

Police posts

The police posts of Gaagwang and Nyerweng have been mentioned under 'History' (above) and are no longer in being.

In 1924 two police posts were formed in Burun area for a two-fold purpose—firstly to protect the Burun from Abyssinian raids (one occurred in 1923)[16]—secondly to make open traffic in arms more difficult.

Kigille post

This post is sited on the Khor Lau at Wursa but is generally known as Kigille from a Burun village of that name close by. Its original garrison was one NCO and twelve men which was supplemented by mounted police during 1927 and 1928 owing to the presence of a district commissioner.

On the withdrawal of the district commissioner it sank to one NCO and four men but has since been increased to the establishment mentioned above.

Daga post

This post was originally at the western end of the chain of Burun villages and so of little use as protection against the Abyssinians. It was moved from there to its present site at Tora Gungara in 1927. Its original garrison was one NCO and twelve men but on the withdrawal of the district commissioner in 1928 sank to one NCO and 8 men. Its present establishment is mentioned above.

Daga and Kigille posts—general

The merging of the protective posts into a district and the subsequent suppression of the latter has rather tended to obscure the original object of their formation. They are essentially frontier control posts and it is

---

[16] *Dajjazmach* Berru sent a tribute collecting force of some 300 men into Koma and Meban country in May 1923 (C. H. Walker, Consul Gorei to HBM Minister Addis Ababa, 12 Sep 1923, NRO Dakhlia I 112/16/102).

unfortunate that an idea has crept in especially among the garrison that their raison d'être is the administration of the Burun.

The posts are relieved as soon as the river Sobat rises (the relief is an arduous task for man and beast at this time of year) and it follows that a new garrison is left isolated for some eight months.

In an attempt to get some sort of continuity and to have an experienced NCO in charge of the non-police work a bash shawish whose work was approved both by the Burun and the district commissioner has been appointed to the area this year.

MEDICAL

The American Mission at Nasir for some time provided the only source of medical treatment but in 1927 a sanitary hakim was sent to accompany the district commissioner on tour.

In 1928 a dispensary was built at Nasir.

The characteristics of this district prevent fixed centres being of much value except along the river and so attempts at curative work requiring long treatment are rather hopeless unless the patient is willing to stay at Nasir.

Despite however the drawbacks from the point of view of the Medical Service the presence of the sanitary hakim with the district commissioner on tour is of very great administrative value.

Owing to the suspicion with which education was regarded by the Jekaing at first the possible source of supply for native dressers is very limited. A start has now been made and it is hoped that a sufficient supply will be attained in the near future.

THE AMERICAN MISSION

The American Mission was opened at Nasir in 1916 and carried on valuable medical work.

It has concentrated largely on building up a supply of teachers and Miss Huffman was responsible for bringing out a *Nuer-English* and *English-Nuer* vocabulary [Huffman (1929 & 1931*a*)].

The Eastern Jekaing did not however take kindly to education and it is only now that their suspicions are beginning to be allayed.

The present heads of the Mission are Mr & Mrs P. J. Smith assisted by the Rev. W. J. Adair, Miss Huffman, and Miss Soule.

TRADE

Internal

The district is a 'closed' one and the system in force is as follows:

A certain number of merchants of repute and with reasonable capital are licensed to trade in the district (in 1930 these numbered twelve). They in turn apply for agents for whom they are held entirely responsible. In practice these agents are not the paid servants of their principals but junior partners who exchanged their efforts for a share of the profits.

The agents go out to various trading posts in September-October and buy grain and hides in exchange for trade goods mostly though occasionally money is used.

A second series of posts along the rivers catch the more distant tribes on their way to the dry weather camps.

From February to April trade is practically at a standstill but then the reverse flow begins and grain is sold back to the improvident at enhanced prices for animals.

Generally speaking the grain bought from the Nuer is sold for province requirements, i.e. police, army, merkaz requirements and the grain resold to the natives is imported. This naturally depends largely on prices but few merchants can afford to keep their capital locked up.

The turnover is small but the profits are large as the grain and hides etc., are bought cheap for trade goods acquired at trade prices and imported grain is sold at a profit for animals valued cheaply. On the other hand the Nuer do not understand price fluctuations and if the price of grain relative to a bull was so much last year he expects it to be the same this year.[17]

The most lucrative trade is in tobacco, supply of which is not equal to the demand; the most speculative is in cattle (including tribute cattle) as they cannot be transported to Khartoum until the Gambeila steamer service is running and prices depend on other sources of supply not having filled the demand.

Apart from the necessary supervision of dealings with the natives the most difficult problem is the allotment of permits since some agents having found good posts wish to reserve them exclusively and others aim at

---

[17] 'Nuer do not regard purchase from an Arab merchant in the way in which we regard purchase from a shop. It is not to them an impersonal transaction, and they have no idea of price and currency in our sense. Their idea of a purchase is that you give something to a merchant who is thereby put under an obligation to help you. At the same time you ask him for something you need from his shop and he ought to give it to you because, by taking your gift, he has entered into a reciprocal relationship with you. . . . As an Arab merchant regards the transaction rather differently misunderstandings arise.' (Evans-Pritchard (1956: 223–4)).

skimming the cream off the market at a series of posts and then moving on to others.

For lists of merchants and agents together with the trading posts see the registers concerned.

External

The Burun have a fairly regular trade in cotton with Abyssinia for Maria Theresa dollars. To acquire these dollars the Abyssinians would like to sell coffee to the merchant at Kigille Post (recently an agent of Limnios Bros) but their own authorities wish to concentrate the trade at Gambeila in order to obtain the dues and pickings usual to trade in Abyssinia. The situation in 1930 was that the coffee trade was a complete failure.

TAXATION

Nuer

Tribute of bulls is paid annually. The assessment is uncertain but supposed to be on the light side, i.e. not to equal 1 1/2%–2% mature animals.

The present numbers originated from a rough and ready method of assessing a large shyeng at ten bulls and others in proportion with many arbitrary alterations since.

Burun

The Burun have been censused and there is an annual tribute of one Maria Theresa dollar to two petrol tins[18] of grain per able bodied male.

Anuak

An annual tax of Pt 10 per hut is paid by the Nasir and Ajungmir colonies.

Others

The standard province rates and taxes apply.

[18] One petrol tin (*safiha*) = 4 imperial gallons, or 18.18 litres, or about 13 kilograms.

Nasir District

NATIVE ADMINISTRATION

The policy with regard to native administration concerns the central government and the governor and therefore the latest minutes should be consulted. It is recommended if an opportunity occurs that the files of the early developments be studied in province headquarters.

It is impossible in any brief note to describe the practical application of the policy to this district since the subject is a very wide one and conditions are constantly changing.

Perhaps the most pithy description of the position can be given by the following verbatim extract from a minute by Major J. W. G. Wyld, district commissioner, Bor, addressed to governor, UNP (SCR/1-C dated 5.8.27):[19]

> This being the case until a functioning machine has been produced administrative effort must be highly centralised upon the DC. It remains for him to decentralise as quickly as he can by making use of chiefs, sifting tribal custom, organising the good, breaking down the bad, and introducing new ones where nothing exists.

The above implies constant, close and sympathetic contact with the native and individuals' efforts vary as to attaining it.

ECONOMIC. NATIVE

Nuer

The Nuer worship their cattle and their life is therefore governed by their herds' requirements.

When the rains have ceased and the rivers are falling, allowing the plain to drain, the coarse grass of the rains is burnt to allow young grass to spring up. It is a gradual process as the waters recede slowly but about December in a normal year the herds move on the new pasture under the charge of the men. At this stage generally only rough wind shelters are erected.

Later an advance party goes on to the dry weather camping grounds, situated near permanent water, and begins to burn the coarse grass there. As soon as it is agreed that the dry weather pastures are suitable the herds are moved to them and are followed by the women and children who have up to now been employed in gathering the crops and preparing for the camps.

The camps are formed of small beehive huts, often built without wood

[19] In NRO UNP 1/44/329

and arranged in the form of a circle round the cattle pickets. Each group has its own grazing area. During the camping season the only food except for merisa is milk and fish so parties are out continually spearing the receding pools or trapping the mouths of the khors. It is also the season for the repair of the cattle barns and the completion of the grass burning to provide pasture for the return trip.[20]

On the approach of the rains the cattle are moved back but this time in a series of jumps until all serious obstacles are behind them. There is then a pause until lack of water outside or the presence of water near the permanent villages induces them to return to the latter. During this stage the cultivations are cleaned and sown.

The permanent villages are better arranged because the cattle have to be protected from biting insects and provided with dry standing. Huge tukls called 'luaks' are built for the cattle and small huts with low doors for the owners adjoin. They are scattered wherever a slight elevation offers a prospect of a dry standing and though therefore there may occasionally be a cluster of huts on some dabba it is more normal to find the 'village' consists of a large number of isolated barns and huts spread over ten square miles of country.

Adjoining villages thus merge into one another until in many cases the name of the village can only be determined by inquiring the name of the hut owner and what his shyeng call their area much as the distinctions between London suburbs are clearer to the inhabitant than the outsider.

With Nuer life ordered by his cattle his livelihood is also affected. They do not sell cows under any circumstances and it is only recently that they have thought of selling bulls though they consider sheep merely a means of acquiring or saving cows (sacrifices) and readily part with them. Incidentally the Gaajak cattle are finer than the Gaajok and among the best in the Sudan.

A certain amount of cultivation is done in the rainy season area and the immediate surplus is sold readily. There is no doubt that cultivation is increasing and the Gaajak now grow a little maize and tobacco as a seluka crop.[21] They take the greatest interest in seed and some maize seed provided by Mr Lee is a topic of conversation to this day.

Burun

The Burun villages deserve no special comment as they are such as would be expected from a sedentary people who have been harried in the past, i.e. tucked away and as far as possible huddled in a small group of huts.

---

[20] For the ecological cycle see Evans-Pritchard (1940a: 95–104).
[21] 'Seluka', refers to land cultivated by the digging stick (Arab., *seluka*).

They are the exact opposite of the Nuer, as being in an area unsuitable for cattle owing to fly or poor grazing they own hardly any animals, though goats are on the increase and poultry are very numerous and large in size.

As they live in the valleys full of alluvial soil they have every opportunity as cultivators. Plots are not large but several crops in a year are obtained. Their main crops are grain, ful sudani [groundnuts], cotton and simsim, and a little maize and beans are also found.

Anuak

The small Anuak colonies are heavy cultivators and are beginning to acquire animals.

JEKAING NUER

The Jekaing Nuer of this district do not comprise the whole of the tribe as part are settled west of the Nile and are included in the Western Nuer District.

No census has as yet been made of the Eastern Jekaing and it is hard to classify accurately the exact importance of the various divisions, sections, shyengs, and sub-divisions of each in a short note.

An attempt below is made to give a general idea of them with the aid of a sketch map [not included in archive].

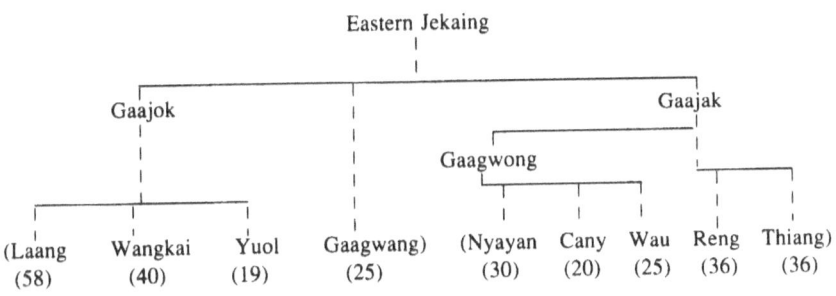

The above table makes the notes easier to follow and so has been inserted first. The figures in brackets under the last row represent the tribute in bulls paid by the section and is included in order to give some comparative standard of importance in the absence of any other.

192   *Chapter 5*

The Eastern Jekaing are divided into two main divisions—Gaajok and Gaajak—though for some time the Gaagwang have been mentioned as if they are a separate section on which subject there is some doubt.

The Gaajok are divided into four main sections if the Gaagwang are included with them.

The Gaajak are divided into one sub-division viz Gaagwong (itself divided into three sections) and two sections.

These sections are sub-divided into shyengs, which are in turn further sub-divided into sub-shyengs. For fuller information the chiefs' and shyeng list should be consulted.

In order to interpret the sketch map[22] intelligently the notes 'Physical Characteristics' and 'Economic. Native' should be read. It will be seen from them that the Nuer drift down in the dry weather to permanent water and also that the villages may merge into one another and the area covered by one depends on the higher ground available.

In the sketch map there has been no attempt at detailed accuracy. The general idea is to show an area which, if visited, will be found to contain the section shown in a majority.

Owing to the fact that newcomers have to take what they find both of higher ground and of grazing, it follows that if a shyeng or sub-shyeng decides to move away from its present neighbours on account of some feud or quarrel, it may have to go far afield, odd shyengs and sub-shyengs will therefore be found in areas far away from the main body.[23]

The sketch map in conjunction with the notes also explains some of the great administrative difficulties of this district. Attention is drawn to two: firstly, except for the Laang section, most of the good grazing near permanent water lies in Abyssinia across the boundary; secondly all the moves to the dry weather areas take place about the same time and it is a physical impossibility with mule transport to catch the sections Wangkai, Gaagwang, Nyayan, Wau and Reng before they reach Abyssinia and at the same time visit the police posts at Kigille and Daga during December and January, i.e. as soon as land transport is possible.

ADMINISTRATION. TOURS

The sketch map attached to the note Jekaing Nuer should be consulted in conjunction with this note.

In view of the fact that only one out of the nine sections of this district

---

[22] See map, p.452 (reproduced from Evans-Pritchard (1940*a*), 58).
[23] The historic pattern of Nuer dispersal in this region is described in Jal (1987).

Nasir District

can be administered throughout the year from a steamer and only part of one other is accessible during the rains, the real administration is confined at present to the months January–May when land transport is possible unless the people choose to visit us in Nasir.

Assuming further that detached police posts must be visited after eight months isolation on the Abyssinian Frontier and that it is desirable at least 'to show the flag' to each section once a year as well as hearing cases and collecting tribute it follows that the practical application of various items of policy depends wholly on what can be accomplished during these five months.

To illustrate the point examples (but not an exhaustive list) are quoted below:

a) Frontier control (arms traffic and poaching)
b) Frontier control (immigrants and protection for Burun)
c) Control of Nuer sections (the government must be prepared to enforce any orders or demands if they are disobeyed)
d) Medical work (peripatetic versus curative centres)
e) Native courts (peripatetic versus fixed centres)
f) Provision of allotment of river transport
g) Provision of remounts for land transport
h) Allotment of police

In order that practical possibilities may be kept in mind when plans are being made a list of the minimum tours necessary illustrated by a sketch map is appended [not included in archive].

1) To Jokau. As soon after the cessation of the rains as possible, Outward journey by steamer, homeward by land.

Reasons: To open the Kigille motor road (the Gaajak still require supervision).

2) To Kigille and Daga. As soon as the road is passable.

Reasons: To visit the frontier police posts which have been isolated for six to eight months.

3) To Koratong.

Reasons: To catch the Wangkai section before they move to their dry weather area: to supervise the Nasir-Akobo road: to clear up Nuer-Anuak cases.

4) To villages north of Nasir.

Reasons: This area is either under water from Khor Wakau flood or without water in the dry season and it is the only chance of the Yuol section, which spend the dry season in the north, seeing the government.

5) To Jokau. Reasons: Cases and tribute from the Gaajak spending the dry season in Abyssinia.

6) To Bar via Kigille from Daga outward and down the Machar swamp on the homeward trip.

Reasons: Burun cases and tribute. Cases and tribute from Gaajak-Thiang section spending dry season on Daga river.

7) To mouths of Khor Makwai and river Gila.

Reasons: Cases and tribute from Gaajok spending the dry season in Abyssinia.

8) Along river Sobat westwards.

Reasons: Cases and tribute from Gaajok-Laang section.

9) To Gaagwang area.

Reasons: To catch the Gaagwang on their return from their dry weather camps for cases and tribute.

In addition to the above minimum there are the following tours which are administratively desirable.

A) Extension of stay in Jokau area (Tour No. 1).

Reasons: To get into contact with Gaajak chiefs but more especially the young men en route to dry weather camps in Abyssinia without always connecting in their mind visits of the 'government' with tribute and cases.

B) Along river Sobat to western boundary (probably between Tours Nos. 2 and 3).

Reasons: Supervision of Nasir-Abwong road: clearing up of cases with Abwong District.

C) Along river Pibor to southern boundary (probably between Tours Nos. 4 and 5).

Reasons: Nasir-Akobo road (Note: A considerable part of this road can only be cleared when the Nuer have gone into their dry weather camps along the Pibor): visiting of camps along river Pibor.

D) To Gaagwang area (probably between Tours Nos. 3 and 4).

Reasons: To visit Gaagwang before the people go to their dry weather camps in Abyssinia (Note: Tour No. 9 is not a good one as the return from the camps is straggling and time is limited by fear of the rains, leave, and relief of police posts).

In addition to the above there has been until the present date the arduous tour to Kigille and Daga as soon as the river opens for relief of the police posts.

Notes on sketch map

1) The routes in red ink represent marching, which, either from lack of water, lack of grain, or lack of people, has to be continuous and is therefore

valueless for administrative purposes. The routes in blue ink represent marching of value.

2) An estimate of the total distance of marching with mule transport (excluding all moves by steamer) is 1050 miles of which 750 miles are mere movement from place to place and useless for administrative work.

3) Grain dumps (either merchants' or government's) are found along the rivers but otherwise grain can only be obtained at Kigille and Daga and then in small quantities only after allowing for the requirements of the police posts.

4) The marching rate at the beginning of the season is very low on account of the unburnt grass, water in small khors, unloading and ferrying at large khors, halts for adjusting saddlery, etc., etc. On a prolonged trip with an average of six hours marching per day it is not safe to reckon on covering more than ten miles per day unless the mud has dried and the grass been burnt.

5) There are only two short strips of motor road of any value to district commissioners: Jokau-Kigille and Nasir-Koratong (Note: The Nasir-Abwong road follows the villages whereas the tours are among camps).

6) The actual number of days spent in marching in 1930 (i.e. excluding all journeys by steamer, cars, and aeroplanes) was seventy-five and the estimated distance covered was 1050 miles giving and average of fourteen miles per day.

Summarising the above it will be seen that the working season is roughly 150 days (x 2 district commissioners = 300 working days).

Of these seventy-five days are taken up with marching of which fifty-five days can be written off as merely devoted to movement.

Out of the remainder has to be found time for steamer travelling (to Jokau etc.), office routine, refits, visits paid and received, special work or patrols, in addition to administration.

Two points deserve to be emphasized: firstly, that the district commissioner here must not be considered discourteous if he wishes to stick to his own programme; secondly, unless both district commissioners are capable of operating independently much has to go by the board and this capability depends both on knowing and being known to the Nuer so cannot be achieved in less than several months.

* * * *

E.D.1.C.

The Governor,
Upper Nile Province,
Malakal

Nasir,
8.3.1931

Reference your 1.C.5 of 23rd February.

The following note will I hope help to give an idea of native administration in this district.

Three years ago there were 48 Gaajok chiefs and 29 Gaajak. Of the Gaajak 10 were held responsible for the whole of the tribute, but for all other purposes all these 77 chiefs considered themselves on a par, though naturally Mr. Lee knew the outstanding men and made use of them more.

The two previous years Mr. Lee had done great work in getting chiefs' courts going and their popularity was increasing by leaps and bounds. With it grew the realisation of the chiefs that it was their job, and in the sincere belief that it was what was expected of them, one and all would troop around with the DC on tour like an enormous brood of chickens.

When faced with 400 odd cases in one spot it was not inconvenient to have a number of chiefs whom one could make up into several courts to sit simultaneously, but it soon became apparent the progress had switched off the right lines. Chiefs were now coming to see what they could get out of it and there was a lot of corruption going on which it was difficult to check as with such an overwhelming number of cases one could not but discourage appeals.

It was about this state that a new suggestion presented itself. The number of chiefs seemed to fall between two stools:
  –they were too many to give the idea that any of them were head chiefs (except in the Gaajak) but too few to enable all communities to feel that they were represented (though their numbers justified it). So a new class of headman was recognised, while everything was done to bring the real chiefs to the front.[24]

This was the main task of last year and the present situation may be summed up briefly in four paragraphs giving the immediate aims, of which the majority at least may be said to be accomplished facts.

  a) The whole of the Jekaing (they should be called Ji Kany, i.e. the people of the rising (sun)) is divided into eighteen sections. These sections are of course according to their existing tribal organisation (and great attention has been paid to their genealogy) and therefore vary in size but

---

[24] This was Armstrong's innovation, introduced within the first six months of arriving in the district (see his 'Jekaing Progress Notes', 8 April 1930, NRO UNP 1/51/4).

average out at sixteen bulls tribute, or (if one must make a guess) 1,200 men each.

b) Each of these sections is to have its chief and his headmen. The bigger sections may have intermediate sub-chiefs.

c) Each section has its local court, of which in theory the chief and his headmen are the only members though of course in practice various local wise-heads will put in their spoke. All cases will normally be referred to these courts, whose decision will be registered. The court will sit at the instigation of the chief and will be in no way dependant on the presence of the DC.

d) The 'chiefs' court' proper has as its members only the leaders of the eighteen sections and at present will only sit when the DC is on the spot. The following cases will be brought before it:

    (i) Appeal from local courts
    (ii) Cases referred to it from local courts
    (iii) Important cases involving two sections

I repeat that this is not yet a perfectly working machine because:

a) Only eleven of the eighteen sections can be said to have single chiefs at their head. Some of them have two outstanding chiefs and at the moment I am not going to encourage factions by drawing distinctions between them and either may sit on the 'chiefs' courts'. Others recognised no one in particular and the best man (in my opinion) has to encourage.

b) This system has entailed that several men who in the past considered themselves chiefs have got to realise that they were really only headmen. This naturally cannot be achieved in a day and requires delicate handling.

On the other hand the stage has been reached where practically every section definitely heard cases on their own last rains. In two sections cases were registered on the spot by boys who could write, and several others have since been registered by me at the request of the chief and headmen concerned.

I should perhaps explain why these eighteen sections were decided on. They are, I think, the largest which are workable at present. The stage above would be to divide the Ji Kany into seven, i.e. into areas of such extent that at present no chief has sufficient influence to summon a representative court on his own. These eighteen sections do not run contrary to these seven divisions and amalgamations may be possible later.

No doubt these notes raise several points of controversy. They are the result of experiments with little knowledge of similar experiments in other Nuer districts and I shall welcome comments thereon.

J. F. Tiernay
Assistant District Commissioner,
Eastern District

CHAPTER 6

Akobo District

E. C. TUNNICLIFFE

BOUNDARIES OF THE DISTRICT

NORTHERN
From a point on the Pibor river, two miles south of Kweichar, due west to Shwailual.

WESTERN
From Shwailual south to Ful Letta following Khor Tuni to Tongadid. From Tongadid in a south east direction to Ful Geni, on Khor Geni, and along the Khor to Mareng. From Mareng approximately due west to Chor Rial, thence along Khor Tuni to the point where a continuation of the line of the Khor would strike longitude 32° 15′. Thence due south following this longitude to its point of contact with latitude 6° 0′.

SOUTHERN
From the point of contact 32° 15′ and latitude 6° 0′ following this latitude due east to the Akobo river.

EASTERN
The left bank of the Akobo river, from latitude 6° 0′ to its mouth. This is the present Sudan-Abyssinian border, but is still unratified.

DISTRIBUTION OF POPULATION

Anuak

The number living in Sudan territory is estimated at 25,000. This is probably less than half the total number of the tribe, the remainder living across the Abyssinian border.

Beir

Colonel Bacon estimated their total population at 50,000. They are divided into six sections. The first four sections living in the following areas—Pibor river, Kangen river, Lotilla river and Veveno river—have been visited and their number estimated, I put their number at 35,000. The last two sections live in the Maruwa Hills and in the neighbourhood of the Boma Plateau, these have not been visited but their number probably brings the total of the tribe to that given by Colonel Bacon.

Nuer

There are only four Nuer villages in the district. Their total number is approximately 800.

TRIBAL ORGANIZATION

Anuak

The Anuak living in Sudan territory may for convenience be divided into two sections:

1. The Akobo or Chiros [Ciro] section.
2. The Upper Akobo river and Adonga section.

The former live on both sides of the Pibor river, covering an area of some fourteen miles north and south of Akobo. They occupy thirty-seven villages. Each village has its own 'Nikkoogo' [*nyikugu*] (deputy chief), the latter has no standing amongst other chiefs but acts as agent for a 'kwero' [*kwaaro*] (hereditary chief), who may exercise authority over a greater or lesser number of villages according to his importance.[1]

The rank of kwero is entirely hereditary and does not depend upon the number of his following. In many cases a kwero may have no following whatever and be living in retirement with his family but by right of heredity he is treated with respect and exercises considerable authority on chiefs' courts. The upper Akobo river and Adonga section may be looked upon as the heart of the tribe. Practically all of the 'Nya' [*nyieye*, sing. *nyieya*] (princes of the royal house) live in this area and the throne and heirlooms are kept there.

---

[1] For further details about Anuak headmen see Evans-Pritchard (1940c: 38–48) and Lienhardt (1957–8).

The throne and heirlooms play such an important part in the organization of the tribe that I give a brief summary of their history.

In the past the procedure in practice with regard to the possession of the throne had always been that the most powerful Nya having captured it by force of arms, retained it until another Nya became sufficiently powerful to capture it in battle.

After the Anuak patrol [1912] the Adonga section was not visited until 1922, when the military administrator visited the village of Utalo, on arrival there he approved the retention of the throne by Nya Sham Akwai [Cam-wara-Akwei], son of Akwai Sham [Akwei-wo-Cam], the leader of the Anuak patrol, on the grounds that Sham Akwai was the hereditary possessor. This was not in fact the case. As will be seen from the family tree of direct descent from Ochoda (attached) any of the nine collateral branches have an equal claim.[2]

On the civil administration taking over I visited all the villages in this area, some thirty Nya were assembled and the question of the custody of the throne was discussed. The general feeling was extremely bitter, they considered that the selection of Sham Akwai was entirely contrary to tribal custom. It was therefore decided that the custody of the throne should be for the period of one year, and that the holder for the succeeding year should be elected by a representative body of his peers. This procedure has worked well.[3]

Chiefs' courts

Were started in 1925, at first although the chiefs were capable of giving sound decisions they appeared to have no idea of seeing that their awards were carried out and were entirely dependent upon the influence of the district commissioner for both the attendance of defendants and compliance with their orders. The formation of the chiefs' police in 1927 greatly simplified the former but it is only recently that, by the employment of an Anuak boy for registration of cases in their own language, chiefs' courts have become an efficient system for dealing with cases, without undue assistance from the district commissioner.

---

[2] Not included in this manuscript, but see Evans-Pritchard (1940c: 92–6 & Appendix 3). The circulation of the emblems was not confined to nine 'collateral branches', but to two major lineages (the Nyindola and Nyigoc) and to a few other minor ones, all tracing descent from Goora, the sixteenth remembered king.

[3] For a fuller history of the circulation of royal emblems among the nobles see Evans-Pritchard (1940c: chs. 3–5 and Appendix 4); and Johnson (1986a: 224–8). See also entries for Akwei-wo-Cam and Cam-wara-Akwei in the Biographical Notes.

Chiefs' police

Every chief in the district has at least one policeman. They supply an invaluable channel of communication between the chief and the district commissioner, particularly in the case of distant areas such as the Adonga, where but for the chiefs' police communication during the rainy season would be non-existent.

Beir

The Beir do not appear to have any paramount chief or chiefs who have authority over the tribe as a whole. They are divided into sections according to the area in which they live. Each of these sections has one important chief, the minor chiefs acting as his agents.

The section living along the Pibor river are all under chief Batlan. They have permanent villages along the banks on both sides of the river, stretching from Pibor Post about forty miles north. In the dry season all the inhabitants go into grazing camps with their cattle, starting in middle January they graze north along the river as far as the junction of the river Agwai, if this grazing is insufficient to last through the dry weather they move across to Khor Geni in the neighbourhood of Lopilod.

A second section lives along the Lotilla and includes the area from Pibor Post as far as Belmorok and Lotimen on the above river.

The third section, living on the Kangen river, are under the authority of chief Kangen [Kengen], the most influential chief in the tribe.

The grazing area for both the second and third sections is east of the Pibor river on the river Kongkong and Khor Kalbat. Last year this grazing area was extended as far as Fulas Jor and Nyanmeda, both the latter are well within the Anuak Adonga country, friendly relations between the two tribes were maintained and the trading of sheep for tobacco between the two was to their mutual advantage.

The fourth section live along the river Veveno. Since the death of chief Batmanan [Burnian] in 1927 [1926] half this section have voluntarily joined chief Kangen's following, the rest remaining under Batinuwi, one of the late Batmanan's minor chiefs. The grazing area for this section is the upper reaches of Khor Geni south of Lopilod.

There are two other sections living in the Maruwa Hills and in the neighbourhood of the Boma Plateau. These do not come under administration.

Chiefs' police

It was extremely difficult to instil any enthusiasm into the chiefs with regard to the starting of chiefs' police. They have however at last come into being, twenty-six being taken on the strength at the end of 1930. They are all young fighting men and in the majority of cases the son of the chief whom they represent.

They are very keen but possibly the novelty of wearing a brassard is largely responsible. If they can be trained to fulfil a similar function to that of the Anuak police they will be a sound proposition.

Chiefs' courts

The Beir are not natural litigants and there is hardly ever a case between two Beir. Cases between Beir and Anuak and Beir and Bor Dinka are always liable to occur.

Nuer

There are four Nuer villages in the district. In most cases they do not belong to any particular shieng but are a collection of oddments from various Mor shiengs.

The following are the villages:

Denjok, at the mouth of Khor Geni. Chief Faragalla Kong (also) known as Faragalla Nuer, he was a bash shawish in the police at one time and has some pretty doubtful incidents in his past. He organizes his village well and grows dura on a larger scale than most; he also derives considerable profit by the cultivation of cotton.

Kana, a village about one and a half miles south west of Denjok. Chief Koryom Kom who is quite energetic and maintains discipline among his followers.

Meir, a village about five miles south of Akobo Post. Chief Nyang Camjok, a senile and pig-headed old man.

Koingai, about three miles south of Meir. Chief Deng Ruair [Deng Rue], a keen and intelligent young chief who succeeded his father, who voluntarily retired on grounds of old age some four years ago.

All these four villages pay tribute to this district, they are assessed on the same basis as the Anuak.

In addition to the above there are two other Nuer settlements in the district:

Kaibui, on the west bank of Khor Geni due west of Akobo. Chief Pac

Ruai [Pec Ruac], a spot Lau chief whose original habitat is Kaikwi and Kurwai.

Welkodni, between Kaibui and Akobo Post. Also of shieng Shan and under the authority of Pac Ruai. The minor chief on the spot is Nyal Kwoth, a nephew of Lual Tiang who retired on age.

Both these settlements live in Anuak territory, and are restricted from making fish weirs, otherwise they would hold up all the fish from the Anuak who bridge the mouth of the khor.

They are administered by and pay tribute to the district commissioner Lau. By arrangement between the various district commissioners at a conference held at Akobo in March 1926,[4] a concession was granted to a sub-section of shieng Maikerr to graze their cattle during the dry season at Beim (Kottome) on Khor Geni. They are not allowed to build there.

Dik Mareng and Fula Geni are also occupied by Lau.

In this connection I would emphasise the fact that the whole of Khor Geni is Anuak and Beir territory, the former from the mouth to Beim (Kottome), the latter from Beim southwards. After the 1917 Lau Patrol this was clearly understood and agreed upon by the military administrator, Sobat-Pibor District and the governor, Upper Nile Province.

Of recent years the tendency has been for the Lau to encroach on the Geni in increasing numbers.

From 1917 until 1924 there were incessant clashes between Anuak and Nuer, the bone of contention being this very point. The Anuak have every reason to resent infringement of their land rights.

I would stress that unless the influx of Lau on the Geni is carefully controlled I see every prospect of this old friction being revived.*
[*Admittedly, but grazing rights can be arranged especially in a dry year like 1931 and if necessary can be paid for.]

REVENUE

Anuak

Tribute is paid by the Akobo (Chiros) section at the rate of 100 m/ms per living hut per annum. The revenue thus derived varies slightly from year to year but averages £ 101.

The upper Akobo river and Adonga section have not previously been called upon to pay tribute. A large number of tribesmen now living in the Chiros section originally moved here from the Adonga for security and as

---

[4] See 'Notes of a Meeting held at Akobo, 2nd March 1926', NRO Civsec 1/2/6.

administration in the Adonga gets a firmer hold, improved conditions there would encourage them to return particularly if by doing so they could avoid paying tribute. It is to the interests of general equity therefore that the Adonga should come into line as regards tribute. I propose to carry out an assessment of this area this year.

Beir

The Pibor river section pay a cattle tribute which is assessed at the customary percentage. The total amounts to fifty-eight head. Now that there is a motor road which serves the Veveno section, I consider that this section should also pay tribute. They will be assessed accordingly.

Nuer

The four Nuer villages which pay tribute into this district are assessed on the same basis as the Anuak and the sum derived is included in the total shown under para 3 (a) above [p.203].

ROADS, BANKS, WELLS, FERRIES

Roads

1) A road was opened in 1930 from Akobo west to Kaibui, length four and a half miles. The road crosses Khor Geni on a ramp containing four culverts. Thence it connects with the Fathai road.

2) A second road was made in November 1929 from Akobo north to the Pibor-Nasir District boundary at Gnorley, distance fifteen miles. This road was constructed with a view of connecting up Akobo and Nasir, this however was found to be impracticable, the section in this district is not therefore maintained.

3) Work was started on the Akobo–Pibor road in November 1930. The alignment followed the Nuer villages south of this post. Thirty kilos of this road had been completed when information was received that the Irrigation Service were about to start grading on a different alignment, work was therefore suspended.

From the sun prints supplied I notice that the Irrigation alignment follows a practically straight line from Pibor Post to Akobo and does not touch any villages en route.* Unless this is modified, apart from getting quickly from one station to the other it will be of little administrative value. [*This is being emended.]

Banks

Apart from the Kaibui crossing there are no banks in the district.

Wells

There is a deep well at Akobo, constructed by the MWD [Military Works Department]. It is surmounted by a 'Hydrohoist' pump and supplies good drinking water for the station.

Ferries

There is a ferry at the mouth of Khor Geni, this will be used to connect up the Akobo-Nasir road, when this is constructed.

ECONOMIC DEVELOPMENT

Agriculture

Dura. Crops are normally good both in the Anuak and Beir country, they only grow enough for their own requirements however and there is at present no surplus for export.

Cotton. Was started in the district in 1926, the yield in that year being only forty-eight kantars. In 1930 the yield had increased to 700 kantars. Should the world market warrant it cotton could undoubtedly be grown on a fairly large scale.

Tobacco. Is grown successfully in the Adonga area. The present supply is only sufficient for internal requirements and for barter with the Beir for sheep. There is considerable market for this commodity and the chiefs will be encouraged to grow on a larger scale.

Livestock

The Beir raise a particularly good stamp of fat-tail sheep.* [*but said not to be worth export.] Their present numbers are not sufficient for export.

BUILDINGS

The permanent buildings at Akobo are good and adequate, particularly since the evacuation of the army garrison. They consist of:

    1)   A MWD concrete block building on piles, previously the commandant's house now occupied by the district commissioner.[5]

    2)   A building built by the MWD with civil labour. The construction of this house is extremely bad. Previously occupied by the district commissioner, now allocated as a dispensary and lying-in hospital. Certain alterations are required to make it suitable for its present purpose.

    3)   A brick building with corrugated iron roof, previously a nuzl [rest house] now used as a general store.

    4)   Squash court, built by the MWD in 1925.

    5)   A corrugated iron roofed building with part brick part zinc walls. Previously the commandant's office, when the necessary alterations have been made, it will be used as a garage, two stall horse stable and harness room.

    6)   A semi permanent dwelling made of concrete blocks with grass roof, allocated to the sanitary hakim.

    7)   Identical to 6) allotted to the mamur.

    8)   Old post office and petrol store, the former is bat-ridden and thoroughly insanitary it will be abandoned on the completion of the new post office. The petrol store will continue to be used as such.

    9)   New type post office, has been recently completed and the fitting of the wireless apparatus is well in hand.

A Bollard type quarter for the post master is approved and included in next year's building programme.

FORESTRY

There is no personnel for the carrying out of forestry on a large scale. During the last two years I have planted some two hundred trees, including the following varieties: mahogany, neem, mango and eucalyptus. They have all done well.

---

[5] This building has withstood the ravages of time and war better than most buildings in Akobo. It subsequently became a rest house and was much neglected in the 1970s. During the siege of Akobo by the SPLA in the 1980s officials and their families took refuge from mortar bombardment by living below the raised floor. In 1988–9 it was the headquarters of Ismail Konye, commander of the pro-government Murle militia, after he was forced to abandon Pibor Post. By 1991 it was once again a rest house and still in surprisingly good condition.

SUNDRY

Gardens

A vegetable garden is run by the district commissioner; this is a private garden and is not subsidised by the government.

The following vegetables do well: tomatoes, turnips, beetroot, artichokes, lettuce, endive, cucumber and parsley. Cabbages also grow but do not produce a heart.

Other vegetables are grown by private enterprise and supply sufficient quantity for the station's requirements.

Merkaz cattle

Sufficient cows are kept in the merkaz for the supply of milk. The present number is ten.

Tribute bulls are sold as soon as possible after receipt to minimise loss by casualties. A small reserve is kept for meat.

OFFICIALS IN THE DISTRICT

Interpreters

There are two Anuak, and two Beir interpreters employed in the district:

Omat Giba. Anuak has been interpreter for some ten years, hard working and sound and honest.

Odol War. Anuak, has been working for two years, young, keen and intelligent.

Lokadi. Beir, dull and slow like most of his tribe but works hard.

Jokor. Beir, not quite so slow, a good worker.

CHAPTER 7

Bor-Duk District

MAJOR J. W. G. WYLD[1]

DISTRICT BOUNDARIES AND DESCRIPTION

The NORTH BOUNDARY is an east and west line drawn through a point two miles north of Duk Fadiat.

The SOUTHERN BOUNDARY, which is also the boundary between Upper Nile and Mongalla Provinces, is an east and west line cutting a point twenty-eight miles south of Bor.

The WESTERN BOUNDARY is the Bahr el Jebel and the EASTERN BOUNDARY, the west bank of K. Geni as far south as Pul Biem thence a vague and undefined line running south westwards to Penko.

The western fringe of the district, along the Bahr el Jebel consists of sudd and swamp in which are found a few scattered fishing camps. Moving eastwards the sudd gives place to open grassy country interspersed with khors. This area is a marsh throughout most of the year and forms the dry season grazing ground for tribal herds.

It is known as the *toic*.

West of the toic the country adopts a more pleasing parklike aspect afforested richly in the south and more sparsely in the north. In this area the permanent villages of the tribes are situated.

The 'Duk Ridge', which is an outstanding feature is a chain of isolated, wooded clumps containing many fine forest trees. It cuts the district northern boundary and comes to an end about ten miles south of Duk Faiwel. The duks stand on low sandy knolls some few inches above the level of the surrounding country.[2]

East of Duk ridge and south of it lies open grassy plain, saved from an utter monotony by belts of heglig and talh forest. The soil is principally cotton soil but tracts of sand appear occasionally. Generally speaking the

---

[1] Handing-over notes, dated 14 November 1930.
[2] Duk is a Dinka and Nuer word meaning low, sandy, wooded knoll. The Duk ridge is not in fact a ridge, but an old river bed. The whole of the area from Duk Faiwel to Mogogh is referred to locally as 'Duk'; sometimes this applies only to the southern end of the Duk ridge, from Duk Fadiat to Duk Faiwel. The Duk ridge does not run as far south as Kongor and Bor, *pace* Collins (1990: 94).

inland portion of the district is a bog in the wet season and excessively parched in the dry.

The many pools which exist are fed by a network of minor khors during the rains. These khors and pools dry up as the season advances and water becomes exceedingly foul if not non existent.

TRIBES AND THEIR BOUNDARIES

The following Dinka tribes inhabit the district:

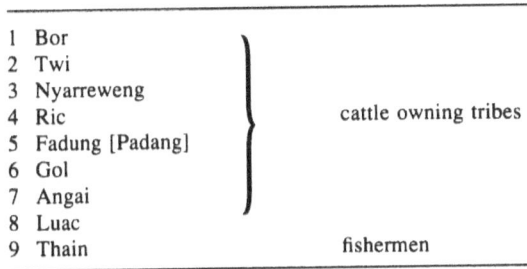

Of these the first five mentioned are descended from Aiwel and claim to be hereditary owners of the country. The remainder (less the Thain) probably came from the west bank of the Bahr el Jebel.

Legend[3]

A story is told of a rope from heaven. The legend runs that a small bird known as the 'atoi' bird [*atoc*, a sparrow] became angry with the inhabitants of earth as they tormented him although he stole neither grain nor meat. He revenged himself upon man by pecking through the rope thus cutting him off from his celestial retreat.[4]

Before the rope was cut there lived one named Aping Diu; his son Aiwel was on earth when the cutting took place.

He had six sons, Bor, Twi, Nyarreweng, Dwar [Duor], Fadung [Padang] and Thoi. Aiwel was a great hunter and travelled far hunting and administering his country. He made his home for a time on the Duk ridge. Duk Ful Aiwel or Faiwel was named after him.

The story goes that all the permanent springs on the Duk ridge are places where Aiwel slept at various times, on his travels. In his declining

---

[3] The ms reads 'legendary'.
[4] For another Dinka version of this story see Lienhardt (1961: 33–4); for Nuer versions Crazzolara (1953: 68) and Evans-Pritchard (1956: 10); there are obvious parallels with the Uduk story of the Birapinya tree (James (1979: 68–72)).

years Aiwel sent out his people to procure food from the sun. He was at this time living near Tithbel. In due course the people returned with a quantity of food. Aiwel fed upon it.

Time went on and he noticed that the store never decreased. He then bade his people eat as much of it as they wanted. For two years they fed upon the sun's food, but like the widow's cruse the supply never ran out.

Finally Aiwel being thoroughly tired of the food took the whole supply and cast it into the Bahr el Zeraf. The sun was exasperated at this and sent word to Aiwel that he would kill him. Aiwel accordingly took precautions. He spent his days in his luak in which for added security he dug a deep pit. Only by night did he venture out for fresh air, and to eat and drink by moon light.

The sun thus thwarted decided to make alliance with the moon. The matter was arranged and the moon made her plans. One night while Aiwel was sitting outside his luak drinking merisa and talking to his people the moon took her fish spear and lowered it over Aiwel's head. When within striking distance the moon thrust and skewered Aiwel to the ground through the crown of his head and body.

Aiwel was not killed and retained the power of speech. He bade his people remove the spear, but they could not. He bade them dig round and under him but water rose where they dug and they could not remove the spear. Then Aiwel's sister addressed the people and told them that there was no good doing anything more, as he was bound to die anyhow. With that they set to and piled earth over him forming a mound. Out of the top of the mound stuck the moon's spear. To complete the job they took Aiwel's drinking vessel and clapped it over the top of the mound. This pyramid with the fish spear sticking out of it is said still to be seen but the spear has become much shortened. It is reputed a spirit centre and is situated at a village (or old village site) called Pwom lying between Paw and Tithbel inland from the river.[5]

Early distribution

Aiwel's sons are the forebears of the various Dinka tribes whose names they bear.[6] The Bor Dinka were originally a small section living on the

---

[5] Stories about Aiwel told by Dinka living south of the Sobat are usually linked to the construction of Puom Aiwel (see Lienhardt (1961: 188–91) and Deng (1980: 150–1)). Versions told elsewhere emphasize the fishing spear and the intervention of women (Lienhardt (1961: 171–88, 191–206)). For Puom Aiwel as a model for Ngundeng's Mound see Johnson 1990.

[6] The Ric, Padang, Nyareweng, Thoi, Rut, and some lineages of the Twic, claim descent from Marbek, a son or descendant of Aiwel, and retained this collective association through the shrine at Luang Deng (Howell in Lienhardt (1961: 99)).

river in the midst of the powerful and more numerous Nyarreweng. In the same way the Twi were an isolated group living near Kongor surrounded by the Nyarreweng.

The Nyarreweng appear to have been the most numerous and important section, they stretched from the Bahr el Jebel to the Khor Geni, an east and west line through Mwot Dit being approximately their northern boundary.

The Ric stretched from the northern boundary of the Nyarreweng northwards to approximately an east and west line through Ayot [Ayod].

The Fadung and Thoi section lost their identity early. The former being absorbed into the Lau Nuer and Jekaing, the latter into the Gaweir Nuer.

Foreign elements

The early distribution while traceable, has altered considerably owing to the incursion of foreign elements, alteration in the position of water holes, evolution and intertribal fighting.

The Gol Dinka are reported to have come from the western bank of the Bahr el Jebel where they were formerly neighbours of the Aliab and lived around Tombe. Originally they became slaves of the Ric, but after tacit agreement in combining to fight the Gaweir Nuer they became an independent tribe superimposed upon the Ric and Nyarreweng.

The Twi Dinka have many foreign elements, but even the rambling stories of origin traceable in other sections are here missing.

From the facts that it is possible to collect it appears that the whole or very nearly the whole of the Liet section are a foreign element from the west bank of the Bahr el Jebel probably from near Shambe.

This section today is by far the wealthiest and most powerful. They are said to have migrated by degrees with a few cattle, owing to blood feuds, bad grazing or other causes.

Being further removed from early incursions of the Nuer the Twi like the Bor have suffered far less from yearly raids and have fattened upon their brother Dinka's misfortunes.

There is no doubt that they regarded the yearly flight for refuge into their country by the Nyarreweng and Ric, as a chance for profit and were in the habit of annexing a large percentage of the herds of these tribes when the latter returned disorganized upon them for support.

A further reason for their present wealth is their fecundity in female children. In past years it was the common practice for the Twi to make expeditions to the Nuer country to sell females of marriageable age for cattle.

The Angai came from about Lake Jor and have been for years mixed with the Gol and Gaweir Nuer. Since the Nuer Settlement they have been mostly concentrated within the district boundary.

The Luac are said to come originally from the Bahr el Jebel; they have for years lived with the element of Ric and Angai on the Khor Fulluth and were moved into the district in 1930 after completion of the Nuer Settlement.

Events leading up to Nuer settlement

It is necessary to have a knowledge of events which led up to the Nuer Settlement of 1929–30 to understand the tribal situation in the north of the district.

In the first half of the nineteenth century, the country east of the Bahr el Jebel, from the river Sobat southwards to Bor, was all Dinka. The Lau Nuer are reputed to have crossed the rivers Jebel and Zeraf and established a footing in this country about 1850. By about 1875 the Nuer had overrun tribal areas of the Rut, Luac, Fadung and Thoi Dinka.

About 1895 the annexation of the Nyarreweng, Gol and Dwar countries had been completed. This last date is fairly accurate, as men who are now about 35 years of age were born in their own country and taken as infants by their refugee parents to Bor or Twi country, where they were brought up.

Those elements of the Dinka tribes that did not become Nuerized took refuge in the case of the Nyarreweng, amongst the Bor Dinka, in the case of the Gol amongst the Twi.

The Gaweir were later in crossing the river. For a time they appear to have occupied a circumscribed area around Ajwong. Later they moved eastward and joined the Lau in their process of annexation. The Nyarreweng claim that the Lau alone had failed to prevail against them, and that it was not until the Gaweir joined in, that they were overcome. Thus Lau bore the heat and burden of the day, but Gaweir came in for many of the 'pickings'.[7]

In 1910 Bimbashi Fox collected the scattered remnants of the Nyarreweng and Gol from Bor and Twi, took them north and re-established them in a portion of their old country, out of which he turned Lau not Gaweir. In the same year he and Mr. Struvé defined a boundary between the Gol Dinka and Gaweir Nuer on the north of the country handed back to the Dinka.[8]

---

[7] Wyld's chronology and dates tend to be supported by other evidence. The Lou and Gaawar fought the Dinka separately (as implied by Wyld), not in a concerted alliance (as later claimed by Coriat). See Johnson (1992b; 1994: 48–50).

[8] Fox and Struvé settled the boundary in 1909, and this was ratified by both provinces in 1910. See K. C. P.Struvé, 'Report on Administrative Boundaries between the Twi Dinkas and Nuers (Mongalla and Upper Nile Provinces)', Appendix C, *SIR* 177 (April 1909).

Since that date these Dinka tribes have been gradually resettling and collecting their scattered elements under guarantee of government protection. In 1914 they were raided by the Gaweir. In 1915 there was a small patrol against the Gaweir which does not appear to have dealt with them very heavily. In 1916 there was a joint rising of Lau and Gaweir.

The Gaweir swept through the Nyarreweng, Gol and Ric countries following much the same route as they did in 1928. After this affair, there was a further raid on the Bor and Twi Dinka. These risings culminated in the Lau patrol of 1917. For their share of the guilt the Gaweir were forgiven and told to behave themselves in future. There followed ten years of comparative peace. The patrol of 1917 had had its effect. The old fighting leaders of both Lau and Gaweir were dead. Their successors, Gwek Wandeng and Dual Diu were both young men and unproved in battle.[9]

Ten years is a long time and the native memory short. In these ten years both Nuer tribes had collected many arms and young men had grown up. The renewal of Nuer disaffection in the rainy season of 1927 and subsequent events does not appear abnormal.

It cannot be said that the disaffection was due to any particular piece of government policy, but rather to Nuer dislike of any policy whatever that is opposed to their traditions of annexation, pillage and robbery. It was not unreasonable to suppose that as soon as a fighting leader should show himself with sufficient personality to kindle the imaginations of the young men, there might be a reversion to tradition. Such a leader was found in Gwek Wandeng. He was the first to show open defiance of government. The tribes were led away with great hopes of loot, raised to enthusiasm by Gwek's 'Kujurial frenzy', and additionally confident in the possession of many arms.[10]

It must be understood that in the old days, when Nuer overran Dinka country, after the preliminary atrocities, in most cases the Dinka settled down happily and became Nuerized.

From this point of view, it might be said that our administration of the country commenced too late or too early. Had we been able to prevent the

---

[9] The Nuer raids of 1916 were organized almost exclusively by the Lou Nuer. The Upper Nile Province authorities objected to hostilities being extended to the Gaawar during the patrol of the following year on the grounds that the Gaawar had been quiet since 1914. This was a source of recurring antagonism between the administrations of the two provinces. Dual Diu, who avoided battle in 1917, had already proved himself as a warrior in 1914. Guek Ngundeng never claimed to be a war leader.

[10] Wyld's attitude towards the Nuer, and his interpretation of events, was commonly held by most subsequent Bor DCs, including the first Northern Sudanese DC at the time of independence. DCs assigned to the Nuer districts tended to take a different view. For events leading to the Nuer Settlement, and Wyld's own role in them, see Johnson (1979; 1994: chs. 5 and 6).

Nuer crossing the Bahr el Jebel the situation obtaining in 1928 would not have occured. On the other hand had we not interfered in native affairs until fifteen or twenty years later, I have little doubt that the whole country would have become Nuerized, as far south as Bor and we should have found that the difficult Dinka-Nuer question in this area had settled itself.

As it was affairs culminated in the Gaweir raid upon the northern Dinka tribes in rains of 1928. In this raid they were joined by considerable elements of Lau. Apart from the attack on the Duk Faiwel merkaz, 87 Dinka men, women and children were killed, 100 were enslaved or missing and 700 cattle were taken. Thirty villages were burnt and the crops destroyed.

The Settlement commenced in February 1929. Gwek Wandeng was killed when attacking a government force of police and mounted rifles. The tribes were then disciplined by enforced concentrations which were carried out in two successive dry seasons. Dual Diu was captured in 1930. Two other notable 'kujurs', Car Koriom and Pok Kerjok gave themselves up during the same year.

The final stage of this settlement was reached when the Gun Lau shens who inhabited the Duk Faiwel sub-district were moved northwards lock, stock and barrel into the Abwong District. Into their place were brought the Dinka sections of Ric, Angai and Luac who had for years inhabited the northern reaches of Khor Fulluth up to the Sobat.

This move took place at the beginning of the rains of 1930. Tribal boundaries were shown on the attached diagram [not included in this copy]. Details of tribal organization and component sections will be found under section five.

TRIBAL LIFE AND BELIEFS

Life of the people

The cattle owning tribes are semi-nomadic.

Their movement depends on grazing and water for cattle. In the height of the dry season, inland waters dry up altogether and the grass dries off and is burnt. In the wet season the people live in their villages. As the water recedes into the swamps the people follow it. In order to facilitate care of the cattle, they are herded into 'morahs'[11] which are placed as near home as is compatible with good grazing and water. Grain for daily food has to be

---

[11] Arabic, *mura'a*, meaning seasonal cattle camp; equivalent to Nuer *wec* or Dinka *wut*. Administrators of this period invariably used the Arabic, rather than the vernacular terms.

carried periodically from the village, similarly water for the aged and sick that cannot move is carried back to the villages from nearest water supply.

In a very dry year morahs are frequently as much as two days trek from the villages or even more in the case of tribes in the extreme north east of the district.

The greater the distance from village to morah, the greater the hardship to the people. The trouble of carrying and the periodical failure of crops, makes the grain supply to distant morahs an uncertain affair. In such circumstances the people often depend entirely on milk for sustenance, augmented by what fish they can spear in the marshes and game they can bring to bag.

Although seasons vary considerably from year to year the following may be taken as a rough programme of their lives:

Dinka Months

(these months do not exactly coincide with our months)

Niet or Anyengol	November	People still in villages, cattle herded in or near village.
Kol	December	Second harvest 'habub'* crop gathered. Cattle with young men move from villages to nearest good grazing.
Akoidit	January	Cattle and villagers move definitely to toic.
Akoithey	February	Everybody in the toic except aged and sick.
Adwong	March	Showers may be expected towards the end of the month, a proportion of the people return to the villages to clean the ground for sowing.
Allabor	April	First sowing should take place, morahs heading for home.
Akoldit	May	General return to villages.
Bildit	June	People remain in villages tending crops.
Bilthey	July	As above, reaping of first harvest should start latter end of month.
Lal	August	First harvest should be completed.
Bor	September	Sowing of second or 'habub'* crop takes place.
Kon	October	Rains finished, inland water still plentiful, road clearing takes place.

* Arab., locally a strong wind, here referring to the late rainy season [*Ed.*].

Beliefs of the people

The cult of Deng is probably the basis of Dinka religion or supernatural belief. Deng is the son of God or Nialic [*nhialic*] as he is styled in Dinka. Deng's wife was named Aciek, the spirits of these two divine persons are the principal ones to which the Dinka give credence.[12]

---

[12] Deng and Arek are ancestral figures. Deng is the son of Garang, son of Nhialic (or the sky) and Abuk, daughter of Apiny (or the earth). His wife was Arek. *Aciek* means 'creator' in Dinka, and is often used when addressing Nhialic (Divinity).

Deng and Aciek had a number of children; Atem and Awol are among the most important. These are regarded as minor spirits or rather semi-divine messengers of impending sickness or other tribulation.

Deng has his representative in every section, the minor spirits are also represented but these have acquired varying degrees of importance in different tribes.

The principal Deng man of a section is known as Bany Tiop [*beny tiop*] which means land chief (Nuer Kwer Mon [*kuaar muon*]). Some of these Deng men claim hereditary descent from the divine Deng, others were seized by the spirit. The popular belief among the Dinka here is that some fifty years ago there was a widespread supernatural descent of the spirit throughout the Dinka and Nuer country. They believe that many of these seizures were genuine while others were fictitious. Some tribes give credence to one, some to another. Amongst the Dinka of this district, Arrak Yak [Rak Yaak], commonly known as Deng Dit, is believed to be the chief, genuine and hereditary owner of the spirit. Deng Dit lives west of Duk Fadiat amongst the Angai Dinka having moved from Fangak District in 1928. As far as I have been able to elucidate, Deng in his truest form is a completely beneficent spirit. The troublesome kujurs who lay claim to the spirit of Deng are all the mushroom growth of not more than two generations standing. Thus Gwek Wandeng derived his spirit from his father only, the latter was seized by the spirit and did not inherit it. The same is true of Car Koriom, Dual Diu, Pok Kerjok, also Garbor Ual Meth [Gatbuogh Wal]. Car's father was seized by the spirit of Deng, he was a Dinka and never practised any malign influence. Dual Diu, Pok Kerjok (Gair), and Garbor (Kerbiel) are none of them more than two generations standing. Their influence was definitely opposed to what is understood by the Dinka as the true spirit of Deng, and their prestige seems to have accrued purely owing to the fact that they preached a policy of aggression and annexation, favourable to those amongst whom they had come to live.[13]

The cult of Deng is not only harmless but inevitable among the Dinka until they are sufficiently sophisticated to require something better. Any

---

[13] The Dinka men of divinity do not all claim seizure by DENG, but from a variety of divinities, including DENG. The main spear-master families claim descent from Aiwel, not DENG. Rak Yaak was the caretaker of the shrine at Luang Deng (see Biographical Notes). Of these Nuer prophets listed, only Guek and Car claimed seizure by DENG. Dual Diu was seized by DIU, Pok by GÄR, and Gatbuogh Wal by KERBIEL. Both Car and Pok claimed that their divinities came to them as gifts from Ngundeng through blessings he bestowed on their fathers. See Johnson (1994: chs. 5 and 6).

malign influence is due to prostitution of the cult on the part of impostors of more or less recent growth.[14]

The actual practices of the cult are not elaborate. A celebration is held in propitious years with dances and sacrifice of bulls and goats. This is comparable to our harvest festival and has roughly the same raison d'être. These festivals are held tribally and not usually in combination with large concentrations of other sections. In the event of rain being late or insufficient, sacrifices will also be made during 'Allabor' (April) or 'Akoldit' (May). Individuals may visit any priest of Deng in whom they have credence for the alleviation of sickness or trouble or because their wife is barren.

An offering of a goat or bull is usually made, whereupon the Deng man retires into his kujurial lair and relief is expected to take place in due course. Should any layman enter the inner recess of the kujurial lair or should he urinate in ignorance on any ground set aside for the worship of Deng, he is believed to become sterile.

The use of amulets and charms is a means employed by minor kujurs, generally of mushroom growth, to increase their prestige. As has been stated the principal priest of Deng in a tribe is known as Bany Tiop, he is therefore a kujurial significance.

Each tribe has also a Bany Luac (Nuer, Kuer Looi [*kuaar loc*, master of the cattle peg, or man of cattle]). The Bany Luac has no kujurial powers, he is the hereditary chief herdsman of the tribe. He decides where and when the herd shall move to new pastures.

In effect Dinka cult or superstitious beliefs does not amount to worship of an almighty 'Deng'. In some tribes, for instance Bor, Deng is now little more than a name. In such cases it will be found that a tribal spirit of paramount importance has been adopted.

These spirits have invariably a symbolic spear which is treated with great respect, housed in a special hut, and tended by its own priest. The Bor spear is known as 'Alier Piou' [Lirpiou].[15] It is probably that these symbolic spears were originally sent out by the high priest of Deng to be his representatives in distant lands.

Every Dinka inherits a number of guardian spirits from his ancestors, some good some bad. These spirits must be propitiated from time to time

---

[14] The idea that there was a subversive 'cult of Deng' associated with the Nuer prophets originated with Willis, in his correspondence with Khartoum. When asked to substantiate this claim, Willis sought corroboration from his DCs. Both Coriat and Lee, who spoke Nuer, denied that any such organised cult existed among the Nuer. Only Wyld, whose ideas are summarized above, agreed with Willis, and presented the Nuer prophets as perverters of a blameless Dinka religion. See Johnson (1985*a*).

[15] See Buttic (1982).

by sacrifices and offerings. Dreams are the medium by which these spirits communicate with their adherents. They are believed to foretell danger and to help in sickness.

As in the case of Deng priests the possessors of certain spirits are believed to be able to invoke their help for other persons and will do so on payment of bulls or calves. The commonest causes for which help is invoked are sickness, or barrenness of women. In the case of illness the skin from the poll of the animal sacrificed is usually cut off and made into a bracelet to be worn on the left wrist of the sufferer.

GENERAL NOTES ON POLICY

In the past principal efforts have been devoted to:
   A.   Obtaining confidence in government
   B.   Obtaining peace and tranquillity
   C.   Reorganization of sections
   D.   Increasing the powers of chiefs
   E.   Opening up communications
   F.   Medical treatment

Results have on the whole been encouraging and foundation has been laid.

It is important that future efforts should be directed to development on the same lines.

Personal touch with individual sections is the best means of retaining confidence.

In past years strenuous chases across the country to get in touch with shy sections who bolted on the approach of the DC took up most of the trekking season; happily this is no longer necessary.

The Nuer elements have been moved from the northern portion of the district. For this reason the work of concentrating and reorganizing into tribal units the scattered parties of Dinka, who have long dwelt amongst the Nuer shens, is greatly facilitated. It is probable, for some years to come, that small parties of Dinka will continue to drift away from Nuer shens in the Abwong District and rejoin their original sections. Such movement is natural and should not be discouraged, but should be carried out by mutual arrangement between the two district commissioners concerned. Care should be taken also to see that there is no sharp practice on either side in the ownership of cattle of personnel so transferred.

In the past, case work has been the instrument through which a close touch has been maintained with the people. While it is undesirable that appeals should be encouraged and although road communications render rapid touring possible, it is of primary importance that this close touch should not be lost. Leisurely trekking through the cattle camps in the toic during the dry season is one of the best ways of getting to know the people. It is suggested that this course is absolutely necessary in the case of all tribes north of Bor whose villages are exceedingly scattered and practically deserted during the dry season.

A further important point to be studied is the employment of people.

Under no circumstances whatever are government police, whether mounted or dismounted, employed beyond the limits of government stations unless accompanied by the DC. That is to say for summoning recalcitrant persons, or any such functions entailing disciplinary, penal or administrative duties amongst the tribes.

The only case in which policemen are employed outside a station unaccompanied by the DC is to supervise the building of a rest house or direct labourers working on a road. In such cases the policeman is sent as a foreman of works only and does not collect labourers.

The foregoing does not of course effect any escorts or police sent with individuals or stores.

Chiefs' police being purely tribal should be used for all cases of summonses, assisting chiefs to enforce judgement, etc. Chief's police should never be taken as carriers or used in menial capacities.

A number of Bor chiefs' police are permanently retained at the merkaz to act as messengers to the tribes. These should not be allowed to live in the suk. They should sleep at their head chief's rest house and be in attendance at the office or chief's court unless employed in some specific tribal work.

Chiefs and tribesmen have been taught to take off their hats if they possess them, when talking to white men or entering an office. They have also adopted the habit of saluting with the right hand extended above the shoulder.

Tribal greetings are preferable to any other form. They are 'cinkeda' in the case of Bor Dinka and 'cinyen' in all other cases.

TRIBAL ORGANIZATION AND CHIEFS' COURTS

Tribal organization

The composition of tribal sections and sub-sections is as follows:

Number	County	Chief	Sub-section

Bor Dinka

Gok Section — *Head Chief Deng Col*

1	Adol	Deng Col	Gol
2	Gol	Jok Ayom	"
3	Abang	Riak Nial	"
4	Gwalla	Deng Ajak	"
5	Abiy	Acok Ngong	Abiy
6	Biong	Deng Agwek	"
7	Palek	Acol Deng	Palek
8	Kuedok	Gogwei Kwei	"
9	Koic	Kang Makwei	Koic
10	Atet	Adol Anyuat	"
11	Dair	Deng Kur	"

Attoic Section — *Head Chief Ajak Bior*

12	Baidit	Ajak Bior	
13	Biong	Lual Kur	
14	Patuyith	Akwei Kur	
15	Alian	Kwain Ateng	
16	Abwodit	Mayan Akwak	
17	Juet	Mabior Deng	

Twic Dinka

Liet Section — *Head Chief Bior Agwer*

18	Kongor	Bior Agwer	
19	Biudit	Deng Yong	
20	Aywal	Bul Kwer	
21	Adiok	Akoi Atem	
22	Deishwek	Deng Lual	
23	Aoolian	Ajak Biar	
24	Abek	Biar Kwek	

Fakerr Section — *Head Chief Majok Ajak*

25	Anok	Majok Ajak	
26	Gol	Majok Ajang	
27	Berah	Akuyen Atem	
28	Cir	Jok Deng	
29	Akinjok	Kunjok Dud	

Ajwong Section — *Head Chief Warabek Aiwel*

30	Abiong	Gag Gwat	
31	Ayolyil	Marier Kwer	
32	Niaping	Warabek Aiwel & Gag Kwain	
33	Kwaj	Deng Koic	

Bor-Duk District

Number	County	Chief	Sub-section

Nyarreweng, Gol, Ric, Angai, Luac and Fadung Dinka

Nyarreweng — Head Chief Deng Malwal
- 34 — Agair — Deng Malwal
- 35 — " — Conkwei Jok
- 36 — Athon — Makwei Gol
- 37 — Kumai — Kuth Yor

Gol
- 38 — Niel — Malwal Mar
- 39 — Pattel — Ayok Gwem

Ric
- 40 — Ringror — Deng Lom
- 41 — Ringbai — Awol Akwei

Angai
- 42 — Afarar — Moinkwer Mabur

Luac
- 43 — Angok — Garrang Weou
- 44 — Aiwel — Kur Tsijuth
- 45 — Mut — Kor Akwe

Fadung
- 46 — — Wer Kwer

NOTE: Chiefs of Angai, Luac and Fadung are subject to further alterations

Thain Dinka

- 47 — Pariak — Aciek Apec
- 48 — Malek — Cabuoc Acok
- 49 — Malwal — Aniang Ameriang
- 50 — Mading (Padeng) — Nguotnyin Der
- 51 — Mading (Famou) — Akol Ajuot
- 52 — Akwak — Dut Ayi
- 53 — Jonglei — Cawoc Akur

Chiefs' courts

General

Chiefs' courts and councils of elders are not a government institution in any way contrary to tribal custom amongst the Dinka.

The fact that this was not generally realized in the early days of administration of the tribe was possibly, to some degree, the cause of the diminution in the power of chiefs, and the long and tedious process that has been necessary to re-establish their jurisdiction in its present form. A second and potent factor in the lack of tribal cohesion and organization which was so apparent in many Dinka sections was the presence of the Nuer. In some cases, as is well known, whole sections had been overrun and reduced practically to the status of slaves. In other cases sections moved bodily, having been relieved of their moveable property, and superimposed themselves on more fortunate sections removed from the immediate scenes of Nuer depredations. It is not surprising that during this time, many acknowledged heads of tribes were either killed or dispossessed of power.

For the above reasons, early administrators of Dinka tribes were faced not only with the difficulty of gaining the confidence of the tribes, but also that of putting their hands on the persons who really carried weight in the tribe. In earliest days internal tribal affairs were settled by the Bany Tiop or land chief, after summoning a council of the elders of the tribe. Intertribal affairs were also frequently subjected to a mixed council. It appears however, that an ultimate decision in important intertribal matters was usually arrived at by force of arms because claimants could not be persuaded to modify their demands for compensation to a reasonable figure. It is common sense to suppose that the first Dinka to get in touch with government representatives, at a time when confidence had yet to be established, were either individuals who were labouring under a grievance real or supposed, against their legitimate chiefs. In the latter case, the government representative was unlikely to hear anything good about the chiefs in question.

Practically all that the Dinka knew about the outside world he had learned from the slave raider and the sole means of communication between himself and the 'Turk' were detribalized outcasts, who had in fact been the creatures of the slave raider. These intermediaries could represent matters much as they pleased.

The first step to be taken by government was naturally an attempt to get in touch with the chiefs. Equally naturally the real chief was reluctant to come forward not knowing what to expect. Instead they thrust forward scapegoats who had not the power to refuse and certainly not the power to carry out any orders they might receive from government for the sections over which they were supposed to be government chiefs.[16]

It was probably the result of having so many bogus chiefs and with a mistaken idea of helping the people, that led government representatives in these early days to attempt to settle cattle cases; although they must have been entirely ignorant of native law and custom and at the mercy of the worst variety of interpreters. The result was to undermine the powers of the real chiefs and to throw established laws and customs into confusion. The abuse was further aggravated by the fact that this early case work was made one of the duties of the mamurs, many of whom found it a safe and rapid method of feathering their own nests.[17]

[16] Deng Malwal was one such scapegoat (see Biographical Notes).
[17] The mamurs all coming from the army at this time, many were also Dinka officers.

The first improvement in the system occured when DCs started hearing cases themselves, but this method proved totally inadequate to deal with the vast amount of case work which government had attempted to shoulder.

The next step was the 'peripatetic' court, which was the first step in the right direction. This form of court was most enlightening. Chiefs were made to tour with the DC and hear cases. Judgements were recorded by the DC in person, he also saw to their fulfilment and heard all appeals on the spot. During this period the suitability or otherwise, the power of control or lack of it, on the part of chiefs, became apparent. At the same time the DC had an excellent opportunity of obtaining an inside knowledge into the native law and custom.

Thus the 'peripatetic' court served its purposes. Its inadequacy lay in the fact that it could not function in the DC's absence and that it monopolized too much of his time.

An example of this, I would quote from my own experience.

On one occasion, in one section of the Twi country, I recorded over 1,000 cases in ten days and some 4,700 in three weeks.

The existing 'lung a bany' or chief's court was the outcome of the system. A separate court was formed for each main section of the district. Care was exercised in the selection of a head chief to preside at each court, who had sufficient hereditary position to justify his appointment and sufficient knowledge and respect of government to ensure a reasonable conformity to our ideas of equity. It would be idle to suggest that the courts were yet beyond reproach, but they are progressing satisfactorily. All chiefs' court judgements are subject to appeal to the DC by either party.

Practically all Dinka cases are concerned with the possession or transference of moveable property in the shape of cattle. These are the cases heard by the chiefs' court. Criminal cases are rare, there are however cases which might be considered criminal from certain aspects, but which are adequately dealt with by the chiefs' courts. These are mentioned later.

Composition and machinery of the courts

The six courts have each a court clerk who records the chiefs' judgements and issues to plaintiff and defendant a tin disk bearing the number of the case.

The fee of 5 Pt is paid by plaintiff for the hearing.

Every clan in the district has two paid chiefs' police. These police work entirely under the chiefs' orders. In addition to their normal work of maintaining order in the villages, they are available for summoning defendants and witnesses and collecting cattle already adjudged from recalcitrant judgement. Plaintiff raises his case in front of the court of the section to which his defendant belongs.

Appeals from the chiefs' court lie to DC.

Appellant must first carry out the chiefs' judgement. He then presents himself with his case disk and the fee of 50 Pt. Should the chiefs' judgement be upheld he forfeits his appeal fee. If the chiefs' judgement is reversed his appeal fee is returned to him. It was found necessary to make the appeal fee as much as 50 Pt to stop frivolous appeals, a Dinka never gives up hope that his oratory will persuade a second court to make a more favourable view of his case. In practice the raising of 50 Pt presents no difficulties owing to the fact that there are invariably many relations interested in the case and prepared to put up the money many times over if they think there is a reasonable chance of the chiefs' decision being reversed. As the courts are held and run entirely tribally, it is unnecessary to have fixed periods of sitting. The head chief and two others form a quorum. The court normally sits at the head chief's village and can be assembled at a few hours notice. From time to time any given court may be made to sit at the merkaz for a given period, so that the DC can reassure himself as to its work.

At the end of the every month the head chief and his clerk present themselves at the merkaz; the head chief then pays court fees into the chest, the money being checked against the number of cases shown in the clerk's book and the number of disks issued. At the same time the head chief is responsible until called for.

Nature of cases heard by chiefs' courts, penalties inflicted, etc.

There is little repugnant to civilized ideas of justice in Dinka laws and customs; nor are there any rituals connected with these which are sufficiently barbarous to be worthy of note here.

Cases are principally confined to those connected with dowries, debts and penalties for adultery. Other cases heard are those concerned with 'blood money', compensation for injuries and for slaughtering cattle the property of another.

Dowry cases and those concerned with debts are frequently involved, if outstanding for any length of time. In the latter a time bar of five years is in force. In the former, if divorce is claimed by the woman the man usually recovers all his wedding cattle. If the man divorces his wife, her relations retain a proportion, 'hag el ferua'.[18] If there are children of the marriage, they become in all cases the property of the man, but he must forfeit 4 head of cattle per child out of his wedding cattle.

---

[18] *Ḥaqq al-farwa* (Arab., property of the hide, or skirt). The hide skirt refers to the married woman's skirt, denoting her change of status from girl to married woman. The deduction is compensation for lost virginity. For the Nuer version (*yang yaatni*) see Coriat (1993: 28) and Howell (1954: 149). The Western Dinka of Bahr el-Ghazal have a different system of repayment in cases of divorce. See John Wuol Makec, *The Customary Law of the Dinka People of Sudan in Comparison with aspects of Western & Islamic Laws* (London, 1988): 77–105.

Penalties for adultery have been standardized throughout the district at 4 head of cattle for an unmarried girl and 6 for a married woman. These cattle are known as 'arok'. In the case of a girl the cattle are payable in the first case to her father, but on the marriage they pass to her husband as compensation for receiving a damaged article.

'Arok' is never paid more than once for any given woman. If a woman commits adultery more than once her husband may divorce her without prejudice to his marriage cattle, but in such a case he must relinquish the 'arok' cattle that he received for the first case. Such cattle will again accompany the woman if she remarries.

Murder cases are outside the province of the chiefs' courts. In my opinion it is desirable that the extreme penalty should be inflicted in such cases. The Dinka are beginning to understand the government is prepared to hang murderers and this is a safeguard against tribal fights. In the past a killing almost always caused a fight. The original death might be avenged, but unless 'honours were easy' at the end of the battle the blood feud remained.

If a fight did not immediately ensue after a killing, relations of the dead man would watch for the opportunity of killing the murderer or some member of his family.

When blood feuds were settled by 'blood money', in the old days when cattle were plentiful, as many as 100 head were paid. Later when cattle became scarce owing to disease and Nuer raids, these large numbers were not forthcoming, with the result that fighting became more prevalent.

The Dinka is beginning to understand the difference between murder and other forms of killing. A murderer promptly hanged satisfies tribal custom and puts an end to a blood feud. Blood money has been fixed for some years past at twenty head of cattle which is considered sufficient for other forms of killing.[19]

Culpable homicide and grievous hurt inflicted with the intention to kill, are the two forms of crime which seem hardest to bring into line with a

---

[19] In common with many earlier administrators Wyld assumed that the bloodwealth rate was a deterrent punishment. Bloodwealth was always linked to the rate of bridewealth, in that the cattle were supposed to enable a murdered man's family to marry a wife in his name; thus continuing his line through her children. Wyld implies here that the Dinka of Bor and Duk were claiming that the customary bridewealth prior to Nuer raids and rinderpest was 100 head of cattle. The Nuer at this time claimed that 50 head of cattle was the ideal rate in pre-rinderpest days. There is as yet no known historical evidence to corroborate either assertion. Following the cattle epidemics of the early 1930s administrators agreed to reduce the amount of bridewealth to be consistent with the availability of cattle, but they insisted on maintaining bloodwealth at a higher rate, again to act as a deterrent. They also found that the execution of a murderer did not, by itself, satisfy custom or end a blood feud. The payment of cattle was still necessary to wipe out the wrong done (Johnson (1986a; 73)).

civilized penal code, because long terms of imprisonment neither satisfy native custom nor act as a deterrent to crime. I personally am in favour of allowing culpable homicide not amounting to murder to be settled by 'blood money' and grievous hurt to be settled by the native custom 'weng keth' (which I will describe later), plus a fine in both cases. I deprecate long terms of imprisonment, firstly because so often the untutored tribesman prisoner dies of a broken heart and loneliness in some distant gaol amongst strangers as fellow prisoners who regard him as an 'abd' [Arab., slave]. Secondly because, should he complete a long term of imprisonment, it is nearly certain that he will have become detribalized in the process and never return to his own village to be a living example of the reformed criminal.

The solution is possibly a penal settlement within the province, where local criminals could carry out useful work living under their native conditions. In view of the fact that no such settlement exists at present and that crime of the nature is not very prevalent, I advocate the alternative, stated earlier, until the Dinka become more sophisticated.

'Wang keth' [cow of the urine] involves the payment of a cow to an injured man, when in the popular opinion the blow inflicted will ultimately cause death.

The popular belief is that should the injured man drink the urine of the cow, his life will be prolonged.

From a practical point of view the merit of this custom lies not in the medicinal virtue of the cow's urine, but in the fact that the payment of the cow is regarded as evidence, when the man dies, of the cause of his death, should no other accident intervene. On death of the injured man, the cow and her progeny are deducted from the total 'blood money' payable. Thus if the man lives 15 years, probably no further payment is necessary, on the other hand should he live but 6 months, the remainder of the 'blood money' cattle become due automatically.

Theft is practically unknown amongst the tribes, but is harshly dealt with under native custom when it does occur. A thief is required to repay approximately six times the value of the article stolen. On the very rare occasions when such cases have occured, I have found that the chiefs' court have referred the matter to me with a recommendation that native custom be not followed, but that the article refunded and the offender be either flogged or fined a bull or calf.

The slaughter of another man's ox, other than his 'fantasia' [Arab., dance] animal is a native custom and not a crime. This act is perpetuated chiefly by young warriors as a sacrifice to their own 'fantasia' ox, with the object of increasing the prestige of animal and owner. A man performing this act is required to compensate the owner of the slaughtered animal by

Bor-Duk District

the payment of a cow calf; no case ensues unless he is behindhand in his payment.[20]

The foregoing is a brief summary of typical Dinka cases. Being entirely governed by tribal law, the chiefs' courts do not inflict either floggings or imprisonment. A scale of cattle fines has been introduced for the following abuses:

1. Attempting to reopen a case already settled.
2. Refusing to carry out the orders of the court and necessitating the employment of chiefs' police.
3. Making libellous statements about chiefs.
4. Attempting to appropriate disputed cattle before the case has been heard in court.

In all the above cases the fine is a bull or a calf according to the aggravation of the offence.

Supervision of chiefs' courts exercised by the DC

Owing to the number of courts and the large number of cases heard the DC does not personally review every case, nor is there any need for him to do so, as litigants can appeal to him, should they so desire.

Apart from the supervision of courts arising through the hearing of appeals, the DC when visiting any given court area, holds frequent meetings of the president and members at which the nature of various cases is discussed and any points of native law which have arisen are examined.

It frequently happens that the president and members while hearing an intricate case, adjourn of their own accord in order to discuss it with the DC before they proceed. In the past, chiefs have been fined for passing palpably biased judgement, but such cases are becoming rarer. In present state of the development of the courts and the close touch maintained between DC and the chiefs, it is inconceivable that any gross miscarriage of justice could arise without its being brought to notice at once, unless the DC was on leave, when he would certainly be informed as soon as he returned.

As has already been stated, flogging and imprisonment do not figure in native custom and are entirely outside the province of the chiefs' courts. Any sentences of flogging awarded by the DC are practically confined to offences committed by the detribalized Sudanese inhabitants of the merkaz. An occasional flogging has to be administered to young tribesmen for offering violence to chiefs' policemen in the performance of their duties, but such cases are rare.

The Dinka woman is not mere chattel. By native custom, no marriage

[20] For a similar custom among the Nuer, see Howell (1948*b*).

can take place unless the girl herself is willing. The more enlightened adhere to this custom, but there is no doubt that the Dinka's inherent cupidity leads to many cases of undue pressure being placed upon the girl to make her select the highest bidder.

Such marriages almost invariably lead to trouble as the girl either runs from her husband after a short period or commits adultery, to which she owns up after it is evident that she is pregnant.

The Dinka woman can and frequently does claim and obtain divorce. In such cases the chiefs' court invariably first orders the woman to return to her husband after having heard her grievances and after having awarded 'arok' when necessary.

If a woman runs away a second time and it becomes evident that she will not live with her husband under any circumstances, a divorce is granted, then, unless neglect on the part of the husband can be proved, the dowry must be handed back in full.

A woman does not possess cattle outright, except in very exceptional circumstances. In the few cases that have come to my notice a curious custom prevails, the woman will herself marry a wife or wives and employ a man to raise offspring from them.[21] In discussing the position of woman amongst the Dinka, it is worthy of note that no odium attaches to a woman for committing adultery once, she is merely regarded as a damaged article in the marriage market until 'arok' has been paid when her value is restored. Cases of adultery are rarely raised unless the girl is pregnant.

Importance of chiefs' courts in the process of devolution

The formation of sectional chiefs' courts has undoubtedly been invaluable in the process of restoring and building up the power of chiefs and giving them a recognized status.

The system has produced the necessary nuclei, on which it has been possible to decentralize the routine work of administration and build up a form of government and control, which though rudimentary at present, is acceptable to the people. The head chiefs tend more and more to assume responsibility and feel themselves to be a part of the government, without assuming an air of officialdom of the 'Jack in office' variety.

---

[21] For a similar arrangement among the Nuer see Evans-Pritchard (1951: 108–9), where barren women who often practice as diviners frequently have enough cattle with which to marry and raise children in their own names.

Bor-Duk District

REVENUE AND RESOURCES

The following is the detail of tribute from the tribes.

Bor Gok

Head chief	Deng Col	£ 33
"	Jok Ayom	10
"	Acok Ngong	29
"	Deng Agwek	29
"	Riak Nial	18
"	Deng Ajak	28
"	Acol Deng	25
"	Gogwei Kwei	25
"	Adol Anyuat	47
"	Kang Makwei	45
"	Deng Kur	30
	Total	319

Bor Attoic

Head Chief	Ajak Bior	£ 71
"	Lual Kur	23
"	Akwei Kur	50
"	Kwain Ateng	25
"	Mayan Akwak	70
"	Mabior Deng	43
	Total	282

Twi Liet

Head Chief	Bior Agwer	£ 62.500 m/ms
"	Deng Yong	17.500
"	Bul Kwer	62.500
"	Akoi Atem	75.000
"	Deng Lual	65.000
"	Ajak Biar	52.500
"	Biar Kwek	20.000
	Total	355.000

Twi Fakerr

Head Chief	Majok Ajak	£ 37.500 m/ms
"	Majok Ajang	17.500
"	Akuyen Atem	15.000
"	Jok Deng	37.500
"	Kunjok Dud	12.500
	Total	120.000

Twi Ajwong

Head Chief	Warabek Aiwel	£ 15.000 m/ms
"	Marier Kwer	10.000
"	Gag Gwat	35.000
"	Deng Koic	10.000
	Total	70.000

Nyarreweng

Head Chief	Deng Malwal	£ 17.500 m/ms
"	Conkwei Jok	10.000
"	Makwei Gol	10.000
"	Kuth Yor	20.000
	Total	57.500

Gol

Chief	Ayok Gwem	£ 21.250 m/ms
"	Niel	17.500
	Total	38.750

Ric

Chief	Deng Lom	£ 28
"	Awol Akwei	5
	Total	33

Angai

Chief Moinkwer Mabur	£ 15

Luac

Chief Garrang Weou	£ 38.250 m/ms
" Kur Tsijuth	4.800
" Kor Akwe	6.000
Total	49.050

Fadung

Chief Wer Kwer	£ 5

NOTE: All these tribes are liable to reassessment during the season 1931.

Thain Dinka

Chief Aciek Apec	£ 5
" Cabuoc Acok	5
" Aniang Ameriang	8
" Nguotnyin Der	8
" Akol Ajuot	5
" Dut Ayi	9
" Cawoc Akur	2
Total	£ 42

Summary of the district revenue

1. Tribute from tribes (as per foregoing lists)	£1,386.300 m/ms
2. Traders tax and licences	88.100
3. Rent of government houses	
DC's house, Bor	30.000
Mamur's " "	12.000
" " Duk	3.600
Sarraf's " Bor	3.600
(X) Agriculturalist's " "	3.600
(X) Dispensary hakim's "	3.600
4. Hikr (ground rent) "	18.960
Total	£ 1,549.760

NOTE: (X) Rent not yet officially fixed.

Chapter 7

COMMUNICATIONS

The attached diagram shows the dry weather road existing in the district [not included in archive].

The annual clearing of roads and maintenance of rest houses is automatic.

Embankments were started in 1929 and 25 miles were completed at varying levels of from nine inches to two feet.

Work of embankment was not continued in 1930 owing to lack of funds. I suggest that the work should proceed as soon as the financial stringency ceases. With about five years properly organized work I consider that it would be possible to keep communications between Bor and Duk Faiwel open for most of the year.

The lists attached show normal payments for upkeep of roads. Chiefs concerned know the limits of their own responsibility in each section.

Aerodromes are cleared yearly at:

Bor	£ 30	cleared by	Bor Dinka	
Kongor	£ 30	"	" Twi	"
Duk Fadiat	£ 25	"	" Nyarreweng, Gol, Angai and Ric Dinka	

Sums allowed for the maintenance of these and the tribes responsible are as shown.

Roads and aerodromes are normally in use from the beginning of December until the beginning of May.

Normal payments for upkeep of roads

Section 1 Mongalla boundary-Bor

Deng Col	£ 2.000 m/ms
Deng Ajak	1.500
Acol Deng	1.500
Jok Ayom	1.000
Acok Ngong	1.000
Gogwei Kwei	1.500
Kang Makwei	1.500
Deng Kur	1.500
Riak Nial	1.000
Deng Agwek	1.500
Adol Anyuat	1.500
	Total £ 15.500

Bor-Duk District

Section 2 Bor-Juet

Ajak Bior	£ 4
Akwei Kur	3
Kwain Ateng	3
Mayan Akwak	3
Mabior Deng	3
Lual Kur	3
Akol Ajuet	1
Nguotnyin Der	1
	Total £ 21.000

Section 3 Juet-Kongor

Jok Deng	£ 3.000
Akuyen Atem	1.000
Majok Ajak	1.000
Kunjok Dud	0.500
Majok Ajang	1.000
Warabek Aiwel	2.000
Deng Koic	0.500
Biar Kwek	1.000
Ajak Biar	3.000
Deng Lual	3.000
Bul Kwer	1.000
Bior Agwer	4.000
Akoi Atem	
Marier Kwer	1.000
Gag Gwat	1.000
	Total £ 23.000

Section 4 Mar-Jonglei

Majok Ajak	£ 1.000
Majok Ajang	1.000
Kunjok Dud	1.000
Deng Koic	1.000
	Total £ 4.000

Section 5 Kongor-Duk Faiwel

Bior Agwer	£ 1
Deng Yong	2
Akoi Atem	3
Bul Kwer	2
Deng Malwal	3
Conkwei Jok	1
	Total £ 13

Section 6 Duk Faiwel-Duk Fadiat

Deng Malwal	£ 3.000
Conkwei Jok	2.000
Ayok Gwem	2.500
Moinkwer Mabur	2.500
Malwal Mar	2.000
	Total £ 12.000

Section 7 Duk Fadiat-Abwong boundary

Awol Akwei
Deng Lom
Garrang Weou } Subdivision remains to be settled later
Kur Tsijuth
Kor Akwe

Total £ 25.000

Section 8 Malek-Abii-Adol-Abodit

Deng Col	£ 2.000
Deng Ajak	1.500
Acol Deng	1.500
Jok Ayom	1.000
Acok Ngong	1.000
Deng Agwek	1.000
Adol Anyuat	1.500
Kang Makwei	1.500
Deng Kur	1.000
Riak Nial	1.000
Lual Kur	1.500
Gogwei Kwei	1.000
	Total £ 15.500

Bor-Duk District

Section 9 Duk Faiwel-Lukluk-Bongil-Faniok

Deng Malwal Conkwei Jok Makwei Gol Wer Kwer Deng Lom	Subdivision to be settled later
Total £ 14.000	

Section 10 Duk Fadiat-Rotit

Moinkwer Mabur	£ 2.000
Total Grant asked	£ 150.000
Payments as per lists For tools special works etc	£143.000 7.000
	£150.000

LABOUR

The labour called for from the tribes falls under the following main headings:
- A. Clearance and maintenance of roads
- B. Clearance of aerodromes
- C. Carriers
- D. Cleaning telegraph routes
- E. Station cleaning etc.
- F. Collection of wood and grass for mud buildings

Normal payments under A and B have already been given. Payments under A cannot be regarded as individual pay to labourers employed but as a reward to chiefs and headmen for collecting their tribesmen and causing the work to be done. Payments under B are considered sufficient to cover the grain supplied to labourers at the rate of two rotls per diem and two per day work per man. If labourers do not put in an average day's work they cannot expect an average day's pay.

C. Carriers are now only supplied for urgent government purposes when the roads are unfit for motor transport. They will not be supplied to tourists, shooting parties etc. In cases where carriers are supplied the rate of pay is 2 Pt per day returning empty or detention, plus 1 Pt per man supplied, dues to the chief providing the carriers.

It is never necessary to employ carriers beyond the limits of their tribal boundaries. For a long trek chief's police are sent ahead to arrange with chiefs concerned for relief carriers to be ready on the boundaries where old carriers should be paid off. Where carriers are retained for more than twenty-four hours they should be supplied with grain at the rate of two rotls per day, for which 5 m/ms may be deducted from their pay.

Fifteen miles is considered a day's carrying. Sixty rotls is the maximum load.

D. The clearance of telegraph routes has to be carried out annually before the grass dries. Chiefs are responsible for arranging this clearance within their own areas, labourers are paid at the rate of 2 Pt per pole cleared. Before this payment is made, linesmen should be sent out to see that the work has been carried out properly.

It is also advisable that orders for the work to be commenced should be sent out in good time.

The replacement of telegraph poles is a periodical work involving hardship to the labourers unless properly supervised as the poles are more than a carrier load.

Owing to the motor road being adjacent to the telegraph line throughout the majority of its length in this district, poles can be dumped by motor lorry thereby reducing the distances necessary for man handling. The Bor merchant Ali Said Ahmed [Ali Sid Ahmed] has special fitments on his lorry for carrying poles.

E. & F. The normal pay for unskilled labour is 2 Pt per day. When labourers are employed at a distance from their homes two rotls of grain should be supplied.

Payment for this grain should be deducted from the total sum earned unless the work is of an arduous nature or entails special hardship.

APPENDIX 1: PERSONALITY REPORTS

Bor Gok

1. HEAD CHIEF DENG COL. Granted 3rd class sword of honour 1926. Continues to exercise a good control over his section and adds to his prestige by ensuring that fair judgements are given by the court over which he presides. There are very few appeals from the Gok court.

Deng Col is a useful asset to government. He is at times apt to be hot headed and has a very good opinion of himself. He gets things done.

2. Jok Ayom. Gives no trouble, has not much personality and is absolutely under the thumb of Deng Col.

3. Riak Nial. Has not great influence over his section. There was an intrigue to depose him in favour of Macar Acamkoc who had been deposed by Richards in 1926. I upheld Riak after hearing all the evidence and punished those concerned. Riak is well disposed but poor in cattle.

4. Deng Ajak. One of the best of the Gok chiefs. He is loyal to government and Deng Col's principal adviser. He is of a retiring nature but carries much weight in the tribe.

5. Acok Ngong. Calls for no special comment, gives no trouble and exercises average control.

6. Deng Agwek. ditto

7. Acol Deng. One of the older chiefs. His section is large and prone to occasional fights. He does what he is told and does his share of court work.

8. Gogwei Kwei. Well inclined somewhat weak although one of older chiefs has not much control over the Pakom section of his tribe who are now urgent in their requests to be treated as a separate unit. This request has a certain justification and will probably be acceded to.

9. Kang Makwei. Quite the best of the young chiefs of the Gok section. Sensible, well inclined and a pleasing personality.

10. Adol Anyuat. A good elderly chief and supporter of government. Does what he is told and is reliable.

11. Deng Kur. Not an outstanding chief but does what he is told and has given no trouble lately.

Bor Attoic

Head Chief Ajak Bior. Granted 3rd class sword of honour 1926. Has considerable influence throughout his section but cannot be relied upon to give impartial judgements in his court with the result that there are many more appeals in his section than amongst the Gok. He has often to be driven in order to get things done. He is too old ever to become an enlightened chief, but has been doing rather better in 1930 than in former years.

Lual Kur. An old man but does his best with little support from his sub-chiefs. I have often been struck by the amount of personal endeavour shown by Lual but his people are somewhat much for him.

Akwei Kur. Not an outstanding figure. Has given no trouble lately but does nothing unless driven.

Kwain Ateng. Deposed by Richards in 1926 for drunkenness and an outburst of temper in the office, in favour of Ko Nial. Reinstated in 1929 by me as he is the hereditary chief and the man carrying most weight in his section, Ko Nial is a sheepish youth of little account. Kwain needs watching and urging to obtain results. Has behaved himself better since reinstatement.

MAYAN AKWAK. An old man and very little use. He has had a lot of urging from me in the past and is rather better than he was but can never be a good chief.

MABIOR DENG. Easily the best of the Attoic chiefs young and hardworking, does what he is told and gets things done.

Twi Liet

HEAD CHIEF BIOR AGWER. Granted 3rd class sword of honour 1929. Very young for his position and still being educated. Is hot tempered and often stupid. There are many appeals from his court. If properly handled and educated will turn out a useful head chief when a little older.

AWOL CHAN. Actually a sub-chief of Bior's own section but given permission to sit on the Liet chiefs' court as a steadying influence to Bior. Well inclined and sensible.

DENG YONG. Used to be a gun runner importing Abu Gigera[22] from the Nuer and for some time under a cloud. Is now quite well inclined and a useful member of the chiefs' court. Has good authority over his people.

BUL KWER. About the best of the Liet chiefs. Finds Bior rather trying at times. His section is somewhat unruly but has given no trouble lately.

AKOI ATEM. Old and fairly useless, if there was anybody better I should have deposed him. His section was the last of the Twi to come into line and have the reputation for wildness. Have given no trouble lately but require watching.

DENG LUAL. Made chief instead of his brother Daw Lual in 1929. Daw was incapable of honesty and younger than Deng. Deng is handicapped by his old father Lual Deng who had great influence in the pre-government days and is still a reactionary. Deng needs helping and urging to get things done.

AJAK BIAR. Eldest son of the notorious Biar Abit. Was an outlaw with his father for many years till the latter was recaptured by me in 1926 after which he behaved himself until he died in 1930. Ajak is well disposed but somewhat less sophisticated than might be expected even of a Twi chief. With time and patience he should become a useful asset.

BIAR KWEK. Made chief in 1928 instead of Goj Bul who was hardly

---

[22] 'Abu Gigera', Sudanese colloquial name for the bolt-action French (1874) Gras rifles commonly available in Ethiopia, where it was known as 'ujijqra' or 'wujigra'.

human and quite useless. His people are somewhat wild and require handling. Biar like most of the Liet chiefs is still in need of tuition.

Twi Fakerr

HEAD CHIEF MAJOK AJAK. The last head chief to be made and has no sword of honour as yet. He is personally well inclined and about the first Twi chief of any section to come into line with government in the early days. He is muddle headed and has curious notions of justice, he tries but cannot exert much influence.

MAJOK AJANG. The best Fakerr chief and mainstay of Majok Ajak. Well disposed and sensible.

AKUYEN ATEM. Has only fair control over a small section. Lazy and lacking in personality but his people have given no trouble.

JOK DENG. A plausible rascal. Disliked by most of his people and has little control over his section which is quite well behaved.

MADING MAJOK. Actually a sub-chief of Jok Deng but made a member of the chiefs' court to counter-balance Jok. Is rather more honest than the latter.

KUNJOK DUD. A crude personality with an extremely offensive odour. His section are really Thain Dinka who have given up fishing for cattle. Kunjok requires periodical urging to get things done. His section gives no trouble.

Twi Ajwong

HEAD CHIEF WARABEK AIWEL. Made head chief in 1928 and given a 3rd class sword of honour in 1929. Has considerable influence and gets things done. Suffers from a temper. His relation Aiwel Malwal is feared as the hereditary owner of the malignant spirit of Muttening Guk [mathiang goh] and is supposed to have caused deaths with this spirit.[23]

GAG GWAT. Not a bad young chief and well inclined. Though somewhat wild his section has given no trouble lately.

MARIER KWER. Not outstanding. Has only a small section who are rather wild but cause no trouble.

---

[23] *Mathiang goh* (or *gok*) is a fetish bundle made up of roots, reputed to give its owner power over those who have wronged him. It appears to have entered the Dinka country of Rumbek from the Jur-Beli people to the west at the beginning of this century. It can be bought and sold and it spread throughout the Dinka and Nuer territories of Upper Nile Province throughout the 1920s and 1930s. Because of the fear it engendered, and the confidence it seemed to give to its owners to defy the orders of chiefs and other government officials, it was outlawed and routinely suppressed (Fergusson (1923), Lienhardt (1961: 65–8), Johnson (1992a: 13–14).

DENG KOIC. Well disposed but possessed of practically no brain. His people give no trouble.

Nyarreweng, Gol, Ric, Angai, Luac & Fadung

HEAD CHIEF DENG MALWAL. 1st class sword of honour granted in 1928. An outstanding personality with a long record of loyalty and honest purpose.

His influence spreads outside his own tribe and I consider him the best president of chiefs' courts in the district. He has been the DC's right hand man in administrative development in the Duk sub-district for many years.

CONKWEI JOK. Well disposed but stupid and often stubborn.

MAKWEI GOL. A well disposed chief of a small section. His people may be expected to increase with the movement of the Lau Nuer from his country. Had a bad reputation in his youth as a fighter and killed several persons in company with his brothers. This was due to the fact that he was reared as a Nuer.

KUTH YOR. Really a Nuer but allowed to remain with Nyarreweng on transference of Lau to Abwong owing to a series of deaths in his family popularly supposed to have been caused by a malignant spirit of the Nuer shen to which he belonged because his relations had accepted government.

Kuth is well disposed and does what he is told.

MALWAL MAR. Made a chief in 1930, on the separation of Gol Dinka from the Angai. He is elderly but well disposed. His people are lazy and require pulling at times.

AYOK GWEM. Made chief in 1930 on the death of Malwal Ayik. Personally well disposed. His people are like those of Malwal Mar. Ayok frequently drinks too much and becomes stupid as a result.

DENG LOM. The only man of the Ric who has enough character to become a good chief. He has been a loyal supporter to government for many years. Until the removal of Lau from the district he lived amongst shen Dung over whom he had a good influence. He obtained information which led to the arrest of Dual Diu. He should be allowed to remain at Faniok as, being considered a personage amongst the Nuer, he is best fitted to watch the boundary between the two tribes.

AWOL AKWEI. Well disposed but controls only a small section. His people are lazy and have given trouble in concentration into their tribal unit. They should be watched for a tendency to split up amongst the Gol.

MOINKWER MABUR. Was formerly accounted a Gol chief until 1930. I separated the Angai from the Gol. He has a hard task in front of him in reorganizing his tribe some of whom have come from Khor Fulluth and others from amongst the Gaweir Nuer.

He is capable of being a good chief with assistance and perseverance. His chief difficulty will be in keeping off drink to which the whole of his section are much addicted. When stupid with drink he is useless. Requires particular attention to the DC to form his character.

GARRANG WEOU, KUR TSIJUTH, KOR AKWE. All transferred at the beginning of the rains in 1930 from Khor Fulluth.

I do not yet know these chiefs at all well. Garrang Weo [Garang Wiu] appears to be the brightest of a very poor lot. He has influence but whether for good or bad remains to be seen and will depend on his handling. Portions of the tribe still have a hankering for the Khor Fulluth and the reorganization and resettlement of these Dinka in their new homes remains to be done during the dry season 1930–31.

APPENDIX 2: CENSUS

A rough census of the people is practically completed and is contained in volumes at district headquarters Bor.

The following is a summary of those listed.

TRIBE	SECTION	POPULATION
BOR	Gok	10,147
"	Attoic	6,699
TWI	Liet	13,056
"	Fakerr	2,737
"	Ajwong	1,935
NYARREWENG		2,316
GOL		1,865
ANGAI		737
RIC		1,080
LUAC		566
THAIN		1,288
	Total	42,286

APPENDIX 3: CHIEFS' POLICE[24]

No.	Chief	Police	No.	Remarks
Bor Police				
1	Deng Col	⎰ Deng Malwal	51	
2	" "	⎱ Aniang Alier	52	
3	Jok Ayom	⎰ Riem Jo	53	
4	" "	⎱	54	
5	Acok Ngong	⎰ Rial-Bek Maich	55	
6	" "	⎱ Kur Col	56	
7	Deng Agwek	⎰ Fakit Ayee	57	
8	" "	⎱ Deng Bol	58	
9	Riak Nial	⎰ Nial Agot	59	
10	" "	⎱	60	
11	Deng Ajak	⎰ Anieth Gog	61	
12	" "	⎱ Aret Malok	62	Gok Section
13	Acol Deng	⎰ Thiong Aiwel	63	
14	" "	⎱ Maich Ding	64	
15	Gogwei Kwei	⎰ Maning Jok	65	
16	" "	⎱ Lueth Thiong	66	
17	Adol Anyuat	⎰ Garrang Aniang	67	
18	" "	⎱ Tiop Lual	68	
19	Kang Makwei	⎰ Garrang Lual	69	
20	" "	⎱ Jil Ayom	70	
21	Deng Kur	⎰ Duoinngok Akol	71	
22	" "	⎱ Deng Tinda	72	
23	Ajak Bior	⎰ Aciek Jok	73	
24	" "	⎱ Akwok Wutic	161	
25	Lual Kur	⎰ Deng Akoul	75	
26	" "	⎱ Tem Wel	76	
27	Akwei Kur	⎰ Deng Aniang	77	
28	" "	⎱ Alith Dut	78	Attoic Section
29	Kwain Ateng	⎰ Ayuen Gut	79	
30	" "	⎱ Garrang Kur	80	
31	Mayan Akwak	⎰ Akwok Kok	82	
32	" "	⎱	81	
33	Mabior Deng	⎰ Garrang Apiu	83	
		⎱ Bior Mayan	84	
Twi Police				
38	Bior Agwer	⎰ Ajang Bul	91	
39	" "	⎱ Bior Deng	92	

[24] This appendix was untitled and unnumbered in the manuscript, which contained no appendices numbered 3 or 4. Appendices 4–7 were originally numbered 5–8. There is no internal evidence suggesting that there is a missing appendix; rather they seem to have been misnumbered.

Bor-Duk District

No.	Chief	Police	No.	Remarks
40	Deng Yong	Thiong Mayan	93	
41	" "	Allak Yak	94	
42	Bul Kwer	Dwet Deng	95	
43	" "	Akuyen Koin	96	
44	Akoi Atem	Deng Raic	97	Liet Section
45	" "		98	
46	Deng Lual	Deng Thiong	99	
47	" "	Yuol Jwaic	100	
48	Ajak Biar	Atem Cieng	101	
49	" "	Daw Yak	102	
50	Biar Kwek	Ngor Agot	103	
51	" "	Giet Akuyen	104	
52	Majok Ajak	Atem Kuot	105	
53	" "	Garrang Abot	106	
54	Majok Ajang	Deng Dut	107	
55	" "	Agwek Mayan	108	
56	Akuyen Atem		109	Fakerr Section
57	" "		110	
58	Jok Deng	Majok Atem	111	
59	" "	Yei Atem	112	
60	Kunjok Dud	Awang Arok	113	
61	" "	Atem Magok	114	
62	Warabek Aiwel	Mabior Kwer	119	
63	" "	Garrang Faniang	120	
64	Gag Gwat	Riak Deng	115	Ajwong Section
65	" "		116	
66	Marier Kwer	Bek Adol	117	
67	" "	Nyingut Deng	118	
68	Deng Koic	Garrang Lueth	121	
69	" "	Awok Kur		

Nyarreweng, Gol & Ric Police

No.	Chief	Police	No.	Remarks
70	Deng Malwal	Kuot Ajok	127	
71	" "	Awol Akol	128	Nyarreweng Section
72	Conkwei Jok	Malith Ayeek	129	
73	" "	Ayak Akwei	130	
74	Makwei Gol	Wal Deng		Athon Section
75	" "	Ter Jong		
76	Kuth Yor	Niort Gai	140	Kumai Section
77	" "	Yak Witha	139	
78	Ayok Gwem	Majok Dwal	123	
79	" "	Gumwel Diu	124	Gol Section
80	Malwal Mar	Majok Aru	125	
81	" "	Baden Awer	126	
82	Deng Lom	Jal Lom	147	Ric Section
83	" "	Lem Rueh	157	

No.	Chief	Police	No.	Remarks
84	Awol Akwei	{ Lem Mayol	131	
85	" "	{ Ayok Ding	132	
86	Moinkwer Mabur	{ Toodel Mabor		
87	" "	{ Rueh Allair		Angai Section
Thain Police				
34	Cabuoc Acok	Cwei Tir	85	Malek
35	Nguotnyin Der	Ngong Aniang	86	Mading
36	Aciek Apec	Deng Macar	87	Pariak
37	Akol Ajuot	Maniel Adit	88	Mading

APPENDIX 4: ECONOMIC DEVELOPMENT AND POSSIBILITIES

Economic development is a very slow process in the district, firstly owing to the people being semi nomadic and therefore poor agriculturalists, secondly owing to their extreme reluctance to part with their cattle which may be accounted their only source of wealth. Unreliable rainfall further militates against agricultural effort with the result that for the last three seasons there has been constant famine in one or other part of the district. It is only in exceptional years that an export of grain is possible and an average year barely produces sufficient for all requirements.

A fair progress had been made with cotton growing in the Bor area and in the rains of 1930 cotton seed was issued to those Twi tribes inhabiting the country adjacent to Jonglei. But in the absence of constant urging in cotton production the results obtained may be considered discouraging.

That there are good possibilities of agricultural development in the swamp area along the banks of the river, there can be little doubt. This, however, entailing reclamation work, must at this stage be experimental and in the hands of government.

It is proved by the small experimental plot at Bor that if cultivation banks are constructed above high flood level many useful commodities can be grown. At the same time it is for experiments to prove whether there is any produce that can be grown economically of sufficient value to cover the high cost of freightage to distant markets.

It has been stated that on an average year the grain produced is barely sufficient for all needs in the district and this is a serious problem.

The Dinka are conservative to a fault and have a deep rooted prejudice against any new food crops. In the rains of 1930 for the first time the Agricultural Department carried out experiments in planting various varieties of dura at Kongor, Duk Faiwel and Duk Fadiat and the results are fairly encouraging especially at Duk Faiwel.

If the seed of the more successful varieties is issued to the more enlightened chiefs during the coming season, I believe there is a possibility that such varieties will be gradually adopted by the tribes.[25]

The rainfall in the centre of the district around Kongor appears to be on the whole steadier than in the north or south also the land appears richer.

Both Bor and Duk areas have been dogged by ill fortune in this respect for the past three years and whole crops have perished either from deep flooding or drought.

Development of the economic value of the herds which are the only wealth of the country at present, can be carried forward in two ways only. Firstly by veterinary effort to eradicate diseases which follow each other with monotonous regularity. Secondly by improvement of the breed which will be a lengthy and expensive process.

I consider that a government experimental farm, run by an experienced person of good sense, in the most favourable part of the country, and following native custom as far as possible, is the best way of forming a nucleus for such development.

APPENDIX 5: BUILDINGS

All buildings in the district, excepting those enumerated later at Bor itself, are classified as mud buildings. The permanent buildings at Bor itself are as follows:

A.1. District office and P&T office (in one building)
2. Prison and armoury
3. District commissioner's house
4. Mamur's   "
5. Sarraf's   "
6. Post master's   "
7. P&T clerk's   "
8.   "   "   "
9. P&T rest house (British officials)
10. Hospital and dispensary
11. Dispensary hakim's house (under construction)
12. Agriculturalist's house
13. Grain store

---

[25] The Dinka proved to be more experimental agriculturalists than Wyld gave them credit for, and cultivation is a far more important economic activity than he realised. In any planting season people plant a combination of drought-resistant and flood-resistant strains of dura, hoping to get the balance right.

14. Egyptian Irrigation Department rest house
15. Garage

Repairs to permanent buildings are carried out by PWD under arrangements by district engineer Juba (not Malakal).

B. Mud buildings at Bor are as follows:
1. Police barracks
2. Clerk's house
3. Hospital ward
4. Three tukls P&T launch crew
5. One tukl district felucca crew
6. Kitchen and outhouse P&T rest house
7. Two stables and two tukls for hamla mounted police
8. Two head chiefs' rest houses

C. Approved but not yet built at Bor:
1. Brick shed with iron roof RAF petrol store
2. Chiefs' court house to be made of locally burnt brick and grass roof

D. Mud buildings at Duk Faiwel are as follows:
1. Office, guard room and prison
2. District commissioner's house
3. Mamur's house
4. Hospital
5. Chiefs' court house
6. Head chief's house
7. Interpreter's house
8. Police barracks
9. Two cattle luaks

E. Mud building at Kongor are as follows:
1. District commissioner's rest house
2. Mamur's rest house
3. Police guard room and prison
4. P&T clerk's house
5. " office
6. Chiefs' court house
7. Hospital
8. Sanitary hakim's house

F. The annual repair of mud buildings is carried out under district arrangements and paid for from an annual grant made by province headquarters. £ 90 is the usual sum allotted.

In addition to buildings enumerated earlier the DC arranges for an annual supply of 600 bundles of building grass to the mission station, Malek. This is cut and delivered to the mission station by the Thain Dinka section of chiefs Aciek Apec, Cabuoc Acok and Aniang Ameriang.

The DC also arranges for any repairs or addition necessary to the leper colony at Malek.

G. Certain of the buildings classified as mud buildings are built of locally burnt brick made at Bor or Duk Faiwel. It is possible by burning bricks locally to construct various new buildings that are required of a more permanent character.

APPENDIX 6: FORESTRY

The tree of the country is the heglig which grows splendidly throughout. It is valuable to the people as an alternative food supply when dura fails.

The only forestry experiments that have been made are of a very minor character. It appears that certain valuable varieties of trees could be grown, and it is suggested that the most suitable area for making a serious experiment would be the area along the east bank of the river between Bor and Pariak.

It is also probable that under certain conditions varieties of eucalyptus would grow well in the marshes on the west bank of the river.

The following varieties of trees are found in the district:

	Local name
Gameiza [*Ficus platyphylia*] of various varieties	Kwil
Nabak [*Zizyphus mucronata*]	Lang
Sunt [*Acacia arabica*]	Angwat
Abu Shutur [*Kigelia æthiopica*]	Rual
Ardeba [*Tamarindus indica*]	Cwey
Dom Palm [*Hyphæne thebaica*]	Niet
Doleb " [*Borassus æthiopum*]	Akot
Talh [*Acacia seyal*]	Bii
Abu Kamir [*Bauhinia fassoglensis*]	Pac[26]
Babanus [*Dalbergia melanoxylon*]	Rit
Heglig [*Balanites ægyptiaca*]	Thou
Bacam [*Grewia salvifolia*]	Kem
Inderab [*Cordia rothii*]	Akoi
Large soft wood [*Butyrospermum parkii, var niloticum?*]	Ariek
Trees growing in the Duks	
Ambac [*Herminiera elaphroxylon*]	Adet
Another large tree growing in Duk area with edible fruit [*Diospyros mespiliformis*]	Cum
Abu Gowi [*Gardenia lutea*]	Dong

[26] Abu Khamir is the *Landolphia florida*; Pac (in Dinka) is *Bauhinia fassoglensis*, or Abu Khameira; see Broun & Massey (1929).

APPENDIX 7: SUNDRY

Garden

The district garden at Bor on west bank of the river was started in 1929 and was extremely productive.

Cabbages, lettuce, beans, tomatoes, carrots and cauliflowers all did well and there seemed to be every prospect of being able to supply post boats in the near future once the area of cultivation was extended.

Unfortunately the exceptionally high river of 1930 inundated and destroyed the value of the vegetable garden and no further cultivation will be possible until flood subsides. In the dry season of 1930 cultivation banks were constructed and bananas planted. These have done exceptionally well and should prove a steady source of income for the garden.[27]

Several small citrus and mango seedlings were also planted on these banks and have done very well.

Tobacco of several varieties has also given encouraging results on the cultivation banks.

The remainder of the garden plot, or as much of it as finances will allow should be banked during the coming dry season. The easiest and most economical method of constructing cultivation banks has been found to be as follows:

Having marked out the banks, the portions between are ploughed up, the tilth is then scraped up by means of large wooden shovels on to the bank area and beaten down. Ploughing is then continued and the building up process repeated until the bank is high enough.

A motor pump has recently been supplied to the district and as soon as the flood has subsided sufficiently should be erected in the garden plot.

As a temporary measure the pump has been erected in the DC's garden from which position it can irrigate the fruit garden on the east bank of the river.

With some work the water could also be made to reach the effendia quarters and the hospital with object of beautifying the station.

The position on the east bank will be the normal position for the pump in the rains and the position in the garden plot on the west bank for the dry season.

Six plough oxen have been trained for work.

The merkaz possesses a plough, a harrow and a rough bull cart.

---

[27] Bananas subsequently became well established in Bor and were a common foodstuff sold to passengers on the steamers until river traffic was suspended during the civil war of the 1980s and 1990s.

Merkaz Herd

The following is a list of merkaz cattle with progeny.

The system recommended for maintaining this herd is for the best female calves to be retained for breeding purposes while bull calves and inferior females should be transferred periodically to the devolution cattle and sold.

NAME OF COW	AGE	PROGENY
Ayan	7	Nanluel 1930
Agok	6	
Ayan	8	
Agok	4	
Rolniel	9	Mareng 1929
Ajak	7	Mamer 1929
Billith	9	Makol 1930
Ayan	5	
Ding	7	
Akol	6	Manjok 1929
Kweibil	5	
Yom	5	
Lou	6	Malou 1929
Yar	13	
Ayan	5	
Aluel	4	

Duk Merkaz Herd

NAME OF COW	AGE	PROGENY
Ajok	9	Manlou 1929
Yom	9	Malwal 1930
Ayan	13	
Bil	9	
Yar	10	
Lau	12	Nanbil 1929
Areng	10	
Niang	7	Nanbil 1930
Akol	8	Makol 1929
Acole	8	Nancole 1929
Niel	8	Nanjok 1930
Cuor	5	Maniel 1929
Ayan	4	
Ajok	6	Makol 1930
Akerlou	11	
Aluel	4	Nanluel 1930

CHAPTER 8

Yirrol District

G. K. HEBBERT

BOUNDARIES OF THE DISTRICT

These are not clearly defined. The rough boundaries may be traced on the sketch attached [not included in archive].

NORTHERN BOUNDARY. Lake Nyibor [Nyubor] to some 10? miles north of Shambe.

EASTERN BOUNDARY. The main channel of the Bahr el Jebel.

SOUTHERN BOUNDARY. From a mile or two north of Tombe to the junction of the Yirrol-Tali and Yirrol-Gnopp [Ngopp] roads, thence to a point some 15 miles S. of Gnopp.

WESTERN BOUNDARY. Roughly 16 miles W. of Gnopp on Gnopp-Mvolo road to a point 7 miles E. of Akot on Yirrol-Rumbek road and thence to Lake Nyibor.

DISTRIBUTION OF PEOPLE AND GENERAL TRIBAL ORGANIZATION

It would appear that the district was originally inhabited by blacksmiths, hunters and fishermen, living in small isolated communities.

Various individuals from cattle owning tribes, such as Nuer, and Bor, were expelled from their own tribes or ran away from them. Settling with the blacksmiths and fishermen etc. they introduced cattle herding. The idea took on. The descendants and hangers on of the newcomers became stronger than the original inhabitants.

Tribal organisation usually took the nomenclature of the newcomers. The original inhabitants were either driven out, scattered, exterminated, or became dependants on or a gol within the tribe of the new.

None of the tribal groups as now distinguished claim a common ancestry.

The process has rather been that a man and his son lived in adjoining houses and tied their cattle in one circle. This is the gol ['cattle hearth', group of agnatic kin].

As men and cattle increased in numbers, they still lived in one village, but several circles were formed in the cattle kraal.

The unit who tied their cattle in the one kraal is known as the diet [dhieth], in which there may be several gols.[1] There is always a chief in charge of the whole diet. Whilst each gol of any size has its head man.

When further expansion became necessary, the diet would split into two or more diets. The whole who were connected by a common ancestry are known as the 'Un', in which in this way there may be one or several diets. The Luaic are an example.

The 'Un' would have a fighting chief common to all the diets, but each diet would have its own independent chief for all other purposes. Though often one of the diet chiefs would be more influential than the others.

The larger units have been formed not by descent from a common stock, but by expediency based on propinquity.

Thus two or more small independent communities live near each other.

At first they fight. Then either one is the stronger and gets the better of the other or they tire of fighting. They intermarry and combine for defence against a common enemy, who lives further away. They invent a name for the group. Examples are the Aliap and the Afak.

The larger divisions of the district are:

A. Atwot
B. Afak
C. Cic
D. Ador
E. Gok
F. Aliap

See Sketch and population [not included in archive]

A. Atwot is merely a name (given probably by outsiders) to the Dinkacised natives living around the toiches of lakes Yirrol and Anyi. They had no common ancestry or organisation and did not combine to fight invaders. However owing to propinquity and inter-marriage they have a common language, which is nearer to Nuer than Dinka.[2]

They have three paramount chiefs or 'beng [*beny*] dit'.

1. Chief Nial Acol (Luaic) has the Luaic who have several diets, the Gillik, Piair and Awanpial.

---

[1] For a description of Western Dinka social and political organisation, see Lienhardt (1958: 106–28).
[2] Throughout the Condominium period, and later, the Atuot were officially classed as Dinka. For the convolutions of Atuot identity see Burton (1981a).

2. Chief Mabor Kacwal has the Akot, who have two diets.

3. Chief Ongwi Bol (Kwek) has the Kwek (several diets), the Dima, Nue, Ajwong (blacksmiths), Balang Joya (hunters).

The Rokaic comprising three tribes, Nyang, Paleu, and Kok, are under the 'beng dit' of the Afak.

B. Afak is a group of tribes who combined under a common fighting chief. They speak Cic Dinka.[3]

The tribes are Awan (two diets), Palwal, Apair, Rwok, Riair, Acok, Aparair.

They are under one 'beng dit' Korriam Awo. He has also under him the Rokaic, as mentioned above, Palul (fishermen) and a tribe of Atwot origin Pakwaic.

C. Cic. This is a term invented by the natives to describe the peoples living between Lau and Yirrol.

They have two 'beng dit'.

1. Chief Cep Aciek has under him a group of tribes of diverse descent, part of whom are known collectively as Kwaic. Kwaic consists of the following tribes: Ding (3 diets), Cirbek (3 diets), Jalwa, Nuen, Pakol, Jar, Ajwong (blacksmiths) and some fishermen.

Cep Aciek has also Pajak (3 diets).

2. Chief Takpin Malwal. His group is also of diverse origin and is known as Ajak. It consists of Dwaur (2 diets) and Cilic (3 diets) and some fishermen.

D. Ador.[4] A group of diverse origin, consisting of the following tribes, united for defensive purposes etc.: Die, Abadon, Angar, Ajwot, Lok, Abwong, Aleu and Ajwong (blacksmiths).

Their 'beng dit' is Attair Bar.

E. Gok.[4] Also a group of tribes, living in the sandy country, known as Gok, inland from Kenisa.

Their 'beng dit' is Raic Amo and he has the following tribes: Lual, Ding, Jagjuair, Arek, Bun, Awan (two of these are small and have only headmen).

F. Aliap is the name of a group, more or less united by conquest.

Within the group are three groups of whom the conquering one is known as Thiang. Thiang consists of Nyingar (3 diets), Apuk, Angwom and Luel.

The other groups are Ajwot (Akair and De), and Balok (Aken and Korriam).

NOTE Angwom and Luel are the names of diets. Originally with De they formed a group known as Ajwot.

---

[3] Normally (and currently) considered a major section of the Atuot.
[4] Later grouped with the Cic.

PLATE 1

Governor Willis with Shilluk guard of honour, on the Kodok light line (Willis)
Sudan Archive, University of Durham (SAD) 210/14/192

Governor Willis on trek, 1927 (Coriat)

PLATE 2

Shilluk review (Willis)

PLATE 3

Murle at Akobo, 1928 (Coriat)

'A Dinka near Khor Fulus mouth on the road to Fadding' c.1928 (Romilly)

SAD 788/1/2

PLATE 4

Nuer building thatched roof over namlia (Willis)   SAD 210/14/139

Nuer building road, Coriat and Willis in background, 1928 (Willis)   SAD 210/14/165

PLATE 5

Coriat, Wyld, Maxwell at Tied Wiot, Khor Atar (after 30 hours march), 1928 (Romilly)
SAD 788/1/12

Captain Romilly (Gaweir March 1928) with 'daughter of sword and honour bloke [chief Guer Wiu]' (Romilly)
SAD 788/1/28

PLATE 6

Gaawar 'who gave false information and had been definitely anti-government being flogged', Gaweir March, 1928 (Eastwood)

Coriat, Romilly, Maxwell, 'looting a hippo harpoon', Nuer cattle camp, Gaweir March, 1928 (Romilly)

SAD 788/1/13

PLATE 7

'Women prisoners on the march with goods & chattels & babies on their heads — one baby was born en route', Nuer Settlement, 1929 (Eastwood)

Pulling car on a raft across Khor Woat, 1930 (Coriat)

PLATE 8

Yoynyang Roman Catholic mission, 1930 (Coriat)

Further Apuk, Akair, Aken and Korriam were originally diets of a tribe Jukom.

In no case in this description of the tribal organisation is the name of a gol mentioned, rarely that of a diet. The names are in almost all cases those of a tribe, according to Dinka ideas.

Every tribal group has a certain amount of blacksmiths and fishermen attached to it.

Chiefs

One or two of the 'beng dits' are fighting chief of their tribe, but otherwise they owe their authority entirely to the government and not to inherent right or native selection. They are selected by the government from the chiefs of diets. The position should not be hereditary, but given to the ablest chief in the tribal group.

Except for two cases every diet has what is known as a *ring* ['Flesh']. This appears to be an ancestral spirit, inhabiting a particular man and giving him wisdom and power to rule the tribe. It is hereditary in one particular gol of the diet. It is quite separate from the rain maker, who is known as a ran e Nyalic [*ran nhialic*], 'man of god'. In some cases there is friction, owing to the fact that the Arab slave traders made any one they chose chief, and many of the chiefs are descended from these, and are up against the tribal ring.[5]

Chiefs of diet are selected by the people, subject to a right of veto by government.

Justice

The following native courts exist, and deal with all civil Dinka cases and criminal cases with the exception of the most serious or if any particular reason renders it desirable that the ADC should see it himself.

In 1929 the courts saw over 1000 cases.
1. Luaic Court
2. Kwaic Court
3. Ajak Court
4. Afak Court
5. Kwek Court
6. Ador Court
7. Gok Court

[5] For Ring, the clan divinity of the Dinka masters of the fishing-spear, and for men of divinity see Lienhardt (1961: chs. 2, 3 & 5).

8. Aliap Court
9. Akot Court

Each court has a Mission trained clerk who writes Dinka in European script.

Appeal cases are seen in Yirrol on the following system:
1. The case must have been seen and recorded by a chiefs' court.
2. A cow calf or £2 is deposited. If plaintiff wins his case this is returned to him, if he loses it, it lapses to the government.

The case is seen by an advisory court of chiefs, other than those who originally saw it. The evidence and the opinion of the court is recorded, the parties are brought before the ADC who reads the record and opinion, may question the parties and gives his own decision.

40 appeal cases were seen in 1929.

Chiefs' police

There is a provision for 100 chiefs' police. This number has been officially accepted. About 20 at a time attend the office for any work that may be on hand. They spend two months in Yirrol and then return to their village, being replaced by others.

Chief headmen etc.

Each of the nine tribal groups is under a 'beng dit', who is president of the tribal court and has his own clerk.

Each diet (if large enough) has its own beng, who wears a red sash with a black 'C' worked on it.

Each gol (if large enough) is in charge of a head man or 'ran e gol nom' who wears a red armlet with 'W' worked on it.

The headquarters of all tribal groups are connected by motor road with Yirrol, and each is provided with a rest house.

RECENT EVENTS OF IMPORTANCE

Yirrol was administered from Rumbek until 1922. There were mamurs at Lau and Gnopp and Shambe.

There was no post at Yirrol.

Originally the Gok and Aliap were under Mongalla. When the Aliap were again taken over about 1925 they applied to join Yirrol.

Tong e Mudir[6]

In the very early days of the government the Afak had a mad rain maker called Awo. He had taken some merchants' cattle and his people had fought and taken cattle from both the Agar and Cic. The governor of Bahr el Ghazal came to visit him and Awo tried to enter his zariba. The governor shot him.

The governor returned, but summoned the Afak chief to send in his son. He refused and the result was the first Afak patrol.

Tong e Den

About 1907? [1909] the chief of the Luaic refused to go in to the mamur at Lau. The mamur came with the Cic chief and a few troops and police. They got the Luaic chief but on their return journey were attacked by his son and some young men. Some troops and Dinka were killed. The chief escaped and the mamur got back to Lau.

In the night the Luaic attacked the Cic villages. Each man took a hut and set fire to the thatch, stabbing all the inmates as they issued. A few months later was the Luaic patrol.[7]

Tong e Maiyen

In 1918 [1917] a policeman named Maiyen was killed after arresting an Afak, by his brothers.

Very shortly afterwards the Luaic and Afak had a fight and the Afak chief was wounded. He went in to Gnopp and was sent off as a prisoner towards Rumbek. He escaped and refused to come in again. His people started brigandage on the road.

The second Afak patrol was sent, in which Capt. Lawton was killed.

---

[6] 'The war of the governor': *tong* (spear) also meaning war. The confrontation between the governor, Sir Henry Hill, and Awo took place in December 1906, and the subsequent patrol in April 1907, after Awo's death was publicly announced (without details) that February ('Annual Report. Bahr-el-Ghazal Province, 1907', *Reports on the Finance, Administration, and Condition of the Sudan, 1907* (London, 1908): 163; SIR 151 (February 1907): 2) (see Biographical Notes). In 1908 it was stated, in the first of many similarly optimistic reports, that 'the Atwot Dinkas who until last year not only held aloof from, but were occasionally even actively hostile to, the government have now since Sir H. Hill's patrol through their country in 1907, come to their senses ... [and] appear to have become loyal subjects of the government.' ('Annual Report. Bahr-el-Ghazal Province, 1908', *Reports on the Finance, Administration, and Condition of the Sudan, 1908* (Khartoum, 1909): 455).

[7] In January 1909 the 'Loitch Atwot Dinkas' were reported to have 'caused some trouble' ('Annual Report. Bahr-el-Ghazal Province, 1909', *Reports on the Finance, Administration, and Condition of the Sudan, 1909* (Cairo, 1910): 599).

The Afak suffered heavily in this both from thirst during the patrol (they were kept away from the river) and from famine after it (they had been unable to sow their crops).[8]

Tong e Aliap

In 1918 there was a mamur at Minkiman. He sent out police and took the Aliap favourite bulls (maur e chen) for taxes. The Aliap killed some linesmen setting up the wire from Tombe to Tali. The men were hanged and 'dia' [Arab.—blood money] was taken. The Aliap attacked Minkiman. The mamur escaped by night to Bor. Major Stigand, governor of Mongalla came with a patrol. The Aliap hiding in the grass ambushed the advance guard and killed Majors Stigand and White. Some 90 of the Aliap were killed. The patrol retreated in disorder. Nothing was done for some time. Then two strong parties of troops arrived. One from the river and one from Rumbek. The river party was attacked by the Aliap, who lost some 50 men. Otherwise the patrol was able to do but little against the Aliap, who had scattered, except that they caught a few with cattle near J. Tindalo.[9]

The Aliap remained unadministered until 1924 or 1925.

The Nuer

Shortly before government times the Nuer attacked the Kwaic Cic, who repulsed them twice. The third time a very strong party of Nuer arrived and utterly routed the Cic, killing many and taking all their cattle. The Kwaic retired to the forest country and bought spears and malodas [iron-bladed digging sticks] from the blacksmiths for grain, and with the iron work cattle from the Nuer.

They returned to Lau, where the Nuer have attacked them in government times, but have not done much harm to the Kwaic.

---

[8] In 1910 chief Acol (father of Nhial Acol) was arrested in a patrol and deported to Khartoum. He was allowed to return in April 1912, promising never to trouble the government again. In February 1917 he refused to pay taxes and evaded arrest. Between June and November 1917 police and troops were sent against him and Dhieu Alam. Dhieu Alam was captured, but then escaped (*SIR*s 271, 275, 277–8, 280 (February, June, August, September, November 1917): 3, 3, 2, 3, 3). A military patrol was sent out to burn villages in April and May 1918, during which Dhieu Alam surrendered. Of this patrol it was said, 'The experience of the three campaigns (1907, 1910 and 1917) has thoroughly engrained in the mind of the Atwot Dinkas the futility of standing up against the modern rifle fire, and at the same time has shown him the greatest possibilities his vast forests afford him for evading contact with the enemy.' (E. D. Bally, 'Notes on the Atwot Patrol 1918', Appendix in *SIR* 286 (May 1918): 5).

[9] See Collins (1967) and Johnson (1982*d*).

The large number of cattle the Kwaic now own they got by acting as carriers in the patrols.

The Ador used to live on the Lau-Shambe road. During government times they were attacked by the Nuer and lost much cattle.

They retired to Falwal, south of the Yirrol Shambe road, where they still are.

The Lek incident

There is a place in Rumbek district where there is ordinarily no water, but after long periods in certain years a lake forms by bubbling up from below.

The Afak chief [Dhieu Alam] believed this to be magic which would help him to defy the government. He did defy Capt. Fergusson and told his people to stop working. He was arrested and died in Khartoum.[10]

On top of the patrols this caused the ill-feeling amongst the family against the government to remain very much alive.

Apparently when Capt. Fergusson was killed the Afak were sitting on the fence and obtained a magic from the Jur for the Nuer, to cause Capt. Fergusson's death.[11]

Kwek

In 1930 a man of the Kwek killed a government policeman. He was caught and hanged.

REVENUE 1930

Nature of Revenue	£ M/M	Remarks
Hut tax	1852.600	
Town Rates	68.737	
Conservancy	19.617	
Water Rate	7.308	
Rent of houses	24.400	
Devolution	810.839	
Auctioneers' licenses	2.750	
Tax on simsim mills	3.000	to be discontinued
Slaughtering fees & butchers licenses	17.000	
Rest house fees	52.735	
Marriage registration fees	.500	to be discontinued

[10] See Fergusson (1924); also S/R 332 (March 1922): 7–8.
[11] See S. H. (1929).

Nature of Revenue	£ M/M	Remarks
Motor car licenses	52.250	
Fees sales of animals	23.870	
Liquor licenses	72.500	
Sale of milk	47.940	
Traders' licenses	27.100	
Traders' Profit Tax	10.800	
Hikr	17.565	
Ivory Royalties	43.013	
Fines	21.200	
Permits to trade in closed district	14.000	
Ivory weighing fees	1.120	
Miscellaneous	3.380	Market fees Jurs bringing produce for sale etc.
Wakils permits to trade	.400	
Firearms licenses	6.000	
Shambe garden	25.390	
TOTAL	3226.006	

COMMUNICATIONS

Roads

These are shown on the sketch [not included].

1. Shambe-Yirrol-near Akot, for Rumbek (about 83 miles).

This road is gradually being metalled and in 1930 cars were able to get from Yirrol to Shambe every month of the year. The embankments will have to be much heightened for the road to be passable at times of really high flood. The toic of the river Lau requires an enormous amount of work.

2. Yirrol to Acol Bol (Aliap) 56 miles. The road is all weather as far as Alel (39 miles). In 1929/1930 the road went from Alel to Pap, the headquarters of the Aliap, but this road was abandoned as it is nearly all through the toic of the R. Gell.

Alel to Acol Bol was constructed in 1930 and will require a little ramping to make it all weather.

3. Acol Bol to Pap (16 1/2 miles). A rather rough road, much of it under water in flood time.

4. Acol Bol to Papiu (14 miles). Rather rough. Would require a good deal of work to make it all weather.

5. Pap to Minkiman (23 miles?). Rough road, only open for three months of the year as it crosses the River Gell, which is not provided with a ferry.

6. A circular road, leaving the Aliap road to Madlar (20 miles from Yirrol) and joining the Rumbek road at Aluak Luak (75 miles). There is no ferry over the River Lau at Gnopp, otherwise the road might easily be made all weather.

A road from Tali joins this road, thus connecting Yirrol with Amadi. A little work on Khor Rora would give communication all the year.

From Gnopp a road branches off to Mvolo for Meridi. Only a few miles of this road are in Yirrol District.

7. A road leaving the circular road at Pul-a-dor and leading to Maguk Ju's village (10 miles) all weather.

8. Yirrol to Lau (19 miles) all weather.

9. Pakujiak (3rd rest house on Yirrol-Shambe road) to Raic Amo's village (25 miles). Road passes through the headquarters of the Ador and at present ends at the headquarters of the Gok.

It will require work to make it all weather.

It might be well to carry this road on to Kanisa[12] later. There is no toic at Kanisa, so perhaps this road would give an alternative port in years of heavy flood.

10. A grant from the Reserve Fund for £150 was approved to construct an embanked road from Minkiman to the river bank opposite Malek.

Nothing has been done about this.

Personally I am against the project for the following reasons* [*see communications (Willis' introduction)]:

(1) I think it bad policy to work the Aliap too hard. This year they cleared a new road of 17 miles. There is much work to be done in improving, ramping and metalling the existing roads.

(2) The road will be entirely over the toic of the main river. It will involve great labour. If it is to stand it would require numerous culverts. £150 would not supply these.

(3) I cannot see that this road will benefit anyone except the Malek missionaries, who by taking their car to Shambe can get anywhere that they want to.

It does not seem to me to be worth disturbing the Aliap, undertaking great labour and spending much money for such a small advantage, particularly when there are many more useful works waiting to be done.

Wells

There are six wells in use at Yirrol. They give very fair water. Only one is covered in.

---

[12] 'Kanisa' (Arab.—church): the site of the old catholic mission station of Heilige Kreuz (Holy Cross), opened in 1854 and closed in 1859, due to the high mortality of missionaries.

Wells also exist at the following resthouses:
(1) Paken (but requires new well, owing to the dropping in of the sides etc.)
(2) Pakujiak (new 1930)
(3) Manyang
(4) Kantok (new 1930)
(5) Aluak Luak (also an Afak well)
(6) Ado
(7) Agoran[13]
(8) Ardeiba. The water is near the surface here and the Kwek have many wells of their own.

The well at Atet has fallen in. Many of wells want linings. None have them at present.

A well is under construction at Falwal.

Near which is an Ador well. Another well is to be dug at Yirrol for the water hoist, and it is proposed to dig a well at Maguk Ju's village.

Wells have been tried but failed at Madbar Yali, Acol Bol, Pap, and Gaiwam.

Ferries

There is a ferry over the R. Lau on the Rumbek road. It is capable of taking Ford Lorries. Two sections were replaced and one added in 1930.

Two roads have no ferries:
(1) The circular road at Gnopp. It is certainly not worth while to provide one capable of taking a car at a time of financial stringency. It is proposed to construct a boat.
(2) The Pap-Minkiman road at the River Gel. It will be years before cars could get to Pap in the rains, so a ferry would be of little use. A boat might be provided later.

ECONOMIC DEVELOPMENT AND POSSIBILITIES

The main product of the district is naturally cattle and hides, sheep & goats. If and when the Dinka acquires a commercial mind there might be certain possibilities in these.[14]

---

[13] In 1992 Aguran became the site of a large camp of displaced persons, mainly Dinka, fleeing from fighting around Yirol and Bor.

[14] Yirol became the centre of a vigorous market and cattle auction, with a Yirol Co-operative Marketing Society involved in the purchase and sale of agricultural products prior to the independence of the Sudan, and Atuot eventually taking a leading role as cattle traders (SDIT (1955: 131); Burton (1978)).

Agricultural

Some cotton is grown each year. With a good market this would bring a little money. But without supervision the Dinka would soon stop growing it. I do not think it will ever bring much profit over the pay of the Agricultural Staff employed in the supervision.

There is a certain surplus in dura, simsim and ground nuts, but this year export to the North has not paid. In fact it pays to import dura to Shambe (but not to Yirrol).

There are plenty of elephants, but the Dinka do not kill many.

Some honey, tobacco and lulu oil are brought in to Yirrol for sale by the Jurs. There have been enormous quantities of locusts this year.

Veterinary

The Aliap and the Gok have lost enormous number of cattle in the last year. The Dinkas say they have three different illnesses which attack their cattle. It would be of great value if a Veterinary inspector could visit the district and explain to the ADC etc. the nature of these illnesses, what, if anything, can be done, how and when to inject. Experiments could be begun with the government cattle, which generally seem to have one or other of these illnesses.

The Aliab sheep have also had a plague and it has even spread to the buffalo and tiang.

Buildings

The medical expert on malaria talks of advocating the removal of the British staff to a place a mile or so up the Tali road, and the building of PWD houses. Perhaps the offices will also be moved.

At present there are the following brick buildings:

(1) The ADCs houses constructed to local pattern at a cost of £600 each with kitchens and servants quarters.

(2) Three Effendia quarters at £150 each. A fourth is to be built.

(3) There is a grant of £500 for the construction of 2 blocks of offices each to contain 4 rooms. One block has been started.

(4) A grain store.

A grant for the construction of a garage to hold three cars was cancelled.

At Shambe there is a rest house and hospital on PWD charge. A house for the AMO is to be constructed by the PWD. There is a corrugated iron and wood erection for the Sarraf and 3 corrugated iron store sheds.

The following mud buildings at Yirrol would better be replaced by brick ones:
(1) Hospital & AMO's house
(2) Guard room and rifle & ammunition store
(3) Prison
(4) Police & district stores
(5) Police lines
(6) Workshop
(7) Rest house

Forestry

Cutting of firewood particularly for brick kilns has depleted the forest round Yirrol, the Forestry Dept. has done the same for Shambe.

There is a certain amount of mahogany in the vicinity of Yirrol. An engine and circular saw has been supplied. A guide table is still required for feeding logs to the saw. This is somewhat expert business requiring a trained hand.

A plantation of mahogany was tried at Yirrol, but I think the trees were transplanted too young. At any rate so far it has not been a great success.

The Forestry Dept. experimental plantation at Shambe appears to have been a complete failure.

Gardens

At present the Yirrol garden consists of fruit trees only, and officials grow their own vegetables. A water elevator has been supplied and it is hoped to make a proper garden shortly.

The Shambe garden supplied a certain amount of fruit and vegetables to the steamers.

Cattle

Chiefs' court fines provide sufficient cattle to supply milk to officials and the hospital. There is often a surplus for sale, particularly when there are a number of Dinka cattle in 'Amanat'[15] with the government, pending cases etc.

At present there are:
government cattle—18 cows and heifers 47.

---

[15] 'Amanat' (Arab.), 'deposit': cattle paid into the court as security until a judgment has been given.

Capt. Fergusson and others 'dia'[16] bulls 3 heifers 25. The last to be disposed of.

Market

A proper place for the sale of meat is very necessary. The auction of butchers licenses provided a clear profit of £19 for 1931.

Hospitals

A hospital at Yirrol has an average of about 20 in and 40 out patients. That at Shambe a slightly large attendance—as the AMO is popular with the people.

The following dressers are stationed with chiefs outside Yirrol:

Cic	2
Afak	1
Kwek	1
Gok & Ador	1
Aliap	1

POPULATION STATISTICS

Summary

Tribal Group	Head Chief or Beng Dit	Population
Luaic	Nial Acol	9920
Akot	Mabor Kacwal	3105
Kwek	Ongwi Bol	5325
Afak	Korriam Awo	12845
Cic Kwaic	Cep Aciek	9455
Cic Ajak	Takpin Malwal	5180
Gok	Raic Amo	3800
Ador	Attair Bar	5060
Aliap	Abyar Kon	13670
	Total	38340

[16] The remaining cattle from those paid as bloodwealth by the Nyuong Nuer for the murder of Fergusson and various of his Dinka companions in 1927.

Beng dit Nial Acol

TRIBAL GROUP	TRIBE	DIET	CHIEF	POPULATION Estimated at 5 persons per house
Atwot (Luaic)	Luaic	Jagbari	Nial Acol	530
"	"	Nyilok	Gaj Mair	1505
"	"	Adut	Mabor Deng	2685
"	"	Airial	Mow Gai	610
"	"	Kun	Mabor Kok	250
"	Jillik	Bang	Gaj Gom	1775
"	Pir	Pir	Kacwol Apokain	640
"	Awanpail	Kulang	Lat	1005
"	Gillik	Thit	Aloin Thowath	280
"	Ajwong	Ajwong	A. An Dal	640
			Total under Nial Acol	9920

Beng dit Mabor Kacwal

TRIBAL GROUP	TRIBE	DIET	CHIEF	POPULATION Estimated at 5 persons per house
Atwot	Akot	Biel	Mabor Kacwol	1770
"	"	Riair	Macek Caping	1335
			Total under Mabor Kacwol	3105

Beng dit Ongwi Bol

TRIBAL GROUP	TRIBE	DIET	CHIEF	POPULATION Estimated at 5 persons per house
Atwot (Kwek)	Kwek	Nang	Ongwi Bol	695
"	"	Thiang	"	125
"	"	Yeth	"	305
"	"	Ajwot	"	760
"	"	Gwarang	"	340
"	"	Juluth	"	730
Atwot	Nue	Nue	Dak Kairjok	500
"	Dima	Dima	Makenj Ilari	705
"	Ajwong	Ajwong	Maguk Ju	760
"	Balang Joya	Balang Joya	Arouping Yak	405
			Total under Ongwi Bol	5325

Yirrol District

Beng dit Korriam Awo

TRIBAL GROUP	TRIBE	DIET	CHIEF	POPULATION Estimated at 5 persons per house
Afak	Palwal	Palwal	Korriam Awo	875
"	Awan	Akaikar	Macar Nijong	1360
"	Awan	Akot	(scattered amongst chiefs)	910
"	Apair	Apair	Majok Gang	1990
"	Acok	Acok	Jong Tong Maic	1785
"	Riair	Riair	Cok Macek	965
"	Aparair	Apairair	Lueth Magot	435
(fisherman)	Palul	Palul	Kok Kaurainyang	500
Rokaic Atwot	Kok	Kok	Gum Acek	2130
"	Paleu	Paleu	Rue Ca Aca	1395
"	Nyang	Nyang	Colel Aiyol	770
			Total under Korriam Awo	12845

Beng dit Cep Aciek

TRIBAL GROUP	TRIBE	DIET	CHIEF	POPULATION Estimated at 5 persons per house
Cic (Kwaic)	Ding	Lith	Cep Aciek	1150
"	"	Aliap	Nyiboi Ngong	675
"	"	Agok	Thuom Amok	500
"	Cirbek	Nam	Riak Manyang	1765
"	"	Alico	Caniyang Maiyan	475
"	"	Kun	Kwiarot Aciran	625
"	Jalwa	Jalwa	Jok Angwac	485
"	Nuen	Nuen	Riak Jam	505
"	Pakol	Pakol	Aceng Pwo	405
"	Jar	Jar	Mamair Majok	435
"	Ajwong	Ajwong	Akuc Kacwal	475
"	Pajak	Aliap	Kot Kanj	1055
"	"	Dikoic	Attair Aleng	345
"	"	Yom	Jieng Agarak	560
			Total under Cep Aciek	9455

Beng dit Takpin Malwal

TRIBAL GROUP	TRIBE	DIET	CHIEF	POPULATION Estimated at 5 persons per house
Cic (Ajak)	Dwaur	Dur	Takpin Malwal	1910
"	"	Alak	Deng Ajoin	1185
"	Cilik	Paiyok	Riel Makoi	855
"	"	Padiet	Awan Bolator	625
"	"	Anyon	Attair Mun	605
			Total under Takpin Malwal	5180

Beng dit Raic Amo

TRIBAL GROUP	TRIBE	DIET	CHIEF	POPULATION Estimated at 5 persons per house
Gok		Jagjuair & Bun	Raic Amo	1070
"		Ding	Matot Acinpwo	1260
"		Awan	Malwal Abongbar	915
"		Lual	Luk Acok	555
			Total under Raic Amo	3800

Beng dit Attair Bar

TRIBAL GROUP	TRIBE	DIET	CHIEF	POPULATION Estimated at 5 persons per house
Ador	Dim	Die	Acek Nuot	650
"	"	Abadan	Ut Jok	1100
"	Angaur	Angaur	Thianic Magok	670
"	Ajwot	Ajwot	Mabor Mangwanjok	700
"	Lok	Lok	Ruen Acilik	585
Gok	Abwong	Abwong	Alueth Kwaiwel	850
Ador	Ajwong	Ajwong	Kong Tong	505
			Total under Attair Bar	5060

Beng dit Abiyar Akon

TRIBAL GROUP	TRIBE	DIET	CHIEF	POPULATION Estimated at 5 persons per house
Aliab	Thiang (Nyingair)	Akwe	Abyiar Kon	2535
"	"	Biri	"	880
"	"	Niyarar	"	945
"	Thiang (Jukom)	Apuk	Kejok Cappa	2285
"	Ajwot	Angwom	"	825
"	"	Luel	Duic Cappa	1055
"	"	Akair (includes fishermen)	Acol Bol	2970
"	"	De	Acol Bol	520
"	Balok	Aken (includes fishermen)	Kenj Dut	910
"	"	Korriam (includes fishermen)	Dut Makoic	745
			Total under Abyiar Kon	13670

CHAPTER 9

Abwong District

BIMBASHI A. H. ALBAN[1]

BOUNDARIES OF THE DISTRICT

NORTHERN BOUNDARY

From Gobjak or left bank Sobat (N lat. 9° 17' E long. 31° 45') and from Bonglai or right bank Sobat (N lat. 9° 20' E long. 31° 54') along the line of the Sobat river. To Wegin or left bank Sobat (N lat. 8° 50' E long. 32° 32') and Luin or right bank Sobat (N lat. 8° 59' E long. 32° 26'). On the right bank of the river is included about 5 miles of territory to the north.

EASTERN BOUNDARY

From Wegin in a south easterly direction to Mankaith on the Khor Nyanding, thence to Yor (N lat. 8° 17' E long. 32° 55') and then south to Ful Letta and Tongadid on the Khor Tuni. From Tongadid in a SE direction to Ful Geni on Khor Geni and along the line of the khor (left bank) to Mareng on the Khor Geni.

Note. The eastern boundary is more political than geographical and it may be necessary to follow cattle camps into the Eastern and Akobo Districts by trips to the mouth of the Nyanding, along to Khor Farak to the Pibor to the Gila river mouth and to Kaibui and the junction of the Khor Kit and Geni near Akobo.

SOUTHERN BOUNDARY

From Mareng through Cor Rial on Khor Tuni to the point where old boundaries of Mongalla, Upper Nile and Pibor Military District met (N lat. 7° 46' E long. 32° 32') and thence westwards to Mankwauka, Fatitet, Juwai on the Khor Fullus.

Note. The southern boundary as defined above is purely geographical. The Lau in the dry season go well south of this (though they are not allowed to build huts there) to Biemm on the Beir border (this place is rented) and into Lang.

[1] Document dated 17 December 1930.

Abwong District

WESTERN BOUNDARY
From Juwai (or Aywai) in a NW direction through Ngit on Khor Kwanjor to a point where the line of 31° 30' E longitude is met. This line is then followed north to approx. where the line E latitude 9° 15' is met. Thence east to the Khor Fullus passing just south of Wunalong to Gobjak on the Sobat river.

DISTRIBUTION OF POPULATION

The tribes inhabiting the district are Lau Nuers (Gun and Mor sections), Ngok Dinkas, Ballak Dinkas.

The *Ngok Dinkas* live on both banks of the Sobat river from a point a few miles down stream of Kurmayom to Bonglai on the right banks and Gobjak on the left where Shilluk country begins. Inland they live along Khor Fullus as far as Wunging a few miles south of Kan, thence to Atoing on Khor Wang Nyaish thence Abwong.

Their grazing rights extend as far as Ful Bwoa 8 miles N of Nyerol. Thence W to Fanyangluel on Khor Fullus thence due west. From Ful Bwoa roughly in a NW direction to the Sobat river W of Kurmayom.[2]

The *Ballak Dinkas* inhabit a few villages on both banks of the Sobat from Kurmayom (Nuer village) upstream to about Wegin. On the right bank they do not go beyond Khor Luin.

The *Lau Nuers* inhabit the whole of the rest of the district, the greater number being contained within a circle of 30 miles diameter from Mwot Tot as a centre.

The rough boundary between Gun and Mor is Waat[3] on the Fathai-Akobo road.

The Mor live to the east of this point, their main centre being Faddoi, and most of their villages are to east of Khor Thul.

The pyramid[4] is Gun Lau country.

One section of Gun live at Kurmayom on the Sobat.

The figures of population are:

---

[2] Kurmayom was the site where E. E. Evans-Pritchard carried out part of his research in 1931.
[3] Chosen in 1946 as the site for a sub-district (subsequently district) headquarters.
[4] Ngundeng's Mound, destroyed by the army in 1928; see McMeekan (1929) and Johnson (1990).

Lau Nuer

	Men	Women	Boys	Girls	Total
Gun Lau	2859	2405	1180	887	7331
Gun Lau (3 shyengs from Duk)	1403				5612
Mor Lau	1732	1627	1420	1303	6082
Total Lau	5994				19025

Note: Gun Lau and Mor Lau figures from census during Nuer Settlement 1929 & 1930. Of these the Mor Lau is the more accurate as the people were actually seen. The Gun Lau figures were rechecked in 1930.

I have put the 3 Gun shyengs which I took over from Duk separately as the women and children were not counted in 1929. The total has been obtained by multiplying the men by 4. I do not know yet how many from these people who claimed to be Dinka remained behind in Duk District.

Dinka

	Men	Women	Boys	Girls	Total
Ngok	2457	1625	1273	1201	6556
Ballak	138	81	83	91	393
Chief Kuth Mayan	41	25	14	17	97

Note: All counted this year

I have included amongst the Ngok any Jweir (Dinka who originally fled here from Duk District) who are remaining here. Chief Kuth Mayan's people are mixed Dinka-Jekaing.

GENERAL TRIBAL ORGANIZATION

Lau Nuers

The tribal organization consists of sub-shyeng or family divisions divided between 20 main shyengs, each shyeng of which belongs either to the Gun or Mor section of the tribe.

The 20 main shyengs are

Gun Lau
1. Falkir
2. Matel
3. Nya Jekaing
4. Dung ⎱ related
5. Dul ⎰
6. Kwaijien
7. Maikeirr

Known collectively as shyeng Rumjok (live in S of district)

8. Shish [Cic] (with sub-sh. Lam)
9. Yuwong (with sub-sh. Manttiep)
10. Lang
11. Thiang
12. Machok

Known collectively as sh. Gadbal & sometimes Yuol (live in N of district)

Mor Lau
13. Jemaic ⎱ related
14. Garliek ⎰

15. Jegar
16. Can Known collectively as sh. Niang [Nyang]
17. Bul

18. Buth
19. Kun Known collectively as sh. Yol
20. Belyu

The sub-shyengs are some 80 in number and each have a chief of their own. These chiefs in the past only listened to a fighting chief who would lead them in war, or to a kujur like Gwek whom they were afraid of. In some cases they live in country occupied by some other main shyeng having broken away owing to a feud or some other cause. The small sub-shyeng and individual feuds are too numerous to keep trace of, but of those that exist between large shyengs the following are known and if not stopped when they break out might cause trouble.

Shyengs	Shish & Yuwong	Shyengs	Lang & Thiang	Gun
	Falkir		Nya Jekaing	"
	Buth		Niang	Mor
	Jemaic (2 sections)		Jemaic (2 sections)	"

The present policy is to keep the sub-shyengs under the main shyeng to which they belong, bring others back who have fled away and to try and produce one head chief from each main shyeng who would be responsible for it. Each chief has his own chief police to assist him. This was begun on Nuer Settlement when the census which was taken showed where every man was and force was available to shift them. Much still remains to be done.

The Mor Lau, who were supposed to be less amenable than the Gun, are in fact much more so. They also have more chiefs of calibre than the Gun. I ascribe this to the fact that partly the Gun chiefs were overshadowed in the past by Gwek and his father Wondeng [Ngundeng] the kujur and secondly they live near to the Dinka and the government both of which have been their natural enemies.

When mention is made of moving people back to their shyengs this means wet season villages (permanent) only. In the dry season in the scramble for water and grazing they can go where they like provided that the chiefs know where their men are.

In this connection it is important to know the configuration of the country and their mode of life. Except for the Nyanding, Lang country and parts of Thul and Fullus water courses, the country consist of a vast treeless cotton soil plain. In the rains most of the country is practically under water and in the dry season with the exception of the main khors, the only drinking supply is in muddy fulas scattered about the country. At the end of the rains (about December) the villages are left deserted except for a few old women to look after the dura, and people and cattle move off in search of water and grazing. At this time of the year there are many rain water pools in the forest. Small bee hived shaped huts of grass are built in a circle and the cattle are tethered to pegs in the centre. Fruit of the heglig trees, milk, dura from villages (if sufficient) and fish (not abundant as the water is still too high for spearing) keeps them alive during this time. About January they burn off the grass near the main watering places on the main perennial fulas, Nyerol, Faddoi, Mwot Tot, Mwot Did, Fadding, Ful Geni etc. and by about February 15th (when the inland pools are dry) move to these places where they remain until the rains are sufficient to return to their villages.

In these big fulas the fish are abundant and by that time of course they are unlikely to have any grain left except for sowing.

Should the year be very dry (such as this year) they are forced further afield, on to the Sobat, mouth of the Nyanding, Pibor, Gila etc.

After the first rains (end of April) as soon as there is enough water near their villages for the cattle, they return there, though people go ahead to start cultivating.

They plant dura (bel wic) which ripens about July. the head is then cut off, some of this dura is sown among the same crop and this and regrowth from the cut off plants forms their second crop (bel pan) which ripens about December.

In bad years many of them go to friends and relatives in Jekaing or amongst Ngok Dinka and cultivate as the land is better there. They also buy dura from these people for goats and cattle. This year was a good year which means that they will have just enough for their own consumption, as their areas of cultivation are small, partly owing to the physical features of the country, partly owing to their disinclination for this work.

On the other hand as regards grazing for their cattle they are most particular and would never think of settling at a place, however good the soil for crops, or the water if it lacked the sort of grass they require. This forms an obstacle to settling them on places where they might be beyond the reach of continual famine, and moving about to look for water.

Ngok Dinka

Consists of 2 main divisions, 10 sections, and 34 headmen:

Sections

1. Ngan	
2. Abi	
3. Deng	
4. Achak	Division of Jok
5. Adong	
6. Ajuba	
7. Baliet	
8. Awir	Division of Yom
9. Dud	
10. Diak	
Thoi (chief Diu Ngor[5])	

These people give no trouble whatever except for their innumerable cases, and petty wrangles between chiefs.

They suffer from a plethora of chiefs.

Each chief has chiefs' police to help him.

Deng Mayan of section Baliet used to be their paramount chief. He was murdered by one of the Ter Akwr [Ater Kur] family (another chief of the same section), who thought they ought to be paramount. His son Riak Deng is coming on very well, and should be able to take charge of them in a few years.

The Ngok are good agriculturalists, grow large crops of dura and pay their taxes punctually in cash. They are settled on permanent water in good dura growing land and own quite a fair number of cattle. They do not

---

[5] Written in the ms as 'Din Ngon'.

migrate like the Lau but some of them send their cattle to dry water camps on the Khor Fullus, where the grazing is better than in their own country.

Ballak Dinka

These people have 5 chiefs, all useless except one,[6] whom I intend to put the others under. They do chiefs' courts with the Ngok. They are a poor tribe who live mostly by fishing, own few cattle and do little agriculture. From an administrative point of view they cause trouble by always mixing themselves up with the Jekaing Nuers, and having trouble with them over fishing and grazing rights.[7]

INCIDENTS OF IMPORTANCE IN RECENT HISTORY[8]

Previous to the present government the only record of any penetration of the Lau Nuer country is that during the lifetime of the kujur Wondeng Bung [Ngundeng Bong] (father of Gwek) who died in 1906, some Turuk (possibly slave raiders) coming from the Sobat raided the Pyramid and carried off a quantity of ivory with which the base and apex of it was adorned.[9]

Oct. 1901	Lau raid the Khor Fullus Dinka.[10]
April 1902	Patrol against the Lau. Blewitt Bey with Bimb. Wilson and Crispin and 160 men of the 10th Sudanese went up the Fullus to the Pyramid, where the Nuers put up a fair fight.[11]
April 1904	The Ngok Dinkas refused to pay taxes (under chief Deng

---

[6] Probably Deng Aiwel Agot, whom Coriat recommended as 'a determined fellow with influence over the others, none of whom are worth calling Chiefs' (Coriat (1993: 73)).
[7] Coriat made the same complaint when handing over the district to Alban in 1929 (ibid.).
[8] This section is based mainly on reports in past issues of the *Sudan Intelligence Report* and Coriat's official reports on Guek and the Nuer Settlement (Coriat (1993: documents 3.2 and 3.3)). It shows how early, and how completely, the distortions of the official history of government-Nuer relations had set in, recasting events which were then still vivid in the memories of the Nuer, but already hazy in the minds of administrators, in a way which fully justified the Nuer Settlement and the suppression of the prophets.
[9] The raid by 'slave raiders' (a claim first made by Coriat (1993: 110)) was in fact the 1902 government patrol under the command of governor Blewitt (Johnson (1982c)).
[10] 'The Nuers from Deng Kurs village made an unsuccessful raid on the Dinkas at Khor Filus on 26th September.' (*SIR* 87 (October 1901): 3). There was later some question about whether a raid ever took place. The Khor Fullus Dinka chiefs were imprisoned in 1904 for manufacturing complaints against Ngundeng and instigating the government patrol of 1902.
[11] According to both the official report and Nuer testimony Ngundeng evaded the patrol and no fight took place at his Mound. The patrol reported only two or three 'demonstrations' by Nuer at Muot Did, where they tried to prevent troops from seizing their cattle. See Johnson (1982c; 1994: 117-8).

1905	Mayan). Wilson Bey reports that the Lau must be subdued before any attempt of administration be made.[12] Post established at Abwong to administer the Ngok, Jweir, Ballak, and Rueng Dinkas. Wilson Bey and Mr. Dupuis (inspector of Irrigation) went from mouth of Khor Fullus to Bor. Report Nuer friendly but irritated by Dinka treachery and lies.[13]
August 1906	O'Sullivan Bey goes to the Pyramid and thence to the Pibor and was well received. Death of Wondeng Bung (or Dengkur) the big Lau witch doctor and creator of the Pyramid.[14]
1911	First administrative patrol in Lau by Miralai? [Kaimakam H. D. E. O'Sullivan] governor of UNP, and Mr. A. J .C. Huddleston, inspector Sobat Valley. They did not go far inland and collected 1 1/2% tribute of mature cattle from any camp they came across. They collected 145 h/c from 9 Lau shyengs. Mr. Huddleston compiled a list of sections of Lau.

These tribute collecting patrols went on for the next few years until, as the influx of rifles from Abyssinia increased, the Lau became reluctant to pay tribute or to hold any friendly relation with government.

In 1911 before the Lau rifles, a small band of Anuaks from the Pibor river, armed with rifles, practically overran the Lau country.[15]

---

[12] Wilson reported about the Ngok: 'The position at the present moment is that Gnok have during my absence in the Rueng district made no attempt to pay their tax, and Deng-Maiung simply told the police officer that he could not pay it. I have started off several of the village Sheikhs to get their tax without reference to the head Sheikh, but I think it is advisable to show the Gnok Dinkas that the Government intends to have the tax paid without further delay. . . . I do not think that there should be much delay or trouble in collecting the Gnok tax . . . ' About the Lou he recommended, 'that any attempt to take in hand the administration of the Nuer country on the Sobat and Pibor rivers before the heart of the Nuer country in Lao has been brought under control would be premature, and only lead to disappointment and failure, and a waste of energy and money. . . . Once the root of the Nuer opposition to the Government has been removed, the various outlying sections of the tribe, which come geographically into touch with the Government, will probably be found to be amenable to control. To work *vice versa* is, I am sure, unsound.' (H. H. Wilson, 'Report on the Situation in the Sobat Valley', Appendix A, *SIR* 117 (April 1904): 8–9).

[13] It was on this march that Wilson met the Gaawar prophet Deng Laka and learned from Nuer as well as Dinka sources that Ngundeng did not sanction any raiding by the Lou. ('Report by El Kaimakam H. H. Wilson Bey on a March from the Sobat (Mouth of the Filus) to Bor', Appendix A, *SIR* 128 (March 1905): 5–9).

[14] H. D. E. O'Sullivan was sent to confirm reports of Ngundeng's death (O'Sullivan, 'Lau Nuers', 13 March 1906, NRO Dakhlia I 112/13/87).

[15] It was partly the government's failure to provide effective protection against Anuak raids, while insisting on the collection of cattle tribute (increasingly by force), which contributed to the estrangement between the Nuer and the government at this time (Johnson (1982a: 195; 1986b: 223–4)).

Chapter 9

1914	The Lau combined with other Nuers and attacked the Anuaks at Akobo post, and a little later talked of attacking Akobo post itself, but after collecting to do so they eventually dispersed.[16]
1915–16	The Lau give trouble by attacking and raiding tax paying Dinkas, both south and north. They also wiped out a small party of the 9th Sudanese who were sent to check a raid near Bor. This brought on the Lau patrol in 1917.[17]
1917	This patrol (under Major Bayly) marched to Faddoi where they encountered 600 of the enemy. They inflicted 100 casualties and captured 16. They also brought away 4–5000 cattle 3000 sheep and goats and 14 rifles. Gwek Wondeng the kujur (son of Wondeng Dengkur), who was said to have directed the attack on the 9th Sudanese, they failed to catch.[18]
May 1917	An attempt was then made to administer the Lau and a post was formed at Nyerol under Bimbashi Godwin with 1 Coy Sudanese. Abwong was used as a base for supplies. They had such a bad time with exceptional floods during this year and difficulties with carriers transport that the post was given up in 1918 [see Struvé's comments in Appendix 1].
	For the next few years the administration of Lau was limited.
1921	Following reports of Gwek's anti-government activities a visit was paid to Dengkur by the then deputy governor of the province [H. C. Jackson] who reported that he had been able to influence Gwek in the right direction and had left the kujur in an attitude entirely friendly to government. At the same time he appointed a half brother Bul Wondeng [Bol Ngundeng] as government chief to represent Gwek in matters affecting his own sub-shyeng and shyeng Shish.[19]

[16] There was fighting between Nuer and Anuak cattle camps reported in January 1914. In April 1914 the Lou, Gaajok and Gaajak combined to attack the Anuak near Akobo, driving them back to the walls of the government fort. The troops opened fire on the Nuer to force them to withdraw. The Nuer attack on the Anuak was later described as pre-emptive, intended to forestall Anuak raids during the forthcoming rainy season (*SIR* 237 (April 1914): 5).

[17] The 1916 raid, in which the Sudanese soldiers were killed, is said by Lou to have been in response to what they claimed to have been an unfair fine of cattle taken off them and awarded to the Dinka by Bor District officials (Johnson (1994: 170)).

[18] For figures see *SIR* 272 & 273 (March & April 1917): 2 & 3. In fact it was Pok Kerjiok who was the target of the patrol. Guek Ngundeng took no leading part in these events, and did not even claim seizure by the divinity DENG until 1918 or 1919 (Johnson (1994: 170–4)).

[19] 1921 was the first year that Guek's name came to government attention. Jackson reported that the reports of Guek's 'anti-government activities' were entirely false (Johnson (1994: 177)).

Abwong District

1922	Reports of disturbances in Lau and rumours of Gwek's activities came to nothing.
1923	Mr. Coriat transferred from Ayod, where he was DC Gaweir, to Abwong and instructed to include the Lau in his administration. He was given a mamur to help him. Owing to the size of the district the Gaweir were taken away in 1927 [1926] and came under DC Fangak. The district remaining as it is at present. The mamur was withdrawn on Mr. Coriat's arrival he found that many of the existing shyengs had not been registered and a proportion of those listed were inaccurate. The majority of so-called chiefs had either been appointed by government in the past or were produced by the shyengs as their leaders. In most cases they were old and decrepit or of the type of tribesmen to be found loitering around a government post for what he can pick up. The people of influence were not forthcoming in dealings with the government. He visited Gwek at the Pyramid and informed him that he was a sub-chief and expected to deal directly with the government (Bul, now political prisoner at Abwong, was then acting). Gwek demurred as he said he was only able to leave his home at the behest of kujur. However he carried out his section duties and visited Abwong in 1925 & 1926. Mr. Coriat hoped if he was successful to be able to appoint him head of shyeng Shish and perhaps all Gun Lau. In 1926 he appeared friendly and harmless.[20]
1927	Chiefs' courts, chiefs' police and roads were now started. In May 1927 at a meeting of Lau chiefs to settle work on the roads, Gwek appeared with a following and objected to the road making. He went off with his following singing lustily.

Later he did not appear at Abwong to meet the governor general and stopped a party of Mor chiefs on their way there. Chiefs of 3 Gun shyengs also did not appear.

On the return of the DC from leave he found the road not made, definite resistance to government by shyengs Falkir, Nya Jekaing, Yuwong and Shish and Gwek's section and that the greater number of section chiefs failed to put in an appearance. Also that Gwek had spread numerous

---

[20] This section, and the section on 1927, summarize information in Coriat (1993: document 3.2).

1928

1929

prophecies about the day arriving when the Turk power was to be thrown off and Dinka raiding begin again, etc. etc.[21] This brought the Lau Nuer patrol S8. A column marched to the Pyramid and blew it up, or the top of it, but failed to catch Gwek, and in fact saw few Nuers. It became obvious that slow moving column of infantry were not suitable for rounding up Nuers who move very fast their cattle.

It however showed that the government was stronger than any kujur.

After the patrol, Gwek fled to Jekaing country at Faweng on the Sobat where he has [maternal] relatives. In August he returned to the Pyramid, built himself 2 huts. He also started again his prophecies about the downfall of the Turk. About this time the attack by Dwal Diu (Gaweir) on Duk Faywil post and the Dinkas took place. The DC was then in Khartoum with a party of 49 Lau Nuer and Dinka chiefs. Dwal had sent messages to the Lau to join him and Gwek endeavoured to get them to do so. Although the chiefs were away he failed in his object. Chief Ding Twil of shyeng Falkir taking a prominent part in stopping him. Certain of the Lau as individuals however joined in.[22]

This brought on 'Nuer Settlement', which was a break away from patrols as known in the past in that (a) It was applied to the whole of the Lau and Gaweir. (b) People were concentrated into areas and a drive by mounted troops took place out of all the country outside. Those who were outside were therefore known to be hostile, those inside could be sorted out at leisure and the guilt brought home to the actual individuals required. Nor could people dodge about from Gaweir to Lau and vice versa. (c) The operations were controlled by the political officers [i.e. the DCs]. (d) A programme of road making, sorting people out into their respective shyengs and making them move there, a census, medical work and other normal administrative duties. (e) In addition as regards this district the moving of all the Nuer in Duk District (3 Gun shyengs) into this

---

[21] Only one such prophecy was reported at the time. For the subsequent life of this prophecy see Johnson (1985b; 1994: 339–47).

[22] For accounts of events in 1928–30 see: Coriat (1939; 1993: 108–48); McMeekan (1929); Johnson (1979; 1994: chs. 5 & 6).

district and the repatriation of certain Dinka (Jweir) back from this district to their original homes near Duk.

On February 8th Gwek gave battle at the Pyramid and was killed together with 3 other witch doctors and chief Lig Lig Kuin [Liglig Kuny] (Sh. Thiang) and 13 Nuer. The Gun Lau concentrated well in their area near Mwot Did, were censused and counted out.

The Mor Lau who were to concentrate near Wegin on the Sobat failed to do so properly, owing partly to their ignorance of government and partly to its being far away from them.

A motor road, graded, was made from Khor Fullus mouth to Mwot Did, and a causeway constructed at Lior about a mile in length. Through motor road communication was established to Bor. All cattle captured were returned to Dinkas as compensation. Hostages were taken from both Gun and Mor, for their good behaviour during the rains, and sent to Malakal. The 3 Gun shyengs from Duk were not moved owing to lack of time for them to build. During this period Capt. Alban took over from Mr. Coriat as DC.

1930　Mor Lau were ordered to concentrate again, at Kaibui or Khor Geni. Also to hish [Arab.—'to weed', i.e. to clear of grass] a road from Fathai to Akobo.

Gun Lau under normal administration.

The hostages were sent to Akobo, and thence to the base camp at Kaibui where they were employed on building a ramp across the Khor.

As a condition of their release two wanted kujurs, Pok Kerjok and Char Koriom both of Gun Lau were first to be brought in.

The concentration was delayed by an outbreak of smallpox of a mild variety which swept through the whole of Lau. However, apart from immunising them in the future, this turned out not to be a disadvantage, as it gave them time to make the road, and to become familiar with the government. As a result when required they concentrated with extreme rapidity and almost to a man, and showed a very friendly feeling.

Pok and Char were not given up as family ties amongst the Nuer are very wide and very strong, but pressure was brought to bear on them and they both gave themselves up.[23]

---

[23] For Coriat's evaluation of Pok Kerjiok after his surrender, see Coriat (1993: 151).

In Gun Lau, the chiefs' courts functioned well. The motor road was regraded by the PWD and a dry season's station built at Fathai.

The 3 Gun shyengs from Duk (Maikeirr, Dung, and Kwaijien) were moved out into this district, north of a line Yuwai, Fatitet, Mankwauka.

The causeway at Lior was increased in height and another causeway over the Khor Fullus built at Fathai, for the Akobo road.

Communication by car was established with Akobo over an ungraded road.

The Mor Lau were properly censused and the Gun Lau lists rechecked. Tribute was re-assessed on the basis of numbers. Chiefs' police were appointed and boys for hospital dressers obtained.

During the rains all the chiefs have been in Abwong and seem to like coming in.

Everything possible is done to look after them. It must be remembered that one of the difficulties of administering the Lau is that Abwong is in Dinka country and very far away from them.

No trouble was experienced in getting the roads hished in November and December.

REVENUE

Lau Nuers

1923	83 bulls	
1928	157 "	
1929	161 "	valued at £2.500 each
1930	153 "	" " " " "
	69 "	" " " " " (From 3 shyengs transferred from Duk Dist.)

These people are on a tribute basis. They were supposed in the past to be assessed on their cattle, at a rate increasing from 1/2% to 2%. When Mr. Coriat came here in 1923 the tribute was 83 bulls.[24] Many of the shyengs were not listed and very little knowledge of how many cattle they

---

[24] Though cattle tribute figures are invariably given in numbers of bulls, the majority of animals taken in tribute were actually oxen.

possessed existed. However it was gradually worked up to somewhere near what it is now. The value of the animals raised from year to year according to the market price, and so did the assessment of each shyeng, not because their cattle increased or diminished as in practice over such a vast area, and with the habits of the tribes and means of the DC's disposal, apart from the political troubles, he could not see half their cattle. The assessment really varied on whether a shyeng was troublesome or not. If it was it paid more, as they cause trouble to get. Also shyengs furthest away from the merkaz were assessed higher so as to make up for the past when the ones nearest, being naturally an easy prey always had to pay, while the others got off scot free.

Taking the figures from Nuer Settlement I reassessed all the shyengs on the basis of 10 Pt per grown up male (for example a shyeng of 200 adult males at 10 Pt = £20. Turning this into bulls at £2.500 per bull, which is my standard price for the cattle account, they would be assessed at 8 bulls). The advantage of this is that the revenue is now on an understandable basis, and not subject to wide fluctuations. The assessment is light, and when the time comes for them to pay in cash or go on a poll tax as they must soon, there will be no revolution either in their minds or those of the Finance Department.

The chiefs received 10% tribute remuneration this year for the first time and were highly gratified. I have not re-arranged the assessment for the 3 Gun shyengs taken over from Duk yet.

Dinkas

	1928	1929	1930	
1. Ngok	355.130	361.400	366.700	
2. Ballak	–	24.900	22.500	(includes chief Kuth Mayan)
3. Jweir	–	87.850	22.000	(chief Diu Ngor only who is remaining)

Note: In 1930 the bulk of the Jweir were transferred to Duk District. Those who have remained will in future be classed as Ngok.

These people were originally assessed in cattle, and in 1924 started to pay cash. They actually collect cash from the people who paid the cattle. For instance some people who used to own cattle, since dead or dispersed, still go on paying the same. Until a census was made it was impossible to work anything out. I have just completed one (see Population Figures). Taking the figure of adult males and putting the Ngok and Jweir on a 20 Pt basis, and the Ballak, who are poor, on 10 Pt, the revenue would be for

Ngok and Jweir £491 instead of £389 this year. The Ngok and Jweir grow large crops of dura, for which they obtain a good price, and 20 Pt poll tax would not press on them. 10 Pt for the Ballak and chief Kuth Mayan would produce £18 instead of £22.500 as at present.

ROADS, BANK, WELLS, FERRIES

Main roads

Malakal-Bor Road

From 5 miles S of Khor Fullus mouth, to boundary of Duk District. Length 120 miles. Graded to Mwot Did in 1929 by SDF. Graded Malakal-Bor in 1930 by PWD.

Fathai-Akobo Road

Length 106 miles.

Malakal-Nasser Road (Made by Egyptian Irrigation Dept.)

From boundary with Shilluk District to my boundary with Nasser District. Length about 65 miles. Graded in 1930.

Country Road

ABWONG-NYEROL ROAD
Length 38 miles.

ROAD ALONG S BANK OF SOBAT FROM KHOR FULLUS MOUTH TO WEGIN
Length about 70 miles. This is more a track for the nas and is kept up rather sketchily at the ends. From Abwong 30 miles in either direction it has a good motorable surface.

Banks

Lior. On main road Malakal-Bor, over Khor Lior. Length about 1 mile. Height about 4 ft. 4 culverts.

Fathai. On main road Fathai-Akobo, over Khor Fullus. Length 530 yards. Height about 3 ft. 2 culverts.

Kaibui. On main road Fathai-Akobo, over Khor Geni. Length 300 yards. Height about 15 ft. 5 culverts.

Wells

There are no permanent wells in this district. In the dry season holes are dug in the beds of Khors in innumerable places.

Ferries

One at Abwong, which can take a Ford lorry (now in use at Khor Fullus mouth).

ECONOMIC DEVOLUTION

The Ngok grow good crops of dura, and sell it freely. Theirs is not a good cattle country. As regards the Lau, their future lies in their cattle. They are unwilling to dispose of them, as their whole social life is bound up in them. It would appear that their means of obtaining cash in the future lies in their cattle producing more milk and the surplus being disposed of in the form of semn [Arab., *samn*, clarified butter]. Grazing is unlimited and good, and the country can hold many more cattle than it does. However the breeding up of cattle should go hand in hand with the inoculation of stock to prevent the ravages of disease like rinderpest and pleuro-pneumonia, which sweep through the country every few years and decimate the cattle.

Two half bred Friesian bulls were sent to this district for breeding up purposes, but both died. These animals are very delicate and require more attention than the DC is able to give. However several cows have been covered and their progeny may turn out a success.[25] Combined with a selection of native cows on their milk records it should be possible to produce better milking animals. Native boys able to keep milk records are not yet available in this district, but soon will be.

Agriculture

The Dinka grow maize as their first crop, and dura (white tall variety, called Ajak) as their second and main crop. This ripens about January. It is very good dura. An experimental plot was started by Agriculture Dept. at

---

[25] Only one Friesian was still alive when Alban took over the district in May 1929. It was used to upgrade the station herd at Abwong only (Coriat (1993: 74)).

Fathai this year and grew many varieties of dura, but this sort (or kind very close to it) did the best.

Bufra (manioc) was also planted and has done well, but it has not yet stood a dry season.[26]

The Nuers grow 2 sorts of dura, one red and one white and short in the stem. It is all planted together in 2 crops. The first (bel wic) about April, the second (bel pan) when the first crop ripens about July, on the same ground and among the stalks of the first crop which also grows again. They are beginning to plant the Dinka variety of Ajak.[27]

A little tobacco, beans are grown by both tribes.

BUILDINGS

DC's house and kitchen Office (combined with guard room & prison) Dispensary AMO's house	Kept by PWD
4 tukls DC's servants Sarraf's house and tukls Dura stores 12 police tukls 3 cattle luaks 2 tukls hospital out patient or tumargis Stable for DC's and govt. animals 4 tukls grooms Tukl for motor driver and women prisoner cook Tukls for servants AMO's house	out of Mud Buildings
Chiefs' court house Tukls for chiefs and chiefs' police	out of Devolution

1 namlia for use of Veterinary Dept. & servant's tukl.

(There are also 4 namlias at Fathai and 2 at Kaibui).

FORESTRY

Higlig [*Balanites ægyptiaca*; Tau in Dinka and Nuer] is the principal tree in this district. There are no forests, but trees occur in favourable places, such as Nyerol, along Khor Fullus, in Lang country and Khor Thul.

[26] Manioc did not thrive in the Upper Nile.
[27] For *Ajak* (or *jak* in Nuer) see above, ch. 2, n. 41.

I have planted some giant bamboo at Abwong obtained from the Mission at Doleib Hill and if it is a success can extend it along the Sobat.

I intend to try teak at Nyerol, but doubt if the rainfall is sufficient in this district, apart from the soil.

SUNDRY

Gardens

At Abwong there is a vegetable garden on the river bank watered by cans, and a tree garden just below the DC's house 200 x from the river (lemon, paw paws, etc.) watered by a hydro hoist pump in the dry weather, and rainfall in the wet. The pump is an old type and very inefficient and the water is obtained not from the river but from an inland Khor parallel to and just behind the river bank. It dries up in January and February and land watering has to be resorted to.

If a petrol pump* was obtained and installed on the river there is quite a large area that could be irrigated as Abwong is on a long ridge which slopes down to the river. [*I don't think it could cover expenses.] Bananas grow on the river bank, but do badly owing to the strong North wind. A few hundred yards up stream from the Meshra there is an island on which excellent water melons are grown in the dry season.

Merkaz cattle

Abwong has a good herd of selected cattle. The receipts from milk come to about £60 a year and go to LPS. I have a separator and hand churns and have trained certain boys to produce butter. There are 3 good cattle luaks and good standings. In the dry season they graze on the opposite bank of the river, where there is a khor running inland.

Other animals

There is a herd of pigs about 20 in number, which seem to do well. They are rapidly increasing.

Horses and mules do well at Abwong, as owing to its being a sandy dubba, it has good drainage and dries directly after rain. Also the wind and absence of grass in the station keeps mosquitoes down.

There is a good brick stable, mosquito proof.

Local boys

4 employed as servants of DC
7   "   " mule syce by DC
1   "   "   "   " government
20 trained as hospital dressers
12 cattle men[28]
4 gardeners and ferrymen
1 motor driver[29]

Every effort is made to try and get as many local boys as possible especially Nuers in to the station. The station herd is essential for this. About 2/3 of the above are Nuer, and the remainder Dinkas. Starting rate of pay 10 Pt a month and dura. No one gets more than 60 Pt. They are made to run their own show as much as possible.

Merchants

22 in the district, of whom 4 at Abwong. Not more than 2 merchants are allowed in one place, and they do not move about but remain there. If they want to shut up shop in the rains they go to Malakal or Khartoum, but are not allowed to come to Abwong. This prevents Abwong from being turned into a gallaba village.

These merchants are all along the Sobat and Khor Fullus, buy their grain from the Dinkas and sell it at Malakal.

The Dinkas are pretty wide awake as to the price. In general it is bought at 2 Pt the ruba, which is fairly high, the price being based on Malakal which is quite close.

In Lau I have established 1 merchant at Fathai, and hope to establish one at Nyerol.

Transport is the difficulty there. During Nuer Settlement use was made of the SDF lorries, and a great deal of surplus grain was sold to the Nuers for cash, and for bulls, which were required for [anti-rinderpest] serum.

The Fathai merchant has got a Ford lorry this year and I am helping him in every way I can. He has also a shop at Kaan on the Khor Fullus road, a useful stopping place on the way up to Lau, and a good centre for dura.

---

[28] 'The Herdsmen are all Tribal and are never allowed to wear clothes' (Coriat (1993: 74)).
[29] Pok Makeir, son of the Ngok Dinka chief Makeir Amoryal (Coriat (1993: 70)).

Cost of building etc.

An ordinary grass tukl £1 to £2 according to size. Cattle luak £4 to £5.

A chief or chiefs is given a tukl to build and makes his own arrangements.

A local thatcher by name Leim Cwol does every work for us. Bricks can be made at Abwong but the difficulty is to get the firewood. It is better to get them from Nasser.

Nyakia, a Shilluk political prisoner, and his 2 boys can build brick edifices (cement etc.) and the 2 boys know how to make and bake bricks, so if a suitable place can be found they can go and make them there, when required. Fadl Mula Jak, one of the merchants, is a very handy man at carpentering or any odd job. He also does all the sewing of clothes for the merkaz police etc. Good sand can be obtained quite close to Abwong (at entrance to Khor Wang Nyaish) at any time of the year as it is dug out of the bank.

Province police

12 of the Southern type who came this year.

Give no trouble, but their wives (Zande and Atwot Dinka) need to be dealt with firmly.

These police are never allowed out of the station except by order of DC and their principal work is to look after prisoners.

Interpreter

Mayan Lam, Nuer, son of chief Lam Tutiang [Tutthiang] who was chief of shyeng Maikeirr and a big man in his day. This chief was deposed many years ago as he was a thorn in the side of the Dinkas near Duk. He now lives at Deeny near Abwong.[30] Mayan is a very good interpreter as Mr Coriat had him as a small boy. He can be relied on to speak the truth, knows all the past history of the district and in addition has influence over the people. Goes to school at Nasser and can read and write.

---

[30] Died in 1931; his mortuary ceremony is described in Evans-Pritchard (1949) and (1956: 147–53).

Chiefs' court clerk

At present I borrow one from Nasser Mission for the dry season. I have two small boys there but they will not be fit for this work for some time.[31] The best teachers at the Mission are Gun & Mor Lau but have been there for years.

Classified officials

I have normally: 1 sarraf, 1 dispensary hakim.

---

[31] The ms. has 'no small boys', but this is clearly a misprint. One of the boys at the Mission at this time was Dak Dei, who had been taken hostage by the government in about 1927 to force his father to appear at court when wanted for homicide. There being no where else to put Dak, he was sent to Nasir. By the time his father was caught and his case tried, Dak had decided he wanted to stay in school. By virtue of this education, and subsequent administrative experience in the 1940s, Dak Dei was one of the few Southerners eligible to enter politics after 1947, eventually being elected to the House of Representatives and serving as a minister in the pre-independence and first independent governments. He died in Malakal in 1976 and was buried in Nasir.

CHAPTER 10

Zeraf Valley District

H. G. WEDDERBURN-MAXWELL[1]

BOUNDARIES OF THE DISTRICT

NORTH BOUNDARY. From Zeraf mouth along right bank of White Nile to Lake No.
WEST BOUNDARY. From Lake No along right bank of Bahr el Jebel to pole 325 (lat. 7° 30′ north).
SOUTH BOUNDARY. The old Upper Nile-Mongalla Province boundary from pole 325 to a point lat. 7° 50′ north, long. 31° 30′ east.
EASTERN BOUNDARY. Along eastern edge of Duk 'Ridge' Fula Gwer inclusive (lat. 8° 38′ north, long. 31° 20′ east) thence along Khor Atar inclusive to lat. 8° 14′ north long. 31° 6′ east; thence along straight line through Jebel Zeraf produced to meet khor 2 1/2 miles to north of jebel; thence along south bank of this khor to Zeraf river and thence along left bank of Zeraf to its mouth.
Note: The Shilluk are peacefully penetrating along both banks of the Zeraf as far as kilo 10 from Zeraf mouth but no objection has been raised as the country is uninhabited. They have been told that they are only allowed there on sufferance.[2]

The eastern boundary is rather vague and no reason has yet arisen for its demarcation.

The southern boundary has been temporarily modified by the creation of a no man's land, whose north boundary runs through Ayod on the Duk 'Ridge' thence through Awoi telephone post straight to the river Zeraf.

DISTRIBUTION OF POPULATION

(Note: The Zeraf Island is the country surrounded by the rivers Zeraf, White Nile and Bahr el Jebel. Distances from the Zeraf mouth are marked

---

[1] Document dated 11 January 1931.
[2] Shilluk encroachments into Nuer and Dinka territory between the Zeraf and Khor Fullus were a regular administrative problem (Coriat (1993: document 1.5); Howell (1941)), and continued after independence.

by iron poles at intervals of 5 kilos, pole no. 1 being 5 kilos from river mouth and so on.)

The Lak Nuer occupy that part of the Zeraf Island which lies north of lat. 9° 2'. A few of shen Nyawar have built on the right bank of the Zeraf at lat. 9° 4'. The Lak are being listed this year. Their population should be about 18,000.

The Tiang Nuer occupy Zeraf Island south of the Lak. Their southern boundary is lat. 8° 41'. One sub-shen lives on the opposite side of the Zeraf about 8 miles east of kilo 90. The Tiang were listed last year. Their population is 7750.

The Gaweir occupy the rest of the district, on both sides of the Zeraf. They were listed last year and their population is 18,000.

The Dinka form a few small scattered communities at Fangak, Fulfam, Alam and Luang Deng. These have been listed and their population is 1360. They are the remains of the original inhabitants of the district and all talk Nuer.

GENERAL TRIBAL ORGANIZATION

The Lak, Tiang, and Gaweir are distinct clans of Nuer, and are divided into shens and sub-shens.[3] There are 150 sub-shens in the district, and most of them have a chief of their own. The population of a sub-shen varies from 1300 to 80. In some cases the chief of a shen acts as head chief of a group of sub-shens, but paramount chiefs have not been appointed. The chiefs are assisted by 170 chiefs' policemen. It is hoped to reduce the number of chiefs with whom the DC has to deal to 30 or 40.

Shens and sub-shens are usually called after an ancestor, but are in fact always in a fluid state; an outstanding personality will gather a large following, and many men will leave their sub-shen (and even tribe) on marriage and settle with their wife's people.

About 30 chiefs' dressers have been appointed. At first it was a case of taking what one could get. Eventually they will be employed one to each group of sub-shens. They are trained by the sanitary hakim and are under their chief for discipline. So far they have been the only source from which clerks can be recruited.

---

[3] Prior to the publication of Evans-Pritchard's interpretation of the Nuer segmentary lineage system (1933–5; 1940a) administrators commonly regarded the Nuer as a single tribe, divided into clans (rather on the model of the Scottish nation). After Evans-Pritchard administrators tended to write about the Nuer as a single people divided into discrete tribes.

RECENT HISTORY

The period from the time the government started administering the district until the end of 1927 may be described as the Cattle and Petition Epoch. I am unaware how the cattle tribute assessment was made; it was quite common for its payment to be refused, in which case mounted police were loosed at the offenders. These police would generally return to the DC with cattle, but the cattle did not always belong to the people who owed them. Atrocities occurred at times owing to the absence of control of these raids by the DC.[4] As regards cases, a few were brought to the DC (usually by Dinka or detribalised Nuer) and the DC gave the best decision he could, though his ignorance of customs and language must have led to some queer decisions.[5] When force was necessary to carry out a decision, the tribute collecting method was used. Most of the Nuer preferred to settle their cases in their own way by taking the law into their own hands. (The above applies to Gaweir only, after they were handed over to this district.)

A mamur reigned for a few years at Longtam, in the Tiang Nuer country.

On my arrival in January 1928 it was the custom of the Lak and Tiang and many Gaweir to decamp on the news of the DC's approach.

Following the murder of Capt. Fergusson in the Western Nuer District [14 December 1927] and the rising of the Lau Nuer on the east under Gwek and Pok, the Gaweir (accompanied by a lesser number of the Lau) led by Dwal Diu and Kurbiel [Kerbiel], attacked their southern neighbours the Dinka of Duk Faiyuil district and after looting and laying waste 30 Dinka villages, the warriors followed the fugitives who had taken refuge at Duk Faiyuil police post. They attacked the police post, but were driven off, losing 40 dead. This brought the whole of Nuerland into the limelight of Khartoum, and resulted in the Nuer Settlement. Under this scheme those Gaweir who elected to obey the government were instructed to concentrate in the more accessible parts of the district where there was ample grazing for their cattle. Columns of police and mounted rifles (each with a political official) made tours throughout the rest of the Lau and Gaweir countries. The main object of these tours was to arrest and intern the young men, and prove to the people that they cannot evade the government indefinitely. Three or four hundred hostages were taken, and kept for periods of from 3

---

[4] Tribute collection began among the Zeraf Nuer in 1908 (*SIR* 168 (July 1908): 4). Cattle were extracted from the Lak Nuer by force (often accompanied by loss of life) in 1912 and 1914, (*SIR*: 213 (April 1912): 4; 236 (March 1914): 4). An account of unsupervised tribute collecting along the Zeraf in 1922 is given in 'Ben Assher' (1928: 291–2).

[5] Cases decided by inspectors prior to the 1920s were usually judged according to the Sudan Penal Code, and not customary law; see Johnson (1986a).

to 12 months. In those cases where the warriors opened fire first, or where it was known that the people concerned were real diehards, the police and troops fired on them; the few casualties thus inflicted had an effect out of all proportion to their numbers. Dwal Diu, after losing most of his family's cattle and receiving a wound in the thigh, fled to Nasser district, where he was arrested by DC Nasser [C. L. Armstrong], in January 1930.[6]

The Nuer who concentrated were allotted work on causeways, porterage etc., and for this they were given grain. As it was a famine year, and the supervision of the work was left to the chiefs (northern police and soldiers with korbags [Arab.—*kurbaj*—rawhide whip] were kept away from all work) the work was not unpopular among the people. The same scheme continued in 1930, but the people showed that they had learnt their lesson, and the troops left after just over 2 months.

The opportunity was taken during Nuer Settlement to get the Nuer to settle their cases by tribal courts, and chiefs' police and dressers were enrolled. Gaweir have always been looked upon as the real he-men of the district, and as soon as they came to heel the Tiang and Lak followed without further trouble.

I am convinced that Nuer Settlement would have had slight chance of success, but for the cooperation of DC Lau [P. Coriat] on the east. The presence of Dinka on the south also helped, as it was impossible for any but individual Nuer to slip away.

The RAF also cooperated, but their main use proved to be reconnaissance.

REVENUE

I have referred above to the cattle tribute system. It had two other disadvantages; the strong family would often leave the production of tribute cattle to the weaker families, and the cattle in any case are not worth much.

Since the people have been listed, it is possible to make each individual contribute annually. The only way they can produce money is by work. The only work they have been taught is the construction of causeways and roads. Owing to the people's ignorance which renders them an easy prey for the average northern accountant, I have been unable to devise any workable system whereby some 10,000 men are given a few Pt each, for

---

[6] It was Wedderburn-Maxwell's pursuit of Dual Diu in his own territory during the wet season (when government officials were usually absent from the district) which convinced the Gaawar that further resistance was futile.

the purpose of paying it in as tribute after various pieces of different coloured paper have been inscribed by a foreigner in an unknown tongue. So in practice no money changes hands, and each sub-shen is required to do a definite piece of work every year under the supervision of its chiefs.

ROADS, BANKS, WELLS, FERRIES

As the district contains some 400 miles of permanently navigable river, I have always looked upon this as the main line of communication. The Zeraf forms a highway through the middle of the district. But unfortunately in most places there is a fringe of floating grass or swamps between the dry land and the waterway. This is being remedied by the construction of banks. It is now possible to land at Ajwong (kilo 225) Laikaich (kilo 195) and Fakwak (kilo 193) without wading through mud and water, and the telephone post at kilo 175 [Tithbel] is also connected with the river by a bank. Rufshendol has been linked up with Fasheir and Ajwong by banks over the Khor Jurwil, but though this place can now be visited dryshod in the summer, a lot of work remains to be done before the journey can be made in comfort in the rains. Another bank has nearly been completed at Fasheir meshra. These banks are intended for animals transport, the only one really suitable for motor transport being at Ajwong. (Ajwong is the only suitable place for a military base in event of operations in the Gaweir country.)

A road is being cleared (but not levelled) this year from Khor Fameir (kilo 158 right bank) to Fula Gwer (lat. 8° 38′ long. 31° 20′). This is intended to join up with the Bor-Khor Fullus road.

The main embankments over khors are being made this year on the Zeraf Island so that a motor road can be made in 1932 or 1933 running from the north end of the island to Laikaich.

The only well in the district is at Awoi. In most years the country suffers from too much water.[7]

A ferry has been provided and will be erected at the most southern place which can be made suitable.

---

[7] Good drinking water was also found at Ayod, where an open well was dug in the 1940s, and a donkey-pump bore hole well installed in the early 1960s. Both wells were destroyed by the Sudanese army in its evacuation of Ayod in 1987.

Chapter 10
ECONOMIC DEVELOPMENT AND POSSIBILITIES

At present the people confine their activities to rearing an inferior type of cattle, fishing and growing a small amount of dura. No economic development is to be expected until agricultural and veterinary experts have had a look round and tried a few experiments, and until the people have been induced to abandon their cast iron conservatism.

The only trade in the past has been in hides, and in a famine year cattle are bartered for grain. The arms trade with Abyssinia via Jekaing and Lau has flourished in the past and probably still continues.

BUILDINGS

There is a DC's house and half a merkaz at Fangak. As this is a most unsuitable place for a district HQ the completion of the merkaz has been stopped. The HQ should be on the Zeraf Island where 3/4 of the population are, but I do not feel qualified to recommend a site until I have seen it in the rains.[8] About lat. 8° 49', long. 30° 45' is the most central position and I foresee no difficulty in finding a good site in this neighbourhood. Approval was given to build a DC's house in the Gaweir, but this house has not been built as the DC was not allowed to reside in Gaweir during the rains on account of lack of communications. In practice the Fangak house is used as a storeroom, and the ADCs live in their tents or in mosquito proof resthouses.

FORESTRY

The district has for many years had to provide wood stations both for the SGS and the Egyptian Irrigation. As far as I know the Department of Forests have not yet planted a single tree in the district, which seems likely to become as bare as the rest of the Upper Nile.[9]

---

[8] The headquarters of the district remained at Fangak until 1976 when 'New Fangak' was opened at the Zeraf mouth and the old station was closed, having been completely surrounded by water since the mid-1960s.
[9] In 1927 thirty feddans of *sunt* (*Acacia arabica*) plantation were sown near the Zeraf mouth, with no result (Booth (1952: 120)).

GARDENS

The occasional visits paid to Fangak do not allow time for gardening.

District cattle. These were obtained from tribute and fines. Cattle tribute having been abolished, the herd will soon diminish.

OFFICIALS EMPLOYED IN THE DISTRICT

The only employees are 2 ADCs.[10] There is not sufficient work to keep a clerk occupied. When a lot of accounting work accumulates a clerk is usually borrowed from the Province Hq, and two or three days is enough to get through the accounts of as many months.

---

[10] The second ADC was F. J. H. Bacon, a probationer who joined the political service in 1929 but who was released in 1931, for reasons of financial stringency.

CHAPTER 11

Western Nuer District

PERCY CORIAT[1]

BOUNDARIES OF THE DISTRICT

The district may be divided into two separate geographical areas divided by a natural boundary, each with distinct features as regards the physical nature of the country.

The Jebel Island area to the south, inhabited by the Nuong [Nyuong], Dok, Jagey, and Jekaing [Jikany] clans, consists for the most part of a low lying black cotton soil plain interspersed by khors, with here and there a patch or ridge of high sandy ground on which palm trees and scrub grow.

As one approaches the Ghazal river to the north, the high ground becomes more frequent and occasional belts of palm and talh [*Acacia seyal*] increase in density. South, in the Nuong country, where the ironstone belt reaches its northernmost extremity, the cotton soil gives way to a hard reddish coloured terrain and sand and the scrub is replaced by well afforested land on which the ameit (*Anogeissus leocarpus*) predominates. Bounded on two sides of the triangle formed by the confluence of the two rivers, by a papyrus swamp of varying width, the country appears to be a vast swamp when seen from the river. Yet the Western Nuer compares favourably with other Nuer districts and to the Nuer is more favoured than either Lau or Gaweir. The high ground affords good sites for villages during the rains, while the numerous khors give ample water and grazing to the herds in the dry season at no great distance from their winter quarters. To the west bank of the Ghazal river in the area occupied by the Leik and Bul Nuer and the Ruweng Dinka, a maze of khors running both parallel to the river and at right angles to it cover the first five to ten miles inland. Interior of this an open treeless plain of hard soil extends to the southern Kordofan border. The Bul country on the lower reaches of the

---

[1] Report dated 1 February 1931. Only the first six sections are reprinted here. For the full report (including sections on buildings, forestry, sundry, notes on district officials and employees, military and intelligence, medical, office organisation, budget, and full annotation) see Coriat (1993: document 4.1).

Bahr el Arab is for the greater part under water during the rainy season but ridges of sand and forest land occur on its northern and western limits.

NORTH

From the junction of the Khors Loll[2] and Bau north between the Ruweng Alor and Ngork [Ngok] Dinka, thence in a semi-circle towards the north of Milleim el Deleibi to the southern edge of Lake Abiad and thence south of Jebel Kurondi. From Kurondi due south to Lake No. From the junctions of the khors on the west the line follows the province boundary as far east as Jebel Kurondi but the limits given above have not yet been ratified.

Along this northern border the neighbouring tribes are Arab.[3]

EAST

From Jebel Kurondi, south to and including Lake No, thence the Jebel river forms the district boundary to approximately Kilo Pole 400.[4]

The Shilluk adjoin to the east of Lake No. From thence south is bordered by the Lak and Tiang [Thiang] and the Gaweir 'toiches' of the Zeraf Island and beyond by the Twi [Twic] Dinka 'toich'.

SOUTH

From approximately Kilo Pole 400 on the Jebel river, southeast to point N. lat. 7° E. long. 30° 30' and due west to long 30° 00'.

Shish [Cic] Dinka are neighbours to the south.

WEST

From point N. lat. 7° E. long. 30° due north to point N. lat. 7° 47', thence west to point E. long. 29° 45' and north west to south of Lake Umbadi.

From Lake Umbadi to Lil (N. lat. 9° 2'. E. long. 29° 45') and west to the southern junction of the Khors Lol and Manding and following the line of the Khor Manding to its northern junction with the Lol. Thence along the Lol to its junction with the Khor Bau.

The Agar Dinka inhabit the country on the western border to its south. Northwards the Meshra Dinka tribes and the Mareig of Tonj adjoin.[5]

The Dok, Jagey and Nuong clans have much intercourse with the Gaweir of the Zeraf Island with whom they are friendly. The few rifles that find their way into the district are brought over by Gaweir.[6]

---

[2] Called Lol by the Dinka, Ngol by the Nuer.
[3] The northern neighbours are Nuba. It is only during the dry season that the Hawazma and Homr come from the interior of Kordofan to the Bahr el-Arab to graze.
[4] This may be a typographical error, as Adok is reference pole 42.
[5] The Rek Dinka gave their name to Meshra el-Rek, the Ngok Dinka live along the border of Kordofan and Bahr el-Ghazal Provinces, and the Twij Dinka were contained within Tonj District, Bahr el-Ghazal Province.
[6] See Coriat (1993: 23).

The Agar and Shish Dinka are hereditary enemies of the Jebel clans.[7] The Jekaing are of the same sub-tribe as the Jekaing of Nasser District and have the same divisions, i.e. Gatjo [Gaajok], Gatjak [Gaajak] and Gatwang [Gaagwang].

DISTRIBUTION OF POPULATION

Jebel River clans

Area & Tribes	Chiefs	River Post	Population
C. Dok	Buom Diu	Adok	11063 (1927)
D. Jagey	Thiey Poich [Thiei Poic]	Tarjath & Ryer	5195 (")
B. Nuong (Northern Gaaliath)	Galwak Nyag [Gaaluak Nyagh]	Nuong	3305 (")
A. Nuong	Won Kwoth [Wuon Kuoth]	Belek	4116 (1929)

Ghazal River clans

Area & Tribes	Chiefs	River Post	Population
E. Jekaing	Badeng Bur (s/chief of Twil Ran of H.)	Yodni	4021 (1927)
F. Jekaing & Kilwal	Gatkek Dwoich [Luop] of Jekaing & Ruai Wur of Kilwal. Both s/chiefs of Twil Ran of H.	Bentiu	2953 (1927)
H. Leik [Leek] & 2 sections Jekaing	Twil Ran* [* Now limited to part of Leik only.]	Yoynyang	3120 (1930)
J. Leik	Nuel Juel	Wathjak	8353 (")
K. Bul		Wagkal	10924 (")
G. Ruweng Dinka	Bilkwey Duot		9000 (1926)
			62060

---

[7] See Fergusson (1921) for an account of warfare between the Western Nuer and the Agar and Cic Dinka.

HISTORY AND GENERAL TRIBAL ORGANIZATION

Nuer mythology traces a common ancestry for the sub-tribes the origin of which was a miraculous descent from Heaven at Kot (a Tamarind [*Tamarindus indicus*] tree) in the Jagey country of Western Nuer, some 300 to 350 years ago.

There are some local variations of the legend concerning the person and manner of origin of the semi-divine ancestor or ancestress but in neither of the tribes does memory appear to go back more than 400 years.[8]

Western Nuer regard their habitat as the home of the founder of the tribe and it is reputed from here that the various sub-tribes migrated.

Whatever their origin, it is probable that the Nuer at one time in their history came from farther to the west[9] and it is credible that when Western Nuer was first inhabited by them, it was as one tribe, which expansion caused to break up into separate clans who turned to the east in search for new homes.

The Dinka are their hereditary enemy and conquest of new land meant conquest of the Dinka. Those tribesmen who elected to remain or were unable to leave the Western Nuer, contented themselves with raids and counter-raids against the Dinka. From 1870 onwards, the sport of Dinka baiting was varied by the advent of the slave raider and in their clashes with the 'Turk' it was not always the Nuer who suffered defeat. As with other tribes of the Nuer they have to their credit one decisive victory when in 1883 the tribesmen attacked the Turkish post and Arab allies at Rumbek and succeeded in massacring the garrison and killing the Arab leader Morgan Ali.[10]

Though the slave-bands never penetrated far into Western Nuer and hardly at all into the Jebel areas, as a consequence of which their tribal organisation was not broken up as in Lau and Gaweir, nevertheless their influence was felt sufficiently to engender a feeling of mistrust of all foreigners. Seemingly it is due to the slave-raider that attempts to attain friendly relations with the Nuer have been difficult and their administration has not progressed smoothly and yet it is not easy to conceive that but for

---

[8] Versions of the tree myth are found in Fergusson (1921: 148–50), Jackson (1923: 70–1), Crazzolara (1953: 8–9, 66–8), Evans-Pritchard (1956: 6, 10), Coriat (1993: 13–14), and Johnson (1994: 45, 50–1). Coriat gives no reasons for his time-scale, which must be treated with caution.
[9] Seligman and Seligman (1932: 207) report a story that the Nuer claim to have come from a waterless country to the west of present-day Bul Nuer country.
[10] Slave-raiding against the Western Nuer began well before 1870. Murgan Ali was one of Emin Pasha's agents, appointed to Rumbek in 1880. Rumbek was overwhelmed by a combined Dinka-Nuer assault in July 1883. See Johnson (1993*b*).

the slave-raider they would otherwise have been docile. Although Casati writes of them in 1880 as 'once a peaceful amiable nation, but to-day jealous, timid and hostile,'[11] the primitive and warlike character of the Nuer could not have been acquired in a few generations. Notwithstanding this it is certain that had it not been for the Turkish era, their administration would have been less unsure.

After the occupation the tribes were a constant source of embarrassment to the government owing to their propensity for raiding their more peaceful Dinka neighbours, but the country was unknown nor was any attempt made to penetrate it. The first record of a visit by an official was in 1913 when a Mr. R. A. Williams [sic] of the Egyptian Irrigation Dept.[12] carried out a survey from Adok (Hillet el Nuer) to Bentiu (Ardeiba). The Nuer reported as not actively hostile but suspicious and unfriendly.

In 1914, the Nuong led an attack against the C.M.S. station at Lau and El Bimb. Bally[13] was sent to Adok for the purpose of reporting on a suitable site for a government post but the project was dropped and no further action was taken until 1922 when Capt. Fergusson was instructed to march through the Nuer country and to get in touch with the tribes with the object of initiating some form of administration.[14]

In spite of tribal raids against the Dinka and many setbacks, he succeeded before his death at the hands of the Dur Nuong in 1927 in establishing a definite system of administration and reorganising the clans under either their own leaders or chiefs appointed by himself.

During this period 1922–1927, there were three punitive patrols, two in 1925 against the Dok and Nuong and one in the Jagey area; all of which

---

[11] G. Casati, *Ten Years in Equatoria and the Return of Emin Pasha*, vol. i (London 1891), 38: '... the Nuer, once a peaceful and amiable nation, but today jealous, timid, and hostile. The frequent raids made on them by the slave dealers of Khartoum have changed their feelings to hatred and animosity.' This passage was also cited by Jackson (1923: 88) and refers specifically to the Western Nuer. For a critique of Coriat's assertion that slave-raiding led to the break-up of Nuer political organization, see Johnson (1993a: p.lv) and Coriat (1993: 157).

[12] Not R. A. Williams, but R. H. Willan. Coriat may have confused the surname with that of a contemporary of his, K. B. Griffiths Williams, director of works in Malakal in the early 1920s.

[13] The Lau post mentioned here was on the Lau river in Rumbek district and has no connection with the Lau (Lou) Nuer of Upper Nile Province. Bimbashi E. D. Bally: second inspector Bahr el-Ghazal Province 1913–16, second inspector Upper Nile Province 1916.

[14] See V. H. Fergusson, 'Summary of Information on the Nuong Nuer in the Northern Bahr-el-Ghazal...', Appendix A, *SMIR* 323 (June 1921): 11; idem, 'Visit to the Nuong Nuers', 6 March 1921, NR0 Civsec 1/2/5; and idem (1930: 113–39).

were the result of disaffection promoted by witchdoctors and raids against the Dinka.[15]

In December 1927, Fergusson was murdered by tribesmen in Dur Nuong. A patrol was despatched and active operations were undertaken against the two Nuong areas. There were few casualties to the Nuer but heavy losses in cattle were reported caused by aircraft bombing fugitive camps located in the swamps.[16]

Galwak Nyag, a young warrior chief of the Northern or Gatliath Nuong who had previously given trouble concerning the return of Dinka cattle raided by his tribe, gave himself up shortly after operations began. Presumably on further evidence he was suspected of having instigated the murder and was arrested and confined.

In 1929, one of the actual murderers [Cuol Weng] gave himself up and after trial was executed in the district. In 1930 an agent effected the arrest of the other tribesman [Gatkek Jiek] concerned in the attack on Fergusson. Evidence obtained at his trial led to conviction of a sub-chief for complicity and a headman [Gaaluak Buth] was remanded. Both these men were from the Dur section of the Nuong and Cag Riang, chief of the tribe was deposed. The sub-chief (Dang Dungjiek) died in hospital shortly after being sentenced and the murderer was executed in the area. Galwak Nyag proved innocent, released and reinstated.

In effect the murder of Fergusson by two tribesmen was the outcome of a plot conspired by a group of Dur chiefs with ambitious ideas and ignorant of government intentions.[17]

During 1928–9 four areas, Bul, Leik, Jekaing and the Ruweng Dinka were visited by a district commissioner with an escort of troops.[18] The tribes were said to have been disturbed and disobedient to their chiefs. In the Bul, which had only twice been visited by Capt. Fergusson and was the most backward area, the intention was to concentrate the clans within an accessible site on the Bahr el Arab. The Bul failed to respond to this suggestion, which appears to have been premature and after a second visit by a district commissioner early in 1930,[19] it was abandoned.

The Ruweng Dinka originally under Kordofan were transferred to

---

[15] There were patrols in March 1923 and January and December 1925. See 'Patrol S.1, Intelligence Reports 1–4', NR0 Intel 2/27/217; Fergusson (1930: 182–5, 212–27); *SMIR* 344 (March 1923): 4; 377 (Dec 1925): 6; 380 (March 1926): 5; and Collins (1983: 40).
[16] Collins (1983: 133–4).
[17] The investigations into the murder and transcripts of the trials of the murderers can be found in NR0 Civsec 5/4/14–15. For a fuller account of the events surrounding Fergusson's murder and its aftermath, see Johnson (1994: ch. 7).
[18] See SR0 UNP 5.A.3/31, and *SMR* 2 (Feb.–March 1929): 4–5.
[19] *SMR* 5 (May–June 1929): 3; Masterman, 'Notes on Bul Nuer 1 930', Nasir END 66.A. 1.

Western Nuer in 1926 but were again placed under the Kordofan administration in 1928. In 1929 they were retransferred to Western Nuer.

Capt. Kidd followed Capt. Fergusson as district commissioner in 1927 and handed over to me on his transfer in 1929. Capt. Masterman was appointed a second assistant district commissioner in May 1929 and was transferred in August 1929 when he was succeeded by Capt. Romilly in November 1930.

The present tribal organisation is as follows:–

Area A. Dur or Southern Nuong

Won Kwoth. A hereditary 'Kwar Mon' [*kuaar muon*—earth-master] (leopard-skin) and chief of the tribe until deposed for malpractices in 1924. Prior to the present administration Won was a warrior leader noted for his successes against the Dinka. After his deposal, Galwak Nyag of the Gatliath Nuong was appointed chief of both his own and the Dur areas.

Early in 1927 the Dur were removed from Galwak's control and placed under Cag Riang who was neither a hereditary chief nor a fighting leader and his rule does not appear to have been successful. He was deposed and succeeded by Won Kwoth in December 1930 after having been tried and found not guilty, owing to insufficient evidence, of complicity in the murder of Capt. Fergusson.

Owing to the trouble of 1927 and consequent changes in the chiefship, the Dur are in more backward state than the neighbouring Dok and Jagey clans but the tribal organisation exists and given an era of peace it should not be long before their administration becomes as little dependent on government resources as the former clans.

Won Kwoth is reputed to dabble in witchdoctory but this should not affect his qualities as a leader if he remains loyal. He is slow in action, peculiarly unexcitable, ambitious and appears now to realise something of the meaning of government. Provided that due allowances are made and a high standard of efficiency is not expected and that Won can maintain a balance among his heterogeneous collection of sub-chiefs, he should succeed.

There are 30 individual shiengs under their respective headmen, including two sections of Angai Dinka living in the country.[20] These are divided into five main groups under sub-chiefs.

---

[20] The Angai (or Angac) appear to have been an independent group until the middle of rhe nineteenth century, when many of them crossed thc Nile to settle with the Ric Dinka in the east. The rest then seem to have merged with the Agar Dinka but intermarried with the Nyuong.

Area B. Gatliath or Northern Nuong

Chief Galwak Nyag. A hereditary 'Ut Ok' [*wut ghok*] (cattle chief) and fighting leader. Paramount of both sections of the Nuong from 1924 to the end of 1926, when he was believed to be exceeding his authority and made trouble over the return of cattle raided from the Dinka and his chiefship was confined to the Gatliath while the Dur were placed under Cag Riang. In 1927 he was arrested on suspicion of having instigated the outbreak in December of that year and was imprisoned. After his removal the area was placed temporarily under Cag Riang who was then also controlling the Dur. In June 1929, Caath Bang a Dok chieftain who had been deported to the Agar country in 1924 for oppressive acts, was appointed to the Gatliath. Caath was killed elephant hunting in August 1930 after he proved himself remarkably able.

After capture of the 1927 murderers, Galwak Nyag was proved innocent and was reinstated in December 1930.

The Gatliath comprise 18 shiengs under headmen and 4 sub-chiefs.

Galwak is young and has complete and unquestioned authority over the clan. Three years imprisonment may have done much to curb an impetuous nature but it may also have embittered him and it is probable he will require some years of restraint before he can be given a freer rein.

Area C. Dok

Chief Buom Diu. A witchdoctor and fighting leader who led the Dok before government control. The Dok have in the past had a tribal organisation which is practically that of the present day and the clan has been less affected by changing conditions than any other of the Nuer tribes.

Buom wields a paramount influence over a populous tribe and administers the area with a minimum of help from government. He is harsh, possibly oppressive at times and little liked but that he realises in greater measure than other Nuer chiefs the meaning of government and the inevitable consequences of misrule, there can be little doubt. His autocratic methods seem best suitable to the people he has to rule and I believe his apparent harshness to be not inconsonant with a sense of fairness.

Buom has under him 42 sections under their respective headmen and 6 sub-chiefs.

Area D. Jagey

Chief Thiey Poich. Hereditary 'Kwar Mon'. Appointed on the death of Mani Kolong the witchdoctor in 1926.

The country occupied by the Rangyan [Rengyan] group of this area is reputed the ancestral home of the Nuer and witchdoctors have become a perennial growth in Jagey, possibly because of this. Thiey has the qualities of a chief but lacks the fighting character needed to make his position entirely secure from the machinations of the wizards. His chiefship is not an easy one but he has done well and has little more need of assistance than Buom Diu of the Dok.

Although a smaller tribe than the Dok, the sections and headmen number 51 with 7 sub-chiefs.

Area E. Jekaing

This area includes 15 Jekaing headmen with their sections under 4 sub-chiefs, the senior of whom, Badeng Bur, is responsible to Chief Twil Ran of area H.* [*Twil has now been removed and 4 subchiefs appointed to run Jekaing.]

The Jekaing on the Ghazal river border have been more harried by slave raiders and more influenced by the Arab than the neighbouring Jebel clans and their organisation is less secure. The petty jealousies of Twil Ran and sub-chiefs has rendered a closer administration necessary, which it has not been possible to give.[21]

I am uncertain whether Badeng Bur the sub-chief of this area is incapable of controlling his headmen or is unwilling to assert himself in the face of cross-currents of opposition to his chief Twil and Twil's apparent untrustworthy method of dealing with his own supporters.

Area F. Jekaing & Kilwal

Gatkek Luop a sub-chief responsible to Twil Ran of H has under him 7 sections and headmen and is assisted by one sub-chief.

The Kilwal, a branch of the Leik tribe are controlled by sub-chief Ruai Wur also responsible to Twil Ran. Kilwal sections are under 6 headmen.

Gatkek is young, able and has the confidence of his sections but is ambitious and independent and has antagonised Twil possibly from over-assumption of his authority.

With the chief and sub-chiefs at cross purposes, the headmen have been able to run loose and the Jekaing of both areas E and F are unsettled.

Ruai Wur with the Kilwal has managed to steer clear of Jekaing intrigues and is competent subordinate leader.

---

[21] It was more than petty jealousy. The Jikany chiefs resented being subordinated to a Leek chief.

Area H. Jekaing & Leik

Chief Twil Ran.[22] Hereditary 'Kwar Mon' and a Leik by birth. Until appointed chief in 1924, Twil was unknown to his people either as a chief or leopard-skin and spent most of his youth piloting and escorting Arab traders and hunting parties around the country. On his appointment he was given control of the Jekaing of areas E and F in addition to the two Jekaing sections in area H and also the Kilwal of F and the Shwak [Cuak] division of Leik of area H. Being a Shwak Leik himself he elected to live in this Area. The Shwak are grouped into 11 sections under their headmen and 2 sub-chiefs.

Twil has a liking for power and is energetic but completely unscrupulous and hardly less untrustworthy. He is sufficiently intelligent to be loyal to government, yet without restraint it is certain that he would abuse any position he held by misrule.

It is probable that the Jekaing will be removed from his chiefship and his authority confined to the Leik.

Area J. Leik

Chief Nuel Juel. Was appointed a chief by Fergusson when the Leik were still little known. Nuel was removed and imprisoned at Malakal for some months during 1928 as he was alleged to have been truculent during the 1927 trouble but was later reinstated. He is crafty and unpleasing and only partially controls the Leik who are in too close proximity to the Bul to be amenable to proper control. Not being a chief by heredity and lacking the instincts of a leader, it is doubtful whether Nuel will last.

Feuds are still prevalent in the area and there is enmity between the Leik in area H and the Leik divisions under Nuel who form 37 shiengs with headmen and 5 sub-chiefs.

Area K. Bul

A paramount chief has not been appointed and is unlikely to be for some years.

The Bul were twice visited by Fergusson but other than the two marches of troops into the area in 1928–9 were left to their own devices until 1930. They have much intercourse with the Arabs from the North and have intermarried with them. The country is difficult of access the greater part

---

[22] By 1927 Twil Ran was already noted to be too strict with his people, but he remained loyal to the government after Fergusson's death.

of the year but if they can be got at their administration should not be difficult.

In 1930 Bul Belyu [Biliu], Teg Jiek [Tegjiek Dualdoang] and Pey Poar were appointed sub-chiefs of the Myindeng, Dijul [Dieng] and Gok Areas respectively. Bul Belyu is half Arab and by far the most intelligent of the trio.

Pey Poar had for some time been treated as head chief but lacked any kind of control and is old and utterly incompetent.

Area G. Ruweng Dinka

The Ruweng Ajiba and Ruweng Alor were in 1930 transferred from Kordofan Province. They were originally within the Western Nuer and placed under Kordofan in 1928 as it was considered unfeasible to administer them from the Upper Nile. For obvious reasons they cannot be administered satisfactorily from the headquarters of an Arab province.

The Ruweng Ajiba, the chief of whom is Mai Belkwey [Bilkwei], have more intercourse with the Nuer than the Alor. Mai's father Belkway Dwot, an old man, is alive and much feared by the Jekaing as a dabbler in the more virulent forms of magic.

For the past four years the Ruweng have been more or less dependent on their own resources. They are quiet amenable people though tiresome when they afford refuge to recalcitrant Nuer. Occasionally there are clashes with the Jekaing and Leik arising out of disputes over some wretched waterhole on the border.

General notes on organisation & judicial system

The administration initiated by Fergusson was developed on tribal lines and has the foundation for an essentially native structure. The chiefs with a few exceptions were tribal leaders in the past and it is noteworthy that it is with the exceptions that there have been failures and greater progress has been evident in areas where the chief was a leader before the present administration set in; that is if progress is to be measured in terms of lessening contact by a district commissioner and dealing direct with the people.

The problem here has been not so much to organise and centralise as with the Lau and Gaweir but to consolidate and secure. The organisation and the chiefs exist, which they did not in the Eastern Nuer and the district commissioner is not impelled to make such contact with the people nor to discipline the young warriors; rather it is his work to check and guide the chiefs and to ensure that the structure remains balanced and is improved where is needful. A closer approach to the work of the district commissioner adviser of the future.* [*I do not agree—I think the chiefs are too powerful and need to be reduced if the system is to stand.]

Headmen throughout the areas were and are appointed by the chief without reference, the only rule being that they should be tribesmen selected direct from the section they are to control. Sub-chiefs are elected by the group of headmen subordinate to them and approved by the chief and district commissioner.

Except where the individual holds a dual position as a government chief or headman and also a tribal functionary, the chiefs, sub-chiefs and headmen are purely administrative, though not precluded from hearing or giving decisions in the settlement of tribal cases. It is only in blood-feuds or in matters concerning tribal rights as also in rites and functions that the hereditary leader is absolute in his authority. Though he is not part of the government machine as such, his duties are distinct and definable and without him there would be a collapse of the tribal system. It rests with the chief to ensure that the 'Kwar Mon' or 'Ut Ok' does not run contra to government authority and it is here that the snag lies as the mantle of a witchdoctor falls more easily on the spiritual guide.

Tribal courts in so far as a bench of chiefs is implied do not exist in Western Nuer. Headmen hear their own people's cases and trivial cases brought against them by outsiders. In more important disputes or where there is question of offence and in cases raised from other tribes the chief adjudicates; sometimes with sub-chiefs or 'Kwar Mon' as assessors, more often alone.* [*This is to be altered—The courts are an important check on the chiefs.]

That the system works is proved by areas such as the Dok and Jagey where there is remarkably little litigation, the people are contented, the few appeals there are do come to light and in the presence of the chief and seldom is there dissatisfaction in cases brought by tribesmen from other areas and districts. More remarkable is this where the Dinka is concerned.

Chiefs' police (1 to 190 population) are enlisted proportionately from the different shiengs and are responsible to their respective headmen within their own sections but are used as a tribal body under the orders of the area chief for the maintenance of law and order generally.

There is an establishment of one clerk to each area chief. This has been in being only 8 months and decisions only are recorded on the hearing of cases. Most of the boys are inefficient and until competent clerks are available it will not be possible to record the full hearing. The clerks are also responsible for keeping a roster of fines.

Chapter 11

REVENUE

The tribes in Western Nuer were not taxed until 1929. During Fergusson's administration they were encouraged to sell their surplus bullocks and cotton growing was made compulsory in order that when the time came for a tax the people would have sufficient money to enable them to pay a poll tax and would avoid the uneconomic and unequable tribute in cattle. A tax of 5 Pt per adult head of population was levied in 1929 and was collected by headmen and made payable as tribute. In 1930 this was revised to 10 Pt per adult male.

	TAX PAID IN 1929	TAX PAID IN 1930
A. Southern Nuong	Nil	£E 141.400 m/ms
B. Northern Nuong	"	88.500 m/ms
C. Dok	£E 221.820 m/ms	254.400 m/ms
D. Jagey	108.150 m/ms	162.300 m/ms
E. Jekaing	120.955 m/ms	152.400 m/ms
H. Leik		42.700 m/ms
J. Leik	43.685 m/ms	183.300 m/ms
K. Bul	39.900 m/ms	Remitted cattle tribute
G. Ruweng Dinka	To Kordofan	Kordofan
Total	£E 534.510 m/ms	£E 1025.000 m/ms

Fines, mostly in cattle are levied by area chiefs and credited to item chiefs' courts in the devolution budget. There is no fee for the hearing of cases. Cattle are sold locally, those from one area being sold in another.

Revenue in fines

1929	1930
£E 565.575 m/ms	£E 662.900 m/ms

ROADS AND COMMUNICATIONS

There are ten river ports in nine of the areas as shown in 'Distribution of Population' and a port will possibly be opened at Lake No for the Ruweng Dinka. Each of these is accessible from the mainland and in addition to a landing stage there are a merchant's shop on each, rest houses for chiefs and quarters for a guard and Agricultural Dept. employee.

Belek the southern Dur meshra on the mainland side of a Lake [Jor] is at times inaccessible from the river owing to sudd blocks at the mouth of the passage into the lake, and Nuong is 4 hours upstream of a side-channel some 3 hours steaming south of Adok. Both these areas are now more approachable from inland via the new road and their only use is for export of cotton and trade goods.

Started in 1929 and completed by the end of 1930 a road now runs throughout the length of the Jebel river areas. Southern roadhead is at Ameij on the Southern Nuong-Shish Dinka border, from whence it runs northwards to Bentiu on the Ghazal river. A subsidiary road from Adok provides an outlet on the Jebel river. It is proposed to maintain a ferry at Bentiu and to continue the road north through the Jekaing and Ruweng to join with the Tonga–Talodi road. With the provision of funds it would also be possible to connect Ameij with Rumbek and Yirrol Districts by clearing to Akot (C.M.S. station) or to a point on the Rumbek–Fakam district road.

A G.R.F. [Grant for Roads and Ferries] grant, originally submitted in 1928 as an estimate for upkeep and erection of river ports, has been used for road work as the amount was in excess of that required for Meshras.

Western Nuer Road

	Interim dist.	Total (miles)
Adok (Jebel river post)		
Kh. Wathlual (ramp)	3.6	3.6
Kh. But (ramp)	5.4	9.0
Kh. Woat (ramp-rest house) junction	1.5	10.5
To Nuong		
Kh. Woat		
Kaati (water at Chir 2 m.)	32.9	32.9
Nyandong (wells—rest house)	24.5	57.4
Ful Shun (water)	12.7	70.1
Kwil (water)	20.3	90.4
Ameij (roadhead-Dinka border)	9.5	99.9
To Ghazal River		
Kh. Woat		
Kui (wells) resthouse proposed		52.4
Dwar (water) ramp		
Kh. Rial (water-ramp)		
Tharlil (water) possible sites for new hqs. post		
Bentiu (Ghazal river post)		87.4

A district headquarters will be built during 1931, possibly at Tharlil.[23]

ECONOMIC DEVELOPMENT AND POSSIBILITIES

The output of cotton could be greatly increased if the crop were of sufficient economic value to withstand the cost of transport.[24] Hibiscus [*Hibiscus sabdariffa*] grows wild inland and it would possibly be feasible to cultivate flax inland. Bananas, sugar cane and sisal grow well by banks of khors and at the edge of the sudd. Sisal should flourish in the waterless areas.

The Nuer is entirely pastoral and cultivation does not appeal to him and it is doubtful whether there will be any inducement to encourage him to farming on a large scale. Cattle are the beginning and end of all things and an improvement in the quality of their herds will eventually tend to better conditions of life in the Nuer country.

Rinderpest is scarce but Pleuropneumonia and Trypanosomiasis are rife particularly in the swampy areas in Nuong.

The amount of trade carried on by the merchants at the shops on the river stages is small and of little value.

The following shows exports for 1929:–

Hides	Ivory	Cattle
1779 pkgs	3138 rtls.	349 head

In 1930 there was a decrease in hides and ivory and a slight increase in cattle.

---

[23] A district headquarters was opened at Bentiu in January 1946.
[24] Compulsory cotton-growing ceased in 1931.

Exports of cotton

	1926/7 Kantars	1927/8 Kantars	1928/9 Kantars	1929/30 Kantars
Area A.	–	–	243.00	237.00
Area B.	–	–	2.00	208.00
Area C.	113.66	356.66	1335.24	1200.00
Area D.	109.23	345.58	816.00	973.00
Area E.	–	632.77	386.49	563.00
Area F.	–	–	294.31	476.00
Area G.	–	61.38	48.66	–
Area K.	–	–	50.00	221.00
Area H.	–	386.05	350.32	824.00
Area J.	–	356.48	385.66	973.00
Total	222.89	2138.92	3910.48	5674.00

CHAPTER 12

Malakal Town

T. F. G. CARLESS

The town of Malakal has suffered rather badly from not being designed in the first instance. Even if it had been, I doubt if the founders would have anticipated the expansion that has occurred in the last few years and the still greater expansion that may be expected in the next decade.

In the first instance the Egyptian Irrigation Department established itself there. Previously a suggestion to put province headquarters there was turned down (NB Malakal proper is down stream and on the other bank).

Later when province headquarters moved from Kodok, they were established in their present position, the interval between them and the Egyptian Irrigation Department enclave being left for the market, etc. Later by the instructions of Lord Allenby the Egyptian Army was moved from Taufikia to the area south of the mudiria and was hemmed in to the south by a small village and cattle camp belonging to an Arab merchant who claimed to have been given the area by Major Stigand.

The labour employed by the Egyptian Irrigation Service and the government departments and by merchants settled to the north of the Egyptian Irrigation Service enclave in what is known as the malakia village.

Roads

Up to the end of 1926 practically nothing beyond i.e. east of what is now the main road through the town.

This road was made in 1927 under the supervision of Mr. E. G. Coryton after whom it is called. It was made by cutting two ditches and throwing the spoil into the middle, and covering the whole with four inches of sand which was worked into the soil by the action of rain and people's feet.

Various bridges were put in and in view of the fact that the landing ground was being made to the north of the town and a good deal of heavy mechanical transport might be expected to traverse the road the bridges were built to take ten tons. With a little patching of sand in places, this road has stood well. The part of the road that goes through the residential area of

Malakal Town 313

Egyptian Irrigation Department has been macadamized by them.[1] The cost is said to be £ 2000 a mile without the cost of transport of material from Khartoum. In the market area some effort has been made both on this road and that on the river front to get a hard surface with brick bats, broken lumps of concrete etc. – and the same has been done to a mild degree over paths joining these two roads through the market area and the officials' quarter, but the paths are not broad enough or numerous enough for convenience in wet weather.

Drains

The main drain which runs southward from a point near the tumergia to the mule lines and then west into the river was built in 1925 and was then designed to surround Malakal and draw all water away from it, from the back. This was supplemented by a few drains e.g. by the zabtieh and the post office to draw the water off the area immediately below the highest point of the bank.

Unfortunately that part of the main drain which ran from north to south never worked satisfactorily and the town continued to spread beyond the confines of the drains.

The Egyptian Irrigation Department has two main drains at each end of the portion of its area that is built over, to carry off surplus water: they also have an elaborate system of irrigation channels for their garden extending up to the so-called polo ground.

The hospital lying immediately south of the Egyptian Irrigation Department has devised a system of drainage of its own; the result is not fully satisfactory.

Owing to the 'deltaic' foundation of the bank and the necessity of keeping all drains above the level of high flood, any drainage system requires to be designed with care and maintained with all possible supervision to avoid drains being cleared out too deep, so that the level drops below the river mouth of the drain. The problem becomes more difficult as the town spreads away from the river. The director PWD has hoped to draft a scheme to deal with the whole problem in the last two years but has not been able to find staff. It is hoped that the district engineer can tackle it in 1930–31.

Meanwhile the problem is complicated by the addition of a dockyard, a benzine store and the serum station to the north of the malakia village. The

---

[1] The remainder of the road, from the official quarter to the air strip, was not paved until 1974, when it was macadamized for the Unity Day celebrations, marking the second anniversary of the end of the first civil war.

conservancy problem involved is already under consideration, and the legal controls necessary have been applied for.

At the south end of the town it is proposed to hand over the Equatorial Battalion barracks to the police and this involves a further increase of liability and an extension of the sanitary problem.

On the river front considerable erosion has already occurred from the action of rain and drain water down the bank. The Egyptian Irrigation Department has been able to terrace the foreshore in front of the colony and so not only check erosion but add considerably to their amenities. It is no doubt desirable to do the same over the remaining frontage, especially in front of the hospital, the market and the mudiria buildings.

Butchers' market etc.

Plans and funds for a new butchers' market, and slaughtering place have been mooted for over two years but owing to pre-occupation of PWD have not materialized.

Town planning

A plan to keep the different sections of the community in their own areas has also been put forward so that the 'gellaba' quarter is defined, next to them are the effendia; south of them the British officials, extending to the boundary of the Egyptian Irrigation.

In practice these limitations have yet to be made as British officials are still living in the effendia quarters, and sufficient funds for the provision of new quarters for them have not yet been available. The houses now occupied by the WT inspector and PWD foreman might advantageously be handed over to e.g. the head clerk and chief accountant. That would leave only the district engineer PWD adjacent to the effendia area and as he lives next to his office and not very near to the effendia, his transfer is not pressing though if he required any extension of office accommodation he would need a house for himself.

The area allotted to British officials is large enough to allow for some expansion but is not unlimited. No consideration was taken at the time of the possible requirements of non-British official residents.* [*The police parade ground might be available when the police take over the military lines.] It should however be considered possible that commercial representatives of Imperial Airways, the Sudan Mercantile or Gellatly, Hankey and Co. and similar firms might at some period need accommodation.

A space now empty south of the hospital has been reserved for commercial buildings of 1st class. Efforts have been made by Sudan Government Railways and Steamers to use the space for a shed, but apart from aesthetic reasons the space will undoubtedly be required at some date and should be reserved.[2]

The SGR&S was asked to state its needs for plots some years ago. More recently it has asked for room for offices and shed, and was told that space was not available. There is ample space in fact on the river front for that type of building but great care has to be used to ensure that local susceptibilities are not unduly outraged. A repetition of Kaka is studiously to be avoided. For the matter of shed, see the correspondence.

When the 'military area' comes under the administration, various houses will fall vacant e.g. the Sudanese officers', translator's houses and it will have to be considered whether the inclusion of non-British residents in this area is acceptable.

Something might be done by limiting them to police officers etc. (and the WT engines staff who are already there). But the allotment of the whole area, barrack rooms stores etc. will need to be carefully examined. Incidentally there is a scheme to grant a small plot on the river bank to Imperial Airways for a restaurant, but not for anything more.

Mosquito brigade and grass cutting

A small gang to do anti-mosquito work was formed in 1928, and a further gang to clear the drains and ditches in 1930. There still remains an enormous quantity of grass which grows in the hoshes and the sites for houses not yet taken up, and the labour of keeping the grass down is disproportionate to the result. From recent researches it is indicated that the control of grass growing along the foreshore is of great importance.

It has been suggested by Mr. Bailey of the Research Farm that an Australian grass can be found which would keep down the higher grass — and this may provide a solution, but unless the land was levelled when the new grass was put in, the water retained by the rough ground would still allow mosquitoes to breed.

Considering the very large area to be controlled and the funds available the results are tolerable. It is going to be more difficult when the military area is taken over and the addition at the north end of the town require to be dealt with on the rates. The matter has been referred as that of conservancy to the Central Sanitary Board.

---

[2] This area subsequently was built up with shops owned by Greek merchants and other well-financed traders.

Light line[3]

A 2' light line runs from the conservancy pits into the market and thence north to join the Egyptian Irrigation Department system and south to the extent of rails available.

There is also a line at present on loan to PWD from the meshra by the main drain to the mule lines to facilitate carriage of materials, and there is a space from PWD to the main line.

An extension of the line to fit in with conservancy scheme for malakia village is needed, and the Egyptian Irrigation Department also proposes to connect their dockyard with their enclave by light line, but it is hoped to avoid putting this line down 'Coryton's road' and so reduce the roadway.

The province originally purchased second hand 2' & 1'6" gauge line. A good deal of the latter is now at Renk. A large quantity of new 2' line was bought against LPS reserve, about 1929, with a turn table and various turnouts. This was actually bought for the malakia conservancy but owing to disagreement of the medical authorities was not used for that purpose.

Cattle luaks

The government cattle used to be kept close to the police lines and mule lines, but were moved in 1929, as was also the zariba of Ahmed Abdallah who was previously south of the military area. The sites are not ideal, owing to bad drainage, but more could be done by putting sand down and by raising the level of the luak floors.

The Baggara cattle which provide the town milk supply are allowed to camp on the 'debba' just north of the malakia village, where there is a corrugated iron shed which used to accommodate mules, now leased as a petrol store.

The serum cattle are accommodated on the island by the landing ground, and steps must be taken to ensure that animals infected with rinderpest for serum work do not infect native owned animals.

The foreshore and shed

For many years a charge of 5 m/ms a packet has been collected from merchants etc. stacking their goods on the foreshore. The reason for this charge was not clear, but as the abolition of it meant raising the rates and as there was no complaint about it, it was allowed to stand but an application

---

[3] This light line, which used hand carts, was too insignificant to be included in the chapter on light railways in Hill (1965: ch. 9).

was made for a shed, in which such goods could be stored and guarded and protected from rain, thus giving a quid pro quo.

A good deal of misunderstanding arose over the shed (for which see correspondence), but it is still proposed to erect a shed on the foreshore and if the SGR&S pays half the cost it will be allowed half the accommodation.

Prison

The Malakal prison is a kind of compromise between a province and zabtieh prison and like most compromises is not very satisfactory. Consisting originally of two rooms in one block, as a substitute for a red-painted corrugated iron shed, it left no place for women or guard room, nor was there any arms store. A building was put up for a women's prison and solitary cell and was promptly appropriated as a guard room and arms store. On further application for a women's prison and solitary cell the suggestion was received coldly, but on explanation a further building was approved and erected: it has suffered the same fate as the first and the women and the kitchen continue to remain in their old semi-permanent building, mainly because they are so filthy it seems a pity to waste a nice clean building on them.

Meanwhile a scheme for making a prison hosh in barbed wire and making native tukls or the like for prisoners was recommended, and a barbed wire fence has been erected and a couple of tukls for 'tribesmen'. The barbed wire needs considerable elaboration to form a real obstacle to escape. Recently a number of prisoners escaped.

The prison is inspected on Wednesday mornings at 7.45 am by the governor if in Malakal.

A weekly inspection of the town by the governor has lapsed as it should hardly be necessary to make a formal inspection so frequently.

The old corrugated iron shed is used partly as a workshop pending the erection of a new one and partly as a store.

Water supply

Pending a scheme of roads water and light supply under consideration by PWD, water was obtained for domestic uses from helical pump by the garden gate. This was allowed to get out of order and water was simply taken from the river. Recently owing to cases of typhoid the Medical inspector made an arrangement with Egyptian Irrigation Department to supply drinking water to British officials from the tap in the hospital which is fed from the water system of Egyptian Irrigation Department. Bath water etc. still is carried by prisoners from the river to British officials. The effendia and gellaba pay local tribesmen a small wage to supply their needs.

Light

When the Egyptian Irrigation Department started its electric plant, a scheme was mooted to connect it with the mudiria and British officials, and others. On enquiry it appeared that the effendia were not prepared to pay for light and the result was that so small a return was to be obtained that the expense (including a cable at £ 800) could not be met. It was perhaps as well as the Egyptian Irrigation Department is already enlarging its plant to meet increased load.

It is still hoped however that electric light can be put in the British officials' houses, some merchants' houses and the offices.

Games

Until 1926 there was one concrete tennis court by the old mess and another in the Egyptian Irrigation Service. In 1926 a place suitable for polo was found on the west bank and this has proved an enormous boon but the business of transporting ponies and players across the river is a nuisance, and involves the provision of a boat and barge. Attempts have been made to find a ground on the landing ground, but the ground was found unsuitable. The Egyptian Irrigation Department has cleared a large space as a possible polo ground on the east side of the colony but so far the surface has been too bad to make it playable.

A squash court was erected by Egyptian Irrigation Department in 1928 and by courtesy of the officials of Egyptian Irrigation Department has been of the greatest value to Sudan government officials.

It is however increasingly felt that the one court can barely meet the needs of the Egyptian Irrigation Officials, especially as the department is enlarging its staff, and then the court will be but rarely available.

Steps were taken to obtain a loan for the building of a second tennis court. An estimate of £ 500 for a concrete court seemed too much to pay and a cheaper court of tarmac at £ 250 required so much maintenance, besides being an experiment that the Club is still being dubious of going further in the matter.

Meanwhile the Club has recognized its duty to its neighbour to the degree of giving the use of the court two days a week gratis to the effendia. This public spirited attitude has got to find its replica in higher quarters: but the need of some adequate means of exercise in Malakal is a question not merely of charity but of hard headed value, as fitness means better and more work.

The addition of a bathing pool would be a very great thing. The site suggested is on the high part of the bank just outside the gate of the governor's garden, adjacent to the tebeldi trees [*Adansonia digitata*, or baobab] there,[4] as this could be fed by the garden pump and drained into the river bank.

If another tennis court were made, the best place for it would be between the rest house and the road along the top of the river bank.

This is sufficiently near for all persons, without being so much identified with one particular official's house to make the use of it almost equivalent to a call on the official in the house!

Malakal is a difficult place to deal with: there seems to be a spirit of inertia that descends on all officials in it, so that it is only with the greatest effort that anything can be finished. The local soil is so stubborn and awkward that buildings such as tukls with mud walls always present a rather disreputable appearance, and the garden repays considerable effort to a disappointing degree. Practically, it is best to concentrate on shrubs and the like in the gardens of officials, though it is possible to grow a few flowers. Vegetables have a constant disappointment actually in Malakal, but are doing better at the head of the island just upstream of Malakal.

A very large proportion of the time of the mamur and sub-mamur is taken up settling the squabbles of the Egyptian Irrigation Department Officials with one another or with their opposite numbers in the Sudan government. The zabtieh staff has practically nothing to do with the Shilluk tribal organization beyond the actual receipt of tribute or the detention of prisoners.

One of the great problems in Malakal is araki. It is drunk by the malakia, the gellaba and the officials. A fairly consistent stream of elderly Sudanese women pass through prison under conviction for making araki but it is always obtainable, and the people of Malakal seem to be very genuinely and seriously addicted to araki. So much so, that the late Sagh Hussein Eff. Farag who had had an experience of some 18 years in Upper Nile Province declared that it was impossible to eradicate araki, whilst the present mamur Sagh Ahmed Eff. Okeil informed me that a really serious and effective campaign against araki would be quite likely to cause open

---

[4] About which see Struvé (1925).

revolt against the government. It cannot be overlooked that a large number of women of the type of those of the XIIth Sudanese harimat live in Malakal, in fact there are quite a lot of that harimat and they were the people who resented the interference with their araki-making so seriously as to pursue in a most dangerous manner the district commissioner of Omdurman and the police officer.[5]

The ultimate solution must lie in education of the younger generation to better habits. The immediate policy is hard to find, unless we are to be contented to carry on with a mildly preventive method which may have a slight deterrent effect but still allows a considerable trade to be carried on sub rosa, and does little or nothing to stop the deterioration of employees of all sorts from the effects of Araki.

---

[5] The brewing of beer and the distillation of araki has long been an activity of army wives in the Sudan, even in very recent times.

CHAPTER 13

The Gambeila Enclave

CAPTAIN J. K. MAURICE[1]

As requested by the governor Upper Nile Province I have compiled these notes to the best of my ability from notes in this office, conversations with local people and personal experience, I am therefore open to correction in some of my remarks and dates.

Gambeila Enclave

Is I suppose in every way a unique post; the original concession granted to the Sudan government by King Menelik [Menilek] was at a spot near Itang. But presumably finding that site quite useless as a trading post, its being cut off entirely from the interior during about half the year, the first parties coming down to establish the post pushed on till they found high ground and established the enclave of Gambeila here.[2]

In 1918 Ras Tafari feeling more secure in his authority after the Liggie Yasu (Lij Yasu) affair, raised the question of our right to the enclave and argued (apparently rightly) that the concession applied to Itang thirty miles down stream.[3]

[1] Report dated 28 December 1930.
[2] The post at Itang lasted one trading season only before it was moved to Gambela in November 1904, with the authorisation of *Ras* Tassama, governor of Illubabor. See H. H. Wilson, 'Report on the Itang trading station', Appendix A, *SIR* 116 (March 1904): 5–9; idem., 'Report on the expedition to Goré, Saiu, Anfilo, Gidami, etc.', Appendix A, SIR 126 (January 1905): 9; Zewde (1976: 227–31).
[3] The emperor Menilek designated his young grandson, *lij* (prince) Iyasu, his successor in 1909. A high-spirited and somewhat unorthodox youth, he came into conflict with the nobility who had supported his grandfather soon after he succeeded to the throne in 1913, and also alarmed the three colonial powers in the region (Britain, France, and Italy) during the early years of World War I. One man whom he particularly alienated was Tafari Makonnen. Iyasu had taken particular interest in the exploitation of the Gambela region, appointing the Syrian freebooter Ydlibi as governor there in 1916. A coalition of powerful nobles and churchmen deposed Iyasu for alleged apostasy in 1916, replacing him with one of Menilek's daughters, Zawditu, and simultaneously appointing ras Tafari Makonnen as heir apparent to the empress. Tafari became *negus* (king) in 1928 and was crowned emperor (taking the name Hayla-Selasse I) shortly after Zawditu's death in 1930. See Zewde (1991: 114–37).

He was successfully bluffed at the time but in 1925 and 1926 he again raised the question. The result being that as from December 1926 the Sudan government agreed not to collect any customs in the enclave, but at the time apparently no mention was made of our leaving the enclave, although Ras Tafari seems to have construed that meaning into the agreement to our not collecting duties.[4]

But again he seems to have been suitably bluffed and things carry on.

The Gambeila boundaries

These under the circumstances narrated above are naturally not defined, but are more or less recognised as follows: triangular in shape the north boundary Sugar Loaf Jebel Khor Jajaba from the Sugar loaf to the main river bounds the east and separates the enclave from the Abyssinian village. The south is bounded by the river Baro from the mouth of Khor Jajaba west to a distance of about seven hundred yards and an undefined line from that point to the jebel bounds the west.

The Abyssinian officials seem quite happy to accept this. Ato Taffara one of Dejazmach Makonen's officials from Sayo did question it in 1929, when I suggested that he should ask permission before camping in the enclave, but I pointed out the limits to him and apparently satisfied him for when he later started the road to Sayo [now Dembi Dollo] he was careful to start from the northern boundary.

The enclave was under the charge of the Customs officials till 1921 when a district commissioner was appointed who took charge of the customs together with his other duties.[5]

The native village behind or I should say to the northern part of the enclave is of medium size and besides the local inhabitants who for the most part are Anuaks, it is used by large numbers of Anuaks from down river when they come in to purchase things or seek work. During the steamer season quite a number of such people stay here for work.

Sheikh Oshan wakil of sheikh Ogilo [Ujulu-war-Udiel?] of Pinkio is the headman.

---

[4] Ras Tafari first raised the question of Gambela customs on his visit to London in 1924. An agreement on customs duties was finally reached in 1928. The Sudan government was less concerned about the revenue than the loss of British prestige along the border should the Gambela enclave be evacuated. See Zewde (1976: 289–96).
[5] J. F. H. Marsh, see Appendix 1.

Ground rents

The bulk of the land on the main part of the enclave and on the river front is let on leases of various years terms, these rents are payable in advance half yearly, and any new leases transfers, or surrenders of land are first authorised by the Director of Lands, Sudan government Khartoum.

The population of Gambeila

Other than the Anuaks mentioned above the population of Gambeila is a mixed one consisting of a district commissioner, a sarraf, a dispensary hakim, a postmaster and his assistant, two electricians of the Post Office, a varying number of the Egyptian Irrigation Department, and twelve police, this completes the Sudan government staff.

In addition the population is composed of Levantines, Gallas [Oromo], and a few old Sudanese subjects.

The Greeks are the traders and store holders or representatives of such. The Galla does the porterage from and to the interior.

Currency

This consists of Egyptian currency and Maria Theresa dollars, and a few Menelik dollars crop up at times but are not popular. Both currencies used to be accepted both in the merkaz chest and the post office; but owing to the drop in the exchange of dollars they are only accepted by approval of the financial secretary who also notifies the district commissioner of the rate of exchange to be accepted. At the present moment the Addis Ababa rate of exchange is dollars 20.25 per pound sterling.

Passports and permits

Gambeila being a closed area all people visiting or settling require a permit to enter the enclave which is granted from the civil secretary's office.

Leaving Gambeila for the Sudan no such permit is required unless persons of whom the district commissioner knows nothing, when they are required to produce passports and necessary particulars and telegraphic approval is requested from the civil secretary before they leave the enclave.

The district commissioner is kept informed of undesirables by the Intelligence Department.

All merchants are required to take out a permit to trade; these are obtainable either in Khartoum or from district commissioner's office at

Gambeila. A merchant's licence costing 50 Pt and his agent's costing 5 Pt all such permits have to be renewed yearly.

Firearms

Anyone in Abyssina, be he trader or savage, can carry arms without let or hindrance. The Greek traders living in Gambeila take out licences, and for the most part those of them living in the interior as their only means of obtaining ammunition is from Khartoum through Gambeila and such permit is not obtainable without a licence.

Exports and imports

Practically all the export is coffee and beeswax, and the imports salt, bales of cloth, empty sacks for coffee and general merchandise.

I fear that the bad price of coffee in Khartoum this year will lessen the trade considerably this coming year. I understand that the merchants for the most part are not buying yet as the price is still kept up in Abyssinia.

The salt monopoly has also very much cut down the trade for only one merchant deals in it and moreover it has put the price of salt up very high even to 7 dollars 75 per kantar.[6]

Steamers

The steamers are able to function between Khartoum and Gambeila during the rains when the river is high, and roughly speaking this season is from the end of May to the middle of October. These steamers carry the mails and bring in the import goods mentioned above and return with the outgoing mails and the export goods of coffee and beeswax.

Some smaller province steamers occasionally arrive before that date, and generally are able to function later, these carry mails and perhaps personnel and light goods.

At the conclusion of the steamer season the mails are carried from Nasir to Gambeila by canoes.

---

[6] The granting in May 1930 of a trade monopoly in salt to the Franco-Ethiopian company, in which the Ethiopian government had 40% shares (most held by negus Tafari himself) caused some diplomatic tension between Ethiopia and European governments. In 1931 trade figures for Gambela reached a record low (Zewde (1976: 296–300)).

Customs dues

Formerly up to the year 1926 the customs dues were collected by the Sudan government, included in these were the share of the Abyssinian government, which amount was paid annually at Addis Ababa. The average share of the Abyssinian government being in excess of £8000.

The Abyssinian officials since taking over control of the customs are very close about how much they collect, but I venture to guess that it is considerably less, a number of official scallywags have to take a picking out of it, and bribery is rampant in the country.

One Ato Fanta [*fitawrari* Fanta] functioned for some years as Abyssinian head man of customs in the Abyssinian village adjoining the enclave.

He always seemed to get on very well with the merchants and was always obliging to myself; unfortunately for him he dipped too deeply into the government funds, or anyway was blamed for it and was arrested and sent to Gore. After his release (the government having got all that they could out of him) he was sent to Addis Ababa.

George Noumeir was appointed chief of customs in Gambeila by the Abyssinian government and took charge in 1927.

During that year he was allowed to live in the enclave and collect his customs there. This was altered in 1928 to his annoyance and he apparently tried every new district commissioner that arrived (and there were three between Captain Pletts leaving and me taking over) for permission to continue in the old way and live in the enclave. He certainly came to me almost directly I arrived.

The trouble then was that the Abyssinian government and Noumeir wished to build a new customs house and to enforce all goods going through this customs from the steamers before entering the enclave, the site for this proposed customs house was to be at a point west of the enclave.

There were very many objections to this and perhaps the first and foremost is that it would give the idea that Gambeila enclave was not an enclave but Abyssinian territory in that goods passed Abyssinian customs when coming into the enclave. Moreover there would be a constant procession of Abyssinian officials and their police crossing the enclave from their village to the customs and back. Again the site is under water a considerable period of the rains. Another drawback is that it would put a lot of work on the merchants carrying their goods from customs to stores a long step away. Steamers moreover would be tying up in Abyssinian territory.

I had many talks with Noumeir both on the subject of his site for the customs house and ways of collecting the duties, and finally he agreed with me or anyway conceded to my suggestions of building the customs house on the east of the enclave over the khor in the Abyssinian village, and that he should live on that side and to receive a copy of the manifests as steamers arrived or departed to enable him to check all the articles without a personal inspection.

The district commissioner therefore sends him a copy of the manifests having previously marked it showing any goods that are genuinely for the enclave consumption.

This system has been functioning for 1929 and 1930 and appears satisfactory and to please everybody concerned. It saves the money for the Abyssinian government in that they don't need the buildings or the number of officials that they would have to have if they checked all through a customs house, it also helps the traders as they are at liberty to send goods as they like without having to accompany them and check them through. I hope myself that this system may carry on for many years.

There is every chance of this being the case as the Abyssinian government while pressing for the buildings to be put up sent no funds to pay for them, and it was with the greatest difficulty that Noumeir at last got permission to take sufficient out of the customs dues to build a house for himself.

The Ethiopian motor transport coy

This enterprise started originally by Danalis in company with Manolis & Comoudis, this partnership was dissolved at the end of 1927 or early in 1928 and the new name as mentioned above was given to the company, Danalis having got a concession for a road from Ras Tafari at some considerable expense; Ras Tafari receives yearly a large gratuity from the company.

The present company has backing by Messrs Gellatly Hankey of Khartoum who have down at road head the headquarters of the company two of their representatives.[7]

Existing situation

As regards the Abyssinian authorities relations are very friendly indeed, there is, and has been for some time now, no trouble. They all seem to try

---

[7] In 1931 Tafari Makonnen (now Emperor Hayla-Selasse) owned 3000 shares in the company, and a further 7000 shares were owned by two of his sons. The major shareholder, with 104,999 shares, was Gellatly Hankey & Co. Ltd., the British trading and engineering firm which had a subsidiary in Khartoum. See Zewde (1976: 353–61).

and help in every way and one and all show a marked improvement in their manners in that any of them passing through or coming to Gambeila for any duties connected with their own village invariably call on the district commissioner at his office, and on these occasions I have found them most friendly.

I should like to be able to suggest a means of helping on the trade this year which at the moment is very stagnant, suffering as it is from two set backs, i.e. the slump in coffee prices and the salt monopoly, but I cannot see any way of improvement at present.

As long as the price of coffee remains at its present rate in Khartoum the merchants here cannot afford to ship unless the price also drops in the interior.

At present the Abyssinian owners are holding up the coffee and refusing to sell at any reduced rate, but some of the merchants seem pretty optimistic about the situation and think that it is only a matter of time and they must sell.

The salt monopoly known as Franco-Ethiopian Co. was granted this year. I understand that this same company are holders of a salt lake near Jibuti and also hold the shares in the railway there.

Messrs Seffarians have I believe a large interest in that concern and therefore they secured the agency for the salt at Gambeila, this is a bit hard on the other merchants as the carrier trouble is always great and carriers do not like returning empty.

Incidentally the Abyssinian officials themselves complained of it to me when they called on me on my return from leave.

There is but little salt going into the interior and what does go is of a high price.

Abyssinian officials

Taking firstly those near the enclave, GEORGE NOUMEIR a Syrian, a most plausible man, educated to an extent, he reads, writes and talks many languages, English, French, Amharic, and Arabic. He is easily excited but I think taken the right way is really not hard to get on with, personally he has given me no trouble and we get along quite well.

He is unfortunately a very sick man, and at the moment away at Gore. We might do much worse than have Noumeir here as the customs official.

FANTA. As I have already stated got into trouble and was removed, I do not think that he will ever come into the picture again so I need not deal with him again.

TEGANI. Arrived here and took over after Fanta's trouble. He is a very quiet fellow, agreeable and obliging, he always is ready to assist and keep things running smoothly and gives me the impression that he is most friendly to us.

ATO RAMDI. A new official who has only been here some three months, I have only seen very little of him, he called on me on my return from leave and I have seen him a few times when he has been here to attend hospital. He appears quite friendly towards us, he is a civil old man to talk to but very delicate and I don't think that he will stand this climate long, in fact I hear that already he is telegraphing daily to get himself relieved.

WALDER GEORGES [WALDA-GIYORGIS]. One of Negus Tafari's men from Addis called at my office the other day, he told he that he was sent down by the Negus to look after some lands in the Gims [Guma or Jimma?] country which fell into the hands of the Negus on the death of Dejazmach Gemini [Ganame].[8]

How long he is likely to be there he does not know but he was extraordinarily friendly and said that as he was down in the near neighbourhood to come in to call.

DEJAZMACH MAKONEN WASSO [MAKONNEN WOSANIE] of Sayo, succeeded Dejazmach Birru [Berru Walda-Gabr'el] as governor of Sayo, I have never met him but have had a good deal of correspondence with him, generally speaking he is almost inclined to be enthusiastic in his letters. And his representative Ato Tafarra always when sent down by him, enlarges on Makonen's friendliness to us and his zeal for advancement.

There was a little trouble in 1929 when he closed the roads for food stuffs, but this although indirectly affecting us was not really aimed at the enclave but at the people of the Abyssinian village with whom there seems to be a permanent feud.

Makonen is at Addis now and it is not known whether he will return or not; in the mean time Fitawrari Ili Georgis is acting in his stead.

ATO TAFARRA. Who styles himself the representative of Dejazmach Makonen for the Anuak country, is a young fellow educated at the American Mission at Sayo and talks English fluently, originally his intentions were to go into medicine and he studied in that line at the Mission. But being a bit swollen headed and very ambitious I understand that he refused to stay on and eventually go and get qualified, but left and got appointed in his present position by Makonen who also uses him as a translator.

---

[8] This is clearly another, lesser, Walda-Giyorgis, client of Hayla-Selasse, and not the famous governor of Kaffa (1897–1910) and later negus (king) of Amhara, Begemder and Semien, who died in 1918. For the fate of the previous governor of Gore, dajjazmach Ganame, see the Biographical Notes. It is not quite clear from this passage when Ganame died, or what estate in his former province had passed to Hayla-Selasse: it could have been in the Guma or Goma area west of Bure, the lowlands of Jimma to the south, or some other territory.

He is a very young man that I don't altogether trust although he appears on the surface to be quite friendly, but I am sure that in reality he has but little use for us.

RAS KABADA MANGESHA [MANGASHA]. Who succeeded Ras Nada [Nadaw] at Gore, I have not yet met but he recently passed through the Sudan having made a trip to Khartoum for treatment.

He is at the moment in Addis Ababa and it seems very doubtful whether he will return to Gore, all his staff and people have been recalled to Addis.

CHAPTER 14

Some Suggestions For The Future

C.A. WILLIS

NATIVE ADMINISTRATION

It is assumed that the objective of the policy of Native Administration is to get the tribes to administer their own internal affairs and their relations with their neighbours in peace with the least possible amount of supervision by government.

The principles on which this administration is to be managed are the traditional customs of the tribes with such modification as local circumstances and public opinion demand.

The two first essentials are reasonably established traditions and chiefs strong enough and honest enough to administer it fairly.

The chiefs' authority

There is a common preconception about the African that the tribes are normally ruled by an arbitrary potentate of absolute power.

I think it is quite likely that when white men came into contact with black tribes, they frequently found they had to cope with a 'dusky potentate', and they drew the inference that this was normal; but I believe that it was the actual intrusion of the whites on the native population that caused the latter to consent to the absolute authority of any man who could lead them and protect them against the alien intrusion.

So far as the Nilotics are concerned there is ample evidence to show that they have numbers of what one must call chiefs, both for want of a better word and because it is the meaning of the name applied to them by the tribesmen. The leopard chief, the land chief, the cattle chief, the chief of the warriors, and of the dance all have their places in tribal life, and their authority varies according to their function and personality. Primarily I think it is probably true to say that the chiefs are derived from families who have hereditary tradition entitling them to perform certain ritual. This ritual is connected in each case with some essential custom of the tribe, and as an individual of the family must perform the ritual if that part of the tribe is to prosper he acquires a certain authority in that particular matter. He cannot, however influential he may become, usurp the right of performing any other ritual, unless he has the hereditary right to it.

It is not infrequent that different functions are performed by one man owing to his family connections. But it can safely be assumed that in each section of a clan there will be several chiefs with various functions, which they perform by hereditary right and so have some authority.

It is from these chiefs that the government normally chooses its mouthpiece, and calls the government chief, and it is obviously to the advantage of the government to select a man whose function is of an executive nature which gives him some authority over the young men and so have some control over their fighting propensities.

The most effective organization the tribes possess is their fighting system. Among the Nuer, for instance, when a boy reaches the age of about 14, he is marked with all the other boys of his age with the tribal marks at a ceremony with considerable ritual and he is 'initiated' to manhood. The lads so marked in a period of several years are combined into one class and that class has a special name, and the only way there is of ascertaining the age of Nuer is to get his age class.

What the subsequent ritual and training is, is a matter about which little is known. But the organization such as it is is for war and training in warlike practices.[1]

Whether such an organization can be diverted to the arts of peace instead of war is a question that has got to be answered. In any case it not infrequently occurs that the chief of the warriors is a useful man to be the government chief as he has influence over the young men in his special capacity.

There are however other points of importance to be made: one is that where the age-class system holds, the chiefs normally come out of the senior age-class. This would not necessarily apply to a chief whose function is purely ritualistic (e.g. rain making), but would be almost certainly the case where his function was executive, e.g. chief of the warriors or the cattle chief.

Equally it may occur that a chief acquires so high a reputation that he retains his position although his age-class has been superseded and his contemporaries have all, so to speak, gone to stud.

---

[1] For descriptions of initiation and age-sets among the Nuer see: Stigand (1918a), Coriat (1993: document 1.2), Crazzolara (1932), Evans-Pritchard (1936a and 1940a), Howell (1948b). Willis is here following Stigand's presentation of the Nuer age-sets as a formalised regimental system, akin to the Maasai, an interpretation which Evans-Pritchard later refuted.

But as a general rule the effective life of a chief in his 'chiefly' authority is the period that his age-class is senior.[2]

Thus the government representative (who is equally known as chief) need not remain in one family at all. When the existing government chief dies or gives up because he is feeling old, there should be a variety of persons of 'chiefly' rank from whom it is possible to select the man best suited to do the government work.

The case of the Ret of the Shilluk is sui generis and the succession is governed by tribal custom.

In the past when a feud had gone on for a long time and had become a public nuisance, the tribesmen had devised a means of ending the feud by getting influential men to bring the parties together and work out a compromise between them and have the matter settled with the proper ritual. This has been adapted to the formation of chiefs' courts which settle up points of dispute, if possible before they become the subject of battle, and also deal with assessment of personal compensation due to aggrieved parties in matters of blood money, matrimony, etc., etc.

The courts work in with the functionaries who are specially required to perform certain rites, and they cannot usurp these functions in any way. For instance the chief whose business it is to put the first spear into the sacrificial bull killed to end a feud must still perform his rite or the feud is not ended: the court only settles the cattle payments to be made which satisfy the parties and enable them to accept the performance of the rite and the conclusion of the feud.

In practice the courts give a good indication of how well a chief is doing his work. If he is playing the tyrant within his own sphere, it is likely to be exposed by the number of appeals that will be made to the court against decisions he has given within that sphere.

Without the check of the court, an individual chief is liable to try and acquire absolute authority and to oppress his people until they are exacerbated to the point of killing him. It has come within my experience to find a chief deliberately exploiting the assistant district commissioner and persuading him to take action against a section for alleged misdemeanour,

---

[2] Willis was wrong to separate the spiritual from the executive authority of the cattle chief (or man of cattle). The reputation of the man of cattle among the Nuer rests as much on the perceived strength of his spiritual power (*ring*) over cattle as on efficient livestock management. This can be achieved by young men and need not be handed on according to seniority. In fact, neither the Nuer nor any other Nilotic peoples of Upper Nile Province had a highly structured succession of offices and age-sets, as found among many other peoples of Northeast Africa. The system Willis outlines here is closer to that found among the Maa- and Oromo-speaking peoples of Kenya (e.g. Maasai, Nandi and Borana), about whom more was known at this time.

Some Suggestions for the Future

when the truth was that the chief had been behaving like a tyrant and he wanted to make the tribesmen see that he could get government force behind him to support his tyranny. In another case, a government chief tried to assume to himself the functions of a leopard chief to which he was not entitled.[3]

In fact therefore, when a chief appears to have absolute authority it is desirable to keep an eye on him as it is likely that he is exceeding his rights.

It is clear that the more knowledge we have of tribal custom, traditional and ritual, the sounder basis we shall have on which to build our native administration.

The government has recognized this by the appointment of Dr. Evans-Pritchard to study the ethnology of the Nuer.

Food supply

One of the first needs of all the Nilotics is a more extensive and stable food supply; in many clans cultivation is limited almost wholly to the women and until the men are able and willing to do their share, the harvest can hardly be expected to meet tribal needs. The need for more cultivation of grain and food-stuffs has been impressed on the tribes, and on the chiefs. If all the tribesmen are scattered in every direction looking for higlig nuts, fish or game, they can hardly be expected to be available to carry out the chief's orders.

It is not however to be expected that a cattle owning people will divert wholly to cultivation, though they may modify their habits, as have the Shilluk to some degree owing to paucity of cattle and the pinch of hunger.[4]

Civil and criminal jurisdiction of the courts

At present the courts do not primarily do more than determine the compensation to be paid for personal wrong by one tribesman to another; but there is a tendency to impose a fine for disobedience of orders, such as a summons to appear before the court. In W. Nuer this system of fining has

---

[3] In fact, the assumption of the duties of the 'leopard-skin chief' was very often a matter of common consent rather than heredity. Numerous 'hereditary chiefs' in the 1920s and 1930s were first or second generation descendants of men who had been given the emblems of chiefly office (the leopard-skin) in the nineteenth century.

[4] The Nuer and Dinka of the province relied far more on agriculture than was immediately evident from their apparent obsession with cattle cases, a fact which was only then being recognized in the aftermath of the Nuer Settlement when the implementation of Willis' policies of segregation and resettlement drastically reduced agricultural production; see Johnson (1991b).

been considerably extended and a number of calves were paid as fines by tribesmen who had omitted to grow cotton.

The idea of a penalty due to society (except in the case of Shilluk blood-money where 5 cows go to the Ret and 5 bullocks to the government) is not yet assimilated by the tribesmen and when they get what they consider is crime, they almost always refer it to the ADC. Still less do the chiefs' courts recognize imprisonment or stripes as a tribal punishment. For these reasons I am sceptical of the wisdom or possibility of giving any criminal powers to chiefs' courts.

Crime however is relatively rare and there are many minor misdemeanours which a chief can appropriately deal with by fining. It is a question however whether it is necessary to legalize these fines any more than it was necessary to legalize the fines imposed by nazirs and omdas in the Northern Sudan until quite recent years.[5]

With custom in its present fluid state and in a period of transition it seems to me advisable to avoid defining these powers too closely as they may develop along unexpected lines.

Tribal custom as the basis of administration

As however custom is the basis of tribal law it is of the utmost importance to see that innovations are absorbed or grafted into custom and not merely superimposed upon it.

The effect of outside influence on the tribesmen is so liable to have a bad effect on their character and morality that it is necessary to stress the importance of keeping them under their tribal rules. The detribalized Nilotic although he may have the externals of a different civilization has in fact only surrendered his proper morality for the shadow of another which has no hold on him.

The essential is that the tribesmen if they do adopt other codes, should only do so as supplementary to their own code. Otherwise the whole tribal

---

[5] Khartoum's proposal to regularise the powers of sheikhs in the northern provinces in 1920 was greeted with some reluctance by provincial governors. The Powers of Nomad Sheikhs Ordinance of 1922 enabled the government to issue warrants to recognized tribal sheikhs, empowering them to deal with most criminal offences. The removal of Egyptian mamurs after 1924 accelerated the process of devolving judicial and administrative authority to tribal leaders in the North, culminating in the 1927 Powers of Sheikhs Ordinance which extended such powers to territorial sheikhs and sheikhs of settled peoples. The Powers of Sheikhs Ordinance of 1928 set up inter-tribal courts. All of these enactments were finally incorporated into one statute, the Native Courts Ordinance of 1932, providing the legal basis for Native Administration throughout the Northern Sudan. The creating of courts and issuing of warrants proceeded much more slowly in the South, following the Chiefs' Courts Ordinance of 1931. See Daly (1986: 360–8, 415).

system is liable to break down. This is not likely to find favour with certain types of religious propagandist, but is a principle to be adhered to with the utmost tenacity.

Inevitably on these lines the progress of the tribes will be slow but it should be sound: and during the period of consolidation it is desirable that the tribesmen should not be given easy opportunity of losing their true custom for an illusory social rise. Thus, if they are employed on any extensive works, it should be made a special condition of such employment that they should not mix with more sophisticated labourers from the North and should be dealt with in their own language through 'gangers' of their own under the control of a British overseer and under the supervision of a British official with proper knowledge of their language and customs.[6]

Tribute

In principle it is right that the tribesmen should make some acknowledgement of their position under government and that they should pay at least something for the benefits they receive. In practice, hitherto, it was found difficult to get anything but cattle: the introduction of cotton-growing provided a means of introducing cash and made it possible to collect the tribute from the individual able-bodied man instead of pooling the individual dues in the value of one animal.

Unfortunately the growing of cotton is no longer economic and unless a substitute can be found, there would seem no alternative but to return to the old method of taking cattle, but I think it is very undesirable to do so, except in certain cases such as serum cattle.

Whilst some cattle have a value either in the market or for making rinderpest serum, many of the cattle from such clans as Gaweir are of little value, and the difficulty and expense of transporting them to a market are prohibitive.

Moreover with clans like Gaweir whose young men have little discipline, it is of great value to insist on individual service by the young men. So long as there are works of public utility such as roads and banks to be made, one means of obtaining value from the tribesmen and at the same time strengthening tribal discipline is to allot sections of the works to the sections of the clans according to their various capacity.

Admittedly this method does not bring in any actual cash to government on the other hand it provided a useful temporary solution to the problem;

---

[6] An implicit reference to irrigation scheme proposals recently under discussion; see below, Appendix 2.

and whilst the works of public utility are being completed, some scheme for the introduction of money values may be worked out.

In practice it should be managed as follows: the chief or more probably sub-chief would be shown a job of work which is worth, say, £20 and would be told that as he has so many able-bodied men in his section, capable of doing this work in, say, 15 days, he would by employing these men at a nominal wage of 2 Pt per diem, expend the sum of £20. The government would certainly have to supply the durra at any rate until local supplies are larger, and this would have to be taken into consideration in estimating the value of the work to government.

At first there would only be a book entry showing expenditure £20 on labour and £X on durra, and revenue tribute £20.

Later on the actual cash would be paid to the workers, and they would pay tribute in cash on demand.

An experiment on these lines is being made in Zeraf Valley this year, and should be observed with care.[7]

Stress should be laid on the fact that there is nothing contrary to the League of Nations Conventions in this matter.[8]

As time goes on the payment of work could be made more individual until it could be left to tribesmen to find the work congenial to them and so earn the cash they required for tribute or any other purposes.

If the Egyptian Irrigation schemes materialize it is likely that considerable numbers of labourers will be required not only for the main works such as the Gemmeiza barrage but for local works for the advantage of the tribesmen to compensate them for alteration of their normal conditions. The execution of such work would normally fall on the local tribesmen.

Tribute in practice has been assessed in an arbitrary sort of way, sometimes on a rough estimate of the herds, sometimes on the population on the basis of the number of huts and sometimes on the number of men fit for work.

In order however to avoid complications over finance we have never tied our hands to any one system.

In practice, I am confident that the best way is to base the dues on the number of adult male labourers: and ADCs have been finding it increas-

---

[7] This experiment was successful, from the administrative point of view, and labour dues in lieu of tribute continued to be levied on the Nuer—at least in the Zeraf Valley—throughout the 1930s. By 1934 the ADC there wrote, after detailing the previous year's completed labour projects, 'The question of the future is not going to be how to make the Nuer work, but how to find him enough to do to save him from boredom.' (Sherratt to governor, 28 Feb. 1934, SRO BD 66.A.1).

[8] A reference to the anti-slavery conventions of the League of Nations, which also attempted to outlaw unpaid labour.

Some Suggestions for the Future   337

ingly necessary to have lists of the men under each headman showing when possible the number of wives and children.

As however no account is taken of infants in arms and the details are often inaccurate, these so-called 'census' lists should be given a less precise name.

The tribal assessment would then work in closely with tribal custom. When the boys came up to be given their tribal marks, a ceremony that is practically universal, the local chiefs' court clerk would add the names of the freshly initiated to the tribal books, and casualties by death would be struck off.[9]

I anticipate that in the long run a system of tallies might be borrowed from Mongalla Province (I think it is also used in Bahr el Ghazal).

LABOUR

In the past all general 'labour' was obtained either by direct recruitment in the Northern Sudan for employment in the South or from the so-called 'malakia' settlements of detribalized Sudanese in places like Malakal.

The Forest Department has always adopted the former policy and the province and other departments including the Egyptian Irrigation Department mostly the latter.

The old slave population that was freed after the battle of Omdurman is now dying out; and the subsequent generation, brought up in more liberal conditions, has not improved on its forebears.

The disbanding of the Sudanese regiments[10] and discharges from the police have increased the population of Malakal and usually these are the heavy drinking cross-bred type, calling themselves Mohammedans but omitting all the weightier matter of that religion.

Apart from the descendants of the old slave population there are individual tribesmen who have left their tribe to attach themselves to town life. Sometimes because they were taken away by the government

---

[9] This would have been applicable to the Nuer and some groups of neighbouring Dinka only, as the Anuak, Murle, Shilluk and most of the northern Dinka did not mark their youths on reaching manhood. In the event the province retained the system of ten-yearly tribal censuses.

[10] The disbanding of the Sudanese battalions in the Egyptian Army, and their replacement by locally recruited territorial units had begun before 1924, but was accelerated as a result of the mutiny of that year. All units in the Sudan were separated from Egyptian control with the creation of the Sudan Defence Force in 1925. The last of the old battalions (the 9th Sudanese) was disbanded in 1930.

officials in a menial capacity and then deserted, sometimes to get away from the results of their own misbehaviour at home.

Both classes have little to recommend them: their work is poor and expensive for what they do, their habits and morals are deplorably low, and as they have no recognizable organization it is difficult to cope with them.

Their women are worse than the men.

A continuance of the policy originally adopted in the Southern Sudan would have been, by degrees, to turn the whole population into 'malakia'; this lamentable prospect was, fortunately discerned but not before a considerable population of this type had collected, and it is constantly increasing as the conditions of life in the Northern Sudan drive the remnants of the 'servile' classes Southwards.

One trouble about them is that they provide an easy refuge to any tribesman who wishes to evade his tribal liabilities and these tribesmen inevitably drift into the lowest dregs of the population where drink and immorality soon destroy their character and probably their health.

For the needs of Malakal town itself, for the building programme of PWD and EID and for such work as water carrying, building tukls and the like, the 'malakia' population of Malakal is sufficient. It is desirable to avoid sending out parties of 'malakia' or so-called 'Eliri' (mostly Baggara from Southern Kordofan) to work among the tribesmen.

As long as the government is dependent on Arabic as its means of inter communication with natives of the Southern Sudan, the employment of malakia or their equivalent from Omdurman is inevitable; whilst the employment of Northerners as smiths, builders and carpenters helps to add to the malakia ranks, as they find local tribesmen to employ (and generally exploit) and impose upon them the externals of a society with which they have little really in common.

If and when the training of crafts reaches the necessary standard, all the 'Ostas' ought to be local tribesmen using English largely as their mutual means of communication with other tribesmen, and they would have little difficulty in bringing in labour of their own type as required.

The malakia would then become what they ought to be, an alien enclave of the relics of the Bad Old Times.

It must be long however before the standard of work attained by native craftsmen can reach the limit required. But in the meanwhile steps should be taken to check the influx of Northerners, and to find means to substitute Southern labour *with its proper organization* for 'malakia'. The root of the problem lies in the difficulty of finding subordinate officials such as gangers, forest overseers, and the like who are not northern-bred.

The UNP has one economic asset that has yet to be exploited in any way and that is a large and increasing population. There should be available large quantities of labour, but it must be handled in the appropriate way and as long as working for government or for any considerable organization means the sacrifice of the tribal ideals, no labour ought, or (except in small numbers) is likely, to be available.[11]

DRINK

One of the chief objections to the malakia as a section of society is the degree to which they drink and the fact that they are greatly addicted to araki. The mild form of beer which is almost a staple food among the tribesmen is of little alcoholic power but when they are introduced to the stronger forms of merisa brewed by the malakia and still more to araki, it has a very bad effect on them and it is very desirable to keep the tribesmen away from either the strong merisa or araki.

The question of araki is already the subject of consideration by the government but the practical means of coping with the problem have not yet been found. But the drink problem is an additional reason for keeping the tribesmen away from centres where they are exposed to this temptation and organizing them as labour outside existing labour centres.

THE ECONOMIC PROBLEM

The great divergence between revenue and expenditure in UNP must naturally be a matter for serious consideration especially in times of financial stringency.

The only revenue which might be capable of expansion at present is the tribute or similar levy from the tribesmen. It was hoped that cotton growing would prove to be a profitable crop which would pay both government and people, but it has failed to do so, and the only assets the tribes have is cattle and of these they have not really enough for their requirements. They do not at present grow enough corn for their own needs. Thus in fact an increase of tribute on any appreciable scale is not practicable.

Experiments in sugar cane were made up the Bahr el Ghazal as a possible raw material for making spirits, but the results if obtained have

[11] As the demand for labour increased in Malakal itself during the 1930s, the government created a 'tribal village' to the south of the town (in the quarter now known as Dengar Shufu) where temporary migrant tribal labourers could be kept segregated from the corrupting influence of the malakia. For a few years the exiled Nuer prophet Dual Diu was appointed 'chief' of the tribal village. This experiment in maintaining native administration within the town was abandoned during the Second World War.

not been divulged to the Province. The possibility of turning the 'Sudd' into cellulose has been put forward, but so far as I know has not been examined as a practical proposition.[12]

The agricultural experiment made by ADC Bor on a plot of land walled off from the flood is full of interesting possibilities.

It is conceivable for instance that an organization like the Shell Co. would think it worth its while to develop the manufacture of raw spirit to take the place of benzine in an area where transport of the paraffin product was unduly high.

It is conceivable that it might be produced in a large scale at so low a price as would make it cut out ordinary benzine over a large part of the hinterland of Eastern Africa, and the government would presumably profit by means of reduced cost of transport, profits on transport, royalty, rent etc.[13]

As long as transport charges are what they are and the difficulties of obtaining barge accommodation remain as they are, any economic development is merely a matter of academic consideration.

It is arguable and to my mind correct to say that if any such economic development were to materialize it could only do so by supplying its own transport and by obtaining bed rock charges on SGR. The syndicate operating the business, wood-pulp or anything else, would have to accept special conditions in the matter of employment of labour and the type of overseer etc. it would use. There would be no reason why such an organization should not work to its own advantage and that of the government and give useful employment to many tribesmen under suitable organization.

The activities of the EID would not materially differ from those of a business syndicate except they would be less profitable to the Sudan government.

TRADE

The system of trading permits issued to merchants postulates a state of affairs that does not in fact exist. In theory an independent merchant draws his own permit and can obtain a permit for an agent to work for him as a shopman.

---

[12] See NRO UNP 1/9/77, 'Cellulose from Sudd' (1928).

[13] The irony of this proposition is that in the 1970s and 1980s substantial deposits of petroleum and natural gas were discovered in the Bentiu, Bor and Northern districts of Upper Nile and Jonglei Provinces.

In fact, there is not an independent merchant in the province. The apparent merchants are really commission agents working for principals in Malakal who are in their turn commission agents for their principals in Omdurman. For instance with very few exceptions the whole of the merchants in W. Nuer are in one syndicate which also has a large combination dominating Yirrol, and the head partner is completely in the hands of his principals in Omdurman.

The result is that unless pressure can be brought to bear on the merchants in Omdurman it is impossible to get any improvement on the trash that is offered to the tribesmen at an absurdly high price.

DC Western Nuer has reported that some of his people refuse to buy shoddy articles; and Messrs Limnios' agent at Daga reported that he had to revise his list of goods and provide much better class goods than he had anticipated.

The merchants in Omdurman have no interest in the improvement of the native, indeed anything that encourages the native to demand value for his money is deplorable to them, and they have a complete hold over their subordinates.

It is argued sometimes that the merchant is the true pioneer of civilization and so he may be, but only if he does his share of providing increased opportunities and facilities to the natives amongst whom he works. The sale of beads brass wire and inferior Manchester goods does not, in my opinion, meet the case. Supposing by some act of Divine justice all the fairly dishonest merchants were removed from the UNP (a situation to compare with the argument over Sodom and Gomorrah) the actual loss to the tribesmen of physical necessities would be negligible, and as the only commodities available for sale by the natives, cattle and hides are drugs on the market, the loss to trade is negligible.

Though such a Divine interference is not seriously to be anticipated, it still remains possible for steps to be taken to reduce the number of permits in out-stations and seriously to reduce the number of so-called merchants in Malakal, many of whom are rogues caught out in malpractices or misdemeanours with the tribesmen and hanging on desperately in the hope of some lucky chance restoring them to more opportunities for knavery, and to consider seriously how a fair and decent trade of sound and desirable objects can be pushed through relatively respectable firms.

The missionaries may not touch it. The government did run 'canteens' to discover that a government official is not a tradesman and when he is, is dishonest or incompetent.

The solution is yet to seek, and lies, I believe, in the possibility of opening up some large economic scheme such as those mentioned in the previous section and getting syndicate to work up local shops from a centre of their own, the shops being managed by tribesmen of the class that has learnt a certain amount in school and appears to have a bent for trade.

Some outlet for the mission school boys other than government service ought to exist and trade is the obvious one. But as they have no capital, that must be supplied from some other source.

The transition period must take time and is likely to cause 'reverberations' in the Northern Sudan where the recipients of 100% on trash will pull every string to retain their trade: and time is needed to obtain the necessary syndicate and the required shopmen from the tribes. But I feel that it should be made a definite plank of the government policy.

There is one solution of the labour and the trade problems which should receive careful consideration. One thing only is a common taste to all the tribesmen of UNP and that is a passion for the acquisition of cattle, and any organization that could provide an adequate number of cows and cow calves for sale in return for wages, would find no difficulty in obtaining labour.

Admittedly it is not easy to get cows or cow calves. To take local ones is only to transfer cattle from one savage to another and what is needed is cattle from outside. The Baggara will not willingly part with their female stock and then only because they think there is something the matter with it. Imported animals would not stand the climate.

Nevertheless it does not seem unreasonable to suppose that a solution can be found, and will be found provided sufficient pressure is brought to bear on the subject.

It is to be hoped that now that the province has the services of a Veterinary inspector it may be possible to protect the tribal herds from diseases like rinderpest and pleuro-pneumonia, and this alone would go far to increasing the cattle population to adequate figures. It is hoped at the same time to improve the breed by selection of breeding animals and elimination of scrub animals. But this must take a considerable time.

ARMS

It has been estimated that the Gaajak have 10,000 Gras rifles among them. The Anuak being divided about two thirds in Abyssinia and one third in the Sudan have no difficulty in obtaining rifles. What they all do have trouble over is ammunition which costs the equivalent of 10 Pt a round.[14]

A man, apparently wearing a full bandolier, will be found as a rule to

---

[14] For the Ethiopian arms trade in the first third of this century see Johnson (1986b) and Garretson (1986).

Some Suggestions for the Future

have one or two genuine rounds which might go off, one or two that have obviously failed to go off and the rest are wooden dummies.

The first thing a tribesman does on obtaining a rifle is to knock the back sights off, as they irk his shoulder and with the exception of a few retired soldiers the tribesmen have no idea of marksmanship.

In tribes further away from the Abyssinian frontier the number of rifles is much smaller. In fact in districts like Yirrol and W. Nuer they are very small and the owners are mostly known. But the capture of a rifle is largely a matter of luck as the owner keeps it hidden and tells no one, not even his wife.

The existence of these rifles is not a serious menace to government as an armed opposition but might with special luck cause the death of an ADC or other government official.

Even this is unlikely unless there has been some serious mistake or miscarriage of justice. But the owners of these rifles have all paid real genuine cattle for them and look on their rifles as easily realizable capital. If the government attempted to confiscate on a large scale in Gaajak, the result would only be to alienate native feeling, drive the natives into Abyssinia where they would raid unceasingly into the Sudan and create a situation on our frontier which would provide an almost insoluble problem.

It is worth mentioning that among the Shilluk who could without serious difficulty have obtained arms from further east, tribal etiquette lays down that the use of firearms in a tribal fight is unfair and not permissible.[15]

Actually in practice casualties by gunshot are rare in any tribal fights, and it seems possible that the rifle will gradually fall into disuse as ammunition is unobtainable. Only a truly malicious or Machiavellian person would issue Mark VII, as this, (provided the tribesmen contrived to get it into the rifle with a rawhide wrapping as the Nuba do) would successfully blow the head off the man who fired the rifle.[16]

---

[15] For the Nuer and Dinka, as well, at this time, there were specific prohibitions regarding the use of clubs and spears in intersectional fighting: the more distant the relation between the sections, the more lethal the weapon allowed. The rationale was not etiquette, but an attempt to avoid fatalities, and thus inhibit the spread of blood feuds between closely-related sections. It was only after the proliferation of firearms during the first civil war in Upper Nile (1964-72) that guns became widely used in intersectional fights.

[16] The standard issue .303 cartridge for the army and police was a smaller calibre than the rifles available to the Nuer. In the Nuba hills, where such ammunition was readily available on the black market, the Nuba wrapped the cartridge in leather to enable it to fit snugly in the breach of their 19th-century single-shot .450 Remington rifles. The result, according to Sir Angus Gillan, former deputy governor and governor of the Nuba Mountains and Kordofan Provinces (1921-32) was that while the bullet rattled around in the barrel a bit, ' . . . anything over 100 or 150 yards you would be very unlucky if you got hit by it, but if you were hit by it at close range it would make a very nasty wound, going spinning around.' (interview with Sir Angus Gillan, 9 May 1979, Oxford Development Records Project, 'The Role of British Forces in Africa—The Sudan Defence Force', Rhodes House, Oxford).

Given a few years more wear and tear the existing rifles can be written off. Whether they will be supplemented from Abyssinia depends on the capacity of that distinguished member of the League of Nations to carry out its obligations. But the trade has certainly languished in recent years, partially because the Abyssinian traders will only exchange arms and ammunition for ivory. This the tribesmen cannot get without ammunition so they get into a vicious circle and can do nothing.

THE FUTURE OF THE DISTRICTS

On the assumption that the chiefs in each clan develop a reasonable authority over their people, and can be checked for their ability and honesty by the cases coming before the chiefs' courts, and that the tribesmen effectively realize that peaceful methods of establishing a claim lead to success and violence only to trouble, the work of ADCs will tend to be more and more a light supervision of the chiefs and courts. The amount of effort involved in starting the organization is very great and has been recognized by the fact that during 'Nuer Settlement' ADCs were doubled.

Already however the second ADC has been dispensed with in Lau; it is anticipated that the second ADC Zeraf Valley can be economized when the road system proposed is brought into being. The second ADC in W. Nuer is justified by a considerable addition of territory to the north.[17]

It is conceivable that further economies could be effected in time by putting the whole Nuer tribe into a sub-administration under, say, a DC and two ADCs who would be sufficiently mobile to reach all points of the Nuer country in a relatively short time, and would be so distributed over the whole area that they would all have some knowledge of the whole.

This can hardly be attained under several years partly because the road system is not completed and mainly because the tribal organization is not sufficiently strong to be trusted to run independently.[18]

The period of time that would elapse till the economy of staff would be possible is likely to coincide more or less with the time that will pass before the irrigation schemes will have sufficiently materialized to begin to make demands on local labour; and the ADCs economized would then be

---

[17] H. A. Romilly, the second ADC at Abwong in 1929–30, was transferred to Western Nuer in June 1930, after the completion of that year's Nuer Settlement patrols. F. J. H. Bacon, ADC Zeraf Valley 1929–31, was 'economized' out of the service in 1931.
[18] It had been Fergusson's ambition to be given charge of an entire 'Nuer sub-province' along similar lines (Fergusson (1930: 160–4)). In fact, the population and territory covered by the Nuer were such that there were never fewer than 6 DCs and ADCs appointed to administer them.

Some Suggestions for the Future 345

available to organize, control and administer the labour—and should be well experienced in the ways of the tribesmen.

By that time, it might equally be possible to combine Bor and Duk district with Yirrol, at least in so far as Dinka are concerned. At present the difficulty of inter-communication from Bor and Malek on the east bank and the Aliab and Cic Dinka on the west bank precludes any possibility of combination. I do not see how any great economy can be effected here, as there is now only one ADC in Duk and Bor (where some years ago there used to be two) and one at Yirrol (where there were two until January 1931) but there should be advantage in their working together and having a common system of courts etc.[19]

In the case of the Shilluk there is undoubtedly a couple of years work for two competent officials to get things into working order: and if the Shilluk are managed by one official, more means of crossing the river by ferry will have to be devised. But the Shilluk and Rueng (Khor Atar) Dinka should make a reasonable unit in time.[20]

Whether it will be possible to bring the Dungjol into the same administrative unit as the Melut Dinka is largely a question of communications and the possibilities have not been fully examined but prima facie there should be means of doing so.[21]

Thus the whole province would include four main native administrations, as above described, (1) Northern Dinka, (2) Shilluk (plus odJments of Dinka), (3) Nuer, and (4) Southern Dinka and Atwot and the fifth would consist of (5) Anuak and Beir.

The development of the last is at present a matter of speculation as there is still a considerable area in the S.E. corner of the province including part of the Boma plateau over which no attempt at administration is made.

The so-called Khoma Burun in the Daga and Kigille area would have to remain an offshoot of the Nasir section of the Nuer administration, unless it proved possible to open up communications between them and the Burun further North. In any case it would seem worth while to consider the advisability of making a sixth unit to include all the Burun of Fung Province and possibly all the variegated negroid tribes such as Ingassana into the UNP and make a definite line of cleavage east and west between the Arabs to the North and the Negroids to the South.[22]

---

[19] Yirol was detached from Upper Nile Province and made a separate district of Equatoria Province in 1936.
[20] The Rueng were in fact transferred to Abwong in 1933, and then to the Zeraf District in 1938.
[21] The Dinka of Renk and Melut were added to the Shilluk District (which already contained the Dungjol) in 1935; the whole was renamed Northern District in 1938 with the addition of the Ngok Dinka, the Meban and Uduk.
[22] With the exception of the inclusion of the Uduk in UNP from 1938 to 1953, such a complete racial division was never attempted.

If the suggestions outlined above materialized, I should urge the advisability of bringing the DCs responsible for each unit fairly constantly into headquarters to make their reports, clear up their accounts and incidentally get a change of life and some normal exercise. This would get rid of a great deal of correspondence, as instead of interchange of letters often ending nowhere there would be a definite memorandum, the result of discussion if necessary, which would be available in the file concerned.

Equally I recommend the practice of tribal gatherings of chiefs to meet and talk with the governor at least yearly and even biennially if this proved practicable. This has proved difficult in the past owing to the lack of tribal organization and poor communications but should be increasingly easy; and it not only enables the chiefs to express themselves with greater freedom than they can in the unfamiliar environment of Malakal, where they are strangers in a strange land.

EDUCATION

A suggestion for the training of 'ostas' has already been outlined. One of the reasons for the maintenance of the Lady Baker in the upper reaches of the Jebel river is to provide a training place for tribesmen in medical work. The systematic working of the courts and the decisions of the chiefs will call more and more for clerks capable of keeping proper records. The educational provision at present dependent on the missions will require to be widely extended and supplemented if it is to meet all demands. Veterinary retainers, and foresters have yet to be found a means of training and if any economic development is found possible in UNP, trained tribesmen will be needed in many capacities.

In the circumstances it would seem not unreasonable to contemplate the possibility of a Stack Memorial School in which all the various requirements of tribal life would be catered for. It would be largely a technical school, and the main medium of instruction would have to be English. It is unlikely that either Loka or Wau would commend themselves to tribesmen of UNP to whom their places are remote and uncongenial, and the population of UNP would justify the establishment of such a school for itself. It is worth remarking that the SMI had to withdraw a number of pupils of UNP origin from the Loka school and to put others under medical supervision owing to the deleterious effects on their lungs of the altitude of Loka. Where best such a school should be located it is difficult in present circumstances to say: certainly not in Malakal and preferably in some sufficiently debatable area not to infringe on the rights of any special mission or to put the school too much under the influence of one denomination.[23]

FUTURE ORGANIZATION OF THE PROVINCE

As time goes on and literacy in local languages increases, the type of translator required at headquarters will tend to be be employees capable of reading Dinka, Shilluk, Nuer etc. and Arabic will be used even less than it is now.

Moreover the local clerks who are working with ADCs or are under training to do so, will form a class by themselves and ought to have liaison at headquarters.

I anticipate therefore that either a separate organization for dealing with Native Administration will gradually be formed or the whole junior clerical staff at headquarters will be supplied from Southern sources and will work on lines somewhat different from those appropriate to employees of the Northern Sudan. Such a staff would be very much cheaper and would presumably stand local climatic conditions much better than Northerners. It would however probably require fairly highly trained and efficient supervision.

One difficulty in the way is that it is not possible to make a gradual substitution of Northerners for Southerners without incurring considerable risk of spoiling the latter as they would inevitably imitate the less desirable traits of the Northerners and would probably expect to be put on an equality of pay with them.

I am assuming that a reformed system of accounts will have been instituted, in English and that accounts in the districts will be kept under the supervision of ADCs assisted by their native clerks, and a small but highly trained nucleus of accountants would compile the results at headquarters.

It is fairly certain that a clerical staff of this sort would not be familiar with the routine methods, the regulations and circulars which form the basis of similar work in the Northern Sudan and it seems probably that the government will find it economical and effective to modify its rules for the Southern Sudan and in effect to build up another administrative system in the South on simpler lines.

[23] A Lee Stack Memorial School (named in honour of the murdered governor-general) had been opened in Wau in 1927, but for financial reasons this was handed over to the Catholic church in September 1931, and renamed St Antony's. The government did not re-enter the field of intermediate education in the Southern Sudan until after the Second World War (Sanderson and Sanderson (1981: 133–4)).

Chapter 14

Already the difficulty of making a fair comparison between demands in the Northern and Southern Sudan must have been felt, and the cleavage is likely to increase rather than decrease. Without attempting to define the government's policy too precisely, I feel that these considerations will have their importance in due course and must affect the lines on which, for instance, education will be tackled and building schemes promoted; and all commitments should be looked at in the light of a relatively independent system growing up on its own lines in the South.[24]

The DCs and ADCs who work in the UNP tend to become specialists. A man who knows Nuer i.e. can speak their language and understand their customs, is so much more valuable in Nuer country than elsewhere that he is liable to be kept in it for a considerable time. The same applies to Dinka, Shilluk and Anuak. Then when the time comes when he must be transferred, he is fairly senior and yet is like as not quite unfamiliar with normal methods of administration or with the legal codes and ordinances.

I suggested awhile ago that a regular system of exchange should be worked out between UNP and Mongalla so that officials who had had a long period of roughing it in UNP could go to some relatively quiet and healthy station in Mongalla for a few years. C.S. did not see his way to doing this formally but said he would work it out as far as could be managed.[25]

I still think it would be sound, but it would probably be best to combine the three Southern Provinces for purposes of exchange.

According to the last quarterly return the distribution of British officials is as follows:

Province	Political Service	Contract	Total
UNP	9	11	20
Bahr el Ghazal	4	10	14
Mongalla	5	9	15
		one vacancy	

It looks as if it might be possible by doing four-year shifts in Bahr el Ghazal and UNP and two year shifts in Mongalla to make the arrangement

---

[24] Clerical staff in the three Southern provinces were never completely Southernised prior to independence, and disparities in pay between Northerners and Southerners holding positions of the same grade was one of the grievances voiced by Southern junior administrative staff at the Juba conference of 1947.

[25] Coriat, the longest-serving Nuer DC at this time, was posted to Juba in Mongalla Province before ultimately ending his administrative career as DC Baggara in Kordofan, one of the most senior (and coveted) postings a DC could have.

whether formally or not. The linguistic difficulties are the chief trouble. If the system of tribal administrations be adopted as I suggested earlier, and applied throughout the South, there will be areas of varying size, importance and difficulty which should provide scope for administrative officials and hope of reasonable advancement, without which there is little incentive for officials to pursue a specialist career in an uncomfortable country.

Admittedly the full development of a scheme would take some years but I feel that unless some possibility of fairly swift advancement is given, it will be difficult to get officials of the proper stamp, or to ensure that they will attain the necessary standard of efficiency in the local tongues.

APPENDIX 1

K. C. P. Struvé, Handing-Over Notes, July–August, 1926

July 25th

Dear Willis,

    I am writing these notes for you on my last journey up the Sobat. As far as I can I am keeping to such matters as you cannot find in the Annual Reports, Province Diaries and files, and DCs cannot very well tell you themselves. It is not easy to gauge what you may most wish to know, but generally I have tried to keep to points in which this province is outside your own experience and peculiar to itself, and to help you to avoid making the mistakes which have been made in the past through ignorance of local conditions. All the DCs except Wyld and McMullen have had such long experience of their districts that on all ordinary matters you can get reliable information from them, and, as I have given you in these notes extremely candid opinions on their respective merits and characters, you may be able to gauge their reliability. What they cannot tell you are the origins and histories of little matters which have influenced systems and developments, though small in themselves.

    I am writing practically without system, mixing up descriptions of people with trains of thought which such descriptions bring up, and which I am afraid of forgetting if I do not put them down at once. So please forgive somewhat disjointed jottings, and please also tear up the confidential notes on the personnel; some of the rest it may help you to keep for a bit.

    Davies will give you a short note on agriculture which may be useful for the annual report; the rest can be got from the diaries, a few reports and Coryton, who has not been on leave, so knows the year's history. Coghlan can tell you of PWD work done; I will ask for a statement to be prepared for you. But I have purposely kept the diaries very full, and most can be got from them. Make the most of our export of dura, which has done good work this year in pulling us out of the rut of non-productive provinces. Future policy in this respect is outlined in my reply to Schuster's circular letter on cotton-growing policy; I think the reference number is 2-M-5. Schuster approved it.

    Re the animals, I have drawn forage and groom allowance up to July 31st and have ordered forage for the next month against you, so you start drawing by proxy from August 1st. I am still in doubt what to do about the pony, but he is decidedly no worse, and as you cannot lose by him, I will leave him for you unless I hear definitely to the contrary. We are leaving a few music books for you, and few other odds and ends which may be of use; anything which is not ticketed (and the ticketed things will probably be taken over by Coryton for their future owners) is yours. I hope you will find all in order.

The 'Hafir' will be left for overhaul and for your return. For some inexplicable reason the SGR officials will never give any assistance to us in improving the steamers. I believe the idea still holds that we use them for joy-riding, and that it doesn't matter what sort of steamer we have. Probably a more likely reason is that a province steamer is not an advertisement, like a tourist or post steamer, or the 'Lady Baker', or the 'Metemma' where the Kaid was able to put in a word; but whatever the reason there is almost an antagonism about it. We get rotten furniture, no clothes for the sailors, repairs scamped, stores' requisitions ignored, and so, as I think I told you, we run our own swindle fund to supply ourselves and carry out such small repairs and improvements as we can. I hope you will have better luck. I have managed to run up against the Havercrofts and Bayleys on matters of departmental administration, and this is perhaps their form of revenge. Criticism of the SGR amounts to blasphemy. Parker and Bramall have been helpful this year on matters of transport and trade, but possibly because the dura shortage exposed their lack of material, and since they went on leave, Havercroft and Bayley have shown signs of intending to go back on what was arranged. There is a letter to F[inancial] S[ecretary] from me about this, with special reference to the transport on the Sobat, which was arranged at the C.E.B. meeting in March, you remember.

Coryton is preparing the budget; he takes great care over this and his talent for detail is a great asset to us. But no matter how carefully it is prepared and explained, there will be no subsequent diminution in the number of telegrams from the Cedar Princes [Lebanese accountants of the Financial Department], somewhere about November and December. The only course is to have a trained giraffe to break the Renk telegraph line from time to time, and meanwhile to reply by letter. I think that game is the most exasperating form of Govt. interference from which you will suffer, because one knows it is both unnecessary and deliberate.

August 9th

I left on the 6th with a great send-off. We tuned up the piano before leaving but you will find the wood swelled a little, making the hammers tend to stick; this will pass off when the drier weather comes, and of course it needs constant attention. The key is at the bottom of the back of the piano under the hanging curtain. The horse I left in Coryton's charge; it is much better and I really hope has quite recovered from the fly, in which case it will be valuable as salted, but if Coryton finds it going back again he will either sell it or destroy it. The mules are now yours and you should find a useful sum of money awaiting you as excess Forage allowance. All the things marked down for you are also in Coryton's charge, put away in the two store-rooms; I hope you will find all in order. If you take over the horse it comes on to your forage allowance from August 1st, but if it is sold at a loss I stand the loss.

Coryton was well on with the budget when I left. The Annual Report awaits you, as there are ample notes for everything and you have only to collate, and here Coryton's knowledge will be of great assistance to you; only arrange with C[ivil] S[ecretary] to give you some law, if necessary, over the usual date. Try to keep Tunnicliffe who is most promising; I fear the SDF will want him back but he is most keen to stay on and I feel sure will justify any efforts you make on his behalf.

I recommend you not to visit the districts until the DCs concerned are back (except of course the northern ones), as there are only sarrafs or less in charge and they will not be able to enlighten you much on matters. But I hope you will give Coryton a chance of getting out as he will have had a very long spell in Malakal at rather trying work and has had no leave. He may be able to get Cann in and go out before you arrive. Coryton's wholehearted work impresses me more and more daily; he is always ready for anything at any minute of the 24 hours, splendidly conscientious.

I saw McMullen at Renk and told him that chances of permanent service were small but that I would ask in Khartoum what the policy is if any. He puzzles me greatly; I think he has the wish and ability to do well but has no will power; a very weak type. One cannot place reliance on him, and he seems unable to live in a lonely station, gets depressed and moody.

Khartoum, 11.8.26

I have sold my typewriter so finish in ms. Off tomorrow early; farewell dinner at the Club to-night. Ask Parr to tell you about McMullen, it unfortunately confirms our impressions.

My best wishes to you.

Yours,

K.C.P. Struvé

STAFF

I explained to you in Khartoum the principle on which we work. Mamurs, with a few exceptions, are not allowed executive authority among the tribes. The exceptions are Hussein Farag, Hussein Said and Talib Ismail, but in those cases only exceptionally, in the absence of the DC.

The district of Fangak has no clerical staff at all, but we send up an accountant-sarraf to Pletts when he asks for one, generally at the end of each month.

Abwong has an accountant-serraf only, and that only when the DC is there, e.g. from December to June inclusive.

Nasser has had a sarraf only, but should have a sub-mamur instead, as the suk there is growing.

Akobo has a sub-mamur, and when he is on leave, a sarraf is sent. A sub-mamur is necessary here, owing to the presence of the army, and it is best that he should be an officer.

The northern districts are better staffed, since there is a considerable revenue and large suks, while the peripatetic trader class needs much control.

When a sarraf or suchlike official is placed in charge of a station, it is in his technical capacity only. He has no authority over the police, and the senior NCO is informed of this quite definitely. He is not allowed to call himself naib el mamur [deputy mamur], and of course has no magisterial powers. Above all, and for those reasons, he gets no 'mamur's allowance'. This is a continual grievance, because apparently other southern provinces are more generous in this respect. Letters are addressed to such officials as mamur, for purposes of filing and registration, but they are not allowed to think that this implies the possible granting of those powers. The system works perfectly well, and prevents friction with the police and possible abuse of them, but DCs must satisfy themselves that both the police and the sarraf are observing this order. I gather that in the BOG such officials are really made acting mamurs, and generally in that province and in the NMP mamurs seem to have very great executive powers. Our system throws much more work on the DCs but it quite clearly defines responsibilities, and we never have the exasperating experience of seeing good work upset by the act of some underling temporarily in power. Incidentally I think the mamurs prefer it. Some of them are none too courageous, and if left alone get windy and start sending in alarmist reports, especially if the alarm is due to their own misdeeds. At Duk Faywil I have had for the moment to put an entirely new sub-mamur, and think it is only too likely that you may hear of fearful threats by Nuers against government until Wyld comes back. Very likely these will come via DC Bor [then part of Mongalla Province]. As Duk Faywil has only just come to us, and the Dinka chiefs there are still accustomed to look at the mamur as their real ruler (Wyld would hardly have had the time to eradicate this long-established principle), they will probably seize on this chance of getting up the old Dinka-Nuer disturbances. If anything of the sort occurs, you had better withdraw the sub-mamur at once, and let the police carry on. We have in any case marked him down for transfer when the road re-opens, and from what Wyld tells me, it seems quite likely that he may commit atrocities while he is alone. But the posting of him there was unfortunately unavoidable.

CHIEFS

We have followed the policy of allowing the tribes to choose their own chiefs unless these are absolutely unacceptable to us, and in any case no chief is appointed by us who is known for any reason to be quite unacceptable to the tribes. The latter type is quite as dangerous as the former to general tranquillity. Both Tunnicliffe and I consider that Bacon's choice of the Sultan paramount of the Adonga Anuaks is a most unfortunate one, and you may have trouble over that. A useless conceited youngster, while there is a particularly fine old fellow who seems to have at least as good a right to the stool whom Bacon did not meet.[1] I mention this since I do not consider we are obliged to back up the present man just because Bacon chose him if he turns out to be unsatisfactory. But the objection must come from the tribe first.

By means of the chiefs' councils there is little difficulty in finding out who are the best men to appoint provided you insist on any objections being voiced at the council and not allow the impression that objections would be unwelcome; this of course is difficult for them to understand but the point is to put the responsibility for the choice on the council. Shilluks and Dinkas are born 'councillors' but the Nuers are bad at it, and seem to fear a trap. Coriat's chiefs have greatly improved in this respect, and Wyld has at least one really outstanding chief. Yol Kur of the Bau-Wom is far and away the most intellectual man in the province and is remarkably good as a magistrate on a court. Of the Shilluk chiefs Afash Kur and Bol Aiwel, two very old men, are outstanding, the latter being a true orator with strong and independent opinions, who does not hesitate to find fault with government measures when necessary, and can be counted on to voice any discontent. His combined loyalty and independence make him a valuable asset. I should recommend you to get Cann to summon a Shilluk council shortly after you arrive; you will enjoy it and will get at the mentality of the tribe readily that way.[2] They have little reserve, and once they take a liking to you will welcome you anywhere.

---
[1] See Bacon (1924), for his account of his installation of Cam-wara-Akwei. The main rival, Cam Medho, turned out to be no less unsatisfactory from the government's point of view (see Biographical Notes).
[2] This meeting was held the following January; see Willis' 'Address to Shilluk gathering January 16th 1927', SAD 212/9/80–81.

POLICE

I gathered from Northcote that the principle of a commandant of police had not worked very well in most provinces, having caused a good deal of friction between the commandant and the DCs. I do not think the system I have in view is likely to do this, and so far as it has been worked, the DCs have appreciated it.

The commandant is not intended to go round and find fault with the drill, etc. His purpose is chiefly for record and unification. He is supplied monthly by the DCs with lists of their police, giving them opinions on the various men, whom they recommend for promotion or dismissal, whom they want transferred, etc. so that he can ensure fairness and continuity of promotion. All suggestions for alteration of drill, equipment, etc. go to him for consideration, to be considered as a whole, but each DC is held responsible for the discipline and smartness of the men immediately under him, and there does not seem to be any possibility of friction. If a DC wants the commandant to visit his district to see the police, he can go, and in certain cases the commandant might consider it necessary to ask the governor to allow him to visit a district in which he thought things were not satisfactory, but the order for this would come from the governor. As the police now number well over 300, and will be still further increased when the BOG Eastern District is taken over, this work is quite one man's job. But the commandant will also be DC for Malakal Town, which is also quite a considerable job. He will not be underworked.

I strongly recommend Tunnicliffe for the post. He takes great interest in and understands Sudanese. Coryton, who has been doing the work most of the time, does not understand Sudanese, and always favours any man who has a tinge of yellow in him. Because he has not the smartness of the 'Pasha's' Arab police at Merowi, Coryton cannot see any virtue in the Sudani's qualities, and denies them even courage. All the same, Coryton has done very valuable work in the record line and he wishes to keep control of the Store, which he manages in such a businesslike way that I strongly recommend approval. It will also be a good check on the sometimes too generous disposition of the DCs towards their police kit.

The mounted police were trained by Coriat in 1925, and by him and Wyld in 1926, while Tunnicliffe was present at his own request to learn mounted drill. This plan has worked well, and when either of these ex-cavalry DCs are available, e.g. when nearly due for or just back from leave with their districts still waterlogged and all the M.P. in Kodok, it would be as well to give the police a turn with them again. The M.P. having the magazine rifle, a month's intensive training at musketry is essential.

Tunnicliffe can do this, which is an agreement with the Kaid, based on which our arming of the M.P. with this rifle was allowed (correspondence in the confidential files).[3]

Coriat has organized the M.P. in sections, and they are divided up among the districts for dry-season work by sections and nothing less. So far the Frontier has had three sections, Akobo District two, and one each for Nasser, Abwong, Duk Faywil and Fangak. The Northern District had one divided between Renk and Melut, but this works badly as the men deteriorate without proper supervision, and I am trying to get these districts worked by chiefs' police like the Shilluk District. M.P. should never be put under mamurs. A really efficient force of M.P. reduces reliance on the Army to such an occasion as a general tribal rising, or to a situation such as might be brought about by a serious reverse of the M.P. Our tribes are no more tranquil than those of other southern provinces, but the M.P. have a preventive effect which patrols after the event can never have, so that we appear to be more orderly. The month of June, when southern districts are closing down, is an excellent time to concentrate the M.P. and deal with any part which has shown marked truculence during the dry season. These Civil patrols have a very good effect generally and require no reference to Khartoum, also they have no disturbing effects on any other part of the country than that immediately concerned; everywhere else the police are treated as friends as they pass through.

All through these Nuer districts, trekking is more difficult than in any other part of the Sudan. There is a tendency in Khartoum, of which you may be aware, to consider that conditions in the Southern provinces are uniform. People joy-ride through the NMP and Mongalla and in the more accessible parts of the BOG, and then, without visiting our inland parts, ask why we don't have roads like those provinces, or rest-houses, or why DCs don't travel in cars or why we can only work from December to May inclusive. Travel through Pletts' district in December, or through Coriat's in March, or anywhere in June, and you will get a most unpleasant object-lesson. I think the reason, apart from soil, is that this part, lying between the two great river systems of the Nile and the Pibor, is only recently retrieved from the lacustrine condition which very recently obtained there. It is lower than any other part. The Nuba Mts. are the western containing system of the Nile Valley, Abyssinia being the eastern; Mongalla is the

---

[3] The .303 calibre SMLE (Short Magazine Lee Enfield) was issued to all arms of the British army in 1907 and had became standard issue throughout the armies of the empire during the First World War. The Egyptian army had been armed with the .450 calibre single-shot, breech loading Martini Henry rifle, later converted as the Martini Enfield to take .303 ammunition. The UNP foot police received their first magazine rifles in 1928, in time to repel the Gaawar attack on Duk Fayuil that August.

northern slope of the Uganda watershed; practically the Nile Valley stretches from the Abyssinian plateau to the Nuba Mts. and the high land of the western BOG, and we are at the bottom. In 1918 the whole country from the Pibor to the Nile was literally under water for 18 months nearly, and temporarily reverted to the lacustrine condition. Vast quantities of game, herds and even people died in the southern Nuer country. The country is cut up by such khors as the Nyanding, Fulus, Kwanjor, Geni, which are simply drainage lines to carry off the layer of water which forms as the rains increase, and do not get dry till the Sobat has fallen sufficiently to allow of free flow. Each of these is a serious obstacle to marching; much more to mechanical transport. There is no material for bridging them and they are generally very wide. In the early days of administration here, trekking was not only difficult but dangerous. Previous years' experience is little guide to what may be found in the same place next year. Heavy rains may make a piece of country almost impassable in early January. Go there next year when the rains have been light, and you may find it equally impassable because a full Nile has run up some feeder khor and flooded the country again. Go there in April and you may find every pool dry and be in grave danger for lack of water. Now the country with the water-holes is known, but even so reliance on good Nuer guides is necessary. And perhaps, as once happened to me, you may find that the country has been swept by severe cattle-plague, and all the pools are full of rotting corpses. The growth of coarse grass is prodigious, and a road cleared in April is lost in September, because there is no material for metalling. However we are getting on, but I do not think it is worth spending money on making roads in this country until there is some very definite and profitable reason for so doing.

A good instance of the difficulty of foreseeing conditions is that of Stigand's attempt to find sites for administrative police posts. After the Lau operations of 1917, he decided on Nyerol for a post. Then came the flood, and Stigand, visiting Nyerol, waded for two days ankle-deep to get there. So he decided on Ayod, as being on the 'Duk Ridge' and therefore above flood-level. And now Ayod, after giving us endless trouble in the matter of transport, has become so dry that the Nuers themselves have abandoned it. Again, to administer Lak and Thiang, he chose Longtam, up the Khor Nwazlyel, because in 1918 he easily reached it by steamer. When I heard of this, I had recollections of walking dry-shod along the said Khor to that very spot! Then the Khor became blocked by sudd and could not be reached by steamer, and with considerable difficulty by land. So we abandoned that in favour of Fangak.[4] Moral, stick to the river for your posts, and teach the natives to come to them. They are doing it well now.

[4] Even Fangak became completely surrounded by water after the floods of the 1960s, and was abandoned for 'New Fangak', a post on the mouth of the the Bahr el-Zeraf.

DCs learn by bitter experience the nature of the country, but I hope as each is transferred you will try to get the successor to have a chance to talk with him at least, and not have to learn himself. Still I think things are better appreciated now, and I hope you will not have all the bitterness of working in a Cinderella province and being told you are in a backward side-show. There are some quite nice bits in the province; all the frontier district, much of Wyld's and Pletts' and even Coriat claims some of his district is attractive, but I think rather on the principle of calling the Black Sea 'Euxine'.

(I really think that part of these notes could be worked up into an article for Sudan Notes and Records!)

DISTRICTS

The *Northern District* (Renk & Melut) requires no remarks; the DC can give all information and the administration is fairly simple.

Shilluk District. We have recently included in this district the west bank of Meshra Meteimer (opposite J. Ahmed Agha) to Kaka. This was formerly practically uninhabited, and utilised by the Seleim Baggara for their winter feriks [Arab., *fariq* — division, section] in theory, but in practice to give them a footing opposite the east bank where they could go and hunt. The territory is really Shilluk, and in order to confine the Seleim to their true country and prevent them entering this province to avoid herd-tax, it was decided to declare it Shilluk country again, and to give the Shilluks the opportunity to settle there, as their numbers are becoming too large for their country. The division is known as Moamo [Muomo], its old name, and it includes Kaka. There are as yet few Shilluk villages in it, but the possession is recognised, though the principle was violently opposed by the Seleim and the WNP. The Ret now allows a certain number of Fellata [West African immigrants] from Kordofan to graze there in the dry season on payment to him of a rent, and the Awlad Hameid are also allowed to pick gum in the area north of Kaka on payment of £E 75 to him.

The Shilluks in Kodok District are well run and give little trouble, but those in Malakal district are decidedly unruly at times, and have thoroughly bad chiefs; this matter is being improved by degrees.

Tonga district has been incorporated in Malakal, and Tonga town is to be administered by the NMP on the same lines as Kaka, i.e. the town only, with no authority over the Shilluks. The province keeps a benevolent eye on both places, and lets the NMP know of any requirements.

I'm rather against the Ret being considered as a chief in the ordinary tax-collecting sense. His authority outside Kodok District still requires some bolstering up, since the old system — prevalent up to 1918 — was to run the Shilluk District on the lines of a northern province, with the mamur as the executive authority. The natural result was that the former Rets, not wishing to be sat on by Egyptians, did as little as possible, and their authority was almost annulled outside their immediate neighbourhood. All through Malakal District great respect is shown to the Ret when he goes there, but if he attempts to enforce some unpopular order, he is liable to be insulted or ignored by the subyan [Arab., youths, young men], because he has no material force at his command. My preference is to give the enforcing of such orders and the collection of taxes (when the chiefs have failed) to the Resident [DC Shilluk], and when things have been corrected, to make the Ret pay a visit with the Resident and tell the people off. I do not wish to expose him to the risk of a set-back. There are weak points in this policy, one being that it inclines the Ret to rely too much on the Resident, but the original fault is our own and it is up to us to correct it. Cann is fully in agreement with this, but it does not find favour with the Bimbashi school of thought, and Coryton I think would like to see the Ret hunted a bit. No doubt when the Ret's police have acquired more authority — which again they can only do by being first supported by the province police — the Ret will be able to do more active work on his own.

Truculence among the subyan should not be taken too seriously. It is purely isolated and spontaneous, and does not mean disloyalty. In all references to Malakal Defence Schemes, etc. I have taken it for granted that the Shilluk tribe could not be a possible enemy. The heart of the tribe is loyal. If there are local grievances, the remedy is to insist on their being aired at the Shilluk Council, but for this better chiefs are necessary in Malakal District. Such grievances can be detected and remedied long before they become widespread and serious, and I have assumed that a general spread of active disloyalty among the tribe could not occur without some grave administrative error which has been suppressed and objections refused. At the Shilluk Council the chiefs are ordered to speak about any matters of importance, and given to understand that they would be considered responsible if trouble occurs which they have failed to warn the government about.

A somewhat exaggerated respect shown to the Ret by us does more good than harm, since Fafiti himself is entirely devoid of swollen head and increased honours only make him more deferential to the power that grants them.

Southern District. This includes the inspectorates of Abwong, Duk Faywil and Fangak. The borders of these three inspectorates are constantly being changed as administrative progression necessitates. At present the idea is that the Fangak District shall include the sub-tribes Lak, Thiang and Gaweir, with the Fangak Dinkas. This is in practice the Zeraf Valley. Formerly Gaweir was under Abwong, then the Shen Raz half was put under Fangak, but now it seems best to put Shen Barr also under that merkaz, since Gaweir is more easily administered from the Zeraf than from the Sobat. A new police post is to be formed at Meshra Rufkwaich, on the east bank at about Kilo 180 (Coriat knows the exact spot), to replace Ayod. The Rueng Dinkas on the Khor Atar, recently under Fangak, are to be put under Malakal, being closely connected with the east bank Shilluks.

Abwong District has the Lau Nuers (except for a small part under Duk Faywil), and the Gnok, Balak and Jureir Dinkas.

Duk Faywil has the rest of the Lau Nuers, the Nyaraweng and Twi Dinkas, and should, when the BOG Eastern District is handed over, have the Bor Dinkas also. I am of the opinion that the Bor Dinkas are more closely connected with the Twi than with the Aliab. This is not the BOG opinion, but then the BOG have never had to administer the Twi. A river may divide tribes only slightly, but it certainly divides them more than an imaginary line.

There is continual friction between the Nyaraweng Dinkas and the Gaweir Nuers of chief Dwal Diu (Shen Barr). This is of very long standing and is due to causes dating back to the slave-raiding days, when the Dinkas played a decidedly treacherous game. The trouble is practically insoluble, but a safe line is never to take a Dinka statement for true till it is proved to the hilt. Mongalla DCs consider me prejudiced in favour of Nuers, and so, I think, does Wyld. The Dinkas are decidedly clever at presenting a good case, while the Nuer is a corresponding damned fool at the game, and prefers the spear as an argument. Consequently he appears to be always the aggressor, and the Dinka uses this fact to the full. Coriat has the Nuer side of the question at his fingers' ends, and has no illusions about Nuers; also his experience and knowledge of the language are great assets, and it would be wise, in the event of further trouble, to send him to investigate although Gaweir is no longer in his district.

Just at present the Nyaraweng, having realised the futility of trying to work patrols against their old enemies, as they did so successfully in the past, are making the most of the danger of the Gaweir accumulating rifles, which they are unable to do themselves. Gaweir have too many rifles and kill too many elephants, but it is not a matter for a patrol. If action is necessary, and a definite order to hand over all rifles unregistered, for example, is only partially obeyed, a general move by the mounted police against the most offending shen would probably suffice, without disturbing the rest of the country. But what the Dinkas want is to be used as friendlies, and be rewarded with captured cattle; whereupon the old trouble returns when the Nuers not unnaturally raid to get them back again. I am afraid that as long as the Dinkas have the remotest hope of using government against the Nuers, there will never be peace on that border.

The two tribes have such very contrasting characteristics that DCs with only experience of one cannot understand the mentality of the other. Both Coriat and I have had long experience with both, so has Pletts, but that is not the case with DCs from the Mongalla side, since the Lau Nuers of Duk Faywil district have become almost Dinka-ized.

Transport in the interior of the Southern District is so difficult that we have found it necessary to put all district headquarters on the river. Fangak is fairly central, and was chosen as the only spot above water in the 1918 flood with dry access to the interior. Abwong is too far north, but Nyerol was a failure, and the Lau Nuers have now learnt to come in there (i.e. to Abwong); it has become quite convenient and has excellent buildings. Duk Faywil seems the least bad of many bad suggestions. But the dredging of the new Nile channel may alter orientation, and it is quite possible that Jonglei or thereabouts may be a better site in the future. Duk therefore is not particularly in need of permanent buildings, but I should recommend Fangak as a definite site, which the Egyptian Irrigation Department should be made to consider permanent and not to be affected by the Channel.

Eastern District. This includes the inspectorate of Nasser, Frontier and Akobo. At present the Frontier DC is based on the Lower Nasser house, in default of any other. If it is eventually decided for him to reside somewhere in his true district, the Lower Nasser house could be reserved for the Agricultural Inspector of that area.

Nasser District proper includes the Garjo [Gaajok] and Gargwang [Gaagwang] Nuers, and is separated from the Frontier District by the Khor Machar and the so-called 'Garjak Swamp', which effectually divides the Garjak [Gaajak] and Gargwang Nuers. These Garjo Nuers show more promise of becoming agricultural than any other Nuers, and as many of them have permanent villages on the very fertile banks of the Sobat, they are the best placed for the purpose. Lee, who formerly had the Garjaks also, has not been able to give as much time as I should like to them, and in future, being relieved of the Frontier District, he will be able to give his whole time to them. His district goes up the Pibor to within a short distance of Akobo, and down the Sobat to Wegin. The country is very rich and fertile, and gives great promise of development, both soil and grazing being first-rate. The chiefs are poor, and the organization of the two sub-tribes most indifferent.

The Frontier District has occupied much attention during the last three years on account of raids and prospects of development in an area only recently discovered. I am inclined to think the raids are now a thing of the past, but the picturesque patrols, etc. which attended their elimination has thrown the district into a prominence which it would not otherwise deserve. The population is tiny, and once public security is assured, administration should be extremely simple. For this reason I decided to throw the administration of the Garjak Nuers into the district, which makes it a reasonable size for one DC. If a permanent house is built for the DC, it should I think be at Kigille or Kushulo, but not at Oshimo. Centrality for administrative action throughout the district with facilities for transport and communication should be considered first, and frontier protection can be now left to a secondary place. The country is far more pleasant to travel in than any part of the province, and life in it is a picnic compared to, e.g. the Lau District. The Garjak country is like the others, and the DC will have to spend more than half his time there. The Buruns can look after themselves with an occasional visit, and active work during the export time, which will be chiefly in February. Chief Oshalla of the Jokau Buruns can safely be made paramount chief of all the Buruns south of Teibo; a thoroughly progressive and intelligent man.

The Garjak chiefs are mostly strong young men of the warrior type, and need careful handling. The whole sub-tribe is more virile than any other, chiefly due to their being on the frontier and in the past constantly at war. Several of the chiefs were our implacable enemies during the 1920 operations, but there is no doubt that at present they consider the government top-dog, a state of affairs for which Lee deserves the entire credit.[5] If any set-back occurred under a new DC Lee might be able to correct it.

The Frontier District is of great interest because of the projects for connecting it with the river by mechanical transport, either via Kigille and the Jokau, or via the Yabus and Melut. This has been much discussed on paper, and I personally am in favour of both routes, but the former to Kigille only, while the latter should deal with everything north of the Teibo River. I do not consider that the country between the Lau and Daga Rivers is practicable for motors without a quite unjustifiable expenditure.

Akobo District is simpler than it appears to be. The only Anuaks taxed are those who have settled on the Pibor, and derive advantages from their proximity to Akobo hqrs. The Adonga Anuaks are not taxed, nor at present do I see any advantage in taxing them; we cannot get their crops out and they own few cattle. Administration of them consists in friendly visits and in organizing the just administration of the Sultans. Taxation may come if development comes. The Beirs on the other hand wish to pay tribute, in

---

[5] This was a view many Gaajak shared, even in very recent times.

order to show their position as Govt. subjects, and they will pay a small tribute in grain and cattle, based on what we can get from their distant country without undue difficulty and expense. They can, for instance, provide Pibor Post with grain. They appear to be a quiet and easily handled people, and all this district wants is a steady and patient DC.

Huddleston told me that he would now welcome a definite statement from us that the army is no longer needed at Akobo. I said that so far as I was concerned I should be prepared to let them go now, provided that we had a garrison of thirty police, and at least 24 mounted police in the dry season. But that I thought you should have full time to form your own opinion, especially with the probability of a change of DCs there.

DEPARTMENTAL PERSONNEL

Agriculture

G. R. DAVIES. Has been in the province about five years and knows it thoroughly. Has worked specially among the Shilluks but has seen the whole, having trekked through from Renk via Jonguls to Melut, from Melut via the Yabus and Daga to the Jokau Mouth, and various treks in the Nuer country with Coriat and Lee.

He is very quiet and diffident, but can get through a lot of work and is very keen and competent. Has carried out the organization of cotton growing almost single-handed, since in the beginning I was too short-handed to help him much with the DCs. The fact that his department complained this year that the province yield had not come up to their expectations was caused by our refusal to press on the cotton growing measures (such as fines, etc.) which would cause it to be resented by the people; we wished to get it grown by desire and for cultivators to realise that it was to their advantage to grow it, and not to enforce it to the neglect of their ordinary forms of cultivation. This has been justified by the continued and parallel cultivation of dura, with great advantage to the province in this year of shortage.

Davies has for his work a tug and living-barge, which is distributed between him and Stewart as may be required. He is greatly liked and trusted by the Shilluks.

STEWART. Only recently appointed. A very silent Scot, very keen and I should think has plenty of technical knowledge. He has been given the special duty of dealing with the Sobat and tributaries, and is generally stationed at Akobo. My particular wish is to encourage cotton growing among the Garjo Nuers on the Sobat, Pibor and Khor Nyanding, but Lee has been rather overcome by their opposition which I think is largely due to merchant propaganda against it, as introducing an enterprise which will tend to spoil their opportunities of keeping the Nuers to dura growing alone, giving them opportunities of making high profits by trading with trade goods only and preventing the introduction of money. As Stewart does not know the language he is at a disadvantage. This year I instructed Lee to press on the cotton growing matter, and seed has been issued to certain villages; but I think there is much to be done and that this very fertile area should have special attention devoted to it. If Stewart could learn Nuer, a lot could be done with that very large tribe.

MUSA EFF. HELU. Has worked almost entirely at Kodok. Talks Shilluk a bit and is much liked and trusted by the Ret. Could, I think, be made more use of and be sent out to live in the Fenikang country, for example, where cotton cultivation has been a complete failure, owing to the attitude of the bad chiefs of that part. (See Shilluk District). The Kodok country can look after itself now. The trouble with all these agricultural people is housing; if they are given houses in one place their attention is confined to that place. The agriculture-forest house is rather a white elephant except as a place where a man can live when at a loose end. The Inspectors must keep on the move. Rest-houses built by the tribes are needed in one or two places where development has not prospered.

The original form of assistance given by the Department was a complete failure, consisting of about six low-class *Egyptians* (!) sent up as overseers!!! They immediately started calling themselves Mamurs, and rapid action had to be taken for removal before spears did the work prematurely. A third inspector was also a failure, since we were unable to arrange for his disposal. I think two are sufficient for full utilisation of their time.

Forests

W. MCBAIN. Has, I believe, got all the requisite technical knowledge, but does not seem to have a high sense of duty. The opportunities for slacking with a large steamer and no supervision seem to obscure that sense. I may be maligning him, but that is our general impression, and if there were no elephants in the province, he might possibly think that work was due from him and not from the DCs.[6]

---

[6] Willis later wrote of McBain, 'There are wood areas being grown up at Nasser, Abwong, Wad Shukaba, all of which are due to the activity of the DC but the forestry dept. does nothing but make a nuisance of itself. MacBain is only concerned to shoot elephant, and does not try to grow anything.' [SAD 212/9/24]. Despite SPS dissatisfacton with McBain, he rose to prominence within the Forestry Department.

TURNER, SUPERINTENDENT. Understudies McBain and looks after the plantations. Seems a thoroughly good fellow, and is competent and sensible with native workmen. Consider he could do the whole job himself and better.

Medical

H. A. CROUCH. Very energetic; and from that point of view the best man we have had on the 'Lady Baker'. Has toured inland extensively, has a good comprehensive knowledge of the tribes and the country generally, and is now in favour of a systematic series of campaigns against yaws particularly, dealing methodically with such areas as are most affected. Has drawn up a scheme for systematic work, which has been neglected in the past, MIs having simply journeyed to any place where they heard there was disease, or, in default, where they pleased. Has incurred reproach as joy-rider, etc., but I consider this entirely unjustified, and largely due to the fact that his somewhat arrogant nature has not endeared him to the other members of his department. He gives some cause to this by an over-fondness for social amenities, which he makes no attempt to disguise, but he doesn't get very much of them. His driving power makes him a valuable asset.

C. E. G. BEVERIDGE. Recently appointed. Very surly and heavy in manner (an Australian), and unfortunately inclined to be always on the lookout for slights and neglect, making desperate efforts to keep his end up when no one has any intention of downing the said end. Is consequently rather difficult, and gives Coryton a lot of trouble by refusing to see that some sanitation measure which he thinks necessary is not practicable because there are no funds, or no laws to enforce it. Very shy and sensitive. On the other hand is most keen, I should think decidedly competent, and has a high sense of duty. I think when he gets to know both us and the nature of his duties as a government official and not only as a doctor better, he will be thoroughly satisfactory.

YERVENT KHATANASSIAN. This altogether admirable MO will unfortunately have gone when you arrive, I expect. I should greatly like to get him a decoration.

The *AMOs* in the province are doing remarkably well, and are kept up to the mark by Crouch. The system of making them travel about with the DCs has proved useful.

In the proceedings of the DCs' meeting at Akobo, you will find a recommendation for putting an extra tax on tribute for a general collective payment for all medical work done among the tribes. But I believe the intention now is to give such treatment free to all. Much better, and could be met by an increase of tribute among the Nuers and more southern Dinkas, which is really too light. I decidedly dislike the existing system of payment by goats, etc. which crowds up the 'Lady Baker', and which brings in a totally disproportionately small revenue to Govt. On the other hand, if free treatment is given to the tribes, I see no reason whatever for giving it to the traders, who are the richest, most lightly taxed and most subversive members of the community generally. If it is given, I hope their taxes will be materially increased.

Wyld at Duk Faywil has done a lot of good medical work, and in recognition of this, I arranged with Crouch that he should have an AMO stationed there during the dry season. This has already been very beneficial and should be continued. When the present totally incompetent Syrian doctor has been removed from Akobo, and when (I trust soon) the MC give up their retention of the medical work there, the DC Akobo should certainly be provided with an AMO to accompany him. The MO now there would be a positive danger if he went out into the district, and the qualities of any successor should be carefully noted before it is encouraged. I mention this because Biggar[7] especially ordered that the MO *was* to go out.

Public works

BIMB. E. M. E. COGHLAN. Extremely nice and capable; gloriously absent-minded. Is always willing to help and cooperate in every way. I hope you will manage to keep him in the province, since we have suffered somewhat in the past.

This year I obtained for him the sole use of the 'Culex', formerly one of our steamers. The history of this is as follows: For years it was our system to assist the PWD in free transport by our steamers for all materials and personnel, e.g. sand from the Malakal village 5 miles downstream, gravel from Renk, bricks from the Sobat and from Nasser, and materials generally to the different stations where work was in progress. This because the SGR charged such iniquitous transport rates that the estimates were swollen thereby to an extent which caused their being turned down. We used to lose perhaps 1/3rd of our building programme, and Stigand especially became so furious over the impasse, that he turned to building by swindle-funds on the lines of Mongalla under Owen. Naturally the buildings

---

[7] Both Yervent Khatanassian and Biggar were part of the SDF (for Biggar, see Biographical Notes); the SMS was only just then taking over full responsibility for civilian health matters from the army.

were rotten. The staff got ill and DCs would not stay, while the province got a bad reputation for health.

By carrying everything ourselves, we apparently cut down estimates, and I succeeded in getting a really good building programme carried out. Then some d–d fool found it out. Macfarlane was under the impression that I myself charged the PWD for transport, and saw no reason why the SGR should not get the revenue instead; he did not understand that it was the free transport that cause the estimates to be low. Then the SGR decided that we might continue to transport, but that we must charge the cost to them! At that I struck, and definitely refused to carry for the PWD any more, having in the meantime got the essential parts of my programme through. So Macfarlane was persuaded to agree to the permanent hire by his department of the 'Culex', and now we get the same value out of her as before, since she carries our personnel when convenient, while we continue to do the same for the PWD when it suits. But meanwhile we have as a result got an additional steamer, the 'Eland'. The UNP is one up. Bollard estimated the saving yearly to the PWD by our free transport at over £E 4000.

TRIGGS, FOREMAN OF WORKS. A very pleasant, quiet, competent little man, who gets on well with his men and gives us no trouble. Acts ably for Coghlan in the latter's absence. Is always at work and is exceedingly good at detail.

I hope he will eventually be marked for promotion as was Bollard, since he seems quite able to carry out a building programme by himself. I hope you will continue to insist on the necessity for permanent buildings everywhere, and not be put off by the clamours for mud buildings because of cheapness. Mud in this province is hopeless. Some of the DCs, notably Lee, have built quite good buildings of red brick and mud mortar very cheaply, and because of this the PWD are inclined to suggest that we should do this everywhere. DCs forget that they may run up a building cheaply but that its upkeep depends on the Mud Building Fund, and the more ambitious the design, the more it costs in the future, while I am on account of it unable to get a good permanent building approved in its place. Press for permanent buildings everywhere and you will get them. I have made PWD understand that in that matter we are worse off than any other province. Mongalla, NMP and most of the BOG have good sandy or hard clay soil to build with, but you can do nothing good with cracked cotton soil, and from the nature of things we are obliged to site our posts on it. Even the tribesmen build with debba soil if they can, and when they are obliged to use cotton soil, they put a loving care into their work which they would scorn to use for us.

Formerly all permanent buildings were built of concrete blocks and corrugated iron roofs. I objected to this at any rate for dwelling houses on account of the property of such houses to absorb and retain heat, and conclusively proved this to Crispin and other medicos on a visit by them. I believe all buildings built of red brick in the province are since 1919, so you will be able to see how we have progressed. Fortunately we got Allenby interested. The exception is the truly dreadful house built for Tunnicliffe at Akobo by the so-called 'Engineer Troops'. Tunnicliffe will supply the expletives in describing it.

IRRIGATION

I think you will find matters have improved in the relations between that department and us. There is a rivalry between the officials who were educated at the Gordon College [at Khartoum] and their Egyptian confrères which is all to the good, as it prevents combination, though it does not by any means mean that the former are loyal to the government. It is due to a wish on the part of the former to keep all the billets to themselves and to get rid of the Egyptians whom they consider no more able technically. But it is an advantage to us.

I understood from Newhouse that no more Egyptians are to be sent here of the ADW [Assistant Director of Works] grade, after the failure of Munib Bey. This was Sirri's policy, and of course may be changed.[8] If not, that variety of official, with considerable executive powers, is a distinct danger, but fortunately generally causes his own destruction. Sudanese workmen soon find their limitations and refuse to work for them.

The Britishers like Waller, Mackintosh, and Newhouse himself have no illusions as to their staff, but Moir is more difficult, being apparently afraid to act against them, and Roberts' attitude you know.

When the dredging for the new channel begins, I think you had better get the whole area declared a reserve at any rate for elephants, since every native official of the grade of engineer takes out an A licence, and I do not suppose that they make any special attempt to observe the game laws accurately. And keep to the principle of making them consider the country as uninhabited, with no reliance on the people to supply them with food, etc. This is the only way to preserve good relations. One of the most dangerous elements is the type of interpreter they employ, some of them aging men who were mixed up in former Dinka-Nuer intrigues and Govt. patrols, who are only too ready to get some of their own back by causing

---

[8] Two Egyptian assistant directors of works were appointed in 1933, after which date the number of senior Egyptian officials rose.

trouble between Nuers and Irrigation parties. I think it will be necessary to have a DC for this area specially who can talk the language, and obviously Coriat is the man, but it is a bit unfair to keep him in that country indefinitely. Apparently the Egyptian Govt. do not consider themselves under any obligation to supply their working parties with rations in a country where game can be shot, which was why Newhouse pressed for permission for any parties working in the Reserve to shoot there, which I refused. My argument again being that under such conditions they should consider the country as desert and rations must be taken. We can supply Irrigation parties with tribute bulls indefinitely and are only too glad to have this market, but this simple way out of the difficulty does not appeal to the Irrigation, British and Egyptian alike, as it definitely rules out the game shooting principle, if successful. With their innumerable steamers it is quite easy for them to keep their parties supplied with our bulls, and there is really no excuse.

When the Irrigation form dumps of dura and other supplies in various places, they often ask for our police to protect these dumps. If absolutely necessary, I have arranged this, but don't like doing so, as our establishment is not framed for such extra outposts, and it is bad for the men so detailed. Generally a ghaffir appointed by them ought to be sufficient. Their argument is that the Nuers may 'attack' the posts, which is precisely why I dislike the police being there. I do not want the Nuers to think that the Irrigation parties are in any way connected with us, and I particularly dislike police being at the beck and call of Egyptian engineers or even Britishers like Bambridge, who is apt to lose his head if he thinks that the Nuers are not showing him proper respect.

PROVINCE PERSONNEL

E. G. CORYTON. Admirably businesslike and a master of detail, in the trees of which he sometimes loses sight of the wood. Has a too great capacity and readiness for fault-finding, and was at first rather hated by the DCs, but I think his straightness and fairness are now fully appreciated. Is bad with police and such excellent persons as for instance Capt. Said Abderrahman [see below], who does not like being screamed at in front of his men, naturally. Is an excellent inspector to send round to districts which have been for some time without a DC in charge, or under a new one, and can be counted on to bring things sharply up to the mark and to unearth scandals. Unfortunately has a most objectionable confidence in a Dongolawi servant who supplies him with suk information etc. and Coryton does not seem particularly inclined to sift what he hears that way. The information is generally wrong or biased, as might be expected. Is a most loyal DG [deputy governor] and seems always to be taking work off one's shoulders. I keep him fully informed of everything confidential, and he is quite capable of carrying on for any length of time at short notice, though he naturally has not the long knowledge of the province history which has helped me.

G. P. CANN. Very slow and solid, fortunately tempered by a keen sense of humour. Coryton has rather a down on him as not being sufficiently shedid [Arab, hard] with the defaulting Shilluks, but though this is sometimes justified, I have found Cann always ready to take up sharply enough any shortcomings which are pointed out to him. He must be given time. I have instructed him that he must give more attention to the Malakal District, and let Kodok look after itself a little.

G. S. PLETTS. You know him fairly well, I think. Is really dreadfully slow at times, but so are the people he deals with.[9] His great asset is his absolute justice, and there is not the least doubt that this is very greatly appreciated. He can be quite stern enough when necessary, and is always grateful for suggestions and advice which he follows to the letter. I think he would do well in Akobo District, because his tactful methods would keep the Anuak Sultans quiet and he would rapidly gain the confidence of such primitive tribesmen as the Beirs. But if he is particularly anxious to remain in his present district which has just been considerably enlarged by the handing over of Shen Barr of Gaweir, I should let him remain there.

J. F. H. MARSH. Was quite useless at tribal administration, and earned a rather bad confidential report from me as a result. This is the only one that has been called for on him, and is entirely unjustified by his subsequent work at Gambeila, where he has absolutely found his vocation. He considers, without joking and with every justification, that his business is to keep British prestige high in Abyssinia for so far as he is locally able, and he certainly does so. It was decidedly low when he went there, after a succession of questionable Customs Assessors, and such peculiar DCs as McEnnery and Ratcliffe. He has a good knowledge of currency problems and trade matters, and has the whole system of local government and details of trade relations with Abyssinia at his fingers' ends. I consider he would make an admirable consul, and would ask you to suggest this if

---

[9] P. P. Howell, one of Pletts' successors, later wrote: 'The reports of people like Pletts are pathetic: He spent his time chasing after the Nuer in hopes they would come and talk to him and they spent their time running away in the hopes that he would not pinch their cattle . . . ' [PPH to FDK, 15 Dec. 45, NRO UNP 1/44/329].

occasion arose, not necessarily in Abyssinia only. Very presentable, a very loyal colleague and most genuine. I have left the C.R. [Confidential Report] on him with you, but please cancel it ruthlessly if you are asked whether it is supposed to represent my considered opinion of him. It was then, it certainly does not now, and I think C.G.[10] knows what I really think of Marsh.

J. M. LEE. Did admirable work in 1920–21 in getting the Garjak Nuers under control single-handed, after the 1920 operations. Is wonderfully patient and careful in dealing with the tribes, and is held by them in great affection. Unfortunately is decidedly tactless in his dealings with his own kind. Has a curious dour conceit which makes him unable to see his own shortcomings or to take a reproof. His own methods are the only possible ones, and his recommendations must be accepted or he must resign, etc. Consequently it is difficult to make him understand that a measure necessary for the province as a whole must be adopted by him even if he disagrees with it, because his district is part of the province and not an independent item.[11] Is entirely wrapped up in his tribal work, and takes little interest in his police, merchants, or merkaz. But his work has been and is so valuable that I can forgive him much.

P. CORIAT. Fiery youthful energy, tempered by an admirable sense of discipline and deference to his chief's views. Has an amazing driving force, which carries everything along with it, till his tribesmen have become a sort of special tribe (? Coriatids), like Nicholson's devotees.[12] Is absolutely tireless at work and should be ordered on leave when necessary, as he puts too much faith in a much-tried constitution, and his keenness carries him away. I have been rather inclined to use him as a sort of knight-errant, and to divert him anywhere where there is serious trouble, always with complete satisfaction to myself. Is a delightful cheery companion, a perfect blend of Latin and Saxon. I hope my glowing opinion of him will find an echo in you.

---

[10] i.e. 'Central Government'.
[11] Willis experienced this attitude that October when Lee protested to him 'against what appeared to be an attempt to tie his hands by Coriat who had written to Malakal suggesting that blood money should be levied on certain rates. He pointed out that the amount must depend on the wealth of the section concerned, and he stated that Coriat himself had raised the fine to 24 animals in a recent case, thereby disregarding his own rule. I pointed out that some general lines to be followed were needed, but that exceptional cases could always be treated exceptionally, but in principle I thought the idea was sound.' [SAD 212/9/48] See document 1.4, Coriat (1993).
[12] A reference to the legendary Indian administrator, John Nicholson (1821–57), after whom a Kashmiri sect, the 'Nikkulseynites', took their name.

E. C. TUNNICLIFFE. Appointed from the XIIth [Sudanese battalion] this year on loan. A quietly competent young officer, who showed marked capacity for understanding and managing Sudanese soldiers, and was recommended for the Civil by me on that account; I think he has quite justified my confidence. He has the gift of sympathy, and has shown ability for tribal work already in the Pibor District. If, as I think advisable, you select him for the police command, I should suggest that he should work with his successor-elect in the Pibor District till about February, and come in to Malakal for his new duty about the beginning of March. He is, I think, not strong constitutionally, and would possibly not last long in Pibor.

C. B. TRACEY. Decidedly clever and correspondingly cocksure, though not offensively so. Picked up his new duties in Renk very quickly, with a marked disregard for the opinions of his predecessors when he considered this necessary, and, I must admit, with a good deal of reason. Improves on acquaintance and responds readily to appreciation of his work. I think him thoroughly sound and a good asset generally.

J. W. G. WYLD. Seems rather brilliant, judging by the remarkable quickness with which he picked up the essentials of entirely new duties in an entirely new country quite alone, and after taking over from a very indifferent predecessor [Capt. H. C. E. Routh]. Has a capacity for rapid movement exceeding even Coriat's and is forceful and energetic, with sound judgment. Decidedly a man to mark. I think under a military style of government, he might be something of a fire-eater, and too prone to force the pace; I sometimes think he chafes a little under the restraint of a chief who has himself got past that stage and seen the futility of it.

G. MCMULLEN. Given a piece of work which interests him, he can do it well, but I have never seen him hard-pressed in this respect. My impression is not very favourable so far. He strikes me as shallow, unreliable, and sketchy; always on the lookout to make a favourable impression rather than to deserve it, and he possesses an attractive personality at first acquaintance of which he seems well aware and regards as a personal asset to be made the most of. I believe on the frontier he would do well, because there is interesting open-air work with no drudgery or boring details of office work, but this will not enable him to disprove the feeling which both I and Coryton have formed about him; that can only be done by trying him in a northern merkaz. The question is whether to employ him where he would be most useful or to give him a fair chance. His manner with native officials is bad; he seems to have adopted the traditional bad type of Anglo-Indian manner (he was engaged in private motor transport work in

India). I feel that he should not be encouraged to think that he may have permanent employment, and as he has applied for that, I shall inform him that it is most unlikely to be approved. But I should like you to have a year in which to form an opinion. My own opinion was very favourable at first, which is why I feel that second summing up to be probably correct.[13]

MAMURS AND SUB-MAMURS. Can be gauged from their C.Rs. which are quite candid.

CAPT. SAID ABDERRAHMAN. Was given a charity appointment by me to avoid the unfortunate impression given by the sight of an officer of the *British* service arriving in the province destitute. Cannot read or write. Has the rank of mamur. I did not expect that he would do more than enjoy the retired life that his previous services entitled him to, and just do enough work to justify his pay. Instead he has shown every readiness to accept any duty given him; has served at the Daga and now is in charge of Pibor Post. Talks Shilluk, is a warm friend of the Ret, and is an asset as being untainted with Egyptian service and being absolutely loyal. I mention him particularly, as new people in the province do not know his history and the reason for his appointment, and are inclined to consider him useless and to hunt him. Coryton is rather an offender in this respect. Put him in charge of a post with a policeman who can read and write, and he will keep order and good discipline, and will very soon get an excellent influence with the surrounding tribes, and carry out orders faithfully and well. Cann knows and understands him thoroughly; so I think do Coriat and Tunnicliffe.

SAGH HUSSEIN EFF. FARAG. I specially mention him for my past knowledge of him. He has practically been in the province since 1906, I think, and was a frequent companion of my DC days. He is an absolute asset for his intense loyalty to the British, though he himself was in the Military School in Cairo. The Irrigation effendia are beneath his thumb (and lash!), and such unfortunate northerners as merchants and baharis [river crew]

---

[13] Willis later wrote of McMullen ('an Australian, with a good physique, but I suspect little brains'): 'I think he has been wrongly treated. Struvé was very kind to him and then gave him a very poor report to me on him, without telling MacM. Coryton disliked him greatly. The dislike was apparently mutual, but even so Coryton did not tell him off for laziness as I think he should if he considered him so. He was never told off for his intemperance, although he himself does not deny the fact, merely claiming that he could do what he liked with his spare time.... My impression is that he is a man with a weak character, but pleasant manners and agreeable, who will gradually go down hill. At present he shows no results of his occasional orgies, e.g. they were so extensive at Khartoum, that he had to be seen by the Gov. Gen and told off. But I think that he cannot or does not try to control himself and he will slip down.' [SAD 212/9/21, 59].

likewise. In 1924 I think, his impending promotion to Sagh necessitated his return to the army, but I warned them that he was too deaf for battalion work, and Lyall got him back to us, to the mutual delight of both. You will find his deafness very trying at first, but forgive it on account of all his other merits.

Generally speaking, I would like to warn you of many old Sudanese, ex-soldiers, police, etc. whose previous services are unknown to the present staff, who consequently have no use for them, but whom I feel should be treated with some consideration to conserve their loyalty to us. They are not without influence, and if turned bitter by slights and neglect, they can do direct harm. Strange old fellows in worn out uniforms may meet you now and then with some entirely footling petition referring to past wonderful services and vague promises by shadowy governors. Deal with them lightly, and you will make firm friends, for they are always in terror that a new chief will ignore them and their little prestige among their fellows be at an end. Cann knows more of them than anyone else, and can sometimes give you information about them. Coryton holds most of them in contempt, and will tell you they drink merissa, on which subject he is something of a fanatic. Hussein Farag also knows many of them. Of such were the little gathering of old cultivators at Kodok who complained to me about the high price of dura, you may remember.

MERCHANTS

There has been rather strong feeling on the part of some of the DCs notably Coriat, against my principle this year of giving almost unlimited numbers of permits to traders for dura in the tribal country. It was a question of the greater need, and certainly I considered that the call for dura everywhere had to be answered, and was decidedly good for the province. Many of the traders were of a thoroughly bad type, but the tribes were carefully instructed about them and all DCs were kept on the qui vive in this matter. Coriat alone took something like £E 200 in fines from unfortunates who had no permits for demand, and all to the good. If you are obliged to flood the country with them, let them be thoroughly downed when the opportunity offers. You gradually get rid of the bad, and the others learn their limitations. Men like Fiki Awadalla el Awad, to whom I introduced you, will help a lot in this respect, and such have been most loyal in informing us when men deported from the province have returned. And of course Hussein Farag, and also Talib Ismail at Melut, are quick to let you know. Tracey, Lee and Coriat keep the heaviest hand on them, and Cann also, but Pletts frequently gets let in; however his district is not a favourite with them. Nicholls put in a plea to C.G. that we should prevent all trade and purchase the entire crop ourselves for Govt. purposes. Of course he knows nothing of local conditions. The idea is preposterous. You would need either to divert your DCs to that alone, or import a whole temporary staff of officials of the katib [clerical] class! The remedy would be 1000 times worse than the evil. The merchants at least are completely under our hands and the trade with them is understood by the tribes, also conditions are decidedly improving. Thousands of tons have been obtained and exported by this means; why alter it and build up an entirely new system? Nicholls had a grudge because some dura we sent him was rather bad. The dishonest agents who go out into the country to obtain dura for their principals frequently sack bad dura, knowing that there is neither time nor opportunity to have all the dura opened and examined. When this occurs and the recipient puts in a good case, I deduct from the total price a percentage according to the recipient's opinion, and inform the principal that he must deduct a corresponding sum from the agent's takings, and if the case is particularly glaring, I insist on the agent's recall, and he is deported. With such a remedy, only the agent is a loser, and Nicholls' proposal becomes unnecessary.

INTERPRETERS

These are a rather important element in the administration. Most of them are drawn from the old soldier class, but recently there has been a good tendency to recruit them from a few tribesmen who speak Arabic, but who have not previously served in government. These are generally more reliable. As a class, interpreters are very unsatisfactory. Actually with the DC they often do good work; when he is, for example, on leave, they only too often put themselves at the disposal of the sarrafs left in charge of a station, and work ramps to recover cattle, etc. for people who bribe them. Or go out into the country, and represent themselves as bearing the DC's orders to get cattle. It is very difficult to hear of such abuses, as the information about them is almost certain to come through the interpreters themselves, and be suitably twisted in the coming. Many have been detected and discharged on this account, and such are an even graver danger if they get back into the country from which they were taken. The Irrigation Department frequently unwittingly engage such as interpreters, with disastrous results. No less than two patrols to my knowledge have been caused by the machinations of such men. With DCs like Lee and Coriat, who know the language, there is little danger, but in the other districts you have to be continually on the lookout for false information of 'asiness' [Arab., *'asi* — rebellious] or disorder, and take nothing for granted till really reliable corroboration of the information is obtained. This makes some DCs thoroughly annoyed, and other officials, but the principle is most necessary. I am sometimes obliged to refuse to back up a DC who has rushed himself into a false position and expects to be extracted without loss of face for himself but at the cost of an undeserved disturbance of tranquillity. However, most of them know now, but with a change of staff you may have the trouble repeated, since these interpreters are always on the lookout for new DCs whom they can get hold of before experience comes.

Some however, are really reliable. One old soldier, ex-sol of the police and now at Abwong, Musa Ibrahim, was with me for four years, and though seriously disgruntled over what he considers his inadequate pension, can be counted on to assist when required, and much appreciates being called on. He is a Dinka. Both Lee and Coriat have good men, tribesmen. Wyld's are rather suspect as being tainted by the old Dinka-Nuer intrigues of that area, and their information cannot be taken for granted. My departure and your arrival will probably be the cause of a lot of stirring of old antagonisms, and attempts may be made to see if you are likely to reverse present policies. Tribesmen cannot understand either continuity or cooperation, and do not believe that we hand over to each other. Most of the chiefs know me personally from my own DC days, and know it is useless to start on to old intrigues which I have washed out, but your appearance will rouse fresh hopes. However I have no doubt you will soon satisfy them in that respect.

I have never made a list of interpreters, ex- and present, but I think it would be a good thing for the commandant of police to have the duty of keeping a record on the lines of the police, including those discharged. Both discharged interpreters and ex-policemen are possible sources of trouble, and records of them should be kept for Intelligence purposes. This we have not yet done, at least not systematically.

APPENDIX 2

Report on Possible Effects of the Sudd Project of Irrigation on Local Populations

No. UNP/97.F.1
Financial Secretary,
Sudan Government, Khartoum

Your H 145 of 26th December, and CS 97–F–5 of the same date:

I enclose herewith three copies of my memorandum. Mr. Roberts is in possession of a copy.

I am fully conscious that much of the information in the memorandum will be found to be vague and indefinite, but the difficulties in the way of obtaining exact information are insuperable and it must be many years before any great precision can be reached.

Mr. Roberts in his questionnaire refers constantly to the reduction of the low level to that of 1922. Unfortunately there is no one in the province, or to my knowledge in the country who is in a position to state how the areas under consideration were affected by that low level.[1]

Again the degree to which some of the tribes, such as the Gaweir Nuer and Aliab Dinka, have been brought under administration is so slight, at present, as to make impossible the provision of precise information as to their distribution and tribal movements. This backwardness in administration is not due to any lack of effort on the part of province officials but to the fact that progress must be slow, new ideas take a long time to be assimilated and their diffusion can best be procured through the more forward tribesmen from whom they gradually percolate [to] the more backward.

It is to be hoped that the rate of progress with these tribes will increase appreciably under the system of 'devolution', but the application of it above all things requires time; and I should view with apprehension any scheme which involved unduly hastening the stages of development of these tribes.

The past season's work has given abundant evidence of the normal

---

[1] No systematic investigation into the local effects of the low river of 1922 was made until 1947, when John Winder collected evidence from the Aliab, Twic, Gaawar, Lak and Thiang. See his 'Notes & Queries', SAD 541/9.

difficulties of administering these tribes. The imposition on to their habit of a project of irrigation involving the most modern machinery and a complicated organization must create disturbance not merely to their material conditions but their moral and mental outlook.

Our policy may be described as bringing the natives from the first chapter of Genesis to the book of Judges, but if we hasten too much, we shall be liable to be plunged into Revelations.

I hope it will be clear from the report that a great deal of work will have to be done throughout the length not only of the project but of the White Nile as well, before the question of the effect of the project could be even tentatively put into more definite form. But until the general policy and alignment of the channel is known, any work in the possible area of the scheme is likely to be wasted, but work on the White Nile could be set in hand, such as contouring etc. with the object of ascertaining the damage likely to be caused or the subsidiary works to be taken.

I am sending with the report one copy of the reply to Mr. Roberts' questionnaire given by Major J. W. G. Wyld, DSO, assistant district commissioner of Bor and Duk District, as the area is particularly important to the scheme approved in principle by the Egyptian government and it gives greater detail on certain points of grazing and cultivation than I have included in my report.[2]

I also send one sheet of the whole area 1/500,000 with the grazing areas marked upon it, and one sheet 1/250,000 with Major Wyld's reply.

C. A. W.
Governor Upper Nile Province
Malakal
31.5.1928

INTRODUCTION

The object of this memorandum is to consider the possible effects of the Sudd Project of irrigation upon the local population.

Normally, when a project of this sort is under consideration, there would be on the one side definite and clear-cut engineering scheme, and on the other more or less precise statistics of population, accurate maps, and returns of production over some years in crops, cattle etc.

In this case the circumstances are different. No less than five different

---

[2] Roberts' questionnaire and the replies to it can be found, along with his report and a copy of Willis' memorandum, in NRO UNP 1/9/83, 'Irrigation Projects on the Upper Nile and their Effect on Tribal and Local Interests'. Other papers relating to this and other irrigation schemes can be found in NRO UNP 1/9/79–82 and 1/10/84–90.

schemes are put forward for consideration [listed below]; it is true that the Nile valley has been mapped with precision by the Egyptian Irrigation Service but outside that prescribed limit the maps have been for the greater part compiled from compass sketches, made by officials and officers passing through the country; many details are lacking, and many villages and water courses unmarked; precise statistics of population are not available only general and vague estimates being possible, whilst there is no legally defined system of land tenure or any means of estimating the productive possibilities of the land, or the actual production in any given year or the number of animals maintained in any given area.

Further, whichever of the schemes may finally be adopted, is to be carried out first on a relatively small scale (though it is a big proposition), and then increased by degrees, till it is colossal; and the effects of the project will thus be constantly varying as it grows in size. Equally, the primitive people who inhabit the area concerned have mostly only recently come under administration and they are likely to develop rapidly in the course of the next fifty years, though the particular lines of growth must be at present a matter of speculation, and the effect upon them of the project will alter as their mental and material progress takes place.

With so many variables and unknowns it appears to me that the only course is to go back to first principles.

The Sudd Project is an integral link of the whole chain of irrigation works, projected and completed, from approximately the sources of the Nile to the Mediterranean which combine to form Nile Control; each link of the chain is dependent on others, and only by a comprehensive survey of the whole chain and the correlation of the parts to the whole can a clear policy be formulated. Until such a policy has been formulated, the discussion of individual schemes for any one link seems to me a work of supererogation as the most carefully thought-out proposal may be upset from its very beginning by the conditions essential to the other links.

The definition of a policy for Nile Control would put the consideration of the different schemes for the Sudd Project in a new perspective from which could be obtained a clear view of what was to be done in the Sudd area to meet the situation. In-as-much-as the administrative problem is fraught with many difficulties and whatever is done requires much time, care and tact for its execution, the provision of one accepted and unalterable policy of construction and administration is of the first importance and the essential condition precedent to any action.

I have endeavoured in the following pages to give some description of the salient points of the area and its inhabitants and the peculiar conditions which are likely to be affected by the schemes, and some indication of the possible effects of such scheme and the difficulties and problems that may arise.

One of the chief obstacles in the way of writing a memorandum of this kind is that both the administrative and engineering rapporteur is liable to assume the familiar facts of his own estimate of local conditions and forget that they may not be known to the other party, and may be sufficiently peculiar to cause grave confusion even to an expert to whom the special circumstances are unknown.

It would have been easy to expend the explanations to a degree that would have made them of impracticable length, and I have tried to concentrate on bringing out the salient features of the problem. Throughout I have worked in the closest co-operation with Mr. Roberts, for whose sympathetic criticism and advice I am profoundly grateful, and without whose assistance this memorandum could not have been written.

CHAPTER I
CHARACTERISTICS OF THE AREA AFFECTED BY THE SCHEME

The investigation of the relative merits of different schemes of irrigation in the Sudd region of the Sudan springs from a pressing need in Egypt for more water to enable her increasing population to obtain more production from existing land and to reclaim new land.

Were the Sudd region uninhibited the problem would be purely an engineering one, but as it contains a not inconsiderable population of singularly backward and primitive natives who have adapted themselves to the peculiar physical conditions of the region and are dependent on them it is unthinkable that the scheme should not be carried out without safeguarding the rights and interests of the native, and it would seem only reasonable that out of the progressive benefits arising from the scheme in Egypt provision should be made for the moral and material growth of the natives whose life is now to be disturbed.

I put this consideration at the forefront of this memorandum deliberately.

I hope to make it clear that the native inhabiting the area affected by the scheme are too numerous to be settled elsewhere, and the whole routine of their life is dependent on the flood regime and any interference with it must be carried out in a very gradual manner to give the natives time to adapt themselves; and as they are very backward they have not the mental elasticity that makes for easy changes, and as they are very inarticulate,

Report on Possible Effects of the Sudd Project

it will be difficult to find out their grievances before they have become oppressive.

To obtain a rough estimate of the outlines of the problem I give below in very round figures an estimate of the population concerned: the areas referred to are discussed in relation to the scheme later.

Population

		Population	Cattle
Group I. Dinka			
Area I	Bor / Twi / Nyarreweng, Ol & Dwar / Lau (Nuer)	64,000	40,000
Area II	Aliab / Shish [Cic]	50,000	85,000
Area III	Atwot*		
[*The Atwot are not Dinka but a group of their own, speaking Nuer, but administratively they group with the Dinka.]			
Group II. Nuer			
Area IV	Western Nuer	60,000	200,000
Area V	Zeraf Island / Lak, Thiang &	66,000	60,000
Area VI	Gaweir		
Group III. Shilluk & Dinka			
Area VII	Rueng Dinka	15,000	8,000
Area VIII	Shilluk	18,000	3,000⁺
		273,000	356,000

⁺(Also 8,000 sheep and goats)

Relation to govt.

It might be in place to mention briefly here the record of these tribes. Of the Dinka of area I the larger part are Twi who have been often described as the most truculent savages in the country. They have been behaving well latterly but that is their reputation. Again the Atwot (area III) have the distinction of having had more patrols against them than any tribal unit in the country, whilst it is the Aliab (area II) who killed Major Stigand and Captain White, in 1921.

In group II, it was a section of Western Nuer who killed Captain Fergusson last year, and the Gaweir are notoriously difficult. The Lau were the objective of the patrol caused by the witchdoctor Gwek. In group III the Shilluk of this area are persistent fighters, intolerant of discipline and with little respect for their own chiefs or any one else. All these tribes have fought against themselves and one another for generations and not infrequently have been in arms against the government.

Tribal characteristics

The tribesmen are tall, thin and very lanky in the leg. The average height of a man must be about six feet and many are much taller, whilst the women are in proportion. The majority wear no clothes at all, except the Shilluk who have a tribal garment consisting of one oblong piece of cotton passing under one arm and knotted over the opposite shoulder, the whole stained terracotta. The Shilluk also felt their hair into two oystershell-shaped pads at the back. The Nuer and Dinka go in for fancy shapes made by mixing the hair with a disgusting melange of clay, urine, and dung ash, which dyes their hair a kind of red.

They all fight with spears, though a certain number of rifles have crept in among the Nuer especially, they do a lot of rough and tumble fighting with sticks but that is only looked on as a game. They are amazingly volatile, ready to fight at one minute and quite happy and laughing the next. They have any amount of animal courage and are very much more hardheaded than their appearance would suggest. They require time to assimilate a new idea or situation, but up to the lights of their knowledge and experience are often surprisingly shrewd. The Nuer are relatively truthful, the Dinka incontinent liars. Their chief failing is a universal terror of magic which makes them an easy prey for the hereditary wizards who with some sleight of hand and 'belly talk' cozen them out of their wits and their property.

Their village life is very communal. Huge huts of conical shapes thatched with grass are the centre of each unit, and in them the cattle are put at night. In the middle is a rough wooden platform under which a dung fire burns to keep off the mosquitoes and maintain warmth; and here all the men live. The women have a separate hut the entrance to which is so small it must be negotiated on hands and knees, and there is generally a little shelter over the entrance where the babies play all day. There may be an extra hut or so for the old men. But this nucleus is repeated as often as is required to accommodate the population of a village, which as a result is prone to straggle for miles so that each family party has its own place and can manage its cattle without fear of infection from neighbours in case of disease. One of the quickest ways of finding death is deliberately to go from an infected cattle camp to a place where the animals are, so far, clear of disease.

That they would be suspicious of strangers from the North is not unreasonable. The tribesmen have not forgotten and probably never will forget the slave raids and the slave trade, which is simply epitomized in the ineradicable habit of the Arabic-speaking Northerner of referring to these tribesmen as 'Abid' (slaves) and having that attitude towards them.[3]

The description of the area

The Nile valley in the area under consideration to the eye presents a completely flat plain and very slight difference of level are of great importance.

In an exceptional flood, such as that of 1917, the whole country is under water and the destruction to life, human, animal and vegetable is terrific. Normally however there is slightly higher ground which remains just above flood level and naturally in these places the permanent villages are made.[4]

The early rains and the first rise of the river more or less coincide so that rain water flows down to the river whilst the flood slowly rises in every direction, filling the beds of the khors and spreading over slightly lower depressions, following the levels, until it reaches its maximum and a vast mass of water is held in the vegetation like a sponge. During this period the tribesmen are confined to the high ground, where if there is enough of it they can grow one crop on the early rains, and a second on the last rains and the water that is retained in the ground.

Special meaning of grazing

The country presents an unbroken expanse of green, but this is not grazing. The coarse tough grass that fills the landscape has to be burnt off, and fresh young grass grows up in its stead which is fit to be eaten. Moreover the khors, which are the most productive source of grazing, are not merely the winding channel that is finally visible as the khor, but a much broader area or bed to which the channel acts as a feed or a drain. The wide bed is

---

[3] Stories about nineteenth century slave-raids were still being told in the 1970s and 1980s; the image of the rapacious Muslim *ansar* had been reinforced by the behaviour of the Northern Sudanese army in the civil war of the 1960s (Johnson (1993b)).

[4] For descriptions of the extent and effects of the floods of 1916–19 see Johnson (1988, 1991b & 1992b).

covered with flood water for a space and grows special grasses that are particularly good for the cattle.

Beside the khors, there is the 'toich' which is a vast area of land extending inland from the Nile banks and covered annually by the flood and gradually exposed as the river drops. For every few inches that the flood goes back, thousands of acres of grass are exposed, either of open plain ('toich') or khors. The coarse grass is burnt off, young grass springs up to supply food for the herds, which can drink from the edge of the flood or from khors going through the 'toich' until the next area is clear of water and the herds move on. So by degrees, the herds ultimately reach the low level banks of the river and there they must remain until the rain has filled the inland pools, so that they can return to higher ground and find the young grass and the water they need.

The khors lying between the highland and the swamp are particularly valuable as grazing land, as the water in the khor serves the needs of man and beasts and the grass adjacent feeds the animals, during the period before the 'toich' has become clear of water.

The main points to appreciate are that a khor implies a wide area of good feeding on each side of the actual channel, and that in the 'toich' the cattle cannot eat the coarse grass, but this has to be burnt off; this obviously cannot be done until the water has fallen and the grass dried. Thus the regime of the flood provides a gradual system of grazing from rains to rains.

If the flood water did not come at all, there would be no grass: if it came but did not fall, the grass could not be burnt: and the rise of the water over the low level banks outwards in thousands of little channels and depressions would not easily find a substitute in a few masonry outlets from an artificial channel, which would deliver the water in unknown directions and over a restricted area, and with results on the swamp and vegetation that no one could predict.

Grazing as a cause of tribal warfare

Apropos of grazing, it must not be forgotten that it is already a constant source of battle. By long series of wars the tribesmen have acquired certain areas where they can graze their cattle in peace, but if for instance one area fails and the natives of that area proceed to encroach on their neighbours, there is immediately serious trouble, and a general upheaval of the grazing system would present an administrative problem of great difficulty and imperil general peace and security.

The government would certainly be confronted with extensive inter-

Report on Possible Effects of the Sudd Project 385

tribal fighting and a considerable probability of bitter opposition to itself and to the scheme.

For this reason, it is essential that alterations must be gradual and gentle. Ample time must be given for the readjustment to new conditions and there must be certainty that the new conditions will provide at least as much grazing as before, and to do so in a way that can be fitted to tribal distribution.

Food supply

Another special feature of this area is the peculiarity of food supply. Anybody who has travelled through it must have been impressed by the enormous number of ant hills, the presence of which make it easy to understand that the storage of grain from one year to another is impossible, even where a surplus exists. Further, the grain is grown near the villages, and when the natives go to their grazing, they can take only what they can carry on their heads, having no other means of transport. As the grazing gets further and further from the villages the natives are less and less able to maintain a supply of grain and become dependent on milk, fish and blood, with occasional edible grasses when they are very hard up. It follows that the supply of fish during the summer months is of great importance. These fish they obtain by spearing them in the channels of the khors with a kind of harpoon or spearing them with fish spears in the grass or by fish-traps. The use of a net is rare, partly because there is not a great deal of water suitable for netting. Here again the flood regime is of importance, as with the dropping river and the corresponding concentration of the fish into the channels of the khors, quantities of food are readily available. If the flood regime were altered, so that all the water ran away prematurely there would be no fish left, or again if the level were maintained high, the fish would be distributed over a vast area of marsh and inaccessible.

Even in existing conditions the natives go hungry for several months in the year, as their general appearance indicates, and it is of great importance that nothing should be done to reduce such food supply as they have.

Cultivation is always chancy; rains may fail, or the land become too water-logged to bear, or the birds may come and eat the whole harvest, but the fish are a great standby.

Predominant importance of cattle to the natives

One other point of tribal importance has to be made and that is the attitude of the native to cattle.

Among the Nuer who form the larger part of the population affected by the schemes, cattle are the be-all and end-all of life. When a boy reaches the age of puberty and is given the tribal marks, he is given a 'name-bull' and is henceforward known by the name of the bull and he must always have a bull of that type in his possession or he loses his 'persona'. For this reason he makes it his business to collect a number of the type in order to be on the safe side and handles and fondles them with loving care. Besides this, cattle represent wealth, position, and putative wives. Every thing is calculated in cattle, and the only thing more prized than a valuable cow would be a rifle, a taste not to be encouraged.

The Dinka whist they do not base their tribal existence on cattle like the Nuer, (though many of them have adopted Nuer custom) centre their lives on the possession of cattle, and are as besotted with cattle as the Nuer; both tribes are definitely a pastoral people whose habits cannot be changed under generations.

CHAPTER II
A BRIEF DESCRIPTION OF EACH AREA AND AN ANTICIPATION OF THE POSSIBLE RESULTS OF THE DIFFERENT SCHEMES ON THEM

Area I

This area extends from Bor in the south to pole 325 on the Jebel river eastwards roughly to the line of the telegraph up to lat. 7° 30'. It is thus a long triangle of which the apex is to the south and the base crosses through the great swamps of the upper Zeraf. From Bor to nearly lat. 6° 45' it is inhabited by Bor Dinka, north of them the Twi Dinka, and in the broader part of the triangle are the Nyarreweng, Ol, and Dwar Dinka and finally certain sections of Lau Nuer. Following approximately the line of the telegraph is a succession of sandy excrescences covered with trees, where water can generally be found in the dry season close to the surface; these 'duks', as they are called, are scattered about more or less along a line in the northern part of the area until they merge into a sandy ridges along which runs the road to Bor. East of this line south of 7° 30' there is no permanent water, so that the permanent villages are compelled to remain on it, as west of it they come very quickly into the flooded area. In the accompanying map [not included in archive] the grazing grounds are shown, that with horizontal lines being available by December or January according to the height of the flood, those marked diagonally in January or February and those marked longitudinally in March.

The water passes through a march just north of Bor and through various outlets on the Jebel river into the Khor Atem, and thence merges into a vast marsh to the north approximately on the latitude of Shambe, whence the water finds a way into area VI.

In the earlier stages of Scheme I[5] the effect would be to make a channel some seventy metres wide running along the main line of villages for some distance till it curved slightly westward into Gaweir country (area VI). For the first half of this distance the result would be to put a barrier between the villages and the grazing and possibly the cultivation; this barrier would be negotiable at a width of seventy metres to men and cattle but obviously present difficulties to women and children and calves. Later when the canal is widened to 200 metres it would prove an obstacle to all classes of men or cattle, and steps would have to be taken to provide facilities in both periods.

The cultivation also provides a problem. This is mostly in the southern part of the area and lies on both sides of the line A.B.

The first crop is sown in the early rains about April or early May and is cut in August by which time the flood water has risen and the rains have continued for several months and the land is liable to become water logged. The erection of a permanent barrier across the line of drainage of the rain water in the early rains might not have a deleterious effect but in the middle and latter part of the rains when the soil is very wet, any check to the drainage of the rain water is likely to interfere with the ripening of the first crop and the sowing of the second crop which is normally sown in September and cut in December or January.

The assistant district commissioner estimates a minimum of eight ferries and twenty-one watering places. I hesitate to offer any such definite figure where there are so many contingent possibilities. His estimate is on the assumption that there is a possibility in the northern part of the area of making some special works which might preserve water in the Khors Awologot, Njanagol (Yanagol in the map) and Wandior, which are connected with the Atem. This might be a solution of the grazing problem referred to above. With regard to grazing in this part of the area, the bulk of it lies between the line of the canal and the Khor Atem, which would therefore supply flood water as usual though presumably the rain water

---

[5] The three proposed schemes discussed here are summarized below under 'Area II' and at the end under 'Summary and Conclusions'.

would not drain down to it, being barred by the canal. It is impossible to say what the result would be for certain, but the reduction of the level to the 1922 basis would probably mean confining the grazing to the areas nearer the Khor Atem and the river, and there would be likely to be constriction. Further north the villages tend to remain on the higher ground east of the line of the canal, and the grazing is mostly but not entirely on the west. The early dry weather grazing would only have the rain water supply and none of the water which normally goes up the khors into these grazing areas, and the effect might be to reduce the grazing very appreciably. Whether it would be possible to supply water from the canal artificially for such large areas and at such a distance from the canal, is problematical, as the works involved would be so extensive and costly.

Although there are certain definite losses to be met and many adjustments to be made, there does not seem to be any convincing reason to suppose that the scheme over this area could not be carried out, subject to reasonable precautions and sympathetic handling.

Scheme I modified takes the canal further west and so leaves a far larger portion of the grazing land on the east of the canal. The area to be put under water artificially in order to provide alternative grazing is so large and the corresponding works would be so extensive that I do not foresee the proposition being acceptable. There is one strip over forty miles along and several miles across and another some twenty-five miles along, which indicates the nature of the problem. Again the area actually left to be inundated by the flood west of the canal is so restricted that there would not be room for the natives concerned; there would be continual fighting and very little hope of controlling any outbreak of cattle disease.

Scheme II and III both postulate high banks on both sides of the river from Bor northwards. At present the grazing grounds derive their water from the river practically all along in little khors and depressions and over the low banks. To substitute for this a series of masonry outlets is to produce an entirely different set of circumstances and until it had been successfully *proved* that the required amount of grazing can be obtained by putting the water on to the land during flood *and* that the water can be drained off at the date or dates required for the successive gradations of grazing, it must be assumed that the high banks will seriously interfere with the grazing. The enormous area fed now by the Khor Atem and its accessory khors and marshes present an irrigation problem almost as big as the scheme.

Area II

This area extends from opposite Bor on the west bank to Shambe. The natives who inhabit the land are the Aliab Dinka and the Shish Dinka. Their grazing lies all along the river for a depth of some miles. Where the river bank is slightly higher, the land is only flooded in high Niles; but the larger part of the grazing is watered in an average Nile.

The Aliab are (except the Moin–Thain [Monythain] Dinka who live in the marshes almost entirely on fish and hippo and are barely human) the most backward of the Dinka and have only recently been brought into administration; any interference with their existing conditions would arouse their suspicion and hostility. The Shish are a much more biddable people; they have suffered from the depredations of their neighbours and are badly off for cattle, and their herds are likely to increase in the future, so that they need to retain all the grazing they can. The soil alters inland and is not suitable for grazing, and the nearest grazing land is thirty or forty miles away and is already occupied by other tribesmen.

Under Scheme I, a barrage is to be made at Bor and flood conditions are likely to be slightly modified and low water to be at 1922 levels. This will mean presumably that some of the grazing which is at present only watered in a high Nile will habitually not be watered and become a permanent loss, whilst it seems possible that a proportion of the area normally flooded, will also suffer.

It is possible that the reduction of the water to 1922 level may expose more grazing ground which would take the place of the higher land lost, but it is also likely that the lower levels are covered with papyrus grass which is negligible for grazing. Thus there is a possibility of permanent loss to the grazing land, for which no immediate solution can be offered.

The same remarks apply to Scheme I modified.

Under Schemes II and III there are to be high banks all along the river through this area, and though it is suggested that several masonry outlets might be made to enable the waters to reach the land, when it is brought to mind that the distance direct from Bor to Scheme is some eighty miles, whilst the river is considerably longer, and that the grazing is several miles deep, it is difficult to credit anything like the same results will be produced artificially in this manner as by normal flooding; and until it has been proved by demonstration that a really satisfactory substitute can be provided, it is right to assume that the execution of Scheme II and III would be wholly destructive of the existing grazing lands. The areas affected are shown in the accompanying map [not included], those cross-hatched being normally flooded and those crossed in single lines only in high Niles.

Area III

Inland of area II some thirty or forty miles from the river lie the grazing lands of the Atwot. They are formed on the banks of a system of rivers the last of which, the Lau, is believed to make its way into the Nile through the marshes north of Shambe.

Whether these grazing grounds are liable to be affected by the manipulation of the flood regime is worth enquiry; for, if it appeared that a lower level in the Nile meant a swifter fall of the inland rivers and less flooding of the inland grazing lands, there must be serious loss to the natives unless it proved to be feasible with subsidiary works to maintain the supply or to substitute alternatives.

The period during which the grazing lands are required is from January to May; and as they are the only grazing lands available for a considerable population who are ever ready to go to war for any encroachment on their rights, I feel that a definite enquiry into the circumstances of the grazing and with it the water, (for grazing and water must be side by side) is required before any opinion with reference to any one of the schemes can be given.

Area IV

The Jebel island is the area lying between the Jebel river to the east and a series of swamps extending from near Shambe along the west side of the island to merge into the Bahr el-Ghazal system somewhere between Yoinyang and Yodni. There is a ridge of high land running more or less north and south down the middle of the island, and the villages are all right inland and can only be reached by causeways extending several miles and crossing several khors. Various sections of Nuer live there, the Nuong, Jekaing (Western), Gwai [Jegai] etc. and they are rich in cattle and cultivate a certain amount of cotton. The general effect is of an island completely surrounded by papyrus or swamp grass, although access to the island by the land from the southwest is possible in the dry weather.

Under Scheme I & I (modified) the normal rise and fall of the river in flood time will be approximated, but a high and low level lower than average is to be anticipated. The effect of this may be to water the useless lowland where the papyrus grows, and not fully to supply the inland khors, on which the natives depend for water and grazing, but an examination of the actual levels would be required to the effects.

Further, as the supply increases from the artificial channel and the Zeraf into the main White Nile, this will tend to hold up the water of the Jebel river and raise it at any rate from some miles back from the mouth of the

Zeraf, reproducing something approaching flood conditions at a time of year when the inland grazing is finished and the cattle normally shift down to the 'toich' land and lower khors. Without an exact knowledge of the levels inland and the contours of the grazing land it is impossible to say what the result would be but it seems likely that the natives living in the northern end of the island would find they had finished their rainy season grazing and had nothing else to go to; and as they are particularly rich in cattle, it would hit them hard. It is conceivable that the effect would be to produce a refilling of the khors or some of them and a restoration of some of the grazing, provided that the water could drain away again, and in this case the effect might be to keep the natives more on their villages and make them more sedentary. The question is a difficult one, and will require careful enquiry and if necessary execution of many subsidiary works to substitute alternative grazing for what may be lost.

Under Scheme II this part of the Jebel river would be used as a waste pipe, and the water level would be presumably dropped rapidly from flood level to 1922 low level but the conditions of the previous paragraph would be liable to apply in the northern area.

Under Scheme III, it is probable that a permanently high level would be maintained in the Jebel river so that the means of draining of the khors and swamp at any rate in that direction would be eliminated and serious disturbance caused to the grazing and possibly the cultivation, but to what degree can only be told by examination of levels and extensive survey.

Area V

The Zeraf island lies between the Jebel and Zeraf rivers, with the main Nile and the north side which forms one side of a triangle of high land the apex of which lies at the point where it meets the big swamps converging from the Jebel and Zeraf. Through this triangle percolates a system of khors fed by both rivers and the marches, and the villages are distributed along the khors over the high land. Thus the Lak Nuer extend right across the north (broad) end of the triangle and remain on the khors until these break up into pools and the people are driven to the 'toich' or the main Nile for grazing and water. The Thiang further south have less area and less khors to provide them with their needs and a number of Thiang villages have been started in the last few years on the east bank of the Zeraf. South of the Thiang are the Razz [Radh] section of Gaweir, and the bulk of their villages are on the other side of the Zeraf, though many cross the river on to the Zeraf island for the sake of their cattle during the dry weather. There is a certain amount of cultivation at the north end of the island, and this tends to keep the people on the high land until they have secured their crops. Thus the maintenance of the khors which forms the water supply of the population is [of] special importance, as without the water supply of the khor they cannot remain to collect their crops.

A reduction of the average high flood may seriously interfere with the native life, by reducing the distribution and capacity of water in the village area, and as this would entail an early move to the low land, possibly before the crops were ripe, and before the grass was ready for burning, further enquiry seems to be indicated to examine the levels and distribution of water. Whatever scheme is taken up affects either the Jebel or Zeraf and what proportion of water from each river goes to the khors of the Zeraf island, no one can say.

Equally the maintenance of a high level of the Zeraf and main Nile and the banking up of the Jebel river towards its mouth will cause a block to the draining of the khors and swamps at the north end of the island, where the main part of the villages lie.

The effect of this might be to maintain the water supply in the villages from rains to rains and if grazing in sufficient quantity were available, this would merely tend to make the natives more sedentary. But several conditions have to be fulfilled, and it can only be said with our present knowledge that the known regime will be disturbed and the alternative has yet to be determined.

Area VI

The main body of the Gaweir section of the Nuer inhabits an area extending from pole 175 on the Zeraf southwards to area I, i.e. the great swamp area about lat. 7° 30'. The villages are mostly at the northern end and some miles inland, owing to the big khors which converge on the river about that part, and the people are hemmed in by Lau Nuer to the east, Dinka to the south whilst to the north the country has little grazing land until the upper waters of the Khor Atar are reached and the boundaries of the Rueng Dinka. Owing to the inaccessibility of the country the people are unsophisticated, warlike and rather truculent, and their great desire is to go south and southeast to raid the Dinka and take over their grazing land.

Under Scheme I, the canal would cut diagonally across their country, leaving on the east side a considerable network of khors which form a very large proportion of the grazing e.g. the Tem, the Keer, the Deng which connect with the Jurwell and ultimately drain back into the Zeraf. The Gaweir have hardly any cultivation or indeed much place for it, and they move in the usual steps roughly December, February, March, till they are distributed all over the 'toich'.

This 'toich' at high flood extends from the banks of the Zeraf inland across the network of khors, and in exceptionally high floods goes right up to the Duk ridge (about long. 31° 20′) and how much of the water covering this area is flood water and how much rain is a matter of speculation.

In so far as it may be rain water, on the east of the line of the canal, the canal will be an obstruction to its draining away, and in so far as that area may have been covered by flood water, it will lose the flood by the interposition of the barrier of the canal.

Scheme I modified goes much further in cutting off the grazing lands of this area, as it contemplates reducing the khor system to a channel system. This appears inconsistent with the formation of 'toich', besides eliminating the grass of the khor beds, and it would make the problem of providing grazing for these people a very big irrigation proposition.

Under Scheme II, the water of this area is to be controlled in the Zeraf channel and possibly in the khors, and its effect is likely to be similar to that described in Scheme I, i.e. much will depend on the relative value of rain as compared to flood supply and the drainage system to be applied, but it seems likely that some of the khors in any case would be seriously affected.

Scheme III makes the Zeraf a subsidiary channel and the result seems likely to be a lower regime and serious interference with the network of inland khors on which the Gaweir depend.

Whatever scheme be adopted the Gaweir grazing seems likely to be seriously affected, and as they are already anxious to spread into neighbouring areas even by force, any restriction will arouse opposition and make difficulties. The provision of subsidiary works to supply some of the important khors and the draining off the water at some point lower down the channel may do what is required, but the problem is difficult nor is it likely that a solution can be found except by experiment and careful investigation when the work reaches the area.

Area VII

From pole 175 on the Zeraf to its junction with the main Nile and inland to the upper waters of the Khor Atar there is an area with comparatively little population, as there are few khors to provide grazing and the bank is too high for 'toich' to be formed.

A certain number of miscellaneous Dinka are settled on the Zeraf near Fangak, and there are some Thiang villages also further north on the bank.

Along the main Nile (area VIII) and up to Khor Atar are the Rueng Dinka, and on the extreme upper waters of the khor there are some Nuer camps.

It appears likely that the water level from the barrage on the main Nile down stream would be maintained at a relatively high level and this might prevent the lower waters of the Atar from draining into the river and leaving the grazing available and water for the cattle. But presumably the upper waters of the Atar would be drained and the effect would be felt in its lower reaches only.

Area VIII

On the banks of the White Nile from the barrage down stream are the Shilluk on the left bank and Rueng Dinka on the right bank. These villages have their only grazing on islands running parallel to the main land and the land lying between the big khors like the Lolle and the Harami and the main Nile. As the flood drops the islands are exposed and provide the only fodder available at that time of the year. Assuming that this is interfered with, there does not seem to be any alternative area to be found for subsidiary works, or other substitution of grazing land. The Shilluk number 18,000 people and have some 3,500 cattle and 8,000 sheep and goats; the Rueng population of 15,000 it is difficult to say what proportion is dependent on this grazing and what on the Atar (see area VII), but it is a considerable part. The Shilluk in this area cultivate dura. They are backward in growing cotton but the industry is being encouraged. The Dinka grow dura but have shown little inclination to develop other form of cultivation; they are more backward than the Shilluk and more dependent on their primeval customs.

Other areas[6]

A channel from some point south of Bor across to the Khor Veveno and so to the Pibor and Sobat[7] would go through an area, part of which is not very well known. The plain of the Veveno is very flat and the Veveno itself only a slight depression in it; it takes a more definite form as it gets nearer the Pibor. The Pibor from Pibor Post northwards has the same characteristics as any khor, i.e. it has a channel meandering along the bed of a wide expanse of grazing. The channel itself is only navigable to a small boat, but

---

[6] There was no heading in the manuscript, but a heading has been added to this section as it begins on a different series of pagination from the previous ones, yet is still contained within chapter II of this document.

[7] See Parker and Mackintosh (1934), and papers in SAD 212/6/1–51.

at high river a steamer leaves the channel altogether and goes straight up the water which is often several miles wide. Below Akobo banks are more defined. In the high flood of 1917, the whole plain of the Veveno and the upper waters of the Pibor was under feet of water and in a normal flood the area under water must be very large, and the effect of putting a channel with artificial banks across the plain might be to cut off a considerable part of the water from flowing down the channel, unless there were abundant inlets and the level of the water in the channel were low enough to allow the water to flow off the plain into the channel.

The maintenance of the Pibor channel at its full capacity from February to May would mean keeping up the level of the tributary khors, such as the Veveno, Lotilla and Geni, unless some means were found of getting the water to them; these supply the grazing of the Beir are mainly on the Pibor and upper Geni and the Nuer on the lower waters of the Geni. The Geni breaks up into pools leaving large areas of grazing, so that the herds have both water and flood (N.B. the Geni is not shown on the sketch map, but runs slightly east of north and joins the Pibor near Akobo).

The Beir are estimated at something between five and ten thousand people; the number of their cattle is mere guesswork but it is estimated that there are 5,000 on the Pibor and 1000 on the Veveno. They are exceptionally fine cattle, much sought after by the Nuer, the Beir also breed fat tailed sheep.

Apart from the Pibor and its higher streams, the maintenance of the Sobat at a high level would have considerable effect on the Nuer and Dinka living on both banks, whose grazing along the khors such as Nyanding, Twalor and Filus would not be cleared of water. This would be very serious as there is no alternative grazing. Already large numbers of the Jekaing Nuer go into Abyssinia to find grazing, and those present a difficulty to administration, in that, when they are in the Sudan, they are inaccessible owing to the conditions of rain, swamp and water, and when the dry weather comes they depart into Abyssinia. It would be most unfortunate to increase the number who do this, and it would be liable to create trouble between the immigrants and the Anuak who live over the border. It is possible that the effect of the scheme would be to render conditions impossible for the Beir, the Mor Lau and the Jekaing living on the left bank of the Sobat, by eliminating, or gravely reducing the size of, their grazing, interfering with the fishing, and rendering impossible the growth of maize and tobacco which is done on the banks of the river when the water has dropped. The Anuak also would suffer from the loss of cultivation.

Precise figures cannot be given, but at a minimum 50,000 people would suffer, and as many cattle, and it might be far more.

It must be born in mind that whatever the effect of this scheme on the Veveno Pibor Sobat line, the regime of the Zeraf and Jebel has still to be reduced to the 1922 level, and so the difficulties of the other schemes apply to it as well, and the total disturbance to native life is much higher than in any other scheme.

One area that will be affected by all the schemes has been neglected. The increase of the output of the Zeraf by 250 metres cube per second, which is the first result of the sudd channel is represented to be the amount that can be conveniently sent down the White Nile from Malakal to Kosti and later when the Lake Albert scheme is complete[8] a volume of water up to an additional 1500 metres cube will be sent down the Zeraf into the White Nile. This must mean that the White Nile will in the first period have a relatively high level maintained through the normal period of low level i.e. February to May, and later will maintain something approaching to flood level. The effect throughout the distance can only be ascertained by examining the levels of individual flooded areas, but some idea of the results can be realized by what would happen at Malakal. There, there are two main grazing areas, about three miles north and south of Malakal which are cleared of water as the river drops and leave adequate and suitable grazing for all the animals kept in Malakal. There is also on the west bank a large area which is flooded annually and then cleared of water, which not only provides grazing for animals of all sorts, but also thatching grass. When it is under water and as it dries up it is a natural breeding place for mosquitoes which are blown across the river into Malakal.

Under the conditions of the sudd project, the grazing will remain under water both north and south of the town and the other bank will become permanent swamp and Malakal will be reduced to circumstances being similar to those of Bor which are notoriously bad. As the Egyptian Irrigation Service will be based on Malakal it will no doubt be specially concerned to see that the loss and inconvenience caused by the higher water at Malakal will be reduced to a minimum: but an examination of the conditions all the way down the river would have to be made to see how far the ill effects of a permanent raising of the water level could be counteracted.

The Shilluk would be the tribe primarily concerned. Already the effect on those 18,000 in the area adjacent to the proposed barrage has been considered; the remainder amount to some 72,000.

---

[8] It was proposed to build a dam in Uganda to raise the level of Lake Albert for use as a large reservoir. The flow of water out of Uganda would thus be regulated, and the sudd diversion canal was intended as a channel for the increased outflow.

CHAPTER III
THE SCHEME IN RELATION TO NATIVE ADMINISTRATION

The assistant district commissioners in their replies can hardly be said to welcome the prospect of the incursion of numbers of Northern folk and wish to make arrangements to avoid any contact between the tribesmen and the incomers. Though they express it in somewhat extreme form, they represent the logical tendency of government policy.

Firstly: the government policy towards the tribesmen is to get them to administer themselves in accordance with tribal customs, through the tribal chiefs.

The Northerner, being as a rule an Arabic-speaking Mohamedan, arrives with a ready-made morality and culture which he assumes is to take precedence of any other that he may meet. He therefore is liable to disregard local feeling which he neither knows nor respects, and hinders the prospects of native administration. He sets up to the negroid an easy means of social promotion, by a nominal adherence to Islam and the adoption of the externals of Mohamedan life as practised in the Northern Sudan; this entails the rejection of tribal custom and discipline, and tends to reproduce indefinitely the detribalized and demoralized type of native who automatically lapses into a state of nominal slavery. The Northerner can, too, provide a nucleus and a refuge for any tribesmen who have had difference with their chiefs.

Secondly: that the government appreciated that unrestricted intercourse between the Arabs of the North and the negroid pagans was undesirable is shown by the fact that there has been legislation on the subject ever since the government began its work, and not only has the legislation tended to reduce the degree of intercourse, but the administrative authorities have made full use of their powers to reduce the number of Northern natives and control their movements. This was the result of experience: for instance when the gellaba (traders from the North) were permitted to roam the villages, nominally in search of trade, there was constant trouble owing to interference with women and sharp practice in trade dealings. By limiting the number of the gellaba and restricting them to market areas, where they can trade but do not mix with the tribesmen, much trouble has been avoided. Again the woodcutters are liable to fall foul of the tribesmen over grazing rights and many small matters, and steps have to be taken to draw a line between the woodcutters and the tribesmen, to preserve the peace. Otherwise there are incidents, such as the killing of two woodcutters at Barboi two years ago.

Thirdly: there is less difficulty in keeping the tribesmen away than might be imagined. Their wants are few and their first instinct is to keep away. Where difficulty is likely to arise is where settlements or working parties interfere with the natives' normal habits and arouse their resentment. This no doubt will be met by the appointment of liaison officials who will work in with the assistant district commissioner of the district and the Irrigation Service so as to adjust matters.

Fourthly: the linguistic difficulty proves a great hindrance to effective intercourse. Even where a native purports to speak Arabic, it is of a 'pidgin' kind and is almost incomprehensible to a Northerner. Whilst in e.g. the southern Dinka area generally one man in a village can be found who can understand a few words of Arabic, further North among the Nuer no one would be available, and the use of interpreters of Dinka origin (no others being available) to cope with Nuer is notoriously unsound and has repeatedly led to serious trouble.

Fifthly: the memory of the tribesmen is quite long enough to recall the old days of slave raids and slave trade, and the Northerner has an ineradicable habit of looking on the tribesmen as 'Abid' (slaves) and treating them as such.

For these reasons it appears to be undesirable to introduce Northern labourers to the area of the scheme.

The alternative would appear to be to employ the local tribesmen. This on the other hand is impracticable.

The native has only one tool, his spear, and is remarkably unhandy in using any other and shows little inclination to learn. Even if were anxious to learn, the difficulty of teaching numbers of natives in any language they could understand is obvious.[9]

Moreover the stimulus to work is lacking: money presents little attraction to the natives who have no pockets, and though they might be induced to work for money as a means of buying cattle, they have shown little desire to do so, so far.[10]

Again the physical development of these natives is not of a kind to render them good material for such work as heavy earth shifting, and although they have astonishing endurance for e.g. getting across bad country without food or water at a remarkable pace, they cannot stand heavy work, and they are temperamentally opposed to the inevitable discipline of gangs and organized labour. Thus the local native is intellec-

---

[9] Compare this statement with the report in 1930 of the 'tribal' ownership of cars among the Shilluk and Cic Dinka, and the training of drivers and mechanics for same (above, ch. 2).

[10] At roughly this same time Willis was arguing for the introduction of enforced cultivation of cotton as a cash crop, as one means of introducing money to enable taxes to be paid in currency (see above, ch. 1).

tually incapable of doing semi-skilled work and physically and temperamentally incapable of unskilled work, and the effort of training large numbers to do the simplest work would be out of all proportion to the results likely to be obtained. Finally there could be no guarantee of being able to keep any labour on the job for more than a short period of time, which would prove a tiresome obstacle to consistent progress.

It would seem thus that the Northern labour will have to be introduced but so administered that the least amount of harm follows. Without going to the extreme of putting the Northerners into a barbed wire enclosure, I think that in practice a kind of enclave for each labour settlement would have to be established and arrangements made in each case to adjust relations with neighbouring villages to avoid clashing, e.g. by arranging to graze the cattle in a particular area or shifting a piece of cultivation.

There would have to be a liaison officer who would be conversant with all the details of the scheme and work out with the local assistant district commissioner a modus operandi. Any attempt to estimate how local adjustments would be made would be useless, but I feel confident that a working method could be found and experience would improve on it.

Any obstruction or mischief by the tribesmen to hamper the work could be dealt with by the assistant district commissioner; but for offences against the tribesmen swift investigation and adjustment would be necessary, to prevent the tribesmen taking the law into their own hands.

Offences as between tribesmen and Northerners would require special treatment. The tribesmen are ruled by their custom administered by chiefs' courts, and the compensation due for any wrong committed is a matter of tradition and is invariably assessed in cattle. One of the commonest offences is and would be adultery, for which the compensation is usually a cow and a bull, with slight variations in different tribes and according to the nature of the offence. I do not think it would be feasible to try a Northerner under tribal custom, but if the offence were one that could come under the Sudan Penal Code he could presumably be tried under that, and the penalty under local custom for the offence could be taken into consideration in the sentence; but I can see obvious difficulties in getting the value of a cow (£5) and a bull (£2) out of a Northern Sudanese drawing, say, 5 Pt a day.

Moreover offences do not always come under the code, and although there may be considerable certainty as to the guilty party, legal proof is not always possible; but a primitive people does not stand on legal niceties, and there would have to be some means of adjusting such cases on lines of common sense. Such cases would find a solution between the assistant district commissioner and the liaison officer, providing they kept in close touch, and had both of them some latitude in authority to deal with them.

It is possible that opportunities would occur of employing local labour for simple jobs of clearing or light banking, and I do not wish to preclude the possibility of their use, but I think that in such cases the work would have to be done through the assistant district commissioner. Firstly I think it a mistake to give the native more than one authority whose orders he is to obey; and secondly such work would be bound up with the tribal organization and division with which only the assistant district commissioner would be likely to be familiar.

It is a matter of experience that small parties of Northerners are liable to get into difficulties either owing to the truculence of the natives or through their own indifference to the rights and feelings of the natives, and if small parties have to be employed, a proper organization for their supervision control and protection by responsible officials would have to be made.

It is easy to imagine that a dredger manned by a British engineer of the grade normal to such with an Egyptian mechanic and a couple of Sudanese greasers might involve themselves in most complicated linguistic knots in endeavouring to purchase e.g. eggs from the natives where eggs do not happen to exist, (as is the case in the larger part of the area included in the schemes), and lead to a practical illustration of the relative merits of a one inch spanner and a spear as a weapon of offence. Again the temptation to remove steel marking poles required by survey parties is one which the Nuer are liable to find too much for them; many instances of possible friction might be given. Exactly what degree of supervision would be required and the regulations that might be necessary, can only be outlined when the scheme is in a far more advanced state, and will actually have to be worked out on the spot by the liaison officer and the assistant district commissioner with the Irrigation authorities. But it should be understood that small parties will require special supervision and attention by properly qualified British officials, working in close conjunction with the liaison officer.

CHAPTER IV
GENERAL PROBLEMS

With a scheme of such magnitude as that contemplated, it would be impossible to cover all the points that might arise in course of and after construction. I have merely attempted briefly to refer to certain problems which occur to me as likely to require consideration.

Ultimate authority

Assuming that the Egyptian government finally selects the scheme best suited to its purpose and the Sudan government has given its sanction with such provisos and safeguards for its own protection as are needed, the next step presumably would be a precise survey of the channel of the canal and the river banks and a definite allotment of works such as spillways, ferries, roadbridges etc.

Naturally it is to the interest of the Egyptian government to keep expenditure down and only to build a minimum of these, and there must be some authority to decide what should be built in the first instance and what provision should be made for further expansion.

To find an authority who could compel the Egyptian government to vote money for expenditure it did not wish to incur is certainly difficult.

Again when the canal is in being and the outlets and spillways exist, the Egyptian Irrigation Service will presumably control the water service: and a difference of opinion might easily arise as to whether any given area had been adequately watered or not. The dates of water service would be important, as well, and in the event of conflicting interests between Egyptian needs for the water and the local demand, some authority must be found to decide between them.

The solution would appear to be a 'gentlemen's agreement' accepted on both sides in perfect assurance of the good faith of both parties; but even so some machinery for the representation of native needs and views would be needed.[11]

Right of way

The Egyptian government will construct a water way through the area concerned and the Sudan government will presumably claim a right of way along the channel, and along the banks of the channel and over any works of the Irrigation Service.

If there are locks, as is likely, the right to go through the locks must be conceded, and the Egyptian government would be responsible to maintain the channel and its banks in a fit and proper state.

---

[11] When construction on the Jonglei canal began in the 1970s the central government in Khartoum gave assurances to the Southern Regional government concerning the number of crossing points and the laying of pipes for the offtake of water for local use. In the end both the Sudanese and Egyptian governments failed to honour these promises. The Jonglei Executive Organ, which was set up to oversee the implementation of development projects along the canal line, was powerless to ensure compliance. See Howell, Lock and Cobb (1988: ch. 19).

Afforestation

Areas for afforestation will have to be allotted, not only for fuel for steamers, but also for the domestic use of the communities that will be required for the maintenance of the works and for native use.

It may prove that wood fuel for steamers is not economical in which case localities for oil tanks or coal dumps would have to be agreed upon.

In any case, however, afforestation should be considered at an early date as trees are slow to grow and the need must arise at least as soon as the forests are grown.

Power

If on the other hand there proves the possibility of getting electric power from e.g. the fall in the canal or any other means the Sudan government should reserve to itself the right to develop this or to be able to make use of the power: this may prove to be the solution of part of the fuel problem.

New staff[12]

The administration of the channel from an irrigation point of view will be a work of great importance demanding high technical skill. It involves a staff, presumably centred somewhere on the canal, a number of settlements at important points such as locks and barrages, besides small posts on individual works of control. There will be clerical staff, minor engineering staff etc. etc.

This inevitably means more administrative work, and the provision of the necessary staff on the part of the Sudan government, with their houses, offices etc. and a considerable amount of additional work will be put on the Medical Service. New post & telegraph stations will be opened, whilst there will be likely to be a telephone service down the line of the canal, and possibly a narrow gauge railway.

The number of officials whose work will be dependent on the canal and whose interests will be in the Irrigation Service plus the merchants who will supply them and the servants and hangers-on that will accompany them, will be so great that there will be a tendency for the canal to become the main pre-occupation of local government instead of the tribes, and an Egyptian-Arabic instead of the Anglo-Sudan system will tend to permeate the whole country.

---

[12] A descriptive sub-heading has been inserted here, as none appears for this section in the ms.

Something can be done to check this, such as the use of English as the official language, and the predominance of English European officials.

I imagine that the bulk of the native population will remain aloof and uninterested, and be rather like the Masai in Kenia who carry on their tribal life undisturbed by planters' demand for cheap labour. Nevertheless there will be some spread of education into the population, and those that achieve anything like a decent education will have acquired it in English.

Land tenure

In other places where schemes of this sort are made the land is 'settled' and a definite tenure is laid down. I presume the Egyptian government would require some legal hold over the land occupied by the canal and its appurtenances; I do not know if there are 'Servitudes' in the Egyptian law but they might be attached to the right on the land.

In any case the legal aspects of the scheme appear complex. How far for instance may the building of a barrage be taken to imply subsidiary works, offices and residences, or when would they become new works?

With an expanding scheme, as this is, there would be constant extension of works which would or might involve a constant intrusion on fresh native rights at present legally undefined.

Law

Presumably the law of the land, whether within the scheme or without, will be the laws of the Sudan.

At present it is true the tribesmen carry on their tribal custom without the sanction of law, but it is to be hoped, and reasonably anticipated, that by the time the scheme comes into being the tribal custom administered by the chiefs' courts will have been brought within the law. The new conditions, however, of an elaborate irrigation scheme will probably entail the drafting of new ordinances to cover the managing and protection of the works.

Compensation

In discussing the possible effects of the schemes on the land it appeared not infrequently that serious and permanent damage would be done to grazing or cultivation, and no alternative method of provision was available. Such cases would normally be dealt with by a cash compensation. With these primitive natives however cash is of no value, and there would be great difficulty in assessing the cash value. Assuming however that the difficulty were got over, it might be possible for the total cash value to be set aside for improving the general conditions of the tribe concerned.

Abyssinia

One feature of the Veveno Pibor Scheme is that it will march with Abyssinia from the mouth of the Akobo to the mouth of the Pibor. The frontier at this point has not been finally delimited and accepted by the Ethiopian government, but there is doubt how far any interference with existing conditions could be made without the consent of the Ethiopian government. Further it seems likely that most of the control required in this section would be on the Abyssinian side of the river.

SUMMARY AND CONCLUSION

Sudd project

The Sudd Project is a plan primarily to reduce the level of the swamp area to the lowest workable level and pass the water so obtained to Egypt. Later the channel used for this purpose suitably enlarged can carry any further supplies of water that can be obtained from other sources.

The area concerned lies between Bor in the south and the junction of the Zeraf river with the main Nile in the north.

Four schemes have been put forward.

Scheme I involves a channel from Bor to about pole 175 on the Zeraf in a more or less direct line, with barrages above Bor and the junction of the Zeraf with the Nile.

Scheme I modified is the same except that the canal is carried nearer the line of the river throughout.

Scheme II postulates a barrage near Shambe and one at Zeraf mouth and a banking of the Jebel river from Bor to Shambe and a channel thence to the Zeraf with improvement of the lower Zeraf channel.

Scheme III relies on improving the Jebel river channel throughout and using the Zeraf as an auxiliary supply.

There is also a suggestion to make a barrage above Bor and divert water up a channel to Khor Veveno and thence to the Pibor and Sobat rivers.

Report on Possible Effects of the Sudd Project 405

The natives; importance of cattle

The country through which the Jebel and Zeraf rivers go is inhabited by tribes of primitive character, whose chief concern in life is the maintenance and care of cattle. They are for the most part warlike and inclined to truculence, and have been constantly at war with one another and sometimes with the government.

Special significance of grazing

Since cattle is their chief care, grazing is of the first importance to them. The grazing consists of (1) young grass growing on the high land inland during the rains, (2) khors, (3) 'toich'. Khors are wide depressions which may be filled by rain or by flood, in the bed of which there is a more or less defined channel; as the water recedes after high flood, the bed is exposed leaving good grazing on each side of the channel which serves to supply water to the herds. 'Toich' is the native name for the low lying land adjacent to the river bank which is flooded at high Nile and clear at low level; it is often very wide in extent and is all covered with grass during the flood. As the water recedes the grass (which is too coarse to form food) is burnt and fresh grass grows up and gives fodder to the animals till a further stretch of 'toich' is dried off and ready for burning. Thus the regime of the river is of particular importance for the supply of grazing.

The regime of the river also affects fishing and cultivation.

General effect of the schemes

All the schemes described above involve certain definite changes to existing conditions:

(i) The reduction of the low flood to the level of 1922 may disclose new grazing areas on the land exposed between normal low flood and that of 1922 but it is likely that much of this will be bad ground producing only papyrus grass etc. which is not fit for grazing, on the other hand the reduction of the high level must inevitably cut off some of the grazing land now regularly flooded. This means a general reduction of grazing available. Moreover the variation of the regime may alter the supply of water to the khors which support the villages on the higher land of the Jebel and Zeraf islands and compel the inhabitants in some cases to evacuate their villages for the 'toich' before they have finally gathered their crops of cotton or dura as the case may be, and in others to lose grazing land which is never uncovered owing to maintenance of high levels.

(ii) The barrage near the Zeraf mouth and the control of the water below that at a relatively high level, is liable to keep permanently under water the grazing land of the tribesmen living along the banks of the main White Nile, Shilluk and Rueng Dinka.

(iii) The maintenance of a relatively high level of water between February and May along the White Nile from Sobat mouth to Jebelein will interfere with grazing conditions, fishing of the Shilluk and possibly the Dinka further north. It will also embarrass the hygiene of Malakal.

Apart from these disabilities common to all schemes:

In Scheme I the canal goes along the main line of villages of Bor and Twi Dinka living some east and some west, and leaves most of the Nyarreweng, Ol and Dwar Dinka and the Lau Nuer villages on the east of the canal. It then cuts diagonally across the Gaweir country to join the Zeraf.

The Bor and the Twi Dinka would find their villages and cultivation separated from their grazing and it is uncertain what effect the barrier that the canal would make would have on the drainage of rain water down to the swamps; possibly serious water logging of the cultivation might be caused.[13]

Most of the grazing lies west of the canal and so would not be affected (beyond the reduction of level to that of 1922), until the Nyarreweng, Ol and Dwar Dinka and the Lau Nuer are reached. They would lose a considerable amount of early grazing, in so far as that is dependent on flood water.

In the Gaweir about half the grazing would be affected: to what degree, depends on the relative proportion of rain and flood water in the area, which is a matter of speculation. Incidentally as the chief ambition of the Gaweir is to raid south and seize the Dinka grazing any interference with their existing grazing will accentuate this propensity.

In Scheme I modified, the canal is carried further west and a far larger proportion of grazing will be cut off on the east of the canal from the flood water and what remains would be inadequate to the needs of the tribesmen. Whilst the Dinka to the south would still have some flooded area left, the Gaweir further north would have practically none and would depend wholly on the (at present) speculative effect of water as the sole supply to their grazing land.

In Schemes II and III the provision of high banks to the canal from Bor to Shambe would seriously affect the grazing of the Bor and other Dinka on the east side of the Nile and the Aliab and Shish Dinka on the west. The possibility of providing an adequate substitute for the present distribution

---

[13] This is in fact what happened to Gaawar and Dinka villages along the line of the unfinished canal during the high rains of 1988–91 (Johnson (1992b: 627, 647–8)).

of flood water by masonry outlets, even in considerable number, is doubtful, and until such substitution can be proved, it is reasonable to assume considerable loss.

(1) The Gaweir grazing east of the Zeraf would also be affected and would present a difficult problem, as the main source of supply to the khors and 'toich' of their country would have been seriously interfered with.

The Veveno-Pibor Scheme is liable to upset the grazing and fishing arrangements of the tribes throughout its length, by holding up the water and thus preventing the disclosure of the khor grazing which is particularly important in this area where there is no 'toich'. It also involves international questions as the channel would be actually on the Abyssinian frontier from the Akobo mouth to the mouth of the Pibor.

(2) Further it upsets the regime along the Sobat where Nuer, Dinka and Shilluk are dependent on the drop in their river for the clearance of grazing land, and the opening up of general communications and the facilities of fishing.

The question of what scheme best fits in with the whole system of Nile Control is beyond my scope nor am I in any way qualified to give an opinion on it, and I am confident that that consideration is one of overwhelming weight.

Relative merits of schemes on local conditions

Simply judging the schemes on their local effects it seems to be clear that Scheme I offers the least amount of disturbance to native conditions; and provided that it be carried out slowly to give time for adaptation to new circumstances and fresh ideas, as well as experimental enquiry to obtain more exact results of the completed scheme, it should be capable of execution.

Scheme I modified presents greater difficulties as the reduction of grazing area would be very serious unless it were found that an alternative could in fact be provided by the rain supply and the manipulation of flood water.

Schemes II and III and the Veveno Pibor Scheme appear to postulate so wide an upheaval of native conditions, and the practical difficulties in coping with the problems appear so great, that they do not seem to deserve contemplation until very strong arguments on the technical side have been satisfactorily proved to justify the complications they would cause.

Nile control

Such arguments would be supplied by an examination of the whole principle of Nile Control and establishing that one particular scheme was the proper complement of other projected Irrigation works both above and below the Sudd Scheme: and it seems reasonable to claim that the Sudd Project should be worked out as a part of the whole Nile policy. There would thus be obtained a definite foundation on which an administrative policy could be based.

Detemination of a settled policy essential

The business of adapting the primitive inhabitants of this area to new conditions must be carried out very slowly and carefully, and the first essential to success in so doing is security from a sudden reversal of general policy which would render all the work done futile.

This defined policy seems to postulate an agreement in principle between the parties concerned.

A gentleman's agreement

As the effect of the project on local conditions is not capable of exact definition and in view of the fact that the progressive nature of the project will have a varying effect extending over many years, anything more than an agreement in principle seems to be impracticable; and it would take the form of a 'gentlemen's agreement' each part admitting the rights and interests of the other and the need of meeting them in a spirit of generosity.

If such an agreement is to work, some ultimate authority would have to be agreed upon by both sides whose decision would be final.

The scheme in relation to native administration

Having reached the point of a clear policy and an agreement, the question of actual construction could be approached, and the provision of labour has to be examined. The tribesmen are physically and temperamentally unfitted for unskilled work and intellectually incapable of semi-skilled work; and labour will have to be imported.

Any considerable intercourse between Northerners and tribesmen is to be deprecated; it may interfere with the development of native administration by introducing a new and opposing set of ideas; it has been shown by experience to lead to friction as the Northerners are prone to despise and disregard local custom, whilst the tribesmen remember the days of the slave trade and are liable to be truculent and obstructive.

This can be met by concentrating the larger numbers of labourers into a sort of 'enclave' and keeping down the number of small independent parties e.g. dredgers, levellers as low as may be, and providing for such parties a careful organization and supervision that would be constantly under the responsibility of a competent British official.

A liaison officer with the necessary staff would be needed who would be conversant with the details of the scheme and work out with the local assistant district commissioner such adjustment as could be made for easy working. He would equally examine the possibility of subsidiary works or other means of providing for existing or future requirements of the tribesmen.

Various other problems will require solution, such as the nature of the tenure under which land would be held within the scheme, the reservation of areas for special purposes such as afforestation, rights of way and power etc. But there would presumably find a solution through the medium of the agreement and whatever ultimate authority were set upon.

It is clear that whichever of the schemes may be adopted, the natives of the Upper Nile Province and the Sudan government are likely to be profoundly affected. The point of first importance is exactly when the Egyptian government passes from the phase of investigation and enquiry to that of execution. There is a school of thought that maintains that the very fact of permission to investigate constitutes a permission to carry into effect, and that the approval in principle of what is called Scheme I at any rate was adequate notice of the transfer to the phase of execution.

The fact that tenders have recently been put out for dredgers and money has been voted for the project might not unreasonably be taken as a cause for enquiry from the Egyptian government as to their position.

It is of the first importance to know whether the Egyptian government is starting on the Sudd Project as an integral part of a much larger scheme, as if that be not the case, there is not justification for the disturbance caused to local conditions in the results likely to be obtained. If on the other hand the larger scheme is the true objective, some reason ought to be produced to show that the larger scheme can be carried out and that the political authorities concerned are agreeable.

It is not within my scope to argue the political side of the problem, but I have felt ever since I came to the province that I had no confidence that the transition from investigation to execution was not going to be made imperceptibly and on assumptions that I did not believe the Sudan government to grant.

It is hardly within my scope to raise such a question as whether the project may seriously interfere with the rainfall of the Sudan by reducing the evaporation area. Nor am I in a position to say anything as to the possible results of raising the level of the White Nile and the main Nile during the low season, though there is to be expected to be an effect on foreshore cultivation.

There are infinite possibilities both for evil and for good in the project, and although it is not possible to give precise and definite figures for either, the object of this memorandum is served if it has shown sufficiently the risk involved in a hasty assumption either of the scheme or its execution. The worst that could happen would be for it to become a matter of political diplomacy instead of weighed on its intrinsic merits.

APPENDIX 3

Biographical Notes

Entries for civil, departmental, military and missionary personnel give full dates of service in the Sudan (where known), and service relevant to UNP, or for the time covered by these documents. Entries on Sudanese personalities summarise what is known from a variety of official and unofficial sources. The spelling of Ethiopian names and titles follows the system employed in Zewde (1991).

Abd el-Aziz Hamad Hassouna (Hassoun): Sudanese civilian; appointed probationary sub-mamur in Kordofan 1924; sub-mamur UNP 1929–32; transferred to Blue Nile Province 1932.

Abd el-Radi Murjan: Sudanese officer, Yuzbashi seconded from SDF 1930; sub-mamur UNP 1930–1; retransferred to SDF 1931.

Abd el-Rahim Abdalla: grandson of the Ngarrotti Murle drum chief Burnian; his father, Munang Burnian, was killed during the Beir Patrol of 1912 and Abd el-Rahim was carried off by Sudanese troops to Malakal; had he returned to the Murle he would have been eligible to suceed as drum chief; instead he was educated, given an Arabic name and became a government clerk; in 1930 he was an ungraded clerk in Malakal District; by 1944 he was employed in the Malakal rates office.

Adair, Rev. W.J.: American missionary at Nasir in the 1920s and early 1930s; worked in the school along with Mrs. Ilda Smith (see P.J. Smith below).

Ahmed Okeil: Saghkolaghasi seconded from SDF to civil administration 1926; mamur Nuba Mountains/Kordofan Province 1926–29; mamur UNP 1929–31; transferred to Dongola 1931.

Ahmed Mohammed Ragab: Egyptian officer in the 10th Sudanese bn., transferred to Sudan government service/1903; Sudan civil administration 1903–24; police officer UNP (Fashoda, Sobat) 1903-04; sub-mamur UNP (Abwong, Melut) 1905-08; mamur Melut 1908–10; transferred to Halfa, 1910; retransferred to UNP (mamur) during World War One; assistant political officer patrol no. 71 1919–20; retransferred to army 1924; for many years the most accomplished linguist in UNP administration, speaking Dinka, Nuer and Shilluk (he married a sister of the reth); educated at al-Azhar before joining the army, his classical Arabic puns in his official telegrams were long remembered among retired Sudanese army officers.

Aiwel Akwei: head chief of the Dungjol Dinka in the 1920s and 1930s; reputedly descended from Ayong Aiwel, the leader who was supposed to have led the Dungjol from Bor to the White Nile in the 19th century.

Ajak Bior: head chief of the Bor Athoic; one of the Bor chiefs raided by the Gaawar Nuer in 1914; dismissed in 1932 for 'lack of scruple amounting to complete irresponsibility'.

Ajak Tor Bil (d.1930): Dungjol Dinka man of cattle and man of divinity; as a man of divinity he displayed symbols associated with the divinity DENG and Aiwel Longar, the first spear-master; much in demand by the Gaajak Nuer, who asked his prayers and blessing for their raids on the Anuak in 1914; in constant trouble with province authorities in 1915–20 for allegedly inciting the Dungjol to tax resistance and for collaborating with the Gaajak, to whose country he frequently fled for protection; reported to have assisted the Gaajak in their opposition to the government during the government patrol of 1919–20; surrendered in 1920 and released in 1921; afflicted with a skin disease, his remarkable appearance is described in Mills (1919).

Akoi Atem: chief of the Aiwal section of the Lith Twic Dinka; refused to pay tribute in the years immediately following WWI; despite the dismissive assessment reprinted here, Wyld's immediate successor declared that Akoi Atem was a 'sterling character' who fulfilled 'all demands on him spite of tippling habits.'

Akwei-wo-Cam (d. 1920): Anuak noble turned border brigand; through hunting and trading with the highland Ethiopians he was able to amass a large number of breech-loading rifles with which he supplied a small army; seizing the Anuak royal emblems from Uliimi-war-Agaanya early this century, he lived an independent life on both sides of the undelimited border, alternately being opposed and supported by highland Ethiopian officials; in 1912 the Sudan government sent a patrol against him, which lost heavily against Akwei's riflemen before forcing them to withdraw into Ethiopia; Akwei's power among the Anuak was unmatched, but his rapacity against Nuer, Murle and Anuak alike limited his popular support; he died in October 1920, passing the royal emblems to his twelve year old son, Cam-wara-Akwei.

Alban, Captain Arthur Hugh, DFC (b. 1892): Sudan civil administration 1921–52; ADC UNP (Daga, Abwong, Akobo) 1929–37; DC UNP (Akobo) 1937–42; H.B.M. Consul, Gore, Western Abyssinia, 1942–52; Nuer ox-name Kotnyangdor (see Bell & Dee: 37).

Ali Sid Ahmed: Omdurmani merchant; arrived in Bor and set up shop in 1911; had permission to trade in Bor town and also hired out his lorry for odd government jobs, such as transporting telegraph poles to other parts of Bor District.

Amer Mohammed Bashir: Sudanese civilian sub-mamur; served in Kordofan, Blue Nile Province, Kassala, and Berber before coming to UNP; sub-mamur UNP, 1931; struck off strength of civil administration 1931.

Armstrong, Cyril Lionel, DSO, MC & BAR (1894–55): Sudan civil administration 1921–41; DC UNP (Nasir) 1929–31; governor UNP 1939–41; invalided out for nervous strain in 1941; Nuer ox-name Kocdhor-Latjor; preferred to be called 'the General' but was generally known as 'Stuffy' (see Bell & Dee: 32).

Ater Kur: Ngok Dinka chief of the Baliet section at Banglai; his father had been leader of the Ngok and a prominent ally of the slavers in the nineteenth century; Ater was recognized as a chief by the British as early as 1904, but he and his family had a feud with the recognized paramount chief, Deng Mayan; Ater's brother, Malo Kur murdered Deng Mayan in 1926, and was subsequently captured and killed by government forces; Ater was described in 1929 as 'a pleasant enough old man' who was 'getting past his working days', but his sons were considered troublesome, spending too much time with the Shilluk, whose territory they bordered.

Biographical Notes   413

Awet Col (d.1935): chief of the Ageir section of Paloic Dinka; Awet Col's father, Col Awet, seized the leadership of the Ageir from the Fayok section with the help of the Mahdist general al-Zaki Tamal in 1890–1, and was recognized as chief of the Ageir by the British as early as 1900; Awet was dismissed in 1923, but was back in favour and reappointed chief by 1930 (see Hill (1967: 65)).

Awir Renk (Oweir Areng): son of Renk de Com of the Abialang Dinka; recognised by the incoming Anglo-Egyptian administration as his father's successor; deposed in 1902 'for malpractices', including adultery, for which he was sent into the army for ten years; succeeded as chief of the Akon section by his brother Padiet Renk.

Awo (d.1907): Afak Atuot chief; recognised as one of the most influential Atuot leaders at the turn of the century; attempted to play the British against the Belgians in 1903, with little success; resisted government orders for some years, and a confrontation with the governor of Bahr al-Ghazal over a stolen post bag early in 1907 resulted in the government's decision to send a punitive patrol into Awo's country; Awo's subsequent death was reported in February 1907.

Awol Akwei: Ric Dinka chief, eventually incorporated in the Ghol Dinka court when the latter was separated from the Nyareweng in 1939; as the nearest Dinka neighbour to the Gaawar, he took an active role in stabilizing Dinka-Nuer relations in the 1930s and 1940s.

Awol Can: sub-chief from Kongor (Lith Twic); another instance where DCs had diametrically opposed opinions, as Wyld's successor thought Awol was 'an almost worthless person', who was at his best only 'when kept to his proper role of second to Head Chief Bior Agweir'.

Bacon, Lt.-Colonel Charles Raymond Kenrick, OBE (b. 1877): EA 1911–25; Sobat-Pibor District (OC Pibor Post 1912) 1911–13; OC 15th Sudanese bn. (Akobo) 1916–18; OC Sobat-Pibor Military Administration and Troops UNP 1918–24.

Badeng Bur (d.1932): Western Jikany chief; remained loyal to the government after Fergusson's murder, and together with Gatkek Luop shared authority over the Jikany after Twil Ran was deposed in 1931; murdered in 1932.

Bakhit Nyok: chief of the Akon section, Abialang Dinka; taken into EA as a boy in the nineteenth century, he appears to have risen to the rank of mulazim (lieutenant) before returning to his home and acting as a minor chief under the then paramount Kak Akwei; continued as a chief during the Mahdiyya and was recognized as such by the incoming Anglo-Egyptian army; at first described by the British as unpopular among the Dinka because of his association with the Mahdists, by 1909 he was described as 'a very reliable and deserving Sheikh' who carried out all his obligations to the government promptly; retired in 1928.

Bally, E.D.: transferred to Sudan government service from EA 1913; inspector Eastern District Bahr el-Ghazal (Rumbek) 1913–15; inspector UNP (Bahr el-Zeraf) 1915–16; acting governor Bahr el-Ghazal Province 1920–1.

Bambridge, Hugh Gordon, MC (d.1969): EID 1912–52; director of works, Malakal 1925–34; inspector of irrigation, Malakal 1935–52.

Bayley, L.B. (d.1964): superintendent of the line, SGR&S, 1926–32.

Bayly, Major Edward Archibald Theodore, DSO (1877–1959): EA 1908–18

(10th and 13th Sudanese bns); OC Sobat-Pibor District 1916–18; OC Lau Patrol 1917.

Beavan, John (1901–32): Sudan civil administration 1926–32; ADC UNP (Malakal, Renk) 1928–31; died at Khartoum (see Bell & Dee: 45).

Berru Walda-Gabr'el (sometimes also known as Berru Habta (or Hayla) Maryam) (c.1887–c.1945): Ethiopian dajjazmach ('commander of the gate', one title below ras); first Amhara governor of Sayo 1916–28; involved in a struggle for control of Gambela with successive governors of Gore; raided the Koma of the Daga valley in the early 1920s; later Minister of War 1931–4.

Beveridge, Dr. C.E.G. (1898–1972): SMS 1925–46; spent only one year (1926) in UNP and was transferred to Wad Medani in 1927; retired as assistant director.

Biar Abit (d. c.1930): chief of the Aulian section of the Lith Twic Dinka, father of Ajak Biar; between 1919–1922 Biar Abit increasingly took the lead in opposing the extension of government control over the Twic, refusing to organize road work and blaming the government road for the introduction of influenza and cattle plague in his country; briefly arrested and exiled to Mongalla in 1919, he was the subject of a punitive patrol in 1921–2 but nonetheless remained at large and a powerful influence until captured in 1926; he died in 1929 or 1930.

Biggar, Lt.-Colonel B.;Royal Army Medical Corps, later Egyptian Army Medical Corps; Principal Medical Officer, SDF, 1924–7.

Bilkwei Duop (d.c.1932): chief of the Rueng Dinka of Western UNP; a chief of the Bibiok section of the Kwil-Rueng in the late nineteenth century, he was captured during the Mahdia and spent some time as a prisoner in the Shilluk country, where he was given the Arabic name Fadl el Mula; returned to his country shortly after the overthrow of the Mahdists in 1898; coming from a chiefly line he already possessed the clan-divinity Ring ('Flesh') but increased his spiritual reputation with a judicious use of a mirror and matches, which he obtained in captivity; armed with a spiritual reputation and backing from the new government, he soon replaced the old chief of the Kwil; considered loyal by government throughout his long life; his son, Makwei de Bilkwei, was interviewed in Deng (1980).

Bior Agwer (d.1992): Twic Dinka chief, long serving court president of Kongor who he retired in the 1970s; even in retirement he was a vocal sceptic about the supposed benefits of the Jonglei canal project, which cut through his territory; in extreme old age he was killed by Nuer soldiers of the Nasir faction SPLA in July 1992.

Blewitt, Lt.-Colonel Arthur (1861–1917): EA 1897–1903; Sudan government service 1900-03; administrator and commandant Fashoda District 1900-02; governor Gezira 1902-03 (see Hill (1967: 81)).

Bol Ngundeng: Lou Nuer, son of Ngundeng Bong and half-brother of Guek Ngundeng; appointed by H. C. Jackson to act as head of the Lou Nuer on behalf of his brother Guek in 1922, Bol had an uneasy relationship with the government; Coriat considered him 'lacking in brains and quite incapable of acquiring any merit as Chief', detained him at Abwong in 1923, and dismissed him in 1924; Guek continued to try to use Bol as an intermediary and sent him as part of a delegation to Abwong in November 1927 to try to sound out the government's intentions;

Coriat detained Bol for a second time, thus convincing Guek and the Lou that the government meant war; still listed as a minor chief in the mid-1930s.

Bollard, Edward G. (d.1964): PWD 1918-44; superintendent of works, Malakal, 1925-6.

Bramall, G.: port manager, Port Sudan, 1930-2; traffic manager, SGR&S, 1932-8.

Broadhurst, J.: Agricultural Department 1926-31; inspector of agriculture, Yirol, 1928-31.

Bul Biliu (Bul Belyu): Bul Nuer chief of the Gek-Gaak-Kuac section; served as a sub-chief under Tegjiek Dualdoang after 1931.

Bul Kwer: sub-chief of the Adhiok sub-section, Aiwal-Lith-Twic Dinka; along with Biar Abit was a leading opponent of expanding government authority after WWI; his arrest and detention in Mongalla in 1919-20 ended his active opposition; Wyld's successor found Bul to be 'unconsciously humorous' but difficult in that he encouraged his people to take their complaints against the head chiefs and even the DC to Malakal; in 1941 he appeared to be suffering from syphilitic skin eruptions and went mad, a madness locally diagnosed as seizure by the divinity DENG.

Buom Diu: Dok Nuer, prophet of TENY; known as a brave but stubborn and hot-headed warrior in his youth, he announced he was seized by the divinity TENY in c. 1921; after leading raids against the Dinka he was arrested by the government in 1923 and deported to Yirol in 1925; on his return he became one of Captain Fergusson's most reliable and trusted chiefs; he protected government property in the aftermath of Fergusson's murder, was thought well of by Coriat, and was presented with a ceremonial spear by Willis in 1931; Romilly deposed him in 1936, charging him with extortion and autocratic behaviour; he was exiled to Akobo and then Yirol, returning home in 1948; his son, John Wicjaal Buom, later joined the administrative service.

Burnian (Batmanan) (d.1926): drum chief of the Ngarotti Murle; held a prominent position during the first quarter of this century but was not as active a war leader as Lom (father of Kengen); his elder son, Munang, was killed during the government patrol in 1912 and a younger son (Poti) was a minor at the time of his father's death in 1926; according Murle custom it was an adopted Majangir boy, Ngapul, bought from the Anuak by Munang's widow, who was selected to suceed Burnian as drum chief; Kengen and Poti alternated as regents in the 1930s and 1940s.

Caath Bang (d.1930): Dok Nuer chief; an early supporter of Fergusson's and became acting chief of the Dok when Buom Diu was exiled in 1923-5; the prophet Kolang Ket was put under his charge in 1925, and Caath is said by Nuer to have murdered him; Cath was himself dismissed and exiled in 1925 but was appointed chief of the Gatliath Nyuong Nuer in 1929; his death while hunting an elephant was also said to be Kolang Ket's revenge.

Cag Riang: Nyuong Nuer chief; an early supporter of Fergusson, he was the first person to accuse Gaaluak Nyagh of planning Fergusson's murder in December 1927; he took an active part in trying to round up the murderers and was even recommended for the British Empire Medal; on the two murderers being captured it was learned that Cag himself was involved in planning the murder, perhaps as a way eliminating Gaaluak; Cag was deposed in 1931 and replaced by Wuon Kuoth.

Camjok Cai: Lou Nuer headman of cieng Lam; lived with the Gaawar until 1928, his section having earlier dispersed among the Gaawar and cieng Lang after a feud with another Lou section; they were reunited under Camjok in 1929.

Cam-wara-Akwei (c.1908–33): son of Akwei-wo-Cam; when his father died in October 1920 Cam was only twelve years old, but because he was in possession of the stool and emblems of Anuak royalty he was able to claim being 'king'; this claim was disputed by a neighbouring noble, Cam-wa-Medho, whose threatened attack on Cam-wara-Akwei was forestalled by Lt.-Colonel Bacon, who arrived at Cam-wara-Akwei's village on January 1921 and formally confirmed Cam as king, adding his own sword to the emblems at the investiture; Bacon hoped by this action that the government would be able to control the circulation of the emblems and the succession to kingship, as part of its closer administration of south-eastern Anuak country and the Adonga Anuak, following a formal agreement on the partition of the Anuak between Ethiopia and the Sudan in 1921; complaints against Cam-wara-Akwei brought by other Anuak nobles led to his detention and deposition in 1927; between 1928 and 1933 he frequently absconded to Ethiopia to avoid court cases in the Sudan.

Cann, Captain George Ponsford (b.1886): transferred from EA to Sudan government service 1918; Sudan civil administration 1918–37; 2nd inspector UNP (Longtam and Nasir) 1919–20; ADC UNP (Shilluk: Malakal and Kodok) 1923–30 (OC Police 1923–25); DC UNP 1934–7 (see Bell & Dee: 28).

Car Koryom (d. 1948): Lou Nuer of the Maiker section of Rumjok; prophet of DENG; seized by the divinity DENG in about 1914 and soon gathered a significant following among both the Nuer and the Dinka living along the UNP-MP border, where he had a reputation for healing and praying for rain; avoided hostilities in the 1917 'Lau Patrol' and tried to do the same in 1927–29 during the campaign against Guek Ngundeng; briefly arrested in 1928, he escaped and remained at large until after Guek's death; was one of the prophets government troops were still searching for during Evans-Pritchard's first field-trip among the Lou in 1930 and gave himself up later that year; allowed to return to his home after a few years' exile, and continued to follow his spiritual calling among the Dinka and Nuer of the border until his death.

Carless, Thomas Frederick Gordon (b. 1897) : Sudan civil administration 1922–45; ADC UNP (Shilluk: Malakal & Kodok) 1930–31 (see Bell & Dee: 35).

Coghlan, Bimbashi E.M.E.: Royal Engineers; PWD 1925–8; district engineer, Malakal, 1925–8.

Colebourne, G.W.: Joined the PWD in 1929; mechanical superintendent of works, civil mechanical transport section, Malakal, 1932–7.

Coriat, Percy, MBE, DCM (1898–1960): Sudan civil administration 1922–42; ADC UNP (Ayod, Abwong, Western Nuer) 1922–31; DC Mongalla (Juba) 1931–3; DC UNP (Malakal) 1933–4; Nuer ox-name Kolang Gierkuei (see Bell & Dee: 40).

Coryton, Edmund George (1889–1980): Sudan civil administration 1914–39; senior DC and deputy governor UNP 1924–27; deputy governor UNP 1930–32 & 1935–36; governor UNP 1936–39; lifelong member of the MCC (see Bell & Dee: 26).

Crispin, Dr. E.S.: SMS 1901–22; assistant director general 1909–15; director 1915–22; was MO for the 1902 'Dengkur Expedition' against Ngundeng.

Crouch, Dr. H.A., OBE, MC (d. 1947): SMS 1923–44; medical inspector Malakal, UNP, 1925–33.

Cuol Weng: Nyuong Nuer, one of the murderers of Captain Fergusson; surrendered in 1929, was tried, pleaded not guilty, but was found guilty and hanged; his testimony was the first evidence which exonerated Gaaluak Nyagh.

Danalis (d.1931): Greek businessman; given road-building concession from Mattu to Gore by ras Tafari (the future Emperor Hayla Selasse) in 1927; died of an illness contracted while building this road.

Dang Dung Jiek: Nyuong Nuer chief; one of a group of Nyuong chiefs who enlisted Cuol Weng and Gatkek Jiek to assassinate Fergusson; Dang Dung admitted this at his trial in 1930, was found guilty and sentenced to be hanged, but died in the Malakal hospital the night after he was condemned.

Davies, G.R.: Agricultural Department 1919–31; inspector of agriculture, Malakal, 1923–8.

Deng Ajak: chief of the Gol section of Bor Gok; related to the priestly caretakers of Lirpiu, the sacred clan-spear of the Bor Dinka (see below, Deng Col); spokesman for the free-divinity Ayiou; considered 'deep and persistent' by Wyld's immediate successor.

Deng Col (b. c. 1883): Appointed head chief of the Bor Gok section in 1925; at first a great favourite of British administrators, he was deposed in 1933 as despotic and having 'a great talent for intrigue'; his son, Joseph Maciek Deng Col (c. 1911–45) was educated at Malek and Loka schools (1925–32) and spent a a few months as a boy clerk at Bor; in the early 1930s he was listed as an 'undesirable', but when elected chief in the 1940s soon demonstrated the value of an educated chief in native administration; assassinated in June 1945, a murder in which the caretaker of the sacred spear of Lirpiu was implicated, leading to the 'arrest' and 'imprisonment' of the sacred spear in the Ethnographic Museum in Khartoum; the spear was subsequently returned to the Bor Dinka by President Nimeiri in 1971 (for Joseph Deng Col see Hill (1967: 220)).

Deng Lom: a Ric Dinka chief who lived among the Lou Nuer prior to the Nuer Settlement of 1929, when his section was transferred to Deng Malwal's jurisdiction; though he urged Major Wyld as early as 1927 to eliminate all of the Lou Nuer prophets, many of his people joined the Lou in their raid on the Nyareweng in 1928; as late as 1938 he complained that his people fled to the Lou whenever he tried to enforce government orders; succeeded by his son, Cuol Deng Lom in the early 1940s.

Deng Lual: chief of the Daicuek section of Lith Twic Dinka; nicknamed Deng a Koc Nok ('Deng the Killer'), he was deemed by Wyld's successor as 'quite capable' but prone to violence and 'a tricky independence of everyone'; Deng's father, Lual Deng, had been an ally of Biar Abit and Bul Kwer in their opposition to government after WWI, and died in 1932.

Deng Malwal (d.1946): Of the Agair section of Nyareweng Dinka, Deng Malwal was orphaned when his parents died in Bor after fleeing the Nuer in the late nineteenth century; his uncle, Lual Ajok, spiritual leader of the Nyareweng, approached the British for protection from the Gaawar Nuer at the beginning of this century and put his orphaned forward nephew to act as intermediary with the government; Deng gained a reputation for loyalty and efficiency among British administrators and in the 1920s was made paramount chief of all of the Dinka on the Dinka-Nuer border (including the Ghol); by the end of the 1930s he was widely respected, even among the Gaawar, who nevertheless thought him unbending and too closely associated with the government; British administrators found him to be intelligent, active, truthful, a painstaking and clear judge, a good road foreman and organizer of labour, though 'not entirely free from the usual Dinka failings of uxoriousness and partiality' (see Hill (1967: 112)).

Deng Mayan (d.1926): paramount chief of the Sobat Ngok Dinka, 1903–26; succeeded his father Mayan Riak when the latter was too old to work; British officials before WWI found him reluctant to collect taxes; he asked to resign and by 1909 was 'relieved of all responsibility' though he was retained as chief; he continued as chief until murdered by a brother of Ater Kur; he was succeeded by his son Riak Deng.

Deng Rue (Deng Ruair): son of Rue Wor; sub-chief of Buth-Mor Lou Nuer and principal chief of the Nuer-Anuak frontier along the Pibor in the 1930s.

Dhieu Alam: Afak (Atuot) leader (fl. 1910–22); a consistent sceptic of government, who in turn considered him cunning, brave, and possessing a strong personality; refused to provide labour for road-clearing in 1910, and was one of the main leaders of the Atuot rising in 1917; submitted to the government in 1918 but was involved in the 'Holy Lake' incident in 1921; arrested by Fergusson and charged with spreading anti-government propaganda, he was sentenced in 1922 to fourteen years in prison and life-long exile.

Ding Twil Kuoth: sub-chief in the Fulkir section, Rumjok Lou Nuer; after the RAF bombed Guek Ngundeng's shrine, the famous Mound (or 'pyramid') of his father, Guek fled inland and in 1928 attempted to recoup some of his losses by organizing a raid against the Dinka on the Lou border; Ding Twil Kuoth, a sub-chief from the border objected to the raid, on the grounds that many of the Dinka were his relatives; Coriat described Ding in 1929 as a man of considerable authority over his section; he was still listed as a sub-chief in the mid–1930s.

Diu Ngor: Thoi Dinka chief; appointed chief of the Thoi living along the Khor Fulluth in 1927; he and his section remained behind when the majority of Khor Fulluth Dinka were temporarily relocated near Duk Fadiat in 1930; became president of a separate Thoi Dinka court in the 1940s.

Dual Diu (Dwal Diu) (d. 1968): son of the nineteenth-century Gaawar prophet Deng Laka (d. 1907), Dual first claimed to have been seized by the divinity DIU in about 1913, the year his elder brother, Macar Diu, rose against the government; when Macar was killed raiding the Dinka in 1914 Dual led the Gaawar retaliation, and gained a reputation as a warrior leader; from 1918–28 he attempted to work with the Sudan government and became a close friend of the first Nuer-speaking DC in the area, Percy Coriat; like Car Koryom, Dual tried to avoid becoming embroiled in the hostilities which developed between the government and the Lou Nuer prophet, Guek Ngundeng in 1927, but was forced into open opposition in 1928 after government troops, supported by Deng Malwal and his warriors, swept through his cattle camp; Dual retaliated by attacking Duk Fadiat and Duk Fayuil in August that year; hunted by Wedderburn-Maxwell, the army, and police for the next two years he escaped to the Eastern Nuer District, where he was finally captured by Armstrong in 1930; he remained in exile until 1953; in 1955, just a

Biographical Notes 419

few months before independence, the new Sudanese provincial authorities feared he was planning to raid the Dinka and arrested him; he was held in Malakal for two years, but on returning home in 1957 married one of Moinykuer Mabur's daughters to help establish peace between the Gaawar and Ghol; he lived to see the beginning of the Sudan's first civil war.

Dupuis, Charles Edward (1864–1943): British engineer and inpsector general of the EID in Khartoum, 1904–12; later advisor to the Egyptian Ministry of Public Works; author of the plans for the Jebel Aulia dam in 1923 (see Hill (1967: 118)).

Ellison, Major John Reynolds: Royal Army Veterinary Corps; EA 1918–25; SDF 1925–8; transferred to Veterinary Department 1920; veterinary inspector 1920–38; did a veterinary survey for the Nuer Settlement in 1929; veterinary inspector UNP 1936–8.

El Sayed Effendi Mohammed Munib: Joined the EID in 1916; assistant director of works (the most senior Egyptian official) Malakal 1925–6.

Fadiet Kwathker (d.1917): 28th Shilluk reth (calculated from Nyikang), son of Kwathker Akwot, who was reth from 1863–70; Fadiet was installed by the British in 1903 after they deposed and exiled reth Kur Nyidok; Fadiet had difficulty being accepted by the Shilluk as long as Kur remained alive, even though he was in exile; Fadiet was the father of reth Dak Fadiat (r. 1946–52), and is grandfather of the current reth, installed in 1993 (see Hill (1967: 122)).

Fafiti Yor (d.1943): 29th Shilluk reth (calculated from Nyikang); r.1917–43; son of Yor Akoc, the reth who was installed with the approval of the Mahdi in 1882, but who was beheaded by the Mahdist general al-Zaki Tamal in 1892; Fafiti's installation was forced by Stigand on the death of Fadiet, against the opposition of the southern Shilluk; survived an assassination attempt by a son of reth Kur in the early 1930s; his long reign enabled the government to build a stable administrative hierarchy around the reth, and at the time of his death he is said to have been 'held in high esteem by all his subjects'; he was father of the 32nd reth Kur Fafiti (r. 1952–74) (see Hill (1967: 123)).

Fanta: Ethiopian fitawrari ('commander of the vangard', title below dajjazmach, often given to officials on the frontier); sent to Europe by Menilek to learn European languages, he was fluent in French and Arabic but spoke only a little English; he took over the administration of Gambela in 1916 as the represntative of the governor of Gore, switching his allegiance to dajjazmach Berru, governor of Sayo, in 1920; he left in 1926 but owned many coffee plantations in Gambela, and returned in 1935 as the head of the 'Game Preservation Department' and agent for the governor of Sayo.

(Mohammed) Farag Ismail: Mulazim Awal seconded from the SDF 1930; sub-mamur, UNP, 1930–1; retransferred SDF 1931.

Fargalla Kong Dungdit (Faragalla Nuer) (b. c.1870): a Gaajak Nuer and veteran of the Turco-Egyptian, Mahdist and Anglo-Egyptian armies in the nineteenth and twentieth centuries; rose to the rank of bash shawish in the UNP police and was posted to Nasir as interpreter during WWI; served as Lt-Colonel Bacon's interpreter during Patrol No. 71 against the Gaajak in 1919–20; transferred to Akobo and later appointed chief of the Lou living along the mouth of Khor Geni, a post he held until his retirement in 1942; particularly efficient in supervising cotton growing schemes and collecting taxes and fines; other DCs thought he was 'worth his weight in gold as a solid rock of sanity in the Chirru bedlam'; still alive at the time the British left the province in 1954.

Fergusson, Captain Vere Henry, OBE (1891–1927): transferred from EA to Sudan government service 1919; 2nd inspector Bahr el-Ghazal (Rumbek) 1920–3; ADC Bahr el-Ghazal (Hillet Nuer) 1923–26; appointed to permanent service 1926; DC Bahr el-Ghazal (Yirol) 1926–7; murdered at Lake Jor 14 December 1927; Dinka ox-name Awarakwei (see Hill (1967: 126), and Bell & Dee: 28).

Fox, Captain Charles Vincent (1877–1928): EA 1908–13; transferred from EA to Sudan government service 1910; 2nd inspector Mongalla (Bor, Duk Fadiat, Twi) 1910–13; political officer Beir and Anuak Patrol, 1912; retransferred to army 1913 (see Hill (1967: 128)).

Gaaluak Buth: Nyuong Nuer chief; one of a group of chiefs (including Dang Dung Jiek and Cag Riang) who planned Fergusson's murder in 1927; because Gaaluak Buth gave evidence against himself as a witness at the trial of others it was felt that the government could not prosecute him, but he was deposed and detained for two years.

Gaaluak Nyagh (c.1896–1938): cattle-master and prophet of the divinity DAPIR from the Dur Nyuong Nuer; rose to prominence raiding the Agar and Cic Dinka in the early 1920s; the object of a series of armed patrols by Captain Fergusson, he finally surrendered in 1925; he subsequently impressed Fergusson, who appointed him head chief of the Nyuong Nuer, but was demoted in November 1927 for embezeling government cattle fines; was wrongly accused of instigating Fergusson's murder that December; though he gave himself up to the government within days of Fergusson's death, he was not fully cleared of the charge until 1930; he was reinstated as chief of the Dur Nyuong in 1930, and proved an efficient chief; appointed head chief of all the Nyuong in 1936; Gaaluak died suddenly in 1938, a death his family attributed to magic used by his main political rival, Wuon Kuoth.

Garang Wiu: Luac Dinka chief; originally settled on the Khor Fullus near the Lou, he belonged to one of the group of Dinka who had moved north with the Gaawar occupied their territory in the late nineteenth century; he was described by Coriat as able with complete control over the Luac; they were moved to the Duk Fadiat area in 1930, but returned to the Khor Fullus at their own request a few years later.

Gatkek Jiek: Nyuong Nuer, one of the murderers of Fergusson; the first to stab Fergusson, he remained at large until 1930 when he was caught partly by a subterfuge of Wuon Kuoth, a relative of his; at his trial he implicated Cag Riang, Dang Dung Jiek, Gaaluak Buth and other chiefs as the real conspirators against Fergusson; he was found guilty, returned to his home, and hanged in front of his section.

Gatkek Luop (b. c.1895): Jikany Nuer chief; appointed sub-chief by Fergusson in 1925; shared authority with Badeng Bur after Twil Ran was deposed in 1931, and became head chief of the Jikany when Badeng Bur was murdered in 1932; government reports noted that he was popular with the people because he saw to their complaints quickly, but unpopular with his sub-chiefs who found him too restricting; as a secular chief he was often in conflict with the earth-masters; still head chief of the Jikany when the Sudan became independent in 1956.

Ganame: Ethiopian dajjazmach; governor of Gore 1914–16; he opposed

Biographical Notes   421

attempts to set up a separate administration over the Anuak and succeeded in taking control of Gambela through his agent fitawrari Fanta in 1916; less than energetic in his support of the Shewan nobility against lij Iyasu, he was imprisoned in 1916 for his association with the deposed emperor; condemned to death, he was later reprieved.

Godwin, Major C.C., OBE: EA 1913–25; Sudan government service 1917–23; inspector UNP (Nyerol) 1917–18; military secretary, Khartoum 1923–4.

Guek Ngundeng (Gwek Wundeng or Wanding) (d.1929): a younger son of Ngundeng Bong, the renowned nineteenth-century Lou Nuer prophet (d.1906); claimed seizure by his father's divinity DENG in about 1919 when the Lou were recovering from the aftermath of the 1917 military campaign against them and the floods of 1918–19; his revival of his father's Mound shrine at Weideang in the early 1920s attracted the attention of the government, who feared that he was planning an insurrection; under Struvé's guidance direct contact was made with Guek and his peaceful intentions established; during the mid–1920s Guek resisted Coriat's efforts to incorporate him into the hierarchy of native administration; voiced the Lou opposition to building a new government road in 1927 when no other chief was willing to speak out on behalf of the people; Coriat did not see him as a serious threat, but at Wyld's urging Willis got Khartoum to approve a military campaign against Guek as the first phase in creating a new administrative system for the Nuer; attacks by the RAF and ground forces in 1927–8 served only to spread disaffection to the Gaawar; Guek was finally cornered at the ruins of his father's Mound in 1929 where, during a brief battle, he was shot and killed (see Hill (1967: 144)).

Havercroft, C.: controller of steamers, SGRS, 1918–20; deputy general manager, SGR&S, 1925–8.

Hebbert, Captain G.K.P., MC (b. 1892): transferred from EA to Sudan government service 1922; Sudan civil administration 1922–32; ADC UNP (Yirol) 1930–32.

Henderson, Dr. L.H.: SMS 1926–43; medical inspector, Malakal, 1926–31.

Hinsley, Archbishop (later Cardinal) Arthur (1865–1943): Rector of the English College at Rome 1917–27; appointed Visitor Apostolic to the Catholic Missions in the British Colonies in 1927; Delegate Apostolic to Africa 1930; Archbishop of Westminster 1935; Cardinal 1936; a strong advocate of cooperation with colonial authorities and of developing education over evangelisation.

Huddleston, Arthur James Croft, KBE, CMG (1880–1948): Sudan government service 1905–32; inspector UNP (Sobat valley) 1910–12; later governor of Khartoum and Gezira 1920–28, and Financial secretary 1928–31; knighted 1933 (see Bell & Dee: 14).

Huddleston, Major-General Sir Hubert Jervoise, KCB, DSO, MC (d.1950): joined the EA in 1909; led the troops who killed Sultan Ali Dinar in Darfur in 1916; commander-in-chief SDF 1924–30; governor-general of the Sudan 1940–7.

Huffman, Ray: American educational missionary who was posted to the American Mission at Nasir in 1925; she produced graded vernacular text-books, a pair of Nuer-English vocabularies, and a book on Nuer customs (see bibliography).

Hussein Farag: Sudanese officer in EA, transferred to Sudan government service from the 12th Sudanese bn 1906; sub-mamur UNP (Quanlualfan,

Abwong) 1906–11; mamur UNP 1911–24; retransferred to army and promoted Saghkolaghasi (Adjutant-Major) 1924; reappointed to civil administration 1924; died before 1930.

Hussein Said: Sudanese officer in EA, transferred to Sudan government service 1914; sub-mamur UNP 1911–25; mamur UNP 1925–30; promoted to Saghkolaghasi and transferred to duty in the Central Prison, Port Sudan, 1930.

Ismail Sirri Pasha: Egyptian minister for works during much of the 1920s and 1930s; a supporter of the sudd-diversion canal project, he was a target of nationalist oppositon to British plans for a series of dams along the Nile in Uganda and the Sudan in 1920, and was replaced as minister in 1925.

Jackson, Henry Cecil (b. 1883): Sudan government service 1907–31; senior inspector (deputy governor) UNP 1920–22; later governor of Berber and Halfa 1924–31 (see Bell & Dee: 18).

Jackson, Major-General Sir Herbert William, KBE, CB (1861–1931): EA 1888–1899; OC Fashoda District 1898–99; later civil secretary and deputy governor general 1900-01, governor of Berber and Dongola 1902–22; knighted in 1919 (see Hill (1967: 188–9); and Bell & Dee: 9).

Kabbada Mangasha: Ethiopian ras ('head', highest title in the Ethiopian nobility, next to that of negus, king); son of Menilek's ally ras Mangasha Atikim; governor of Wallo 1916–26; removed for trading in slaves; governor of Gore 1930–1 but arrived in his new province a sick man and went to the Sudan for treatment before returning to Addis Ababa and a new appointment in highland Ethiopia; the British did not trust him and reported that he caused a boom in the slave trade during his short governorship of Gore; died during the Italian Occupation.

Kengen (Kangen): Ngarotti Murle chief (also known as Baatalaan); son of Lom, the renowned war-leader against the Dinka in the late nineteenth and early twentieth centuries; though chief of the Nyangkobal (Veveno) territory, he was not a major drum chief, and served as regent to Burnian's adopted grandson, Ngapul, in the 1930s; arrested and temporarily deposed in 1942 for obstructing the resolution of a murder case; reinstated as territorial chief in 1944; regarded by Bacon as the cleverest of all the Murle chiefs, and by Alban as 'The Old Fox'.

Kavanagh, Major (Bimbashi) G.C.M.: Royal Engineers; as captain commanded the engineers in operations against the Nuer, 1928–30; commandant, engineer troops, SDF 1930–3.

Kerbiel (Gatbuogh Wal) (b. c.1880): Nuer prophet from the Gaakuar section of the Bar Gaawar; announced seizure by a divinity in 1927 and took the ox-name Kerbiel ('Kurbiel' in government records); reported to have proclaimed his intention to raid the Dinka early in 1928, he was visited by Wedderburn-Maxwell, Romilly and a few policemen, who then all had to retreat in the face of the overwhelming numbers of Kerbiel's following; Kerbiel subsequently joined Dual Diu's raid on Duk Fayuil and remained at large until his surrender in 1931; assumed to be an incurable epileptic, he was exiled to Wau, where he lived out the remainder of his life.

Kidd, Captain Herbert Frederick, MBE (b.1888): transferred from EA to Sudan government service 1920; Sudan civil administration 1920–32; Bahr el-Ghazal

(Yirol, Western Nuer) 1920–28; DC UNP (Western Nuer) 1928–9 (see Bell & Dee: 34).

Kippax, Jack: Australian chemist and missionary with the Sudan United Mission, arrived in the Sudan in 1929 and was joined by his wife Nell in 1930; they served among the Dinka at Rom before returning to Australia in the 1940s.

Kur Nyidok (r.1892–1903): 27th Shilluk reth (calculated from Nyikang); a son of Nyidok Nyakwac, the longest reigning reth in the nineteenth century; after the Mahdist commander al-Zaki Tamal's armies killed reth Yor Akoc in 1891–2, Kur was installed by the Mahdist government and was given the Arabic name, Abd al-Fadil; was reth when Marchand's French force arrived at Fashoda in 1898 and signed a treaty with him, a fact he later denied when Kitchener appeared with a larger Egyptian force; the British were never convinced of Kur's loyalty because of these earlier associations, and contrived his exile in 1903; father of the 30th *reth*, Anei Kur (r. 1944–5), and grandfather of the 33rd reth, Ayang Anei (r. 1975–92).

Kolang Ket (d.1925): Jagei Nuer, prophet of MAANI; established himself as the leading prophet of the Western Nuer in the early years of this century, his influence extending to the Bul, Jikany, Leek, Dok and Nyuong; a very elderly man and nearly senile by the time the government contacted him in 1921, he agreed to curtail raids against the Dinka of Bahr el-Ghazal; lost the support of many young men, including his son Majok, who died while raiding the Cic Dinka in 1922; moved by public opinion to resist the government in 1923–5; surrendered in 1925 after his people were defeated in battle and was detained in Adok, where he was reportedly buried alive by Caath Bang; his daughter, Nyaruac Kolang, was seized by her father's divinity after his death and achieved the same spiritual eminence he had until her death in 1973.

Lam Tutthiang (d.1931): Lou Nuer magician from the Rumjok section of the Lou, bordering on the Dinka and Gaawar; reluctant to implement the 1910 border agreement and was arrested and briefly detained in Malakal in 1911; an enthusiastic supporter of the government after the 1917 Lau patrol; eventually moved from Rumjok to settle near the government posts at Nyerol and Abwong; one of his nephews was Car Koryom; as a young man Lam had refused Ngundeng's summons to give up his magic and later transferred this hostility to Ngundeng's son Guek; after his death Captain Alban described him as the greatest chief the Lou ever had; his son, Mayan Lam, was a government interpreter at Abwong.

Liglig Kuny (Lig Lig Kuin): Lou chief; appointed chief of the Thiang section of the Gun Lou Nuer on the death of his brother in 1928; supported Guek, with whom he had marriage ties; died alongside Guek in 1929.

Lee, John M., MBE (b.1889): transferred from EA to Sudan government service 1919; Sudan civil administration 1919–29; ADC UNP (Longtam, Sobat, Nasir) 1920–9; DC (Nasir) 1929; invalided 1929; Nuer ox-names Carbiel, Wadh Bilieth (see Bell & Dee: 34)).

Lual Wal: chief of the Niel section of Paloic Dinka; his father, Wal Lual, had been recognized as chief by the British as early as 1900, but was considered 'quite incapable of dealing with the people of the district, who are notorious cattle thieves.'

Lyall, Charls Elliott, OBE (1877–1942): Sudan government service 1901–26; civil secretary, 1921–6 (see Hill (1967: 219); and Bell & Dee: 11).

Mabior Deng: appointed head chief of the Bor Athoic in 1932 to replace Ajak Bior; Wyld's immediate successor had a low opinion of his abilities and strength of character.

McBain, W.J.: Forestry Department 1921–46; inspector forests, White Nile, 1923–4; assistant conservator of forests, White Nile 1925–8; conservator of forests, Malakal, 1942–6.

McEnnery, J.J.: Bimbashi EA, transferred to civil administration 1916; inspector UNP (Nasir) 1916–18; inspector Gambela 1919; retransferred to EA 1919.

Macfarlane, D.: director of works, PWD, Khartoum, 1923–6.

Mackintosh, W.D., MC: Joined the EID in 1919; assistant director of works, Malakal, 1923–6; technical assistant to the inspector of irrigation, Malakal, 1927–34; personal assistant to the inspector general of irrigation, Khartoum, 1935–8.

MacMichael, Sir Harold, GCMG, DSO (1882–69): Sudan civil administration 1905–34; assistant civil secretary 1919–25; civil secretary 1926–34; knighted 1938; known to his colleagues affectionately as 'Macmic', and less affectionately as 'Horrible Harold' (see Bell & Dee: 15).

McMullen, G.: Australian appointed to Sudan government service in 1925; ADC UNP (Renk) 1925–7; struck off strength 1927.

Maffey, Sir John (1877–1969): Indian Civil Service 1899–1924; governor-general of the Sudan 1926–33; 1st Baron Rugby 1935.

Mahmud Osman el-Sheikh: Sudanese civilian, appointed sub-mamur (on probation) Mongalla 1924; sub-mamur UNP, 1930–3; the last sub-mamur in Bor District in the 1930s.

Mai Bilkwei: chief of the Bibiok section of the Kwil-Rueng Dinka; son of Bilkwei de Duop; appointed chief of the Rueng while his father was still alive; confirmed as chief in 1933 after his father's death; deposed in 1934 as he lacked his father's influence and spiritual authority and was seen as ineffectual; replaced by his younger brother Makwei de Bilkwei, who was made chief of the Kwil-Rueng in 1935.

Majok Ajak: head chief of the Faker Twic Dinka; his career as chief in the 1930s was marked by personal doggedness but also an unproven suspicion of the use of magic.

Majok Ajang: sub-chief of the Faker Twic Dinka; another man about whom DCs disagreed; Wyld's successor thought him 'weak, querrulous but rather attractive'.

Makonnen Wosanie (Makonen Wasso): Ethiopian dajjazmach, governor of Sayo 1928–32 (replacing dajjazmach Berru); continued Berru's attempt to take control of Gambela; a strong ally of the emperor Hayla-Selasse, but considered anti-foreign and anti-missionary by the British; appointed governor of Walamo in 1932 and fought in the Italo-Ethiopian War of 1935–6, submitting to the Italians in 1937.

Makwei Gol: a Nyareweng Dinka chief who played both sides of the border; his small section was increased by the addition of Dinka forcibly removed from the Lou Nuer after the Nuer Settlement, but in 1937 he formally asked to be allowed to return to the Lou, in part to escape a case pending against him by Deng Malwal.

Malek Agwer (born *c*. 1860): son of Agwer Alai, a sub-chief of the Paloic

Dinka at the beginning of this century; appointed chief of the Abuya section of the Paloic Dinka in c. 1905 on the dismissal of his brother as chief.

Marsh, J.F.H., DSO: transferred from EA to Sudan government service 1920; 2nd inspector UNP (Renk, Nasir) 1920–1; ADC Gambela 1922–7.

Masterman, Captain John: Sudan civil administration 1929–32; ADC UNP (Western Nuer/Ghazal River) 1929–30; OC Police Yirol 1931–2; Nuer ox-name Kerialbegh; nicknamed 'Pink Eye' by Coriat.

Maurice, Captain J.K., MBE, MC (1883–1953): EA 1916–25; Sudan civil administration 1927–49; ADC UNP (Gambela) 1928–32; DC Gambela 1932–49; known as 'Mori' to the Anuak, many of whom regarded him as a friend and protector, his name has since been applied retroactively to all British officials who preceded him (see Bell & Dee: 53).

Mayan Lam: Lou Nuer, son of Lam Tutthiang; hired as an interpreter by Coriat at Abwong in the 1920s, he was responsible for translating into Dinka and Arabic as well as Nuer; active in providing information on Guek's activities in the lead up to the patrol against the Lou in 1927; won the trust and confidence of a succession of British DCs.

Mohammed Abd el-Rahman Burhan: Sudanese policeman; appointed police officer 1929.

Mohammed Sabr Idris: sub-mamur (civilian) MP, 1922–9; mamur UNP 1929–30; transferred to Kordofan 1931.

Moinykuer Mabur: son of Mabur Ajuot, one of the government's earliest allies among the Dinka of Upper Nile; Mabur was a constant enemy of the Nuer prophets, Ngundeng Bong and Deng Laka, and was finally repatriated to the then Mongalla Province border with a section of Angai Dinka; while Mabur gained a reputation for intrigue and agitation among administrators of UNP, his son Moinykuer soon won a reputation for diplomacy; as a sub-chief under Deng Malwal in the 1920s and 1930s he was active in improving relations with the Gaawar; appointed court president of the Ghol Dinka court when the latter was made independent of the Nyareweng in 1939; the Gaawar prophet, Dual Diu, married one of Moinykuer's daughters in 1957, shortly after being released from detention; until recently his sons continued to fill the post of court president of the Ghol.

Moir, S.B.: joined EID 1914; assistant director of works, Malakal, 1925–6; technical assistant to inspector of irrigation, Malakal 1927–34; director of works, Malakal, 1935–9.

Mulholland, Major P.D.: controller of steamers, SGR&S, 1928–32.

Nadaw (c.1867–1929): Ethiopian ras; sent by Menilek to France to study, he combined a diplomatic career with provincial administration; represented Ethiopia at the League of Nations in 1923; in 1924 he visited Britain with ras Tafari, was made a K.B.E. and appointed ras; governor of Gore c.1920–9; enthusiastic about road-building, he was considered 'progressive' by British and Ethiopians alike; died in 1929 and was succeded by ras Kabada Mangasha.

Nayel Ali: Officer in the SDF, seconded to Sudan civil administration in 1929; sub-mamur UNP (Bor) 1929–18.08.31; retransferred to SDF 1931.

Newhouse, Major Frederick: joined the EID in 1905; inspector of irrigation, Malakal 1923–28; inspector general of irrigation, Khartoum, 1932–37.

Ngundeng Bong (d.1906): Lou Nuer prophet of DENG; son of a Bul Nuer earth-master, he grew up among the Gaajok north of the Sobat in the mid-nineteenth century; announcing his seizure by DENG he went to live among his mother's people, the Lou, in the 1870s; there he combined the attributes of the Dinka divinity DENG with the symbols of the first Dinka spear-master Aiwel Longar and the attributes of a Nuer earth-master to fashion a new idiom of prophecy among the Nuer; noted for his prohibitions against feuding and raiding, he remained aloof from all governments who entered the region; declared hostile by the Anglo-Egyptian administration he was raided by them in 1902 and died in 1906; he is best remembered for constructing a large mud mound in imitation of Aiwel's Mound on the Bahr el-Zeraf; see above, Guek Ngundeng.

Nicholls, William P. (b.1882): Sudan civil administration 1907–32; governor White Nile Province 1922–6; governor Berber 1926–32.

Northcote, Major Cecil Stephen, CBE (1878–1945): seconded from EA to Sudan government service 1912; Sudan civil administration 1912–28; governor MP 1918–19; governor NMP 1919–28 (see Hill (1967: 296); and Bell & Dee: 21).

Noumeir (also Neumair), George: Syrian; ras Tafari's customs representative in Gambela in the 1920s; introduced a 7% customs duty on top of that levied by the Sudan government in 1921; dismissed (or withdrawn) in 1924 prior to Tafari re-opening negotiations with Britain over the customs agreement at Gambela; returned to Gambela after agreement was reached in 1928.

Nuel Juel: Leek Nuer chief; man of cattle, appointed government chief in 1925 but deposed in 1926 for abusing his power; appeared 'truculent' in the aftermath of Fergusson's assassination, was arrested and threatened with permanent exile to Malakal in 1928, but was reinstated at the end of the same year; never succeeded in making a good impression on the DCs and was finally deposed in 1934 after numerous complaints from his own people.

Oshalla (d.1931): 'Burun' (Koma) leader at Pil on the Abyssinian border; held the Ethiopian title of *grazmach* ('commander of the left', a title below fitawrari) and assisted Abyssinian tribute collecting patrols and raids on Koma villages as far inside the Sudan as Maiwut; in 1923 Lee described him as 'a crippled medicine man' and replaced him with Sheila Kong because of Oshalla's collaboration with the Abyssinians across the border; Sheila Kong was killed in an Abyssinian raid a week later and Oshalla continued as 'chief' of the Koma along the border, making his final peace with the Sudan government after the establishment of the frontier police post at Kigille in 1926; many Anuak settled near him, becoming his followers and paying tribute to the government through him; he died in June 1931.

O'Sullivan, Major-General Hugh Dermond Evan, CBE (1870–1948): EA 1901–11; Sudan government service 1905–11; senior inspector UNP 1905–07; governor UNP and OC UNP military district 1910–11.

Owen, Lt.-Colonel Roger Carmichael Robert, CMG, OBE (1866–1941): seconded from EA to Sudan government service 1903; Sudan civil administration 1903–18; governor and OC Military District, MP 1908–18 (see Hill (1967: 300); and Bell & Dee: 12).

Padiet Renk: chief of the Akon section of Abialang Dinka; son of Renk de Com; replaced his brother Awir as chief of Akon in 1902; as chief he appeared to the British to be lacking influence and untruthful; deposed in 1913.

Biographical Notes 427

Parker, A.C.: assistant general manager, SGR&S, 1922–5; general manager, SGRS, 1925–32.

Parr, Martin Willoughby (1892–1985): Sudan civil administration 1920–42; private secretary to the governor-general 1928–9 and 1931–33; deputy civil secretary 1934; governor UNP 1934–6; governor Equatoria 1936–42 (see Bell & Dee: 29).

Pawson, Albert Guy, CMG (1888–1986): Sudan civil administration 1911–34; 2nd inspector UNP (Renk), 1916–17; governor UNP 1931–4 (see Bell & Dee: 23).

Pec Poar (Pey Poar) (d.1931): Bul Nuer chief; appointed sub-chief of Gok Bul in 1930 when he was already an old man; considered old and incompetent by both Coriat and Romilly, retired in 1931 shortly before he died.

Pec Ruac: chief of the Can Mor Lou; in 1927 Pec was one of the newly appointed Mor chiefs to urge Coriat and the government to suppress Guek (of the Gun Lou) before he attracted support from the Mor; in 1929 Coriat judged Pec to be a promising young chief who none the less lost his head 'very easily'; by 1946 many of Pec's section had moved out of his district to join Lang section of the Gaajok Nuer.

Pletts, Captain G. S. (b.1882): transferred from EA to Sudan government service, 1921; Sudan civil administration 1921–8; 2nd inspector and ADC UNP (Gambela, Fangak) 1923–8 (see Bell & Dee: 37).

Pollen, Walter Michael Hungerford, MC (1894–1968): transferred from EA to Sudan government service 1921; Sudan civil administration 1921–38; 2nd inspector and ADC UNP (Ayod, Malakal, Renk) 1918–23; knighted 1959 (see Bell & Dee: 27).

Pok Kerjiok: Nuer prophet of the divinity GÄR from the Nyajikany section of the Rumjok Lou; descended from a Ngok Dinka immigrant, he claimed a clan relationship with Dual Diu of the Gaawar (whose father also came from the Ngok); rose to prominence among the Lou during the years coinciding with WWI and won a stunning victory over a party of Sudanese soldiers during a raid against the Twic Dinka in 1916; he was the main object of the 'Lau Patrol' of 1917 and, though defeated in a single battle, managed to elude capture; his reputation never fully recovered from this defeat; in 1927–29 he alternately sided with Dual Diu and Guek Ngundeng and became a fugitive once again on the latter's death in 1929; surrendered to the government in 1930 and was exiled to Wau in 1931, where he died shortly thereafter.

Porter, W.A.: Joined Agriculture Department in 1925; inspector of agriculture in Bahr el-Ghazal Province 1927–8; the first government official to learn of and report the news of Fergusson's assassination and subsequently served as political officer to the punitive patrol sent against the Nyuong Nuer in 1928; inspector of agriculture UNP Nuer area 1929; inspector of agriculture Malakal 1934–8.

Price, Cecil Livingstone (1899–1961): born in India into a CMS missionary family, he attained a B.A. in Engineering at Queen's College, Cambridge in 1921, and joined the CMS that same year; served in the Sudan 1923–35, mainly in Malek, but also Juba and Loka.

Pschorn, Fr. E: Verona Father missionary at the Shilluk stations of Detwok and Lul in the 1920s and 1930s.

Rak Yaak (b. *c*.1900): Rut Dinka caretaker of the shrine at Luang Deng;

succeeded his uncle, Deng Agwer, as caretaker in the early 1920s, long before the latter's death in the 1930s; maintained close relations with the Gaawar, among whom he lived, and was active as caretaker until his death in the 1960s.

Ratcliffe, W., DSO: Bimbashi EA, transferred to civil administration 1919; inspector Gambela 1919–20; transferred to Kordofan 1920; returned to army 1922.

Reid, Wing Commander George R.M., DSO, MC: commander No. 47 squadron RAF in Khartoum.

Renk de Com (Areng Com): Abialang chief in the late nineteenth century; taken into slavery as a child to Karkoj on the Blue Nile; brought back to his home by Bakhit Nyok; rose to prominence during the Mahdiyya; was murdered by a man from the Pittio section of the Paloic Dinka, who accused him of adultery, in c.1898; the town of Renk on the White Nile is named after him.

Riak Deng Mayan: son of Deng Mayan, whom he succeeded as paramount chief of the Ngok Dinka on the Sobat in 1926; when first appointed he was considered shy and quiet, but rapidly grew in stature and authority and began to display a 'fiery temper'; both Coriat and Alban considered him to be potentially a strong chief.

Richards, Captain Manuel Glasbrook, MC (1889–1950): seconded from EA to Sudan government service 1919; Sudan civil administration 1919–37; appointed to permanent service 1925; ADC Mongalla (Bor) 1925–27; ADC Bahr el-Ghazal (Bor, Tonj) 1927–37 (see Bell & Dee: 29).

Rimmer, Keith: New Zealand missionary with the Sudan United Mission; trained at the Los Angeles Bible College, served in the Sudan 1922–30, mainly among the Dinka; he founded the SUM station at Rom in 1924, but left with his wife in 1930 when the latter contracted blackwater fever.

Roberts, W.D.: EID 1903–27; inspector general of irrigation, Khartoum 1923–7; presented the first proposal for a canal to be cut from Bor to the Bahr el-Zeraf in 1925, and was dismissed by the Egyptian government as a scapegoat when the Sudan government objected to the scheme; was then hired by the Sudan government to undertake a study on the probable effects of the canal scheme on the local area, submitting his report in 1928.

Romilly, Captain Herbrand Alan, MBE (1894–1968): EA and SDF 1923–9; Sudan civil administration 1929–46; ADC UNP (Abwong, Western Nuer) 1929–36; DC UNP (Nasir) 1936–46; Nuer ox-name Jangwan (see Bell & Dee: 29).

Routh, Captain H.C.E. (1894): Sudan civil administration 1919–27; ADC Mongalla (Duk Fayuil) 1924–5 (see Bell & Dee: 29).

Said Abd el-Rahman, Captain DCM: Shilluk soldier, served in the King's African Rifles in East Africa, where he won the DCM; taken on locally by Struvé in UNP as a police officer in the early 1920s, served throughout the rest of the decade as police officer and sub-mamur; with Coriat he arrested a group of rebellious Egyptian officers in the Nuba Mountains in 1924; commanded Pibor Post 1925–8; struck off strength as a sub-mamur in 1931 but reappointed as police officer later that same year.

Salim Banga (Salem Banga): chief of the Giel section of the Abialang Dinka; a minor chief during the Turkiyya and Mahdiyya, he 'was first on the spot at Fashoda' when the British arrived and was thus recognized as head chief of the Giel; British administrators subsequently described him as 'very slack'; deposed in

1906 for forcing a girl to marry another man against her parents wishes; still alive in 1909 and though elderly, continued to exert influence among his kinsmen.

Schuster, Sir George: Financial secretary 1923–8; barrister and financier responsible for reforming the Finance Department; credited with financing the Gezira scheme, plotting the Sudan government's strategy in the Anglo-Egyptian negotiations of 1924, increasing the number of British administrators in the Sudan, and cutting the budget for education in the Southern Sudan.

Shaw, Archdeacon Archibald (1879–1956): CMS missionary to the Southern Sudan 1905, where he helped to open Malek mission station; secretary of the Gordon Memorial Sudan Mission, 1907–36; Archdeacon of the Southern Sudan, 1922–40.

Smith, P.J. (1877–1961): American missionary at Nasir 1916–49; both his wife (Ilda) and his daughter (Dr. Mary) were also missionaries at Nasir; another daughter (Ellen) later worked in the American Mission's school for girls in Khartoum North.

Soule, Cora Blanche (1875–1945): American Presbyterian missionary at Nasir 1921–45; worked as a nurse and with orphan girls; died in Malakal (see Hill (1967: 342)).

Stewart, J.B.: Joined the Agriculture Department in 1925; inspector of agriculture UNP 1927–1932, ADC Shilluk 1932–4; he was one of the first British officials to learn Shilluk, reportedly being determined, after Willis failed him in his Arabic exam, to learn a language for which Willis would be unable to serve as examiner; later served on the Gash Board.

Stigand, Major Chauncy Hugh (1877–1919): EA 1910–19; Sudan civil administration, 1910–19; 2nd inspector UNP (Nasir) 1915–16; Senior inspector UNP 1916–17; governor UNP 1917–19; governor MP 1919; killed in the Aliab Dinka rising 8 December 1919 (see Hill (1967: 346)).

Struvé, Kenneth Chetwood Price, OBE (b. 1876): Sudan civil administration, 1901–26; 2nd inspector UNP 1906-08; senior inspector UNP 1908–10; governor UNP 1919–26 (see Bell & Dee: 11).

Takpiny Malwal (Takpin Malwal) (d.1943): chief and magistrate of the Adar section, Cic Dinka (see Hill (1967: 355)).

Talib Ismail: Sudanese officer in EA, transferred to Sudan government service in 1920; sub-mamur UNP from 1920.

Tegjiek Dualdoang (b. c.1877): Bul Nuer earth-master; appointed sub-chief of Dieng section Bul Nuer by Fergusson c.1927; appointed head chief Bul Nuer 1931.

Thiei Poic (Thiey Poich) (b. c.1895): earth-master of the Rengyan section of the Jagei Nuer; appointed chief of Jagei by Fergusson in 1926 on the dismissal of his brother, Jeic Poic; throughout the late 1930s Thiei appeared to be constantly suffering from various spiritual threats and even proposed to resign his chieftainship in favour of the prophetess Nyaruac Kolang Ket; his family continued to fill the court presidency of Jagei up into recent times.

Tiernay, James Francis (1902–74): Sudan civil administration 1925–52; ADC UNP (Renk, Akobo, Nasir) 1927–32; deputy governor Equatoria 1945–7; governor Equatoria 1949–52; Anuak name Peitut; Nuer ox-name Bilrial (see Bell & Dee: 44).

430   Appendix 3

Tracey, Christopher Birdwood (1898–1984): Sudan civil administration 1923–48; ADC UNP (Renk, Gambela) 1924–27.

Trudinger, Ronald (1887–1968), BSc, MB: medical doctor and Presbyterian missionary from Adelaide, one of the Sudan United Mission's first missionaries in the Sudan; served in the Sudan 1913–53 (joined by his wife, Lima, in 1918), first at Melut and Rom (staying on at Rom after it was handed over to the SIM in 1938), and then with the American Mission from 1944–53; he translated the New Testament into Dungjol Dinka, and wrote a dictionary, grammar, and school books in the same dialect; on leaving the Sudan he worked among the Aboriginal people of Central Australia.

Tunnicliffe, Captain Eric Charlton (1897–1953): lent by SDF to Sudan government service 1925; Sudan civil administration 1925–37; OC Police UNP 1926–27; ADC UNP (Pibor) 1927–34; OC Police UNP 1934–7; Anuak name Othiri; Nuer ox-name Wancar (see Bell & Dee: 48).

Turner, L.: Forestry Department 1921–42; appointed superintendent (later assistant conservator) of forests, Wau in 1934, he ended his career in the Sudan as conservator of forests, Singa (1939–42).

Twil Ran (b. c.1885): Leek Nuer earth-master and chief; appointed chief of the Jikany, along with the Lak and Kilwal sections of the Leek Nuer by Fergusson; was already noted in 1927 as being inclined to be too strict; was one of the chiefs who remained loyal after Fergusson's death, but also falsely accused Gaaluak Nyagh of instigating the murder; deposed as chief of the Jikany in February 1931, and several minor cases continued to be brought against him as late as 1934; was one of Fr. Crazzolara's main informants.

Ujulu-wuru-Ubulu (Ogilo): Anuak kwaaro (headman) of Pinykeu on the Baro, one of the most powerful kwaari in the Upeeno district of Gambela, who also worked closely with the British authorities in Gambela in the 1930s.

Waller, E.S., MC (d. 1963): EID 1911–53; director of works, Malakal 1923–29; acting inspector of irrigation, Malakal, 1930–1; inspector of irrigation, Malakal, 1932–4; assistant inspector general of irrigation, Khartoum, 1939–53.

Wedderburn-Maxwell, Henry Godfrey, MBE (1897–1972): Sudan civil administration 1922–46; Fung, White Nile 1922–26; ADC UNP (Daga, Fangak) 1927–32) Blue Nile/Fung 1932–37; DC UNP (Western Nuer) 1937–46; Nuer ox-name Dhuoryian (see Bell & Dee: 36).

Wheatley, Lt.-Colonel Mervyn J. (1880–74); seconded from EA to Sudan government 1907; Sudan civil administration 1907–28; Sudan civil administration 1907–28; governor and OC Bahr el-Ghazal 1921–28; knighted 1952 (see Bell & Dee: 19).

Willan, R.: EID; assistant director for works, Malakal, c. 1913–6.

Willis, Charles Armine, CBE (1881–1975): Sudan civil administration 1905–31; assistant director of intelligence 1915–19; director of intelligence 1920–26; governor UNP 1926–31; generally known by his nickname, 'Chunky' (see Bell & Dee: 16).

Wilson, Captain Horace Hayman (1874–1915): EA 1899–1909; Sudan government service 1901–1907; inspector UNP 1901–05 (the first administrator to make direct contact with the Gaawar prophet Deng Laka); assistant civil secretary 1905–07; assistant adjutant general 1907–09.

Biographical Notes

Wuon Kuoth (Won Kwoth) (b c.1898): Nyuong Nuer prophet of DIU; he was one of the first Nyuong leaders to make peace with the government in 1923; cooperated in Fergusson's cotton growing schemes but was deposed for unfairness in 1925; he helped to capture his relative, Gatkek Jiek, one of Fergusson's murderers, and was reappointed a chief of the Dur Nyuong after Cak Riang was deposed; served as a headman under Gaaluak Nyagh and was one of those accused by Gaaluak's relatives of causing his death by magic in 1938; he had ambitions to be made chief of all the Nyuong, but was promoted only to head chief of the Dur in 1941; he was known to have good relations with the Dinka, but also to deal in magic roots; his and Gaaluak Nyagh's families continue to be political rivals within the Nyuong to this day.

Wyld, Major J.W.G., DSO, MC (1896–1968): Sudan civil administration 1925–51; ADC Mongalla (Duk Fayuil) 1925; ADC UNP (Duk Fayuil, Bor & Duk) 1926–31; Dinka ox-name Kurjok.

Yol Kur (c. 1868–1942): Bawom Dinka, sub-section Mangnok; appointed chief of the Bawom section in 1904 as successor to Awir Renk; it had been thought that his uncle had been head chief of the Abialang prior to Renk de Com, but later it was recognised that Yol had no hereditary claim to any paramountcy; appointed president of the Abialang Court (combining the Bawom and Giel Dinka) 1936; endeared himself to the government through his strength of character, intelligence, knowledge of Arabic, Shilluk and Nuer, and his loyalty towards the government itself (see Hill (1967: 385)).

APPENDIX 4

Steamer Transport in Upper Nile Province, 1926–31

Main source: Hill (1970 & 1972)

Anuak: Oil-burning steam stern wheeler, powerful tug with limited passenger accommodation (length 150 ft., beam 33 ft., draught 5 ft., 450 h.p.); built during World War I for use in Mesopotamia; bought by SG 1921 and commissioned 1925.
Atbara: Stern-wheeler; commissioned 1929, the third steamer of this name.
Beatrice: Small stern-wheel steamer (length 70 ft., beam 16 ft., 60 h.p.) with limited passenger accommodation; commissioned 1906; named after Princess Beatrice, daughter of Queen Victoria; sister ship to *Margaret*; scrapped in the 1920s.
Culex: Single cylinder stern-wheel steamer with living accommodation for one (length 60 ft., beam 12 ft., 40 h.p.); commissioned by SG 1905; named after a type of mosquito; used by the Slavery Repression Department and later by the Wellcome Laboratory of Gordon Memorial College until 1915; a scale model is on display in the Wellcome Institute in London.
Eland: Small, single-deck stern-wheel steamer (length 65 ft. 6 in., beam 10 ft., draught 4 ft., 25 h.p); built at Khartoum North Dockyard; commissioned 1914; scrapped 1941.
Hafir: Originally a steam stern-wheel gunboat, commissioned 1885 as *El Teb*, similar in design to *Abu Klea*, *Metemma* and *Tamai* (all named for battles during the Suakin and Gordon Relief expeditions of 1884–5); used in the 1896–8 reconquest of the Sudan; wrecked twice, renamed *Hafir* in 1897 to change her luck; converted to civilian duty after 1899, re-hulled and rebuilt 1925 (length 86 ft. 6 in., beam 18 ft., draught 4 ft 8 in., 100 h.p.); sank in the Bahr el-Zeraf 1941.
Kerreri: Stern-wheel steamer, built at Khartoum North 1903 (length 100 ft., beam 22 ft., 100 h.p.); purchased by SG from Sudan Development and Exploration Company 1912; of the same type of vessel as *Lady Baker I* (formerly *Atbara II*); was for many years the floating headquarters of the DCs of Eastern District, Bahr el-Ghazal (later Western Nuer District, Upper Nile).
Lady Baker: Originally commissioned 1903 as the *Atbara II*; a stern-wheel steamer (length 100 ft., beam 22 ft., 100 h.p.) belonging to the Sudan Development and Exploration Company; purchased by SG 1912 and converted to a hospital ship 1922 for use by the Sudan Medical Service; named after Florence Baker, Sir Samuel Baker's Armenian wife; the first *Lady Baker* was scrapped about 1929; a second *Lady Baker*, also a stern-wheeler hospital ship, was commissioned 1929 (length 86 ft. 6 in., beam 17 ft. 6 in., draught 4 ft. 3); renamed *Wad El Nugomi* after independence.
Lord Kitchener: Stern-wheel, semi-diesel vessel, commissioned 1927; her engine was too weak to move against strong currents; renamed *Kerreri* after independence and given a new engine 1964.

Steamer Transport, 1926–31   433

Margaret: Stern-wheel steamer commissioned 1906; sister ship to *Beatrice*; sank in a storm at the mouth of the river Jur 1907 but refloated; scrapped about 1931.

Shabluka: Stern-wheel steamer; built with a new hull and a boiler and machinery salved from Mahdist steamers; commissioned 1904 (length 60 ft., beam 10 ft., 25 h.p.); nicknamed "Shabbyloo" by those who travelled on her; scrapped about 1930.

Sir Reginald Wingate: Stern-wheel steamer (length 100 ft., beam 21 ft., draught 4 ft. 4 in.); commissioned 1926; in the late 1940s was used by the Agriculture and Forests Department; renamed *Osman Digna* after independence; scrapped 1964.

Archival Sources on Upper Nile Province

The Sudan

The main collections of archival material on Upper Nile Province in the twentieth century are to be found in the National Records Office, Khartoum, and the Southern Records Office, Juba.

NATIONAL RECORDS OFFICE: various files in classes Cairo Intelligence (Cairint 3: 21 from 1898–1905), Intelligence (Intel 1: 20 from 1901–24; Intel 2: 40 from 1910–24), Civil Secretary (Civsec: 56 from 1914–54), Interior (Dakhlia I: 29 from c.1929–51), Mongalla Province (MP: 4 from 1908–12), Bahr el-Ghazal (BG: 4 from 1910–37) and Upper Nile Province (UNP: 362 from 1911–61). Reports of general ethnographic interest are found in classes Dakhlia I 112 and Civsec 112.

THE SUDAN COLLECTION, UNIVERSITY LIBRARY, UNIVERSITY OF KHARTOUM: copies of *Sudan Intelligence Reports*, *Sudan Monthly Intelligence Reports*, and *Sudan Monthly Record*; the *Sudan Government Gazette*, the governor-general's annual report from 1902 to 1914; and the 'Upper Nile Province Diary' for the 1940s–50s.

SOUTHERN RECORDS OFFICE: In 1981–3 files were systematically transferred from district and province headquarters in Jonglei and Upper Nile Provinces to the Southern Records Office in Juba. These included Akobo (230 from 1933–79), Bor (140 from 1925–73), Nasir (8 from 1914–65), New Fangak (48 from 1926–71), Pibor (193 from 1912–72), Yirol (1 notebook, c. 1933–40); and province headquarters files from Malakal (c. 900 from 1909–69, including c.65 files dealing with Gambela and the Ethiopian border, 1909–56). The majority of district files dated from the 1940s to 1972. The province files from Malakal covered all aspects of administration, mainly from the 1930s on.

The Southern Regional Government was dissolved in 1983 before all records in the SRO could be properly housed or re-catalogued. It is not currently known in what state the files are. Many administrative records refering to the early independence (and even some on the late Condominium) periods were retained in district headquarters. All those left in Bor, Akobo, Nasir and Yirol are known to have been destroyed or lost during the fighting in the second civil war (beginning 1983). Those at Pibor, Fangak and New Fangak are likely also to have been destroyed. There is no information at this date concerning the state of administrative records in Bentiu, Kodok, Malakal and Renk. It is known that prior to 1983 Shilluk administrative records at Kodok were sometimes pilfered by administrators and local researchers.

Britain

THE PUBLIC RECORDS OFFICE, KEW: Copies of some official reports were forwarded by the central government in Khartoum to the Embassy in Cairo and the

Foreign Office at Whitehall. The majority of these documents will be found under classes FO 141 and 371. Such files usually referred to specific problems of public security or general problems of development (including the Jonglei Canal scheme).

THE SUDAN ARCHIVE, UNIVERSITY OF DURHAM: The largest collection of Sudan-related papers in Britain, composed of donations of personal papers from former officials employed in a variety of capacities in the Sudan throughout the Condominium period. All papers are classed under individual donations. They include copies of official records and unofficial papers (letters, diaries, memoirs, photographs, etc.). The most important donations concerning Upper Nile Province are: J. H. Dick (400/1 & 6: notes on Northern District and Maban, 1942); P. P. Howell (Dinka, Nuer and Shilluk administration, Jonglei Investigation Team, Southern Development Investigation Team, c.1925–32 and 1942–54); H. C. Jackson (465/4: Safaria Notes, UNP, 1920-2), R. T. Johnston (639/12/1–79: Bor and Duk District Handing Over Report, 1934); H. H. Kelly (132/7, 133/3–4, 182/2: Sudan-Abyssinian border, 1912, plus photographs); John Longe (642/1–3, 5–7, 10, 643/2: Upper Nile Province, Northern District and Malakal during the Second World War; handing over notes and annual reports by governors Corfield and Longe and assistant governor Donald, 1950–53); J. G. S. Macphail (403/9: Malakal, 1938); J. W. Robertson (527/15, 528/12, 529/2–3, 5, 9–11, 14, 530/4 & 9: correspondence with district and provincial officials, 1949–52); H. A. Romilly (pocket diaries and photographs, 1923–48); G. W. Titherington (636/12/1–33: personal letters, 1920–36); J. Winder (104/13–17, 541/2, 4, 8–10: UNP, Gambela, Jonglei Canal investigation, 1936–54); F. R. Wingate (correspondence with various officers, but especially 266/5, 8, 12, 269/1, 270/1, 271/7–8, 275/2–3, 5, 276/5, 301/3 which contain correspondence on conditions in the Upper Nile, 1898–1905, 1911; and 181/1–2, 199/1–2, 200/6, 290/1, on military patrols 1910–16). There is also the four volume ms 'The Sudan: A Medical History' by J.F.E. Bloss and A. Cruickshank (E//S649), which has some account of medical work in the Upper Nile. The record of service of many British, Egyptian and Sudanese officials can be found in the *Sudan Government Gazette* (1899–1908, 1918–1932, 1940 to independence and beyond), and various Monthly, Quarterly and Half-Yearly Sudan Staff Lists. Copies of the *Sudan Diocesan Review* (catalogued up through 1973) are invaluable for obituaries, especially the later issues.

The C. A. Willis MSS contain the following papers (not included in this handbook): 209/12/1–42 & 209/13/1–73: personal letters, May 1926-May 1931; 210/14/1–244: uncaptioned photographic negatives, including some of Southern Sudan (nos. 106–214 have been given provisional captions by the editor); 212/6/1–51: correspondence and reports on Bahr el-Jebel and Veveno-Pibor canal schemes, 1931; 212/9/15–92: notes on tours of the province before taking over, and within a year of taking over as governor (including comments on Struvé's handing over notes), April 1926-April 1927; 212/10/1–13: two surveys of Upper Nile Province administration, 1927.

RHODES HOUSE, OXFORD UNIVERSITY: Papers of Percy and Kay Coriat, 1920–60 (Mss Afr. s.1684 & 1684 (1)); and H. A. W. Morrice (Director of Irrigation in the Sudan), 1936–59 (20 vols., Mss Afr. s.1457).

INSTITUTE OF SOCIAL AND CULTURAL ANTHROPOLOGY, OXFORD UNIVERSITY (ISCA): E. E. Evans-Pritchard MSS (EP 1/8/46, Anuak grammar; 1/

8/49, P. P. Howell, Observations on the Shilluk of the Upper Nile); B. A. Lewis MSS on the Murle (BAL 1/1/1–13, 1/2/14–17).

CMS ARCHIVES, UNIVERSITY OF BIRMINGHAM LIBRARY, MANUSCRIPT COLLECTION: CMS Précis Books, Sudan Mission, 1905–34 (G3 S/P1); original incoming letters, reports and papers, 1905–34 (3 boxes, G3/S/O).

Italy

ARCHIVO STORICO DELLA CONGREGAZIONE DEI MISSIONARI COMBONIANI (ROME): The archives of the Comboni (or Verona) Fathers, catalogued in two volumes by S. Luciani and I. Taddia, *Fonti Comboniane per la Storia dell'Africa Nord-Orientale*, vols. I & II, Fonti e Studi per la Storia dell'Africa 1 & 3 (Bologna & Cagliari, 1986 & 1988); contains correspondence and station diaries from Detwok, Kodok, Lul, Malakal, Tonga, and Yoinyang (1901–56), papers of Frs. Banholzer, Crazzolara, Kohnen, Mlakic, Pschorn, Tappi and others; and ethnographic and linguistic material on the Anuak, Nuer and Shilluk.

USA

The records of the AMERICAN MISSION stations at Doleib Hill and Nasir used to be kept at the United Presbyterian Church of North America headquarters in Philadelphia. The present headquarters of the American Mission is Presbyterian Church (U.S.A.), 100 Witherspoon St., Louisville, Kentucky 40202–1396.

Records of the SUDAN INTERIOR MISSION have been deposited in the Billy Graham Library, Wheatley, Il, USA.

Australia

Enquiries concerning the record of the Australian and New Zealand missionaries with the SUDAN UNITED MISSION can be directed to ACTION PARTNERS, Australian and New Zealand Branch, P.O. Box 327, Baulkham Hills, NSW 2153 Australia.

BIBLIOGRAPHY

The Upper Nile Province in the Twentieth Century

The following is a comprehensive (though not complete) bibliography of publications on various aspects of the Upper Nile Province in the twentieth century (both before and after the date of this handbook). Only primary sources or works based on primary research are included (excluding contemporary reports in such official publications as *SIR*). Articles which were subsequently incorporated in anthropological monographs (e.g. by Burton, Evans-Pritchard, and James) have been excluded.

Development, Natural Resources and Hydrology

NB: For a full development bibliography, see Howell, Lock & Cobb (1988).
BOOTH, A. F. (1952), 'The Forests of Upper Nile Province, 1862–1950', *SNR*, 33/1.
BROUN, A. F. & MASSEY, R. E. (1929), *Flora of the Sudan*, London [includes vernacular names of plants, including those from Anuak, several dialects of Dinka, Nuer, Shilluk].
CRISPIN, E. S. (1902), 'The "Sudd" of the White Nile', *Geographical Journal*, 20/3.
EL-SAMMANI, M. O. (1984), *Jonglei Canal: Dynamics of Planned Change in the Twic Area*, Khartoum.
GARANG, J. DE M.(1981), 'Identifying, Selecting and Implementing Rural Development Strategies for Socio-Economic Development in the Jonglei Projects Area, Southern Region, Sudan', Ph.D. thesis, Iowa State University.
GARSTIN, W. (1901), 'Report as to Irrigation Projects on the Upper Nile, &c.', (*Blue Book*) Egypt No.2.
GIRGIS, S. (1948), 'A List of Common Fish of the Upper Nile with their Shilluk, Dinka and Nuer Names', *SNR*, 29/1.
HASAN MUTWAKIL (1947), 'Types of Dura used by Shilluk and Dinka', *SNR*, 28.
HOWELL, P., LOCK, M., & COBB, S. (eds) (1988), *The Jonglei Canal: Impact and Opportunity*, Cambridge.
HURST, H. E. & PHILLIPS, P. (1938), *The Nile Basin. Volume V. The Hydrology of the Lake Plateau and the Bahr el Jebel*, Cairo.
JONGLEI INVESTIGATION TEAM [JIT] (1946), *First Interim Report*, Khartoum.
—— (1947), *Second Interim Report*, Khartoum.
—— (1948), *Third Interim Report*, Khartoum.
—— (1952), 'The Equatorial Nile Project', *SNR*, 33/1.
—— (1954), *The Equatorial Nile Project and its Effects in the Anglo-Egyptian Sudan*, 4 vols., Khartoum.
LAKO, G. T. (1985), 'The Impact of the Jonglei Scheme on the Economy of the Dinka', *African Affairs*, 84/334.
MEFIT-BABTIE SLR. (1983), *Development Studies in the Jonglei Canal Area*.

Techincal Assistance Contract for Range Ecology Survey, Livestock Investigations and Water Supply. Final Report, 9 vols., Glasgow/Khartoum/Rome.

PARKER, P. and W. D. MACKINTOSH (1934), 'The Veveno-Pibor-canal project survey', Geographical Journal, 84.

SANDON, H. (ed.) (1951), 'Problems of Fisheries in the Area Affected by the Equatorial Nile Project', SNR, 32/1.

SHERWOOD, J. H. (1948), 'Upper Nile Province', in J. D. Tothill (ed.), Agriculture in the Sudan. Being a Handbook of Agriculture as Practised in the Anglo-Egyptian Sudan, London.

SOUTHERN DEVELOPMENT INVESTIGATION TEAM [SDIT] (1955), Natural Resources and Development Potential in the Southern Provinces of the Sudan. A Preliminary Report by the Southern Development Investigation Team, 1954, London.

STRUVÉ, K. C. P. (1925), 'The Age of Tebeldis', SNR, 8.

SUTCLIFFE, J. V. 1974, 'A Hydrologicial Study of the Southern Sudd Region of the Upper Nile', Hydrological Sciences Bulletin, 19.

—— & PARKS, Y.P. (1982), A Hydrological Estimate of the Effects of the Jonglei Canal on Areas of Flooding, Wallingford.

—— & PARKS, Y.P. (1987), 'Hydrological Modelling of the Sudd and Jonglei Canal', Hydrological Sciences Journal, 32.

WRIGHT, J. W. (1951), 'The White Nile and the Sobat', SNR, 32/1.

Ethnography

ALBAN, A. H. (1940), 'Gwek's Pipe and Pyramid', SNR, 23/1.

THE AMERICAN MISSION (1932), Some Nuer Diseases and their Remedies, Nasir.

—— (1938), Nasir District Sub-Divisions and Native Nuer Chiefs, Nasir.

ANON. (1922), 'The Ujang Tribe', SNR, 5/3 [Majangir].

ANON. [a Shilluk student] (1956), 'Installation of a New Shilluk King', SNR, 34.

E. F. N. B. (1918), 'Divination', SNR, 1/2 [Padang Dinka].

EL WATHIG KAMEIR (1980), 'Nuer Migrants iin the Building Industry in Khartoum: A Case of the Concentration and Circulation of Labour', in V. Pons (ed.), Urbanization and Urban Life in the Sudan, Hull.

BACON, C. R. K. (1921), 'Kingship amongst the Anuak', SNR, 4/3.

—— (1922), 'The Anuak', SNR, 5/3.

—— (1924), 'The Investiture of an Anuak Nyera or Sultan', SNR, 7/2.

BEDRI, IBRAHIM (1939), 'Dinka Beliefs in their Chiefs and Rainmakers', SNR, 22/1.

—— (1948), 'More Notes on the Padang Dinka', SNR, 29/1.

BURTON, J. W. (1978), 'Ghost Marriage and the Cattle Trade among the Atuot of the Southern Sudan', Africa, 48.

—— (1980), 'Atuot Totemism', Journal of Religion in Africa, 11.

—— (1981a), 'Atuot Ethnicity: An Aspect of Nilotic Ethnology', Africa, 51.

—— (1981b), God's Ants: A Study of Atuot Religion, St. Augustin.

—— (1981c), 'The Moon is a Sheep: A Feminine Principle in Atuot Cosmology', Man, (N.S.), 16.

—— (1981d), 'The Proverb: An Aspect of Atuot Collective Thought', Folklore, 92.

Bibliography

—— (1981e), 'Sacrifice: A Polythetic Class of Atuot Religious Thought', *Journal of Religion in Africa*, 12.
—— (1981f), 'Some Observations on the Social History of the Atuot Dialect of Nilotic', in M. L. Bender and T. Schadberg (eds.), *Nilo-Saharan*, Leiden.
—— (1982a), 'The Divination of Atuot Philosophy', *Journal of Religion in Africa*, 13.
—— (1982b), 'Figurative Language and the Definition of Experience: The Role of Ox-Songs in Atuot Social Theory', *Anthropological Linguistics*, 24.
—— (1982c), 'Lateral Symbolism and Atuot Cosmology', *Africa*, 52.
—— (1987), *A Nilotic World. The Atuot-Speaking Peoples of the Southern Sudan*, Westport CT.
CANN, G. P. (1929), 'A Day in the Life of an Idle Shilluk', *SNR*, 12/2.
CORFIELD, F. D. (1938), 'The Koma', *SNR*, 21/1.
CORIAT, P. (1923), *The Gaweir Nuers* (Khartoum) [reprinted in Coriat 1993].
—— (1939), 'Gwek the Witch-Doctor and the Pyramid of Dengkur', *SNR*, 22/2.
—— (1993), *Governing the Nuer. Documents in Nuer History and Ethnography, 1922–31*, with notes and introduction by D.H. Johnson, JASO Occasional Papers no. 9, Oxford.
CRAZZOLARA, J. P. (1932), 'Die Gar Zeremonie bei den Nuer', *Africa*, 5/1.
—— (1933a), *Outlines of Nuer Grammar*, Vienna.
—— (1933b), 'Pygmies on the Bahr-el-Ghazal', *SNR*, 16/1.
—— (1950–54), *The Lwoo*, Verona.
—— (1953), *Zur Gesellschaft und Religion der Nueer*, Vienna.
DAVIES, H. R. (1960), 'Some Tribes of the Ethiopian Borderland between the Blue Nile and Sobat River', *SNR*, 41.
DENG, F. M. (1973), *The Dinka and Their Songs*, Oxford [mainly songs from the Dinka of Bahr el-Ghazal and Kordofan, but some from the Atuot, Bor, and Ngok of Upper Nile].
—— (1980), *Dinka Cosmology*, London [contains transcripts of interviews with some Rueng and Bor Dinka chiefs].
EVANS-PRITCHARD, E. E. (1932), 'Ethnological Observations in Dar Fung', *SNR*, 15/1.
—— (1933–35), 'The Nuer: Tribe and Clan', *SNR*, 16/1, 17/1, 18/1.
—— (1936a), 'The Nuer: Age-Sets', *SNR*, 19/2.
—— (1936b), 'Customs and Beliefs Relating to Twins among the Nilotic Nuer', *Uganda Journal*, 3/3.
—— (1937–38), 'Economic Life of the Nuer: Cattle', *SNR*, 22/2 & 21/1.
—— (1940a), *The Nuer. A Description of the Modes of Livelihood and Political Institutions of a Nilotic People*, Oxford.
—— (1940b), 'The Nuer of the Southern Sudan', in M. Fortes & E. E. Evans-Pritchard (eds), *African Political Systems*, London.
—— (1940c), *The Political System of the Anuak*, London.
—— (1947), 'Further Observations on the Political System of the Anuak', *SNR*, 28.
—— (1949), 'Burial and Mortuary Rites of the Nuer', *African Affairs*, 48/190.
—— (1953), *Kinship and Marriage among the Nuer*, Oxford [paperback edition, with introduction by Wendy James, issued 1990].

—— (1956), *Nuer Religion*, Oxford.
—— (1962), 'The Divine Kingship of the Shilluk of the Nilotic Sudan', in E. E. Evans-Pritchard, *Essays in Social Anthropology*, London
—— (1965a), *The Position of Women in Primitive Societies*, London.
—— (1965b), 'Nuer Modes of Address', in Evans-Pritchard 1965a.
—— (1965c), 'Imagery in Ngok Dinka Cattle Names', in Evans-Pritchard 1965a.
—— & A. C. BEATON (1940a), 'Folk Stories of the Sudan, I', *SNR*, 23/1 [Anuak].
—— & A. C. Beaton (1940b), 'Folk Stories of the Sudan, II', *SNR*, 23/2 [Anuak].
—— & T. H. B. Mynors (1941), 'Folk Stories of the Sudan, III', *SNR*, 24 [Anuak].
FERGUSSON, V. H. (1921), 'The Nuong Nuer', *SNR*, 4/3.
—— (1922), 'The Holy Lake of the Dinka', *SNR*, 5 [Atuot].
—— (1923), 'Mattiang goh witchcraft', *SNR*, 6/1.
—— (1924), 'Nuer Beast Tales', *SNR*, 7/1.
S. H. (1929), 'The Trial of a Jur "Witch-Doctor"', *SNR*, 12/1.
HEASTY, J. A. (1937), *English-Shilluk, Shilluk-English Dictionary*, Doleib Hill.
HOFMAYR, F. (1925), *Die Schilluk*, Vienna.
HOWELL, P. P. (1941), 'The Shilluk Settlement', *SNR*, 24.
—— (1945a), 'A Note on Elephants and Elephant Hunting among the Nuer', *SNR*, 26/1.
—— (1945b), 'The Zeraf Hills', *SNR*, 26/2.
—— (1947), 'On the Value of Iron among the Nuer', *Man*, 47/144.
—— (1948a), '"Pyramids" in the Upper Nile Region', *Man*, 48/56.
—— (1948b), 'The Age-Set System and the Institution of "Nak" among the Nuer', *SNR*, 29/2.
—— (1952a), 'Observations on the Shilluk of the Upper Nile', *Africa*, 22.
—— (1952b), 'The Death and Burial of *Reth* Dak *wad* Fadiat', *SNR*, 33/1.
—— (1953a), 'The Election and Installation of Reth Kur wad Fafiti of the Shilluk. With an Account of the Final Ceremonies by J.O. Udal', *SNR*, 34/2.
—— (1953b), 'Some Observations on "Earthly Spirits" among the Nuer', *Man*, 53/126.
—— (1954), *A Manual of Nuer Law*, London.
—— & B. A. LEWIS (1947), 'Nuer Ghouls: A Form of Witchcraft', *SNR*, 28.
—— & W. P. G. THOMSON (1946), 'The Death of the Reth of the Shilluk and the Installation of his Successor,' *SNR*, 27.
HUFFMAN, R. 1929, *Nuer-English Dictionary*, Berlin.
—— (1931a), *English-Nuer Dictionary*, London.
—— (1931b), *Nuer Customs and Folklore*, London.
HUTCHINSON, S. (1985), 'Changing Concepts of Incest among the Nuer', *American Ethnologist*, 12.
—— (1990), 'Rising Divorce among the Nuer, 1936–1983', *Man*, 25/3.
—— (1991), 'War through the Eyes of the Dispossessed: Three Stories of Survival', *Disasters*, 15/2.
—— (1992a), '"Dangerous to Eat": Rethinking Pollution States among the Nuer of the Sudan', *Africa*, 62.
—— (1992b), 'The Cattle of Money and the Cattle of Girls among the Nuer, 1930–1983', *American Ethnologist*, 19.

—— (1996), *The Nuer in Crisis: Coping with Money, War, and the State, 1930–1992*, Los Angeles.
JACKSON, H. C. (1923), 'The Nuer of the Upper Nile Province', *SNR*, 4/1 & 2.
JAMES, W. (1971), 'Beer, Morality and Social Relations among the Uduk', *Sudan Society*, 5.
—— (1972), 'The Politics of Rain Control among the Uduk', in I. Cunnison & W. James (eds), *Essays in Sudan Ethnography, presented to Sir Edward Evans-Pritchard*, London.
—— (1977), 'The Funj Mystique: Approaches to a Problem of Sudan History', in R.K. Jain (ed.), *Text and Context: The Social Anthropology of Tradition*, ASA Essays in Social Anthropology vol. 2, Philadelphia.
—— (1978a), 'Ephemeral Names: the Uduk Case', in R. Thelwall (ed.), *Aspects of Language in the Sudan*, Coleraine.
—— (1978b), *'Kwanim Pa: The Making of the Uduk People. An Ethnographic Study of Survival in the Sudan-Ethiopia Borderlands*, Oxford.
—— (1980), 'From Aboriginal to Frontier Society in Western Ethiopia', D. L. Donham and W. James (eds), *Working Papers on Society and History in Ethiopia: The Southern Periphery from the 1880s to 1974*, Cambridge African Studies Centre [Koma].
—— (1988), *The Listening Ebony. Moral Knowledge, Religion and Power among the Uduk of Sudan*, Oxford.
—— (1994), 'War and "Ethnic Visibility": the Uduk on the Sudan—Ethiopian Border', in K. Fukui & J. Markakis (eds), *Ethnicity & Conflict in the Horn of Africa*, London.
JOHNSTON, R. T. (1934), 'Religious and Spiritual Beliefs of Bor Dinka', *SNR*, 17/1.
KIGGEN, J. (1948), *Nuer-English Dictionary*, London.
KURIMOTO, E. (1992), 'Natives and Outsiders: the Historical Experience of the Anywaa of Western Ethiopia', *Journal of Asian and African Studies* (Tokyo), 43.
LEWIS, B.A. (1947), 'Murle Folk Tales', *SNR*, 28.
—— (1951), 'Nuer Spokesmen. A Note on the Institution of the *Ruic*', *SNR*, 32/1.
—— (1972), *The Murle. Red Chiefs and Black Commoners*, Oxford.
LIENHARDT, R. G. (1954), 'The Shilluk of the Upper Nile', in D. Forde (ed.), *African Worlds: Studies in the Cosmological Ideas and Social Values of African Peoples*, London.
—— (1955), 'Nilotic Kings and their Mothers' Kin', *Africa*, 25.
—— (1957–58), 'Anuak Village Headmen', *Africa*, 27/4 & 28/1.
—— (1958), 'The Western Dinka', in J. Middleton and D. Tait (eds), *Tribes Without Rulers. Studies in African Segmentary Societies*, London.
—— (1961), *Divinity and Experience. The Religion of the Dinka*, Oxford [mainly about the Western Dinka of Bahr al-Ghazal, with some references to Padang, Bor and Nyareweng Dinka].
—— (1970), 'The Situation of Death: An Aspect of Anuak Philosophy', in M. Douglas (ed.), *Witchcraft Confessions and Accusations*, London.
—— (1975), 'Getting Your Own Back: Themes in Nilotic Myth', in R. G. Lienhardt & J. H. M. Beattie (eds), *Studies in Social Anthropology, Essays in Memory of Evans-Pritchard by His Former Oxford Colleagues*, Oxford.

—— (1982), 'The Dinka and Catholicism', in J. Davis (ed.), *Religious Organization and Religious Experience*, ASA Monograph no. 21, London and New York.

—— (1985), 'The Sudan—Aspects of the South: Government Among some of the Nilotic Peoples, 1947–52', *JASO*, 12/3.

LOGAN, M. H., 1918, 'The Beirs', *SNR*, 1/4 [Murle].

LYTH, R. E. (1947*a*), 'The Suri Tribe', *SNR*, 28.

—— (1947*b*), *Murle Grammar*, Juba.

—— (1956), *A Murle Vocabulary*, Khartoum.

MILLS, W. L. (1919), 'A Dinka Witch-Doctor', *SNR*, 2/1 [Dungjol].

MLAKIC, S. (1943–44), 'Nuer Religion', *The Messenger*, 12/8–13/4.

MOSTYN, J. P. (1921), 'Some Notes on Burun Customs and Beliefs', *SNR*, 4/4 [Meban].

MUNRO, P. (1918), 'Installation of the King of the Shilluks', *SNR*, 1/3.

NIKKEL, M R. (1992), 'Aspects of Contemporary Religious Change among the Dinka', *Journal of Religion in Africa*, 22/1.

NUNN, N. (1942), 'A Dinka Public Health Measure', *SNR*, 25/1 [Padang].

—— (1950), 'A Dinka Sacrifice', *SNR*, 31/1 [Padang].

O'SULLIVAN, H. D. E. (1910), 'Dinka Law', *JRAI*, 40.

—— (1921), [Anon.], 'The Reason for the Beir's Hatred of the Dinka', *SNR*, 4/1.

Oyler, Mrs. D.S. (1919), 'Examples of Shilluk Folk-Lore', *SNR*, 2/3.

Oyler, Rev. D.S. (1918*a*), 'Nikawng and the Shilluk Migration', *SNR*, 1/2.

—— (1918*b*), 'Nikawng's Place in the Shilluk Religion', *SNR*, 1/4.

—— (1919), 'The Shilluk's Belief in the Evil Eye', *SNR*, 2/2.

—— (1920*a*), 'The Shilluk's Belief in the Good Medicine Man', *SNR*, 3/2.

—— (1920b), 'The Shilluk Peace Ceremony', *SNR*, 3/4.

—— (1926), 'Shilluk Notes', *SNR*, 9/1.

PAUL, A. (1952), 'The Mar of the Shilluk', *SNR*, 33/1.

PERNER, C. (1992*a*), 'Living on Earth in the Sky', *Journal of Religion in Africa*, 22/1 [Anuak].

—— (1992*b*), 'Anyuak Religion and Language, *Journal of Religion in Africa*, 22/2.

PUMPHREY, M. E. C. (1937), 'Shilluk "Royal" Language Conventions', *SNR*, 20/2.

—— (1941), 'The Shilluk Tribe', *SNR*, 24/1.

RICHARDS, M. G. (1927), 'Medical Treatment by Bor Witch-Doctors', *SNR*, 10.

SELIGMAN, C. G. (1911), 'Cult of Nyakang and the Divine Kings of the Shilluk', *Wellcome Research Laboratories Fourth Report*, vol. B.

—— with BRENDA Z. SELIGMAN (1932) *Pagan Tribes of the Nilotic Sudan*, London.

SHAW, A. (1915), 'Dinka Songs', *Man*, 15/3.

—— (1919), 'Dinka Animal Stories (Bor Dialect)'', *SNR*, 2/4.

SHISHAGN, S. (1986), 'The Economic Basis of Conflict among the Nuer and Anuak Communities', *Proceedings of the Third Annual Seminar of the Department of History*, Addis Ababa.

SOULE, C. B. (1931), *Some Nuer Terms in Relation to the Human Body*, Nasir.

STEVENSON-HAMILTON, J. (1920), 'The Dinka Country East of the Bahr-el-Jebel', *Geographical Journal*, 56/5.

STIGAND, C. H. (1918*a*), 'Warrior Classes of the Nuers', *SNR*, 1/2.

—— (1918*b*), 'Dengkur Earth Pyramid', *SNR*, 1/3.

— (1919), 'The Story of Kir and the White Spear', *SNR*, 2/3.
— (1922), 'Notes on the Burun', *SNR*, 5/4 [Meban].
— (1923), *A Nuer-English Vocabulary*, Cambridge.
SVOBODA, T. (1985), *Cleaned the Crocodile's Teeth. Nuer Song*, New York.
THEIS, J. (1990), 'Zerströng und Wiederherstellung eines Volkes. Geschichte und Ethnographie der Koma (Gokwom) im Sudan-Äthiopischen Grenzgebiet', Ph.D thesis, Free University of Berlin.
THOMSON, W. P. G. (1948), 'Further Notes on the Death of a Reth of the Shilluk (1945)', *SNR*, 29/2.
TRACEY, C. B. (1940), 'Two Ghost Stories', *SNR*, 23/1 [from the Malakia of Renk].
TRUDINGER, R. (with AYONG DENG) (1942), *English-Dinka Dictionary*, Sudan United Mission [Padang].
TUNNICLIFFE, G. W. (1932), 'Anuak Vocabulary', Pibor Post (MSS in Tylor Library, Institute of Social and Cultural Anthropology, Oxford).
WEDDERBURN-MAXWELL, H. G. (1936), 'The Maban of Southern Fung', *SNR*, 19/1.
WESTERMANN, D. (n.d., c.1911), *A Short Grammar of the Shilluk Language*, Philadelphia and Berlin.
— (1912), *The Shilluk People*, London and Philadelphia.
WHALLEY, R. C. R. (1936), 'Notes on the Adonga Anuak', *SNR*, 19/2.
WILLIS, C. A. (1922), [D.I.], 'Conspiracy against the Mek of the Shilluk', *SNR*, 5/2.
— (1928), 'The Cult of Deng', *SNR*, XI.
WILSON, H. H. (1905), *English-Dinka Vocabulary*, London.

History

BELL, G. and DEE, B. D. (n.d.), *Sudan Political Service, 1899–1956*, Oxford.
COLLINS, R. O. (1960), 'Patrols against the Beirs', *SNR*, 41.
— (1967), 'The Aliab Dinka Rising and its Suppression', *SNR*, 48.
— (1971), *Land Beyond the Rivers. The Southern Sudan, 1898–1918*, New Haven and London.
— (1983), *Shadows in the Grass: Britain in the Southern Sudan, 1918–1956*, New Haven and London.
— (1990), *The Waters of the Nile. Hydropolitics and the Jonglei Canal, 1900–1988*, Oxford.
DALY, M. W. (1986), *Empire on the Nile. The Anglo-Egyptian Sudan, 1898–1934*, Cambridge.
— (1991), *Imperial Sudan: The Anglo-Egyptian Condominium, 1934–1956*, Cambridge.
GARRETSON, P. P. (1986), 'Vicious Cycles: Ivory, Slaves, and Arms on the New Maji Frontier', in Donald Donham & Wendy James (eds), *The Southern Marches of Imperial Ethiopia. Essays in History and Social Anthropology*, Cambridge.
HILL, R. L. (1965), *Sudan Transport. A History of Railway, Marine and River Services in the Republic of the Sudan*, London.
— (1967), *A Biographical Dictionary of the Sudan*, 2nd ed., London.
— (1970 & 1972), 'A Register of Named Power-Driven River and Marine Harbour Craft Commissioned in the Sudan 1856–1964', *SNR*, 51 & 53.
JACKSON, H. C. (1960), *Pastor on the Nile. Being Some Account of the Life and*

Letters of Llewellyn H. Gwynne, CMG, CBE, DD, LLD, *Formerly Bishop in Egypt and the Sudan and Deputy Chaplain-General in France in the First World War*, London.

JAL, G. G., 1987, 'The History of the Jikany Nuer before 1920', Ph.D. thesis, History, SOAS, London University.

JOHNSON, D. H. (1979), 'Colonial policy and prophets: the 'Nuer Settlement', 1929-1930', *Journal of the Anthropological Society of Oxford*, 10/1.

—— (1981), 'The Fighting Nuer: Primary Sources and the Origins of a Stereotype', *Africa*, 51/1.

—— (1982a), 'Tribal Boundaries and Border Wars: Nuer-Dinka Relations in the Sobat and Zaraf Valleys, *c.* 1860-1976', *Journal of African History*, 23/2.

—— (1982b), 'Evans-Pritchard, the Nuer and the Sudan Political Service', *African Affairs*, 81/323.

—— (1982c), 'Ngundeng and the "Turuk": Two Narratives Compared', *History in Africa*, 9.

—— (1982d), 'An Account of the Aliab Uprising' [document], *Heritage: A Journal of Southern Sudanese Cultures*, 1/2-3.

—— (1985a), 'C. A. Willis and the "Cult of Deng": A Falsification of the Ethnographic Record', *History in Africa*, 12.

—— (1985b), 'Foretelling Peace and War: Modern Interpretations of Ngundeng's Prophecies in the Southern Sudan', in M. W. Daly (ed.), *Modernization in the Sudan: Essays in Honor of Richard Hill*, New York.

—— (1986a), 'Judicial Regulation and Administrative Control: Customary Law and the Nuer, 1898-1954', *Journal of African History*, 27/1.

—— (1986b), 'On the Nilotic Frontier: Imperial Ethiopia in the Southern Sudan, 1898-1936', in Donald Donham & Wendy James (eds), *The Southern Marches of Imperial Ethiopia: Essays in History and Social Anthropology*, Cambridge.

—— (1988), 'Adaptation to Floods in the Jonglei Area: An Historical Analysis', in Douglas H. Johnson & David M. Anderson (eds), *The Ecology of Survival: Case Studies from Northeast African History*, London and Boulder CO.

—— (1989), 'Enforcing Separate Identities in the Southern Sudan: The Case of the Nilotes of the Upper Nile', in J-P. Chretien & G. Prunier (eds), *Les Ethnies ont une Histoire*, Paris.

—— (1990), 'Fixed Shrines and Spiritual Centres in the Upper Nile', *Azania*, 25.

—— (1991a), 'From Military to Tribal Police. Policing the Upper Nile Province of the Sudan', in David M. Anderson & David Killingray (eds), *Policing the Empire: Government, Authority and Control, 1830-1940*, Manchester.

—— (1991b), 'Political Ecology in the Upper Nile: The Twentieth Century Expansion of the Pastoral "Common Economy"', in J. G. Galaty and P. Bonte (eds), *Herders, Warriors and Traders. Pastoralism in Africa*, Boulder CO [reprinted from *Journal of African History*, 30/3, 1989].

—— (1991c), 'Criminal Secrecy: the Case of the Zande "Secret Societies"', *Past and Present*, 130.

—— (1992a), 'On Disciples and Magicians. The Diversification of Divinity among the Nuer during the Colonial Era', *Journal of Religion in Africa*, 22/1.

—— (1992b), 'Reconstructing a History of Local Floods in the Upper Nile Region of the Sudan', *International Journal of African Historical Studies*, 25/3.

Bibliography 445

—— (1993a), 'Percy Coriat's Life and the Significance of his Work', in Coriat 1993.
—— (1993b), 'Prophecy and Mahdism in the Upper Nile: An Examination of Local Experiences of the Mahdiyya in the Southern Sudan', *British Journal of Middle Eastern Studies*, 20/1.
—— (1994), *Nuer Prophets. A History of Prophecy from the Upper Nile in the Nineteenth and Twentieth Centuries*, Oxford.
MAXWELL, J. L. (n.d., c. 1953), *Half a Century of Grace. A Jubilee History of the Sudan United Mission*, London.
MAWUT, L. L. (1983), *Dinka Resistance to Condominium Rule, 1902–1932*, Khartoum.
MORRISON, G. N. I. (n.d., c.1942), *The Upper Nile and the War (1940–1941)*, Khartoum.
SANDERSON, L.M. PASSMORE & N. (1981), *Education, Religion & Politics in Southern Sudan, 1899–1964*, London.
SANDES, E. W. C. (1937), *The Royal Engineers in Egypt and the Sudan*, Chatham.
SPARTALIS, P. J. (1981), *To the Nile and Beyond. The Birth and Growth of the Sudanese Church of Christ, being the work of the ANZ Branch of the Sudan United Mission*, Homebush West, NSW.
WARBURG, G. (1971), *The Sudan under Wingate. Administration in the Anglo-Egyptian Sudan (1899–1910)*, London.
ZEWDE, BAHRU, (1976), 'Relations between Ethiopia and the Sudan on the Western Ethiopian Frontier, 1898–1935', Ph.D. thesis, History, SOAS, London University.
—— (1991), *A History of Modern Ethiopia, 1855–1974*, London/Athens, Ohio/ Addis Ababa.

Memoirs

BACON, C. R. K. (1923), 'Days and Nights on the Akobo River', SNR, 4/1.
'BEN ASSHER' [C. BORRADAILE] (1928), *A Nomad in the South Sudan*, London.
BYAM, W. (1963), *The Road to Harley Street*, London [Anuak patrol 1912].
COMYN, D. C. F. FF (1911), *Service and Sport in the Sudan. A Record of Administration in the Anglo-Egyptian Sudan. With Some Intervals of Sport and Travel*, London and New York.
CRUICKSHANK, A. (1962), *The Kindling Fire. Medical Adventures in the Southern Sudan*, London.
DENG, F. M. and DALY, M. W. (eds) (1989), *'Bonds of Silk'. The Human Factor in the British Administration of the Sudan*, East Lansing.
DUNCAN, J. S. R. (1948), 'A Dry Season Trek', *Blackwood's Magazine*, 1597, November.
—— (1949), 'Antrycide, 1949', *Blackwood's Magazine*, 1603, May.
—— (1957), *The Sudan's Path to Independence*, Edinburgh.
EVANS-PRITCHARD, E. E. (1973a), 'Fragment of an Autobiography', *New Blackfriars*, January.
—— (1973b), 'Genesis of a Social Anthropologist: an Autobiographical Note', *The New Diffusionist*, 3/10.

—— (1973c), 'Operations on the Akobo and Gila Rivers 1940–41', *The Army Quarterly*, 103/4.
—— (1976), 'Some Reminiscences and Reflections on Fieldwork', in *Witchcraft, Oracles and Magic among the Azande*, abridged by Eva Gillies, Oxford.
FERGUSSON, V. H. (1930), *The Story of Fergie Bey, Told by Himself and Some of His Friends*, London.
HENDERSON, K. D. D. (1987), *Set under Authority. Being a Portrait of the Life of the British District Officer in the Sudan under the Anglo-Egyptian Condominium, 1898–1955*, Somerset.
JACKSON, H. C. (1954), *Sudan Days and Ways*, London.
KENRICK, R. (1987), *Sudan Tales. Recollections of some Sudan Political Service Wives, 1926–56*, Cambridge and New York.
KINGDON, F. D. (1945), 'The Western Nuer Patrol, 1927–1928', *SNR*, 26/1.
MCMEEKAN, G. R. (1929), 'The Demolition of a Pyramid', *Royal Engineers Journal*, 43.
ROUSSEL, P. L. (1955), 'Last Days in the Sudan', *Time and Tide*, 6 August.
'SARTEK' (1932), 'Fantasia', *Blackwood's Tales from the Outposts*, Edinburgh [review of the Akobo garrison by Sir Lee Stack].
THESIGER, W. (1987), *The Life of My Choice*, London.
VANDEVORT, E. (1968), *A Leopard Tamed*, London.
WILLIAMS, C. R. (1986), *Wheels & Paddles in the Sudan (1923–1946)*, Edinburgh.

Politics

ALIER, A. (1990), *Southern Sudan. Too Many Agreements Dishonoured*, Exeter.
DE WAAL, A. (1990), *Denying 'the Honor of Living'. Sudan: A Human Rights Disaster*, an Africa Watch Report, New York/Washington/London.
—— (1991), *Evil Days. 30 Years of War and Famine in Ethiopia*, an Africa Watch Report, New York/Washington/Los Angeles/London.
DUANY, W. (1992), 'Neither Palaces nor Prisons: the Constitution of Order among the Nuer', Ph.D. in Political Science and Public and Environmental Affairs, Indiania University, Bloomington.
GARANG, J. (1992), *The Call for Democracy in Sudan*, edited and introduced by Mansour Khalid, London.
HUMAN RIGHTS WATCH/AFRICA (1994), *Civilian Devastation. Abuses by all Parties in the War in Southern Sudan*, New York/Washington/Los Angeles/London.
JOHNSON, D. H. (1988), *The Southern Sudan*, Minority Rights Group Report No. 78.
—— & PRUNIER, G. (1993), 'The Foundation and Expansion of the SPLA', in M. W. Daly and A. Sikainga (eds), *The Civil War in the Sudan*, London and New York.
WATERBURY, J. (1979), *The Hydropolitics of the Nile Valley*, Syracuse.

Travel

ARTIN, Y. (1911), *England in the Sudan*, trans. G. Robb, London.
AUSTIN, H. H. (1902), *Among Swamps and Giants in Equatorial Africa*, London.

BULPETT, C. W. L. (1907), *A Picnic Party in Wildest Africa*, London.
DOMVILLE-FIFE, C. W. (1927), *Savage Life in the Black Sudan*, London.
GROGAN, E. S. (1900), 'Through Africa from the Cape to Cairo', *Geographical Journal*, 16/2.
GWYNN, C. W. (1901), 'Surveys of the Proposed Sudan-Abyssinian Frontier', *Geographical Journal*, 18/6.
JESSEN, B. H. (1905), 'South-Western Abyssinia', *Geographical Journal*, 25.
KELLY, H. H. (1914), 'Some Aspects of Abyssinia with Special Reference to the Western Frontier', *The Army Review*, 6/1.
LANDOR, A. H. S. (1907), *Across Widest Africa*, vol. i, London.
MILLAIS, J. G. (1924), *Far Away up the Nile*, London.
TANGYE, H. L. (1910), *In the Torrid Sudan*, London.
WILSON, H. H. (1902), 'A Trip up the Khor Felus, and Country on the Left Bank of Sobat', *Geographical Journal*, 20/4.

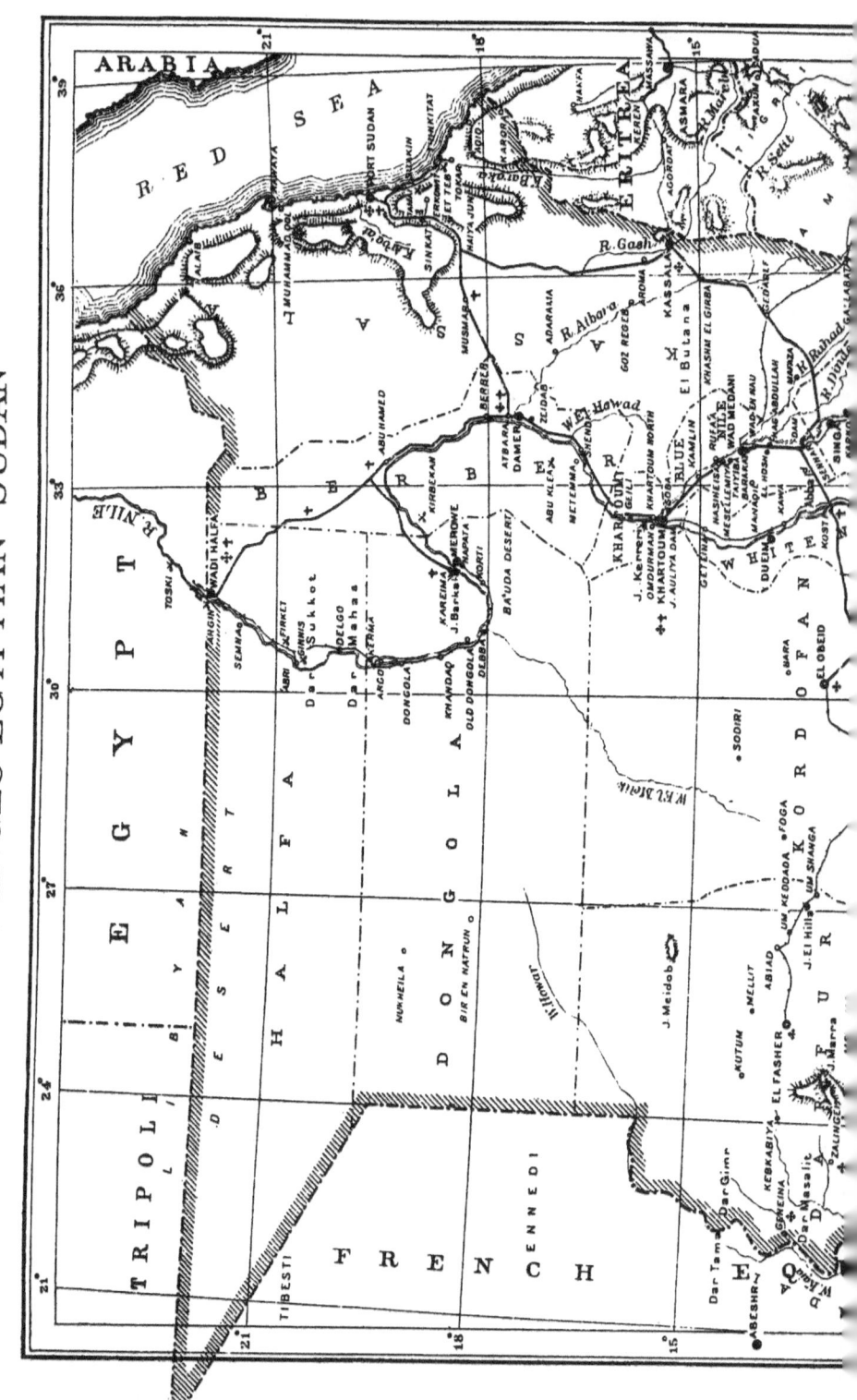

THE ANGLO-EGYPTIAN SUDAN

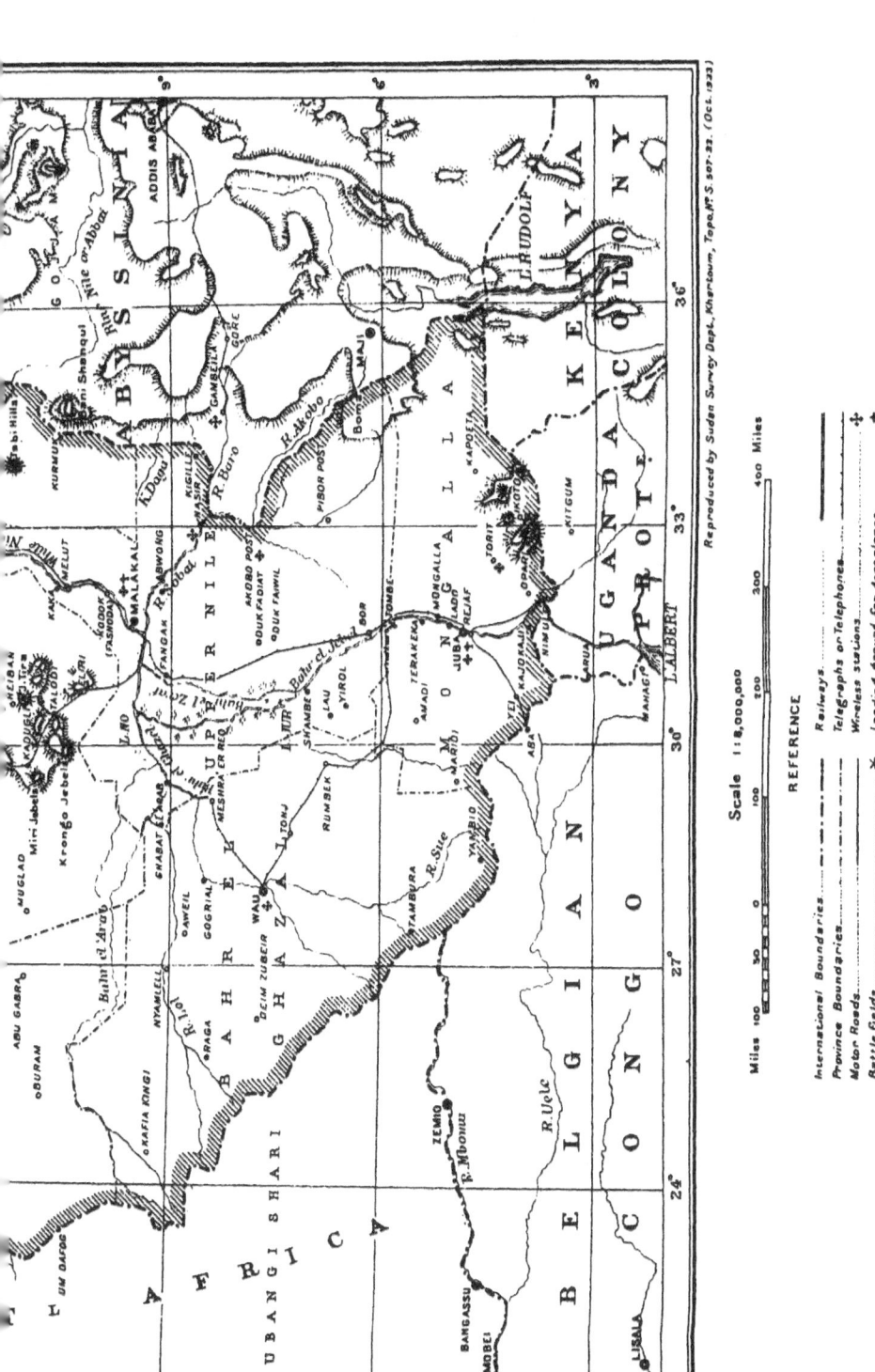

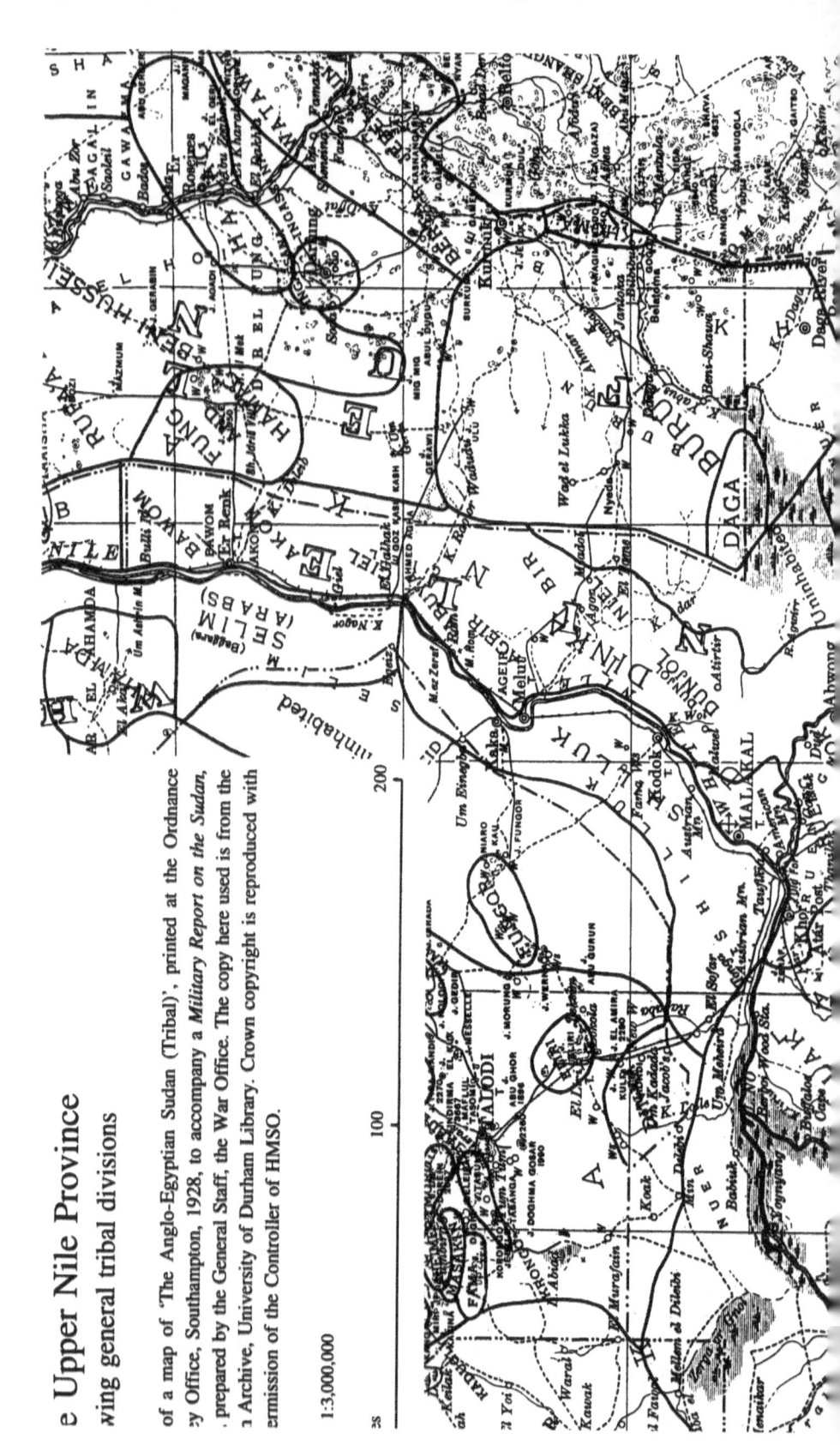

Upper Nile Province showing general tribal divisions

of a map of 'The Anglo-Egyptian Sudan (Tribal)', printed at the Ordnance Office, Southampton, 1928, to accompany a *Military Report on the Sudan*, prepared by the General Staff, the War Office. The copy here used is from the Archive, University of Durham Library. Crown copyright is reproduced with permission of the Controller of HMSO.

1:3,000,000

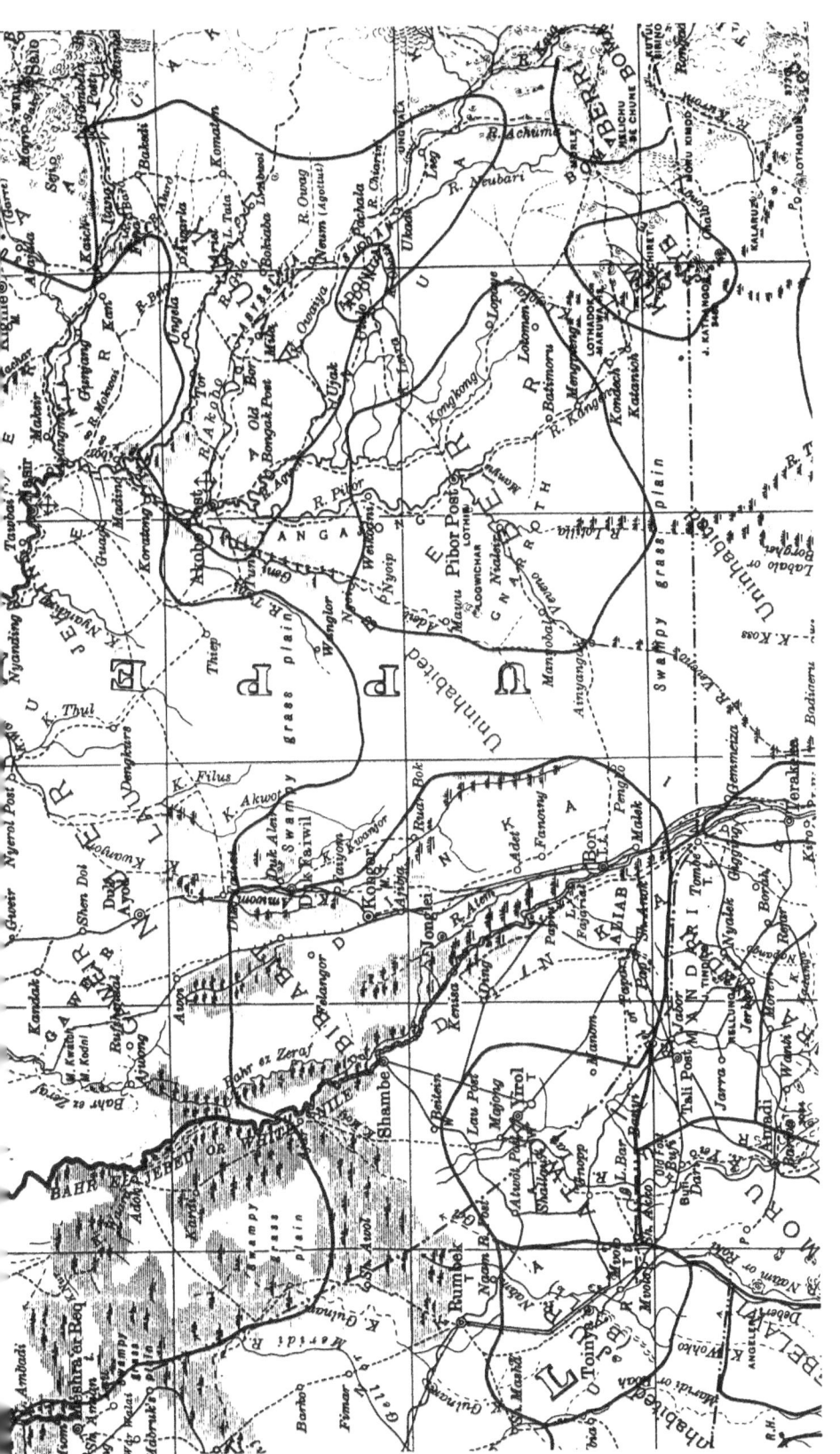

Sketch-map to show distribution of the Eastern Jikany tribal sections
(arrows point from area of villages to dry season camps)
(after Mr. C. L. Armstrong)

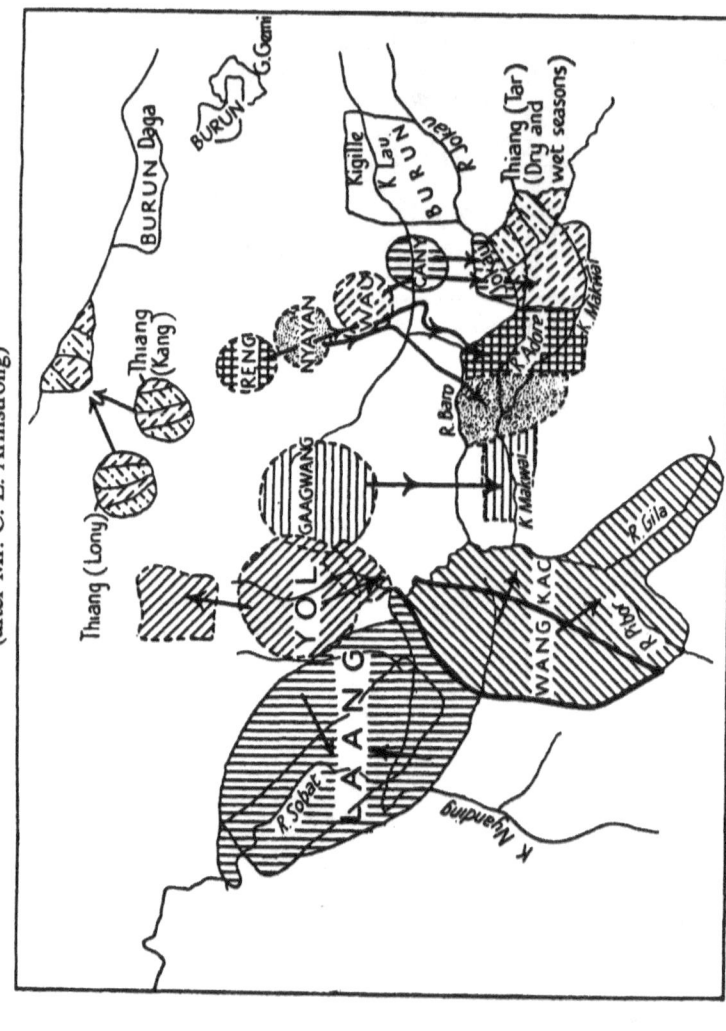

Reproduced from E. E. Evans-Pritchard, The Nuer
(first published 1940), by permission of Oxford University Press

Index
of persons, peoples and places (towns and villages)

A. An Dal 264
Abanima 170
Abbas Seleim 100, 151
Abd el-Aziz Hamad Hassouna
  (Hassoun) 100, 151, 411
Abd el-Gadir (Abdel Gadir) Lutfi 100, 151
Abd el-Gelil (Abdel Gelil) Omer 100
Abd el-Mutalab (Abdel Mutalab)
  Mustafa 100
Abd el-Nabi (Abdel Nabi) Fadl el
  Mula 100, 151
Abd el-Radi Murjan 100, 411
Abd el-Rahim Abdalla 100, 411
Abd el-Rahman (Abdel Rahman)
  Abdalla 99
Abd el-Wahab (Abdel Wahab)
  Mahmud 100, 151
Abdulla Ahmed Ibrahim 99
Abialang Dinka 413, 426, 428, 431
  Akon section 143, 144, 145, 152
  Bawom section 143, 144, 145, 152
  Giel section 143, 144, 145, 152
  in Mahdiyya 144
  Mangnok section 144, 145
  Piti section 145
  population 27, 152
Abiangyai 170
Abii 234
Abodit 234
Abu Bakr Ali Tayeb 100
Aburu 170
Abwong 49–51, 65, 103, 269
  as administrative base 361
  administrators posted to 277, 411, 412,
    416, 422, 428
  brick making 287
  buildings 81, 137, 138, 284
  in Dinka country 280
  dispensary 137
  district headquarters 102
  experimental herd 141, 283, 285
  felucca at 93
  ferry 283
  founded 275
  garden 285
  Guek Ngungdeng visits 277
  landing stage 94
  merchants 286
  pigs 141, 285
  police 2, 124
  postal service 98
  road 77, 194, 282

  supply base 276
  well 80
Abyar Kon (Abyiar Akon) 263, 267
Abyssinians 177, 178
Acek Nuot 266
Aceng Pwo 265
Aciek Apec 221, 246
  chief's police 244
  tax 231
Aciek Jok 242
Acok Ngong 220, 242
  personality report 237
  road work 232, 234
  tax 229
Acol 256 n.8
Acol Bol 258, 260, 267
Acol Deng 220, 242
  personality report 237
  road work 232, 234
  tax 229
Acoli (Acholi) 23, 107
Adair, W. J. 186, 411
Addis Ababa 34, 323, 325, 329, 422
Ado 260
Adok (Hillet Nuer) 3, 74, 109, 420
  and Dok Nuer 298
  Kilo pole at 297 n.4
  landing stage 94
  road 309
  survey 300
Adol 234
Adol Anyuat 220, 242
  personality report 237
  road work 232, 234
  tax 229
Ador (Cic Dinka) 252, 266
  attacked by Nuer 257
  court 253
  dresser stationed at 263
  headquarters 259
  population 263
  tribes and diets of:
    Abadan (Abadon) 252, 266
    Abwong 252, 266
    Ajwong (blacksmiths) 252, 266
    Ajwot 252, 266
    Aleu 252
    Angaur (Angar) 252, 266
    Die 252, 266
    Dim 266
    Lok 252, 266
    well 260

Index

Adung Okeich (murderer) 169
Afak (Atuot) 251, 252, 413, 418
  court 253
  dresser stationed at 263
  patrols against 255–6
  population 263
  tribes and diets of:
    Awan 252, 265
    Acok 252, 265
    Akaikar 265
    Akot 265
    Apair 252, 265
    Apairair 252, 265
    Pakwaic 252
    Palwal 252, 265
    Riair 252, 265
  well at Aluak Luak 260
Afash Kur 354
Afuki 115
Agaibi Fam 101
Agar Dinka 143, 255, 303
  and Angai Dinka 302 n.20
  and Nuer 297, 298
Agordo 170
Aguran (Agoran) 260
Agwek Mayan 243
Agwer Alai 424
Ahmed Abdallah 316
Ahmed Mohammed Ali 100
Ahmed Mohammed Ragab 158, 411
Ahmed Okeil 100, 319, 411
Aiwel (Aiywel) Akwei 158, 411
Aiwel Longar (legendary figure) 209–10, 412
Aiwel Malwal and *mathiang goh* 239
Aiyadajo 170
Ajak Biar 220, 243
  personality report 238
  road work 233
  tax 229
Ajak Bior 220, 242, 424
  biographical entry 411
  personality report 237
  road work 233
  tax 229
Ajak Tor Bil 159, 411–12
Ajang Ajwang (Ibrahim) 143, 145
Ajang Bul 242
Ajang Kwathker (Kwatkeir) (Shilluk king) 156
Ajungmir 178, 188
Ajwong 81, 103, 212
  landing stage 94, 95, 293
Akobo 202, 203, 268, 361, 395
  administrators posted to 412, 419, 429
  buildings 137, 138, 206
  dispensary 137
  founded 3

  garden 207
  garrison 4, 14
  herd 207
  landing ground 97
  Nuer attack on 276
  police 124
  postal service to 180
  roads 64–5, 74, 76, 77, 78, 133, 180, 194, 204, 205, 269, 279, 280, 282–3
  staff 100–1
  steamer service to 90, 179
  wet weather post 122
  well 80, 205
  wireless 98–9, 180
Akoc (Akoic) 156
Akoi Atem 220, 243
  biographical entry 412
  personality report 238
  road work 233
  tax 229
Akol Ajuot 221, 231, 244
Akol Kak 144
Akot 250, 258
  mission and school 105, 107, 109, 309
  road 75, 77
Akot Atuot 252
  court 254
  diets of:
    Biel 264
    Riair 264
  population 263
Akuc Kacwal 265
Akurwa 170
Akuyen Atem 220, 243
  personality report 239
  road work 233
  tax 230
Akuyen Koin 243
Akwei Kur 220, 242
  personality report 237
  road work 233
  tax 229
Akwei-wo-Cam (Akwai Sham) 200
  biographical entry 412
  death 416
  fighting the government 12
Akwok Kok 242
Akwok Wutic 242
Akwot 157 n.3
Alam 290
Alban, A. H. 182 n.13
  takes over Abwong from Coriat 279, 283 n.25
  biographical entry 412
  knowledge of vernacular 22
  on local chiefs 423, 428
  manner of administration 26
Alel 258

Index

Aliab (Aliap) Dinka 2, 62, 143, 251, 345
  administered from Mongalla 254
  administration of 114, 377
  backwardness of 389
  and Bor Dinka 360
  cattle loses 261
  court 254
  effect of irrigation schemes on 406
  and Ghol Dinka 211
  headquarters at Pap 258
  population 27, 263, 381
  port of entry to 94
  punitive patrol against 9–10, 256
  road work 259
  sheep 261
  tribes and diets of:
    Ajwot 252, 267
    Akair 252, 253, 267
    Aken 252, 253, 267
    Akwe 267
    Angwon 252, 267
    Apuk 252, 253, 267
    Balok 252, 267
    Biri 267
    De 252, 267
    Jukom 253
    Korriam 252, 253, 267
    Luel 252, 267
    Niyarar 267
    Nyingair (Nyingar) 252, 267
    Thiang 252, 267
Ali abd al-Latif (Abdel Latif) 53 n.21
Ali Abdel Rahman 171
Ali Ibrahim 100, 173
Ali Sid (Said) Ahmed 236, 412
Alier, Abel 34
Alith Dut 242
Allak Yak 243
Allel 170
Allenby, Lord 312
Aloin Thowath 264
Aluak Luak 259, 260
Alueth Kwaiwel 266
Amadi 259
Ameij 74, 75, 77, 309
Amer Mohammed Bashir 100, 412
Anei Kur Nyidok 157 n.3, 423
Angai Dinka 209, 216
  chiefs 221, 240–1
  chief's police 244
  history of 211–12
  population 241
  repatriation of 214
  road and landing ground work 232, 234, 235
  tax 231
  in Western Nuer 302
Aniang Alier 242

Aniang Ameriang 221, 231, 246
Anieth Gog 242
Anong 75
Anuak 63, 107, 395, 420, 421, 426, 429
  administration 345
  Adonga Anuak 3, 9, 199, 200, 201, 203, 205, 362
  attack Lou Nuer 275–6
  chiefs' police 125, 201, 202
  Ciro (Chiros) Anuak 199, 203
  as food producers 127, 191, 205
  in Gambela 322
  international border and arms trade 3, 342
  lack of initiation 337 n.9
  language 23
  movement into Ethiopia 35
  nobles (*nyieye*) and headmen (*kwaaro*) 9, 23–4, 119–20, 199–200, 412, 416, 430
  and Mor Lou 203
  and Murle 201
  and Nuer 177, 178
  population 27, 198
  punitive patrols against 3, 9, 200
  royal relics 26
  tax 188, 203
Aping Diu (legendary figure) 209
Arabs 53, 62, 63 n.c, 112, 345
  Arabic-speaking Northerners 83, 397
  Awlad Hameid 358
  Baggara 'Eliri' 338
  bordering Nuer 297
  and cattle 342
  and Dinka 128, 144
  of Fung Province 141
  and gum 148
  introducing cattle disease 163
  labourers 155
  and simsim 162
  Ta'aisha (Taaisha) Baggara 142–3
  traders in Western Nuer 305
  and wells 161
  White Nile (Seleim) 142, 146, 358
Ardeiba, *See* Bentiu
Aret Malok 242
Armstrong, C. L. 176 n.1, 418
  arrests Dual Diu 292
  biographical entry 412
  and headmen 196 n.24
  knowledge of vernacular 22, 52 n.18
Arok Thon 35
Arouping Yak 264
Atakdok 147
Atem Cieng 243
Atem Kuot 243
Atem Magok 243
Ater Kur (Ter Akwr) 273, 412, 418

456 Index

Atet 260
Atia Tadros 99
Ato Ramdi 328
Ato Taffara 322, 328–9
Atoadwai 170
Atoing 269
Atokong 170
Attair Aleng 265
Attair Bar 252, 263, 266
Attair Mun 266
Atuot (Atwot) 62, 264–5
  administration 345
  cattle trade 260 n.14
  chiefs' police 126
  and education 109
  grazing lands 390
  identity 251
  language 23, 251
  and Nuer 115
  police wives 287
  population 27, 263, 381
  punitive patrols against 9–10
  tribes and diets of (*See also under* Afak, Akot, Kwek, and Luaic):
    Ajwong (blacksmiths) 252, 264
    Balang Joya (hunters) 252, 264
    Dima 252, 264
    Kulang 264
    Nue 252, 264
    Thit 264
Awad el-Karim (Awadel Kerrim) Osman el Karm 100
Awad Girgis 99
Awadalla el Awad 374
Awan Bolator 266
Awang Arok 242
Awarajok 170
Awet Col (Oweit Shol) 143, 413
Awin 157 n.3
Awir Renk (Oweir Areng) 145, 413
Awo 255, 413
Awoi 99, 289, 293
Awok Kur 243
Awol Akol 243
Awol Akwei 221, 244
  biographical entry 413
  personality report 240
  road 234
  tax 230
Awol Can 413
Ayak Akwei 243
Ayang Anei 423
Ayod 11, 13, 35, 211, 277, 416, 427
  abandoned 357
  no man's land 289
  police post 5
  road 76 n.2
  well 79

Ayok Ding 244
Ayok Gwem 221, 243
  personality report 240
  road 234
  tax 230
Ayong Aiwel 411
Ayuen Gut 242
Aywai *See* Juwai
Azande 9, 287
Aziz Michael 101

Baatalan, *See* Kengen
Bacon, C. R. K. 4, 199, 416, 422
  biographical entry 413
  choice of Adonga Anuak sultan 354
  and local chiefs 416, 422
Bacon, F. J. H. 137, 295 n.10, 344 n.17
Baden Awer 243
Badeng Bur 298, 420
  biographical entry 413
  Coriat on 304
Bailey, Mr. 315
Baker, Sir Samuel 3
Bakhit Nyok 144, 145, 413
Ballak Dinka 54, 275, 360
  chiefs 274
  country 269
  mix with Jikany 274
  population 270
  tax 281–2
Bally, E. D. 300, 413
Bambridge, H. G. 369, 413
Banglai 154
Bany, William Nyuon 35
Bar 194
Barboi 75, 131, 397
Batinuwi 201
Batlan 201
Batmanan, *See* Burnian
Bayley, L. B. 351, 413
Bayly, E. A. T. 276, 413–14
Beavan, J. 414
Beim (Beimm) 203, 268
Beir, *See* Murle
Bek Adol 243
Belek 298
Bellal (Billal) Ahmed 100, 151
Belmorok 201
Bentiu 27, 34
  and Western Jikany Nuer 298
  road 74, 309
  survey 300
Berber 173
Berru Walda-Gabr'el (Berru Habta (Hayla) Maryam) 419, 424
  biographical entry 414
  collects tribute from Koma and Meban 185 n.16

Index

governor of Sayo 328
Beveridge. C. E. G. 365, 414
Biar Abit 238, 415, 417
  biographical entry 414
Biar Kwek 220, 243
  personality report 238-9
  road 233
  tax 229
Biggar, B. 366, 414
Bilkwei de Duop (Bilkwey Dwot) 298, 424
  biographical entry 414
  feared by Jikany 306
Billal Allagabu 100
Bior Agwer (Agweir) 220, 242, 413
  biographical entry 414
  personality report 238
  road 233
  tax 229
Bior Deng 242
Bior Mayan 242
Biu 170
Blewitt, A. 274, 414
Bol (Shilluk village) 170
Bol Aiwel 354
Bol Ngundeng 276, 277, 414-15
Bollard, E. G. 367, 415
Bongil 235
Bonglai 268, 269
Bongo x
Bor 29, 208, 212, 247, 256, 389, 394, 396, 404
  administrators posted to 412, 420, 428
  agricultural experiment at 129-30, 244, 248
  buildings 138, 139, 245-7
  dispensary 137
  district headquarters 241
  EID in 134
  fighting around, 1992 260 n.13
  garage 84
  herd 249
  landing ground 97, 232
  launch 90, 93
  1983 mutiny at 31, 34
  police at 55, 124
  postal and telegraph service 98-9
  rent 231
  reoccupied 1
  resthouses 81, 82, 133
  roads 64, 66, 73, 74, 75, 76, 140, 161, 232-3, 279, 282, 293, 386
  staff 101
  transferred to Mongalla Province 2
Bor Dinka 2, 3, 143, 209, 251, 417
  Athoic (Attoic) 220, 411, 424
    Abwodit sub-section 220
    Alian sub-section 220

    Baidit sub-section 220
    Biong sub-section 220
    chiefs 237-8
    chiefs' police 242
    Juet sub-section 220
    Patuyith sub-section 220
    population 241
    tax 229
  chiefs 220
  chiefs' police 125, 126, 219, 242
  cotton 127
  country 386
  cultivation 127
  dialect 23
  effect of irrigation schemes on 406-7
  Gok 220, 417
    Abang sub-section 220
    Abiy sub-section 220
    Adol sub-section 220
    Atet sub-section 220
    Biong sub-section 220
    chiefs 236-7
    chiefs' police 242
    Dair sub-section 220
    Gol sub-section 220
    Gwalla sub-section 220
    Koic sub-section 220
    Kuedok sub-section 220
    Palek sub-section 220
    population 241
    tax 229
  and Murle 202
  origins of 210-11
  population 27, 241, 381
  in regional government 34
  road and landing ground work 232-3
  sacred spear Lirpiou 217
  take in refugees 212
  transfer to UNP 360
Bramall, G. 351, 415
Broadhurst, J. 415
Bruce, James 143 n.5
Bul Biliu (Belyu) 306, 415
Bul Kwer 220, 243, 417
  biographical entry 415
  personality report 238
  road 233
  tax 229
Bul Nuer 94, 415, 425, 427, 429
  and Arabs 305
  contacted by government 301, 305-6
  country 296-7
  original home 299 n.9
  population 27, 298
  sections:
    Dieng (Dijul) 306
    Gok 306
    Myindeng 306

tax 308
Buom Diu 298, 304
  biographical entry 415
  personality report 303
Bure 328 n.8
Burnian (Batmanan) 201, 411, 422
  biographical entry 415
Burun (*See also* Cai, Koma, Meban, Uduk) 23, 177, 178, 182
  administration 345, 362
  and cultivation 190–1
  protection of 193
  tax 188

Caath Bang 303, 415, 423
Cabuoc Acok 221, 246
  chief's police 244
  tax 231
Cag Riang 420, 431
  biographical entry 415
  and murder of Fergusson 301, 302
Cai 177 n.4
Cam-wa-Medho 354 n.1, 416
Cam-wara-Akwei (Sham Akwai) 200, 354 n.1, 412
  biographical entry 416
Camjok Cai 416
Can (Shan) Kak 145
Caniyang Maiyan 265
Cann, G. P. 352, 373
  biographical entry 416
  knowledge of Sudanese 374
  knowledge of vernacular 22
  and merchants 374
  and Shilluk council 354
  Shilluk Resident 359
  Struvé on 370
Car Koryom (Char Koriom) 216, 418, 423
  biographical entry 416
  surrenders 214, 279
Carless, T. F. G. 416
Casati, G. 300
Cawoc Akur 221, 231
Cep Aciek 252, 263, 265
Cic (Shish) Dinka 62, 143, 345, 429
  biddable people 389
  carriers 87
  courts 253
  diets of:
    Agok 265
    Alak 266
    Aliap 265
    Alico 265
    Anyon 266
    Dikoic 265
    Dur 266
    Kun 265
    Lith 265
    Nam 265
    Padiet 266
    Paiyok 266
    Yom 265
  effect of irrigation schemes on 406
  fight Atuot 255
  invented name 252
  not really Dinka 114
  and Nuer 297, 298
  population 27, 63, 263, 381
  road 309
  tribal lorry 82, 398 n.9
  tribal groups (*See also* Ador and Gok):
    Ajak 252, 253, 263, 266
    Kwaic 252, 253, 256–7, 263, 265
  tribes:
    Ajwong 252, 265, 266
    Cilik 252, 266
    Cirbek 252, 265
    Ding 252, 265
    Dwaur 252, 266
    Jalwa 252, 265
    Jar 252, 265
    Nuen 252, 265
    Pajak 252, 265
    Pakol 252, 265
Coghlan, E. M. E. 350, 366–7, 416
Cok Macek 265
Col Awet 413
Col, Joseph Maciek Deng 106, 417
Colebourne, G. W. 75, 105, 416
Colel Aiyol 265
Conkwei Jok 221, 243
  personality report 240
  road 234, 235
  tax 230
Cor (Chor) Rial 198, 268
Coriat, P. 31, 52, 56, 369
  and administration of Lou Nuer 48–50
  biographical entry 416
  chiefs 354
  and chiefs' police 125 n.36
  district 356, 358
  and Fergusson 43
  and Guek Ngundeng 17–18, 277, 421
  interpreters 376
  knowledge of the Nuer and Dinka 360–1
  knowledge of vernacular 11, 22, 375
  and Mayan Lam 287
  and merchants 374
  and Nuer chiefs 414–15, 418, 420, 425, 427, 428
  Nuer Settlement 292
  and Said Abd el-Rahman 373
  Struvé on 371
  subsequent career 348 n.25
  trained mounted police 355–6
  treks among Nuer 363

and Western Nuer   74, 119
and Willis   15
Coryton, E. G.   350, 372, 373
  attitude towards Shilluk king   359
  attitude towards Sudanese   355, 374
  biographical entry   416
  budget   351-2
  and main road in Malakal ('Sharia Coryton')   312, 316
  Struvé on   369-70
Crispin, E. S.   274, 368, 416
Crouch, H. A.   134-5, 365, 417
Cuol Deng Lom   417
Cuol Weng   301, 417
Cwei Tir   244

Daga   345, 412, 430
  administrative tours to   192, 193, 194
  grain at   195
  landing ground   97, 180
  mail service to   98
  merchant at   341
  police   122, 124, 172, 185-6
  road   78, 193, 195
Dak Dei   288 n.31
Dak Fadiat   157 n.3, 419
Dak Kairjok   264
Dal Aiwel   143
Damawt   170
Danalis   326, 417
Dang Dung Jiek   301, 417, 420
Davies, G. R.   172, 363, 417
Daw Lual   238
Daw Yak   243
Deeny   287
Delal Ajak   170
Dembi Dollo (Sayo)   322
Deng Agwek   220, 242
  personality report   237
  road   232, 234
  tax   229
Deng Agwer   428
Deng Aiwel Agot   274 n.6
Deng Ajak   220, 242
  biographical entry   417
  personality report   237
  road   232, 234
  tax   229
Deng Ajoin   266
Deng Akol   144
Deng Akoul   242
Deng Akwoi   144
Deng Aniang   242
Deng Bol   242
Deng Col   106, 158, 220, 242
  biographical entry   417
  personality report   236
  road   232, 234

and sub-chiefs   237
  tax   229
  Willis on   113
Deng Dut   243
Deng Kak   143, 145
Deng Koic   220, 243
  personality report   240
  road work   233
  tax   230
Deng Kur (Dinka chief)   220, 242
  personality report   237
  road work   232, 234
  tax   229
Deng Kur, See Ngundeng Bong
Deng Laka   418, 425, 430
Deng Lom   221, 243
  biographical entry   417
  personality report   240
  road work   234, 235
  tax   230
Deng Lual   220, 243
  biographical entry   417
  personality report   238
  road work   233
  tax   229
Deng Macar   244
Deng Malwal   53, 54, 221, 222 n.16, 424, 425
  biographical entry   417-18
  chief's police   243
  personality report   240
  road work   234, 235
  tax   230
  Willis on   113
Deng Malwal (chief's policeman)   242
Deng Mayan   273, 274-5, 412
  biographical entry   418
Deng Raic   243
Deng Rue (Ruair)   202, 418
Deng Thiong   243
Deng Tinda   242
Deng Yong   220, 243
  personality report   238
  road work   234
  tax   229
Dengjok   176
Denjok   202
Detwok   427
  dressing station   137, 168
  embankment   161
  European population   155
  Roman Catholic mission   108, 109, 168
  school   106, 168
Dhieu Alam   256 n.8, 257, 418
Dik Mareng   203
Ding Twil Kuoth   278, 418
Dinka (See also Abialang, Agar, Aliab, Angai, Ballak, Bor, Cic, Dungjol, Duor,

Ghol, Jureir, Luac, Ngok, Nyareweng, Paloic, Ric, Rueng, Rut, Thain, Thoi and Twic Dinka) x–xi, 4, 6, 12, 13, 22, 41, 42, 45–6, 177, 411, 422, 428
administration of 62–3
and 'Anyanya' 33
Arabicized 112
in the army and police 5, 222 n.17
born 'councillors' 354
bridewealth and bloodmoney (Bor District) 225 n.19
and cattle 59, 61
chiefs' courts (Bor District) 221–28
chiefs' police 125, 126
country 83
and education 106, 107, 108
as food producers 127
grain 283–4
and gum 148
as an imitative people 52–3
initiation 337 n.9
labour duties (Bor District) 235–6
language 23
literacy in Dinka 347
law (in Bor District) 224–7
and merchants 286
merisa 171
missions among 108
months 215
Nuer Settlement 292
political organization and chiefs 9, 20, 24–5, 32
raided by Nuer 52, 54
religion 215–18
semi-nomadism 214–15
sheep 141
and tax 11, 39, 49
use of rifles in inter-sectional fighting 343 n.15
villages 73, 75
Diu Ngor 273, 281, 418
Dok Nuer 302, 303, 415
compared with Jagei 304
and Gaawar 297
litigation 307
location 296
population 27, 298
punitive patrols against 9, 300
tax 308
Doleib Hill 285
American Presbyterian Mission 105, 108, 109
dressing station 137
European population 155
road 160
school 106
Dual (Dwal) Diu 41, 216
arrest of 240, 292

biographical entry 418–19
friction with Nyareweng Dinka 360
and government 13, 17, 18
and Kerbiel 422
in Malakal 339 n.11
marries Moinykuer Mabur's daughter 425
and Pok Kerjiok 427
raids Dinka, 1928 118 n.33, 213–14, 278, 291
Duic Cappa 267
Duk Fadiat 208, 216, 418, 420
agricultural experiment at 128–9, 244
buildings 81, 82, 138
landing ground 98, 232
police post 2
road 64, 73, 75, 234, 235
wireless 99
Duk Fayuil (Faiwel, Faiyuil, Faywil, Paiwel) xv, 208, 418
administrators posted to 428, 431
agricultural experiment at 244
buildings 246, 247
dispensary 137
headquarters of Dinka-Nuer district 2
herd 249
named after Aiwel 209
Nuer attack on 41, 214, 278, 291, 356 n.3
police at 55, 124
possible abandonment 361
post and telegraph service 98
rent 231
road 232, 234, 235
sub-mamur at 101, 353
Dungjol (Dunjol) Dinka 53–4, 142, 173, 411, 430
administration of 113, 158–9, 345
cattle 162–3, 172
chiefs' police 125, 126
country 144
cultivation 127
education among 106
food producers 162
and Jikany Nuer 178 n.6
medical work among 110
origin of 143
population 27, 155
tax 160
Duoinngok Akol 242
Duor (Dwar) Dinka 54, 209
absorbed by Lou Nuer 212
country 386
effect of irrigation schemes on 406
population 113, 381
poverty of 60
Dupuis, C. E. 275, 419
Dut Ayi 221, 231

Index 461

Dut Makoic 267
Dwal Diu, *See* Dual Diu
Dwar 309
Dwet Deng 243

Eastern Jikany (Jekaing) Nuer 46–8, 63
    n.d, 177 (see also under Gaajak, Gaajok
    and Gaagwang Nuer)
  absorb Dinka 211
  arms trade with Abyssinia 294
  and cattle 189–90
  chiefs' police 125
  cultivation 187, 272
  division into sections 191–2, 196–7
  and education 110, 186
  Guek Ngundeng flees to 278
  and medicine 186
  and other Nuer 182
  population 27, 62
  punitive patrol against 9–11, 47, 51 n.1
  same sub-tribe as Western Jikany 298
  tax 181
Eliri 74, 155
Ellison, J. R. 163, 419
El Sayed Ahmed el Hag 100, 173
El Sayed Mohammed Munib 368, 419
El Shafia Ahmed 100
Evans-Pritchard, E. E. 19, 25, 290 n.3, 333
  field work among Nuer xii, 21, 269 n.2
  relations with Willis 21
Ewart, J. M. 16

Fabur 170
Fadding 272
Faddoi 269
  dispensary 137
  landing ground 97
  perennial water 272
Fadiang 170
Fadiet Kwathker (Kwathkeir) 35, 156
  biographical entry 419
  and British 8–9
  reign 158
Fadl Mula Jak 287
Fadung, *See* Padang Dinka
Fafiti Yor 156, 158
  biographical entry 419
  Struvé on 359
Fafoijo 154, 160
Fahim Hanna 101
Fakit Ayee 242
Fakwak 293
Fakwar 170
Falo 170, 173
Falwal 257, 260
Fangak 45, 51, 52, 66, 109, 427, 430
  alternate spelling xvi
  buildings 137, 294, 361

  Dinka at 290, 393
  dispensary 137
  experimental herd 141
  felucca 93
  flooded 357 n.4
  garden 295
  police 124
  road 75, 77
  telephone 99
Faniok 235
Fanta, fitawrari 325, 327, 421
  biographical entry 419
Fanyangluel 269
Fanyidwai 170
Farag Ismail (Mohammed Farag
    Ismail) 101, 419
Faragalla Fleet 171, 173
Faragalla Kong Dungdit (Faragalla
    Nuer) 202, 419–20
Fasheir 293
Fashoda (*See also* Kodok) 2, 4, 411
  ceremonial visit to 157
  Fashoda incident ix, 1–2
  holy place of Shilluk 117
  Mahdist attack on 145 n.7
  origin of name xv
  renamed Kodok 2–3
  village feud 170
Fathai 83
  agricultural experiment at 128–9, 284
  causeway 280
  dispensary 137
  embankment 80
  merchant at 286
  namlia 81, 284
  road 74, 75, 76, 77, 204, 269, 279,
    282–3
  wireless 99
Fatitet 268, 280
Fatma (lunatic) 170
Faweng 278
Fellata 358
Fergusson, V. H. 55, 60, 64 n.27
  assassination 4, 41, 167 n.6, 291, 300–1,
    302, 382, 415, 417, 426
  biographical entry 420
  bloodmoney for 263
  and Bul Nuer 305
  and chiefs 305, 415, 418, 420, 429, 430
  first contacts Nuer 300
  holy lake 257
  method of administration 43–5, 47, 51–
    2, 56, 61, 306–7
  Nuer sub-province 344 n.18
  and prophets 44 n.5
  and taxation 308
  and Willis 15, 43
Fox, C. V. 212, 420

Fuad Araman 99
Fuad Bishara 99
Fuad Dagher 99
Fulfam 290
Fung (Funy) 143 n.5, 144, 156

Gaagwang Nuer (Eastern Jikany) 177, 191–2, 361
  administration of 194
  tax 181
Gaagwang Post 181, 185
Gaajak Nuer (Eastern Jikany) 35, 46, 62, 361, 419
  administration of 193–4
  and Ajak Tor Bil 159, 412
  cattle 190
  chiefs 196, 362
  chiefs' police 125–6
  country 177
  courts 117–18
  cultivate extensively 126, 190
  former leaders of 112
  and Meban 178 n.6
  rifles 342
  sections of 191–2
    Cany 191
    Gaagwong 191, 192
    Nyayan 191, 192
    Reng 191, 192
    Thiang 191, 194
    Wau 191, 192
  tax 181
Gaajok Nuer (Eastern Jikany) 46, 62, 361, 426
  administration of 194
  cattle 190
  chiefs 196
  country 177, 181
  courts 117
  and Mor Lou 178 n.7
  sections of 191–2
    Laang 191, 192, 194
    Wangkai 191, 192, 193
    Yuol 191, 193
  tax 181
Gaaluak Buth 301, 420
Gaaluak Nyagh (Galwak Nyag) 298, 415, 430, 431
  appointed chief of Dur and Gatliath Nyuong 302
  biographical entry 420
  personality report 303
  suspected of Fergusson's murder 301
Gaawar (Gaweir) Nuer 11, 52, 240
  absorb Dinka 212
  arms trade 297
  blood-money 118
  cattle tribute patrols 291

chiefs 411, 413, 417, 418, 422, 427
chiefs' police 125 n.36
and civil war 35
compared with Western Nuer 296, 299, 306
country 387, 392–3
discipline of young men 335
dryness of country 80
effect of irrigation schemes on 406–7
fight Dinka 41, 42, 211–14, 356 n.3
and government 17, 214
lack of administration 45–6, 377
Nuer Settlement 291–2
population 27, 62, 290, 381
punitive patrols against 9, 16, 41, 81
rifles 360
road 75
sections:
  Barr 360
  Radh (Raz) 360, 391
toic 297
transferred to Fangak 277, 360
Gag Gwat 220, 243
  personality report 239
  road work 233
  tax 230
Gag Kwain 220
Gaiwam 260
Gaj Gom 264
Gaj Mair 264
Galla, See Oromo
Gallabat 85
Galwak Nyag, See Gaaluak Nyagh
Gambela (Gambeila) 35, 45, 321ff
  administrators posted to 419, 421, 424, 425, 426, 427, 428, 430
  boundaries 322
  coffee trade 188, 324
  currency and revenue 323, 325–6
  dispensary 137
  EID in 323
  established as a trading enclave 2, 321
  Greek merchants 323, 324
  police 124
  population 323
  postal service to 180, 324
  river discharge 133
  road 78
  steamer service to 90, 187, 324
  well 80
  wireless 98–7
Gameiza 77, 336
Ganame, dajjazmach 328, 420–1
Ganza 177 n.4
Garang, John 35
Garang Wiu (Garrang Weou) 221
  biographical entry 420
  personality report 241

Index 463

road work 234
tax 231
Garrang Abot 243
Garrang Aniang 242
Garrang Apiu 242
Garrang Faniang 243
Garrang Kur 242
Garrang Lual 242
Garrang Lueth 243
Gatkek Luop (Gatkek Dwoich) 298, 413
  biographical entry 420
  personality report 304
Gatkek Jiek 417, 431
  arrested for Fergusson's murder 301
  biographical entry 420
Gaulo 170
Gaweir, *See* Gaawar Nuer
Geigar 65, 142, 143, 144
  groundnuts 128
  population 153
  road 64, 74, 77, 147
Gelhak 78
  market 65
  population 153
  roads 64, 142, 147
George V 157 n.4
Geteina 144
Ghol (Gol) Dinka 54, 209, 418, 425
  chiefs 221, 240
  chiefs' police 243
  country 386
  effect of irrigation schemes on 406
  history of 211–12
  Niel section 221
  Pattel section 221
  population 27, 113, 241, 381
  poverty of 60
  road and landing ground work 232, 234
  tax 230
Giet Akuyen 243
Girgis Buctor 101
Glanville, W. H. 141 n.45
Gnorley 204
Gobjak 268, 269
Goc Deeng 144
Godwin, C. C. 276, 421
Gogwei Kwei 220, 242
  personality report 237
  road work 234
  tax 229
Goj Bul 238
Gok (Cic Dinka) 251, 266
  administered from Mongalla 254
  cattle loses 261
  court 253
  dresser stationed at 263
  headquarters 259

  population of 263
  tribes and diets of:
    Arek 252
    Awan 252, 266
    Bun 252, 266
    Ding 252, 266
    Jagjuair 252, 266
    Lual 252, 266
Gol, *See* Ghol Dinka
Goora 200 n.2
Gordon, C. G. 180 n.8
Gore 325, 329, 412, 417
  Ethiopian governors of 414, 419, 420, 422, 425
Goz Ajwang 153
Goz Fami 147, 153
Goz Gerbanat 147, 153
Goz Nabbuk 142
Guek Ngundeng (Gwek Wanding/ Wundeng) 13, 40–1, 42, 46, 274, 426
  biographical entry 421
  and brother Bol 414–15
  death 279
  and government 17–18, 277, 291
  mistaken for Pok Kerjiok 276
  operations against 117, 125, 213–14, 278–9
  and other Nuer chiefs 271, 22, 418, 423, 425
  and other prophets 416, 418, 427
  proposed removal of 49, 57
  and road 47 n.11
Gulbaing 170
Gum Acek 265
Gumwell Diu 243
Gurbana (well) 80
Gwer (lunatic) 170
Gwogol (landing stage) 94

Hassan Sid Ahmed 99
Havercroft, C. 351, 421
Hayla Selasse I, *See* Tafari Makonnen
Hebbert, G. K. P. 22, 421
Henderson, L. H. 135, 421
Hill, H. 255 n.6
Hillet Nuer, *See* Adok
Hinsley, A. 109, 421
Huddleston, A. J. C. 275, 421
Huddleston, H. J. 42, 421
Huffman, R. 182, 421
Hussein Farag 319, 353
  biographical entry 421–2
  and merchants 374
  Struvé on 373–4
Hussein Said 353, 422

Ibrahim Said 100
Ibrahim Zaki Shawki 99

Ili Georgis 328
Ismail Hashem 100
Ismail Konye 206 n.5
Ismail Sirri 368, 422
Itang 35, 321
Iyasu, lij (Liggie Yasu) 320, 421

Jackson, H. C.
  biographical entry 422
  and Bol Ngundeng 276, 414
  deputy governor 11–12
  disagreement with Struvé 12 n.23
  and Guek Ngundeng 17, 276
Jackson, H. W. 2, 145, 422
Jagei (Jagey) Nuer 302, 303, 390, 423, 429
  and Gaawar 297
  litigation 307
  location 296
  original home of Nuer 299, 304
  population 27, 298
  punitive patrol against 9, 300
  Rengyang (Rangyan) 304
  tax 308
Jal Lom 243
Jeic Poic 429
Jekaing, *See* Eastern and Western Jikany Nuer
Jieng Agarak 265
Jil Ayom 242
Jok Angwac 265
Jok Ayom 220, 242
  personality report 237
  road work 232, 234
  tax 229
Jok Deng 220, 243
  personality report 239
  road work 233
  tax 229
Jokau 2, 87, 362
  administrative tours to 193, 194
  road 74, 78, 195
Jokor 207
Jong Tong Maic 265
Jonglei 101, 244, 361
  mosquito house at 81
  police post at 2, 55
  road 233
Juai Bor (CMS mission) 105 n.15
Juba 139, 246, 416, 427
Juet 233
Jum Jum 177 n.4
Junker 180 n.8
Jur 257, 260
Jureir (Jweir) Dinka 54, 275, 360
  mixed Dinka-Jikany 270
  repatriation of 113
  tax 281–2
Juwai (Yuwai) 268, 280

Kaan (Kan) 269, 286
Kaati 309
Kabbada Mangasha (Kabada Mangesha), ras 329, 422, 425
Kacwol Apokain 264
Kaibui 202, 203, 268
  concentration of Mor at 279
  embankment 205, 283
  namlia 284
  road 204
Kaikwi 203
Kak Akwei 144, 413
Kaka 62, 144, 148, 149, 315
  administered by NMP 358
  roads 64, 66, 74, 160
  store shed 87
  Sudanese population 155
  telegraph line 98
Kana 202
Kang Makwei 220, 242
  personality report 237
  road work 232, 234
  tax 229
Kanisa (Kenisa) 131, 252, 259 n.12
Katalok 147
Kavanagh, G. C. M. 75, 422
Kejok Cappa 267
Kengen (Kangen) Lom (Baatalan) 201, 415, 422
Kantok 260
Kenj Dut 267
Kerbiel (Gatbuogh Wal) 41, 216
  and Dual Diu 291
  biographical entry 422
Ket 75, 97
Khalifa Abdallahi 1, 144–5
Khartoum 97, 103, 414, 421, 424, 425, 428, 430
  cattle trade to 187
  coffee prices in 324
  as centre of government 1, 11, 12, 14, 15, 17, 19, 32–3, 66, 291, 352, 401 n.11
  Director of Lands 323
  Episcopate of 109
  lack of knowledge of Southern provinces 356
  material brought from 313
  merchants 286
  and native administration 334 n.5
  in nineteenth century 144
  Nuer chiefs visit 278
  permits to trade 323
  research laboratory at 72
  road 75
  steamers from 324
Khawaga Yakoub Apkarian 171
Khershawal 153

Khojali al-Hassan 178 n.5
Kidd, H. F. 55, 64 n.27
  biographical entry 422–3
  succeeds Fergusson 302
Kigille 345, 362
  administrative tours to 192, 193, 194
  coffee trade 188
  grain at 195
  mail service to 98
  police 122, 124, 185–6
  road 74, 78, 193, 195
Kingdon, F. D. xii
Kipling, R. 51
Kippax, J. 169, 423
Kippax, N. 169, 423
Kitchener, H. H. 1, 8, 145, 423
Ko Nial 237–8
Kodok 61, 63, 65, 110, 137, 154, 173, 416
  buildings 138, 163–5
  dispensary 136, 167–8
  embankment 161
  garden 86, 130, 166–7
  garage 84
  herd 167, 174
  idiots 170–1
  landing ground 97
  landing stage 94
  light line 88
  liquor 171
  in nineteenth century 144, 145
  police 85, 121, 124, 124, 172
  postal and telegraph service 98–9
  province headquarters moved from 312
  pump 139
  resthouse 81
  road 75, 77, 160
  school 169
  and Shilluk police 117, 123, 125, 157
  staff 101
  Sudanese and European populations
    in 155
Koingai 202
Kok Kaurainyang 265
Kolang Ket 303, 415, 423
Koma (Khoma) 177, 426
  'Burun' at Daga and Kigille 185–6
  in civil war 35
  language 23, 177 n.4
  and Nuer 178 nn5 & 6
  population 27
  raided by dajjazmach Berru 185 n.16
Kong Tong 266
Kongor 2, 101, 113, 208 n.2
  agricultural experiment at 244
  buildings at 246
  landing ground 97, 232
  police at 55
  post, telegraph and telephone 98–9

road 76, 233, 234
  and Twic Dinka 211
  well 79
Kor Akwe 221
  personality report 241
  road work 234
  tax 231
Koratong 176, 193, 195
Korriam Awo 252, 263, 265
Koryom Kom 201
Kosti 396
Kot Kanj 265
Kudit 157 n.3
Kui 309
Kulang Majok 125 n.36
Kunjok Dud 220, 243
  personality report 239
  road work 233
  tax 229
Kuot Ajok 243
Kur Col 242
Kur Fafiti 156–7, 419
Kur Nyidok (Nyadok) 8, 156, 419
  appointed 158
  biographical entry 423
Kur Tsijuth 221
  personality report 241
  road work 234
  tax 231
Kurbiel, See Kerbiel
Kurmayom (Kormayom) 77, 269 n.2
Kurmuk 64
Kurwai 203
Kushulo 362
Kuth Mayan 270, 281, 282
Kuth Yor 221, 243
  personality report 240
  tax 230
Kwain Ateng 220, 242
  personality report 237–8
  road work 233
  tax 229
Kwama 177 n.4
Kwathker Akwot 156, 419
Kweichar 198
Kweikun Akoc (Akoich) 156
Kwek Atuot 257, 264
  dresser stationed among 263
  population 263
  tribes of:
    Ajwot 264
    Gwarang 264
    Juluth 264
    Nang 264
    Thiang 264
    Yeth 264
  wells 260
Kwiarot Aciran 265

Kwil 309
Kwoishung 170

Laikaich 75, 94, 293
Lak Nuer 45, 118, 357, 360
  census 290
  country 391
  Nuer Settlement 292
  population 27, 62, 381
  road 75
  tax evasion 291
  toic 297
Lam Akol 35
Lam Tutthiang (Tutiang) 287, 423, 425
Lat 264
Lau 252, 255, 256
  mamur at 254
  Nuer attack CMS mission at 300
  road 257, 259
Lau, See Lou Nuer
Lawton, Captain 255
Lee, John 12, 361, 426
  biographical entry 423
  and chiefs' courts 196
  credit for winning over Gaajak to government 362
  interpreters 376
  knowledge of vernacular 11, 52, 181 n.12, 375
  and maize seed 190
  and merchants 374
  Struvé on 371
  treks among Nuer 363
Leek (Leik) Nuer 301, 305, 426, 430
  country 296
  Cuak (Shwak) section 305
  Kilwal section under Jikany 298, 304, 305
  population 27, 298
  tax 308
Leim Cwol 287
Lem Mayol 244
Lem Rueh 243
Ler (Leiro) 77, 105 n.15, 108
Lewis, B. A. 24
Liglig Kuny (Lig Lig Kuin) 279, 423
Lil 297
Limnios, Messrs 341
Loka 99, 346
Lokadi 207
Lom 415
Longtam 416, 423
  isolated 357
  mamur at 291
Lopilod 201
Lou (Lau) Nuer 12, 17, 40, 42, 48, 65, 414, 417, 421, 425
  absorb Dinka 211–12
  administration of 117
  in Akobo district 199, 202–3
  arms trade with Abyssinia 294
  and civil war 35
  chiefs' police 51, 59, 125
  compared with Western Nuer 296, 299, 306
  country 269, 386
  dry season movements 298
  and Duk Fayuil 360–1
  effect of irrigation schemes on 406
  encroaching on Khor Geni 203
  fight Dinka 212–14, 274, 276
  Gun 46, 62, 277, 423
    chiefs' courts 280
    concentration of 279
    country 269
    population 270
    sections (See also Rumjok):
      Cic (Shish) 271, 277
      Gadbal (Yuol) 271
      Lang 271
      Machok 271
      Thiang 271, 279
      Yuwong 271, 277
    teachers 288
  Mor 46, 62, 178 n.7, 202, 427
    census 280
    chiefs 277
    concentration of 279
    country 269, 395
    more amenable than Gun 272
    population 270
    sections:
      Belyu 271
      Bul 271
      Buth 271
      Can 271
      Garliek 271
      Jegar 271
      Jemaic 271
      Kun 271
    teachers 288
  population 27, 62, 270
  punitive patrols against 16, 96–7
    1902 Dengkur Patrol 9, 274
    1917 Lau Patrol 51 n.1, 213, 276, 357, 414, 416, 427
    Nuer Settlement (1929–30) 42, 74, 81, 212, 214, 278–9, 291
    S8 Patrol (1927–8) 41, 278, 416
  removal from Bor and Duk District 240, 270, 278–9
  road 74
  Rumjok 46 n.8, 416, 418, 423, 427
    sections:
      Dul 271
      Dung 240, 271, 280

Index

Falkir 271, 277, 278
Kwaijien 271, 280
Maikerr (Maikeirr) 203, 271, 280
Matel 271
Nya Jekaing 271, 277
shyengs (sections) 270–1
tax 204, 275, 280–1
Luac Dinka 209, 420
 chiefs 240–1
 history of 212
 population 241
 repatriation of 214
 sections:
  Aiwel 221
  Angok 221
  Mut 221
 tax 231
Luaic Atuot 251
 court 253
 patrols against 255
 population 263
 tribes and diets of:
  Adut 264
  Airial 264
  Awanpail 251, 264
  Bang 264
  Gillik 251, 264
  Jagbari 264
  Nyilok 264
  Pir (Piair) 252, 264
Lual Ajok 417
Lual Deng 238, 417
Lual Kur 220, 242
 personality report 237
 road work 233, 234
 tax 229
Lual Tiang 203
Lual Wal 143, 423
Luang Deng 210 n.6, 290
Luel 75
Lueth Magot 265
Lueth Thiong 242
Lugard, Lord xii
Lugbara 115 n.29
Luin 268
Luk Acok 266
Lukluk 235
Lul 427
 dressing station 137
 embankment 161
 European population 155
 school 106, 108, 168
Luo 23
Lwoo languages 23
Lyall, C. E. 374, 423
Lythe, R. E. 24

Mabior Deng 220, 242

biographical entry 424
personality report 238
road work 233
tax 229
Mabior Kwer 243
Mabor Deng 264
Mabor Kacwal 252, 263, 264
Mabor Kok 264
Mabor Mangwanjok 266
Mabur Ajuot 425
Macar Acamkoc 237
Macar Diu 418
Macar Nijong 265
McBain, W. J. 364, 424
Macek Caping 264
McEnnery, J. J. 370, 424
Macfarlane, D. 367, 424
MacIntyre, A. B. 141 n.45
Mackintosh, W. D. 368, 424
MacMichael, H. 20–1, 42, 424
McMullen, G. 351, 352
 biographical entry 424
 Struvé on 372–3
 Willis on 373 n.13
Madbar Yali 260
Madlar 259
Maffey, Sir John 42, 424
Magara 151
Maguk Ju 259, 260, 264
Mahdi Omer 101
al-Mahdi, Sayyid Abd al-Rahman
 ('S.A.R.') 32–3
Mahmud Osman el-Sheikh 100, 151, 424
Mai Bilkwei (Belkwey) 306, 424
Maich Ding 242
Maiyen 255
Majangir 415
Majier, Martin 35
Majok Ajak 220, 243
 biographical entry 424
 personality report 239
 road work 233
 tax 230
Majok Ajang 220, 243
 biographical entry 424
 personality report 239
 road work 233
 tax 230
Majok Aru 243
Majok Atem 243
Majok Dwal 243
Majok Gang 265
Majok Kolang 423
Makeir Amoryal 286 n.29
Makenj Ilari 264
Makonnen Wosanie (Makonen Wasso),
 dajjazmach 322, 328, 424
Makwei de Bilkwei 414, 424

Makwei Gol 221, 243
  biographical entry 424
  personality report 240
  road work 235
  tax 230
Malakal 42, 62, 63, 97, 172, 352, 411, 429
  administrators posted to 414, 416, 427
  Agricultural and Forestry
    departments 417, 424, 427
  araki 319, 339
  army 5, 85, 86
  bridges 79
  buildings 137–9
  Dinka tribute paid in at 159
  district engineer 246
  drains 313–14
  EID 132–3, 312, 313, 314, 318, 319, 413, 419, 424, 425, 430
  effect of irrigation scheme on 396, 406
  electricity 318
  forestry 131
  founded 3
  garage 84
  herd 316
  hospital 135, 167, 168
  Imperial Airways site 134
  laboratory 136
  landing ground 97
  light line 88, 316
  market 314
  malakia 80, 83, 101, 108, 134, 313, 319, 337, 338–9
  merchants 286, 341
  milk 174
  mosquito brigade 315
  mutiny 33
  Nuer prisoners sent to 279, 305
  police 55, 121–2, 123, 124, 171
  polo 85
  postal and telegraph service 98–9
  prison 317
  PWD 65, 313, 314, 316, 317, 415, 416
  rates 133
  rest houses 81, 82
  roads 64, 74, 75, 76, 77, 160, 161, 282, 312–13
  schools 108, 346
  serum station 61, 72
  SGR&S depot 96, 315, 317
  SMS 136, 417, 421
  squash court 318
  staff 108
  steamers, launches and ferries 66, 69, 93, 94
  stores 87–8, 173
  Sudanese population 155, 319–20
  tennis court 318–19
  town planning 134, 314–15
  lack of 312
  town survey 140
  water supply 317–8
  wireless 180
  workshop 120–1
Malek 66, 114, 259
  buildings 246
  leper station 109, 247
  mission and school 34, 105, 107, 108, 427, 429
  road 74, 76, 133, 234
Malek Agwer (Agweir) 143, 424–25
Malith Ayeek 243
Malo Kur 412
Malwal Abongbar 266
Mamair Majok 265
Manam 170
Mandari 114
Mangasha Atikim, ras 422
Maniel Adit 244
Maning Jok 242
Mankaith 177, 268
Mankwauka 269, 280
Manyang 260
Mar 233
Marchand, Captain 1, 8, 145 n.7, 181 n.9, 423
Mareig 297
Mareng 198, 268
Marier Kwer 220, 243
  personality report 239
  road work 233
  tax 230
Marroum, Lewis 99
Marsh, J. F. H. 181 n.11, 322 n.5,
  biographical entry 425
  Struvé on 370–1
Masterman, J. 94, 302, 425
Matot Acinpwo 266
Matthews, G. E 9–10, 14, 28
Maurice, J. K. 425
Mayan Akwak 220, 242
  personality report 238
  road work 233
  tax 229
Mayan Lam 287, 423, 425
Mayan Riak 418
Mayom (well) 80
Meban 177 n.4, 345 n.21
  hariq cultivation 143 n.2
  in civil war 35
  language 23
  raided by dajjazmach Berru 185 n.16
  SIM mission 110 n.22
Megaga 81
Melut 159, 362, 411, 430
  administrative centre 142
  buildings 149, 150

Index

chiefs' court 143
cotton 87
dispensary 136
felucca 93
ferry 66
garden 150
landing ground 97
police 121, 124
resthouse 81
roads 64–5, 66, 73, 74, 75, 77, 78, 94, 147
staff 101, 151
SUM mission 108, 110, 169 n.7
telegraph and telephone service 98–9
well 80
Mengistu 180 n.8
Menilek II 419, 422, 425
  grant of concession near Itang 321
  territorial claims 1
Meridi 259
Meshra el-Rek xvi, 88, 297
Meshra Rufkwaich 360
Mialek 147
Milleim el Deleibi 297
Minkiman (Minkeman)
  mamur 256
  road 66, 76, 258, 260
Mogogh 208 n.2
Mohamed Ahmed (lunatic) 170
Mohammed Abd el-Rahman Burhan 100, 425
Mohammed Ali Hamdi 151
Mohammed el Dinkawi (idiot) 170
Mohammed (or Mahmud) el Sayed el Hanafi 100, 151
Mohammed Fahmi 99
Mohammed Hamdi 100
Mohammed Ismail 99
Mohammed Mahd Abu el Naga 99
Mohammed Sabr Idris 151, 425
Mohammed Safwat 99
Mohy el Din el Geneidi 100, 151
Moinykuer (Moinkwer) Mabur 221, 244, 419
  biographical entry 425
  personality report 240–1
  road work 234, 235
  tax 231
Moir, S. B. 368, 425
Mongalla 2, 416
Moro 160
Mow Gai 264
Mubarak Nasr el Din 100
Mudather Gabr el Dar 100
Mulholland, P. D. 93, 425
Murgan (Morgan) Ali 299
Murle (Beir) 3, 25, 63, 97, 345, 412
  and Bor Dinka 202

cattle 395
chiefs and government 9, 24, 120, 200–1
chiefs' police 202
country 395
cultivation 205
lack of initiation 337
interpreters 207
militia, 1991 206 n.5
  and Mor Lou 203
Ngarrotti 411, 415
population 27, 199
punitive patrols against 3, 9, 412, 420
sheep 141, 205
Surma language group 23
tax 204, 362–3
Munang Burnian 411, 415
Musa Ibrahim 376
Musa Helu 364
Mustafa Bakri 99
Mustafa Khalifa 100
Mwot Dit (Did) 211
  concentration of Gun 279
  perennial water 272
  road 64–5, 75
Mwot Tot 269, 272
Mvolo 250, 259

Nadaw, ras 329, 425
Nagdia 62, 74, 154, 160
Nairobi 75
Nalder, L. F. xi–xii
Nasir (Nasser) 11, 68
  administrators posted to 412, 416, 423, 424, 425
  American Mission 105, 107 n.18, 109, 182, 186, 288, 411, 421, 429
  Anuak 178, 188
  buildings 81, 137, 138, 182–3
  dispensary 137, 186
  felucca 93
  ferry 66
  landing ground 97, 180
  malakia 182
  Nasir faction of SPLA 35, 414
  old Nasir 76, 181
  part of Pibor River Province 3
  police 124, 184–5
  postal and wireless service 98–9, 180, 324
  pump 80
  reoccupied in 1898 1–2, 181 n.9
  roads 64–5, 74, 75, 76, 77, 78, 194, 195, 204, 205, 282
  school 106, 108, 287
  staff 100, 184
  steamer service 179
  visits in rainy season 193
  wood station 131

470   Index

Nasir Ali   180 n.8
Nayel Ali   101, 425
New Fangak   294, 357 n.4
Newhouse, F.   368, 369, 425
Ngapul Burnian   415, 422
Ngit   269
Ngok Dinka   54, 143, 275, 360
  chiefs   113, 412, 418, 427, 428
  country   269
  cultivation   127, 272, 273, 283
  of Kordofan (Ngork)   53 n.20, 297
  population   27, 270
  refuse to pay tax   274–5
  sections:
    Jok   273
    Yom   273
  sub-sections:
    Abi   273
    Achak   273
    Adong   273
    Ajuba   273
    Awir   273
    Baliet   273
    Deng   273
    Diak   273
    Dud   273
    Ngan   273
  tax   281–2
  transferred to Northern District   345 n.21
Ngong Aniang   244
Ngopp (Gnopp)   255
  mamur at   254
  road   250, 259, 260
Ngor Agot   243
Ngundeng Bong   421, 423
  attacked by 'Turuk'   274
  biographical entry   425–6
  death   275
  overshadowed chiefs   272
  pyramid (Mound)   46, 49, 57, 269, 274, 278, 275
Nguotnyin Der   221, 231, 244
Ngwer   76
Nial Acol   251, 256 n.8, 263, 264
Nial Agot   242
Nicholls, W. P.   375, 426
Niel   230
Nimeiri   417
Niort Gai   243
Niyiyar   170
Nordeng (Noor)   180, 181
Northcote, C. S.   355, 426
Noumeir (Neumair), G.   325–6, 327, 426
Nuba   155, 161, 162
  border Nuer   297 n.3
Nuel Juel   298, 305, 426
Nuer (See also Bul, Dok, Eastern and Western Jikany, Gaawar, Jagei, Lak,

Leek, Lou, Nyuong, Thiang, and Western Nuer) x–xi, 42, 43–5, 48, 177 n.4, 411, 412, 422, 431
  absorb Dinka   222
  administration of   51–2, 62–3, 67
  age class   331
  and 'Anyanya'   32
  in army and police   5
  attack Cic Dinka   256–7
  and cattle   59–60, 61
  and chickens   141
  in civil war   35
  country   83
  cultivation done by women   126
  and Dinka border   2, 14, 18
  and education   106–7
  as food producers   127
  grain   284
  gifts to chiefs   49–50
  language   23
    literacy in Nuer   347
  missions among   108, 109
  political organization and chiefs   9, 20, 25, 32
  as security threat   15, 32
  tax   11, 39
  tribal land   134
  use of rifles in inter-sectional fighting   343 n.15
  warlike tribe   51
  in Yirol District   250
Nun   77, 79
Nuong, See under Nyuong Nuer
Nyakia (political prisoner)   287
Nyal Kwoth   203
Nyalwingi (lunatic)   171
Nyandong   309
Nyang Camjok   202
Nyareweng (Nyarreweng) Dinka   54, 209, 210 n.6, 413, 417, 424, 425
  Agair section   221
  Athon section   221, 243
  chiefs   221, 240
  chiefs' police   243
  and civil war   35
  conflict with Nuer   212–14
  country   386
  effect of irrigation scheme on   406
  history of   211
  intrigue against Gaawar   360–1
  Kumai section   221, 243
  population   27, 113, 241, 381
  poverty of   60
  road and landing ground work   232, 234
  tax   230
Nyaruac Kolang   423, 429
Nyatuk (lunatic)   171
Nybodo   170

Index

Nyeda 64, 78
Nyerol 103, 269, 421
  failure 361
  flooded 357
  forestry 285
  merchant 286
  perennial water 272
  post opened 276
  road 64–5, 73, 74, 77, 282
Nyerweng (police post) 181, 185
Nygir 170
Nyiboi Ngong 265
Nyidok (Nyadok) Nyakwac 156–7, 423
Nyikang 155–7
Nyingut Deng 243
Nyith Guer 125 n.37
Nyngaro 170
Nyuong (Nuong) Nuer 42, 45, 302–3, 309, 390
  and Angai Dinka 302
  assassination of Fergusson 300, 301
  attack CMS mission at Lau 300
  bloodmoney 263 n.16
  chiefs 415, 417, 420, 427, 431
  Dur section 300, 301, 302, 303, 309
  chiefs conspire to assassinate Fergusson 301
  and Gaawar 297
  Gatliath section 298, 301, 302, 303
  location 296
  population 27, 298
  punitive patrols against 9, 97, 300–1
  road 74, 309
  tax 308
Nyuyudu 170

Oashi 170
Ochoda 200
Odok (Odhok) Dedigo 169, 173
Odol War 207
Ogon 170
Omat Giba 207
Omdurman 144, 145, 320
  battle of 181, 337
  merchants 341
  as source of labour 131
Ongwi Bol 252, 263, 264
Opari 107 n.19
Oromo 323
Oshalla 426
Oshan 322
Osman Abdel Wahab 100, 151
Osman Nurel Medina 99
O'Sullivan, H. D. E. 111, 275, 426
Oweir Areng, *See* Awir Renk
Oweit Shol, *See* Awet Col
Owen, R. C. R. 366, 426

Padang (Fadung) Dinka 209, 210 n.6
  absorbed by Lou Nuer 211–12
  chiefs 221, 240
  tax 231
Padiet Renk 145, 413, 426
Paken 260
Pakkam (Fakam) 75, 309
Pakujiak 259, 260
Paloic (Paloc) 147, 169 n.7
Paloic Dinka
  Abuya section 143, 144, 146, 152
  Ageir section 143, 144, 146, 152
  Beir section 143, 144, 146, 152
  chiefs 413, 423, 424–5, 428
  hariq cultivation 142 n.2
  Niel section 143, 144, 146, 152, 157
  population 27, 152
Panaru (Fanaru) 159
Pap 258, 260
Papiu 94, 95, 258
Pariak 247
Parker, A. C. 351, 427
Parr, M. W. 352, 427
Paw 210
Pawson, A. G. xii, 26, 31
  biographical entry 427
  reverses Willis' policies 22
Pec (Pey) Poar 306, 427
Pec Ruac 202–3, 427
Penko 208
Pibor Post 201, 363, 394, 428
  dispensary 137
  dry weather post 122
  founded 3
  landing ground 97
  mail service to 98
  police 124, 172
  road 74, 76, 77, 78, 133, 204
Pletts, G. S. 45, 325, 361
  biographical entry 427
  district 356, 358
  and merchants 374
  Struvé on 370
Pok Kerjiok (Gär) 47 n.11, 216
  biographical entry 427
  and government 276 n.18, 291
  surrenders 214, 279
Pok Makeir (driver) 286 n.29
Pollen, W. M. H. 86, 427
Port Sudan 415
Porter, W. A. 92, 427
Poti Burnian 415
Price, C. L. 105, 427
Pschorn, E. 106, 109, 427
Pul-a-dor 259
Puom (Pwom) Aiwel 210

Raic Amo 252, 259, 263, 266
Rak Yaak (Arrak Yak) 216, 427-8
Ratcliffe, W. 370, 428
Reid, G. R. M. 42, 428
Rek Dinka xvi, 297
Renk 6, 15, 21, 144, 352
  administrative centre 143
  administrators posted to 414, 424, 425, 427, 429, 430
  buildings 137, 138, 149-50
  commercial development 29
  dispensary 136
  EID 134
  excluded from Closed Districts Ordinance 29 n.63
  felucca 93
  Gabarona 153
  garage 84
  garden 150
  Kumshowar 153
  landing stage 94, 95
  landing ground 97
  light line 88
  lorry needed at 65
  in Mahdiyya 145
  malakia 101, 142-3
  police 2, 121, 124, 172
  postal and telegraph service 98-9
  pump 139
  Radif 153
  rates 133
  resthouse 81, 133
  roads 75, 142, 147
  staff 151
  store shed 87, 88
  Suari 153
Renk de Com 413, 426
  biographical entry 428
  in Mahdiyya 144-5
Riak Deng (chief's policeman) 243
Riak Deng Mayan 273, 418, 428
Riak Jam 265
Riak Manyang 265
Riak Nial 220, 242
  personality report 237
  road work 232, 234
  tax 229
Rial-Beck Maich 242
Ric Dinka 209, 210 n.6, 413, 417
  chiefs 221, 240
  chiefs' police 243-4
  history of 211
  population 241
  repatriation of 214
  Ringbai section 221
  Ringror section 221
  road and landing ground work 232, 234, 235

tax 230
Richards, M. G. 55, 237, 428
Riek Mashar 35
Riel Makoi 266
Riem Jo 242
Rimmer, K. 169, 428
Roberts, W. D. 29-30, 368
  biographical entry 428
  questionnaire 377-8
Rokaic (fishermen) 265
tribes of:
  Kok 252, 265
  Nyang 252, 265
  Paleu (Palul) 252, 265
Rom 144, 428, 430
  dressing station 137
  European population 155
  road 78
  SUM mission 106, 108, 110, 169
Romilly, H. A. 137, 415, 422, 427
  biographical entry 428
  knowledge of vernacular 22, 41
  transferred to Western Nuer 302, 344 n.18
Rotit 235
Routh, H. C. E. 114, 372, 428
Ruai Wur 298, 304
Rue Ca Aca 265
Rueh Allair 244
Ruen Acilik 266
Rueng (Ruweng) Dinka 113
  administration of 159, 275, 301-2, 345
  chiefs' police 125
  country 296, 394
  of Khor Atar transferred to Malakal District 360
  population 27, 298, 381, 394
  road 309
  sections:
    Ajiba 306
    Alor 297, 306
    Kwil 414, 424
    transferred from Kordofan 306
  tax and tribute 160, 308
Rufshendol 45, 95, 293
Rumbek 256
  administered Yirol 254
  administrators 413, 420
  attacked by Dinka and Nuer 299 n.10
  as place of exile 115, 255
  road 74, 75, 109, 250, 258-9, 260, 309
Rut Dinka 210 n.6, 212, 427
Ryer 298

Sabah al-Khair 5
Sadik Ali 99
Said (Sayed) Abd el-Rahman 101, 172-3
  biographical entry 428

and Coryton 369, 373
Struvé on 373
Sa'id Sughaiyir 145 n.7
Salim (Salem) Banga 145, 428–9
Sayo 322, 328, 414
Schuster, G. 350, 429
Schweinfurth, G. xi
Seffarians, Messrs 327
Shambe 211, 250, 389, 390, 404
  buildings 139, 261
  cost of transport to 127
  cotton 129
  deforestation around 262
  dispensary 136
  garden 258, 262
  Imperial Airways site 134
  landing stage 94, 95
  police 122
  post and telegraph office 98
  resthouse 81
  road 65, 66, 74, 76, 77, 79, 257, 258–9
  store sheds 88
  wood station 131
Shaw, A. 429
Sheila Kong 426
Shilluk xi, 55–6, 177 n.4, 416, 427, 429, 431
  administration of 62–3, 115–16, 345
  and 'Anyanya' 33
  in army and police 5, 59
  bloodmoney 334
  border with Dinka 269
  border with Nuer 297
  born 'councillors' 354
  and cattle 59, 61, 162–3, 172
  Christian convert 110 n.20
  and chickens 141
  and civil war 35
  cotton 127, 128, 129
  council 359
  country 83, 394
  cultivation 126, 127, 162, 333
  and education 168–9
  effect of irrigation schemes on 396, 406
  encroachment on Dinka land 289
  forestry 130–1, 166
  king (reth) and kingdom 8–9, 23, 32, 59, 156–7, 172, 173, 332, 358–9, 411, 419, 423
  lack of initiation 337
  language 23
  literacy in Shilluk 347
  medical survey of 135
  merisa 171
  missions among 108, 109 (See also under Doleib Hill, Lul and Tonga)
  police 116–17, 123, 125
  population 27, 63, 154, 381, 394
  religion 20
  roads 73–4
Shilluk/Dinka boundary 154
  tax 11, 39
  trade 163
  tribal land 134
  tribal lorry 82, 398 n.9
  use of rifles in inter-sectional fighting 343
  village feuds 169–70
Shwailual 198
Shyita 177 n.4
Singa 430
Sirel Khatm Hasan Taha 101
Smith, E. (Mrs. Theobald) xiv, 429
Smith, I. 186, 411, 429
Smith, M. 429
Smith, P. J. 107 n.18, 186, 429
Soule, C. B. 186, 429
Stewart, J. B. 363–4, 429
Stigand, C. H. 181, 312, 366
  on arms and security 13
  biographical entry 429
  choosing sites for administrative posts 357
  death of 114, 256, 381
  forces election of Fafiti Yor 419
  on Nuer age-sets 331 n.1
  Nuer vocabulary 7 n.11
Struvé, K. C. P. xii n.7, 51 n.16, 276
  approach to Nuer leaders 17
  on arms and security 12–13
  attitude towards Willis 13–14
  biographical entry 429
  and civil administration 10–13, 32
  first civilian administrator in UNP 4, 6
  character 14
  defines Nuer-Dinka boundary 212
  and Guek Ngundeng 421
  on mamurs and interpreters 7
Sudanese 63 n.c, 374
  in army and police 1, 5, 337 n.10, 355
  and detribalization 337
  as labour 337–9
  and malakia 60, 101, 337
  Nineth battalion 276
  in Shilluk district 155
  Tenth battalion 274
  Thirteenth battalion 181
  Twelfth battalion harimat 320
  woodcutters 131

Tafari Makonnen, ras (Hayla Selasse I) 417, 424, 425, 426
  and Ethiopian Motor Transport Coy 326
  and Gambela concession 321–2
  interests in Gambela region 328
  and lij Iyasu 321 n.3
Takpiny (Takpin) Malwal 252, 263, 266

biographical entry 429
Tali 39, 250
  road 259, 261
  telegraph line 256
Talib Ismail 353, 374, 429
Talodi 98, 159, 309
Tarjath 298
Tassama, ras 321 n.2
Taufikia 3, 181
  forestry 131, 165
  housing for officials 137
  launch at 90, 93
  ox-ploughing at 86, 130
  Sudanese population 155
Tayeb Mukhtar 99
Tayiba 144, 153
Tegani 327-8
Tegjiek Dualdoang 306, 429
Teibo 362
Tem Wel 242
Ter Jong 243
Thain (Monythain) Dinka (fishermen) 209, 389
  chiefs' police 244
  labour duties 246-7
  population 241
  sections 221
    Akwak section 221
    Jonglei section 221
    Mading section 221, 244
    Malek section 221, 244
    Malwal section 221
    Pariak section 221, 244
  tax 231
Tharlil 309
Thiang (Tiang) Nuer 45, 118, 357, 360
  Nuer Settlement 292
  population 27, 62, 290
  road 75
  tax evasion 291
  toic 297
  villages 391, 393
Thianic Magok 266
Thiei Poic (Thiey Poich) 298
  biographical entry 429
  personality report 303-4
Thiong Aiwel 242
Thiong Mayan 243
Thoi Dinka 209, 210 n.6, 418
  absorbed by Gaawar Nuer 211
  among Ngok 273
  overrun by Lou Nuer 212
Thuom Amok 265
Tiernay, J. F. 137, 176 n.1, 182 n.14
  biographical entry 429
  knowledge of vernacular 22, 52
Tiop Lual 242
Tithbel 210

landing stage 94
telegraph line 98-9
telephone post 293
Tombe 211, 256
Tong 144
Tonga 62, 159
  administered by NMP 358
  buildings 165
  dressing station 137
  embankment 161
  resthouse 81
  road 64-5, 66, 74, 76, 79, 160, 309
  Roman Catholic mission 109
  school 106, 108
  Sudanese and Europeans in 155
  telegraph and telephone 98-9
  wood station 131
Tongadid 198, 268
Tonj 428
Toodel Mabor 244
Torakit (Tworokit) 154
  dressing station 137
  Sudanese in 155
  wood station 131
Torakwac 150
Torit 33
Tracey, C. B.
  biographical entry 430
  and merchants 374
  Struvé on 372
  on Willis 15
Triggs 367-8
Trudinger, L. 430
Trudinger, R. 106 n.16, 110, 136, 137
  biographical entry 430
Tunnicliffe, E. C. 352, 373
  on Anuak Sultan 354
  biographical entry 430
  knowledge of vernacular 22
  recommended for commandant of police 355-6
  Struvé on 372
Turner, L. 365, 430
Twic (Twi) Dinka 54-5, 143, 209, 210 n.6, 414
  administration of 114
  Ajwong section 220
    Abiong sub-section 220
    Ayolyil sub-section 220
    chiefs 239-40
    chiefs' police 243
    Kwaj sub-section 220
    Niaping sub-section 220
    population 241
    tax 230
  and Bor Dinka 360
  chiefs 220
  chiefs' police 242-3

Index

and civil war 35
cotton seed 244
country 386
court cases 223
effect of irrigation schemes on 406
Faker (Fakerr) section 220, 424
  Akinjok sub-section 220
  Anok sub-section 220
  Berah sub-section 220
  chiefs 239
  chiefs' police 243
  Cir sub-section 220
  Gol sub-section 220
  population 241
  tax 230
history of 211
Lith (Liet) section 211, 220, 412, 413, 414, 415, 417
  Abek sub-section 220
  Adiok sub-section 220
  Aulian (Aoolian) sub-section 220
  Aywal sub-section 220
  Biudit sub-section 220
  chiefs 238–9
  chiefs' police 242–3
  Deishwek sub-section 220
  Kongor sub-section 220
  population 241
  tax 229
population 27, 241, 381
punitive patrol against 9
road and landing ground work 232–4
source of wealth 211
take in refugees 212
toic 297
wealth in cattle 60, 113
Twij Dinka (Bahr el-Ghazal) 297 n.5
Twil Ran 298, 304, 420
  biographical entry 430
  personality report 305
Tworo 170

Uduk
  and civil war 35
  inclusion in UNP 345 nn21&22
  language 23
  SIM mission 110 n.22
Ujulu-wuru-Ubulu (Ogilo) 322, 430
Uliimi-war-Agaanya 412
Ut Jok 266
Utalo 200

Waat 35, 269
Wad Akona (wood station) 131, 142, 150
Wagkal 298
Wal Deng 243
Wal Lual 423
Walda-Giyorgis 328

Waller, E. S. 368, 430
Wangkai (landing ground) 97
Warabek Aiwel 220, 243
  personality report 239
  road work 233
  tax 230
Wathjak 298
Wau 139, 173
  Episcopate of 109
  as place of exile 427
  medical service at 136
  St Antony's school 347 n.23
Wedderburn-Maxwell 41, 51, 52, 182 n.13, 418, 422
  biographical entry 430
  knowledge of vernacular 22
  pursuit of Dual diu 292 n.6
  request for transfer 15 n.36
Wegin 177, 268, 269, 361
  concentration of Mor at 279
  road 282
Welkodni 203
Wer Kwer 221, 231, 235
Western Jikany Nuer 301, 390, 413, 420
  and Arabs 304
  chiefs resent subordination to Leek 304 n.21
  location 296
  population 27, 298
  road 309
  same sub-tribe as Eastern Jikany 298
  sections:
    Gaajak (Gatjak) 298
    Gaajok (Gatjo) 298
    Gaagwang (Gatwang) 298
  tax 308
Western Nuer (*See also* Bul, Dok, Jagei, Leek, Nyuong and Western Jikany Nuer)
  administration of 3–4, 118–19
  cattle 310
  cattle fines 333–4
  chiefs' courts 59, 307
  chiefs' police 126, 307
  cotton 127, 129, 311
  country 296
  and Dinka 299, 300–1
  meshras of 81, 309
  original home of Nuer 299
  population 62, 381
  tax 308
  and Turks 299–300
Wheatley, M. J. 41–2, 430
White, F. R. 114 n.114, 256, 381
Wiao Kak 145
Willan, R. H. 300 n.12, 430
Williams, K. B. G. 300 n.12
Willis, C. A. x–xiii, xv, 7, 40 n.1, 350, 415

achievements as governor 31–32
administration of UNP 4–5, 14–18
biographical entry 430
and British staff 15–16
character 14
on character of Northern Sudanese 397
on character of tribesmen 382–3
director of Intelligence x, 7, 13, 16
and economic development 28–31
and Evans-Pritchard xii, 21
and irrigation projects 29–31, 40, 377ff
on native administration 19–22, 397–400, 408–10
and 'S.A.R.' 32–3
on Struvé 10, 32
suppression of Nuer prophets 16–18, 421
suspicion of missionaries xii, 21 n.50, 106 nn 15–16, 107 n.18
Wilson, H. H. 6
biographical entry 430
on Dinka 275
Dinka history 143 n.5
Dinka vocabulary 7 n.11
on 1902 patrol 274
on Nuer 275
Wunakir 154
Wunalong 269
Wunging 269
Wuon Kuoth (Won Kwoth) 298, 415, 420
biographical entry 431
personality report 302
Wyld, J. W. G. xv, 17–18, 30, 31, 350, 353, 417
biographical entry 431
chiefs 354
on disarming the Nuer 13, 16
district 358
on Guek Ngundeng 49, 421
influenced by Dinka intrigue 360–1
knowledge of vernacular 22
lobbying on behalf of Southern Sudan 33
medical work 366
on native administration 189, 218–219
on removing Nuer from Bor District 218
response to Roberts' questionnaire 378
Struvé on 372
trained mounted police 355

Yak Witha 243
Ydlibi 321 n.3
Yei Atem 243
Yervent Khatanassian 365–6
Yirol (Yirrol) 252
 administrators posted to 415, 420, 421, 423
 appeal cases 254
 buildings 138, 139, 261–2
 Co-operative Marketing Society 260 n.14
 dispensary 136
 fighting around 260 n.13
 forest 262
 garage 84
 garden 262
 hospital 263
 landing ground 97
 police 121, 122, 124
 roads 65, 66, 74, 75, 76, 77, 81, 109, 250, 257, 258–9
 sawmill 120
 well 79, 260
Yodni 81, 390
Yoing 170
Yol Kur 53, 143
 appointment as chief 145
 biographical entry 431
 Struvé on 354
 Willis on 112
Yor 268
Yor Akoc 156, 419, 423
Yoynyang, 390
 dressing station 137
 road 75, 77
 Roman Catholic mission 105, 109
 school 107, 108
Yukwan, Savario 167
Yuol Jwaic 243
Yuwai, See Juwai

Zaki Faris 99
al-Zaki Tamal 144, 413, 419, 423
Zarzur (wood station) 131, 150
 re-afforestation 165
 Sudanese at 155
Zawditu 321 n.3
Zein el Abdein Gaafar 99

www.ingramcontent.com/pod-product-compliance
Lightning Source LLC
Chambersburg PA
CBHW021113300426
44113CB00006B/132

9780994363107